JAMES DILLON
A BIOGRAPHY

James Dillon

A Biography

Maurice Manning

WOLFHOUND PRESS
Celebrating 25 Years

Published in 1999 by
Wolfhound Press Ltd
68 Mountjoy Square
Dublin 1, Ireland
Tel: (353-1) 874 0354
Fax: (353-1 872 0207

British Library Cataloguing in Publication Data
A catalogue record for this book is available from the British Library.

ISNB 0-86327-747-0

Cover photograph reproduced courtesy of the Dillon family.

Cover design by Slick Fish Design
Printed and bound by ColourBooks Ltd, Dublin

For Mary

CONTENTS

ACKNOWLEDGEMENTS

THIS BOOK HAS taken two parliaments – and long parliaments, at that – to write. That was a longer time than was ever intended, and the process has taxed the patience and tried the tolerance of my family and friends, for which tolerance I am grateful. I make no apology, however; after all, had I not been writing, I could have been up to something much worse.

In particular, I owe a great debt to the Dillon family, whose complete co-operation I have enjoyed from the outset. All of James Dillon's papers were made available and all my many queries were diligently and enthusiastically researched. John Blake Dillon and his wife, Clodagh, made me welcome in their home on many occasions and their help, hospitality and friendship is much appreciated. Their daughters, Lee and Tara, gave me fresh insights into the character of their beloved grandfather. I owe a particular debt to Professor John Dillon, who acted as a wise mentor and helpful guide, and I am particularly grateful for his compiling of James Dillon's *Memoir*. I am also grateful for the warm common-sense of Jean Dillon throughout. Most of all, however, I want to thank the late Maura Dillon, who encouraged me to write this book and shared with me many memories of her late husband.

Among the wider Dillon family, I want to thank my good friend Marie-Therese Farrell for making available the papers of her father, Theo Dillon; and her husband, Professor Brian Farrell, for his friendship and encouragement. Dr Patrick Nugent and James Nugent SC, were of great and enthusiastic help, as were the sisters of the late Maura Dillon, Sr Joseph Ignatius and Mrs Ellie Shee. Fr Dom Christopher Dillon OSB was a helpful gadfly, reminding me of the passage of time at useful intervals.

The late Hector Legge, one of James Dillon's oldest friends, along with his late wife, Thelma, deserve special thanks, and I am sorry the book did not appear in their lifetimes.

I want to thank the staff at various libraries and archives. Dr Seamus Helferty at University College, Dublin, was, as ever, helpful, as was Dr Bernard Meehan in Trinity College, Dublin. In the National Archives, Caitriona Crowe and Ken Halligan, and Dr Gerald Lyne of the National Library, gave me invaluable help. Dr Patrick Melvin and Seamus Haughey provided sanctuary and assistance in the Oireachtas Library. The Clerk of the Dáil, Kieran Coughlin, helped me with some procedural matters. I am indebted also to Eamon MacHale, who made his private collection available, and Dr Harry Spain, the pioneer of the Parish Plan.

There are many to be thanked among my friends and colleagues. Stephen Collins, Conor Brady, Moore McDowell and David McCullagh read the text and made helpful suggestions; Mike Burns, the late and much missed Patrick Lindsay, John Coakley, Tom Garvin, Richard Sinnott, Michael Mills, Tim Ryan, Mary E. Daly and TP O'Connor all had helpful things to say along the way. John Horgan, Eunan O'Halpin and Breandán Ó Cathaoir provided me with useful leads, generously sharing some of their own research. Ann Carville made available her excellent thesis on Monaghan politics, while in that county James Holland, his daughter Bridie, Patrick Macklin, John F. Conlon and many others gave me help and hospitality. I also had discussions with civil servants who served under James Dillon. All were helpful and, in the best civil service tradition of the time, prefer not to be named.

I have had many formal and informal discussions about James Dillon over the years with past and serving members of the Oireachtas from all sides. May I thank in particular Liam Cosgrave, TF O'Higgins, the late Jack McQuillan, Declan Costello, Jack Lynch, Charles McDonald, Jim Dooge, Garret FitzGerald, the late Neil Blaney, the late Brian Lenihan, Paddy Harte and Dick Barry.

I would also like to thank the late Olga Koenigs, for many years private secretary to James Dillon.

I am grateful also to Brian Kelly of Ballaghaderreen, who made available useful financial records from Monica Duff's, and Laurence Crowley for his analysis of these records.

Help in finding photographic material and permission to publish it was generously offered by RTE, *The Irish Times, Dublin Opinion* and the *Examiner*. May I thank in particular Lilian Caverley of the *Examiner* for help above and beyond the call of duty.

My publishers, Seamus Cashman and Emer Ryan, were constructive and never pressurised me. Peter Malone was a model of editorial tact, while Rosemary Dawson was all that a good agent should be.

My very special thanks go to Marie Burnell, who is a great friend and a pleasure to work with.

And, finally, thanks to Nicholas and Mary. If they were discommoded during the writing of this book they have yet to tell me, and for that, and, as they know, for a great deal more, I am grateful.

Maurice Manning
September 1999

INTRODUCTION

FOR THIRTY-SEVEN years James Mathew Dillon was an ever-present figure in Ireland's political and parliamentary life, and rarely far from the centre of any of the great controversies of his day. One of the country's most colourful politicians, and perhaps the finest orator ever to speak in Dáil Éireann, he had a distinctive contribution to make on all the major issues of his time. But then, everything about James Dillon was distinctive. Impeccably groomed, with a broad-brimmed black hat, his cigarette clasped in an elegant cigarette-holder and his lower lip protruding, he moved in stately fashion, his bearing invested with innate *gravitas*. He was solemn, indeed some said he had been born so, and throughout his life everything he did was invested with a sense of high-minded purpose. He was neither frivolous nor familiar. To most people he was 'Mr Dillon', a form of address he reciprocated. Some, who professed familiarity where none existed, might call him 'Jim', but to his close friends and senior colleagues he was James.

Courteous, courtly and formal, he would not have been out of place in the Palace of Westminster at the close of the nineteenth century, and there were many amongst his opponents who said that such indeed was his rightful home and that it was the great regret of his life that he had been denied the chance of attending there. And in his private moments he may occasionally have had such regrets, such was his admiration for Westminster and his great reverence for the whole concept of the central role of parliament in the world of civilised politics.

Westminster might have suited James Dillon and provided him with a bigger stage for his talents. Perhaps. The suggestion, however, ignores the fact that at the centre of his father's and indeed his grandfather's life was the burning ambition to break the link with Westminster and to establish in Dublin an independent Irish parliament – the very House in which James Dillon deemed it such a privilege to serve.

In that parliament James Dillon was different. He was a nationalist, but stood outside the nationalist consensus of Sinn Féin. He distrusted England and English politicians, but for most of his life was a passionate advocate of the Commonwealth of Nations, seeing it as the framework within which the problem of partition would be resolved, and looking to the Commonwealth rather than to Europe for Ireland's long-term development. He was a free trader in an age of protection, an internationalist in an age of isolation, an enemy of overly strong government and intrusive executives just as these were becoming the norm. He was, in fact, an enemy of compulsion in any form, whether it came in the shape of government directives to grow wheat or the imposition of the Irish language. Most of all, he was different in having the courage to stand outside the overwhelming national consensus which kept Ireland out of the Second World War, standing then, as one opponent spat at him, 'abhorred by [Fianna Fáil], cast out by Fine Gael, avoided by Labour, spurned like a plague by Clann na Talmhan ... alone, in abject isolation'. Alone maybe, but never abject, his stance one of the rare examples of sustained moral courage in modern Irish politics.

He was different, too, in his style. He was probably the best orator of this century. The word along the Dáil corridors that 'Dillon was on his feet' was enough to attract politicians from all parties to the chamber. Dillon, speaking at a public meeting – in an age when public meetings attracted huge crowds – was always the highlight. He revelled in the heckling and gloried in the put-downs. Politics, he knew, was no place for the faint of heart.

In the long run Dillon's reputation as an orator did him harm. The sheer bravura of his performances, and in later years his tendency to fall back on well-tried formulae, invoked the suspicion that behind the showman there was less than met the eye, a man in whom form triumphed over substance. Such an assessment was unfair. His speeches show a command of principle, a wide-ranging knowledge, independence of spirit, and a capacity to ridicule and hurt his opponents.

Dillon was a tough politician in an age of tough politics. He had no time for those who looked down on party politics or deprecated the rough and tumble of everyday political warfare. He said harsh things and had harsh things said about him. And he saw, like Bagehot before him, that without party, politics was impossible. While he started political life as an Independent, and would later spend a decade on the Independent benches, he helped found two political parties and led Fine Gael, one of the two major parties in the state.

In one very real way James Dillon's life sought to vindicate the work and memory of his father. Few political fates were more cruel than that of John Dillon, swept aside at the very moment he might have inherited his political kingdom; not just summarily rejected, but rendered irrelevant as a younger, impatient generation set about building the new Irish state – and won little more for their pains than his aborted Home Rule Bill would have provided. It would have been easy and certainly it must have been tempting for James Dillon to turn his back on the new politics, to devote his talents to business or the professions, to follow his own leaning towards the study of medicine. That he chose not to do so owed much to his unshakable belief that as John Dillon's son he belonged in politics. He was conscious of his debt, in many ways a debt of honour, to that inheritance.

Throughout his political life certain key beliefs underpinned his political philosophy. He was an old-style liberal in his defence of free trade, his abhorrence of colonialism, his belief in parliament, his passion for free speech, his defence of the individual and his suspicion of all governments and all bureaucracies. He was a constitutional nationalist who took pride in his country's past, especially that with which his family was associated, and who wanted to see his country reunited. No charge could be more false than to say that he was in some way 'West British'. He was an internationalist who saw the influence Ireland could have in an international community loosely based on the old English-speaking British Empire, because of the Irish influence in the former colonies and the growing power of the Irish diaspora in the USA.

At another level, he never lost his sense of the primacy of land or his innate belief in the moral and social superiority of the rural over the urban way of life, and his ingrained suspicion of the desirability of rapid economic development was to blunt his effectiveness in a time of economic change. He began his political life as both a moderniser and a defender of a tradition which had been sidelined in Irish political life; he ended it neither fully understanding, nor much liking the forces of change and modernisation he saw all around him, but knowing that change there must be. When he left politics and relinquished the leadership of Fine Gael he was happy to do so, and to spend the last years of his life preparing himself, among other things, for a return to the fundamental understandings of his Catholic faith. In that happy retirement he was proud to say, 'I have never regretted a single moment of political activity. In politics I found what I am convinced I was meant by Providence to attempt.'

More than that, as he looked back on fifty years of political activity, his belief in the nobility and centrality of politics was as strong as it had been when he read the words of Tom Kettle, written in 1905. These words had inspired Dillon all his life, and summed up the essentials of his own philosophy and the primacy of politics among the great vocations:

Politics is not as it seems in clouded moments, a mere gabble and squabble of selfish interests: it is the State in action. And the State is the name by which we call the great human conspiracy against hunger and cold, against loneliness and ignorance; the State is the foster-mother of the arts, of love, of comradeship, of all that redeem from despair that strange adventure which we call human life.[1]

CHAPTER ONE

THE DILLON TRADITION

*His real and lasting significance may be less in what he did than what
he was ... the embodiment of a type or style of nationalist rare in any
country, and of incalculable value to the Ireland of his day.*
FSL Lyons on John Dillon

FROM HIS EARLIEST days, James Dillon was conscious of his father's
eminent position in national life. His father's world was his, the
world of politics. His *Memoir*, dictated nearly eighty years later,
captures the intensely political atmosphere in which he grew up:

My earliest recollection is curiously related to politics. In the general election
of January 1906, when Sir Henry Campbell-Bannerman was the Leader of the
Liberal Party and Mr. Arthur Balfour was the Leader of the Tory Party in
Great Britain, the *Daily Telegraph* published a cartoon every day in the shape
of a ladder. On each side of the main page was a cut-out figure, one of
Campbell Bannerman, in a frock coat, and another of Arthur Balfour, simi-
larly attired. As general elections in those days took about ten days with the
results coming in from the constituencies over the whole period, (because each
constituency took a poll on whatever day suited them, within a certain fixed
time range), if you hung up two ladders you were able to advance Sir Henry
on his ladder and Mr. Balfour on his, day by day as the results came in. These
two ladders were hung on the wall in the front bedroom, which at that time
was my father's dressing room, and my eldest brother Shawn, who was
regarded as the politician of the family, would register each morning the
progress of the two Leaders. There was great rejoicing in our household when
it became clear, as the days passed, that Sir Henry Campbell-Bannerman was
having a sweeping victory.[1]

When he was nine, James was taken to hear his father speak at the
unveiling of the Parnell monument in Sackville St, now O'Connell St,
Dublin. The following year, 1912, he watched from the windows of the
United Irish League's headquarters as his father, John Redmond and several
of the other Irish Party leaders spoke from different platforms to the crowd
which filled Sackville St from the Parnell monument to O'Connell Bridge.
He met the daughters of JFX O'Brien, the former Fenian, who had the

macabre distinction of being the last man ever to be sentenced to be hanged, drawn and quartered.

James and his brother Brian had also seen the procession of King George V when he visited Dublin in July 1911. His father had not approved of the royal visit, but consented to the boys watching the event from the balcony of a house in Merrion Square belonging to Sir Christopher Nixon, Senior Physician in the Mater Hospital and a friend of the Dillon family.

James Dillon knew his mother hardly at all. He was four when she died in 1907, and to the end of his days he only had two memories of her:

I have a vague memory of seeing her getting ready in her own bedroom for going out somewhere, in the costume of violet cloth, wearing a hat that was trimmed with violets. I also believe that I recall her standing on the rug in front of the fire in the drawing room on another occasion, ready to go out in an evening dress covered with black sequins, with a train on it. But these memories are so vague that I am virtually certain that if I were to meet my mother on the street tomorrow morning I would not recognise her.[2]

There is, however, one memory which did remain with him all his life:

I have a clear recollection however of what I now know must have been the day on which she died. We were sitting on the nursery floor, which had a cork surface, such as was quite common in those days, and Dr. Michael Cox who, in addition to being our family Physician, was my father's oldest and most intimate friend, came in, sat down on the sofa and gathered the family around him, with Maria, who was our nurse. It was in the evening, and I have little doubt that the purpose of the assembly was to break the news to the children that their mother was dead. My father was not present at this gathering.[3]

By all accounts Elizabeth Dillon was a remarkable woman. Her marriage to John Dillon lasted only eleven years, during which time they had six children. James, born in Dublin on 26 September 1902, was the fifth in line. His brother Shawn had been born in 1896 and sister Nano in 1897. Theo arrived the following year and Myles in 1900. Brian, the youngest, was born in 1905. These years were undoubtedly the happiest in John Dillon's life. He had met Elizabeth Mathew in 1886 when she was twenty-one years of age. She was the daughter of Sir James Mathew, an Irish-born judge of the High Court in London and a nephew of the famous Franciscan apostle of temperance, Father Theobald Mathew. Elizabeth was highly educated, proficient in a number of languages, particularly Latin, and had travelled widely. She had grown up in a politically aware milieu, in a family with strong Liberal connections, but she herself was a passionate Irish nationalist and a benefactress to Pádraig Pearse, whom she aided by selling Irish produce to Harrods to help him equip and furnish his school at St Enda's. Her death from pneumonia and medical incompetence in 1907 did not mean the end of the Dillons' association with the Mathew family. James, whose second name was Mathew, was very close to his grandmother, Lady Mathew, and spent much of his time with the family when he went to work in London.

Life for the Dillons revolved between their house at 2 North Great George's St, Dublin, originally the home of Charles Hart, and what to most of the family was their 'real home' in Ballaghaderreen in Mayo. The living conditions in North Great George's St were spacious but spartan. There was no water above the ground floor so that water for bathing or washing had to be hauled up six flights of stairs. The dining room was never heated and while there was always a fire in John Dillon's study during the winter, James and his brothers recalled 'how we used to leave father's study, when we were old enough to come down stairs to dinner, and go into the frigid dining room where no fire ever burned, and have our meals in desperate cold, after which we returned to the study and thawed out. Father used to take a small glass of whisky at dinner, but we had no such consolations.'[4]

The family ethos was one of formality and propriety. The children looked on their father with a mixture of awe and affection. James later recalled that:

> We grew up in a household where there was no mother, and from which my father was absent most of the time, at Westminster or elsewhere. He returned periodically, always with a new supply of tortoiseshell pen-knives, blue pencils, and large brown envelopes, which were items which he invariably purchased on his visits to London. These piled up on his desk and were still there at his death. Another problem was the newspapers. Father received five daily papers every day, and these piled up on a large table in the middle of his study, whether he was in town or not. Periodically the family would revolt, because at a certain stage you could no longer see whether he was in the room, and purged the papers.[5]

Their mother's warmth would undoubtedly have softened the formality which was so much a part of the Dillon children's upbringing, but her absence did not mean there was no feminine presence in the house. One of the main influences in James's upbringing was Lia – Maria O'Reilly – a formidable figure who spent sixty-three years with the family and became virtually a second mother to him. She had little formal education but was intelligent and politically aware, and though strict and critical, her warmth and love had an enormous influence on him, to the extent that he later claimed it was to her he owed his simple Catholic faith.[6]

There were other strong figures in the household. Winnie Forde, the parlour-maid at Ballaghaderreen, doted on James, while Jenny Penderleath, the under-nurse in North Great George's St, a Scottish Presbyterian who later became a Catholic, spent her entire life with the family. The one discordant note was struck by his governess, Miss Fitzsimons. She was a wonderful teacher and James got a good educational foundation from her, especially in French and German, but he found her extremely unsympathetic and looked back on the time he spent with her with 'unalloyed dismay'. He felt she disliked him and could be cruel, while she lavished affection on his brother, Brian. One family explanation was that she was jealous of the relationship between James and the parlour-maid Winnie, and compensated for this by indulging Brian.[7]

The world inhabited by the young Dillons was in every respect out of the ordinary. Their father, though much loved, was remote, formal, and frequently absent. Comfortable though they were in the material and financial sense, there was an abhorrence of frivolity or extravagance. They were taught to be self-reliant and encouraged from an early age to engage in formal debate. It was not unusual to have one or other of the brothers declaiming from a chair or table as if addressing a public meeting. James, who had something of a stutter, overcame it by adopting an exaggerated, almost theatrical style of delivery, which was to stay with him all of his life.[8]

As youngsters they were particularly conscious of the Dillon name, the sense of their father's position as one of the pre-eminent leaders of nationalist Ireland and their grandfather's role in history. The name Dillon was heavy with history and pregnant with possibilities, and made them different in their own eyes and the eyes of others.

JAMES DILLON liked occasionally to boast that his great-grandfather, Luke Dillon, was 'the irregular offspring of the 11th Viscount Dillon of Loughlynn', a man whose dissolute behaviour led to his being disowned by his family. The truth is almost certainly more prosaic, but Luke is at least the first member of the Dillon family about whom we can be certain. He was born at Lissiane, about three miles outside Ballaghaderreen, in around 1756. He was a tenant farmer on the Waldron estate, holding approximately 150 Irish acres at Blenaghbane in the townland of Lissiane, making him, in the context of the time, a farmer of substance. Family tradition has it that he was a member of the United Irishmen and had some part in the rising of 1798, though there is no evidence to support this view. We are on firmer ground in believing that Luke had considerable renown as an athlete and it was this athletic prowess which recommended him to Arabelle (Anne) Blake of Dunmacrina, Co. Galway, whom he married in 1797.

In 1812, Luke Dillon lost his land, in all probability a victim of the prevailing system of land tenure. When the Waldrons proposed to raise the rent, Luke refused to pay, and when a family called Clarke offered to take the holding, he was evicted. Luke must have had some resources to fall back on, however, because the family now moved to Ballaghaderreen, where Luke operated as a successful merchant and local postmaster until his death in 1825. The Dillons settled in an area known as Tullynahoo, and opened their shop in the town's main square. After a few years Luke bought the nearby Hughes house and established the Dillons there. A third storey was added to the building in the 1870s. This house, which dominated the town of Ballaghaderreen and which was known for most of its lifetime as Monica Duff's, remained the Dillon family home until the death of James Dillon in 1986.[9]

Luke and Anne Dillon had seven children. John Blake, James's grandfather, was the fourth child, born in 1814. Of the other children, Andrew became a medical doctor, Valentine became Crown Solicitor for Sligo and lived to 1904, Jane married a man called McDonagh, apparently not a very happy marriage, while the baby of the family, Bridget became a Sister of Mercy in Derry. Luke's son, Thomas, did much to build up the family enterprise before moving to set up another business in Ballina, Co. Mayo, when he transferred the Ballaghaderreen business to his sister, Monica, who was by now widowed

The family business was carried on under Monica Duff's name for over a century. Monica, born in 1798, was the eldest of Luke Dillon's daughters. She married a tanner from Fishamble St in Dublin called Arthur Duff, a marriage which, according to family tradition, was not particularly happy. In spite of this, Monica proved a highly competent businesswoman and under her name the former Dillon shop became the dominant commercial force in the area. She was widowed early, but not before she had four children. Of these, John Duff went to Australia, Patrick became a doctor practising in the Midlands, Mary married a Dr McCormack, and Anne, later to be Mrs Deane, remained in Ballaghaderreen where she inherited and ran the family business.

Anne Deane was a woman of character, organisational skills and good business instincts. An obituary notice in 1905 gives us a picture of a formidable lady, even allowing for the pietistic exaggerations of the time: 'carefully and methodically educated by private tutors, getting a thorough and business-like education, eschewing the frivolities of mere drawing-room accomplishments'. She knew most of the leading political and ecclesiastical figures of the time, including Anthony Trollope, who frequently stayed at her house. President of the Ladies Land League in 1891, she was noted for her charity and had, apparently, strong nationalist views on most of the major issues of those years. She excelled at business, and by the time of her death in 1905 Monica Duff's had expanded to cater for every need in the community: grocery, haberdashery, millinery, footwear, hardware and bar. There was a builders provider's section, a bakery, bottling plant, mineral water factory, piggery, egg-exporting business and farm, plus whiskey and tea blending and a profitable Guinness agency.[10]

Anne Deane's business success was not matched by matrimonial happiness. Her husband, Edward Deane, was 'no good' according to family tradition, and in fact the relationship was short-lived as he died early in the marriage. Childless, Anne Deane came to regard her nephew, John – James Dillon's father – as if he were a son, especially so after his mother's death in 1872. It was she who encouraged and indeed financed much of his career in politics, urged him to marry, and left him the family business on her death in 1905.

The first Dillon to achieve prominence in politics was Luke Dillon's fourth son, John Blake, James Dillon's grandfather. His story has been frequently told, most notably in Breandán Ó Cathaoir's fine biography, *John Blake Dillon: Young Irelander*.[11] Although John Blake Dillon died almost forty years before James was born, he was always conscious of the political legacy he inherited from his grandfather.

John Blake Dillon was born in 1814 and educated privately, mostly by country classical masters of the hedge-school tradition. He went for a short time to Maynooth to try his vocation for the priesthood and then transferred to Trinity College, where he read ethics and mathematics before proceeding to law, being called to the Bar in 1841. While at Trinity he became a close friend of Thomas Davis and others who founded the Young Irelanders, and his first article in the very first issue of *The Nation* concluded on a theme which was to underpin the political philosophy of both his son and grandson: 'Land reform should hold the first place in the thoughts of every man who wishes to better the conditions of the people.'

His early writings and speeches indicate enormous concern for the appalling conditions of the peasantry, and anger at the evils of a kind of landlordism which, he said, 'neglected the common duties of humanity'. He was an early advocate of some form of Land League and wanted 'a domestic and democratic government'. Although he was later to fall foul of the Catholic clergy and develop a deep distrust of the ultramontane tendencies and sheer bigotry of many ecclesiastics, he saw the priests as 'the natural advisers of the Catholic people'. He detested the Irish tolerance for 'rascality' in public life, and was a supporter of Father Mathew's temperance crusade and a strong advocate of the revival of the Irish language. An intensely high-minded young man, John Blake Dillon was described by his biographer as having 'a strong, logical mind, a passion for social justice and grave charm. He was an enlightened, compassionate, if unoriginal thinker.'

In 1847, John Blake Dillon married Adelaide Hart, daughter of Charles Hart, a prominent Catholic solicitor and a man of advanced nationalist views. Dillon took a leading part in the uprising of 1848, in itself an insignificant affray, but which later assumed great symbolic importance. As Breandán Ó Cathaoir has written, 'when their hour of destiny arrived a fatal paralysis overcame these men of the pen. But their courage would live in the minds of the people and the Young Ireland tradition contributed to the evolution of the Irish nation.'[12]

Dillon was a wanted man after the 1848 Rising. He escaped to the USA, where he remained until 1855. In February 1849 his first child, Rose, was born and in September of that year Adelaide joined him in their Long Island home. He became a respected but unfanatical member of the Irish community, built up a successful law practice, and found himself excluded from Catholic business because of his opposition to the wave of Catholic sectarianism which swept through the immigrant community at this time.

Following his return to Ireland in 1855, and in spite of his own best intentions, John Blake Dillon found himself drawn once again to political activity. The condemned rebel of 1848, who was still deeply hostile to the ethos of Pope Pius IX, was at one with Cardinal Paul Cullen and the Catholic establishment in his advocacy of the disestablishment of the Church of Ireland. In 1863 he was elected to Dublin Corporation for the Wood Quay Ward and in 1865 he was elected MP for Tipperary.

As an MP he returned to fundamental Dillon themes. He believed, as he had outlined in his first political writings, that the relationship between landlord and tenant was the cause of most of the country's ills, and he introduced a Land Bill which interested and influenced Gladstone. In parliament he gravitated to the company of the Radicals and became friendly with John Bright and John Stuart Mill. He supported moves for the extension of the franchise and opposed any suspension of habeas corpus. The first Dillon to enter parliament showed an instinctive liking for it, but his promise was not to be realised for he died suddenly on 15 September 1866, struck down during an epidemic of cholera; family folklore has it that he was the last person to die from cholera in Ireland. His character was best summed up by John Mitchel: 'I have known in my time many good men, but one nobler, more generous-hearted, more pure and gallant than John Dillon I never knew or hope to know.' Mitchell could hardly have offered higher praise, and this in spite of thinking that Dillon was 'all wrong, about almost everything'.[13]

In a celebrated passage written in 1880, Sir Charles Gavan Duffy wrote of John Blake Dillon:

In person he was tall and strikingly handsome, with eyes like a thoughtful woman's, and the clear olive complexion and stately bearing of a Spanish noble. His generous nature made him more of a philanthropist than a politician.

And of Dillon's political philosophy he wrote:

he desired a national existence primarily to get rid of social degradation and suffering which it wrung his heart to witness without being able to relieve. He was neither morose nor cynical, but he had one instinct in common with Swift, the villanies of mankind made his blood boil.[14]

Adelaide survived him by only six years, dying in 1872 aged forty-four. There had been seven children, but only three lived past the age of twenty. Two girls, Rosalie and Christina, died of consumption at the ages of eighteen and twenty, and two boys, Charles and Thomas, died as young children. The three surviving members were William, Henry, and James Dillon's father, John.

William, born in Long Island during his father's exile, was the godson of Thomas Francis Meagher, who attended his baptism shortly after escaping from penal servitude in Australia. William trained in Dublin and London as a lawyer, but in 1880 moved to the US when he was threatened with tuberculosis. He worked intermittently as editor of the *New World*, the newspaper of the Catholic archdiocese of Chicago, where, according to the official history of that paper, he generally sided with Labour and supported reform legislation to break trusts and monopolies. He was later the first Dean of Loyola University Law School, received honorary doctorates from the University of Notre Dame and the National University of Ireland, and spent much of his later life in Colorado.

The story of his marriage best sums up his independence and sense of honour. He wished to marry Elizabeth Ratcliffe, an Episcopalian, who had agreed the children would be raised as Catholics, but Dillon refused to have her sign the agreement then required by the Catholic Church, believing that her word was her bond. In any event, William, who had spent some time as a young man 'testing his faith by studying various Protestant teachings', was content that there was nothing 'under the teachings of Christ or Canon Law which imposed such a requirement'. When the Catholic archbishop refused the couple permission to marry, William pointed out to him that 'the Episcopal Bishop of Denver could perform as valid a marriage ceremony in the eyes of the Catholic Church as the Archbishop', and took Elizabeth by horse and buggy to Denver. Ten children were born of the marriage and all were raised as Catholics.

William remained in close contact with Ireland, paying many visits home and writing a respected biography of John Mitchel. He corresponded on a regular basis with his brother, John, and later with James. He lived to the age of eighty-five, dying in 1935 in Chicago, where his son, Bill, had set up the successful law firm of Concannon Dillon.[15]

Henry was born in 1856 after John Blake Dillon's family had returned permanently to Dublin. He also studied law and practised for a short time before entering the Franciscan Order, where he took the name in religion of Nicholas. He also lived to a good age, dying in 1939 aged eighty-three at Multyfarnham, where he is buried. He remained in close contact with the family throughout his life, frequently dispensing spiritual and political advice, the quality of the former certainly better than that of the latter. He was a formidable character, renowned for his ferocious pursuit of the ideal of poverty, and mortified himself by wearing a hair-shirt. He was a preacher of note, as little given to compromise in matters spiritual as he was in matters political.

The third brother, John, James Dillon's father, was the single most important influence on James's ideas, character and philosophy. The story of John Dillon has been frequently and well told, most definitively in FSL Lyon's magisterial biography, so all that is necessary here is to indicate the main features of his life and politics.

Born in 1851, he was just fifteen when his father died and his education, like that of his brothers, was supported by his mother's family, the Harts and the O'Haras, and by his aunt, Anne Deane. Unlike his brothers he chose to study medicine and qualified as a doctor, attending the Catholic University and becoming auditor of the Literary and Historical Debating Society, where he emerged as a strong advocate of a National University but was highly critical of clerical interference in politics. From his earliest days he was an enthusiast for the revival of the Irish language, later joining the Gaelic League and encouraging his children to learn Irish.

He entered politics in 1880 as MP for Tipperary, a seat his father had won in 1865, and remained in the House of Commons until 1918, though he moved at an early stage to represent East Mayo. The dominant themes of his political life reflected those of his father: land reform, the end of landlordism, and self-government for Ireland – Home Rule. His interests ranged widely. He was a voracious reader and had a passionate interest in foreign affairs, was regarded as a leading expert on Egypt and Persia, and had a good grasp of political economy. His contributions to the Commons covered virtually every major area of political life.

The political story of John Dillon is well known. The long and bitter land war, imprisonments and hardship which triumphed in the shaping of a great parliamentary movement and the conversion of Gladstone to Home

Rule; then the epic battles in the House of Commons to bring about the land acts, which reshaped the social, economic and political map of Ireland as tenant farmers became landowners. Most of all there was the agony of the Parnell split, followed by years of disunity and bitterness, and the postponement of Home Rule on the eve of the First World War. After the 1916 Rising, John Dillon pleaded for leniency for the rebels, then suffered the ignominy of seeing his party, one of the greatest parliamentary machines of all time, swept away by Sinn Féin's 1918 victory. No political fate could have been more cruel than that meted out to John Dillon in 1918.

Dillon was not an easy man. Even with his own family he was remote, formal and unemotional. According to Lyons he had little social ease, 'no small talk, he ate and drank sparingly and was fastidious in his personal tastes and morals'. From the earliest days he treated his children as if they were adults, answering their questions with studied seriousness. His view of human nature was fundamentally pessimistic, a view heightened no doubt by his tendency towards hypochondria and by his political experiences. But he was also a man of the deepest courtesy, kind, cultivated and extraordinarily widely read, and with an unappeasable appetite for knowledge.

His most striking quality, even his harshest critics conceded, was his integrity, his absolute incorruptibility. His hatred of servility was the core of his life-long hatred of landlordism. For an Irish nationalist, one whose life-work was to achieve a native Irish parliament, he had an extraordinary affection, indeed almost a reverence for the House of Commons. He quickly mastered its procedures, spoke on a wide range of issues, and was treated with respect on all sides, though as a member of a minor party he never held office during all of his thirty-eight years in the House. Yet he never lost his sense of parliament's central importance, nor did the respect he felt for it weaken in the face of setback and rejection, and he inculcated this regard for parliamentary democracy in each of his children.

In summing up John Dillon's life his biographer, FSL Lyons, says:

by any standards John Dillon's life must be reckoned a tragedy, scarred by personal pain and grief, and ending in the ruin of all his hopes for his country. Yet he himself, though beyond question deeply hurt by his rejection in 1918, lived long enough to be able to reach a certain serenity, and to look back with pride on the achievement of the Great Movement in which for forty years he had played so notable a part. What, at the end of all, were those achievements and what precisely was his part? The list, though since 1916 it has been fashionable to ignore or to decry it, is undeniably impressive. It includes the creation of a famous Parliamentary Party – in its prime one of the most remarkable phenomena in modern political history – and its recreation after the Parnell split; the building of successive popular organisations which gave to the Irish people, so long debarred from participation in Government, valuable experience in the democratic process and in the business of managing their own affairs; the virtual solution of the land question and the re-instatement of the evicted tenants; the winning of other substantial reforms – chief among them the Congested District Board, the Irish Local Government Act and the National University; finally, and the *raison d'être* for the whole movement, the formulation of the demand for Home Rule, its elevation into a major issue in British politics and its eventual embodiment in legislation – a triumph of sustained pressure and negotiation which not even the later disasters can ever wholly obscure.

After 1918 all was utterly changed. Ireland turned in a new direction and John Dillon was left alone and disillusioned, presenting to history the spectacle – melancholy, but not without nobility – of a fiercely honest man who loved his country, but learned through harsh experience that patriotism was not enough.[16]

THE DILLONS inherited with their family story a sense of place, an identity which found its fullest expression in their home in Ballaghaderreen. Ballaghaderreen was the centre of the universe for the Dillon family. Christmas and Easter were invariably spent there and every summer John Dillon would retire to the Mayo town for what was the happiest part of the family year. For John Dillon, Ballaghaderreen was home, and in later years James would always signal his arrival with the words, 'It's grand to be home.' There was about Ballaghaderreen a sense of secure and unchanging values, the traditional values of a rural and Catholic society. The small farmers were the men the young Dillons' father fought for and most cherished, as James did, too, throughout his career.

The Dillons dominated Ballaghaderreen, though not in the style of so many of the strong merchant families of the time. Their economic importance was part of the reason for their high standing. More significant was the respect with which 'Honest' John Dillon was held as a national figure, a man whose name had brought honour to his town and constituency. There was also the perception of the Dillons as the antithesis of the 'gombeen' merchant. The Dillons were seen as fair and honourable in business, and Monica Duff's was a byword in the West of Ireland for value and straight dealing.

The family's arrival each summer was a momentous occasion. James Dillon remembered

the old Station Master, Mr. Walsh, who was a devoted friend and admirer of my father, when the train was coming in from Kilfree junction, he would have firecrackers on the rails, and we would arrive into Ballaghaderreen with these bangs going off, to be received by the staff with two horses and two drays to carry the luggage and a carriage driven by Dominick Cryan. Father would get into the carriage with Nano, and the rest of us would get into the trap and we would all proceed solemnly from the station to the house. The luggage would arrive on a large dray drawn by a black horse, or sometimes two of them.[17]

After the spartan surroundings of North Great George's St, the house in Ballaghaderreen was very comfortable. John Dillon was revered by the large staff, many of whom had been with the family for up to fifty years. The Dillons invariably arrived for the hay-making. Here James and his brothers were happiest, and would spend summer days shooting and horse riding. The countryside round about was still partly Irish-speaking, and Dillon's store was referred to by some of the older people as *'Teach Mhonica'*. But still they were a family apart, a relationship best summed up by James's brother, Theo, who said: 'what an irony of fate it is that in my father's house there should be the last remnants of feudalism, in its best sense, left in Ireland'.[18]

Many of the great figures of the time visited the house, others were known by repute, and the daily conversation centred on the issues and personalities of the day with an intimacy few could match. Whether in Ballaghaderreen or North Great George's St, the world of politics and political ideas was an ever-present fact in the Dillons' lives.

Home Rule seemed inevitable, and when it came John Dillon would be one of the leaders, if not the prime minister of a self-governing Ireland. As the young Dillons grew up and John Dillon grew to an old age, few would have disputed that his life's work would soon reach its crowning achievement.

CHAPTER TWO

SCHOOL TO UNIVERSITY

*'I declare most solemnly ... I am not ashamed to say it in the House of
Commons, that I am proud of these men'.*
John Dillon, House of Commons, 11 May 1916

J OHN DILLON'S ATTITUDE to the education of his sons was unconventional. Most Catholic and nationalist families of his class would have
chosen to send their boys to the Jesuits at Clongowes Wood or one of
the other vigorously Catholic schools then beginning their domination of
middle-class education, like Belvedere, Blackrock or Castleknock. Or, like
many of the more established Catholic families, he might have sent his sons
to school in England, at Downside or Ampleforth, but he was in principle
opposed to Irish boys attending English schools, especially when there were
good schools available in Ireland.

James's early schooling was entirely at the hands of his governess, Miss
Fitzsimons, and his father seems to have taken quite some time in making
up his mind as to where he should go then, because he stayed with Miss
Fitzimons until he was thirteen. Belvedere College was just across the road
from the Dillon home at North Great George's St, and his older brothers
Theo and Myles went there as day-boys before going as boarders to Mount
St Benedict in Gorey, Co. Wexford. His father toyed with the idea of sending James to Pearse's school in Rathfarnham, due in part to his late wife's
enthusiasm for the Gaelic League and her interest in Pearse. In deference to
her, John Dillon drove out to St Enda's in a cab to inspect the school and
interview the principal. However, according to the family story, as they
drove up the avenue Dillon saw boys in a playing field, 'playing hockey in
skirts', a sight which so dismayed him that he ordered the cab to turn
around there and then.[1]

If St Enda's was an unorthodox option, Mount St Benedict was hardly
less so. The school had been established in 1907 by a strong-willed, eccentric Benedictine monk, Fr John Sweetman.[2] Located in a big house
standing on 500 acres near Gorey, the regime there was spartan, but there
was little of the institutionalised atmosphere then the norm in other
schools. It was a small school with rarely more than fifty students. Much of

the teaching was quite haphazard, but exam results were good, and St Benedict students won many scholarships to university. One student recalled that 'a surprising feature of life was that the studies and the discipline seemed to run themselves, with the absolute minimum of direction from above'. Another curious feature concerned the teaching of Christian Doctrine. 'Once you were confirmed, it was presumed that your natural interest in religion would make you acquire a reasonable knowledge of the faith, and strangely enough the system worked well.'[3]

The school survived for under two decades and ended its life in a row between Fr Sweetman and the local bishop, Dr Codd, a battle inevitably won by the bishop which resulted in Fr Sweetman having his spiritual faculties withdrawn. In fact, the intervention of James's brother Brian, then a Benedictine monk, with Papal Nuncio Dr Pascal Robinson, helped Fr Sweetman return to full ecclesiastical standing shortly before his death.

All of that was in the future. For the present, the school the thirteen-year-old James Dillon arrived at in September 1915 was not much to his liking. He suffered intolerably from home-sickness and felt he did not fit in very well because he was not a conformist, 'and therefore I used to have fairly stormy times with my school fellows'.[4]

His description of life at Mount St Benedict's recounted sixty years later gives a vivid picture of the school:

> Life was in general most austere. Mount Saint Benedict was on a hill, and it was very cold. There was a most elaborate central heating system, but it was never turned on ... Getting up in the morning was never pleasant. There were enamel basins and jugs for washing, and I can remember breaking the ice in the jug on many occasions during the winter in the dormitory where we were all sleeping.
>
> Theoretically, we got a bath once a week, but owing to the scarcity of fuel and coal you frequently shared the bath with other customers, and if you happened to be sixth or seventh in the bath, it was no longer possible to see the bottom of it. But we did not seem to mind these little difficulties in the least.
>
> The diet was particularly austere. Father Sweetman in those days (1915 and 1916), had developed a passion for growing wheat. The quality of the wheat was absolutely appalling. He ground it on the premises and it was converted into bread of a nature which is beyond belief. But we ate the bread and in my recollection we got very little else but bread. We did get meat once a day, and if the meat held out you were very welcome to a second helping. But our diet consisted very largely of bread and tea. You could buy jam, if you had pocket-money, or if your parents sent it to you, and again with pocket-money, you could buy eggs. In those days eggs were very cheap – you could buy two eggs for one old penny – and these would be boiled for us if we brought them back to school.[5]

The school was dominated by Fr Sweetman and the matron, Miss Keogh. Both held strong, if not always consistent political views. One student remembers Miss Keogh, 'her hair close cropped like a boy, which was very unusual in the early years of this century. As relaxation she would take an axe and sally forth to the woods to fell a couple of trees, smoking one of Father Sweetman's pungent home-grown cheroots ... she had a passion for Wild West stories, of which she had a magnificent collection.'[6]

According to James, Miss Keogh had started out as a Loyalist but by 1916 was a rabid Republican, and cycled to Dublin to take part in the Rising. She was briefly arrested by the British, but according to one account so intimidated the arresting officers that she was released against her wishes and sent back to Gorey. Between James and herself there was no rapport; she resented his championing of the Irish Party, but according to him, 'at Father Sweetman's direction she forebore any active interference'.[7]

Fr Sweetman gave the school much of its distinctive character. James later wrote of him:

Father Sweetman was a remarkable man. When I first met him, he was extremely pro-British, and most enthusiastic to persuade anyone who was available to join the British army. But later – I think it was probably after 1916 – he became strongly anti-British, and it was from then on that he became more and more violently Sinn Féin. However, he was quite prepared to argue with you. He was not tyrannical in his views.[8]

Mount St Benedict had a tradition that for special celebrations students could set a blaze on Gorse Hill behind the school:

Accordingly, if the Irish Party won a by-election I would lead a tribe of friends and supporters and set fire to the Gorse Hill, and I can recall an occasion (possibly one or other of the by-elections in early 1918, which our side won), on which Father Sweetman and his supporters set fire to one side of the Hill while we set fire to the other. There were no hard feelings about it.[9]

The staff was largely recruited from graduates of Oxford and Cambridge. Fr Sweetman himself was frequently away:

He would be away for two or three days, and when he was away a kind of peace descended upon the school. When he returned, anything might happen. He was extremely arbitrary and exercised discipline very largely by roaring out through the window of his sitting room, which surveyed the playing fields and the lawn tennis courts in front of the house.[10]

Despite his nationalist sympathies, Fr Sweetman was devoted to cricket, and though he tried to introduce Gaelic football to the school, he was not much interested in it. 'To do him justice, he did not have much enthusiasm for compelling people to play games that they did not enjoy,' James recalled, 'But he would expect you to take some other form of exercise. The whole discipline on that side however was very loose. He was always furious, though, if you were not enthusiastic about cricket, and regarded you as an inferior kind of being if you did not take part in cricket, but apart from that he bore you no ill will.' James was not enthusiastic about cricket – he could not see the ball – and was eventually exempted from playing it.[11]

One of Fr Sweetman's other foibles was to grow tobacco, which he used to dry and cut to make cigarettes. 'Sometimes he would summon a select group from among the boys and set them to work to make cigarettes. I often spent a long and weary afternoon making by hand cigarettes of Ballyowen tobacco. The smell of it was dreadful, and the taste of it was worse.'

The school set a strict rule against smoking, 'but if you were caught smoking a Ballyowen cigarette no sanctions were invoked against you, whereas if you were caught smoking a Players cigarette, you were in very serious trouble indeed.'[12]

In the winter months the boys might be called out to the fields to snag turnips. 'The cold was indescribable, and when you came back to the school, if you had not got a room of your own where you could light a fire, you were as cold in the school as out in the turnip field.' The senior boys had their own rooms and could chop logs for the fire.[13]

James Dillon claims he learned very little at Mount St Benedict, but he was a keen member of the debating society and devoted a great deal of time to preparing his contributions. Mount St Benedict was a highly political place at a time of high political tensions, and debating had a very important part in the life of the school. Every Sunday morning meetings were held in a loft over the stables and all were welcome to attend, whether masters, boys, workmen or local people. Any subject could be discussed, and with Fr Sweetman presiding debate could be a rough and tumble affair.

The majority of the boys at Mount St Benedict came from a background of law, medicine, property and business. James's contemporaries included Owen Gwynn, a son of Stephen Gwynn MP, who died at the age of sixteen; the four Sweetman brothers from Glendalough, sons of Roger Sweetman, later a Sinn Féin TD; and Conor Carrigan, with whom he corresponded for many years afterwards. Carrigan later became a successful stockbroker in London and a leading member of British Intelligence during the Second World War. Another contemporary was Sean MacBride, whose father was executed for his role in the 1916 Rising. In later years

MacBride became Chief of Staff of the IRA, and later still sat at at the cabinet table with James Dillon.

THE EASTER Rising of 1916 changed the lives of the Dillon family as profoundly as it changed the history of the country. James Dillon later claimed his father had some premonition that all was not well in Dublin as Easter 1916 approached, but nothing could have prepared him for the scale or the intensity of the uprising as the Volunteers seized the GPO and declared a Republic. Living in North Great George's St, just up the road from O'Connell St, he and his family found themselves at the very centre of events. James, then aged thirteen and home for the Easter holidays, had vivid memories of that day.

> I remember coming back from the Zoo on that particular Monday. We were on the top of an open tram, and at Dorset St, on the way down from the North Circular Road, we found ourselves in the middle of the Lancers, who were riding down to the Post Office to put an end to what was thought to be some kind of riot. We got off the tram at Findlater's Church, and before we got up to North Great George's Street we could hear the firing down in the City. When we got home, J.G. Swift McNeill was there, and I still remember my sister Nano being in the study with my father and myself – and I imagine Myles and Theo – and Swift McNeill, who was an old fashioned Victorian gentleman saying, 'My God, John, if there weren't ladies present, I'd say these fellows are *rascals*!' That indeed was the general feeling. After the surrender, I recall going out on the streets and overhearing various groups of citizens confidently telling each other that it was John Dillon who had made the peace, that he had gone down himself to the G.P.O. and arranged everything. It was not unnatural that people should suppose this, but in fact my father had never left the house and had been quite unable to influence the course of events.[14]

That had been John Dillon's great tragedy. Besieged in his house, prey to the wildest rumours, John Dillon realised the significance of the Rising, saw that 'physical force was not dead but stunned, and needed very little to wake it into fresh life'.[15] When the government responded to the revolt with summary executions, he witnessed the reaction this policy produced in favour of the revolutionaries, and sought to prevent it becoming a reaction against parliamentarians also. He made strenuous efforts to persuade the government to change its course, and countless interventions with the authorities on behalf of individual prisoners, but found himself ignored and overruled.

When the House of Commons finally debated the Rising and its consequences over a month later, on 11 May, his frustration and anger boiled over in a bitter, passionate speech. 'You are letting loose a river of blood, and make no mistake about it, between two races who, after three hundred years of hatred and strife, we had nearly succeeded in bringing together.' He spoke to a hostile and uncomprehending House about the impact the government's policy was having on constitutional nationalism. 'We are held up to odium by the men who made this rebellion … you are washing out our whole life's work in a sea of blood.'

He condemned the Rising, but not the men:

> I declare most solemnly … I am not ashamed to say it in the House of Commons, that I am proud of these men … I said I am proud of their courage, and if you were not so dense or stupid, as some of you English people are, you could have had these men fighting for you … It is not murderers who are being executed; it is insurgents who have fought a clean fight, however misguided.

And he understood fully the consequences the political situation could have for his party:

> These men, misguided as they were, have been our bitterest enemies. They have held us up to public odium as traitors to our country because we have supported you at this moment and have stood by you in the Great War, and the least we are entitled to is this, that in the great effort we have made at con-siderable risk … to bring the masses of the Irish people into harmony with you, in this great effort at conciliation, I say we are entitled to every assistance from the members of this House and from the Government.[16]

His speech outraged the House of Commons and shocked many of his own colleagues, but in almost every respect it was probably the finest speech he ever made, in its courage, its humanity, its passion, and most of all its realism and wisdom. Had he been heeded, the Irish Party might well have reasserted its authority. Had his further calls for the release of prison-ers and the restoration of due judicial process been followed, many of the factors which fuelled the growth of Sinn Féin would not have arisen. Had the government listened to his urgent plea that a Home Rule settlement was not just possible but politically imperative, and most of all had he been listened to two years later on the issue of conscription, then it is possible that the leadership of nationalist Ireland would have remained with the Irish Party. It was not to be, and as he felt himself increasingly betrayed by Lloyd George and Asquith, as Sinn Féin began its rise and the Irish Party its decline, Dillon became an increasingly marginalised figure.

The Rising of 1916 had a profound effect on James, who expressed vigorous loyalty to his father's cause when he returned in the autumn to

Mount St Benedict. Even here the atmosphere was running in favour of the revolutionaries. In a letter to his father in November 1916 he described how, with the connivance of Fr Sweetman, 'a large number of the boys are now wearing huge Sinn Féin badges. This contagion has spread even to the prefectorate, two members of which are to be seen with very large rebel badges.'[17]

James accompanied his father to the election convention at Bailieboro, Co. Cavan, for a by-election in 1917. The election was won by Sinn Féin's Arthur Griffith, whose cause was helped immeasurably by being arrested and jailed on trumped-up charges during the course of the campaign. The result was another sharp reminder to the Irish Party of the growing support for Sinn Féin, though as yet few saw the full extent of that threat.

When John Redmond died on 6 March 1918, John Dillon was the unanimous choice to succeed him, but it was a bitter inheritance with no sense of joy or promise about it, and Dillon felt very keenly the betrayal of Redmond by the British politicians in whom he had placed such trust. Dillon threw himself into the fight against conscription, appearing on the same public platform as de Valera in Ballaghaderreen, helping to produce a sense of nationalist unity, but in an irony which did not escape him, doing so to the benefit of Sinn Féin and at the expense of his own party. Dillon, however, did not accept the inevitability of a Sinn Féin victory, and in the three by-elections of 1918 – in South Armagh, Waterford city and East Tyrone – his party held off the Sinn Féin challenge. Then came conscription, and with it the surge to Sinn Féin which helped bury the Irish Party. James's first direct political involvement arrived in time to witness the defeat.

He offered his services to the Irish Party candidate in North Wexford, Sir Thomas Esmonde, in the 1918 general election. He was only sixteen, but his family name attracted considerable attention in the press, and he spoke at meetings in Gorey, Castlebridge, Bree and Davidstown. His notes, written in Irish and English, still survive. He argued for the continuity of the Irish Party as the rightful inheritors of the nationalist tradition, and attacked Sinn Féin as an obstacle between Ireland and its true destiny. Sinn Féin's campaign was flying in the face of all that Parnell had achieved; the real beneficiary of their work would be the Unionists of Ulster.[18]

James spent the entire campaign in the constituency with John Bolger from Ferns, involved in much of the detail of organisation and campaigning. Unlike other parts of the country, among them his father's constituency of East Mayo, Wexford was relatively calm, though on one occasion they had the tyres of their car slashed outside the courthouse in Gorey by a woman who later became a valued friend, Máire Comerford. She was, and remained, an avid supporter of Sinn Féin and vehement in the expression of her views.[19]

With the enthusiasm of the neophyte, on 2 December Dillon wrote to his father brimming with optimism, predicting that 'Sir Thomas will win by 2-1'. In the event, Sir Thomas Esmonde became one of the army of Irish Party casualties in that landmark election. James's father was another.

James returned to Ballaghaderreen to be with his father on polling day. One of the memories which remained with him throughout his life was of his father, standing on the front steps of the house in Ballaghaderreen on the eve of polling day and saying: 'James, the profession of politics I regard as the noblest vocation after the priesthood, but if you do not want anything out of it but votes, get out. Above all, never expect gratitude. I have just yesterday returned the last evicted tenant in this area to his holding, but tomorrow he and many others in this county whom I have helped will vote to end my political career.'[20]

Left with only a handful of parliamentary seats and no role in the emerging political drama, the Irish Party soon spluttered out of existence. There was about the whole episode an air of finality rare in the history of political parties, a finality which John Dillon, ever the realist, accepted, though he was uncomprehending sometimes, and ungracious.

John Dillon's ultimately futile struggle to save the Irish Party had a profound affect on James, who felt deeply for the honour of his father. There is, however, one puzzling aspect about his attitude to Sinn Féin. He had taken to writing verse during his schooldays, and compiled a hand-written volume, most of it political.[21] One poem, meant to be sung to the air of 'The Wearing of the Green', told how his father averted conscription:

For when Johnny Redmond took to flight
Up stepped Dillon the bold
And to the British Government
The plainest truths he told

There were many other verses in similar vein, and altogether sixteen poems. They included a lampoon of Kaiser William ('A savage fighter is the Hun/He ravages the land'); 'Erin's Address to England' written on 29 April 1916 ('To thee I owe a debt of hate/which ne'er can in my soul abate'); an 'Ode to Belgium' ('Oh, grief and sorrow is thy lot/ sad country of destruction') and one to Russia. Other verses dealt with schoolmasters and contemporaries, including an attack on his brother, Shawn: 'A fierce pro-German is old Shaun/And he's ashamed to say it.'

The collection was no more than the effort of many schoolboys at that age, though clearly reflecting James's political interests, but one poem stands out from all the others: 'The Rebels of 1916 AD'.

Like Larkin and O'Brien
Fell McDonagh, Pierse (*sic*) and Clarke
Each courageous as a lion
And happy as a lark

Happy for they felt they fell
For the land that gave them birth
Proud to be able to rebel
And thus to Erin prove their worth

McDermot fell with Plunkett too
Both as gallant as the rest
For each man well and truly knew
That for Erin it was best.

Like his father, James hated Sinn Féin, but no more than his father, he was not blind to the personal nobility and idealism of its leaders.

JAMES REMAINED at Mount St Benedict until the summer of 1919, when he took a grind with an old gentleman called McDonagh at a cramming school in Blackrock to prepare him sit the matriculation exam for university. The cramming obviously worked, and in the autumn of 1919 he went to study commerce at University College, Dublin.

His secondary education may have been unorthodox and lacking in formal structure, but James was widely read, competent in Latin and French, had a good grasp of history and a highly developed sense of public affairs. Much of this he ascribed to the influence of his father rather than to his formal schooling. The house at North Great George's St was stimulating, because of the people who visited it and the personality of his father, who had 'the extraordinary gift, of which he was quite unconscious, of not differentiating between our age and his'. John Dillon's outlook helped broaden his family's horizons, but the relationship had its drawbacks too. There was little intimacy or natural warmth, and John Dillon was quite unaware of the stresses in his teenage sons' lives, 'the last person on earth to whom we would have applied for any advice on the kind of problems adolescents have', in James's words.[22]

There was one further intellectual influence on Dillon at this time: Tom Kettle. Kettle was a romantic, if tortured personality; an economist, nationalist, essayist, poet and Irish Party MP. A friend of John Dillon's, he died in the Battle of the Somme in 1916, his own epitaph written in the trenches just six days before his death.

So here, while the mad guns curse overhead,
And tired men sigh with mud for couch and floor
Know that we fools, now with the foolish dead,
Died not for flag, nor king, nor Emperor,
But for a dream, born in a herdsman's shed,
And for the Secret Scripture of the poor.

Kettle inspired Dillon for the rest of his life. His romanticism, heroism and his constitutional nationalism appealed as much to Dillon when he was eighty as when he was eighteen. Kettle's book of essays, *The Day's Burden*, was never far from his side, while the poet's definition of politics – 'the great human conspiracy against hunger and cold, against loneliness and ignorance ... the foster-mother of the arts ... all that redeems from despair that strange adventure we call human life' – became central to his own beliefs.

In September James started at University College, Dublin, then based at Earlsfort Terrace and 86 St Stephen's Green. He was there to study commerce, a clear indication that he was the one who would inherit the family business. Already the other members of the family had made their choices: Shawn was studying for the priesthood, Myles was on the way to becoming one of the country's leading Celtic scholars, Theo had chosen medicine, and Brian, still at Mount St Benedict, would later read law. James, who had already shown a deep interest in politics, accepted that he should prepare himself for a business career. His decision bore a strong sense of duty: had he had a free choice, he would have chosen medicine. Indeed, it remained his lifelong interest, and he frequently exasperated his brother, Theo, by 'borrowing' his medical textbooks. Business was what his father expected of him, however, and he accepted this course without demur.

The university at this time was small, with no more than a thousand students and all faculties in close proximity to one another. It was an almost entirely nationalist and Catholic college, treated with disdain by its largely Protestant and Unionist neighbour, Trinity College. James had not been accustomed to a disciplined academic life at Mount St Benedict, and this was to change little in the relaxed and undemanding regime which characterised UCD at the time. The commerce faculty had little to recommend it, and Dillon's own memories of it are scathingly dismissive. It was 'grotesque', he later wrote, 'a madhouse'. The senior professor was 'a decent man who had as much capacity for teaching as an acrobat'. Another lecturer used 'to read in a quite inaudible tone out of a book of notes which he had been using for twenty years'. In addition 'there was a very cracked character who was an accountant in Westmoreland Street; he used to teach accountancy and was offensive and monstrous'. Long before the end of his two years at UCD, James was convinced of the uselessness of the courses he was following and never sat for his degree.[23]

Nonetheless, UCD was a time of great experience and discovery for James. A contemporary, the late CS (Todd) Andrews, has left us this vivid description of him as he entered UCD. He was

> the most colourful of our first-year men. As a first-year student he appeared to us a sort of *Stupor Mundi* in his self-assurance, his conversation, and his apparent breadth of knowledge. In his dress he was equally egregious; his wide black hat, an expensive walking stick rather than a cane, rimless glasses and very well cut clothes, gave him a dandified appearance quite different from the rest of us. Unlike the rest of us, too, he had a poor opinion of games, except Bridge, and unlike most of us he was a pacifist and an advocate of law and order. While we were devising a way of prolonging the excitement of the Trinity riot and had decided to demonstrate in the Theatre Royal that same evening, he issued a solemn warning – everything he said was either solemn or portentous – about the dangers of clashing with the police and finding ourselves in jail. He certainly did not lack moral courage, as one might expect from his family tradition … His oratory commanded the admiration one gives to an accomplished actor. As a man he was friendly and decent.[24]

James quickly became a college character and was soon involved in university politics, particularly the debates of the Literary and Historical Society. The L&H was the hub of student activity, attracting four or five hundred spectators to its weekly meetings. Many students were involved in the War of Independence and were later to take sides in the Civil War, and much of the excitement and bitterness of the time spilled into their discussions. The mood in the college was pro-Sinn Féin, and from the start Dillon found himself an increasingly lonely defender of an old, unfashionable order. He shared the role with John Hearne, later ambassador to the USA and legal advisor to de Valera on the 1937 Constitution. The pair became known as 'the last frontiersmen of the Irish Party'.

James's first major speech was made 'amid hostile interruptions, defending the Irish Party, his father's reputation, and the cause of peaceful and constitutional reform'.[25] The theme was more than appropriate: as a student at the old Catholic medical school, his father had been auditor of the L&H in 1870. Outspokenness was one of James's strongest characteristics, and he relished the advocacy of unfashionable and minority causes. Most striking of all was the sheer force of his eloquence. A contemporary wrote that 'it was difficult at times to say, so intimate was the marriage between mind and speech, whether he had a command of language or language a command of him, or whether they had then reached their present perfect harmony'.[26] His eloquence won him several awards, including the society's gold medal in 1920.

He found further scope for his debating skills in the more sedate Commerce Society, and took part in the campaign to elect the Irish language writer and family friend, Una Ní Fairceallaig (who wrote under the name Uan Ulaidh, the lamb of Ulster), to the college's Governing Body; her other supporters included Professor Douglas Hyde, later President of Ireland. A leading Irish Irelander and Irish language pioneer, Una Ní Fairceallaig encouraged James to continue his efforts at learning to speak and write in Irish.[27] He was an enthusiastic supporter of the language, and among many of his friends he was known as Seamus. He joined an Irish language group, 'Gragaire', and made many visits to Gortahork in the Donegal Gaeltacht. He enjoyed céilís in the Mansion House and dances at '86', often dancing through the night and, as was the custom with so many students at the time, finishing up by attending 6 o'clock mass in Clarendon St Church.

In June 1920, James visited Paris and toured some of Europe's battle-fields, climbing to the top of Vimy Ridge to witness the scale of the devastation of the Great War.[28] In the autumn he returned to university, where his diary chronicles a hectic round of activities – Students Council, Commerce Society, L&H, notes of horses worth a bet, frequent meetings with a lady called Miss Dodds and later a Miss Potter. He had many girl-friends with whom he corresponded, his letters courtly, gallant and humorous, stilted and affected by today's standards, underlain with innocence and propriety.[29] He also got involved in the theatre and acted in a number of plays, but declined an invitation from the Arts Club to take to the boards. Cards was also a favourite occupation, and he was a regular at the card schools located in the college basement.

He became Todd Andrews' election agent in the Student Council election and, as Andrews later wrote, 'I was elected by, as Dillon boasted, more votes in the ballot box than there were on the register.'[30] James did not share Andrews' Sinn Féin outlook, but he drew his friends from across the political spectrum. His father wrote, at about this time: 'James is engaging energetically in politics, sometimes rather to my alarm, because he is very outspoken, but astonishingly enough he seems to get on with both sides very well.'[31] It may well have been his very outspokenness, the obvious honesty with which he held and expressed his opinions, which allowed all sides accept his bona fides. Brian McNeill, son of Eoin McNeill, who was later killed fighting on the anti-Treaty side in the Ox Mountains, was a bosom friend. Other friends included Kevin Barry, a medical student who was hanged for his part in an ambush in the city, and Frank Flood. James walked home with Flood the night before he was arrested and subsequently sentenced to death for his IRA activities. Deeply upset, Dillon persuaded his father to intercede with the authorities for Flood's life, but to no avail: he was hanged in Mountjoy.[32]

The one feature absent from Dillon's diary was any reference to lectures, and by June 1921 he was clear that, academically at any rate, UCD had little to offer. He was already involved in the detail of running Monica Duff's and he persuaded his father that he would learn more by studying the rudiments of business outside the country. He may have wanted to see something of the world, or to get away from a political situation which held no role for him; for whatever reason, his father agreed to his request to leave UCD and travel abroad to gain experience.

CHAPTER THREE

THE VIEW FROM AFAR

Collins seems to be in the devil of a mess. If he gets all the troops cleared out the Republican IRA will play hell and if he doesn't the whole IRA will say that Lloyd George has bucked and made a fool of him.
James Dillon to his father, 5 February 1922

OR THE MOST part, James Dillon followed the events of the Civil War from afar. No more than the country at large, it was not a happy time for the Dillon family. The Irish Party no longer existed. As Ireland entered a new era, John Dillon, for so long centre-stage, did not even have a supporting role. There were no longer pronouncements on the issues of the day, the management of an important political party, or attendance at the House of Commons. John Dillon was a lost leader, cheated by history, his attitude to the new politics 'one of fascinated incomprehension, lit now and then by flashes of penetrating insight'.[1] Of his old colleagues, only his arch-rival Tim Healy survived into the political life of the new Irish state. All others, including Dillon, were swept away by an impatient and singularly unappreciative younger generation. He could hardly bring himself to look with favour on those who had undone his life's work.

His brother, Fr Nicholas, maintained an unrelenting hatred of Sinn Féin and what it had done to his family. John Dillon was too much of a political realist to allow his judgement to be distorted by such passions. However, his views over the coming years, confided in particular to his old parliamentary friend TP O'Connor and to James, reveal a gradual swing away from the grudging support he initially gave the new government to one of complete antipathy. He thought the Treaty was 'a very good settlement and, if well handled, could be made the basis of a truly united and free Ireland',[2] and in January 1922 he urged support for the new government. In the subsequent period, as the government began to assert its authority, he felt Collins showed courage and ability in considerable quantities but was lacking in political judgement. The turning point, however, came in December, when the cabinet sanctioned the execution of Rory O'Connor and his three companions. He was outraged. There was, he said, 'no precedent for such a proceeding in the annals of any modern civilised government'.[3]

His dislike of the new regime, especially as it grew more established, may also have had an element of sour grapes, a sense that Sinn Féin had taken his rightful place. Nonetheless, he developed a sneaking respect for de Valera, who was he believed at least consistent, and though Dillon himself opposed the Republic, he criticised Cosgrave for abandoning it.

James Dillon arrived in London in the autumn of 1921 to start his apprenticeship at Selfridges. He was no ordinary emigrant. He had been introduced to Gordon Selfridge by TP O'Connor, he had access to a privileged segment of London society through his grandmother, Lady Mathew, and his father's reputation ensured his recognition in some areas of politics. James Dillon shared and reflected his father's views, and for the next two and a half years he followed events at home with consuming curiosity and interest.

He felt lonely at times, but he was particularly fond of his grandmother, Lady Mathew, a formidable lady of eighty-four who, according to James, was pre-Victorian in her outlook. Lady Mathew's Sunday afternoons 'At Home' were something of an institution, and James attended them regularly. He admits that Lady Mathew was somewhat of a snob, always pleased if Lord Justices of Appeal and Law Lords turned up, or a few members of the peerage. 'Once I ventured to opine,' Dillon recalled, 'when she asked my opinion of a visitor, that he seemed to me to be a bit of a snob. "He can't be a snob, my dear," she replied. "He comes of a very good family."'4

The Mathew family welcomed him. His spinster aunt, Kathleen, was particularly devoted to him, while he found companionship among his cousins, especially Charles, who was then at Trinity College, Oxford, and who invited James there a few times. Another relation, his uncle Charles, was Labour MP for Whitechapel and tipped to be Attorney-General in Ramsay McDonald's government, but died after an operation in January 1923.

James's purpose in London was to learn the wholesale and retail business, and he spent a period in each of Selfridges departments under the supervision of the store's Education Section which, to his chauvinistic surprise, was headed by a woman. He began his training with a stint in Goods In, moving through the Checking Out section to the Letter Order department, then Stocktaking and Accounts, before spending time working at the counters. It was a good, thorough training and he seems to have made a favourable impression on his supervisors. His father, never one to lavish praise, noted in a letter in December 1922 how very glad he was 'to hear you stand so well with the authorities in Selfridges'.5

James's father also took a keen and naive interest in his social activities. When James told his father he intended spending the weekend at Oxford, he was warned of the incipient dangers: 'I trust you will not join in any of the revels which I hear go on … your only safety is to plead tee-totalism.'[6] Nor was his father the only source of advice. His old nurse, Lia, bombarded him with her counsels. Now that he was earning £1 a week, 'please God you will be wise … spend it carefully … learn not to become extravagant.'[7]

No longer a member of parliament, John Dillon now had few reasons to visit London, and James only remembers one such visit during his time there, though there may have been more. His father brought him to the House of Commons for lunch, along with TP O'Connor, who was still MP for Liverpool, and Samuel Insull of Chicago, later a controversial figure in US politics, who became a good friend to James when he went to Chicago the following year. James remembered two stories in particular from the lunch:

> There was a Greek gentleman at the luncheon who was an agent for the arms dealer Sir Basil Zaharoff. The talk turned to the incorruptibility of the members of the Irish Party, on which my father and TP expatiated for a while. Then the Greek gentleman interposed, 'Well they aren't all incorruptible!' My father was most indignant and challenged him on that. The Greek declared that he could name at least one that he had bribed himself and, on being pressed, did so. Father and TP thought that over.
>
> 'By God,' said father, 'it's true that X did not turn up for that division.' 'Well,' said the Greek, 'that is why he didn't.'[8]

The men also talked about Parnell.

> I recall another conversation between father and TP concerning how Parnell had degenerated in his personal habits in his last years. Father alluded to how he let his beard grow, neglecting to trim it. 'Beard is it?' said TP in his broad Athlone accent, 'Sure, you couldn't stay in the room with him by the end of it. The man smelled! I do not believe he had a bath above once a year.'
>
> Father looked at TP in embarrassment and said, 'Did you notice that too, TP?' It was not the sort of thing that Father would normally have alluded to, but it seems that it was noticeable. Whether or not Mrs. O'Shea noticed it is not recorded.[9]

From his arrival in London, James visited the House of Commons at every possible opportunity. He looked in on some of the major debates and met up from time to time with survivors of the Irish Party, including Willie Redmond, Joe Devlin and Tom Harrison. His opinion of the calibre of the Irish Party's members was not high, and he was particularly censorious of their excessive drinking: 'the sooner this remnant of the party ceases to exist the better it will be for the reputation of the Irish Party as it was'.[10] Visiting the Commons brought him near to the heart of politics. On one such occasion, he recounted in a letter on 9 January 1921, just as the Dáil was ratifying the Treaty, 'Wiltshire [a waiter] of the House of Commons dining room has just told us that [Lloyd] George, Birkenhead, Churchill and Greenwood had dinner in a private room, and that he himself attended them. They agreed in his own hearing to inform Collins and Griffith when they came over that the whole negotiations were over and that an expeditionary force will be despatched immediately to Ireland to put the whole thing down. He swears that he heard them arrange that, and he was quite sober.'[11]

The Treaty was narrowly ratified by the Dáil in January 1922, but Sinn Féin then split into pro- and anti-Treaty factions. From London, James followed events with compulsive interest. His views were strongly felt but not always consistent, and there was about them a sense of displacement and resentment, with little that was positive to say. In January he predicted a rough passage for the Treaty, which he described as 'never a very seaworthy vessel', and said it would be rejected 'by 9 or 10 votes' in the Dáil. He was wrong, of course. 'I am alarmed to find that my exile tends to drive me towards extreme views, possibly it is really my loathing for Griffith and Collins, who are now the spokesmen for moderation. I think Valera (*sic*) acquitted himself better than Griffith by a long way in their struggle.' But his admiration for de Valera did not last long: 'he has undoubtedly made an unholy fool of himself in even producing Document No. 2 ... when he had survived that I thought he would win altogether.'[12] After the assassination of Sir Henry Wilson in London, he wrote home about 'the great anger in the tubes and buses', and noted with distaste 'Cockneys exulting in the Irish Civil War'. And on 7 July 1922, after Cathal Brugha had died in a hail of gunfire rather than surrender, he wrote: 'I must say that mad as poor Cathal Brugha's last stand was, it stands out as the bravest thing that was done during the whole thing.'[13]

Following the outbreak of the Civil War the situation in Ballaghaderreen soon began to give cause for concern. In July, John Dillon wrote of 'depredations' being wrought in the area by the Republicans, 'conscripting men and threatening to shoot anyone who deserts the colours'. He told James that 'all the shops in town have been mercilessly plundered ... The Republicans are everywhere living on the country without paying for anything.'[14]

James followed the Civil War from his weekly copy of the *Roscommon Herald*, noting with anxiety the burnings in Ballymote and Colloney and hearing from Bob Partridge, a senior manager at Monica Duff's, of the raid on the Post Office at Duff's and the burning of Kilfree railway station. Myles and Brian had been sent to Ballaghaderreen to try to control the situation, and James took comfort in the belief that his college friend Brian

McNeill, one of the Republican leaders in the area, would see that the house remained intact.[15] In late July, while visiting Mrs John Redmond in her London apartment, he read the news of the evacuation of Ballaghaderreen. James attributed the survival of the Dillon home to McNeill. Shortly afterwards, Free State troops commandeered the house and occupied it until late 1923.

For the future inheritor of the business this was ominous news. The house incurred substantial damage; nails were hammered into the mantelpiece and bullets fired through the ceiling. When the question of compensation arose, 'Honest' John Dillon found himself a victim of his own scruples. He had the damage professionally assessed and a figure of £4,000 was arrived at. The county judge in Boyle, however, worked on the assumption that all claims were grossly inflated, and promptly divided the Dillon claim by half.[16]

The Dillon family was not monolithic in its hostility to the Free State. James was astonished at Shawn's enthusiasm, something he found incomprehensible – Shawn confidently predicted to him that 'by the time you resume residence in Ireland our Parliament will be in full swing'.[17] James was outraged by Shawn's 'extremely immoral' defence of the Free State, but in some ways Shawn's political judgement was sharper than his brother's. He wrote to James in September 1923 that the government should drop the Oath of Allegiance, and by doing so weaken the Republican cause. He saw that the Boundary Commission would end as a fiasco, and added the sardonic observation: 'it amuses me to see all the old frauds turning up amongst the Republicans; obviously the Free State had not enough jobs to go around.'[18]

John Dillon, for his part, could sometimes be magnanimous. When James wrote criticising his old enemy, Tim Healy, for accepting the role of Governor General of the new state, his father's reply surprised him: 'I do not agree with your view. He was always a very brave man, physically and morally. And I am sure he is delighted with himself ... for he loves being in the limelight ... and he has no political judgement. He is, of course not responsible for the executions.'[19]

AFTER A year at Selfridges, John Dillon began to think of the next step in his son's training. Early on, James had decided that this should be in the USA, and on his father's suggestion he opted for Chicago rather than New York. He left Selfridges at the end of 1922 and on 2 February 1923 set sail from Liverpool for New York on the SS *Celtic*, his departure, according to Theo, 'accompanied by much sound and fury'.[20] He brought with him introductions from Gordon Selfridge and his father's advice to 'stick closely to your work for over a year and return a fully qualified businessman'.[21]

He spent the next year and a half in the US. After a short stay in New York he worked in two of Chicago's leading department stores, The Fair and Marshall Fields. He was unhappy at The Fair. The boss, DF Kelly, was 'a cold hard businessman', James recorded in his diary, 'dedicated to the dollar'.[22] He was angry at the treatment of the workers 'in this slave-driving city', and the 'inhumanity, exploitation, and injustice in pursuit of the dollar'. One incident remained with him all his life. It concerned Pat Behan, an old floor-sweeper who had been loudly and violently abused by the personnel manager, 'a very offensive person from somewhere South of the Mason-Dixon line'. Dillon could not understand why Behan had taken this in silence.

'I went over to Pat in a rage and said, "Good God, Pat, why didn't you hit him with the broom?" Pat looked at me. "Well," he said, "if I did that, I'd be out of a job, and I'd have the choice of going down to the poor-farm, or sitting down on the kerb-stone and die of starvation."'[23]

The experience gave Dillon an insight into the conditions of labour in the US, but also hinted at how little he understood the insecurity of a working man in a hard age. Remarkably, Dillon learned later that Pat Behan's father had pulled an oar on the boat that brought his grandfather, John Blake Dillon, to the Aran Islands when he was 'on the run' after the 1848 rebellion.

James stayed four months at The Fair, leaving 'this dirty, cruel place'[24] in July to spend the best part of a year in the more congenial surroundings of Marshall Fields, where he divided his time between the main areas of retailing and store management.

All the while he experienced at first hand aspects of Irish-American politics, an arena familiar both to his father and grandfather in their time. Because he was his father's son, he found himself something of a celebrity when he arrived in New York, where he was taken under the wing of James McGurrin, an old family friend and a powerful figure in Irish-American politics in the city. McGurrin introduced him to some of the New York's leading Irish-American figures. He was invited to address a dinner at the Astor Hotel, attended by a hundred or so of the most powerful Irish-American politicians at a time when the Irish were the most powerful political group in New York. For a twenty year old, this was daunting stuff, made worse by the fact that James suffered a bad nosebleed shortly before his speech. We have no record of what he said, his diary only records 'having got through' the evening, but if other entries of this time are any guide, he was unlikely to have been very supportive of the new Free State.

Dillon spent considerable time with two of the dominant figures in Irish-American politics, the old Fenian John Devoy and Judge Daniel Cohalan.

Devoy's overwhelming passion, Dillon found, was his great hatred of de Valera and what amounted to an obsession with the circumstances of de Valera's birth. Devoy was also bitterly critical of what he said was de Valera's bungling of a plan to have him speak on the floor of the US Senate. Dillon's diary records Devoy as a great talker with a memory as clear as if he were thirty rather than eighty years of age.[25] Cohalan he found interesting and able, 'very fond of having his own way, with a passion for having the best of an argument'. Cohalan, he felt, was dominated by an unreasoning 'cold passion of anti-Britishism'. After a later meeting he noted that Cohalan's 'desire for the destruction of the British Empire is a much stronger incentive in his public life than his longing for Ireland's freedom'. With the lofty condescension of a twenty year old, he concluded that the judge's 'fanatical hatred of the British Empire' was an interesting study, but 'quite unworthy of as intellectual a man as Cohalan'.[26]

These meetings were also a learning experience for Dillon, however. He found very quickly that his dismissive attitude to the Free State did not find easy acceptance amongst these men, who had taken the trouble to find out about conditions there for themselves. Cohalan spent time in Ireland in the summer of 1923 as part of a tour of Europe, and in a letter to Dillon he put Ireland into a wider European perspective:

> She has become again a European country so that she is affected by the spirit of general unrest which has swept over all of that continent … With all of this I am satisfied that Ireland has turned the corner and is on the road to peace, prosperity and economic growth. I was well impressed in the main by the men whom I met in responsible positions, and I think they have done very well in face of the difficulties which confronted them.[27]

Cohalan spoke well of WT Cosgrave, as did another senior Irish-American, Lindsay Crawford, who ran the Irish Trade Commission in America. He had been a supporter of the Irish Party, but told Dillon that 'unlike you, I have confidence in the sound common sense of the Irish people … and in Cosgrave's ability and judgement. He has revealed qualities of leadership which have astonished those who knew him best.'[28] How much James took from these words we do not know, but it was important for him to be told that the Free State was now established and, however he might regret it, there could be no going back to an old order.

Life, however, was not all work and politics. Like all young men, he fell in and out of love. He confided to his diary in March about the delights of being in love, but added there was little he could do to pursue his claims since 'the object of my adoration is affianced to another man'. He had no shortage of lady friends, but there is no evidence of any sustained relationship nor evidence that he sought such, with one intriguing exception. His brother, Theo, wrote to his father in November 1923 about James's 'love affair'. 'Is she rich? It seems to me that he couldn't do better than to marry and settle down in America. Ireland is too small for his personality.'[29] At this period, James's diary tells us that he was at times lonely and had pangs of doubt about his American experience: 'profoundly depressed tonight thinking that this whole adventure is insane, and that the occupation I have chosen for my life is about as suitable as it is romantic'. And he experienced the humiliation of being put down by a too-clever contemporary, Farrar, a twenty-six-year-old Yale graduate and editor of *The Bookman*. Farrar, according to James's diary, was 'unquestionably the most remarkable person I have ever met', but he was so 'unpardonably patronising' that James felt humiliated, and then angry at his own 'ridiculous jealousy'. He vowed to overcome it, and in time Farrar and he became quite reasonable friends.[30]

He attended parties with socialites and film stars, and met Jack Johnson, the boxer, 'a more loathsome sight it has never been my misfortune to see'. Most of all he indulged his passion for opera, attending Carnegie Hall and the Metropolitan Opera House while in New York, and going to every major performance in Chicago, noting in his diary after seeing *La Bohème*, 'nothing can describe the exhilaration of having heard the opera; it wipes out all the sordidness, meanness and dirt of The Fair.'[31]

His move to Chicago brought him in touch with the other branch of the Dillon family. His cousin Bill, son of John Dillon's eldest brother, William, was head of the prosperous law firm of Concannon Dillon. There James enjoyed the utmost hospitality. His family, and the friendship of TP O'Connor's old friend, Sam Insull, gave him an entrée to the social life of Chicago, then 'still quite an intimate city'.[32] He also spent time in Colorado on his uncle William's ranch, where his cousin, Richard, taught him to ride. His uncle was well-connected politically, being on friendly terms with Robert Lincoln, son of the late Abraham Lincoln, and acquainted with President WH Taft. William retained a vivid, if slightly eccentric interest in Irish politics, and was thought of as the most accomplished classicist in Colorado. James recounts that in his later years his only reading consisted of the *Odes of Horace* and the *Saturday Evening Post*. When he was knocked down by a car as he crossed the road translating one of the poet's odes, he forfeited what might have been a substantial claim for damages by admitting to the ambulance men, 'I am entirely at fault. I was translating an *Ode of Horace*, and failed to look where I was going.'[33]

By the summer of 1924, James had begun to feel that he had learned as much as he was going to usefully learn of business, and decided to return home. During his absence, Shawn had been ordained, Nano had become engaged, and Theo had shown symptoms of the TB which was to lead to his early death. He had been away for two and a half years.

He frequently recalled in later life the strange but not uncharacteristic welcome he received at North Great George's St: 'If one did not know my father one might have been dismayed at the welcome I received. I arrived to North Great George's Street, let myself in, and found him in his study reading the paper. He lowered the paper. "Ah," he said, "you're back." Then he raised the paper. But he was pleased to see me in his way.'[34]

CHAPTER FOUR

INTO POLITICS

Remember of what blood thou art and (so far as in you lies) strike Sinn Féinery down.

Fr Nicholas to James Dillon, November 1931

W HEN JAMES DILLON returned to Ballaghaderreen in late 1924 the Free State was beginning to find its feet. The Civil War was over and most prisoners had been released. De Valera was at his lowest point politically, with Sinn Féin demoralised and the foundation of Fianna Fáil still two years away. The political climate was turbulent and violence never far beneath the surface, and the government, still establishing its authority, found itself obliged to make a series of harsh decisions over a range of areas, few of which helped win it popularity.

Neither James nor his father were inclined to give the new regime much credit. James was delighted to read of a series of resignations from the Dáil, including that of Cumann na nGaedheal's Minister for Industry and Commerce, Joe McGrath, following an unsuccessful attempt at a mutiny by a small group of officers in 1924 and by the subsequent attempt to challenge the government in a series of by-elections. 'It makes the paper worth reading for the first time in a long time,' he told his father.[1] His brother, Theo, who was convalescing in Switzerland, had begun to move in a different direction: 'I don't think ever in the history of our country has any group of men ever fallen so low, mentally, morally and in every other way as the Republican Party. If I were in Ireland I believe I would almost become a Free Stater.'[2]

For the Dillons, however, politics was something of a luxury just then. A more immediate and pressing problem was the business at Ballaghaderreen, which was in serious financial trouble. The outgoings from Monica Duff's had been substantial during John Dillon's years at Westminster. The business had sustained and funded his political career and educated his family at a time when MPs were not paid a salary, a burden Mrs Deane had accepted during her lifetime and which continued when John Dillon inherited Monica Duff's on her death. In spite of the appearance of prosperity, the underlying financial realities had been distorted in the boom of the post-war years, but now there were problems. The accounts for the period have not survived but it is clear from John Dillon's correspondence that he believed Monica Duff's was heading for bankruptcy. The task of putting the business on a firm footing fell to James.[3]

Monica Duff's was almost one hundred years in existence and had become something of an institution in the West of Ireland in that time. Conditions for the workers were strict and discipline firm, even if things had mellowed somewhat from the code which ruled in the last days of the old century. We have a written account of Monica Duff's from Bill O'Dowd, who served his time in the shop in the early 1920s. Conditions were good by the standards of the day. The food was wholesome – 'four meals a day and the produce came from their own farm' – and unlike some other business 'there was no interference with staff regarding religion or political beliefs, and all were free to join the union if they wished'.

'It was the aim of most boys and girls in Ballaghaderreen to work in Duff's,' O'Dowd said. 'Very few left or were sacked and they were the envy of all other assistants in the town. Hours were 8.30 a.m. to 6 p.m. and there would be 35 to 40 sales staff working there at any given time.'

O'Dowd remembers James working in all departments, and he recalled: 'There was great trust and honesty in the firm. Credit was given freely, and pass books were very much in evidence.'[4]

Relations between employers and workers in Ballaghaderreen, however, were about to take a turn for the worse. James returned to find that his father and the owners of the town's other main businesses – Flannery's, Beirne's and Gordon's – had come to the conclusion that 'the disastrous slump of the past two years' threatened financial ruin unless significant savings were made.[5] The area identified for savings was staff wages, and in late 1924 the employers told their workers that from the beginning of 1925 the agreement they had made with the union in 1920 would be altered and wages reduced, by thirteen per cent in some cases and forty per cent in others. The employers justified their decision on the basis of the low levels of business and the fact that the rates of pay in Ballaghaderreen were above the national average.[6]

Not surprisingly, the workers called in the Irish Union of Distributive Workers and Clerks, which objected to the absence of consultation and to the fact that the proposed wage cuts would fall disproportionately on the most junior assistants. In January 1925, union organiser J. Hunt asked for the cuts to be postponed for six months in the hope of finding a satisfactory compromise. Possibly believing that the workers had no stomach for a strike, the employers rejected this proposal. On 16 January 1925 the union served notice of a strike in Flannery's. The employers answered that a strike at one shop would lead to the closure of all.

When picketing began at Flannery's on 23 January, the employers closed their businesses and sent their staffs home. Three weeks later they changed their tactics and, with heavily depleted staff, re-opened for business. Pickets were strengthened in response and tension increased, though as the *Roscommon Herald* noted on 28 February, the pickets were largely ignored by the substantial numbers of country people who now rushed to buy supplies and were allowed do so without interference from the striking workers. Matters continued to deteriorate, however, and attitudes harden. The pickets became noisy and abusive. Public meetings were held and propaganda leaflets issued. James Dillon was accused of being self-opinion-ated, of being putty in the hands of Doyle, the owner of Flannery's, and of trying to impose 'London and Chicago methods' in Ballaghaderreen. He had new spectacles, and one leaflet proclaimed that 'It was not the efforts of men whose faces are disfigured with tortoise-shell glasses that built up the gigantic business of Duff and company; men of this type will, however, quickly dissipate it.'[7] Trouble came to a head in April when picketers were charged with breaching the peace; they were acquitted after giving under-takings not to break the law in future.[8]

The strike dragged on through most of 1925 and ended in defeat for the workers, most of whom returned in dribs and drabs throughout the year. Surprisingly, the episode left little permanent bitterness in Ballaghaderreen. There can be few doubts that the employers behaved in a high-handed way and made no effort to resolve the matter through conciliation, while all the available evidence suggests that the union was prepared to compromise. James Dillon and his father had a deep-seated antipathy to the union, however, and a tendency to see dangerous left-wing tendencies where none existed. The union organiser, Hunt, was a moderate and sensible man who desperately wanted to reach an agreement, yet the employers saw him as some sort of Bolshevik, a modern-day Trotsky sent to subvert the established order of Ballaghaderreen.

John Dillon saw the strike as part of the general demoralisation of the past six years, and the union – all unions – as being in the vanguard of a worldwide socialist conspiracy under Bolshevik control. His total opposi-tion to socialism had, as FSL Lyons noted, 'a doctrinal cast interesting from one who so often in his career had been at odds with orthodoxy'.[9] James undoubtedly shared this hatred of socialism, or as he would say, 'doctrin-aire socialism'. It became a fixed point in his thinking: he saw socialism as incompatible with freedom, and understood the strike in similar terms. His misreading of the situation, which was a reasonable reaction by employees faced with wage cuts imposed in a peremptory manner, is reflected in a letter he wrote to Bishop Morrisroe in June 1925 when the bishop sought to intervene in the conflict: 'The truth is that this present dispute is no ordinary strike ... but part of a deliberately organised plan to take control and management of our business completely out of our hands, and hand that control over to the union.'[10]

With the petering out of the strike, life in Ballaghaderreen returned to normal. James set about reorganising the running of the shop, introducing changes in the stock control systems and the drapery department, and modifying the accounting practices. He contracted out the firm's laundry and assured his anxious father that Duff's reputation for providing the 'best tea in the West' would be maintained. He also turned his attention to matters which had not been covered in London or Chicago: running the farm, buying and selling pigs, cattle and sheep, reorganising the piggery and, to his great delight, discovered a highly successful specific for liver fluke.

An analysis of surviving business accounts from the late 1920s to the end of the 1940s paints a picture of a business run efficiently along conservative lines. There were steady profits, but no great highs or lows; the financing of the business was sound, with consistent use of bank overdrafts. The farm yielded a modest income, and James had plans to build up a pedigree herd, but like farming in general it had its ups and downs. The Dillon investment portfolio, again of modest proportions, was traded with the usual mixture of success and failure. There was no evidence of any serious loss on investments during the 1929 economic crisis or later.[11]

But the business, once it was stabilised and well managed, could only absorb so much of Dillon's energy. More and more, politics claimed his interest. He read almost all current political publications, noting in late 1924 how the IRA was organising 'with members being signed up every night', and urged his father to keep him abreast of political happenings in Dublin.[12]

John Dillon regularly came down to spend the weekend with him. If his political advice to his son was sometimes astute, his unworldliness could on occasion be carried to extremes:

> One evening, in tones of awe, he said to me, 'James, is it true that you are married?' I said to him, 'What do you mean?' 'Well,' he said, 'the last time I was down here you weren't here, and a young woman came in and asked to see me, and when she came in, she told me that you had married her in this room; and had got the Bishop to conduct the ceremony.' 'In the name of God,' I said to him, 'what are you talking about?' 'Well, her name is —. She's the daughter of Pat —.' She was a girl who had been in the lunatic asylum in Ballinasloe, and everyone belonging to her was in the lunatic asylum, and she must have been out on holiday when she rambled into father. 'Why in the name of God,' I said, 'would I get married in this room to Pat —'s daughter?' But the main thing that shocked him was that a son of his aged twenty-three would even contemplate matrimony.[13]

In September 1926, the National League Party was founded by Captain Willie Redmond in an attempt to bring the remnants of the Irish Party into Free State politics and break the Civil War mould in which they had been cast. Dillon, who also saw the need for a new, non-Republican party, sent his good wishes to the movement's founders. At one level the party was the first he could contemplate joining, but he was sceptical of the National League's chances of success. He thought its manifesto was 'insipid' and that 'it had no one to lead it; it would have a great chance if there was such a man forthcoming'. He saw other problems too, not least being the 'universal hostility among the priests. It's support the Government or away with you, as far as they are concerned.'[14]

A month after the National League was formed Dillon was approached to stand. Whether because he felt himself too young (he was just twenty-four), or had such little confidence in the party and its leadership, he turned down the offer, 'as gracefully as I could'.[15]

As a publican (albeit a reluctant one) he was affected like other publicans by Kevin O'Higgin's draconian Intoxicating Liquor Bill of 1927, which excited violent opposition from the vintners. The National League seized upon the issue to attack the government, but Dillon decided on his father's advice not to join in the protest, though he noted that Redmond had done well as a result – indeed it gave the National League much of its early momentum.[16]

Pressure to become involved, either as a candidate or as a supporter, intensified as a general election drew nearer, but in March 1927 he told his father that 'nothing could induce me to stand for any constituency at present'.[17] He did, however, agree to support the party, and in the June election campaigned actively for Daniel McMenamin in Donegal and for other National League candidates in Mayo and Clare. Although he was still a political neophyte, his presence in the campaign was noted. Patrick McGilligan, the sharpest wit in the Free State government, paid him the tribute of a full-frontal assault at a Cumann na nGaedheal rally in Donegal. He pointed out that 'Mr Séamus Dillon' (as he was referred to in all newspaper reports) had attacked McGilligan's Shannon Scheme and 'condemned the Government for seeking expert teaching from the Germans in matters they could not learn at home'. However, said McGilligan, the same Mr Dillon had 'gone to Selfridges in London to learn his own business on the same principle, but even that great house could not supply brains, with the result that Mr Dillon could not understand the simple financial position of the Free State when he came home.'[18]

It was harmless enough, but the very fact of the attack indicated that Dillon had made his presence felt. Another organisation which was to play an important part in his life now began to show its interest in him. The

Ancient Order of Hibernians, which had long associations with the Irish Party and was particularly strong in the border counties, invited him to speak at an AOH demonstration on 15 August. On his father's advice he politely declined, but in a way which left open the possibility of the offer being repeated in the future.[19] He was also beginning what would become a life-long friendship with the most influential and effective of the Hibernians, John D. Nugent, a former Irish Party MP now working for the National League in Donegal.

The National League, whose campaign was more vehement in its opposition to the Cosgrave government than to de Valera's party, did surprisingly well in the election, winning eight seats, including McMenamin's in Donegal. In the Dáil, the National League went into opposition, but with Fianna Fáil still absent Cosgrave was comfortably re-elected as head of government and began his second term as President of the Executive Council. Shortly after this, however, came the assassination of Kevin O'Higgins, followed by the enacting of the Electoral Amendment Bill to force Fianna Fáil into the Dáil or out of politics. As the Oath became an 'empty formality', Fianna Fáil – to its own great, if private, relief – entered Dáil Éireann for the first time. Cosgrave's government was now in a minority in a parliament dominated by Fianna Fáil, the National League, a large Labour Party, eleven farmers and twenty Independents.

Discussions began with the intention of establishing a Labour–National League government supported by Fianna Fáil, with the Labour leader, Thomas Johnson, as President and Redmond taking the Department of External Affairs. Such a government was unlikely to prove stable, however. Indeed, the very fact that Redmond was prepared to enter government with a Labour Party whose policies were at such variance with his own, and seek support from the more radical of the Sinn Féin parties, seemed to underline Dillon's initial doubts about his judgement. In the event, the proposed political coalition never came about due to the defection of one National League member (Vincent Rice) and the celebrated absence of another (Alderman John Jinks of Sligo) during the vital Dáil vote.

Following this débâcle, and after some by-election successes, Cosgrave called a general election for September 1927. The credibility of the National League had been severely dented and it now won only two seats, those of Redmond in Waterford and James Coburn in Louth.[20] That was the effective end of the party, though it did not formally dissolve until 1931. Cosgrave was re-elected to form his last administration. Fianna Fáil was now an increasingly hungry opposition.

Thomas O'Donnell, Secretary of the National League, wrote to Dillon on 19 October and again on the 25th, assuring him that 'it was the National League which had forced Fianna Fáil into the Dáil and buried the

gun as a force in Irish politics forever'. He sought to justify the party's decision to seek office with Labour. There was no question that the alliance
would 'hand the country over to the Bolshies'; what they wanted was a government which would bring peace, in place of a government intent on
'debasing and enslaving our minds'.[21]

Despite the intense political excitement of those months, James had
taken no part in the September election. The summer was a time of great
personal sadness for him and his family. For much of the previous year
John Dillon had been seriously unwell, and after consulting one of the
leading authorities on gallbladder trouble, he went to London in August
for an operation. It was not a success and John Dillon died, it is believed, of
post-operative shock, on 4 August 1927, at the age of seventy-six.[22] James,
Brian and Nano were with him in Lady Carnarvon's home in Portland
Place when he died, and returned with the body to Dublin's Gardiner St
Church. Dillon was buried alongside his wife in Glasnevin cemetery.

If confirmation were needed of the extent to which John Dillon had
become a marginal figure in Irish politics, it can be found in the newspaper
coverage of his death. Even allowing for the atmosphere of fevered political
activity following the death of Kevin O'Higgins, and as Fianna Fáil
debated whether or not to enter the Dáil, press reports of his life and death
were slight to the point of being perfunctory. Tributes were sparse, and
there was no official tribute whatsoever. There was little generosity in the
attitude of the new generation of politicians towards the leader of the old.
However, even though his family had asked for the funeral to be strictly
private, many of John Dillon's surviving colleagues from the House of
Commons turned up, as did President Cosgrave's aide-de-camp, the leader
of the opposition, Eamon de Valera, the Ceann Comhairle, Michael Hayes,
and the Chief Justice, Hugh Kennedy.[23]

John Dillon's death was a great blow to James. Though their relationship
had been heavily formal, they had grown closer in the past few years,
especially since his father had come to depend more and more on him in
matters of business. John Dillon's letters, especially to TP O'Connor, show
the confidence he had in James's business competence, while their personal
correspondence reveals how closely father and son saw eye-to-eye on
contemporary events and personalities.

There is no direct evidence that John Dillon wanted James to enter politics, but it is clear that the question did exercise his attention. He hated the
new regime to such a degree he confided to TP O'Connor in June 1925
that if he were thirty years younger he 'would be getting ready to take the
field'.[24] It is unlikely that he would not have wanted his son to enter
politics; though his advice had been to say 'no' to the National League and
AOH, this was on the grounds of tactics and timing rather than principle.

In the autumn James decided to study for the Bar, and travelled to Dublin each week, staying in North Great George's St with his brother Myles, then a lecturer in Trinity. He was called to the Bar in 1931. He became auditor of the Bar Debating Society, of which his grandfather John Blake Dillon had been a founder. His inaugural address to the society in December 1930 was a scathing attack on housing conditions in Dublin, conditions he could see every day in the inner-city neighbourhood of North Great George's St. He presented a well-researched paper which advocated spending £7 million on clearing the slums and relocating thousands of slum-dwellers to satellite towns. He recognised that this would involve substantial extra taxation, which he saw 'not just a duty but a wise investment, for in addition to the economies that will be possible on the public health and similar accounts, the city of Dublin will stand forth as one of the very few in Europe in which no slums exist, while the increased revenue derived from rates on the properly developed sites of erstwhile slums will materially help to compensate for any losses on the new accommodation.'[25] He delivered his speech, according to one contemporary account, in 'sonorous, reverberating, re-echoing tones', and led both the Chief Justice, Hugh Kennedy, and Justice George Gavan Duffy to write him very complimentary notes.[26] Gavan Duffy told him that the 'only thing wrong with your inaugural was the audience, which was much too comfortable and prosperous to care about those who are not'.[27] An internal memo in the Department of the President also noted the speech, and dismissed the proposal as 'too fatuous to merit any attention, but file, so it can be turned up if the President ever desires to refer to it'.[28]

The enthusiasm he had had for the Irish language and the revival movement in his UCD days a decade earlier was not much in evidence now. It may be that its association with the new 'official' Ireland, and the introduction of compulsory Irish in schools and as a prerequisite for all public appointments, had led to disillusionment. Certainly his hatred of compulsory Irish and the identification of the language with a narrow kill-joy philosophy was to be a consistent theme of his political life. He showed considerable interest in local history, and in February 1931 was appointed local secretary of the Royal Society of Antiquaries of Ireland in North Mayo.[29]

While reading for the Bar he began his lifelong friendship with Peter Nugent, the son of John D. Nugent, National Secretary of the AOH. Peter was to remain James Dillon's closest friend, but their relationship was also to have important political implications. Dividing his time between the business and his legal studies, James also wondered whether or not he should consider seeking a career in politics. He became active throughout the west of Ireland as a leading supporter of the Farmers and Ratepayers

Association, which campaigned for the prudent and more efficient use of public monies and promised to contest the next local elections on the issue. The question of a political home engaged the whole family and in particular James's uncles, Fr Nicholas and William. Together they looked at his options: to throw in his lot with Redmond's National League, join one of the Sinn Féin parties, or run as an Independent. All three choices were considered.

The National League option was easily dismissed: James had little respect for Redmond, dating back to his experiences of him during his time in London. In any event, in 1931 the party's two TDs, Willie Redmond and George Coburn of Louth, joined Cumann na nGaedheal, against whom Redmond had campaigned with such passion just four years earlier. Fr Nicholas was characteristically scathing about his behaviour when he wrote to James in November 1931: 'Of course it wasn't hard to guess Redmond's line of action so far as concerns himself ... I rejoice at the prospect of your now having the opportunity of definitely and absolutely separating yourself from Redmond and his League ... he has likely arranged for himself to get a place in the murder arson Ministry. For the future I hope to see you ploughing a lonely furrow.'[30]

Curiously, the Sinn Féin option was not dismissed out of hand. James Dillon would have been a valuable acquisition for either Cumann na nGaedheal or Fianna Fáil. With the demise of the National League, Cumann na nGaedheal was becoming the natural party for members of the Irish Party reluctant to embrace Fianna Fáil's increasingly strident nationalism. Yet de Valera had always shown great respect for John Dillon; the two men had met on several occasions, once when de Valera had apparently intended asking Dillon to intervene in London after the Treaty negotiations, to see if the Oath of Allegiance could be removed. John Dillon himself had preferred de Valera to Cosgrave. For Fianna Fáil, desperately in search of respectability, James Dillon would have been a great catch.

Overtures were made by both parties, and in the end both were rejected. A letter from Fr Nicholas in December 1931 refers to James's decision not to accept an invitation, apparently issued by Cosgrave, to stand for Cumann na nGaedheal, and praised him for his determination to keep the matter private.[31] He had also been approached by Fianna Fáil as early as 1929, and had met with de Valera and Sean T. O'Kelly in O'Kelly's house in Anglesea Rd. Their meeting was 'most amicable', but 'I told them that I had no intention of joining any party that was a section of Sinn Féin ... and we parted on that understanding.'[32]

That, however, was not the full story. He had clearly given some thought to the Cosgrave invitation and had put the proposition to his uncle William in Colorado. William had adjudged Cosgrave's visit to the USA in

1928 to be a 'decided success', and on that occasion had written to James that he felt it was in the best interests of the Irish people that his government should continue in office.[33] In December 1931 he wrote that he felt Fr Nicholas's extreme position was politically unrealistic: 'The issue in Ireland is now between Cosgrave or some man of his way of thinking, or of de Valera. If de Valera wins the coming election it will mean not only practical ruin for Ireland for a considerable time to come, but a gross breach of faith in the repudiation of a solemn Treaty.'[34]

In the event, Fr Nicholas's advice won the day. In June 1931 he had told James that his 'vocation was to contest Donegal' in vindication of his father's memory, though the prospect he held out was less than enthusiastic: 'you are the only member of his family destined to dabble in the stinking waters of Irish politics'.[35] He developed this theme further in November: 'the word and actions of your father in face of the infernal Sinn Féin business give you a magnificent chance to strike a blow for God's truth and for Ireland. Remember of what blood thou art and (so far as in you lies) strike Sinn Féinery down.'[36] And in January 1932, just weeks before the election, he warned against the advice being proffered by William: 'Your father's idea: the domination of sniper Cosgrave and company is a necessary evil which must go on for a time until the people kick them out ... your father never hinted at the possibility of any decent man associating himself politically with such a crew.'[37]

The approach to run in Donegal had come from John D. Nugent of the AOH, who said he was in search of a candidate to represent the nationalist tradition, which was still strong in the county. Nugent was a first-class political organiser who had at his disposal the resources of the AOH, and he told James that if he agreed to run he would undertake to take care of the organisation. Having agonised as to whether or not he should enter politics, he was unlikely to get a better offer. Here he could run as an Independent, be sure of strong traditional support and need have no truck with either of the Sinn Féin parties. He had no difficulty in accepting the patronage of the AOH, which had strong traditional ties with the Irish Party: it was an organisation with which he was to be intimately, if for the most part titularly, associated for the remainder of his political life. The fact that he had only visited Donegal to learn Irish and while working for Daniel McMenamin in 1927 did not deter him at all, and was seen as no obstacle by his new supporters.

Donegal in 1932 had eight Dáil seats. Over the previous decade Cumann na nGaedheal had generally won three or four of these, Fianna Fáil usually two or three, with Major Myles, who represented the Protestant/Unionist interest, holding a safe seat. The constituency had also returned Daniel McMenamin as a National League TD between June and September 1927, when it had elected a Labour member and a Farmers' candidate. Now, in 1932, Cumann na nGaedheal had attracted the Farmers' TD to its ranks and, making a strong bid for support from members of the AOH and the Irish Party, put McMenamin forward as its candidate. His selection had the approval of Major Myles, who urged his supporters to continue their preferences for Cumann na nGaedheal.

Dillon was nominated by acclamation on 24 January 1932 in the AOH Hall in Stranorlar as an Independent Nationalist candidate.[38] His election address touched on many themes which were to become familiar. He called for a 'New Departure' based on reconciliation, arguing that there could be 'no enduring progress while the bitterness of the past 13 years endures'. He defended the historic role of the Irish Party and repeated his repudiation of Sinn Féin, which was, he said, wrong in 1918 and wrong now:

> But the past is gone and should now be relegated to history. It will be suffi-
> cient if we record our convictions and resolve that our views on matters of
> historical interest shall no longer vitiate our judgement and bedevil our
> councils when we are faced with the hard facts of providing for the future.[39]

High on his list of priorities for that future was 'co-operation with our fellow countrymen across the border to foster and encourage the growing feeling in favour of reunion between the sundered fragments of Ireland'. He wanted no further tampering with the Constitution without the consent of the people (by this stage the Constitution had been amended sixteen times by ordinary act of parliament). He opposed agricultural tariffs because they hurt the consumer, urged rehousing of slum-dwellers, the establishment of a central roads authority and protection for the fishing community from marauding trawlers. He reiterated his support for the survival of Irish with a complicated proposal for a Gaeltacht-centred approach. On the vexed political question of the land annuities, he favoured neither Fianna Fáil, which urged non-payment, nor the govern-ment, which insisted on honouring the debt. Payment should continue, but only until the appointment of an independent international tribunal by the President of the USA to decide the matter.[40]

His final word to his electors was that he would surrender his indepen-dence to no party, a theme he was to reiterate throughout the campaign. In Murlogh on 10 February, the *Irish Independent* reported, 'Mr. Seamus Dillon emphasised his determination to maintain absolute impartiality between the parties, saying he "belonged to neither and never would".' At Inch the following day, Dillon noted that both Cosgrave and de Valera – anxious perhaps to capture the Irish Party vote – now recognised the value of Redmond's and John Dillon's work. Dillon supported good relations between all parties, he said, and indeed hoped that Cosgrave and de Valera would consent to form a National Government, but he would not join either of the major parties. He made it clear that if he were elected, he would support the claim to government of the party with the highest number of first preference votes.[41]

He campaigned hard, from the first meeting he addressed under a lamp-post in the village of Ballintra, just south of Donegal town, right up to polling day. His supporters even managed a rousing song of execrable literary quality set to the air of 'God Save Ireland'. And as the results came in, more slowly in Donegal than any other constituency, it became clear that both the hard campaigning and his choice of constituency had been vindicated. He was elected on the first count, second only to Major Myles and some few hundred votes ahead of the Fianna Fáil candidate, Neil Blaney. In spite of his family's reservations about Leinster House, it was a heady and historic moment. After an absence of fourteen years, there was a Dillon back in national politics.

He gave two reasons for his emphatic win. The first was John D. Nugent, the 'genius for political organisation' who had provided a band of experienced campaigners to organise his support. But the main factor was his father's name. He illustrated the point in later years by recalling in his *Memoir* a visit to the polling station in Gweedore:

and as I was leaving I met an old man and an old woman, who had just come out from voting, and I asked them, quite jocularly, 'Who did ye vote for?' The old man stopped and looked at me (he hadn't the faintest idea who I was). 'Who would I vote for,' he said, 'but John Dillon's son? Herself and meself walked seven miles down from the mountain to vote for John Dillon's son, and we'll walk seven miles back, and it's not much thanks for all he did for us.'[42]

Fr Nicholas had mixed feelings about the result:

I fear I should only be telling you a lie if I were to congratulate you on your introduction to the pestilential atmosphere of Leinster Lawn but I can and do congratulate you on your tremendous success. There is little fear of my bothering you with remarks as to politics.[43]

He was almost as good as his word.

Overall, Cumann na nGaedheal, to its own surprise but not to any independent observer, lost its majority, dropping from sixty-two seats to fifty-seven, while Fianna Fáil, with seventy-two seats, a gain of fifteen, was in a position with the help of Labour's seven seats to form its first government. The visiting *New York Times* correspondent contrasted Cosgrave, 'cold and unromantic, with no attraction for Irish youth,' with the de Valera campaign, 'arousing emotions and enthusiasms strangely like those Adolf Hitler is spreading through Germany'. The American correspondent pondered the secret of de Valera, 'anything but a firebrand, this mild academic, lean and tight-lipped, who lectures his audience and leaves it to his lieutenants to revive emotions of more troubled times'.[44]

Thus the first phase in the history of the Irish Free State came to an end. It was a period of substantial and under-rated achievement when, as the *New York Times* writer noted, 'only those with first-hand knowledge of Cosgrave's difficulties can appreciate the greatness of this little tawny-headed man who has been in office longer than any Prime Minister in Europe'.[45]

Cosgrave was not bitter in defeat. As far back as 1928 he had gone on record as saying that a change of government would be good for the country. 'We have been in power too long. When one party remains in office five years, it brings upon itself heaps of exaggerated and inflated criticisms ... what I would like to see before long is the present government stepping down and the other fellows taking the reins.'[46] He told the *New York Times*, however, that he would have 'preferred as President one of de Valera's lieutenants, like Sean Lemass, whom he regarded as a practical politician, rather than de Valera, whom he looks upon as an impractical dreamer and a coiner of dangerous phrases'.[47]

If Cosgrave was sanguine as he faced opposition for the first time, it is doubtful if many others shared his equanimity as the Free State sailed into uncharted and potentially stormy waters. But for Dillon at least there was a sense of exultation. Congratulatory letters poured in, mainly from supporters of the Irish Party and admirers of his father. Most struck a backward, even negative note. One, from a Longford solicitor, was typical: 'I was very glad indeed to see that even in these degenerate days, a son of John Dillon can knock blazes out of the rabble, in which unfortunately this country seems to abound.'[48]

These, however, were the voices of a world that was lost and would not return, and for a young, newly elected and energetic politician they offered no way forward. His father's legacy had got him into the Dáil and would help sustain him there, but not indefinitely. From now on, James Dillon was on his own.

CHAPTER FIVE

ENTERING THE FRAY

'Wherever I was in 1916, I was not murdering my neighbours.'
Dillon, Dáil Debates, 22 April 1932

DÁIL ÉIREANN in 1932 was no place for faint hearts. It was a parliament as bitterly divided as any Irish parliament would ever be. The political landscape of the Free State was changing, the balance of power shifting dramatically. De Valera had spent the five years since the last general election building his party into a formidable electoral machine, with an army of militant branches backed by the uncompromising propaganda of the party's daily newspaper, the *Irish Press*. Its radical social, economic and political policies gave the party a momentum which was spurred even further by its sense of righteousness, while opposing it was a government party with an impressive record of achievement, but achievements which for the most part did little to stir the blood and were in many cases won only at the cost of electoral unpopularity. And Cumann na nGaedheal had grown accustomed to government. It had neglected to build, in many cases even to set up local organisations. More than that, it had in a decade become closely identified with the established classes: business, farmers, professionals, ex-Unionists even. It was a party on the defensive, defending the status quo at a time of deep if uncertain change.[1]

In many ways Irish politics were more bitter in 1932 than they had been a decade earlier. In the years since the Civil War distrust had hardened and deepened, grievances had become more certain. Memories festered. It was not a happy country, nor was it going to be, and it was into this political maelstrom that a young, self-confident and politically inexperienced James Dillon arrived on 9 March 1932. Determined to have no truck with either of the Civil War parties, he was set upon inhabiting the lofty middle ground, and was not be the first or last to discover that such a place was hard to find and even more difficult to sustain. He discovered very quickly that the choices in the Dáil left no hiding place for an Independent TD.

Fianna Fáil's election manifesto proposed an economic and constitutional revolution. The party intended to abolish the Oath of Allegiance and suspend payment of land annuities immediately, actions certain to result in political conflict with Britain. Fianna Fáil also planned to embark on an ambitious policy of tillage at the expense of the livestock industry, and put in place a regime of economic self-sufficiency through the imposition of a wide range of tariffs on imports and the fostering of indigenous industry. The party also promised to release all IRA prisoners. Each one of these measures was controversial; taken together they made for a lethal cocktail, especially when presented in language which left little room for compromise.[2]

Dillon's description of his first day as a member of an Irish parliament has become part of political folklore:

> The feeling in Dáil Éireann when I first arrived in it in 1932 was quite extraordinary. A very considerable number of the Fianna Fáil party arrived in the Dáil on the day Mr. de Valera was first elected, armed to the teeth. They thought there was going to be a putsch, that if Mr. de Valera was elected Mr. Cosgrave wouldn't hand over Government. They had a completely illusory notion of the standards and character of Mr. Cosgrave, who, of course, had brought – indeed forced – Fianna Fáil into Dáil Éireann in order to establish normal political functioning in the country. So they were swaggering around the place with revolvers bulging out of their pockets. One old gentleman was assembling a machine-gun in a telephone booth.[3]

Even if the reality was somewhat less dramatic, it was nonetheless a day of high political tensions. A report in the *Irish Press* on 26 February alleged that the transfer of power would be obstructed by a 'cabal of Ministers' in association with the army and a new secret organisation. The paper had no evidence for this story, and none was ever subsequently produced, but in the fevered atmosphere of the time rumours travelled swiftly. Fianna Fáil were certainly apprehensive, though whether this anxiety translated into the type of armed precautions described by Dillon is open to question. In the event such fears proved groundless. There may have been wild talk in some quarters,[4] but Dillon was not aware of it, and he recalls that before the vote for President, 'far from being engaged in any frantic plotting', Cosgrave was upstairs, playing pontoon with the outgoing Education Minister, John Marcus O'Sullivan.[5]

The only candidate proposed for President was de Valera, and in his maiden speech Dillon confirmed that he would vote for him. As the candidate whose party got the highest vote in the election, de Valera was clearly the people's preference, but he warned that insofar as he threatened to 'lead our people into war, economic or actual, with friendly nations or among ourselves, I shall oppose him with all the vehemence I can command'.[6] De Valera was elected by eighty-one votes to sixty-eight, and immediately began to implement an election manifesto which promised a dramatic intensification of the party's nationalist agenda.

One interesting footnote to this historic day in politics surfaced in the diary of the influential British Civil Servant, Tom Jones. He recounted a conversation he had had with Stanley Baldwin on 27 February 1932, when Baldwin quoted the London representative of the *Chicago Tribune*, who had been in Ireland for the election and come back with 'weird prophecies' – 'When de Valera would be put up for President, Labour would combine with Cosgrave and defeat him, then a dark horse would be trotted out in the shape of John Dillon's son, and he would be elected.'[7]

Dillon quickly settled in to the routine of Dáil life. He sat in on all major debates, learning the detail of procedure, observing the cut and thrust of debate, exploiting the potential of parliamentary questions to tackle issues in his Donegal constituency. He tried to bring together in informal alliance the three Independents who had voted for de Valera – JF O'Hanlon, JJ O'Shaughnessy and himself. This group even appointed a Whip and the *Irish Independent* felt it might eventually develop into a new party.[8] In addition, Dillon spoke on every major issue as it arose, maintaining his pledge to vote as a 'free' man on each one. This was particularly true on the Bill to remove the Oath of Allegiance from the Constitution.

Fianna Fáil had long opposed the Oath of Allegiance to the King as head of state, prescribed under the Treaty as a prerequisite to entering the Dáil. Because of it, the party refused to take its seats in the House before 1927, regarded it as 'an empty formula' between 1927 and 1932, and vowed at all times to remove it at the first possible opportunity. The Fianna Fáil manifesto declared that 'this Article is not required by the Treaty. It stands in the way of national unity and of willing obedience to law. Government by coercion is the result.'[9] Cumann na nGaedheal claimed no love for the Oath either, but saw it as part of a binding international agreement between two sovereign states, which could not be abolished unilaterally. This was also the view of the British government, expressed in the House of Commons by JH Thomas.[10] Fianna Fáil was not deterred, and on 20 April introduced a Bill to abolish the Oath.

Dillon entered the debate at second stage on 27 April. As far as the Oath itself was concerned he would not shed a tear at its removal, he said. It was 'an archaism of evil memory, of intolerable present obligation'. He acknowledged that Fianna Fáil had clearly stated its intention to remove the Oath during the general election, 'and with that intention I was, and am, in entire accord'. If the Bill was simply to remove the Oath he would support it, but as he saw it, the Bill was fundamentally different to what had been promised: 'Sections two and three are a total, unnecessary and flagrant breach of the Treaty.' For the first, but not for the last time he told de Valera he would have been better off to be straightforward and do what he had promised, rather than be as devious as he was apparently being in this matter.[11]

It was strange for Dillon to be cast as the defender of the Treaty, and the irony was not lost on him that he was upholding the integrity of 'the unlovely offspring of the Sinn Féin Party, which means little to me … But what does mean a lot to me is the solemn undertaking of an Irish leader to the Irish people. President de Valera told the Irish people that if they committed the destinies of government to his hands he would not compromise the Treaty position … This Bill is a betrayal of that undertaking … a betrayal to which I will not be a party.'[12]

He opposed the Bill's second stage, while at committee stage he voted twice with the government and twice against. In the event the Bill passed all stages in the Dáil but on 7 June was defeated in the Senate by thirty-two votes to twenty-two, which in effect meant it would not become law for eighteen months. This was the first act of defiance by the Senate of the new government, and coming as it did on a major piece of legislation, it deepened even further Fianna Fáil's antipathy to the Upper House, and its feeling that the party's democratically won mandate was being frustrated by unelected, reactionary elements.[13]

The Bill also saw Dillon involved in two heated committee stage incidents which highlighted his continuing antipathy to the Sinn Féin parties. He was bitterly attacked by Batt O'Connor, a Cumann na nGaedheal TD who was a veteran of 1916, a friend of Michael Collins and regarded as a brave and honourable man, who accused him of 'gloating at the Sinn Féin split'. O'Connor may well have had a point, for Dillon had not taken too much trouble to conceal his pleasure at the fact that the Sinn Féin party which ousted his father had not managed to stay united.[14]

Exchanges across the floor quickly got out of hand. O'Connor invoked the memory of 1916 and demanded to know of Dillon where he had been during the Rising, to which Dillon, who was thirteen years old in April 1916, spiritedly but perhaps unwisely replied that wherever he was, 'I was not murdering my neighbours'. An outraged O'Connor claimed that the Irish Party had cheered in Westminster when the first three 1916 executions were announced. Amidst disorder in the chamber, Dillon accused O'Connor of telling 'a damned lie', and refused to withdraw the phrase. Alfie Byrne, a former Irish Party MP, and James Coburn, also from the Irish Party tradition, supported Dillon, while O'Connor stuck by his allegation. When Cosgrave intervened and said the allegation was not true, Coburn thanked him, saying 'you were always an Irish man', but threatened to kill anyone who repeated the slander.[15]

Later, O'Connor made a generous retraction, which Dillon accepted with equal grace. The matter ended there, but it was a reminder of just how much outside the mainstream Dillon was, and an indication to the rest of the House that he would fight to defend the name and honour of his father's party. As he put it: 'I am in the presence of two loyalties. I have a loyalty higher to the memory of these men than I have to this House,'[16] in itself a strange statement, indicating a less than full acceptance of the full legitimacy of the Dáil.

And he needlessly gave a hostage to fortune later during the same debate, with remarks that were used against him as an example of his 'unsoundness' on the national question in many subsequent campaigns. Arguing that the symbolism of the Oath was offensive to many members, he likened it to his own attitude to the national anthem: 'I will not stand up when you play the "Soldier's Song" because I detest it ... it is associated in my mind with horrors.'[17] It was honest, but hardly calculated to endear him to the heirs of 1916. Incidentally, Dillon was later to say that his preferred national anthem would have been 'A Nation Once Again', and his national flag blue, with a golden harp.[18]

Despite his lack of diplomacy, one common thread running through Dillon's interventions in his first parliamentary year was his appeal to the major parties to move away from the bitterness of the Civil War. He attacked Cumann na nGaedheal's opposition to the Army Pensions Bill, which provided pensions for some who fought on the Republican side in the Civil War, and castigated Fianna Fáil for its continual talk 'about Cumann na nGaedheal playing England's game'. Men had given 'the best years of their lives to the service of this country', he said, and he asked de Valera and Cosgrave 'to forget the bitterness that parted them in the past and to sit down together for the nation that claims them both'. His words fell on stony soil. His plea met with jeers from the Fianna Fáil back-benches and sneers from the Parliamentary Secretary to the Minister for Finance, Hugo Flinn, who had formed an early and deep-seated dislike of Dillon.[19]

The next, defining issue arose within weeks of the government taking office. This was the land annuities, which quickly developed into a full-scale economic war between Ireland and Britain.[20]

These annual payments were made by Irish farmers to repay sums lent to them for the purchase of their land under the various Land Acts. The money was collected by the Free State government, and as regards land purchased before the Treaty, was paid over to the British National Debt Commissioners. The figure involved was about £3 million per year, and the outstanding sum was about £76 million. The government declared the annuities were neither legally nor morally due and on 30 June defaulted on the £1.5 million then due for payment. The British government reacted within days with the Free State Special Duties Bill, and on 12 July the Treasury made an order imposing a twenty per cent value added tax on a wide range of agricultural produce from the Free State, to commence three days later. The opening shots had been fired in the Economic War.

De Valera reacted immediately, introducing the Emergency Imposition of Duties Bill in the Dáil on the 15th also. The Bill gave the government wide fiscal powers to retaliate against Britain. In a debate of quite extraordinary intensity and bitterness, Dillon spoke immediately after McGilligan, who had made a brilliant but vituperative attack on the government. Dillon opposed rushing the debate, as the government was doing, saying it could precipitate a trade war whose consequences would be incalculable. He believed the matter could still be resolved by arbitration. He voted against the Bill because 'it was being rushed through the Oireachtas to the jeopardy and destruction of peace'.[21]

The Bill passed by sixty-eight votes to fifty-seven, but once again the Senate refused to sanction a Bill as sent to it from the Dáil, and insisted on making a number of amendments against the wishes of the government. The Dáil was recalled from the summer recess on 22 July. During the debate Dillon elaborated on his views, and disagreed with the government's opinion on the legality of the annuities. 'I have not the slightest doubt that the annuities are legally due,' he said. 'I am equally certain that the annuities are not equitably due.' He argued that if negotiations proceeded, with the Irish government claiming there was no legal case for the retention of the annuities, the British government would probably win any legal battle. There was a different and a stronger case to be made, 'a case based on equity and justice as between nations in the light of present day affairs'. He made a plea for national unity on that basis, and attacked the way the matter was being handled by the British, 'but even with that we must still do everything to prevent an economic war between two countries which would revive all the old bitterness and take years to repair'.[22]

When it came to vote on this occasion, he sided with Fianna Fáil in rejecting the Senate amendments, but condemned both sides for their obsession with Civil War issues and their inability to come together. He was particularly critical of McGilligan for what he saw as needless point-scoring, and pledged himself to 'do anything the President would ask, provided it be morally justified, to help him make a friendly and final settlement of outstanding differences'.[23]

Following the passing of this legislation in Dáil and Seanad, the government imposed duties on British imports, including coal, cement, electrical goods, steel and iron. But while the Free State imported £32 million worth of goods annually from the UK, this was just eight per cent of the UK's total trade, while Britain was the Free State's only foreign market, accounting for

ninety-five per cent of all its exports, £31 million in 1931. It was an
unequal battle, and it did not take long for its effects to be felt. The trade
figures for August showed a drastic drop in all agricultural exports from the
Free State to Britain. The first effects were felt in the cattle trade, where
exports were down by over £900,000 on the same month a year earlier,
while two-thirds of the market for bacon and hams was lost, butter exports
were halved, and one-third of the egg market disappeared.[24] The result was
a sense of panic and outrage in the farming community, especially among
the large cattle farmers, and this in turn led to a nationwide campaign
against the government's policy. It was as yet uncoordinated and largely
local, but it was to gather momentum and eventually be the main factor in
the establishment of the National Centre Party.

Dillon, too, was finding himself more and more at odds with the government as it put its programme before the House in the first months of the
new Dáil. He opposed Fianna Fáil's policy of industrial protection, not on
principle – that was to come later – but because it meant a sharp increase in
costs, especially of the essential requisites of the agricultural community
such as Indian meal, galvanised iron, rakes and artificial manures.[25] The
Control of Manufactures Bill of June 1932 set off some alarm bells, more
for its practical effects than on any question of principle. Dillon was
critical of attempts to restrict the activities of foreign capitalists and investment as part of the government's policy of achieving majority Irish control
in as much industry as possible, and he was sceptical of Sean Lemass's
enthusiasm for industrialisation.[26] He was willing to give Fianna Fáil's
economic policy 'a fair chance', but in a passage which was to be especially
relevant thirty years later, he added: 'I am not as great an enthusiast as is the
Minister for the industrialisation of this country. I am not sure it will be as
unqualified a blessing as he seems to think it will.'[27] In the event, he voted
against the Control of Manufactures Act, and would come in time to
campaign passionately for its repeal.

He was in head-on opposition to the government's policy of compulsory
tillage, especially as it would impact badly on the cattle trade. Fianna Fáil's
proposal to grow wheat on a major scale, and to use compulsion if need be,
he saw as the ultimate gambit in putting Sinn Féin's economic policy into
practice. He argued that it would do great damage, a point he repeated
relentlessly all through the decade. Now, in November 1932, he began to
contrast Fianna Fáil's agricultural policy unfavourably with Cumann na
nGaedheal's during the previous decade.[28]

He was increasingly critical also of the government's handling of another
controversial issue, the compulsory use of Irish in schools, which he felt
would ensure that 'the Irish language, which we are most anxious to see
revived, will come to stink in the nostrils of the people' and would damage

the educational standards of children in other subjects. He warned, with prescience, that without public good-will no amount of zeal or enthusiasm would make the scheme work. His intervention was roundly attacked by the Minister for Education, Thomas Derrig.[29]

Dillon was also increasingly irritated by the government's tendency to legislate through ministerial order and statutory instrument, an issue which was to remain an obsession throughout his career. He was constantly on the look-out for examples of what he saw as an insidious undermining of the prerogatives of the Oireachtas: 'the Oireachtas makes laws, not Ministers, and it is our job to try to keep Ministers in their places'.[30] But though he was critical of most points of government policy in his first term in Leinster House, the first signs of a real parting of the ways with Fianna Fáil came on a motion arising out of the land annuities.

In November, Cosgrave introduced a motion censuring the government for having led the country into a disastrous economic war. Dillon told the House that up to now he had responded to de Valera's appeal to make no public comment which would undermine the government's position in the Anglo-Irish negotiations; he had told de Valera privately of his own disquiet, but felt Fianna Fáil was entitled to have its chance to prove its policies before the country. He was certain, however, that in this war there could be no real victory. If England won it would mean untold economic and financial hardship in Ireland; but even if Ireland won it would result in 'a bitterness and resentment which will injure us far more in the long run than the annuities can ever compensate us for'.[31]

There was more to it than that. He was beginning to see differences of a fundamental nature between himself and the government, which he now believed was using the annuities as a measure whose 'final aim' was the removal of the Free State from the Commonwealth of Nations. This was more than he could stand for. 'I aim at political freedom. I believe the securest political freedom and the securest economic freedom are to be found within the Commonwealth of Nations, as co-equal members, as independent and sovereign States.' He asked de Valera directly whether the dispute was 'an excuse to lead the Irish people whither they never authorised him to lead them?'[32] He received no answer, and voted against the government which he had helped to elect just eight months earlier. The government won by seventy-five votes to seventy.

DURING HIS first term in the Dáil, Dillon was drawn to another Independent, Frank MacDermot, whom he had in part helped to elect through his involvement in the Farmers and Ratepayers Association. Apart from that campaign in Roscommon, they had a great deal in common in terms of their backgrounds and shared views on most of the major issues of the day. As Independents their working lives in the Dáil were interwoven; over the next few years their careers would become inextricably linked.

MacDermot came from a family with a distinguished political lineage in moderate nationalist politics, dating back to the United Irishmen of the eighteenth century. He was, as he was proud of saying, 'the MacDermot of Coolavin'. His father had been Solicitor-General and Attorney General in the governments of Gladstone and Rosebery. Born in 1886, MacDermot had been educated at Downside and Oxford and before the 1914-18 war had been an active supporter of Home Rule, speaking at meetings in the north of Ireland and in Scotland in the two general elections of 1910. He joined the British army on the outbreak of war and served in Flanders. Afterwards he made a career for himself in merchant banking, living in London and the USA, but for some reason Irish politics fascinated him, and while on his way back to Ireland in 1927 he met Lady Lavery, who introduced him to Cosgrave, Kevin O'Higgins and Desmond FitzGerald.[33]

When MacDermot expressed his interest in getting into politics, Kevin O'Higgins took him seriously, and in an exchange of letters in 1927 confided to him some of the party's problems in getting good, electable candidates. O'Higgins advised MacDermot to 'go East rather than West', to stay with his friend FB Barton at Straffan, Co. Kildare, join the central branch of Cumann na nGaedheal and seek a Dublin nomination – where O'Higgins was particularly critical of some of the candidates on offer. The only real recipe for political success, O'Higgins added, was at all times to 'keep near the people'.[34]

MacDermot did not contest the 1927 election but was in contact with O'Higgins immediately afterwards. He found the Cumann na nGaedheal minister in a particularly black mood. He felt the bad result had damaged economic confidence, which in turn would impede the country's progress towards unity. He believed the *Irish Independent*'s negative attitude to the state had done terrible harm and that right-wing elements had played into de Valera's hands. They had 'gone near to destroying the Treaty, in particular Redmond's appeals to the ex-servicemen and Sir John Keane and O'Callaghan Westropp holding the Farmers Union against us: all those wretched little parties vigorously sawing the bough they are sitting on is a sight to make angels weep and devils grin.'[35]

After O'Higgin's murder in July 1927, and contrary to O'Higgins's earlier advice, it was suggested to MacDermot that he might seek a nomination from Cumann na nGaedheal in Roscommon for the forthcoming September election. An acute attack of jaundice on his way down to his putative constituency put paid to this plan, and with politics now out of the question, at least in the short term, he set up home in Paris with his

American wife. In 1929 he was invited by the northern Nationalist MP (and friend of John Dillon) Joe Devlin to stand for West Belfast in the Westminster election. He agreed, and experienced at first hand the playing of the Orange card by his Unionist opponent. He was not elected, but he did well, showing campaigning flair and clearly enjoying the experience. The political bug had bitten.[36]

By now, and it is not clear why, he had abandoned the idea of running for Cumann na nGaedheal, though not of running for the Dáil. Returning to Roscommon in 1932, he was influenced by Monsignor Cummins of the Farmers and Ratepayers Association, and by Dillon, who actively encouraged him and used his influence to have him selected as the association's candidate in North Roscommon. The association was keen to remain independent of the major parties; it wanted to move political debate away from the Treaty and Civil War and instead to give greater urgency to agricultural issues. The urbane, sophisticated MacDermot was a bizarre choice as candidate. He knew nothing about farming, and attracted the nickname 'the Paris farmer', but to everyone's surprise, not least his own, he was elected.

As a TD, MacDermot wasted no time in establishing a reputation for outspokenness and independence, but soon found it difficult to maintain a balance between the major parties in face of the government's decision to release IRA prisoners and in particular its prosecution of the Economic War. More and more his speeches and his votes reflected his opposition to Fianna Fáil, although, like Dillon, he had a good personal relationship with de Valera.

As the effects of the Economic War began to bite through the summer and autumn of 1932, the National Farmers and Ratepayers Association became the main vehicle of protest against government policy. The NFRA was more a loose federation of local groups than a developed national organisation, however, and it soon became clear that it was inadequately equipped to lead the campaign. At a meeting in Dublin in early September the association declared a state of national crisis, and throughout the country meetings were held almost daily to rally support for immediate action. This process culminated in a 'convention' in Dublin on 16 September at which a decision was taken to set up a new political organisation (not yet called a political party) to represent the interests of farmers and to seek an end to the Economic War. The leading force behind the drive to politicise the farmers' movement was Patrick Belton, an energetic political maverick who had previously been a Fianna Fáil TD for Dublin County and was now an Independent. Though controversial and energetic, Belton was not seriously regarded as leadership material, and as a result MacDermot was invited to take on that role. He was elected President of the standing committee of this new organisation, which was still answerable to the NFRA. His job essentially was to set up what amounted to a new political party.[37]

Dillon had stood aside from these developments in spite of strong pressure from MacDermot to get involved. He was not altogether opposed to the idea of joining a party, but had deep-seated reservations about the quality of some of this one's leading personnel, the timing of the initiative and about the overall strategy which would be followed. He wrote to MacDermot three days after the Dublin convention.

The meeting, he wrote, 'was a great mistake. It was organised by people in whom I have no trust whatever, and with whom I would not be seen dead in a ditch.' Two of the leading members, he said, were 'twisters of the lowest type', another was a decent man but 'a complete silly billy who represents nobody', yet another was 'a decent ass, but his whole connection is the old Ascendancy gang, and he has as much national feeling as the wandering Jew'. There was 'a publican who would not know the difference between a bullock and a goat'. Apart from the quality of those involved he objected to the passing of resolutions calling for an end to the war on the eve of de Valera's departure for Geneva, where he was to chair the League of Nations. 'He should have been allowed to make his case there if the British did not meet him before that, and if he came back empty handed from there then I believe there would have been a very good chance of starting a Peace Party. As it is, I feel there will be a violent reaction from the new movement you have started, and its coincidence with Cosgrave's *démarche* lends colour to the suggestion that it is a sort of alliance to down de Valera.' He went on to warn:

Make no mistake about this, if de Valera is downed, we shall pass through the worst ten years this country has ever known, and what will survive is a question I would not care to have to answer.

He then posed a question to MacDermot:

Suppose your new movement succeeded in depriving de Valera of his majority in the morning and that you were faced with the question of choosing a new administration, what would you do? There would be only one alternative and that is Cosgrave. The election of Cosgrave as President at this juncture, would be a first-class catastrophe, and would be immediately followed by a state of affairs approximating to civil war ... You know my mind, but I confess I don't quite understand what it is you have in view.[38]

Efforts to set up the new party proceeded, though the exercise was accompanied by a fair amount of confusion, especially since it was not clear whether MacDermot had in mind a completely new and broadly based party such as Dillon might have supported, or whether, as many of his colleagues would have preferred, it was to be a strongly farmer-dominated party, a revival of the farmers' parties of the 1920s. Others wondered if the group was a prelude to a merger with Cumann na nGaedheal, the only other party opposed to the Economic War. It may well be that MacDermot himself was not fully clear and was heading in a number of directions at once.

MacDermot's plans were not surprisingly engaging the attention of Cumann na nGaedheal also. At a meeting of the parliamentary party on 17 November, the North Mayo TD, Michael Davis, reminded them that in a speech in Wicklow MacDermot had said that since the policies of Cumann na nGaedheal and the Farmers Party (as the MacDermot party was generally called) were at one on the annuities, the Farmers Party should not endanger Cumann na nGaedheal because both had the same objective and depended on Cumann na nGaedheal for its ultimate attainment. The meeting set up a committee of Ernest Blythe, Richard Mulcahy and Patrick Hogan to find out from deputies what the position of the Farmers Association was in each constituency before deciding on further action.[39] The following day, Cosgrave told his colleagues to ascertain whether they really had differences with the farmers; it was essential, he warned, not to divide the forces opposed to the present government.[40] When the party returned to the issue a week later, opinions were sharply divided. Sidney Minch, the Kildare TD and maltster, vehemently opposed any alliance with MacDermot, and claimed that he had attacked Cosgrave and Cumann na nGaedheal in Minch's own constituency. This view was opposed by Denis Gorey, a former Farmers Party leader, who said that ninety per cent of MacDermot's support was spontaneous and to attack him without a clearly defined objective would damage Cumann na nGaedheal.

It was generally agreed that attacking MacDermot would only increase his prestige, and a number of references were made to the contradictions and divergences in the farmers' movement in different parts of the country. Dr TF O'Higgins pointed out that in some counties the local farmers' organisation was 'foul-mouthed in its attitude to Cosgrave and the party', while in others – and he named Kilkenny and Tipperary especially – the opposite was the case. It was decided that the committee should 'feel the pulse of the 26 counties' before making a final decision.[41]

In truth, the possibility of a merger or an arrangement with MacDermot and his ill-defined movement was not all that high on the Cumann na nGaedheal agenda at this stage. The bigger reality was that the political situation was deteriorating rapidly, and not to Cumann na nGaedheal's advantage. Fianna Fáil's election victory had unleashed passions that would not easily be restrained. From mid-1932, Cumann na nGaedheal meetings were disrupted with increasing frequency, the lead being taken by many of the released IRA prisoners, who saw it as their right to deny 'free speech' to the 'traitors' of the old regime. Cosgrave, McGilligan, Mulcahy and O'Higgins all had meetings wrecked, and received no expressions of regret or concern from a government which itself felt beleaguered.[42] Levels of political abuse inside the House increased in intensity, culminating in Finance Minister MacEntee's branding of Cosgrave as 'one of the great traitors of Irish history', and prophesying that 'we will have his name spat upon'.[43] Then in August 1932 came the founding of the Army Comrades Association (ACA), made up at first of ex-servicemen loyal to the old administration. The association's stated purpose was to protect Cumann na nGaedheal speakers at public meetings, but it was seen by Fianna Fáil and the IRA as portending something new and ominous in Irish politics.[44]

As the effects of the Economic War were being felt with increasing severity by the bigger farmers, their anger and concern came up against a wall of governmental indifference; this after all was a government of tillage, not livestock, and if the Economic War speeded up the demise of the ranchers, then that too was according to plan. MacDermot was not left outside the fray. Much as he sought the middle ground, he found soon enough that Fianna Fáil was in no mood to respect 'principled neutrality' in what it increasingly saw as a fight to the finish. Soon enough his meetings would be disrupted, while to MacEntee he was an unwelcome intruder, 'a Castle Catholic: more Castle than Catholic'.[45]

Though nothing of consequence was done to build opposition party unity before the end of the year, talk of some sort of regrouping was in the air, and on New Year's Day 1933 the politically astute Lord Mayor of Dublin, Alfie Byrne, made what became known as the Mansion House appeal for the establishment of a new national party. Byrne's political background was Irish Party, but he had supported the Treaty and was personally close to Cosgrave, and his appeal was for the formation of a party made up of all parties other than Fianna Fáil. He laid out four priorities: an end to the Economic War, friendly relations with Britain, the full working of the Treaty, and the unity of the country – a combination not designed to suit Fianna Fáil, and with little attraction either for Labour.[46]

Byrne's initiative, warmly welcomed by the anti-Fianna Fáil *Irish Independent* and *Irish Times*, never got a chance to get moving. On the very next day, 2 January, de Valera took all parties by surprise, including his own, when he dissolved the Dáil and called an election for the end of the month. He had called the election, he said, because he needed an overall majority to strengthen his hand in the negotiations with Britain, to dispel doubts about the country's stability, which prevented investment in new industries, and because he was faced by a hostile Senate.[47]

Coincidentally, and independently of de Valera's 'snap' announcement, (though he may have been aware of the way things were moving and wanted to forestall them), a meeting of the standing committee of Cumann na nGaedheal had been convened for that evening to consider the Mansion House call. The meeting authorised Cosgrave to make such arrangements as he thought fit with the Farmers and Ratepayers Association, and with any other organisation, with a view to strengthening anti-Fianna Fáil forces in each constituency.[48] The following day the full parliamentary party welcomed the Lord Mayor's proposal and promised full co-operation in giving effect to it.[49]

De Valera's timing had been brilliant, nipping in the bud any real possibility of opposition unity. For Cumann na nGaedheal, which had been in government for the past decade, to merge as equals with a party which did not as yet exist, with an inexperienced and somewhat bizarre leader, and which in some constituencies at least had been hostile to Cumann na nGaedheal, was unthinkable. For the new party a merger meant a loss of identity, absorption in the bigger party before it even had an independent life of its own.

It came as no surprise that when MacDermot and Cosgrave met again on 3 January they quickly concluded that there was little point at this stage in proceeding further. This was confirmed almost immediately by the standing committee of Cumann na nGaedheal, which welcomed Byrne's initiative but felt that the suddenness of the election made it impossible to pursue.[50] The standing committee of the NFRA, which in any event was unlikely to have agreed to a merger with Cumann na nGaedheal, now formally gave the go-ahead for the establishment of a new party, to be called the Centre Party.[51]

Dillon was once again invited by MacDermot 'to collaborate in the formation of the new party, which would be independent of all existing parties'.[52] He still had well-founded doubts about some of the leaders of the new movement, and was uneasy about the speed with which major decisions were being taken; yet he was convinced that Fianna Fáil's policies were profoundly wrong and could only be defeated by organised political opposition. The new party ensured he would remain independent of either of the Sinn Féin parties and so, with a certain reluctance, he agreed to support MacDermot. At his insistence the name of the party was extended to include the word 'National' – the National Centre Party. He wanted the new party to be a broadly-based movement rather than a single-issue farmers' party, and meant to emphasise that the nationalist tradition was still central to his political philosophy. And so with Dillon's support the National Centre Party was launched on 5 January 1933, in MacDermot's words, 'embarking as a frail boat in a stormy sea'.[53] Dillon was no longer an Independent. In the all-engulfing intensity of 1933, independence was not really an option.

His decision to join the party was seen as giving it a much-needed boost, and his own stature was such that within a short time he was seen as the *de facto* deputy leader. The new party's programme, devised principally by MacDermot and Dillon, gave prominence to constitutional and economic issues, including the revision of the Treaty by consent to allow the Free State leave the Commonwealth if it so wished, the abolition of partition, an end to the Economic War, the development of new export markets, the encouragement of capital into the country, and the development of agriculture in all forms.[54] But despite this attempt to present a broadly-based policy the National Centre Party was seen as a farmers' party, which indeed it was. This perception was confirmed as it began to select its candidates.

In all, the National Centre Party ran twenty-six candidates. They were a disparate bunch. They included FB Barton of Straffan House, Co. Kildare, a large landowner who had extensive vineyards in the South of France. A cousin of RB Barton, one of the Treaty signatories, FB Barton lived in almost feudal splendour in Straffan where, it was reported, an ox had been roasted for the local tenantry on the occasion of his marriage. In Meath the candidate was George, the Duc de Stacpoole, Downside educated, a papal knight, World War veteran and also a large landowner. A third and very different personality was WR Kent, a Fianna Fáil candidate who decided instead to run for the National Centre Party in East Cork, to the intense anger of the local Fianna Fáil organisation.[55] Most of the other candidates, however, were products of their local farming organisation, or as MacDermot later described them: 'nice fellows, farmers pure and simple'. And like many new parties, it began its life with a split. This one occurred in west Limerick, where some leading local members left because of MacDermot's alleged opposition to the policies of Arthur Griffith.[56]

The Centre Party had no time to prepare for the election and could not match the financial and organisational resources of the major parties, each of which spent heavily on newspaper advertising, postering and pamphleteering. While Cumann na nGaedheal had a film featuring Cosgrave shown all over the country, the Centre Party managed only two half-page advertisements in the national dailies.

The election campaign was probably the most bitter in the history of the state. Disturbances were instigated by supporters of Fianna Fáil and the IRA, who broke up Cumann na nGaedheal meetings in different parts of the country, where some of the party's leading members were unable to get a hearing. In response, the Army Comrades Association (ACA) emerged as the self-appointed protectors of freedom of speech and assembly for

Cumann na nGaedheal members.[57]

The Centre Party did not escape the prevailing violence. On 15 January, the police had to restrain Fianna Fáil supporters from breaking up a Dillon meeting in Raphoe. Even more than the attack, Dillon was angered by the fact that de Valera, who was present near by, made no attempt to restrain his supporters.[58] MacDermot's meetings were disrupted at Arigna and Roscommon, while a Roscommon Fianna Fáil TD, Dan O'Rourke, charged that 'support for the Centre Party was support for the British Empire'.[59] The National Centre Party, which had discussed an alliance with Cumann na nGaedheal, was hardly neutral between the parties, and on 17 January MacDermot advised voters to give their lower preference votes to Cosgrave's party.

MacDermot had predicted twenty seats for his party and with it the balance of power, which he would use to force the formation of a 'national' government.[60] His prediction proved wildly optimistic, but the party did win a respectable eleven seats from a base of four outgoing TDs, more than the Labour Party and nine per cent of the national vote. Dillon got something of a fright in Donegal, where his first-preference vote dropped from 7,645 to 5,317, but strong transfers from Cumann na nGaedheal won him the fourth of eight seats. Most of the elected candidates were farmers, and the party polled badly in all urban areas. MacDermot and Dillon had done well, but they had not broken the Civil War's grip, nor provided a third force in Irish politics. What they had done was to revive a farmers' party tradition which had surfaced at various times in the 1920s and been given renewed life by the Economic War.

1933 was the make or break election. For Fianna Fáil it was the turning point, a dramatic confirmation of de Valera's strategic boldness, which won them a further five seats and for the first time an overall majority. Despite the crisis in agriculture, higher unemployment and political turbulence, the Fianna Fáil vote increased in virtually every constituency, giving de Valera a clear mandate to continue his policies. For Cumann na nGaedheal the result was a disaster, losing nine more seats and bringing its total loss of seats to seventeen in just under a year. The easy expectation that Fianna Fáil would prove unequal to the task of government – an illusion parties long in power frequently nurse about their opponents – was now shattered, and a party psychologically and organisationally unready for opposition had to ask itself some very searching questions. The fact that it had opened discussions with MacDermot indicated that some of its leaders at least were looking at new possibilities. For MacDermot and Dillon, just a year in Free State politics, here was the opportunity, however slight, of breaking the Civil War mould of Irish politics.

CHAPTER SIX

BREAKING THE MOULD

'So long as you confine your idea of nationality to what is Catholic or what is Gaelic, or to what is persistently, and on principle anti-English, you will not master the elements of the problem.'
Frank MacDermot, Dáil Debates, 1 March 1933

MacDermot AND DILLON began the new Dáil as if their previous discussions with Cumann na nGaedheal had never taken place. The party was assigned three front-bench positions, with the speaking rights and privileges of the third largest party in the House, and began the first session of the new Dáil on 8 February 1933 with a robust declaration of the party's independence.[1]

In a trenchant speech, MacDermot told the Dáil they would not support de Valera for President because of the bitterness he had created between different classes of Irishmen and between Ireland and England, which in turn had hardened feelings in Northern Ireland in favour of permanent partition. Neither could the Centre Party see why Fianna Fáil's aim of building the Free State's home market was any reason for throwing away the greater part of the country's export trade. Nor could they accept Fianna Fáil's propaganda that there was something disreputable in raising, buying or selling livestock, or that those connected with the business should be placed under a cloud as far as their citizenship and patriotism were concerned.

But if MacDermot could not vote for de Valera, he could not vote against him either. There was, he said, no realistic alternative to his government at present. MacDermot's unwillingness to vote against Fianna Fáil was striking in view of his anger about the way in which the party had fought the election – 'a jingo election; with intimidation and much of the lowest kind of personally abusive propaganda' – and his stance provoked the immediate scorn of William Norton, leader of the Labour Party, who declared the Centre Party 'the new abstentionist party of Irish politics'.[2] Labour voted with Fianna Fáil to elect de Valera by eighty-two votes to fifty-four.

Three weeks later the Centre Party introduced its first private members motion in the Dáil, in an attempt to change, or at least clarify, government policy on Northern Ireland. The effects of the Economic War would have been closer to the real concerns of party members, but MacDermot, and to a lesser extent Dillon, believed that the Northern question demanded a new and urgent approach.

MacDermot's views were far in advance of the conventional thinking of the time. He told the near empty late-night Dáil that 'so long as you confine your idea of nationality to what is Catholic or what is Gaelic, or to what is persistently and, on principle, anti-English, you will not master the elements of the problem and all hope of a union of the Irish nation founded on good-will is an idle dream. The more you teach the Ulster Unionists to believe they cannot claim to be Irishmen at all, the more insoluble your problem becomes.'[3] The Centre Party, he insisted, was a constructive nationalist party:

> It is not the constructive side of Irish nationalism that stands in the way of reunion: it is the side that, even if the North did not exist, we should be better without – jingoism, bitterness, intolerance, narrow mindedness, a love of what is tawdry and superficial. Fanatics on both sides of the border have much the same mentality, but we are the people who want reunion, and it is for us to give the lead in propagating charity and common sense.[4]

Dillon's emphasis was different. The key to ending partition, he said, lay in full participation in the Commonwealth: 'the truest form of freedom can be secured as a united and independent country in association with the other countries of the Commonwealth of Nations'. This, he argued, could only happen if partition ended, and this process could only begin if the factions in the Free State could make their own reconciliation, stop harping on the past, forget the word 'traitor' and give up the agitation for the Republic, which repelled Unionists and made their participation in the politics of the country impossible.[5]

In response, de Valera dwelt on the Treaty, which he saw as having made partition permanent. The Unionists would get equality of treatment within a united Ireland, he insisted: 'We want them to enjoy the advantages of a free Ireland, the same as everybody else. We want no privilege for anybody and we are denying no equality to anybody.' It was not 'a question of holding out inducements to the Unionists – we could hardly go back to the Act of Union,' de Valera went on, and finished impatiently: 'We are talking in the air and wasting our time.'[6]

Exasperated, MacDermot challenged de Valera to say how he intended to abolish partition. The President's answer was as tortuous as it was sterile:

> The only policy for abolishing partition that I can see is for us in this part of Ireland to use such freedom as we can secure to get for the people in this part of Ireland such conditions as will make the people in the other part of Ireland wish to belong to this part.[7]

MacDermot's speech had obviously made no impression. He reflected pessimistically that as long as the de Valera view remained dominant, there would be no meeting of minds with Unionists and little possibility of reconciliation between North and South.

While the Centre Party failed to influence Northern policy, the same cannot be said of its next major intervention just four weeks later, when it succeeded in bringing about an unprecedented display of party unity in the House. The matter arose on a government Bill to introduce temporarily a range of pay cuts across the public service, and in the course of the debate the Centre Party proposed that the cuts – which they supported – should also apply to members of the Oireachtas. Dillon introduced the party's amendment, arguing that if sacrifices were being asked of public servants, the politicians should pay their share also.[8]

If Dillon and MacDermot were hoping to make an impact on the Dáil, they succeeded. It was as if the heavens opened. Norton accused them of talking 'eyewash': 'well endowed with the world's goods, they propose to set a standard for others to follow'.[9] Although MacDermot was seen as the chief mover, having already told his Roscommon electorate that he saw no need at all for a parliamentary allowance (and in fact donated his to the local St Vincent de Paul Society), both men were charged with a perverse form of snobbery. A particularly strong attack came from John A. Costello, who spoke with some passion of the straitened circumstances of so many ordinary deputies and the heavy demands made on them from so many different sources.[10] De Valera was more civil – hardly surprising since the Centre Party was supporting the Bill overall – but he also disagreed with the amendment. Civility disappeared when McGilligan, 'a sparse figure with a lean impassive face, leaning forward over the opposition front bench and calmly uttering the most incisive sentences in a Northern accent which adds an extra barb or two to every arrow he lets fly,' rose to speak. In a scathing speech he condemned the Centre Party TDs for their snobbery and vulgarity in seeking to impose sacrifices which meant little to them on those to whom it meant a great deal, and for trumpeting their virtue in so doing.[11]

When the vote was called the Centre Party did have a victory of sorts: for the first time since the state was founded they succeeded in getting Fianna Fáil, Cumann na nGaedheal and the Labour Party into the same lobby. The amendment was defeated by seventy-nine votes to eight.

Just two weeks into the Dáil sitting, de Valera dismissed General Eoin O'Duffy as Chief of Police. No reason was given for the government's decision, but it did not come as a complete surprise. The IRA had been loudly campaigning against O'Duffy since 1932, and on the day de Valera was re-elected a number of English newspapers had carried reports that

O'Duffy would resign or be sacked. Fianna Fáil had little confidence in O'Duffy, who was closely identified with the old regime and widely regarded as politically partisan.[12] Even so, his sacking was abrupt and sensational. The *Irish Independent* described the government as 'ungrateful, unfair and unjust',[13] while Cumann na nGaedheal, which had itself been planning to replace O'Duffy had it won the election, identified the move as the first in a series of purges which would inevitably follow.

When the matter was debated in the Dáil on 14 March, the Centre Party voted against O'Duffy's dismissal. Dillon argued that O'Duffy deserved better, that the least he was owed was an explanation so that in common justice his name could be vindicated.[14] With Labour abstaining, the government had a comfortable majority when the Dáil voted on the decision, but that of course was far from the end of the O'Duffy story.

O'Duffy's summary dismissal made the Centre Party uneasy about the government's attitude to law and order, especially when, within a few months, its leaders began to experience at first hand what had been common to Cumann na nGaedheal speakers over the previous year. On 14 May, a group of IRA supporters at Ballybofey accused Dillon of having 'insulted the national flag and national cause', and described his party as 'a motley collection of Freemasons, Orangemen and all enemies of the national cause'. An attempt to attack Dillon was only forestalled by the intervention of the police.[15] Similar scenes occurred a week later at Newtowncunningham.[16] When the debate on the Justice Estimate came round on 1 June, Dillon attacked the government angrily, charging that intimidation was being used to break up political meetings throughout the country. But for the police, in the last few months 'no man could speak his mind in this country if he was not prepared to bow down before the doctrine of the IRA or Fianna Fáil'.[17]

The political temperature rose significantly throughout the first half of the year. The Army Comrades Association, which had been active at Cumann na nGaedheal meetings in the general election, had decided on 14 February to extend the scope of its activities and to adopt a distinctive uniform, a blue shirt, which made its first appearance at an ACA meeting in Kilkenny in April. The ACA continued to insist that it was non-party political, but nobody accepted that it was other than wholeheartedly committed to Cumann na nGaedheal and utterly hostile to Fianna Fáil and the IRA.[18]

The Blueshirt movement, new and unpredictable, was attacked by de Valera, who warned that any attempt to follow continental patterns would be unsuccessful. The IRA, busy with its 'Boycott Bass' campaign, declared war on what it dubbed the 'White Army'.[19]

MacDermot, too, had reservations:

We have in this country at this time two semi-military bodies. There is a great difference between these two bodies; one exists for the express and clear purpose of crushing individual liberty ... I have had my own individual liberty interfered with by members of that body calling itself the IRA. The other body came into existence for the express object of defending liberty for the individual, and for securing freedom of speech, and on the whole I think it has done a useful and perhaps absolutely indispensable service. I doubt very much whether there would have been anything like freedom of speech at the last general election had it not been for the existence of that body.

MacDermot, however, did not like this new development:

I do not like the existence of any political army in principle and I am extremely nervous that developments may occur here such as occurred in Germany ... the ACA in its present form came into existence as the result of the IRA ... One violence produces another.[20]

Less than a week after MacDermot's remarks, on 19 July some of the ACA's leading members invited O'Duffy to take over as leader, an invitation he accepted. The association's name was changed to the National Guard and its programme was broadened to include the first tentative introduction of corporatist ideas into Irish politics.[21] O'Duffy told the *Irish Independent* on 31 July that it was not a fascist movement and not unfriendly to Fianna Fáil and Labour.[22] On 2 August he assured the Senior Minister of the Dublin Hebrew Congregation that 'the National Guard was absolutely free from all anti-Semitic tendencies'.[23] However, the National Guard's assertion of political impartiality was simply not credible, and as the movement grew in the wake of O'Duffy's arrival, tensions heightened further.

Conditions in the country had also deteriorated as the continuing trade war with Britain hit business, agriculture and employment. On 23 June, Dillon outlined some of its effects in what the *Irish Independent* called 'one of the best speeches he has made since coming into the Dáil'.[24]

'This country seems to think it can cut itself off from the rest of the world, and by doing that save itself absolutely from the consequences of its own economic folly,' he began. Describing the doctrine of self-sufficiency as madness, he illustrated the state of the market. Pigs were 15 shillings per hundredweight (cwt) lower than in Northern Ireland; demand had collapsed and they could expect a glut of pork at catastrophic prices. He quoted the price of fat cattle, between 35s and 39s per cwt before Fianna Fáil came into office, now 24s per cwt. The price of old cows had dropped from 24s per cwt to 8s (which included a government bounty). Springer cows which were being sold at £18 10s were now going for £7. Three-year-olds which were £15 per head could not be sold at any price. He poured scorn on the government's attempts to find alternatives to the British market. To date this had yielded no more than a single German buyer, whose arrival had been the subject of considerable government publicity and glowing articles in the *Irish Press* – and who was buying at even lower prices than those quoted. He was paying 25s per cwt for prime heifers, while that same day in Belfast 'the despised and contemptible John Bull came over and paid 41s per cwt'.[25]

Dillon's facts were accurate, and his speech gave vent to his deep-seated anger at the doctrinaire destruction of the country's main industry, and the apparent indifference of the government in the face of what was happening.

Meanwhile, the Blueshirts were spreading rapidly, drawing their main strength from traditional Cumann na nGaedheal supporters, and from farmers and their sons who increasingly found themselves in the front line of the Economic War. Dillon had his first experience of the Blueshirts at a Centre Party meeting in Macroom on 23 July. He described the event to the Dáil when it reconvened in the autumn:

There were 1,500 people in the square. About 80 or 90 supporters of President de Valera came into the square and deliberately attempted to break up our meeting. The Civic Guards did all in their power to make an end of that disturbance. They went to these men and tried to get them out of the crowd, but everyone who had to be ejected kicked up a row with the object of breaking up the meeting. Subsequently 50 members of the National Guard went over to these people and said to them, perfectly peaceably, 'Will you go away and stop interrupting the meeting?' Then the National Guard withdrew for a while to let them go. And when they did not go away these 50 members of the National Guard simply wiped the square of Macroom with President de Valera's 70 or 80 men. If they had not wiped the square with these 80 men, they would have made it impossible for the 1,500 people assembled there to hear us. There is no use in Ministers saying that there is no threat to free speech. Everybody knows that during the last election every meeting that was not in favour of Fianna Fáil was interrupted by followers of the President, and he knows that well himself.[26]

Against this background, he and MacDermot re-examined their outlook on the other parties. Dillon had first entered the Dáil as an Independent, but as issue followed issue he had found himself unable to support Fianna Fáil's policies and more often than not ended up in the opposition lobby. The Centre Party was now in a similar situation. While it might support some elements of the government's programme, on most of the major issues it was at one with Cumann na nGaedheal, in spite of the prickly feeling between them.

Talks had gone on behind the scenes to see if the earlier discussions could be revived, and a lead was given by Senator Arthur Vincent, who wrote to the honorary general secretary of Cumann na nGaedheal, Michael Tierney, expressing his high opinion of MacDermot and his colleagues, and contrasted their work with the lacklustre performance of Cumann na nGaedheal. He proposed that they form a 'new party, on broader lines, a new national party which will dissipate all the older ideas of class and religion'.[27]

Cosgrave was receptive to the idea[28] and under Vincent's persistent prodding a meeting was held in June to see if there was any basis for a merger. The meeting, attended by Cosgrave, Hogan, MacDermot and Dillon, took place secretly at a neutral venue in Dublin's Mount St Crescent, and was presided over by the Cathaoirleach of the Senate, TW Westropp Bennett. Subsequent meetings followed, bringing in Sean MacEoin, Richard Mulcahy, Michael Tierney and TF O'Higgins from Cumann na nGaedheal, and PF Baxter, Charles Fagan and O'Donovan of the Centre Party.[29]

In spite of the secrecy surrounding these meetings, events were moving rapidly. O'Duffy announced on 25 July that he intended to lead a commemorative parade to Leinster Lawn on 13 August in honour of Griffith, Collins and O'Higgins. This was the revival of a parade which had been held annually under the previous government, but in the fevered atmosphere of the time O'Duffy's plans were seen by many of his opponents as sinister. While no evidence existed, the government could be forgiven for suspecting O'Duffy had more in mind than he claimed, whereas to the opposition the parade was no more than an expression of their constitutional rights to free speech and assembly.

On 30 July the government suddenly revoked the licences of guns held by ex-ministers and some leading Cumann na nGaedheal supporters, most of which fell due for renewal the following day. The guns had been issued for self-protection and those affected included McGilligan, Blythe and Gearóid O'Sullivan. Ironically, McGilligan's house at Lansdowne Rd had been the target of an armed IRA raid just a week earlier. The police, under government instruction, now set about collecting the guns. The only reason given was that they were required for routine 'stock-taking', an excuse which convinced nobody, and heightened the sense of vulnerability of those affected.[30]

The following day, O'Duffy, who had initially predicted a crowd of 20,000 at his Dublin parade, said that because of the economic conditions prevailing he would only 'accept' a small contingent from each county, 3,000 to 4,000 in all. He dismissed as preposterous any suggestion that he intended staging a coup and accused the government of deliberate scaremongering.[31] The government's actions over the coming week indicated that it was indeed preparing for a possible coup, though no evidence that such an act was being planned has ever emerged. It is more likely that the government wanted to prevent a march which it believed would lead to bloodshed between the rival factions. It also wanted an early opportunity to face down this new organisation.

The confiscation of politicians' guns was the subject of an extremely bitter Dáil debate on 1 August. Dillon emphatically refused to believe the reason the government gave for the seizures:

> It surpasses my comprehension of justice and reason to take arms from law-abiding citizens who were given them to protect themselves, while leaving arms in the hands of men who deny the authority of the State and who deliberately declare that anyone in politics in this country who does not agree with them is a traitor and deserves a traitor's fate.[32]

De Valera, angry and under pressure, declared that they were 'not going to allow a force to develop to subvert the will of the people', that there would be 'no new dictators from any side' and 'no private armies'.[33]

On 2 August, O'Duffy's own gun, which he had refused to hand in, was seized by the police, and on the following day heavily armed police patrols made their appearance at Leinster House. They were augmented over the weekend, giving Leinster House 'the appearance of an armed camp ... something similar to Stormont'. By 6 August there were 300 police on duty at the building, 'operating in pairs, carrying heavy revolvers and holsters in their belts'.[34]

The government's case was amplified on 9 August when Justice Minister PJ Ruttledge told the Dáil of a report which O'Duffy had given the government in September 1932, when he was still Chief of Police. According to the report, the ACA had access to arms 'should it at any time desire to adopt other than constitutional methods', sufficient 'to render it a very formidable insurrectionary force and a source of extreme danger to the peace and stability of the country'. The report commented that 'certain members of the organisation hold extreme views and would be prepared to urge the use of force in pursuit of their policy'.[35]

Whether the government believed the report or not – and given its source they would have been foolish not to – it could be used to justify the confiscation of arms. But it did not satisfy MacDermot or Dillon as to why the arms of the National Guard, a legal organisation with no designs on the state, were being confiscated, while the IRA, with its stated rejection of the state, could arm and drill openly. Dillon had put the question directly to de Valera on 1 August, when he asked him to clarify his attitude to the IRA.

De Valera replied, in essence, that because the Oath of Allegiance to the British crown had been removed, there was now a free parliament capable of achieving full republican objectives, and therefore no need for the IRA. He had been working to persuade the IRA of this until the ACA, 'not a body which has any roots in the past, not a body which can be said to have a national objective such as the IRA can be said to have', sprang up.[36]

Time was to show very clearly that the IRA remained stubbornly resistant to de Valera's persuasions and unconvinced by his arguments even after the ACA had disappeared, but the comparison de Valera drew between the IRA and the National Guard, not a single one of whose members had yet been charged with a breach of the peace, infuriated Cumann na nGaedheal. Patrick Hogan accused de Valera of 'trying to justify his anti-democratic past' and said the purpose of the raids was to persuade people that the National Guard was a paramilitary organisation similar to the IRA. 'We were always democrats,' he said, referring to the discredited *Irish Press* stories of the previous year which had claimed that the army and police would not be loyal to the new regime.[37]

It was in this highly charged context that O'Duffy, on 8 August, confirmed that he would go ahead in 'his sacred duty' to lead the National Guard parade in spite of the government's warning, and chose also to make his views on parliament and political parties known. The parliamentary system was un-Irish, he said, and he had found great support for the idea 'that party politics had served their period of usefulness and the sooner a change was effected the better'.[38] He was later to elaborate on these ideas, which amounted to a limited form of corporatism, a concept then popular with both Catholic and fascist political theorists.

His remarks were discussed during the Dáil adjournment debate on 9 August. As usual, MacDermot tried to steer a middle course:

> When the ACA was still the ACA and already in blue shirts and berets, with ex-Ministers marching about in procession with them, the Government paid little or no attention. I might say then that the ACA, or some of them, were making speeches or declarations that personally I very much disliked.[39]

MacDermot objected to any fascist influence creeping into Irish politics. Strangely, he felt that O'Duffy's arrival had been a change for the better, even if he had given the organisation a military sounding name – which 'frankly I wish he had not done'. At the same time, however, he dismissed the government's fears as incomprehensible and ridiculous. O'Duffy's objectives for the National Guard 'took it out of the category of a private army', MacDermot said. He was unable to understand the enrolling of extra police and wondered if some members of the IRA were among the new recruits.[40]

MacDermot may not have been quite so sanguine the following day when O'Duffy elaborated on his constitutional proposals, admitting that part of his proposed changes did borrow from fascism, but only as far as the corporate state was concerned, and asserting again that 'party politics had served their period of usefulness, and the sooner a change was affected the better'. MacDermot by now clearly had reservations, which he was to bring with him to the subsequent negotiations.[41]

On 10 August, as Dublin sweltered in a Horse Show week heatwave, the Cumann na nGaedheal parliamentary party met to discuss the possibility of a fusion with the Centre Party, and for the first time issued a public statement about a potential merger.[42] The negotiations, however, were merely a backdrop to the real drama of the week. Early on Saturday morning, 12 August, the government banned the Blueshirt parade at almost the last possible moment, accusing the National Guard of setting out to destroy parliamentary institutions by violence if necessary. The government decision took O'Duffy by surprise. Trains had been laid on, routes planned, stewards were at the ready. He protested that no coup was planned or even contemplated and that his was an unarmed, law-abiding organisation. He was strongly supported in this by Cosgrave, who threw the full weight of his authority as former President behind his denunciation of the government's action: 'Attempts are being made to suggest to the public that a *coup d'état* is being contemplated. This is nothing but fantastic nonsense, unless the Government themselves have one in mind ... We have commemorated every year the work of three great Irishmen whose adherence to the democratic system was sealed with their lives ... We oppose all *coup d'états* and conspiracies, whatever their origin.'[43]

It was to no avail. O'Duffy now faced a situation in which Government Buildings were held in a virtual state of siege. Going ahead would be certain to result in conflict. He bowed to the inevitable and called off the parade, but arranged church parades for the following Sunday, 20 August. The government countered that if such parades were held the National Guard would be banned. The parades went ahead, and on 21 August the Executive Council issued an order proclaiming the National Guard and re-establishing the Military Tribunal. In the Senate, Ruttledge repeated his charge that the National Guard was anti-democratic and heavily armed.[44]

The ongoing confusion was well reflected in an *Irish Times* editorial just three days before the ban on the National Guard's commemorative parade:

On the one hand General O'Duffy has brought to public affairs a spirit of energy and discipline, which when it has found its proper place, will be a national asset of the first importance. On the other hand the policy of the National Guard remains in doubt. Its organisation is distinctly Fascist, but its professions are democratic. It is constitutional but it desires large and as yet vague changes in the present system of parliamentary Government. Some of the most active minds in Mr. Cosgrave's party seem to have allied themselves with the National Guard. The result is three oppositions which today have few points of contact and no common policy.

It went on to urge the three parties to get together as a matter of national urgency, a point the newspaper repeated with even greater force after what it called the government's 'cynically inconsistent' banning of the National Guard.[45]

The Cumann na nGaedheal and Centre Party negotiators had reached early agreement on the need for a merger, and that it should be a genuine merger, not the swallowing of the smaller party by the bigger; the new party would have its own name. Dillon insists in his *Memoir* that he was not enthusiastic about the merger but that MacDermot was: 'Frank, I think, felt that he would naturally rise to the top of any organisation of which be became a member, and thus would eventually become the leader of the new party which would emerge.'[46] MacDermot recalled events differently: he was reluctant, Dillon enthusiastic. But events were moving rapidly. The banning of the National Guard gave the negotiations a new urgency, convincing some of the negotiators that de Valera, having outlawed one part of the opposition, would soon move to ban the remaining parties. From today's perspective this prospect may appear far-fetched: in the prevailing climate it carried its own credibility.

The banning also introduced a new factor into the equation. O'Duffy was now isolated and his new movement highly vulnerable. Though he had asserted his independence of all parties, even proclaimed his contempt for the very notion of party, the protection of a larger organisation looked more attractive. And in the confusion which surrounded the merger talks, which at times came close to panic, the possibility of O'Duffy joining in suited those who wanted not just a bigger, more dynamic opposition, but wanted also a new leader and a new style of leadership.

Cosgrave's low key, undramatic leadership was seen by some of his colleagues as part of Cumann na nGaedheal's electoral difficulties. De Valera excited passions; Cosgrave did not. Fianna Fáil exuded energy; Cumann na nGaedheal was staid. It was argued that Cosgrave's qualities had served the country well in its hour of need, but now something different was required. It was time for somebody new and dramatic, somebody with energy and organisational skills who would beat de Valera at his own game.[47]

MacDermot had made it clear that Cosgrave would not be acceptable to him as leader: it would give the impression that the Centre Party had been subsumed into Cumann na nGaedheal. MacDermot favoured Patrick

Hogan as the best available leader, as indeed he might have been, but Hogan refused.[48]

Cosgrave had no reason to expect loyalty from MacDermot, but he might have expected more from some of his senior colleagues. At this point, O'Duffy, strongly backed by Blythe and Tierney, emerged as the preferred choice as leader of the proposed new party. It was an act of catastrophic ill-judgement in every respect. O'Duffy was affable, energetic, a self-publicist famed for his organisational skills. He had a record for bravery in the War of Independence and was seen as a martyr to Fianna Fáil. But he had no political skill or experience, his behaviour had earned him the suspicion of Cosgrave's cabinet, he was neither a profound nor an original thinker, and he had no seat in the Dáil. To cap it all, he was now leader of a banned political organisation.

O'Duffy was approached by an 'unofficial' delegation from Cumann na nGaedheal, and then later met with Blythe and O'Higgins, who pressed him to accept the leadership. When he indicated that he was willing to do so, the steering committee which had been conducting the merger negotiations approached him formally.

Cosgrave was not only willing to stand down, but prepared to propose O'Duffy for the leadership. As far as Dillon, who had never actually met O'Duffy, was concerned, that was sufficient for him. MacDermot had never met O'Duffy either, but he too made no objection.[49] Tierney and Dillon were asked to visit O'Duffy formally. 'O'Duffy received us cordially and indicated he would accept the leadership,' Dillon recalled.[50] In hindsight, the fact of accepting as their leader a man not personally known to either MacDermot or Dillon reflects strangely on their political judgement, and even more strangely on the judgement of those in Cumann na nGaedheal who did know him.

Now that a leader had been found, all that was needed was a new party. MacDermot would have little difficulty persuading his organisation, which instinctively favoured Cumann na nGaedheal over Fianna Fáil, and would make little distinction between Cumann na nGaedheal and O'Duffy's organisation. Nor was he jettisoning a party with any real prospects of success. The Centre Party was essentially a two-man band with little real development potential. MacDermot was never a man for the long haul, and the offer of deputy leadership of the main opposition party after just eighteen months in politics was a tempting one. And, as Dillon had noted, there was always the possibility of the leadership.

MacDermot did, however, have two problems. The first was O'Duffy and his flirtation with fascist ideas. MacDermot had already made clear, and would do so with force and clarity throughout his political career, his utter opposition to fascism in any form and his antipathy to uniformed movements. He believed, however, that O'Duffy's attachment to fascism was superficial and that he could be persuaded to renounce his autocratic leanings. This was to be a binding part of the formal agreement amongst the parties, and the presence of constitutional heavyweights like McGilligan and Cosgrave would he thought ensure that O'Duffy kept to his word. He also felt the merger was justified by the government's tolerance of the IRA and the state of widespread intimidation which existed in the country.[51]

MacDermot's second problem was Dillon. From the outset he had been disdainful of both Sinn Féin parties, and it was less than a year since he had refused to join MacDermot's proposed new party because of the danger of its eventually being subsumed into Cumann na nGaedheal. Admittedly, he had made common cause with Cosgrave's party on many of the major issues of the day, and in particular had come to doubt the government's even-handedness on law and order, but now he was being asked to take on a major leadership role in a new joint party. It was not something Dillon could easily have envisaged just two years earlier and he had some explaining to do, not least to himself.

For his part, Cosgrave's approach to the merger was typically understated. Having decided to step down, he did just that. As soon as the Árd Comhairle of Cumann na nGaedheal gave the go-ahead for the merger talks, he left Dublin on 16 August to holiday in Carna, where he remained until the end of the month. This was not the act of a man who feared for his position. Had he insisted on holding the leadership, many – indeed most – of his colleagues would have stayed with him. Cosgrave knew that if he stayed on neither MacDermot nor O'Duffy would enter the new party and thus the opposition would continue to be divided. When he said that 'he didn't care who leads – his concern was what was going to be done about the unity and prosperity of the country,' Cosgrave was undoubtedly genuine.[52] He would have been less than human, however, had he not been hurt at the readiness of some of his Cumann na nGaedheal colleagues to pass him by.

If Cosgrave had reservations they never surfaced, but the way in which the new party was developing did not please everybody. Professor James Hogan, brother of Patrick Hogan, voiced misgivings, but for the moment he seemed to be on his own and kept his views more or less to himself.[53]

The proposed merger would make O'Duffy the leader of the state's second biggest party. If he, or some around him, had ambitions to use the new movement as a vehicle for fascist policies, these ideas were not apparent to others, and the undertaking given by O'Duffy to work strictly along democratic lines was accepted in good faith. Given his subsequent behaviour, however, it seems that O'Duffy's understanding of the deal was very different from that of the other parties.

Among O'Duffy's admirers were some who doubted the wisdom of what he was doing. The maverick TD Patrick Belton, of whom Dillon had been cuttingly sceptical when the first moves were being made by MacDermot to form a new party in 1932, wrote to O'Duffy on 5 September:

> I am very uneasy about the 'fusion'. MacDermot is a chancer from the word go, and Dillon has dirtied himself irretrievably in his remarks about the national anthem and the flag. The furthest fusion conditions we should have is President and Vice President for you and Cosgrave. I will not support anything else. The front bench must be selected on their merits ... men who know finance, agriculture and industry and should not be made up of Professors, Lawyers etc. I should much rather see you out on your own ... you are going to carry a dead weight that will pull you down and that you will never shake off. Beware, your enemies call you a Dictator openly, pseudo friends whisper it, and if later some friends charge you with it, it might be disastrous.[54]

And so, on the basis of a working document presented by MacDermot, and against a background of further raids on the National Guard's headquarters in Dublin and a growing number of cattle seizures from farmers who had failed to make their annuity payments, negotiations were intensified. The four essential points outlined by MacDermot were straightforward and found ready agreement. They were that (i) the party would be known as the United Ireland Party, (ii) O'Duffy was to be the leader, (iii) Cosgrave would lead the party in the Dáil and (iv) the executive committee was to consist of twelve members to be nominated by O'Duffy, Cosgrave and MacDermot. The main details of policy were to be prepared jointly and as a matter of urgency after formal agreement was reached.

The standing committee of Cumann na nGaedheal, in the absence of Cosgrave, who was still on holiday, formally ratified these proposals on 1 September,[55] and on the same day the standing committee of the National Farmers and Ratepayers Association – which was still the executive body of the Centre Party – met at their headquarters at 23 St Stephen's Green and likewise recommended the merger to its members.[56] It now remained for the local associations to accept or reject the proposal, and at meetings over the next few days all counties reacted positively, with the exception of Wexford and Cavan. The only TD to dissent was WR Kent, but he did not threaten active opposition, going quietly to the Independent benches, and did not contest any subsequent elections.[57] In spite of his earlier reservations, Dillon was clearly active in lobbying county associations and was very much in evidence on 8 September when the final decision was taken, persuading waverers and in general drumming up support.

Both parties met in separate conventions on 8 September. At the

Cumann na nGaedheal convention Cosgrave outlined the background and the need for a new party, and told his colleagues that it was unimportant to him who led: his concern was the unity and prosperity of Ireland. O'Duffy was then invited to address the convention, which received him enthusiastically.

Later that day a similar procedure was enacted by the Centre Party, where MacDermot explained his reason for the new departure. Dillon did likewise, after which O'Duffy was introduced, though to a less enthusiastic reception than earlier.

For the first time, Dillon explained his decision. His preference, he told the convention, had been to maintain the identity and independence of the National Centre Party. It had been difficult for him to enter a party with men who had been his political adversaries and with whom he had had many a hard encounter. He found it hard to swallow his prejudices. Yet his former opponents had had similar personal views, and if in the interest of the country they were prepared to sink their prejudices, why should he not do likewise?[58]

Dillon's volte-face appears to have been reached without any great soul-searching. A decision taken in the fevered political climate of the time, once taken it was enthusiastically embraced. Never once did he subsequently doubt the rightness of his decision, or for that matter regret it.

That, essentially, was the start of the new party. No attempt was made that day to have a joint meeting. Two days later the officer board was announced: the original panel of twelve had swollen to eighteen, and there were six vice-presidents instead of the three initially intended.

In addition to Cosgrave, Dillon and MacDermot, the other vice-presidents were Michael Tierney, nominated by Cosgrave; Peter Nugent, by the Centre Party; and James Hogan, by O'Duffy. Tierney, Professor of Greek at University College, Dublin, was a blunt, forthright personality, who in his later career as President of UCD developed a reputation for combining the visionary with the authoritarian. He had briefly been a TD for Mayo and was in charge of Cumann na nGaedheal publicity in the 1932 election. He was impatient with Cumann na nGaedheal's lack of energy and ideas, and had a keen interest in contemporary Catholic political thinking, especially the ideas contained in the papal encyclical *Quadragesimo Anno*. This interest he was shortly to translate into a vigorous series of articles in the new party's newspaper, *United Ireland*.

Hogan was Professor of History at University College, Cork. A brother of Patrick Hogan, he was an outstanding scholar. Frustrated with Cumann na nGaedheal, he wrote to Tierney in September 1933 saying that 'we are in our present plight because we never equipped ourselves with a self consistent political philosophy'.[59] Like Tierney, he looked to *Quadragesimo*

Anno for inspiration. He had also an obsession with communism, out of which came a book published in 1935, which was to be important at the time, called *Could Ireland Become Communist?* a danger Hogan clearly believed was real.

It was almost certainly the first occasion when practising intellectuals were given a formative role in shaping a new and major party, and from the outset the two men saw the party as a vehicle for bringing new ideas into Irish politics, though it is by no means clear that their designs were widely known.

The third of the new vice-presidents was very different. Peter Nugent, a leading member of the AOH, had been Dillon's election agent in Donegal. He was Dillon's personal nominee, his presence confirming Dillon's determination to establish a link, however tenuous, with the remnants of the Irish Party.

The party's national executive was a strange blend of experienced politicians and political neophytes. O'Duffy's nominees contained only one established politician, O'Higgins, while the other five – Commandant Ned Cronin, Col. Jerry Ryan, Capt. Padraig Quinn, Sean Ruane and barrister Charles Conroy – were entirely new to politics and three had a strongly military background. Cosgrave's nominees – Costello, Mulcahy, O'Sullivan, Fitzgerald-Kenney and Blythe – were all former and trusted colleagues who, with one exception, Dan Morrissey, had government experience. The Centre Party nominees had only one elected politician, E. Curran, and one former TD, Patrick Baxter, while its other members – FB Barton, EJ Cussen, Robert Hogan and ER Richards-Orpen – were totally devoid of political experience, unknown and almost exclusively farmer oriented.

It was a potentially unstable and incompatible executive from the start. Thirteen of the twenty-four members had never been in the Dáil and most had little political experience of any kind, something which was also true of the three new vice-presidents. In calmer times the combination might have achieved balance and stability, but the times were not calm, and neither was the new party leadership.

For Dillon, however, the formation of Fine Gael,[60] as the new party soon came to be known, opened new possibilities and put him centre stage in Irish political life – all within a year of entering politics and before he had reached his thirty-first birthday.

CHAPTER SEVEN

O'DUFFY, TURMOIL AND CHAOS

'I am sorry to have to talk so bitterly, because I think the situation is getting past us ... this country cannot last unless we all pull up and take stock of the situation.'
Patrick Hogan, Dáil Debates, 28 September 1933

S EAN LEMASS was engaging in political point-scoring when he described the diverse elements which combined to create the United Ireland Party as the 'Cripple Alliance', but there was an element of truth in his taunt also. Of its component parts, Cumann na nGaedheal had been born out of the need to give political life to the new Free State; the Centre Party had been a product of the Economic War; and the Blueshirts, in their own minds at any rate, had come into existence to protect freedom of speech and assembly. Now, with little time for gestation or reflection, all three had merged into a new political movement under a leader who had never been a member of a political party and was devoid of parliamentary experience.

From the outset the United Ireland Party was a strange mixture of experience and immaturity, of people drawn together because of necessity more than natural coherence. It was formed in an atmosphere of fear, apprehension and anxiety, when many of its members felt themselves under threat, physically from the IRA, financially from the Economic War, politically from a hostile government. Yet not all of the reasons which brought the party into being were negative, and its founding provided a platform for a number of men who wanted to bring new ideas and issues into Irish political life.

The party's first year was acted out against a background of dramatic intensity and bitterness deeper than anything experienced even in the depths of the Civil War. Over the course of these twelve months the government tried to outlaw the Blueshirts through the courts, and on every occasion failed, though some of its leaders were jailed and there were several unsuccessful attempts to put O'Duffy behind bars. The government then tried to introduce legislation to make the wearing of the blue shirt illegal, only to have its efforts frustrated by the delaying power of the Senate. Thus provoked, the government moved to abolish the Upper

House. Throughout this time the Military Tribunal was used against both the Blueshirts and the IRA, and farmers who either refused to, or could not, pay their rates. Political intimidation was widespread all over the country, political meetings were regularly interrupted, and political debate continued to rake over every unforgiving memory of the previous decade.

For the new United Ireland Party, however, the year was dominated by the unpredictable, mercurial and erratic leadership of Eoin O'Duffy. Remembered largely as the erstwhile leader of the United Ireland Party/Fine Gael and for his Blueshirt's participation in the Spanish Civil War, O'Duffy has sometimes been depicted as a buffoon and at other times as a fascist. Both are caricatures, very wide of the mark. There was nothing sinister about O'Duffy. He had a distinguished reputation from the War of Independence and had shown great energy and flair in building up the Garda Síochána from August 1922, when he was appointed Commissioner by Kevin O'Higgins at just thirty years of age. In personality he was open, bluff and garrulous, and he had a capacity to inspire loyalty. But if he had great virtues, he also had faults. In his book *Guardians of the Peace*, Conor Brady describes O'Duffy as 'vain, domineering, constantly in search of publicity, intolerant of the shortcomings of others and slow to credit their virtues'. He adds that, while O'Duffy's qualities were well suited to the crisis conditions of the early 1920s, 'it was not until very much later that the Governments of the Cosgrave era were to realise just how difficult a man Eoin O'Duffy could be'.[1] Indeed, by a strange irony, had Cosgrave been re-elected in 1932, O'Duffy would almost certainly have been removed as Chief of Police and moved to a less sensitive position.[2]

As a political leader, O'Duffy's great defect was his judgement, which lacked all subtlety. His views on Northern Ireland were robustly closer to Fianna Fáil than to Cumann na nGaedheal or the Centre Party, yet he saw no need to compromise on expressing them. His ideas as to what constituted legitimate political action and his willingness to tolerate illegal activities sat uneasily on the shoulders of a former Chief of Police and current leader of a constitutional party, yet he seemed to see no inconsistency in this. He had no fundamental problem with the intrinsically anti-democratic nature of all fascist movements, and could not see the incongruity of a democratic politician lauding the activities of Hitler and Mussolini. His judgement of people was also flawed, and he drew around him a group of hot-headed and irresponsible men of little political competence.

Interestingly, the first warnings about O'Duffy came not from local observers but from the special correspondent of the *New York Times*, Clair Price. He wrote on 10 September 1933: 'Much reliance had been placed on General O'Duffy to win over popular support from Mr. de Valera, but somehow the General's leadership has fallen short of the achievements expected of it. General O'Duffy, it is felt, has been inclined to speak too freely to the press and to announce courses of action from which he has been frequently obliged to recede, all of which has meant loss of prestige ... he must show greater judgement and astuteness if he is to lead the party to victory against such able and experienced a tactician as de Valera.'[3]

A week later the same correspondent wrote again. Noting that Cosgrave 'was as devoted to parliamentary institutions and constitutional methods as any old-fashioned liberal, and only admitted the ACA on condition that it remains an unarmed body,' he predicted that with O'Duffy's arrival 'the turbulent spirits of the ACA would be withdrawn from the influence of the scrupulous Mr. Cosgrave'.[4]

Price was to prove an accurate prophet, but in the short term O'Duffy brought new vigour to the movement. His immediate task was to organise the party – much of his early reputation had been built on his ability as an organiser, first of the Garda Síochána and later of the 1932 Eucharistic Congress, and he set about the work of party-building with enthusiasm. New branches were established and old ones reactivated. By the Árd Fheis in February 1934 the party had 1,038 branches as against Fianna Fáil's 1,800.[5] Public meetings were held on a major scale; by March 1934 O'Duffy had spoken in twenty-three of the twenty-six counties.[6] Dillon also put in a hectic schedule of appearances throughout the country. The presence of Blueshirts was a regular feature at all of these meetings, acting as stewards, providing guards of honour and involving themselves in clashes with interrupters, real or potential. Clearly, if spirited leadership was what the new party wanted, it was getting it from O'Duffy. For all his activity, however, there was one recurring difficulty: the problem of establishing a unified organisation while allowing for the diversity each party, and especially the Blueshirts, sought.

ONLY THE principles of policy had been agreed upon when the party was established; the working out of the details was handed over to a special committee. The lead in policy development was seized by the intellectuals James Hogan and Michael Tierney, disenchanted Cumann na nGaedheal supporters who were anxious to move the party in a new direction. They became the prime movers behind the new party's corporate programme, which they later elaborated in a series of articles in the party newspaper *United Ireland*.[7] Their correspondence at this time shows that they wanted to go very much further than what the politicians eventually agreed. Their ambition was to upgrade the Senate significantly and make it a Supreme Economic Council in a new system, with legislative functions only slightly inferior to those of the Dáil. They also wanted to abolish proportional representation, believing that the type of changes they envisaged would be unlikely without strong parliamentary majorities, which were difficult to achieve under proportional representation.

What Hogan wanted most of all was a strong and distinctive statement of policy. Writing in September he argued that there was 'a need for a strong political statement to unite the UIP. If this is not done when the iron is hot, it will be immensely difficult to do it later. If policy is left over to the future, I can see the different elements in United Ireland cancelling each other out ... ending up with the amorphous utilitarianism of the Cumann na nGaedheal sort ... I think you will agree that we are in our present plight because we never equipped ourselves with a self-consistent political philosophy. The Cumann na nGaedheal Party is the strongest of the component elements of United Ireland and we should not forget that in power its leaders dreaded principle like a cat dreads water.'[8]

The policy when it appeared was inevitably a compromise, but it was nonetheless wide-ranging, and novel in places. In spite of O'Duffy's desire for a Northern Ireland policy closer to that of Fianna Fáil, the voices of Cumann na nGaedheal and the Centre Party prevailed, calling for reunification 'as a free and equal member of the British Commonwealth of Nations', though MacDermot did not get his wish to spell out in detail how this might be done. Tierney and Hogan won a commitment to abolish proportional representation and to reform local government – in any event, Cosgrave had long come to the conclusion, as de Valera would later, that proportional representation was particularly unsuited to Irish conditions. There were traces, too, of the influence of the American New Deal in plans for dealing with unemployment and reconstruction. Hogan and Tierney had invested some considerable thought on this issue, and proposed, for example, the setting up of a reconstruction corps for the unemployed. The most interesting part of the programme, however, was the proposal to set up industrial and agricultural corporations with full statutory powers.

This was the first time a major Irish party had adopted ideas then popular in continental Europe, but what was even more significant was their modest scale as they appeared in the new programme, and the extent to which O'Duffy's earlier proposals were excluded or diluted. There was no mention, for example, of his plan to re-model the Dáil, no echo of his claim that all parliaments 'gabble too much', nor is there any mention of his view that suitable fascist methods and models might be applied to the Irish situation. The programme declared in emphatic terms its total opposition to any form of dictatorship and its utter allegiance to the democratic system.[9]

Time was to show that keeping the General and some of his supporters to their word was more easily written than achieved. The strange nature of Fine Gael's leadership soon became obvious as the party organised its Dáil

strategy. For the first time a major political party was led by a non-parlia-
mentarian, and though O'Duffy chaired the meetings of the new
parliamentary party (or at least was entitled to do so), his absence from the
Dáil made for a sense of unreality. He was removed from much of the real
action and debate, and was not in a position to defend himself against
charges made in the House. More than that, he was free from many of the
procedural constraints and disciplines of the Dáil, a feature increasingly
reflected in his platform speeches. The new front bench led by Cosgrave
included Costello, McGilligan, Mulcahy, John Marcus O'Sullivan,
O'Higgins, MacDermot and Dillon, who was assigned the agriculture
portfolio.

The absorption of the Blueshirts in a new political party did not lessen
the government's hostility to the movement or change its mind about its
objectives. On 15 September the premises of the National Guard in
Dublin were raided by the police, who seized documents and blocked up
the doors of the building. Fine Gael appealed to the Military Tribunal,
arguing that the National Guard was a legitimate political organisation, but
after a three-day hearing the appeal was turned down without any reasons
being given.[10]

The summer had seen more violence associated with the Economic War,
and a number of county councils were suspended because they refused to
collect rates due from farmers. The IRA's dissatisfaction with Fianna Fáil
was also becoming more manifest, and it stepped up its own economic war
with Bass ale as its main target. Publicans who continued to sell the beer
were intimidated, and on one day in September sixteen pubs were raided
and their owners brutalised, some of them tarred and feathered.[11] Nor was
there any abatement in political violence. Dillon spoke at a meeting in
Limerick on 24 September which was totally wrecked by hostile interrupters.[12] Thirty-three people were injured, some of them seriously. Two
days later the deputy leader of the Blueshirts, Ned Cronin, had a warrant
issued for his arrest by the Military Tribunal.[13]

This was the background against which the Dáil reconvened on 27
September 1933. One of the first items taken was a motion censuring the
government over its use of the Military Tribunal. It was the first of many
angry debates that session.

Lemass led the way for the government, describing O'Duffy as a bitter
political partisan and incompetent when he was Chief of Police. He
attacked Dillon, accusing him, in heated exchanges, of inciting farmers not
to pay their rates.[14] This was not the first time the charge had been made,
and in particular Dillon was accused of saying one thing from party platforms and another in Leinster House. This charge Dillon vehemently denied.

If farmers 'have the wherewithal to pay', he said, the government had every right to insist on the rates being paid, but the policies of the present government, he argued, had reduced a large number of farmers to a position where they were simply unable to do so.[15] He was supported by WR Kent, whose speeches in this period showed him to have been ruggedly independent. He denied any campaign by Dillon or MacDermot, and said that 'any man in a position to pay rates is not worthy of being called an Irishman if he does not do so voluntarily,' but he was adamant that many farmers just did not have the money.[16]

The debate took a bizarre turn when de Valera charged Mulcahy with what amounted to treason, accusing him of having had a secret meeting with a British War Minister in Glasgow, a charge which proved to be totally without foundation but from which neither de Valera nor the *Irish Press* ever fully retreated.[17] The Dáil discussion did nothing to calm the general situation, which continued to worsen. Military intervention was necessary to restore order at a Fine Gael meeting in Cork on 1 October, while a week later the worst disturbances to date took place at an O'Duffy meeting in Tralee, Co. Kerry.[18] An IRA group, which included Stevie Coughlan, later a Labour TD, had planned to assassinate O'Duffy on his way to Tralee, but failed largely as a result of their own incompetence.[19] When he arrived in the town, however, O'Duffy received a nasty head wound when he was struck by a hammer on his way to the meeting; his car was burned, the hall was besieged by a stone-throwing crowd, and a Mills bomb was thrown through the skylight – had it exploded there would have been carnage. The following day a further unexploded bomb was found in the hall. Two hundred police were unable to deal with the crowd, and it was not until soldiers dressed in battle kit arrived from Cork late that evening that order was restored. O'Duffy and Cronin had to be escorted to the county borders by a large force of police.[20]

The Tralee incidents were the worst so far, and de Valera unequivocally condemned them some days later,[21] but by now the pattern was being repeated in other parts of the country. The military had to intervene again at a meeting in Kilkenny on 22 October,[22] and a week later a Bandon Blueshirt, Hugh O'Reilly, was taken from his home in the middle of the night and beaten to death.[23] Side by side with these incidents was the growing unrest associated with the non-payment of rates. Each passing week, more and more farmers were brought before the Military Tribunal and charged with forcibly resisting demands for rates and annuities. The government insisted that non-payment was part of an organised conspiracy, while Fine Gael pleaded that the farmers were genuinely unable to pay.

Dillon, whose particular interest was the plight of the farmers, was the principal speaker at a 'victory' celebration in Waterford on 12 October 1933 to welcome home farmers acquitted by the Military Tribunal.[24] He headed up a special party committee in January 1934 to look after the welfare of jailed farmers.[25] Virtually every one of his Dáil speeches returned to the economic and social damage being caused by the Economic War, and he vigorously defended the stand taken by Fine Gael councillors who refused to strike a rate:

> That was a perfectly legal thing to do, and there were perfectly proper methods of going about having that matter tried out in court and a verdict got. They took a certain course of action that the circumstances justified. They were entitled as public men, if they believed it to be in the public interest, to decline to strike a rate. They did it on the grounds that the Government in withholding a large part of the agricultural grant after the original rate had been struck, was doing a gross injustice and was doing something manifestly contrary to the will of the people.

He contrasted the farmers's behaviour with that of the IRA when charged with an offence: 'They went to court. They recognised it. They did not shout "Up the Republic," and they abided by its verdict.'[26]

He denied the charges repeatedly levelled by Fianna Fáil that he was inciting farmers not to pay their rates, and challenged Agriculture Minister Jim Ryan to repeat the allegation outside the House. Fianna Fáil's accusation culminating in a vituperative attack on Dillon in February by MacEntee, who accused Dillon of a 'wink and nod' approach to the farmers' action. In spite of much bad-tempered bluster, MacEntee never produced any specific evidence to substantiate his claim.[27]

Shortly after the government banned the National Guard in August 1933, it had reconstituted itself as the Young Ireland Association. In December the government banned the new association, declaring it an illegal organisation. Fine Gael responded by dissolving the Young Ireland Association and setting up the League of Youth as an integral part of the party. In the confusion of events which unfolded, Fine Gael meetings were banned and O'Duffy was arrested at a huge public meeting in Westport and arraigned before the Military Tribunal. Other leading Blueshirts were also arrested, among them Ned Cronin, who was sentenced to three months detention in Arbour Hill. Fine Gael lawyers succeeded in having O'Duffy released and began a legal action to establish the legality of the League of Youth.[28]

The situation was bizarre and uncertain. The main opposition party, many of whose members had been government ministers just a few years earlier, now found itself in a position where its newspaper, *United Ireland*, was banned, its meetings disrupted and some of its leading members subjected to police harassment. Violence was by now the norm at Fine Gael meetings, and in the new year two members of the Blueshirts were killed in Cork and another Blueshirt sympathiser was killed in Dundalk.[29] The extraordinary state of affairs is captured in the minutes of the standing committee of Fine Gael for 30 November which, after reporting a number of decisions, noted that: 'at this stage it was announced that the homes of General O'Duffy and Mr. Blythe were being raided and also the offices of the Young Ireland Association. It being necessary that the people concerned should be present at these raids, the Committee adjourned.'[30] As Fine Gael reacted to this generalised sense of threat, even moderates like James Hogan began to believe that 'it is evident we are up against a more corrupt tyranny than even we imagined'.[31]

In these circumstances Fine Gael closed ranks, and the growing unease within the party at O'Duffy's behaviour was hidden from public view. James Hogan, writing to Tierney in late November, confessed he did not like the way things were developing.

> I think the Army Tribunal decision [not to allow Fine Gael reopen its premises] a bad blow. It gives de Valera the cue he was looking for. As far as the IRA's attitude towards us is concerned his point of view seems to be *'orne messieurs, les assassins commencent.'* The worst of it is that we laid ourselves open to this repulse through sheer carelessness, for which O'Duffy is to blame. As I said, we have many leaders but no leadership. I have no confidence in O'Duffy and only wish Dillon was at the head of things. Honestly I think O'Duffy has made every conceivable blunder since coming on the scene, and it seems to me it was an ill day he got control of the ACA in July ... It is a great pity. I think we should pin our faith more and more on Dillon. He is progressive and has judgement and personality.[32]

Hogan's views, which were shared by his brother, Patrick, were not to surface publicly for almost a year. He was not alone in having doubts about O'Duffy's style. In November, Dillon and MacDermot insisted, unsuccessfully, on being represented on the committee of the Young Ireland Association, and early in the new year Dillon sounded a warning bell about the financial chaos beginning to develop under O'Duffy's stewardship.[33] For his part, O'Duffy complained bitterly at a meeting of the Fine Gael parliamentary party in January 1934 about the poor support he was getting from the party's TDs. The gulf between elected and non-elected members was widening, and after that encounter O'Duffy stopped attending parliamentary party meetings completely.[34]

A further indication of a difference of opinion, if not yet a rift, came in February when EJ Cussen, a Cork farmer and leading Blueshirt activist, and a member of the Fine Gael national executive, called for 'direct action' by farmers faced with seizure of their goods. By this presumably he meant open resistance to the police, and for this statement he was reprimanded at a private meeting of the standing committee of Fine Gael.[35] For the moment, however, the need for solidarity in the face of an increasingly vindictive enemy stilled any public expression of these divisions.

The first Dáil debate of 1934 showed just how deep was the gap between the parties. *The Irish Times* wrote that 'for sheer vitriolic ill-feeling on both sides of the House nothing before has been seen in the Dáil to compare with the savage exchanges yesterday'. The murder of the Cork Blueshirt, Hugh O'Reilly, was raised, and in heated argument O'Higgins accused MacEntee of 'laughing at the murder', to which MacEntee retorted that 'any Deputy with the name O'Higgins had no right to talk about murder in this House'.[36] Dillon found himself sucked into this atmosphere in spite of having no Civil War baggage of his own. On 7 February he accused de Valera of hypocrisy and of stirring up hatred, and blamed him for banning the League of Youth, which he said stood for the maintenance of law and order and for the rights of the Irish people to chose who were to be the governors of the country.[37]

The government made its most determined attempt yet to outlaw the Blueshirts with the Wearing of Uniforms Bill introduced in late February. Fianna Fáil charged that the Blueshirts represented the militarisation of Irish politics, and that their very existence would create disorders which would lead to anarchy and civil war. The government case, put most trenchantly by Lemass and MacEntee, insisted that O'Duffy was anti-democratic and dictatorial, and that 'while his hazy and indeterminate ideas had been picked up on a Mediterranean cruise, they were none the less dangerous for all that'.[38] It was also alleged that the Blueshirts represented a cynical change of policy by a party which had lost two elections and was unlikely to win back power at the polls in the near future. Noting that bitterness was now more intense than in 1924, Lemass put the blame for this on 'the loud-mouthed opposition politicians, who went around the country deliberately fanning the flames of bitterness for party purposes'.[39]

De Valera was strangely conciliatory. He appealed to the opposition 'to quit the tom-foolery of Blueshirtism'. 'I have listened to expressions from the opposition benches which make it quite clear to me that they have none of the irresponsibilities which O'Duffy has been guilty of on platforms,' he said, 'but they are not able to restrain him.' He paid an extra-ordinary tribute to the loyalty and integrity of the institutions inherited from Cumann na nGaedheal, built up by 'people who regarded us as deadly enemies until a few years ago'.[40] Such magnanimity was rare in the 1930s.

The case for the Blueshirts was as predictable and passionately argued as the case against them. It was put at its most vigorous by Patrick Hogan

who, despite his own reservations about O'Duffy, said the Uniforms Bill
was a deliberate attempt to destroy a lawful organisation. Fianna Fáil had
introduced militarism to recent Irish politics: 'they were fed on it ... used it
to destroy the State, to corrupt and intimidate the country. They did it and
gloried in it up to two years ago.' Fine Gael had 'not been allowed exercise
its legal rights, had been subject to every form of blackguardism and intimidation', while not a single Fianna Fáil meeting had been attacked. He
accused the government of 'going around the country naming us as traitors
and telling the country that there is a war with England and that we are
supporting the English enemy – saying "they are traitors", and left it to
their followers to draw their own conclusions.'[41]

His speech was echoed by many others, all of whom denied any fascist
influences in the Blueshirts. Even MacDermot took a hard line, goaded by
the intemperate tone of government speakers, and in particular MacEntee,
whose remarks he saw as a virtual incitement to murder. He quoted, as
typical of many others, a statement by Fianna Fáil's Leitrim TD, Ben
Maguire: 'Frank MacDermot is betraying this country in exactly the same
way as Judas Iscariot betrayed Our Lord.' He gave examples of widespread
intimidation, of Fianna Fáil collusion with the IRA, and quoted a Kerry
TD who had said in de Valera's presence that 'the IRA are the real people
who ought to be in control of this House and this country'.[42]

It was the strongest party speech MacDermot ever made in the Dáil and,
coming from him, it was particularly telling. Dillon, for his part, fought
the proposed Bill vigorously. He told the House that the Blueshirts had
restored the right of free speech and existed to prevent intimidation. They
were no danger to the state. He was critical, rather, of what he saw as the
government backbenchers' 'dependence on the IRA to retain their seats by
intimidation'. Taunted by MacEntee about his new colleagues, he retorted:
'any colleague I have got I am proud of him'. Martin Corry, destined to be
Dillon's lifelong sparring partner, called him a 'little pup who was stuck
under the bed from 1916 to '31 and who then came out of it to tell this
House that he would neither take off his hat to the "Soldiers Song" nor kow-
tow to the flag.' He was involved also in exchanges with the Labour leader,
William Norton, who referred to Dillon's 'anti-trade union activities' during the Ballaghaderreen strike.[43] Dillon gave as good as he got, and was
developing into a formidable political street-fighter.

The Uniforms Bill was 'guillotined' through the Dáil on 14 March but
was refused a Second Reading by the Senate a week later. The Bill could not
now become law for a further eighteen months, so the whole thrust of the
legislation was frustrated. The Senate paid a high price for this act of
defiance, for the very next day de Valera introduced a Bill to abolish the
Upper House.

Dillon saw this as a further example of de Valera's move to complete dictatorship, and threw himself into the controversy. He was in an angry frame of mind because his home at Ballaghaderreen had been attacked by political opponents the previous Saturday night and daubed with offensive slogans. 'The Senate is not prepared to lend a hand in this oppression of President de Valera's political opponents in this country, and because it would not lend a hand in that work, the Senate is going to be destroyed,' he thundered.[44]

Lemass answered from the government benches: 'It is about time the Irish people became masters in this country. This is a Bill to make them masters,' and he went on to attack the influences of former Unionists – 'the Jamesons and Granards' – in the Senate.[45] Frank Aiken went even further, referring to 'British agents in the Senate'.[46] Their comments were criticised by Dillon and even more emphatically by MacDermot, who said that 'the Fianna Fáil mentality as exposed by Corry (crudely) and Lemass (less so) will amount to deporting ex-Unionists from the Free State and will re-enforce partition'.[47] In spite of this, the Bill passed comfortably in the Dáil, was defeated not surprisingly in the Senate, and became law eighteen months later, by which time the Senate had ceased to have an effective influence in any case.[48]

As 1934 moved from spring to summer, the government remained unable to find alternative markets for agricultural exports. With a glut of cattle appearing on the market, the government embarked on its calf slaughter scheme, a scheme which was to live on in farming folk-memory for decades to come. Its purpose was to reduce cattle numbers by slaughtering 200,000 calves a year. The governments' impotence was summed up by the Minister for Agriculture, Jim Ryan: 'perhaps it is a calamity to see the calves slaughtered, but if there is no other way out of it, if we can't consume the beef ourselves, if no other country is prepared to take it from us, the only solution is to cut down the number ...'[49] By the end of April, calves were being slaughtered at a rate of 25,000 a week. The government paid a bounty to the farmer, while the meat was given away under the free beef scheme or fed to animals. In some cases the carcasses were simply buried in the ground.[50] Dillon thought the whole scheme was an outrage. It was more than that, he believed, it was a deliberate attempt to destroy the cattle industry and replace it with intensive tillage, crushing the hated 'ranchers' and putting land in the hands of Fianna Fáil supporters.

Against this volatile background, O'Duffy now faced his first electoral trial, the local elections of June 1934, which, against the advice of more experienced colleagues, he chose to make a test of his standing in the country. Up to this point Cumann na nGaedheal had never taken local elections seriously, leaving them essentially to commercial interests, unlike Fianna

Fáil which had used the elections of the late 1920s as a means of building up party support. Now O'Duffy determined that Fine Gael should do likewise; indeed, Dillon ran for Roscommon County Council and subsequently served for a full period, though not with any great enthusiasm. It was a good political strategy which O'Duffy backed up with tireless countrywide campaigning, but he could not resist the temptation to make foolish claims, and predicted that his party would win control of twenty of the twenty-three councils being contested.[51] In the event, Fianna Fáil won a majority on fourteen councils, Fine Gael took six and three were tied. Overall, Fine Gael won 596 seats to Fianna Fáil's 728.[52] Objectively it was a reasonable result, but by O'Duffy's self-proclaimed standard it was not and did little to support the belief that he could outbid de Valera electorally, no more than had Cosgrave.

In spite of his pre-election bluster, O'Duffy appeared to regard the results as merely a minor setback and the spate of Blueshirt activity increased in the immediate post-election period. Leading Fine Gael figures were now involved in the anti-rates activities and four TDs had goods and livestock seized by bailiffs. Prominent Blueshirts were being called before the Military Tribunal and some were subsequently jailed. A member of the Blueshirts, Patrick Kenny, was killed in Tipperary in June, and in August came the controversial shooting of the unarmed Michael Lynch at Marsh's Yard in Cork.[53] The language from public platforms became angrier and increasingly reckless.

O'Duffy, losing patience with the Fine Gael parliamentary party, saw it more and more as a continuation of Cumann na nGaedheal and not the radical departure he had envisaged. He made an attempt to distance the new movement from Cumann na nGaedheal at a meeting in Cavan in July: 'Cumann na nGaedheal ... did its work well while in power but Cumann na nGaedheal is no more and we had best forget it. I don't try to take credit for the achievements of Cumann na nGaedheal; neither do I shoulder responsibility for its mistakes.'[54]

His closest supporters and those with whom he was most at home, believers in direct action, chafed at the constraints and timidity of the politicians. More ominously, O'Duffy had returned enthusiastically to public approbation of Mussolini and Hitler and deprecation of the parliamentary system. Patrick Hogan had already publicly disassociated himself from these views while his brother, James, had written to Tierney on the matter. On 9 July, MacDermot wrote to O'Duffy from a nursing home in London where he was recovering from surgery:

> The time has come when I feel obliged to make a more formal protest than I have yet done, against the tendency of certain speakers and writers of our

Party to attack the Parliamentary systems of Government and to imply that it is our official policy to replace it by a Blueshirt ascendancy modelled on Fascism ... I do not believe that more than a small fraction of our Party desire to discard Parliamentary Democracy, but a steady propaganda is going on which may have demoralising consequences and which meanwhile is playing straight into the hands of our political opponents.[55]

A few days later MacDermot wrote to Tierney, warning that in a country like Ireland, propaganda such as O'Duffy's could result in violence, anarchy and civil war. He added that since O'Duffy 'is not sparing in his broadsides against others, he cannot expect his sensibilities to be regarded as the only thing that matters'.[56]

THE BLUESHIRT Conference, held at the Mansion House on 18 and 19 August 1934, shortly after the Marsh's Yard shooting, triggered off a crisis in Fine Gael. The holding of a separate Blueshirt conference, emphasising their autonomy within the Fine Gael organisation, was in itself significant. The subsequent problem stemmed from the third part of a motion dealing with the agricultural crisis, which called on farmers not to pay their annuities unless the government agreed to suspend collection during the current depression and to set up an independent tribunal to resolve the Economic War. According to Michael Tierney, 'the resolution in question was put up by the Westmeath County Executive, which appears to be as wild as Cork if not wilder. It was passed unanimously, the only person speaking against it being O'Higgins.'

Tierney pointed out the dilemma the resolution posed for the party: 'reject the resolution and weaken O'Duffy, or accept it and take part in an organised campaign of resistance to payment which I do not think any responsible political party could dream of standing over. I do not know whom we have to thank for putting us in this unnecessary dilemma, but I suspect the resolution was not altogether spontaneous.'[57]

Dillon gave his opinion in a letter to MacDermot a few days later. 'This is a resolution to which I categorically refused to be a party. It is morally indefensible and politically indefensible.' Dillon's instinctive antipathy to the non-payment of legally due annuities was such that he immediately sought advice from a senior Catholic cleric as to the moral integrity of the motion, and he was assured that his view of its moral indefensibility was correct. He takes up the story: 'I discovered the resolution had been virtually railroaded through the convention at the insistence of the County Cork delegates. O'Duffy, dazzled by the superficial enthusiasm, welcomed the resolution without fully appreciating the implications, and finds himself committed to it. He now finds that virtually all his colleagues who count are resolutely opposed to it.'

Dillon felt it was essential to gain time and not to precipitate a split if this could be averted. He argued that the only way out was to refer the matter to a specially summoned national convention of Fine Gael, which would provide an opportunity to 'let loose the members of the National Executive on the country with the full knowledge of where Cosgrave and I stand'. This move would also 'slaughter' the allegations that Fine Gael had been conspiring secretly to foment rates and annuities strikes, and 'will demonstrate a readiness to risk our political existence in order to keep our left wingers within the law in spite of the unscrupulous provocation of the government' as at Marsh's yard. It would also 'give us an opportunity to demonstrate our strength at a national convention and will dissipate forever the idea that all power in the country and even in the Blueshirts rests with their present leaders (O'Duffy, Blythe and company). It will also give O'Duffy an opportunity to get out of the dilemma without climbing down.' He admitted that he had not yet broached the matter with O'Duffy, but concluded, 'if this course is not pursued I can see no hope of avoiding a split, and we are informed that de Valera is sitting back, confidently anticipating'.[58]

The controversy broke into the open less than a week later, at a meeting of the Fine Gael national executive in Dublin on 30 August, when the 'no rent' issue was raised. Under pressure from the executive, O'Duffy agreed to withdraw the motion, but James Hogan had had enough and resigned from the executive 'as the strongest protest I can personally make against the generally destructive and hysterical' leadership of O'Duffy. He gave two reasons: the 'no rent' manifesto and O'Duffy's 'increasingly destructive pronouncements on Ulster'. Hogan, who had mistrusted O'Duffy from the start and fought with him at a meeting of the national executive as far back as September 1933, concluded his statement by saying that 'it was about time the UIP gave up its hopeless attempt to save O'Duffy from his errors'.[59]

Tierney gave a full account of the national executive's meeting in a letter to MacDermot on 4 September:

The new executive is a very heterogeneous body, containing far more people who should never be allowed on such a body than the old one did. All the Fine Gael type of people were dead against the resolution, as being doubtful to say the least in its moral aspect, certainly illegal and wildly inexpedient. The Blueshirt delegates, of whom there were many ... were all out for acceptance and some very curious speeches were made. The General himself began mildly but gradually an atmosphere developed with which I think you are familiar –

a suggestion that any criticism was an attack on the Blueshirts or himself.

Of course most of the speeches were pretty irrelevant, and scarcely anyone addressed himself to the real problem – how to rescind the resolution and at the same time save the General's face by keeping the movement together.

Tierney continued:

The general atmosphere was that anyone who did not like the resolution was hostile to the Blueshirts and was dishonouring the dead. I 'got in bad' by saying that our position for some time had been that of men sitting harmlessly in Dublin and letting every lunatic in the country decide their policy for them. Quinn of Kilkenny and a new recruit from Arklow were very hot in their desire for action. The latter even thought there was no reason why we should not de-rail trains; in fact all he needed was a beard and a bomb to make him a kind of comic cinema anarchist. At last, when everybody had spoken for and against, an agreement was reached that the officers of Fine Gael and the League of Youth should meet in the morning to put up a formula.

When the officers met, a compromise was drafted by a Fr Nolan of Monaghan, which contained an expression of sympathy with the farmers and an intimation that our members should help in seizure cases in every way they could 'consistent with the moral law'. I tried to improve the phase by deleting the word 'moral'. Would you believe it, I was foiled by Cosgrave, who liked it because he is keen on morality! At the general meeting afterwards its deletion was strongly urged by Paddy Hogan and Costello.

At this stage, the incident with James Hogan took place. Tierney recalled that

[Hogan] was talking in a rambling way and happened to say, for some unknown reason, that he respected Quish and Cronin among the Blueshirts. The inference may not have been obvious to Hogan himself – in fairness I do not think it was – but it was to O'Duffy like the last red rag to a long tortured bull. He sprang up, denounced Hogan as a villain who had always been trying to oust him, and after a torrent of painful vituperation refused to allow him to explain himself. When Hogan did get to speak he did the only thing open to him, resigned there and then.

The debate went on and was wound up by a long speech from O'Duffy in which he represented himself as foully ill-used and finally proposed to withdraw the obnoxious resolution altogether – exactly what most of us had wanted except we were trying to gild the pill. The net result of it all is that we are back a good deal behind where we started, with considerable damage done to O'Duffy's prestige – I should think as far as the saner members of the Executive are concerned, irreparable damage – and with Hogan gone. To make matters worse he seems to have gone off in a rage and called up the Press and stated his case in the form which would damage O'Duffy most.

Tierney believed that the root of their difficulty was their failure to have a constructive party policy, and as a result

> there is enormous pressure on the Blueshirts to take the law into their own hands. It comes partly from Cork, where Cussen has being playing what I can only call a thoroughly sinister game in organising a farmer's defence league for direct action; and partly from people like Blythe and Cronin who fear that if anybody takes the lead in direct action except themselves and O'Duffy, all is lost. Things being so, I fear the whole organisation is going to drift irredeemably into violence.[60]

Tierney, in fact, had also resigned at the executive's meeting, but his resignation was not made public, and O'Duffy nominated him to the new standing committee knowing, according to Tierney, that he had 'no sympathy with Hogan's *démarche*'. Tierney, however, insisted to MacDermot that his resignation would stand: 'I am not going to be responsible either for Cosgrave's inaction or for Cussen, Blythe and Cronin's activities.'[61]

Tierney's secret resignation and Hogan's public one had little immediate impact, and every attempt was made to play down their importance. A statement from the national executive on 1 September simply said that Hogan had resigned for personal reasons and that O'Duffy had the full confidence of the League of Youth.[62]

That, however, was far from being the case. By now Dillon was fully aware of O'Duffy's unsuitability as leader and of the crisis about to engulf the party. He was particularly concerned with the rashness of O'Duffy's behaviour and the recklessness of his public utterances. He was later to tell Elizabeth Bowen that he decided to get rid of O'Duffy when, 'standing behind O'Duffy on a Cork balcony he heard the General passing over into Hitlerian convulsions of speech'. Dillon claims that he 'felt something dangerous was getting loose'.[63] Whether that was *post factum* rationalisation or not, with no sign of Cosgrave intervening and MacDermot out of the country, Dillon now took the initiative.

He had two meetings in O'Duffy's office on 5 September, with Cosgrave and Cronin also present. They reached agreement on a formula designed to ensure a better understanding between the officers of the organisation. It provided for a weekly meeting of the president and the vice-presidents to discuss all matters arising from the activities of the League of Youth, while the league's divisional officers were to invite the local TDs to their monthly meeting. All officers of the organisation were to commit to writing what they had to say in public and then adhere strictly to their manuscripts; interviews with the press would be given in manuscript form and only after consultation; and, finally, there would be a meeting held in the Mansion House to clarify the party's stance on all critical issues. The bulk of the formula was Dillon's, and he was particularly keen that the Mansion House meeting should be held to clear the air.[64]

Any hopes that the problems were about to be resolved were dashed next morning when Cronin told Dillon and Cosgrave that the divisional officers objected to the proposal that TDs attend their meetings. Cosgrave and Dillon, who believed that Cronin genuinely wanted to sort out the party's difficulties, waived this condition; they felt they still had sufficient agreement to prevent a split and bring O'Duffy under control. O'Duffy was in no mood to be controlled, however, and nor were those around him. To Dillon's surprise, when he came into his office on Saturday morning to prepare his speech for a meeting at Mitchelstown the following day, he was informed by Cronin that 'O'Duffy contemplated resignation' and had only been deterred from handing it in by Blythe and Cronin, 'who had persuaded him, with great difficulty, to postpone a decision until the following Tuesday'. On this somewhat dubious basis, Dillon told the Mitchelstown meeting that there was no split in Fine Gael and 'that they were prepared to go forward together under O'Duffy's leadership'.[65]

Dillon spent the next week doing everything in his power to prevent a split. The Tuesday deadline proposed by O'Duffy was postponed until Friday to allow Cosgrave and O'Duffy attend the funeral of John Jinks, the former TD whose celebrated absence from the Dáil saved the Cosgrave government in 1927. The Friday meeting, when it came, went peacefully. There was no talk of resignation and much of the time was spent making arrangements for the conference in the Mansion House.

By now, however, Dillon had seen enough of O'Duffy not to be fully satisfied with the new assurances. He felt there was still too much that was ambiguous and uncertain, and demanded an urgent meeting to 'clear things up'. A meeting of the standing committee was arranged for 10.30 the following morning. That, however, was not enough for Dillon, who went directly to O'Duffy and told him frankly that enormous damage had been done by his speeches and that this was the unanimous opinion of his colleagues and supporters. O'Duffy was less than pleased, especially since Dillon insisted that this view was widely held, and he attacked Dillon about the tone he had adopted at the national executive meeting during the 'no rents' debate. The interview ended inconclusively, but O'Duffy had at least been forewarned. The full meeting went ahead at 10.30 am. Dillon takes up the story:

> When we reached the room where we were to meet I immediately put the
> question of O'Duffy's speeches to the issue by stating that I had seen the

General in his room and by repeating what I had said to him. The General very obviously avoided this discussion and brought forward the general question of the land annuities and their attitude to Northern Ireland. A very long discussion ensued, and it became abundantly clear that O'Duffy had given no consideration to either question, but had made up his mind that it would be a popular thing to do something dramatic in respect of either or both of them, and that therefore his proposal for a 'no rent' manifesto and for the appointment of a Commissioner of the Blueshirts for Northern Ireland would be popular and should be adopted without reference to the consequence that might follow from either decision. The end of the discussion was that he professed to accept our view and to suggest that his proposals were little more than gestures made with a view to precipitating some definite action by the national executive of Fine Gael. We then reverted to the question of the indiscriminate nature of these speeches and of the safeguards that would be necessary to provide against their recurrence, and we parted most amicably under the impression that all was well, having agreed to meet on the following Wednesday (19 September) at 8.30 with a view to making final arrangements for the meeting at the Mansion House preparatory to having them confirmed by the Standing Committee which was to meet on Thursday.[66]

Dillon wrote to MacDermot immediately after that Saturday meeting and filled him in on some of the personality clashes. Patrick Baxter of Cavan he described as 'knowing nothing and in any case is like a jelly that is not yet set'. Tierney was 'in a state of mind that believed something ought to be done but does not know what'. He also informed MacDermot that 'the party now has no money and that none was coming in', and on the more substantive issue of whether O'Duffy would accept the terms as agreed with the vice-president, he already had some doubts. 'Paddy Belton is now trying to engineer a split and I had to attack him pretty savagely at the standing committee when it met yesterday. As I told you two years ago, he is a dirty dog.' He concluded by telling MacDermot that the situation was 'complex' and under no circumstances should he intervene without first coming home.[67]

If matters were 'complex' at this stage they were to become even more so. On Tuesday, the General Secretary of Fine Gael, Liam Burke, received a letter from O'Duffy announcing his resignation from the party. This was seen by Dillon as an attempt by O'Duffy 'to blackmail us into subservience to himself'.[68] O'Duffy's resignation was submitted to the standing committee on Thursday morning and it was agreed to summon the national executive of Fine Gael and the central council of the League of Youth by telegram for the following afternoon. From this point on, confusion is all.

Cronin and Blythe met O'Duffy, who told them that he intended to retire from public life altogether; however, if he was called back in six months he would be prepared to come, but on his own terms. Then, when the League of Youth's central council met, O'Duffy attended and read a long valedictory message into which he interpolated long spoken paragraphs indicating that, while he had resigned from Fine Gael, he had not resigned the Director-Generalship of the League of Youth and was still prepared to lead them.

O'Duffy did not attend the meeting of the Fine Gael national executive, but was kept in touch with the event through regular phone-calls from Thomas Gunning and visits to his house from Blythe and Patrick Belton.[69] Dillon did not offer the benefit of the doubt to either: 'Belton was of course working for a split, in which he had an eager ally in Thomas Gunning, who you may remember started as O'Duffy's secretary and later was supposed to be in charge of publicity. He is a bad lad.'[70]

When the national executive met again that evening, Belton told the meeting that O'Duffy was now prepared to withdraw his resignation. This news, according to Dillon, was not welcome as both the national executive and the central council were by now anxious that O'Duffy's should quit. At this point events became even more bizarre:

> It then became pretty clear that O'Duffy, having been informed by Gunning that he could not split the League of Youth from Fine Gael, had given him instructions to split the League of Youth itself; and it was only when this became apparent to Cronin that Cronin challenged Gunning in the presence of the other members of the Central Council, with having urged him, after his release from Arbour Hill, to murder O'Duffy. Gunning was unable to deny this and shortly afterwards the Central Council unanimously accepted the resignation.[71]

Cronin was immediately appointed Director-General of the League of Youth, but the question of filling the leadership of Fine Gael was postponed until proper procedures could be followed. Dillon predicted to MacDermot that 'O'Duffy's resolution to retire quietly from public life is already beginning to waver and he is apparently making ready to stump the country.'[72] Indeed he was, and the next few months were to see him try to regain leadership of the Blueshirts and then, with the help of Belton, set up a rival movement and eventually a new political party, the National Corporate Party.[73] Dillon had no doubt that the party been right to eject O'Duffy. While he resolved not to comment publicly on the controversy, or, if obliged to do so, only in magnanimous terms, his true feelings, as confided to MacDermot, revealed that for him the break had become inevitable:

> From what has happened during the last week I am now convinced that O'Duffy made up his mind after the local elections that constitutionalism did

not pay, and that he was deliberately preparing the ground for a split between Fine Gael and the League of Youth, and that he intended to precipitate this on the land annuities question. He made the cardinal mistake of tendering his resignation, and, but for this, he might have succeeded. As it is, he has certainly failed to divide the two organisations, but it is much too early to say whether he will fail in splitting the League of Youth itself. Whatever happens the situation will be critical and difficult, but I think we may reasonably hope that out of what seems at first glance to be evil, good will come. One thing is certain, that in view of the information which we now have of his activities for the last couple of months, the parting was inevitable, and on the whole it has taken the least undesirable form that was possible. I was extremely reluctant to face the parting, but I was finally convinced that it was inevitable by O'Duffy's conduct after his resignation had been sent in and by a speech which he delivered in Fethard about a fortnight ago and which I had not seen until a few days ago on account of the newspapers strike. Two passages from the speech read as follows:

'His followers could allow no person to say they were traitors. They could not have that. They must break the skull of anyone who said they were traitors.

'Outlining his policy on the Corporate System of State Government he said that if Mr. Norton could name one Labour man living in Germany or Italy who would vote against Hitler or Mussolini, he would retire from public life . . . No power in the world could induce the people of Germany or Italy to change. Hitler had done more for Germany than any other leader in the world had done for his country.'

There was a lot more 'ráméis' of this kind and I believe that what he actually said was much worse.

It is impossible to go fully into every detail of all that has happened, but you may take it that I was determined to avoid a split if it were possible, and that it was only when I became convinced that there was no longer any possibility of carrying on that I consented to recommend acceptance of the resignation to the organisation.

It is extremely difficult to foresee the immediate future. The resignation will undoubtedly shake the organisation very severely. On the other hand, public distrust had reached enormous dimensions and there will undoubtedly be great relief in the minds of an immense number of people that O'Duffy has retired. One possible consequence would be that the saner elements in Fianna Fáil would react to this development by pressing de Valera to be more reasonable; we must only hope that that may happen. It is odd to notice how the situation develops in the absence of newspapers, and, of course, this circumstance has been invaluable to us. I cannot think what would have happened if the last three weeks' proceedings had been going on under the glare of newspaper publicity.[74]

A few days later Dillon again wrote to MacDermot, reminding him of the appalling state of the party's finances – it was £8,000 in debt and had virtually no income – and relating that

Belton has opened a scurrilous attack on you and me at a meeting of North Dublin Executive Fine Gael. I hope he goes on with it because he will be expelled from the party if he does, and that would be a great blessing … The general situation was difficult and delicate, with O'Duffy on the rampage and already showing signs of self-destruction. As the papers are due to re-appear tomorrow, (after the strike) it is pretty certain that he will explode himself pretty soon. He will not capture more than 5% of the Blueshirts and they will come alright in time.[75]

Tierney, who also wrote to MacDermot the same day, was not so sanguine. He thought O'Duffy's attempt to return to lead the Blueshirts was 'grotesque', but reckoned he would get enough support at least to cripple the whole movement as an effective opposition. His own disillusionment with politics he now sought to transfer to MacDermot, advising him to abandon politics altogether. 'I have lost hope in the old gang completely. They will never move until the electorate exterminate them.' He advised MacDermot, if he did go back to the Independent benches, 'to take none of the big farmers with you. Leave them and all the relics of the Farmers Party where they are. They are a liability to any movement, and my own view is that Cussen of Cork is probably more responsible for our present state than any other single person.' And Tierney ended by warning MacDermot, 'you may take it as verb. sap. that you have few friends in the UIP as it stands'.[76]

In mid-October, Dillon told MacDermot: 'You are well out of the mess here. We are still afloat but little more. O'Duffy is on the rampage with a vengeance. The Blueshirts are split from stern to stern and the morale of Fine Gael is shattered.' Belton, he said, was involved 'in every form of treacherous activity', and a motion for his expulsion was now on the agenda. 'It is grimly amusing to observe all the Blythe propaganda amongst the Blueshirts "against the politicians" recoiling on him and Cronin now like boomerangs. Cronin is a decent man, but he will never provide the leadership necessary to hold the Blueshirts together. It is far better, however, that they should learn that themselves than for anyone to tell them at present. Cronin is working like a Trojan to keep them together, but he will have a tough job.'[77]

He had other news for MacDermot: he had led a deputation of five Fine Gael TDs to meet de Valera to press for a trade agreement with England, an equitable allocation of cattle export-quota licences, and a tribunal before which farmers might ventilate their grievances before the sheriff was authorised to seize their goods. Dillon sought a private meeting with de Valera beforehand, to ask him to suspend seizures pending the reception of the deputation. 'I was coldly, almost uncivilly received. I wish you had been there to see a de Valera I had never seen before. At the end of the interview he inquired most anxiously and cordially about you and asked me to mention his anxiety for good news of your convalescence. But for that more cordial interlude, I think the icicles could have formed about us.'[78]

At first sight it would appear that this visit made little impact on de Valera, and this certainly was the impression he wished to convey. In fact the discussion was of some importance, and much of the substance put forward by the Fine Gael deputation was to appear in the Coal-Cattle pact negotiated by the Irish and British governments early in 1935. It was a first, significant step towards ending the Economic War.

The O'Duffy episode was Dillon's first major political crisis, and he was one of the few to come out of it with his reputation enhanced. He had shown good judgement early on in cautioning MacDermot against some of those behind the Centre Party. His decision to accept O'Duffy as leader of Fine Gael was influenced in part by the advice of Cosgrave and by his belief that the desperate situation demanded opposition unity, but he was never beguiled by O'Duffy. He quickly sought representation on the central council of the Young Ireland Association to counter the influence of the extremists, and he was the first to spot the incipient financial crisis which was being caused by O'Duffy's extravagance. In the end, he was the one who demanded absolute clarity from O'Duffy on the key policy issues. At a time when some of the more prominent ex-Cumann na nGaedheal members had either temporarily abdicated responsibility, or compromised themselves (like Blythe), or were simply not to be seen, Dillon had shown great firmness, especially against the Blueshirt hotheads. He also fought hard to allow O'Duffy retreat with dignity, but when faced with the inevitable, he had been decisive. He had also shown great loyalty to his new colleagues, something which would be an abiding political characteristic throughout his career.

But Dillon was also being shaped by the political legacy of the Civil War, becoming utterly convinced that Fianna Fáil was anti-democratic and suspicious of its every move. In that tense year, few opposition politicians felt any different. Each party's certain belief in the bad faith of its opponent had become a fundamental fact of Irish life and would take decades fully to eradicate. James Dillon, just two years into national politics, was now as much its prisoner as anyone.

CHAPTER EIGHT

THE PARTY MAN

'It is hard for anyone who feels the same reverence for these parliamentary institutions as I do, to listen to Deputy MacDermot's consistent sneers at the capacity of his fellow countrymen in regard to the carrying out of parliamentary institutions.'
Dillon, Dáil Debates, 13 December 1935

THE O'DUFFY EPISODE knocked the stuffing out of Fine Gael. After a year in existence the party had an embarrassing leadership débâcle and was tainted with the fascist proclivities of O'Duffy and some of his supporters – indeed was left in the longer term asking some very awkward questions as to how the whole episode had ever been allowed to happen. De Valera's position was greatly strengthened, and with the main opposition in disarray he could begin his rapprochement with Britain and move stealthily but firmly against his one-time allies, the IRA.

As time passed it emerged that Fine Gael's problems were deep and extensive, but for the moment the urgent need to restore some semblance of unity hid the fact. Patrick Belton was expelled in late October after he made an attempt to have O'Duffy return as leader.[1] In November O'Duffy announced his intention of forming a new Blueshirt party, which he did with Belton's help in early 1935. The National Corporate Party proved as hostile to Fine Gael as Fianna Fáil, but had a short and undistinguished life.[2] Though the Fine Gael leadership found it difficult to bring the wilder Blueshirt elements under control, with the reassertion of constitutional leadership the Blueshirt movement lost much of its earlier political dynamism, and as 1934 became 1935 it was limited to sporadic attempts to frustrate the sale of seized goods by government agents by blocking roads and intimidating sales personnel.[3]

Dillon, Cosgrave and their colleagues could and did contrast the severe – and effective – assault by the government on the perpetrators of these crimes with its 'softly, softly' approach to the IRA. They contrasted the willingness of Blueshirts and farmers (and they were by no means always the same) to recognise the courts with the refusal of the IRA to do likewise. And they argued that the government had deliberately provoked the farmers into illegality by destroying their livelihoods. But after all was said, they were clearly uncomfortable with a campaign which they did not control and which was at times outside the law, and embarrassed when confronted with this by Fianna Fáil TDs in the Dáil. There was little they could say to Norton's taunt that 'the Frankenstein they had created had simply become uncontrollable'.[4]

It is hard to know what precisely slowed down the Blueshirt and farmer activity in 1935 – probably a combination of the government's hard tactics, including the use of 'flying squads' of armed police and the Military Tribunal, and the self-conscious withdrawal of support by the Fine Gael leadership. By the middle of 1935 the campaign had virtually ended, though the Blueshirt movement itself did not disappear until it had been through one more split in 1936.[5]

A normality of sorts returned to political life, and at the Fine Gael Árd Fheis in March Cosgrave was elected as leader, a position he had in effect held since O'Duffy's departure. Dillon, MacDermot, Cronin and O'Higgins were named as the new vice-presidents. MacDermot used the Árd Fheis to emphasise that Fine Gael was not simply the old Cumann na nGaedheal in a new guise. Dillon was more forward looking, seeing Fine Gael's task as developing the institutions set up twelve years earlier, and in this his support for Cosgrave was unstinting and genuine.[6] He had come a long way from his dismissal of those achievements during the 1920s.

Cosgrave's leadership signalled the party's return to its conservative roots, and what was true of Cosgrave was even more true of some of his senior colleagues. Ernest Blythe, whose role in the Blueshirt adventure did him little credit, was now virtually out of politics and never again ran for office. Desmond FitzGerald was still active but markedly less effective in opposition than in government. Patrick Hogan had all but retired from politics, concentrating now on his Galway law practice, and he died tragically in a car accident in 1936. Like Hogan, after ten years in government most of the other members had been obliged, through sheer financial and family necessity, to go back to their businesses and professions. There was also a sense of 'burn-out', a feeling perhaps best illustrated by the Labour leader, William Norton, who pleaded in the Dáil for retirement allowances for ministers: 'This State has been well served … I do not think I am breaking any confidence when I say that many of these people are poor by reason of the fact that they served the State during that period. Some … found it was not easy to adjust themselves to private or commercial life.'[7]

Ten difficult, dangerous years had taken their toll on politicians' spirit and stamina. Fine Gael's finances were also badly strained: O'Duffy had been extravagant. As early as January 1934, Dillon had warned the standing committee of the need to reduce the number of organisers 'to a point where outlay will not exceed expenditure'.[8] In April the question was again raised, and in late June Mulcahy had spoken sternly to O'Duffy on the matter. In July, half of the eighty-six party organisers were let go, but by now, Dillon reported to MacDermot, the party was heavily overdrawn with little money coming in.[9]

Dillon's participation in all aspects of the party's work was impressive, and his front-bench status was strengthened in October 1934 when Cosgrave assigned him the agriculture portfolio, the single most important policy area of the time. The position filled Dillon with delight.[10] In 1935 he was appointed to the only Dáil committee of any significance, the Public Accounts Committee, again an appointment which greatly pleased him. He was also a welcome addition at Fine Gael meetings, and weekend after weekend saw him standing on party platforms up and down the country, surrounded by crowds which greatly prized good oratory. The Dillon name and the elegant, studied appearance marked him out. He spoke in a booming voice, using robust language to make his point and colourful characterisation to ridicule his opponents, punctuating his delivery with dramatic pauses and vivid invective. He had a solid grasp of a wide range of subjects and could take on any heckler in verbal deftness.

His reputation was growing fast. The Independent of 1932 was now entrenched in the party, almost as if he had never been anywhere else. He made the transition with none of the prickliness or half-heartedness of MacDermot. In a way, this should not have been a surprise, since the Dillon tradition had been to such a great extent based upon a belief in party politics. In the Dáil, too, he had begun to assert his authority. The *Irish Independent* parliamentary correspondent, 'JAP', wrote of him in March 1935: 'The member for Donegal is indefatigable. Having listened to him since he first entered the Dáil, I find it difficult to think of any subject on which he would not be prepared to hold forth at length – and generally to advantage.' In June the same observer noted Dillon's 'very good speech which covers the whole ground with his usually uncanny comprehensiveness'.[11]

He also had his critics. Sean T. O'Kelly referred to his 'funereal countenance and sepulchral tone',[12] while Frank Aiken opined: 'Deputy Dillon is a very mournful sort of person. The worst is always going to happen tomorrow and if not tomorrow the day after, and if not the day after, next year.' Aiken also alleged that Dillon was frequently out of line with his Fine Gael colleagues and that he used abusive language at by-election meetings, but 'worst of all is that he was trained to sit, act and talk in another assembly, and he has been forced to come in here instead'.[13] On another occasion Aiken, stung by Dillon's merciless attack on his use of Irish – Aiken had read from a Civil Service script in Irish he did not understand – attacked Dillon's lack of military record: 'he was quite a young man when this country required soldiers ... where was he then?'[14]

In those early days, his sharpest exchanges were with Sean Lemass. Lemass was the clearest and most forceful of the Fianna Fáil ministers, with a sure grasp of his brief and impatient to put his plans into effect. For one who later did all in his power to move away from the legacy of the Civil War, his speeches could be cutting, as they had been in the Uniforms Bill debate, or when in January 1933 he accused Cosgrave of 'treason by any standards' because of his stand on the annuities issue. There was little instinctive rapport between the two men. Lemass felt Dillon was patronising, as indeed he was at times, such as when he described Lemass (five years his elder with far greater political experience) as 'an energetic and enthusiastic young man, and under prudent guidance he can do very useful work in this House'.[15]

Between them there was an instinctive clash of style, personality and philosophy. Dillon's orotund tone irritated the plain-spoken Lemass; Lemass's urban, industrial bias and apparent hostility to the traditional values of rural Ireland offended Dillon (and indeed aroused the suspicion of some in his own party and cabinet colleagues). Lemass's no-nonsense manner and *modus operandi*, which involved extensive use of statutory instruments to achieve his objectives, seemed to Dillon to take parliamentary procedures for granted, while Lemass objected to what he saw as Dillon's obstructive parliamentary tactics. The passage of time did little to change the pair's early roles.

Dillon's sallies were not just against frontbenchers, and his mixture of eloquent insouciance and hard-hitting argument struck home from time to time. He so irritated the Longford–Westmeath Fianna Fáil TD James Victory in January 1934 that Victory warned that 'if the Civic Guard protection was taken off you, we know where you would be'.[16] Another Fianna Fáil TD, Paddy Smith, threatened to knock in his 'baby face'.[17] On a gentler note, a colourful Dublin TD, Alderman Tom Kelly, poked fun at Dillon's seeming omniscience: 'On every conceivable subject he is on his feet – on buttons, flanelettes, pigs, malt, whether liquid or otherwise, beet, wheat and so on, every conceivable subject ... He is like Peter Pan, the boy that never grew up. How old can he be, I wonder?'[18]

Though there were many heated exchanges in the Dáil chamber, in the 1930s Leinster House was a relatively relaxed and uncomplicated place. Dominated at its Kildare St entrance by the ugly statue of Queen Victoria, it still had the air of a temporary rather than a permanent seat of parliament. It had not in fact been the first choice of the Free State government as their home, and had only reluctantly been loaned to the state by its owners, the Royal Dublin Society, in 1922. The main exhibition hall was transformed into a temporary Dáil chamber and the old ballroom, the most beautiful room in the building, was eventually assigned to the Senate.

The problem of finding a permanent home for the Oireachtas was entrusted to a special joint committee by Cosgrave in 1923. The committee set about examining the various possibilities on offer, but it is difficult not to conclude from a reading of their report that the members had no intention of ever moving from this most central of addresses. Of the other possibilities examined, they concluded that the old parliament – the Bank of Ireland at College Green – was no longer big enough, and in any event they would not have been happy to displace the bankers as this would have involved a major question of compensation. Dublin Castle would have been suitable, but because of the destruction of the Four Courts the courts now operated from there and it was felt improper to ask them to move. The third possibility – apparently Cosgrave's preference – was the Royal Hospital at Kilmainham. In might have been an inspired choice, combining a building of great distinction with plenty of space to expand, but the committee (for reasons subsequently believed to have more to do with the location of its members' clubs) concluded that they could not recommend it owing to 'the existing difficulties of access by the business and professional life of the city' and because the 'expenditure of so large a sum as seventy thousand pounds did not commend itself as a business proposition, more especially in view of the inconvenience of the location'.[19]

The Royal Dublin Society fought hard to stay at Leinster House. It pleaded loss of members, the 'jeopardising of its existing work', and perhaps most of all the loss of a marvellous city club. The RDS concluded its submission to the Oireachtas Committee in 1924 by stating that, if the occupation of Leinster House continued, 'the Society must necessarily become disintegrated'. Their pleas fell on stony ground: in May the committee recommended that the entire premises 'should be taken for the temporary accommodation of the Oireachtas', subject to compensation to the RDS, and 'upon the distinct understanding that Leinster House should be vacated at the earliest possible date consistent with the acquisition of a permanent home for the Oireachtas'.[20]

Yet Leinster House was where they remained, and when Dillon entered it in 1932 its organisation and facilities were still very basic. There was a wooden shed at the entrance gates, which Dillon likened to a 'dog kennel', while the main entrance hall, a room of noble proportions, was disfigured by the presence of unsightly wooden structures – 'temporary' waiting rooms which were still serving in that capacity well into the 1940s. Members were paid a salary of £360 per year and had free rail travel to and from their constituencies. There were no offices, secretaries, telephone or postal facilities. Members worked from the single room assigned to each party or from the library. Even party leaders did not have rooms; Dillon, as a vice-president, shared an office with Cosgrave at Fine Gael party headquarters.

The restaurant was situated over the main boiler room and was unbearably overheated – Dillon advocated moving it to the back of the building where the restaurant would open onto a terrace overlooking Leinster Lawn. A bar was introduced in 1928 despite de Valera's opposition, though at his insistence it was shut off from the restaurant. De Valera warned his deputies against socialising with the opposition, and the tradition of the parties sitting at separate tables became an accepted feature, and eventually extended to the refusal of Fianna Fáil members to take part in the inter-party golf competition which had been played annually up till then. It was quite some time before some of the self-imposed – or de Valera-imposed – ordinances began to break down.

The Senate held many ex-Unionists among its members. When Dillon arrived at Leinster House in 1932, the Upper House included Sir John Keane, the Countess of Desart, Sir Edward Bellingham, the Earl of Granard, Henry Guinness, Andrew Jameson, Major-General Sir William Hickie, Sir Edward Coey Biggar and Sir John Purser Griffith. It is not clear whether there was much social mixing between the Houses, but it seems doubtful.

One factor which hugely reduced the pressure on the politicians of that period was the nature of the media. There was no media: there was the press. Small in number, essentially respectful of parliament, the newspapers reported fully on its debates, carrying detailed division lists and rarely indulging in analysis, apart from the parliamentary sketch which was usually well written but anodyne. There was no such thing as 'investigative' journalism, no lobby system, no over-mighty columnists, no opinion formers beyond the politicians themselves. In that pre-television age, most politicians could travel the country without being recognised.

The parliamentary timetable was borrowed largely from Westminster. The Dáil met between eighty and one hundred times each year. Generally it sat on Tuesday, Wednesday and Thursday from 3 pm to 10.30 pm and, if it met on Fridays, from 10.30 am to 2 pm. There were no committees of consequence apart from the Public Accounts Committee. Constituency work was a fraction of what it would later become: there were no clinics and only a trickle of constituency queries. Dillon was fastidious about replying promptly to constituency matters, though the directness of his replies was not always guaranteed to win votes. From the outset he was a great believer in the parliamentary question as a means of eliciting information on constituency matters and, while he used the device sparingly enough, he always regarded it as one of the great weapons of accountability to be used in the interest of the lowliest citizens.

Dáil divisions were called by the ushers ringing hand-bells. There was a high level of missed votes on all sides, particularly on the opposition benches; except on vital issues it was usual to have up to one-third of the members absent. The minutes of the Fine Gael parliamentary party show that the Whips had quite a problem in this regard, but there was little effective sanction open to them even against habitual offenders. Dillon took his voting seriously, as he did his attendance at parliamentary party meetings, initially held once a week but later with less frequency.

Dillon continued to live in Ballaghaderreen and in North Great George's St. His visits to Donegal were not particularly frequent, though he did keep in touch with what was happening in the constituency through a team of supporters and through the AOH, who regarded him as very much 'their' man. He was not unusual in living outside his constituency: others who did likewise included de Valera, Ryan, Derrig, Ruttledge, Boland, Cosgrave, FitzGerald, JM O'Sullivan, Frank Aiken and Mrs Redmond. 'Clientelist' politics had not yet arrived. At a time of simple government there was little need to make representations, and little expectation that such efforts would really do much good.

The Revision of Constituencies Bill which appeared in mid-1934 posed an entirely unexpected problem for Dillon. The Bill was frankly designed to help Fianna Fáil by reducing the size of the constituencies, abolishing seven- and eight-seat constituencies altogether. Dillon saw it as 'a cheap gerrymandering Bill devised to strengthen Fianna Fáil's electoral position' and claimed that its chief architect was the Fianna Fáil general secretary, Seamus Davin.[21]

From Dillon's point of view its effects were potentially disastrous. Donegal was to lose one of its eight seats, and would then be divided into two constituencies, one with four seat and the other with three. Dillon objected on the grounds that three-seat constituencies made genuine proportional representation impossible to achieve, that the county was a natural unit and should not be divided, and because he felt it would lead to the isolation of the Gaeltacht areas. He moved an amendment at committee stage to have Donegal retained as a seven-seat constituency, but lost by one vote. It turned out that a 'paired' Fianna Fáil Deputy had voted, giving the government its one-vote margin, but Dillon accepted that this had been unintentional and he did not pursue the matter. His verdict on the Bill was 'Craigavon wins', and in spite of further spirited resistance its passage through the Oireachtas was inevitable.[22]

Dillon's real objection was more personal than he had stated. As a non-resident, non-Donegal native he had no 'natural' base, no geographical area with which he had strong ties. His vote was spread fairly evenly across the existing constituency, and in a smaller area his position would be significantly weakened to the point where he was unlikely to retain his seat.

Cosgrave was well aware of the implications of the new Bill for many of his TDs and held consultations with each of them in 1935, when the possibility of having Dillon run as a candidate in Monaghan arose. After Ernest Blythe had lost his seat there in 1933 he showed no inclination to return to the Dáil, and Senator Barney O'Rourke of Inishkeen approached Cosgrave to find a candidate as they could get no local man to stand. Dillon describes the situation in his *Memoir*. The exact date is not certain.

> Now that was a strange situation, because there were several obviously eligible persons in the constituency. But a very peculiar atmosphere obtained. Dr. Con Ward, who was the senior Fianna Fáil Deputy, had established in the constituency a positive reign of terror, with the result that no local man was inclined to face the music of a contest in 1937 on account of the extraordinary violence of the atmosphere which had been created by the Ward political machine. So Mr. Cosgrave asked me if I would leave Donegal and stand in Monaghan. I felt it was quiet opportune for me, if Mr. Cosgrave wanted me to stand in Monaghan that I should go to Monaghan.[23]

IN LEINSTER House and outside, political life was returning, albeit reluctantly, to some sort of normality. In January 1935 the government announced a Coal-Cattle pact with Britain, under which Britain agreed to take 150,000 more cattle from the Free State, which agreed to import its coal from Britain. The pact would not end the Economic War, but it did point a very definite way out of the impasse. Dillon welcomed it. He told an audience at Kilsaran a few days later that, when he had served a memorandum on this issue to de Valera, he had replied that it was not worth discussing, yet two of the things suggested had now been put into operation.[24] It was a genuine welcome on Dillon's part and he promised full Fine Gael co-operation if de Valera set out in a positive way to find solutions to all of Ireland's differences with Britain. Dillon wanted more than an end to the Economic War, which he saw as only one element that needed to be dealt with if prosperity was to be achieved.

Despite the change in Fianna Fáil policy, Dillon remained critical of the government's over-dependence on wheat in a single-crop economy. 'Unless you have a livestock industry side by side with a wheat-growing economy,' he insisted, 'the thing becomes utterly impossible and cannot be carried on, for two good reasons: the land would become impoverished and the by-products of wheat production will be unconsumable'.[25]

He was emphatic that prosperity could only be based on the cattle trade and unapologetic about the importance he gave the British market: 'I will go to that market under no inferiority complex and I would put out to them the advantages of linking their economy to ours. I would put out to them the hopelessness of offering to our people any material considerations with a view to inducing them to compromise their rights to sovereignty and independence.' He felt, however, that de Valera had a vested interest in keeping the issue alive, for the present at least: 'He wants to keep boiling in this country a war spirit and a war hysteria in order to distract the minds of the people.'[26] Certainly if the reaction of a prominent Fianna Fáil TD, Donnchadha Ó Briain of West Limerick, just two days after the Coal-Cattle pact was signed is typical – and almost certainly it was – the gap between the parties on the importance of the British market was still enormous. Ó Briain poured scorn on the pact, declaring 'the Government in Great Britain must be in a sorry plight when they have to come like a huckster looking for a market for their coal to a little country like Ireland'.[27] Not for the first time, Fianna Fáil was intent on having it both ways.

The Coal-Cattle pact did not bring the Economic War disturbances to an end, nor was it likely to. Livestock prices were still disastrously low. On 5 January 1935, the *Irish Independent* reported ten cattle being sold for a total of £14.10s at Camolin and thirteen bullocks being sold for £30.1s at Edenderry. A month later five cows were reported sold for 25s at Dowra. Hardly surprisingly, then, resistance to cattle seizures continued throughout the year. Over a dozen Cork farmers, some of them Blueshirts, Cussen among them, but others having no connection with the movement and including a former – and future – TD, Brooke Brasier, were sensationally arrested and brought before the Military Tribunal on land annuity charges. After a month in custody, most of the charges against them were dismissed, but the action, and the ongoing sale of seized goods, ensured the temperature remained high.[28]

The opposition was incensed at the killing of a landlord, Richard More O'Ferrall, shot in a maverick IRA operation in Co. Longford in February 1935. Once again the opposition contrasted the government's 'soft' attitude towards the IRA with its determined sweep against the farmers and Blueshirts. On the day the plight of the Cork farmers was raised in the Dáil, an angry Mulcahy asked 'how many of the murderers of More O'Ferrall were among those arrested at Cork?' MacDermot was particularly enraged and according to the *Irish Independent* made a 'formidable indictment' of the government's handling of the issue.[29] The violence, however, was by no means one-sided. In May the home of a Cork Fianna Fáil TD, PS Murphy, was burned to the ground. Two months later a prominent Cork Blueshirt and later a Fine Gael TD, John L. O'Sullivan, was jailed for five years for the offence.[30]

But the government's stance on the IRA was also changing. In March, forty IRA men were arrested in Dublin and a few days later de Valera spoke out against the organisation.[31] A de Valera meeting was attacked by members of the IRA in July.[32] De Valera was coming to the conclusion that he was not going to succeed in persuading the IRA to give up its illegal methods and follow him into constitutional politics, as he had propounded so frequently when challenged on his attitude to the IRA between 1932 and 1934, and from this point on the line he took was increasingly severe. De Valera's opponents, however, saw it differently: that de Valera, having won power with the help of the IRA and having condoned their attacks on his opponents, was moving against them now that it was safe to do so. For once the IRA and Fine Gael were at one in their view of de Valera, but that mattered for little as the Fianna Fáil leader tightened his grip on both Blueshirts and the IRA, and in the process hastened the return to political normality.

Some sense of this can be seen in the two by-elections held at the end of June in Galway and Dublin county, during which the campaigns were intensive but peaceful. This was Fine Gael's first Dáil electoral test since its foundation and the party held its Dublin seat with little change in the combined Cumann na nGaedheal/Centre Party vote of 1933. One Fianna Fáil reaction to Cecil Lavery's comfortable victory was to declare that 'the Empire speaks today; the Republic will speak tomorrow in Galway'. And indeed, as expected, Fianna Fáil held its Galway seat with a comfortable but reduced majority, with the result that no party could claim very much either way.[33]

A further, if still slight shift in political attitudes can be seen in the greatly improved relations between Fine Gael and Labour. In 1932 and indeed 1933, Labour, which voted consistently with Fianna Fáil, had been unrelentingly hostile to Cumann na nGaedheal. By 1935, however, there was increasing evidence of voting solidarity between the two parties. Labour clashes with Fianna Fáil ministers had taken on a new sharpness and culminated in a particularly bitter row between Lemass and Norton in late July.[34] As an indication of the new Fine Gael-Labour friendship, Cosgrave announced to the party's standing committee on 1 August 1935 that he was setting up a committee to liaise with the Labour leaders on 'Labour questions and Labour policy generally'. Somewhat surprisingly, Dillon was made a member of this group.[35] Dillon was doctrinaire in his opposition to socialism and had taken a strong anti-Labour Party line on many Dáil issues. More than that, some of his most personal confrontations had been with Norton and TJ Murphy of West Cork, whom he accused of 'cheap demagogic fraud' in June.[36] Dillon had the capacity to leave these clashes behind him once he left the Dáil chamber, but his public utterances made him a somewhat unlikely member of a committee to liaise with Labour. The setting up of the committee, however, was significant.

As in most parliaments, most of the Dáil work was routine business of the day. The Criminal Law Amendment Bill 1934 proposed, almost as an afterthought, that the importation and sale of contraceptives would hence-forth be illegal. This Bill, to be such a source of controversy and divisiveness in later years, slipped almost unobserved onto the Statute Book. Dillon, like virtually all others, did not even speak in the debate. That does not mean he was unaware of the measure – he was scrupulous about examining ail proposed legislation in detail – but his silence indicates his approval of the proposal, which was in line with his own very orthodox and conservative Catholicism. Like most men of his time he felt that some matters were not fit topics for public discussion, certainly not in mixed company, and this was one such. Contraception never became a seri-ous political issue during his time in the Dáil, but there is no doubt that on this topic his views did not change with the passing years; later, he warmly supported Pope Paul VI's encyclical, *Humanae Vitae*, which reaffirmed traditional Catholic teaching on such matters.

An example of his prudishness or sense of delicacy in dealing with sexual issues is seen when he spoke in early 1936 on the vote for the Army. He accepted that 'forces which are organised along militaristic lines in this and every other country, have found it necessary, where bodies of men were brought together under military conditions, to impart certain instructions in hygiene of a character that is not familiar to the average young man or youth in rural Ireland.' He was talking about preventative measures against sexually transmitted diseases, but this was in a pre-explicit age, which in this case obliged the word 'hygiene' to do duty for more direct language. Dillon's main worry was that the new part-time volunteers should not be given such instruction, because of the 'evil' which might 'accrue from infor-mation of that character being disseminated widely throughout the country by impressionable youths who only attend short periods of train-ing'. It was a pompous, if not precious contribution, for which he got short shrift from Aiken.[37]

He was conservative, too, in his attitude to the Local Elections Bill 1935, which proposed to extend the franchise in local elections to all voters rather than just ratepayers and their families. Dillon did not see the issue as one of democratic principle but of sound husbanding of public finances and value for ratepayer's money. He argued that 'it was manifestly undesirable where you are raising considerable sums of money from one section of the community, to be spent largely by another section of the community, to give universal franchise'. He felt that human nature being what it was, there would be enormous pressure on ordinary members of local authorities 'to indulge in extravagance and in the improvident distribution of the resources of the community' in pursuit of popular support, and that it would all lead to 'the scattering of public money for the purchase of votes'.[38]

It was at about this time that his life-long antipathy to the *Irish Press* began in earnest. His distrust of the *Irish Press*, indeed his contempt for the paper, was for him a matter of principle, and it was not until Michael Mills became political correspondent in the 1960s that he would even speak to its journalists – at least on the record. He likened the *Press* to *Pravda*, seeing it as little more than a propaganda organ for de Valera and Fianna Fáil. In this he was undoubtedly right. No opposition politician could expect or get fair play from a paper whose controlling editor was Eamon de Valera, from its foundation until 1959, though it was only much later that the full extent of de Valera's daily involvement with the paper was revealed.

From the outset Dillon said de Valera's close association with the *Irish Press* was inappropriate for a prime minister. One of his first skirmishes took place when he attacked an *Irish Press* campaign which aimed to remove 'indecent films' from the country. Dillon, who was a keen cinema-goer, felt the campaign was 'hypocritical and fraudulent', that the censor was doing his work and general standards were above reproach. He accused the paper of a reckless campaign against a highly respected public servant, of starting a reckless and uninformed agitation of a morbid and hypocritical character, and of attempting to portray themselves as 'super purists':

> The same hypocritical business underlies the policy of Fianna Fáil – the idea of setting themselves up as the only patriots, as the only angels, as the only persons of virtue ... that is the kind of nauseating, hypocritical, slushy fraud we have eating the very soul out of this country, and we are all afraid to oppose it lest somebody get up and say 'He voted against the resolution, therefore he must be for dirty films.'[39]

He was even more forthright a few months later when he referred to the *Irish Press* as a 'kept' paper. He charged de Valera with avoiding 'the thrust and parry' of debate in the Dáil, and using the *Press* to put across his views instead. He accused him of direct editorial interference, alleging he had written the editorial of 12 December: 'I can see his hand in every line of it.' Worse still, the particular article was 'plastered with falsehood, that detestable prevarication designed to deceive' and he alleged that the *Press* 'stoops to deception of its own readers by half-truths, suppression of the truth and prevarication'.[40]

It was rough stuff and Dillon's views were not to relent. Yet, whatever the good points of the *Irish Press* – and there were many – it was an unashamedly Fianna Fáil paper, partisan, bitter and uncompromising in the way it treated those opposed to the party. Dillon was right, too, when he spoke of de Valera's iron grip on all aspects of the paper's policy.

Dillon's overall assessment of de Valera was taking its final shape, and was to change little over the passing years. It will be remembered that John

Dillon had preferred de Valera to Cosgrave in the 1920s, and de Valera had once approached James about standing for Fianna Fáil. Dillon had voted for de Valera after the 1932 election and supported some of his policies. The two men treated each other with courtesy – there was even an element of personal cordiality between them – but by 1935 Dillon was convinced that de Valera's policies were not just ruinous for the country but were fundamentally dishonest. He reserved his strongest criticism for what he saw as de Valera's deviousness, his fraudulent republicanism and his flawed relationship with the IRA. He was convinced that much of de Valera's behaviour was motivated by a compulsion to justify his past, especially his role in the Treaty and Civil War. Dillon contrasted the de Valera of the 1920s, who denied legitimacy to many aspects of the state, with the Fianna Fáil leader's current expectation that his opponents should put all that behind them and give him full support. He thought de Valera ran his party in an authoritarian way and was critical of what he regarded as an absence of independent thinking in Fianna Fáil. He despised the constant playing of the anti-English card, in particular the branding of any opposition to de Valera as 'playing England's game'.

As far as Dillon was concerned, de Valera's deviousness had no end, and he had little difficulty in identifying de Valera's true mentor:

> The President is, and always has been, a close and scrupulous student of Niccolo Machiavelli. He will remember that Machiavelli recommended to him the stirring up of disturbance until he got into office, and to stir it up with all the exterior appearance of benignity, magnanimity, justice, truth and religion. He will remember that Niccolo Machiavelli further advised him, having got into the saddle, to take mighty good care he stayed there.[41]

He saw the republicanism espoused by de Valera and Fianna Fáil as shallow and bombastic, a hollow substitute for real policies:

> Whenever I think of President de Valera and the Republic my mind inevitably gets back to *Alice Through the Looking Glass* ... how Alice, whom I always identify in my mind with the Vice-President (Sean T. O'Kelly), plaintively asks the Red Queen when she might expect to have jam for tea; and the Red Queen replied: 'We always have jam for tea.' Then Alice enquired: 'Why haven't we jam for tea now?' and to that the Red Queen replied: 'We always have jam yesterday; we always have jam tomorrow; but we never have jam today.' Let me substitute for the word jam, the word Republic.[42]

Dillon argued that there was nothing to stop de Valera declaring a Republic, but that such a Republic would do little to restore the unity of the country. The real reason he believed the Republic was left undeclared was because it suited de Valera's domestic strategy. He told the Dáil in July 1935:

> Whenever the Government is brought dead up against the reality of the existing situation, hasty research is made for the green flag. The persons who get up to speak are wrapped in it and they are instructed to embrace Kathleen Ní Houlihan for the edification of the populace at large.[43]

What annoyed him most of all, though, was the constant misrepresentation of the opposition and the undermining of their patriotic bona fides. He cited as one example among several the views of the Sligo–Leitrim TD, Ben Maguire, that those who opposed Fianna Fáil were 'Judases, spies, informers, traitors, Carey.'[44]

He warned de Valera that his ambiguity towards the IRA could have unpleasant consequences. This point was borne out in May 1935, when the IRA's new hostility to the government meant that police protection for de Valera and his ministers had to be dramatically augmented. Dillon commented:

> The Government have seen turned against themselves the very self-same methods of insolence, aggression and intimidation that they rejoiced to see turned against us in the past ... In the past the blackguard and the intimidator were clearly shown that they had the sympathy of the Government so long as they confined their activities to attacking ordinary citizens who were members of our organisation. It was not until the Minister for Defence was pelted with rotten eggs in Tralee and until the President was insulted on the streets of Dublin that the Fianna Fáil Government began to sit up and take notice. Now you are reaping the whirlwind you yourselves sowed in the past few years.[45]

IT IS ironic that just as Dillon's hostility to de Valera was hardening, Dillon's first political ally, MacDermot, was moving in exactly the opposite direction, and was to end up as one of de Valera's nominees to the new Senate in 1938. But this was not to happen before MacDermot finally broke with Dillon and Fine Gael in 1935.

Throughout his life Dillon's attitude to MacDermot was one of exasperated affection. He genuinely liked him – their friendship survived until MacDermot's death in 1975 and during much, though not all of this time they corresponded on a regular basis. Despite their closeness, Dillon regarded MacDermot as one of the most egotistical men he had ever met, imbued with a sense of personal superiority which led him to believe that 'he would naturally rise to the top of any organisation of which he became a member'. This, of course, included the political parties he joined.[46]

As Dillon later remarked, MacDermot had about 'as much chance of becoming leader of Fine Gael as I have of becoming a ballet dancer, but one could not persuade him of that'. Indeed, one of the inducements MacDermot held out to Dillon when he was setting up the Centre Party in September 1932 was that, since most of the other TDs were 'duds', it would be 'all the easier for us to make the show just what we want it'. While MacDermot undoubtedly had a higher view of his new Cumann na nGaedheal colleagues, Dillon remained certain that the question of leadership still remained high on his agenda.

Fianna Fáil's actions during the Blueshirt period ensured that party solidarity remained high, even as far as MacDermot was concerned, but from time to time he slipped the leash, such as when he attacked aspects of O'Duffy's behaviour at a public meeting in Roscommon in late summer 1934, much to Cosgrave's discomfort. That particular episode never surfaced in public, largely because of the national newspaper strike, and a second more damaging disagreement was overshadowed by the Blueshirt split and O'Duffy's resignation.

MacDermot was out of the country during the O'Duffy crisis, having left Ireland in July 1934 to undergo surgery in London. He kept in touch with political developments at home through a number of correspondents, especially Dillon and Tierney. Shortly after leaving he wrote to Dillon, chiding him in an avuncular way about a reported speech in Ballina: 'I hope you did not say at Ballina that we would drive de Valera out of public life and that if you did you won't say it again. Ridicule, Ridicule, Ridicule, that's the stuff to give them, but ridicule of their humbug, clap-trap and inconsistencies, not personal stuff.'[47]

Ten days later he told Dillon that he was 'cogitating an article for a newspaper here. Thereafter I should do my best to forget politics and think about family, friends and literature.'[48] A few days later he had lunch with Lord Hailsham and met Geoffrey Dawson, editor of *The Times*, and put to each of them the proposal which had emerged from his 'cogitations'. He felt he had not succeeded very much in changing Hailsham's point of view, but Dawson 'was most sympathetic', and promised to publish MacDermot's 'cogitations' as a letter to *The Times* at the earliest opportunity.[49]

MacDermot's letter, dated 20 July 1934, was written from Brooks Club, an indication, along with his ease of access to Hailsham and Dawson, of the extent to which he was an Establishment figure in London, or at least knew his way around that particular world. From an end-of-century perspective his letter to *The Times* combines insight, originality and a largeness of vision. That, however, was not how it was seen in 1934.

It opened dramatically:

In Ireland itself the Anglo-Irish Treaty is dead and its remains, carefully embalmed and exposed to view, are an embarrassment to those who favour the British connection and not to those who oppose that connection.

He went on to argue that the most valuable asset of those who advocated separation from Britain is 'the impression that we are under external compulsion in the matter. Of this compulsion the Treaty is the emblem. As such the present Government exploited it to the full.' He felt it was time to call the Republican's bluff:

> I suggest that Great Britain would be as wise to abandon the Treaty as would the United States of America to abandon the collection of War Debts. If I were an Englishman I should face with entire composure the possibility of the Free State converting itself into a Republic. As an Irishman on the other hand I strongly object to leaving the Commonwealth of Nations for a variety of reasons, but most for the sake of the unity of Ireland, which I firmly believe can be attained and can only be attained within the Commonwealth.

MacDermot went on to suggest that the British government should take an early opportunity to assure the Irish government it had the right to secede from the Commonwealth without any subsequent economic or punitive measures being taken against it. He referred to the accommodating reply in the Senate from MacEntee on 18 July on the nature of voluntary membership of the Commonwealth, and saw this as an 'immense advance in the political education of Fianna Fáil'.[50]

If MacDermot expected a response he had not long to wait. Dillon first learned of his friend's opinions when *The Irish Times* carried a report. He wrote from Ballaghaderreen on 25 July:

> I have already implored you to abstain from active participation in politics while you are away, but without effect. For the vice-president of Fine Gael to inaugurate a correspondence on Irish affairs in *The Times* is bad enough, but to deal with the Treaty on the lines represented in *The Irish Times* is appalling insanity.
>
> How you could justify going to see Hailsham surpasses me to understand. The only conceivable reason he could wish to see you would be because you represent the organisation of which you are vice-president, and it is nothing short of fraud to pretend that in meeting him and the editor of *The Times* that you do. You are labouring under a wild illusion if you imagine that MacEntee's speech has made any material impression on the political situation here. It has evoked no comment whatsoever. The situation herewith in our own party is critical and extremely delicate, irretrievable damage could easily be done. Dismiss from your mind any idea that you can meet Hailsham without the Government here getting to know of it and in any case it is an

absolutely indefensible thing for a leader of the Opposition to do at the present time. If you feel bound to intervene actively in Irish politics at present you ought to come home and do it in Ireland, in consultation with your colleagues. Spasmodic interruptions in the English press can do nothing but harm and make the position here virtually impossible.

I am no lover of the Treaty, but to refer to it with cold and apparently studied contempt in *The Times* when the brothers and friends of your colleagues died to defend it, it is really beyond the beyonds.[51]

It was a sharp and angry letter and Dillon was not to change any part of it. MacDermot was equally trenchant in his reply:

You need never shrink from expressing complete disagreement provided you do me the honour to mention just what it is you disagree with. I thought every word of my letter would have commanded your assent unless your views have recently changed. But if we do differ on such fundamental matters, it is important that we should both realise it. Some of our Cumann na nGaedheal colleagues have never in their hearts accepted the heads of policy which we laid before them in the pre-merger conferences and which are now the official party policy and it may be that you have adopted their point of view. If I could go back to April 1932, I would in fact take a more decided and persistent line than I have done, and I am more inclined to say with Michael Tierney that my motion in the Dáil didn't go far enough than to say it goes too far. My greatest mistake has been paying too much attention to 'prudent' advice.[52]

He followed with a more comprehensive response four days later, when he argued that he had taken a purely personal initiative in the national interest and had been in no way disloyal to his colleagues, but was merely recognising the reality that the Treaty had outlived its usefulness and the division of politics into pro- and anti-Treaty factions worked only to the advantage of de Valera. Finally he rounded on Dillon, describing him as 'impregnated with party spirit – and Cumann na nGaedheal spirit at that'.[53]

The differences between Dillon and MacDermot were sharp but not particularly personal. MacDermot began a letter of 22 August by telling Dillon: 'I give you very high marks for good temper. Our correspondence does not upset me at all.' And he finished the letter with a flourish of genuine affection: 'Good luck to you old James! You are a swell fellow. You can preach to me as much as you like and I will just preach back.'[54]

In truth, MacDermot was already restless and impatient. He was convinced that his initiative in meeting Hailsham, Dawson and Lord Danesfort offered a way out of the Anglo-Irish impasse. Hailsham had assured him that the only objection to the declaration of an Irish Republic was that recognition of it would destroy Britain's legal basis for using Irish harbours as coastal defences. Hailsham had also felt that if de Valera attended the next Imperial Conference and asked for a declaration of a right to secede, he would win it.

MacDermot's analysis was so far ahead of its time as to be irrelevant in the conditions of 1934. Neither the British government, Fianna Fáil, nor indeed Fine Gael were ready for it, a fact he blithely refused to recognise and which casts some doubt over his judgement. His deepening sense of malaise shows through in his letters to Tierney, whose resignation encouraged MacDermot to contemplate doing likewise. He was much interested to hear what Tierney had to say about Cosgrave's leadership (unflattering) and, considering his own prospects, thought that: 'I could not work effectively under Dillon, a man fifteen years my junior, and the old gang would not as yet accept me, even if my health was yet equal to it.' He concluded on a plaintive note: 'If you were in my shoes I wonder what you would do – stick to the sinking ship, abandon politics entirely, or return to the cross benches.'[55]

He wrote to Tierney again in the autumn and warned: 'I expect I shall go independent a little later and before the Dáil reassembles (unless it involves sitting next to Belton!).' He enjoined Tierney not to mention his intentions to anyone,[56] but clearly from this point on he was detached from Fine Gael. Neither Cosgrave or Dillon were under any illusions about his long-term intentions, even though he was re-elected a vice president of the party at the 1934 Árd Fheis, and when Cosgrave announced his front bench in October he was given the important Finance spokesmanship, ahead of people of proven ministerial experience such as McGilligan. With the re-allocation of offices at 3 Merrion Square after O'Duffy's departure, he was given Cosgrave's old office, and he continued to make regular contributions to Dáil debates and to speak at Fine Gael meetings throughout the country.

His heart, however, was not in it. His attendance at parliamentary party meetings became more and more patchy and on more than one occasion his speeches attracted critical attention from his party colleagues. It was only a matter of time before the final break came. The issue that precipitated it was de Valera's speech at the League of Nations in Geneva in September 1935, when, defending the concept of collective security, he condemned Mussolini's invasion of Abyssinia. De Valera saw the crisis as 'the final test of the League and all it stands for', and his strong speech was widely praised.[57]

The Fine Gael reaction was narrow and ungenerous. O'Higgins, speaking at Thurles on 22 September, averred that de Valera should have used the Geneva crisis as an opportunity for settling Ireland's troubles with Britain.

This outraged MacDermot. He threatened resignation unless the standing committee passed a resolution endorsing de Valera's stand. Such a motion, he declared, was 'the price of my keeping my mouth shut'. The motion was not accepted and MacDermot, in some anger, went straight to a meeting in Dublin of the League of Nations Union at which he strongly endorsed de Valera's position. His speech was virtually ignored by both newspapers and public.[58]

On 4 October, Cosgrave outlined the Fine Gael position at a special meeting at the party's headquarters. While he certainly approved of de Valera fulfilling our international obligations, he had missed an opportunity to represent to Britain how important world peace was to her; how much stronger would be her and Ireland's moral positions as upholders of peace if we made peace between ourselves; how much better de Valera could answer for Ireland if the people were not being destroyed by tariffs. Cosgrave thought de Valera had lost a great opportunity for bringing these points home to Britain.[59]

As expected and, no doubt, intended, MacDermot's action had clearly annoyed the Fine Gael hierarchy. When O'Higgins took a verbal swipe at him,[60] an outraged MacDermot told Dillon his speech referred to 'my baby talk', 'to my being so completely cosmopolitan as to forget to be Irish'. On the following day, MacDermot handed Cosgrave a letter of protest which, according to MacDermot, the standing committee meeting that evening 'considered must, if published, involve my resignation'. Published it was next morning and 'I duly put my resignation at the disposal of the National Executive who are meeting on Thursday 10th. I did not attend and it was unanimously accepted and a resolution passed approving of Cosgrave's speech of the 4th.'

Thus MacDermot's resignation from Fine Gael, long anticipated, came to pass.[61] It excited little surprise. Dillon was out of the country – on holiday in the Holy Land – and only learned the details of the final break when MacDermot wrote to him in Gibraltar from the Kildare St Club.

It is doubtful, however, if he would have tried to persuade MacDermot to change his mind, since for some time he was convinced that MacDermot's mind was already made up and that he was temperamentally unsuited to the rigours and constraints of party politics. He almost certainly agreed with the Fianna Fáil Minister for Lands, Senator Joseph Connolly, who had warned MacDermot more in sorrow than in anger during a parliamentary exchange in June 1935 that he would never succeed in Irish politics 'because he did not understand the psychology of the Irish people', or the even harsher view of Dan Morrissey in a later debate that MacDermot 'is a very superior sort of person, too superior altogether for this House, this Parliament, this country'.[62]

When the Dáil reassembled in October, MacDermot took his place on the Independent benches. While still personally friendly with Dillon, a new sharpness had entered their relationship, and on one occasion at least Dillon was openly and effectively contemptuous of his former colleague.

For Dillon, the MacDermot interlude in his life was coming to its political end. Ironically, on the issue which precipitated MacDermot's resignation, he was right and his Fine Gael colleagues wrong. When Dillon spoke on the question in the Dáil in November, his line was closer to that of MacDermot when he praised de Valera's upholding of the obligations of the Covenant 'in terms both eloquent and appropriate'. All of which brought a wry smile to MacDermot, who talked of Dillon bringing back 'some of the Mediterranean sunshine' and noting that if 'Dillon's speech had been delivered a month ago, I would not be tasting the joys of independence at the present time.'[63]

That is unlikely. As we have seen, his mind had long since been made up and he had lost the trust and confidence of his senior colleagues. McGilligan was particularly dismissive of what he saw as MacDermot's self-importance: 'So much a matter of his imagining himself like one of the old Classical deities, governing the winds, and finding in fact that he could not unloose the storm.' MacDermot, said McGilligan, had 'a detachment few of us in life can get because our condition in life does not allow us to attain it'.[64]

Dillon, on the other hand, had grown secure in his new political setting. The support of his new colleagues was well illustrated during a rancorous Dáil debate on the 1916 commemoration ceremonies, which the opposition alleged Fianna Fáil was hi-jacking. In Dillon's first months in the Dáil, his father's role in 1916 had been attacked by Batt O'Connor. Now, in spring 1935 the Parliamentary Secretary to the Minister for Finance, Hugo Flinn, a man whose invective occasionally spilled over into scurrility, returned once more to the charge, questioning James Dillon's own role as well as that of his father. There was no shortage of colleagues eager to defend him, the strongest being Gearóid O'Sullivan:

> I would refer him to three generations of Dillons in Irish history. Yes, and the men on this side, and on the other side of the House know that the first man who raised his voice for the protection of the men who were in prison was the father of Deputy Dillon.[65]

THE YEARS from 1932 to 1935 had been of crucial importance in determining the future shape of Irish politics. By 1935 most of the major battles had been fought and won by Fianna Fáil. Fine Gael was beginning its years of decline, while Labour remained on the margins. Tensions between the parties may have begun to ease, but other issues were not long in emerging: the Spanish Civil War, and the threat to international peace brought on by the rise of Nazism in Germany, while the new constitution of the Free State and its relationship with the Commonwealth were debated against the background of deteriorating economic and social conditions at home. For Dillon, these matters were closer to the heart of politics than the fevered adventures of his first years, and during the last part of this Dáil they increasingly absorbed his attention. He was one of the few frontbenchers fully to shoulder his share of parliamentary work and his speeches at this stage convey the impression of somebody very much enjoying himself. He ranged from the deprivation of inner-city Dublin to penal reform, farming problems and the health service, and maintained a very keen interest in the major international questions of the day.

To begin with, however, the Economic War was still raging. He made a plea in February 1936 for a sane ending to a conflict which was still doing enormous harm to businesses and agriculture. He described what had become of the monthly fair:

> It used to be a monthly occasion of fun ... now it's a monthly horror, a standing nightmare ... farmers cannot pay their shop debts or buy stock to replace what they sold. They are quarrelling with their wives and children, and depriving them of things they want to give them.[66]

He argued that the notion of 'war' was now a nonsense, since there was in fact the closest daily consultation between the two countries. The British had reached a stage where they were not going to drive a hard bargain, he said, but a settlement was being held up because of the government's need to save face. Dillon's pessimism was uncharacteristic, and his anger was genuine:

> We have to sink or swim according to our own exertions, and the spectre that haunts me and everybody whose people and whose property are indissolubly wedded to this country is that it will be brought down and that we will all be brought down with it. The reason we are so anxious about and want a settlement is because we cannot get out of the country. Personally if I could get out I would have got out long ago. It is legitimate and right that we should want to see our country and our people happy and for that reason we want them provided with the wherewithal to meet their obligations and to stand on their own feet. This cannot be done if the Economic War is not ended.[67]

The Economic War dragged on for another year, causing massive unemployment and emigration in a decade that came to be known as 'the hungry '30s'. Poverty was widespread; Dillon, who lived a large part of his life in Dublin, saw it every day on his doorstep. He had indicated his concern about the city's slums in his Law Society inaugural in 1929, and in April 1936 he told the Dáil that this concern grew from having been born and reared 'in the middle of the slums of this city, and knowing them well'. He felt that the job was too big for the local authorities and wanted the government to take it on:

> Counting myself a conservative person in regard to financial policy, I took the view that it was sound finance to abolish the slums and to count the cost afterwards ... no person in this country or in any other Christian democratic state wants to see individual wealth existing side by side with destitution and misery.[68]

Two other social problems also exercised his mind, as they would throughout his political life. He took a keen and enlightened interest in penal reform and made a point of visiting jails and reformatories to see conditions there for himself. He wanted more humane court procedures for dealing with juvenile offenders and made a strong case for greater use of in camera procedures. He favoured a lessening in the formality of the courts so as to ease the psychological stress on children. He called for the humanising of reformatories and special treatment for young female offenders, and appealed for community policing before that phrase had been invented.[69]

As poverty grew more widespread, tuberculosis became a killer disease and a source of great phobia. Dillon's own brother, Theo, was an early victim and there was scarcely a family in the country free from its ravages. Throughout the 1930s and 1940s, Dillon urged greater emphasis by the state on precautionary measures; he followed medical advances against tuberculosis, and identified poor housing conditions as a primary cause of the disease. There is no evidence that his views were listened to.[70]

One fixed and unchanging part of Dillon's political year was the annual AOH parades on 15 August. The AOH, a conservative Catholic and nationalist organisation, had been an inheritance for Dillon and a source of political support. It played an important part in having him elected in Donegal, but in national terms it had ceased to be in any way a significant force by the 1930s. Its traditional links had been with the Irish Party and much of its political *raison d'être* disappeared with it. It continued to be loyal to the memory of the party and ran a modest range of benevolent insurance schemes for its members. The organisation provided shelter and a rallying point for surviving members of the Irish Party tradition. Dillon's own involvement was born out of loyalty and necessity: the Order gave him electoral support, especially in his early days. He became a national vice-president and continued to be an active member until his death.

The AOH was, in Dillon's words, 'emphatically Catholic and Nationalist', and for this he made no apology. 'It recognises fully the rights of those who want to organise for the purpose of promoting other ideas, but the AOH will continue regularly to demonstrate on the Feast of the Assumption every year its unalterable devotion to its unchanged and unchangeable ideas of Faith and Fatherland.' By 'Faith' essentially was meant fidelity to traditional Catholic beliefs and the pre-eminence of the papacy as the teaching authority of the Church, while 'Fatherland' Dillon defined as 'the united 32 counties, in which a free people can mould its own destiny'.[71]

The AOH was neither a young nor particularly virile organisation, and came to life largely around the 15th of August parades, which were loud and colourful, well attended and peaceful, with none of the menace and triumphalism associated with the Orange parades north of the border. Dillon used the annual platform usually in Donegal and Monaghan to adapt the underlying principles of the Order to contemporary events, with particular emphasis on the dangers communism and Nazism posed to Catholicism and freedom. He addressed these themes at Clones on 15 August 1937, and stressed the importance of a victory for Franco in the Spanish Civil War:

> Valencia and its government are trying to conquer Spain for Moscow and the philosophy of Marx; Burgos and General Franco are trying to prevent that. On that issue our place is behind Franco, and until that issue is disposed of there should be no doubt in anyone's mind which is the right side. After the Communist attempt at conquest has been smashed, then Spain must work out her own destiny in her own way.

On Nazism he was uncompromising. He could not stomach its contempt for democracy and its glorification of dictatorship, its hatred of the Christian churches, its racialism 'Let us remember that all men and women belong to the universal brotherhood of man, which implies the universal fatherhood of God, whether they are Gaels or Arians.' His remarks on Nazism's 'excessive nationalism' had a certain relevance to events at home: 'a nationalism or patriotism which lives on hatred of its neighbours in the community of nations is a horrible travesty of real patriotism, and can lead to nothing but misery and endless strife.'

The Spanish Civil War was at its most fierce when Dillon made his Clones speech. In Ireland, as in every other European country, passions ran deep, and a brigade from Ireland fought on each side in a conflict which some saw as a fight to the death between communism and fascism, others as a fight between communism and Catholicism. Dillon had no doubt about how he saw it: 'The issue in Spain, the fundamental issue, is God or no God.' He felt that Ireland, as 'one of the very few nations left in the world today that is not afraid to proclaim that it is a Catholic country', must stand foursquare behind Franco; while our material support was insignificant, 'our moral support throughout the world could be immense'. In saying this he repeated that as a democrat he detested 'Hitlerism, Mussolinism and Stalinism equally'.[72]

On the practical aspect of the war, however, his approach conveyed a certain confusion. He supported the principle of non-intervention, but opposed the government's Bill to put this into effect. The principle, he said, 'will in the long run redound to the advantage of General Franco and the Burgos Government', but he objected to the government's approach on two grounds: it favoured the communists because it prevented the sending of troops to Spain, 'ninety per cent of whom would go to Franco', and our ambassador was still 'accredited to the Caballero Government', which implicitly conferred legitimacy on the Republican regime. He told de Valera to 'recall your ambassador and we are prepared to co-operate in whatever we believe will be effective to prevent intervention'.[73]

Dillon's non-intervention was essentially tactical. In principle he believed that 'in this time when everything we have been accustomed to look upon as permanent is crashing about us, it is more vital than it ever was before that we should, with courage ... testify to our faith.' He was conscious of the dangers such a stand presented, especially of being labelled 'a fascist' as a result, but that was a risk which he felt had to be taken.[74]

The Spanish Civil War episode reveals Dillon's outlook on Ireland as 'gloriously and notoriously, a Catholic country'.[75] In this he was very much of his time and at one with the values expressed by de Valera in Bunreacht na hÉireann. The depth of his beliefs do raise question marks about his understanding of Northern Unionists' feelings, and how they might be accommodated within the Irish unity to which he was committed. Dillon always denied any taint of sectarianism. In his Clones speech he attacked the Brookeborough concept of 'a Protestant government for a Protestant people', and insisted that 'although in this country they were ninety per cent a Catholic people they did not want a sectarian government'.[76]

The Spanish Civil War was merely a foretaste of terrors to come. Dillon had grown increasingly gloomy about the likelihood of a major European or World War: 'Everything we have been accustomed to looking upon as permanent [is] crashing about us,' he had said in Clones. He had little confidence in the League of Nations, which he saw as 'an ineffective protector of small nations', and thought that Ireland could hope for very little material help from that source.[77]

As early as June 1936, Dillon had thought through his position as far as a future war was concerned, and did so with a clarity and prescience which still stands the test of time. For a start, he had no doubts as to the issues which would be involved:

> Anybody looking around the world today sees that democracy and individual liberty are losing out on one front after another. We stand for these two funda-mental doctrines … and unless the nations of the world who believe in these fundamental principles are prepared to draw closer together for their mutual advantage they are going to be destroyed one after another, by dictatorships that want to destroy them.[78]

He did not think that Ireland would be able to remain aloof in a global conflict: its geographical position was now of increased importance because of air transport. 'It might very well suit one of the dictatorships of Europe to seek an opportunity of annexing at least a part of our territory in order to provide themselves with a jumping-off ground for the maintenance of transatlantic contact by air with the US.'

Nor did he believe Ireland was in a position effectively to defend itself against attack. 'I believe that, in the event of an attempt being made by a Continental power to overwhelm this country by an assault based on a naval invasion, we would be absolutely powerless to defend ourselves, if we had not a guarantee of assistance from Great Britain.'[79]

His willingness to accept this point showed Dillon at his most coura-geous. Anti-English sentiment was at an all time high in the Free State. Over the previous four years the Fianna Fáil government and the IRA had stirred up such feeling on a wide scale. Cinemas which showed newsreel films of the Coronation were attacked, poppy-day celebrations had been virtually abandoned, boycott Bass campaigns were commonplace and any expression of friendship towards Britain was loudly proclaimed as 'traitor-ous' and 'anti-national'. Dillon cut through all of this. In the Dáil, on 18 June 1936, he objected strongly to 'the annual repetition of the lamenta-tions about the [Treaty] ports and about the misery we are enduring in regard to our ports.'[80] It was his view that 'nobody gives two hoots about the ports'. He made the point in more fundamental terms the following week:

> I speak of the solemn obligation there is upon us to keep the liberty that has been won for us. For seven hundred years we tried to make allies of Britain's enemies. But time and time again, in the hour of crisis, the enemies of Britain abandoned us when it suited their hand. The French failed to stand behind us to fight for our liberty, when it no longer suited them to do so. And the

French fleet went home, and left us and our poor people to the hanging and the pitch-caps of the British Government. In 1916 ... the German Government ... left us to bear the brunt of the battle. I want our people for the first time in our history to make allies of England's friends. We could establish an understanding of mutual respect, founded on the recognition that neither is a potential enemy of the other.[81]

He believed that the Commonwealth could be the framework 'into which can be fitted every sovereign democratic nation ... that is prepared to co-operate against tyranny and against violence such as are represented by the dictators of the Right and of the Left on the Continent of Europe at the present time'.

He wanted Ireland to play a leading role in the Commonwealth, promoting greater co-operation between the nations of the Commonwealth and the United States of America. He wanted no part of the growing insularity and political isolationism in which Irish politics was wrapping itself: 'I believe we might hope to lend a hand in breaking down that modern curse of Babel, economic nationalism, through such an approach [and] build up economic ties between the USA and the nations of the Commonwealth, which would lead to bigger things in the future.'[82]

The Commonwealth had been of central importance in Dillon's political thinking from the very start of his career. He explained his admiration during a debate on the Department of the President on 23 June 1936:

It is because I have seen with admiration a body of Irish statesmen able to convert that mighty organisation into an exquisite instrument of constitutional development, which has held together through the shocks and horrors of this extremely difficult period, when other states have been shattered; it is because this extraordinary constitutional conception, for which our people are largely responsible, has weathered the storm ... as no other association of people in the world is doing, that I do not want to exchange our place in it for a Republic whose voice in world affairs would count for nothing, whose trade would be precarious in the last degree and which would be open to the attacks of any power which wanted to assail it, because we would have nobody joined to us to defend our interests.[83]

He thought the Commonwealth could play a crucial role in the event of national unity. He argued that even if Britain favoured a thirty-two county Republic, 'it is my convinced belief that our people would have to go out and fight a civil war against our fellow countrymen in the four north-eastern counties in order to establish a Republic, and I say that no Republic and no national reunion would be worth a civil war of that character.'[84]

Dillon attended the coronation of King George VI and the Empire

Parliamentary conference in London in May 1937. The event, hosted by Stanley Baldwin, Clement Attlee and David Lloyd George, was attended by delegations from fifteen of the Commonwealth countries; Dillon was the only senior politician from the Free State to go. Fianna Fáil boycotted the event, as did Labour, and had Dillon not attended Fine Gael might well have ignored it also. Dillon, however, saw no need to hide his strong and positive feelings for the Commonwealth, and was not going to bow before the taunts his visit provoked or the political ammunition it gave his enemies.

In the same month, de Valera introduced his draft Constitution to the Dáil. Dillon's participation in the debate was limited, in large part because he felt the Constitution was 'grotesquely irrelevant'. In one sense his comments on draft article 5, which declared that the state was 'sovereign, independent and democratic', summed up his overall view: 'It is. It was made so by the predecessors in office of this Government ... and every member of the Fianna Fáil party stumped the country to denounce as a traitor and West Briton anyone who said so.' In short, Fianna Fáil was now accepting as reality what they had dismissed for over a decade. The Constitution made little difference to that reality.[85]

A number of the points he did make are worth noting. He felt that, for all its 'hifalutin' language, the Constitution would do little for women. On the divorce proposal, while he thought 'would seem to represent accurately the unanimous view of our people', he saw legal minefields ahead. He accurately forecast a future conflict between Church law, where 'the Pauline privilege' (nullity) operated, and the absolute state ban proposed in the Constitution. He felt that great damage could ensue from 'loosely drafted documents' dealing with such fundamental matters.[86]

He was greatly angered by proposals from MacEntee (which were later modified) that would have brought restrictions on the freedom of the press. 'If constitutions have any worth at all,' Dillon held, 'their purpose is not to restrain reasonable men, because they do not require restraint. Their purpose is to act as a check on reckless men who might precipitate great evils ... the longer I live the more I am convinced that the most effective way to destroy falsehood is to drag it into the open and place it before the people.'[87]

He and Costello raised the matter – little noted at the time but destined to be enormously important later – of the judicial interpretation of the Constitution. He argued that unless de Valera 'is prepared to take cognisance of the well-established principles of judicial interpretation of such documents, the result of what he writes or what this House puts into the Constitution, may be entirely different from what he intends.' He argued that subsequent judicial interpretation could permit serious incursions that neither the House nor the country intended to permit,[88] a view which generations of later politicians would heartily endorse.

Like most others at the time, Dillon failed to appreciate the strength and depth of de Valera's constitution. He saw it as making little change, and was contemptuous of its Republican language, which nonetheless stopped short of declaring a Republic. Neither he, nor others, foresaw the extent to which the human rights elements of the Constitution would develop and be developed by adventurous jurists, nor the extent to which judicial review of the Constitution would turn the Supreme Court into a major political force, striking down laws and curbing executives. An interventionist Supreme Court may have been on de Valera's agenda, or that of his advisers, but if so, it was not something he shared with the public.[89] It is hard to know how Dillon would have reacted – one part of him supported curbs on overmighty governments and intrusive executives, but another part vigorously championed the supremacy of parliament. In the event, he was not called upon to make a judgement. His priorities remained focused on Ireland's constitutional and political development within the Commonwealth, a Commonwealth he saw more and more as the main bulwark of western civilisation against the growing menace of the totalitarians of right and left.

CHAPTER NINE

MONAGHAN AND THE WAR

*'I believe that, bad and all as are the conditions of the world, decency,
tolerance and freedom are going to prevail over the medieval barbarism
of the dictators.'*

Dillon, Dáil Debates, 11 February 1939

1 937 WAS THE YEAR de Valera consolidated his hold on Irish politics and
began his long period of ascendancy, even if he did so without any
emphatic electoral endorsement, though that would follow. By 1937
Fianna Fáil was the only party capable of winning enough seats to form a
single-party government. Fine Gael was not yet in decline, but there was no
evidence of any significant resurgence and the gap between it and Labour
was too wide even to contemplate the possibility of a coalition. By 1937,
too, the Blueshirts were no more, and the Economic War was coming to an
unlamented end; the programme of economic self-sufficiency was well in
train, though as yet unattended by any obvious signs of success. De Valera's
constitution was ready, awaiting popular endorsement.

The election, held on the same day as the Constitution was endorsed,
was indecisive. In a Dáil reduced from 153 seats to 138, Fianna Fáil and
Fine Gael each lost nine seats on their pre-dissolution numbers. The
Fianna Fáil popular vote was down four per cent, as was that of Fine Gael,
which on thirty-four per cent was four per cent down on the combined
Cumann na nGaedheal and Centre Party votes of 1933. Labour made
modest gains, now standing at eleven per cent of the vote and thirteen
seats. Labour once again supported Fianna Fáil, though this time with
genuine reluctance, and for the third successive time de Valera was elected
President of the Executive Council. Soon that title would give way to
'Taoiseach', but in the meantime Fianna Fáil's majority was unstable and
few doubted that a fresh election was far off.

1937 was Dillon's first experience of Monaghan, a constituency in which
he knew no more than a handful of people. He could, however, claim one
direct historical link with the county. In 1880 the first Monaghan branch
of the Land League had been established in Scotstown by his father just
after he returned from the USA with Parnell and Davitt. The county had a
strong AOH presence, much though not all of which had remained loyal to

the Irish Party tradition, and which now enthusiastically supported Dillon, as it would do for the rest of his political life.

Monaghan had been strongly pro-Treaty, especially since the large Protestant population (over twenty-five per cent) had been advised by its leaders to vote in its favour. Sean MacEntee, one of the two Sinn Féin MPs elected in 1918, had in effect been driven out of Monaghan after he opted against the Treaty and had to seek a seat elsewhere. In the Pact election of 1923 the vote had been 19,862 for the pro-Treaty candidates, 5,747 against. The boundary settlement of 1925, however, seriously damaged the Cumann na nGaedheal position, which was not greatly helped either by the dour gracelessness of its leading candidate, Ernest Blythe. In the June election of 1927 Fianna Fáil moved ahead of Cumann na nGaedheal, and after that the gap widened until in 1933 Blythe lost the sole Cumann na nGaedheal seat and the constituency was represented by two Fianna Fáil TDs and one 'Independent Farmer', Alexander Hasslett, the Protestant candidate and an active member of the Orange Order.[1]

When he was invited to stand in Monaghan, Dillon was surprised that there was no strong local candidate available. This point is disputed by some local survivors, who claim Patrick Macklin was ready, willing and electable but that at Cosgrave's request he made way for Dillon.[2] Dillon put the absence of local candidates down to the personality and political style of Fianna Fáil TD, Dr Conor Ward, who had been prominent in Monaghan politics since before 1918. That year he had been selected to contest North Monaghan for Sinn Féin, but had stood down in favour of Blythe. He was a senior member of the IRA during the War of Independence and had represented the IRA on the Border Liaison Committee in 1922. He was first elected to the Dáil in 1927 and appointed Parliamentary Secretary to the Minister for Health and Local Government in 1932, a position he held until he resigned in 1946.[3]

Dillon attributed almost daemonic political powers to Ward. In his *Memoir* he claims that Ward had established in the constituency 'a positive reign of terror' with the result that no local man was prepared to face a contest in 1937 on account of the extraordinary violence of the atmosphere which had been created by the Ward political machine. He described his arrival in Monaghan for the first campaign:

Senator Barney O'Rourke drove me from Dublin to Carrickmacross, and when we arrived in Carrickmacross the only house where we were made welcome was the house of Paddy Lonergan, which was the hotel. He was a very staunch supporter of Fine Gael. Originally a Tipperary man, he had married a Monaghan woman and made his life in Carrickmacross, where he had lived for 20 or 30 years. From there we went to Castleblaney, and in Castleblaney the only house where we were received was Hugh Malone's, the Corner House. From there we went to Monaghan town, where our only friend was Paddy Macklin on Dublin Street. Then we went on to Clones, and really the only certain supporter I had there was Baldwin Murphy, who had been a boyhood friend of mine, as he and all his brothers had gone to Mount St. Benedict. From there we went on to the fifth town in the constituency, Ballybay, and our only real supporter there was a man called Paddy Coyle. So we were in a strange situation when I started in Monaghan – there were only five houses in the constituency where I could safely call.

I remember my first meeting, held, I think, in a village called Donaghmoyne, in a blizzard. I was introduced there by Paddy Lonergan, my friend in Carrickmacross. We simply went from chapel gate to chapel gate, and gradually supporters emerged, manifesting their support at these meetings.

But the atmosphere was extremely violent and the meetings were very stormy. Strenuous attempts were made by Fianna Fáil supporters to break up the meetings, but as the campaign proceeded our strength began to gather, and I was elected, I think, on the third or fourth count.

From the perspective of 1980, it is strange to recall the sort of techniques which were used in those days for breaking up a meeting. Physical violence, not infrequently; it usually started from my having a crowd of anything from 40 to 100 people after Mass, and a crowd of from 20 to 40 Fianna Fáil supporters hanging about 15-20 yards away, who would begin barracking me when I was speaking, and gradually approach the verge of the meeting. Jostling would begin, and, of course, to continue a speech with these kind of goings on was not easy, so that they confidently expected that the meeting would break up in disorder. However, by this time I was an experienced political speaker, and I had the advantage of having a microphone, and I was usually able to shout hecklers down.[4]

Ward was a tough political operator and a man of very considerable ability, who in different circumstances would have been a member of the cabinet. He was a dour political opponent, a strong organiser, and in the Fianna Fáil ethos of the day saw the conflict with Fine Gael as a fight to the finish, with little time for social or political niceties. Dillon and he each thought ill of the other and rarely saw good in one another's motives. Exchanges between them were often personal and frequently abusive, though in light of subsequent events it is important to note that Dillon never accused Ward of personal impropriety, merely of political jobbery and intimidation on a major scale.

Dillon's reception as the Fine Gael candidate was not as unanimous as he later recalled. To many he was an 'unknown quantity' who had voted for de Valera in 1932. In addition, the AOH had split some years earlier, with some members now supporting Fianna Fáil, while old Sinn Féin families like the Macklins and Toals had their reservations about the Irish Party tradition.

In the event, Dillon did well in his first Monaghan election, polling 7,653 votes against 12,275 for Ward. He won a seat for Fine Gael at the expense of the Independent, and this seat he held for the next thirty-two years. He had mixed views about his new constituency:

> I have often said that Monaghan is a unique county, in that it contains some of the best people and some of the worst people in Ireland. My experience was that if the Monaghan people became your supporters and friends, their loyalty was boundless; but if they were opposed to you, and regarded you as unorthodox, the lengths to which they were prepared to go, in order to shout you down and attack you, were almost unbelievable.[5]

Nor was he apologetic about being a non-resident TD:

> It is strange, perhaps, in view of the prevailing custom in politics now, that I managed to survive for over 30 years representing two constituencies, Donegal and Monaghan, in which I never took up residence, and that I was never prompted to stand for Mayo or Roscommon, where I did reside and where I had ancestral connections. In fact, one of the few pieces of political advice my father gave me was – never reside in your constituency. It will kill you. Your constituents will never leave you alone. This is advice that few men would dare to follow now, but I got away with it. I did make it a rule, though, always to answer correspondence promptly, and I was attentive to my constituents in all other ways. I held regular clinics in the five chief towns of the county, and I was glad to entertain my constituents in Leinster House – never, though in the bar. In that way, I believe, lies destruction, and I have seen many follow it. I entertained them to tea, and they had to be satisfied with that.[6]

Dillon's description of his attention to constituency detail is borne out by surviving memory. He was punctilious in personally answering all constituency correspondence and persistent in following-up queries, especially if he felt there was a case of bureaucratic bullying or denial of rights, but equally he was blunt with those constituents who in his view did not have a genuine case. His strictures against frequenting the bar tally almost exactly with those of de Valera, who never approved of having a bar in Leinster House and discouraged his TDs, not always with great success, from availing of its services.

De Valera's hold on power was tenuous, and the life of the Dáil lasted only eleven months, collapsing on a Labour Private Member's motion on 25 May 1938. Short as it was, however, it saw a number of significant developments, and Dillon continued to play an active and energetic part.

When the government Whip sought Fine Gael's support in April 1938 for an 'agreed' presidential candidate, someone who would be 'above' party politics, Dillon and O'Higgins were the Fine Gael representatives, given full power by the parliamentary party to come to a decision.[7]

Having abolished the Senate in 1934, de Valera proposed to establish a new 'Seanad' under the 1937 Constitution. The government was open about the new Senate's composition and electoral system, and adamant that it should have no real power. Certain principles were laid down, especially that the House should be 'vocational' in its composition, though there were few specifics as to how this concept could be achieved. Dillon was appointed to a special all-party committee, which included de Valera, Lemass, Costello, McGilligan and Norton, set up to examine the proposed electoral system, and when the committee failed to reach agreement, the eventual decision was taken by the Fianna Fáil majority.

Dillon argued that if what was desired was a 'vocational' Senate, as de Valera said it would be, then the electorate should be drawn from vocational interests. He thought the Senate should be free of party politics, a place 'whose members would run amok as far as party discipline is concerned', which would not happen if the political parties dominated the electoral college. He wanted an assembly which would act in a more or less advisory capacity to the sovereign political assembly in the Dáil, and he demanded a much stronger position for Labour, which he believed was under-represented in parliament. These proposals were defeated, however, and the new Senate developed almost exactly as Dillon had predicted, 'under the political thumb of the Government'. The putative vocational Senate, which he described as 'a most valuable experiment in the science of Government', never got off the drawing-board.[8]

On 2 February 1938 the government announced that it was about to begin negotiations to resolve the issues still outstanding in the long-running trade war with Britain. Dillon immediately and spontaneously offered to postpone a Fine Gael Private Member's motion on the issue until 'these matters were brought to what he hoped would be a happy conclusion'. The offer was gratefully accepted;[9] indeed, the year saw a general improvement in day to day relations in the Dáil. When de Valera returned triumphantly to the House in April 1938 to announce the end of the Economic War, the elimination of the special restrictions on Irish agricultural exports, the ending of annuity payments and the return of the ports, Dillon rejoiced in the result, though he was scathing about the damage it had inflicted upon the country: 'It was a return to economic and political sanity, but it has cost the country £50 million to educate Fianna Fáil.'[10] Nonetheless, the Economic War had resulted in a diplomatic victory for de Valera, and the return of the ports was soon to acquire enormous political and military significance.

The ending of the dispute disguised the fact that the government's self-sufficiency programme was not working. Through the Control of Manufactures Act 1932, Lemass had led and directed the campaign to create a self-sufficient industrial sector under native control, and brought great energy and determination to this task, encouraging the establishment of new industries through the use of tariffs, quotas and exclusive licences. Yet, though new firms were given monopoly status to guarantee their investments, the small home market, combined with shortages of capital, technology and expertise, restricted development from the start, while exports proved elusive, with often sub-standard products being produced for world markets which had themselves grown increasingly protectionist.

From his earliest days in politics Dillon had opposed these policies, at first because of their practical consequences, but by now on the basis of principle: 'No greater curse ever descended upon a nation than the loathsome delusion that national self-sufficiency was a desirable end ... It is absolutely impossible of realisation and every step you take involves your people in untold suffering and hastens the dissolution of all civil inter-relationships between states.'[11]

Nor was Dillon's scepticism lessened by his view of the way Lemass sought to implement the policy. He resented what he saw as Lemass's arbitrary and authoritarian methods, his bypassing of parliamentary scrutiny, his keeping the details of policy secret. Dillon reserved his strongest condemnation for the way import licences were awarded, apparently at the sole discretion of the minister and his departmental officials. Dillon charged that this led to croneyism and the creation of a new privileged class, and worked against the consumer by promoting a climate of quotas, market sharing and non-competition. He was particularly concerned with what he saw as 'cabals' in the flour milling and artificial manure industries, and critical too of the decision to concentrate all importing of cement in the hands of a new company, Cement Ltd. Dillon went so far as to suggest that if there must be monopolies then at least they should be in the hands of the state, 'so that the taxpayer will derive the benefits of any profits ... Bad as socialism is, it is better than a monopoly in the hands of private capitalists.'[12]

Dillon was frequently prepared to believe the worst where the granting of licences was concerned, and was not slow to allege favouritism. In reality, there was plenty. Lemass chose firms which he felt would best attain his economic objectives, but he deeply resented the claims by Dillon and others that he was motivated by party political considerations. Lemass did not help his own case by treating Dillon's interventions with hostility, suggesting that Dillon was ill-informed and too easily influenced by people who came to him with personal grievances.

In hindsight, Lemass invited much of the criticisms. His single-minded determination to make his Department of Industry and Commerce a power-house for change had the same effect on some of his colleagues – especially MacEntee, Aiken and Derrig – as it had on Dillon.[13] And unlike his policies in the 1960s, his strong-arm tactics in the '30s could not easily be excused on the grounds that they were crowned with obvious success. The reality was that development based largely on native industry was not a success. In spite of the official rhetoric favouring native firms, in 1938 'a majority of output and employment was probably derived from firms that were dependent on foreign expertise, capital and trademarks. Indeed the camouflaging of this problem postponed an awareness of the inherent drawbacks.'[14] In addition, the long-term efficiency of protected firms was further hindered by the lack of economic competitiveness.

Though it was not obvious at the time, the end of the Economic War marked the end of Fianna Fáil's economic radicalism, and the eroding of the ideological divisions between the two major parties on economic issues. But if that dispute was over, another, more ominous war was looming. The debate on the handing back of the Treaty ports in April 1938 gave Dillon his opportunity to raise in the Dáil the worsening international situation.

De Valera asserted, and with considerable justification, that the return of the ports, which had remained under British control in the Treaty settlement, now made it possible for Ireland to plan for its own defence, and that it would be for the Dáil to say in any given situation whether or not Ireland would remain neutral. There was as yet no certainty of a European war, nor any inevitability about the shape it would take, but governments everywhere were planning and putting contingencies in place. Dillon raised one such question, as to whether it would be possible to remain neutral and to continue to supply foodstuffs to Britain. De Valera replied that 'the truth is that in modern war there is not any neutrality'[15] – a proposition he was to juggle with successfully for the next six years. Dillon's focus, however, was the larger question of Ireland's future alignment. He, at least, had no doubts that hard choices would have to be made:

> We have to make up our minds whether sovereign independence and national unity can best be achieved in the Commonwealth of Nations or out of it. If we make up our minds that these things can best be achieved in the Commonwealth of Nations it is idle nonsense to pretend that we can be in the Commonwealth ... and stand indifferently by if that Commonwealth of Nations is attacked or jeopardised. We cannot. The Prime Minister knows that. The difference between him and me in that regard is that I tell the people perfectly plainly now that if the Commonwealth is attacked, we as part of it will defend it. It is perfectly true that if that Commonwealth went Nazi or ... Communist ... it might become our duty to secede from it.[16]

Dillon attacked de Valera's Northern Ireland policy, or absence of policy, in the same debate. He accused him of saying different things to different groups and in particular of exploiting the feelings of Northern nationalists by pretending that he alone could solve partition, when clearly he could not.[17] An outburst from Fianna Fáil TD Martin Corry two days later convinced Dillon of Fianna Fáil's lack of integrity on the Northern question. Corry, speaking in the Dáil, said that, while there might be wildly divergent views as to how unity would be achieved: 'I personally am in favour of storing up sufficient poison gas so that when you get the wind in the right direction you can stand at the border and let it travel and follow it ... One of the ways and means by which we can finish the job we set our hands to in 1916.'[18]

Corry was invariably intemperate in his speeches, but the fact that he was not reprimanded by his party leaders or forced to withdraw his remarks convinced Dillon that whilst some of the Fianna Fáil leaders might take the high road, the party was not going to leave the low road unoccupied either.

On 25 May 1938, the government was defeated by one vote in a Labour Private Member's motion on arbitration in the civil service. The defeat in itself was not particularly significant and de Valera could have continued as Taoiseach; however, the fact that only fifty-one of Fianna Fáil's sixty-nine TDs turned up for the vote would indicate that the government was looking for an excuse to go to the country for a fresh mandate. Its position had been considerably strengthened by the ending of the Economic War, the return of the ports, and the country's general unease in face of the worsening international situation. On 26 May de Valera dissolved the Dáil and called an election for June. The result vindicated his strategy: Fianna Fáil won seventy-seven seats, giving it a decisive victory and an overall majority. Fine Gael's vote dropped slightly, to thirty-three per cent, with a loss of three seats. Dillon was comfortably re-elected in Monaghan, but the only real consolation for Fine Gael was the return of Mulcahy, who had lost his seat a year earlier. There was no sign of new talent emerging, however.

Dillon was the only Fine Gael speaker on the election of the Taoiseach on 30 June, which de Valera won by seventy-five votes to forty-five with Labour abstaining – the final rift between them was not far off. Dillon's speech was low key, accepting the inevitability of de Valera's election. He stressed Fine Gael's duty to be vigorous in its opposition, but there was a sense of anti-climax in his tone. Fianna Fáil had fought and won the major battles, and in the process had made their own of the very institutions which both they and Dillon had so excoriated fifteen years earlier – a point not lost on Dillon when he paid tribute to 'this parliament, established by Mr. Griffith and Mr. Collins'.[19] Now however, with a secure majority, major policy lines established and ministers behaving more and more like permanent civil servants, secure in their tenure and fixed in their views, parliament's role was increasingly marginalised by government. The 1938 Dáil lasted its full five-year term, its life dominated by war and the maintenance of Ireland's policy of neutrality. Preoccupied with the war and afflicted with rapidly failing eyesight, de Valera paid less and less attention to a Dáil over which an air of torpor had descended.

Dillon had characterised the 1938 election campaign as the freest and most honest in the history of the state,[20] and as the new Dáil sat it turned its attention to redressing some of the burdens which had been placed on its members in previous years. The Ministers and Parliamentary Officers Bill of 1938 effectively brought ministerial salaries back to their 1932 level, provided pensions for former ministers for the first time, and paid an allowance to the main opposition parties, £800 to Fine Gael and £500 to Labour. Dillon supported the measure, but roundly attacked Fianna Fáil for reducing the salaries in the first place, and in particular for having campaigned in 1932 on the basis that 'Cumann na nGaedheal had robbed the country for ten years and had lived in luxury off the people.'

> These were the men who were held up to public ridicule by de Valera as having robbed the country and battened on the State. Now we were told he had made a mistake – just a little error of judgement ... But it was an error of judgement which blackened and slandered honest men.[21]

Dillon was adamant that politicians should be paid a proper allowance: 'If you allow the standard of ability and independence of the public man to fall as a result of financial exigencies, sooner or later you are going to be confronted with the horror of corruption in public life.'[22] He returned also to an earlier theme, the poverty of some of the remaining MPs of the Irish Party. He wanted some small state help for men 'who had done as much for the sovereignty and independence of this country as anybody else ... When Ireland had nothing they served her for nothing and never expected a reward.' Twenty-one former Irish Party MPs were still alive; most were over seventy-five years of age and of these five or six were destitute.

When Dillon had raised this issue in 1933 his was a lone voice, but now he had support from all sides.[23] His plea was enthusiastically backed by Labour's William Davin, and Sean MacEoin called upon 'the old Sinn Féin members of this House' to apologise to these men for all the things they said about them: 'We blackguarded them up and down the country because we were not aware of the facts.'[24] And the minister responsible, Sean MacEntee, admitted that there was indeed a case to be met, 'an historic obligation' to see that these men were not allowed to die in penury.[25]

Nothing in fact was done. Two years later Dillon drew attention to the death of Thomas Sexton, 'the silver tongued orator', who lived in a tenement room on the Vauxhall Bridge Rd and 'went home at night to poverty and sometimes hunger'. Dillon pleaded with the government 'to secure these men against destitution – as the son of one who was privileged at one time to lead them, I think it is my duty to do it.'[26] Dillon did help some men privately, keeping in touch with them and seeking to raise funds on their behalf, but more fundamentally he believed there was a debt owed by one generation of nationalist politicians to an older and now needy one. The debt, despite sympathetic noises, was never acknowledged.

Meanwhile, Dillon's fascination with de Valera's personality and political skills continued. He was to be a lifelong student of the subject, and was taken in particular by what he saw as de Valera's apparently bemused innocence and unworldliness, which Dillon said masked the sharpest and most calculating political brain of the century. He warmed to this theme in the External Affairs debate of 1939:

> I often pity him in this wicked world, so innocent a child, battling with the evil wiles of nasty detractors all around him, and I would remind him that our mutual friend and acquaintance Niccolo Machiavelli has advocated the assumption of that exterior in every crisis.[27]

A film, *The March of Time*, which claimed to be an objective look at modern Ireland, but which, according to Dillon, was little more than pro-de Valera propaganda, had recently been released. When Dillon raised the matter, de Valera professed to being barely aware of the film's existence. Dillon, an avid film-goer, filled de Valera in on the details:

> De Valera, sitting at the Cabinet table where he presented a very creditable appearance and made a very modest claim for fame. He then handed the running over to the commentator and there was a selection of pictures of Trinity College, Guinness Brewery, and the Shannon Electricity works, and we were led to believe, as we sat lost in admiration, that the modest gentleman who had introduced the proceedings from the head of the Cabinet table had just tossed these off as a few of his achievements during his term of office, and that they were only a promise of what was to come.[28]

He was also critical of attempts by de Valera, or some of his supporters, to represent him as a great mathematician. There is no doubt this image was cultivated, and Dillon turned to it during the debate on the establishment of the Dublin Institute of Advanced Studies. Dillon supported the Institute but was critical of the decision to include mathematical physics as part of its remit. This proposal, he said, was 'for one, and one only silly childish purpose, and that is to lend verisimilitude to the myth that the Taoiseach is a great mathematician, which he never was, and never will be. The myth has to be created... that we have a scholar prime minister ... It is all cod.'[29]

Northern Ireland continued to occupy his mind, but unlike most politicians of the time, Dillon did not see partition as the root of the problem; it was, rather, a symptom. In May 1939, he attacking yet another appeal to Britain to intervene in the North and thereby end partition:

> No intervention by Britain can satisfactorily terminate Partition unless Partition is terminated with the goodwill of the people of Northern Ireland. Rightly or wrongly our people in Northern Ireland – unhappily – look upon England as their protector. When I say 'our people' I mean our Orange and Protestant fellow countrymen who are our people, who are just as Irish as we are – every bit ... We have got to win, not only the barren acres of Ulster, but the hearts of the people who live in it ... Whether we like it or dislike it, the Craigavons, the Brookes and the other ministers of the Northern Government are as Irish as the de Valeras, the Lemasses, the Cosgraves, the Dillons – every bit. They were born in this country and they have spent their lives in it.[30]

A month later he returned to this subject:

> Ulster, with a resentful, bitter, disillusioned minority in it, would be far more a liability than an asset ... We have had one civil war in this country. God forbid that, by our ineptitude, we should precipitate another ... The only satisfactory basis upon which we can get rid of partition is to reach the masses of the people of Ulster, and create here in Eire such a state of affairs as will induce the plain, ordinary people of Ulster, to forbid Craigavon to keep them out of their native country any longer.[31]

In saying this, he had no illusions about the nature of the Northern regime:

> I do not deny that Sir Basil Brooke's language is outrageous. I do not deny that when a Northern Premier speaks of a Protestant Parliament for a Protestant people it is an outrage on our people, but there is no use in meeting that sort of language with the same sort of language ... that way we shall only deepen and intensify the bitterness that already exists.[32]

The approach of war, however, was dominating his concern. By mid-1938 the Hitler-Mussolini axis was in place, Austria had been absorbed into Hitler's Germany, Czechoslovakia was under imminent sentence of death, while all the time Germany built up its military might. The democracies dithered and wavered, though war, if not yet certain, was highly likely. In July 1938 the Dáil focused its mind on the possibility of an armed invasion of the country. As the Dáil debated the army vote, the general tone was gloomy, almost fatalistic. The reality was that the Irish state was without the wherewithal to defend itself. Its army was small and lacked equipment; it had no air force or navy worth talking about. To those who thought about it, Ireland might not want war or any part in it, but if the needs of others so dictated it was unlikely to have any real choice in the matter. John A. Costello reflected this sense of gloom and inevitability: he was not proposing a common defence policy with Britain, he said, but such might ultimately be in our best interest.[33] Aiken, however, bluntly dismissed any such possibility, certainly so long as partition remained.[34]

Dillon, who shared Costello's view about Ireland's inability to repel a powerful invader, nonetheless warned that any invasion force would meet with resistance, including 'the mobilisation of the Irish race worldwide'. He did not see Britain as a threat, but warned that she could not take Ireland for granted. 'We are not prepared to authorise you to come in and take over the defence of this country under any circumstances, any more than the French would permit you to come in and take over the defence of her country.'[35]

Dillon was neither a pacifist nor a fatalist as far as a possible invasion was concerned. He was a realist who saw that without a large, well-equipped army, we would merely be 'sending gallant men out to be butchered', and thought that resistance 'other than passive moral resistance' would be futile. That did not mean that every effort should not be made in the meantime to make the army as effective as possible, and in particular he urged the building up of an air force.

It was not until seven months later that the Dáil again had a major debate on the international situation. Neither Dáil debates nor newspaper reports suggested any great sense of public concern or official urgency. It may well be that, since Ireland had no capacity to shape events, most people felt there was little that could be done. Dillon, however, was having none of this and tried to inject a note of realism into the mood of complacency which prevailed. He ridiculed the idea that, if the League of Nations disapproved, then the major European powers would not invade Ireland if it suited them:

> We are in the astonishing position of a very poor, very small and very sparsely populated country which enjoys its sovereignty and its independence against all comers at the present time. Is there any other nation in the world, not to mind Europe, which can say so much? Austria, an independent State, disappears overnight. Czechoslovakia, a powerful independent State, with great defences, a great army, great equipment and a corresponding low

standard of living in order to build up its military strength, disappeared overnight, and all that defence money was wasted. Ireland, with no defences, no money and practically no population, is issuing ultimatums from Leinster House to all and sundry that she will not touch anybody with a forty foot pole and that she is prepared for all comers. To what is this due? Is it not due to the certainty of any political antagonist that an attack upon us would be an attack upon the entire Commonwealth of Nations.[36]

At this stage Dillon was interrupted by Norton, who asserted that the only danger of invasion came from Britain, a view widely held at the time. Dillon, however, had no intention of subscribing to the conventional wisdom:

I want to say quite deliberately and speaking personally ... something which may shock some of my friends about me. I believe the vital interest of every member of the Cabinet at the present time is to keep Britain a great power. Britain, at one time one of the most bloody and predatory of nations ... a poisonous scourge in the world —

He was interrupted by a Labour TD, Jeremiah Hurley: 'She has changed now? Has she?'
Dillon answered:

Look at the world today. Judge it by every standard ... The Commonwealth of Nations, now a group of great, sovereign independent States, living their own lives, running their own countries and absolutely independent of Britain ... The Empire, a bloody beastly institution, is gone. The Commonwealth of Nations is here. We had a part in creating it.

He followed with a passionate, eloquent speech on the loss of liberty in European countries, and concluded:

Our vital interest is to keep England great so long as England behaves herself ... if she embarks on a foreign policy that is antipathetic to our conception of national probity, what we can do, we will do to upset her.[37]

Dillon's view that the nature of the conflict ahead, especially should it be between the democracies and the dictatorships, would make it difficult for Ireland to remain neutral, was uniquely his own. Fine Gael showed little enthusiasm even to debate the issue, and the party's official policy was non-interventionist and neutral. As far as all Irish parties were concerned, events in far-off countries were best left to others to sort out, and there was little welcome for anyone who said otherwise. Dillon was an exception. He neither modified or toned down his arguments, nor altered his conviction that a neutral stance was simply not possible.

There could be no neutrality because of the issues involved. It was a question of 'decency, tolerance and freedom' against 'the medieval barbarism of the dictators. I want Ireland to declare, in no uncertain way, on the side of liberty, decency and freedom.' Thus he urged that in the event of war 'we should give to the US and Britain any facilities they wanted'. He even wondered aloud, if a situation arose where 'great fundamental values, which mean everything to us' were at stake, whether we should think of sending an expeditionary force abroad, though he concluded that Ireland did not have the resources.[38]

Following its own maxim that England's difficulty was Ireland's opportunity, in January 1939 the IRA began a bombing campaign in Britain which was to claim at least seven lives and leave 200 wounded during the course of the year. De Valera now had to face the prospect of the IRA, not just thwarting his authority at home, but threatening his recently established relationship with Britain, where anti-Irish feeling was intense. He responded with the Offences Against the State Bill 1939, in essence the revival of much of the Cosgrave anti-IRA legislation of the 1920s, which de Valera described at the time as the most rigorous public safety statute which Ireland had known in a long history of coercion. He ensured that the phraseology of the 1939 Bill was different, but the end result was to confer on the police wide powers of arrest and detention and to set up special courts. De Valera's embarrassment at having to revert to the very measures he had castigated a decade earlier was underlined by Norton, who told him 'the chickens have now come home to roost'.[39] Cosgrave supported the Bill, but Dillon brought the issue a little further:

> I was brought up in the school of 19th century liberalism, and I am a radical liberal today. But I do not close my eyes to the fact that we are not living in the Victorian age and that the type of dangers that democracy has to face today are quite different from the types it had to face in the 19th century.[40]

Particularly conscious of the failure of democratic institutions to defend themselves against Hitler in the Weimar Republic, he balanced the encroachments which the Bill made on individual liberties with the reality that democracy must be capable of defending itself against its enemies:

> The powers in this Bill can be abused and we are in this dilemma that we have either got to surrender to the forces of the left or the right for destruction, or we have got to put in the hands of the Government powers capable of abuse, which we can only pray to God that the elected Government of the Irish people will not, in fact, abuse.[41]

He was unhappy: 'My instinctive sympathies are with those who are against this Bill, but you cannot govern a country by instinct.'[42]

He was influenced in coming to his decision by information made public by the Minister for Justice about the nature of the conspiracy against the state. Despite this real threat, he felt it had to be balanced against the danger that the powers now being written into law would grow insidiously. He sounded the 'radical liberal's' warning against any threat to freedom of speech:

> The more profoundly we differ from a man, the more scrupulous we must be to see that man is given the fullest liberty to speak his mind, lest our own prejudices should sway us to take away any iota of a right to preach a policy which, we say, he should not use physical force to advocate.[43]

With these reservations he supported the Bill, as did Fine Gael, though Sean MacEoin abstained. Fine Gael support, however, masked a deep difference of opinion in the party. At the parliamentary party meeting on 1 March, Belton – once more back in Fine Gael – moved that support of the Bill be rescinded and that Fine Gael oppose it. He lost, but only by two votes, a clear indication of the widespread unease within the party.[44]

In the event, the only opposition to the Bill came from the Labour Party, and the nastiness of the exchanges, especially Aiken's heavy-handed charge that some Labour statements were 'calculated to incite people to take up arms against the State', ensured the final breach in the once friendly relations between Labour and Fianna Fáil.[45]

As the situation in Europe grew grim, in early May the Dáil had what proved to be its last debate on the worsening situation before the outbreak of the war. It was a strange debate, with little sense of the enormity of the difficulties soon to be faced. The fact that Ireland's policy of neutrality was ultimately successful has, not surprisingly, influenced the subsequent writing of this period, but in 1939 there could be no guarantee whatsoever that the policy would succeed or that Ireland would be left with its sovereignty unimpeded in the event of an Axis victory. Dillon was alone in raising these questions and in imagining the unimaginable:

> God forbid we would ever get the dark awakening of the experience. What would happen to a small nation like Ireland, if the particular methods of diplomacy employed by the German Reich were the order of the day here? What would happen if, when a small nation such as we are, made its protest, or made representations that its interests were being interfered with, the reply was given that it was very lucky to escape incorporation in the Reich, and if the condition of a continued independent existence was that all our legislation and that all our future international relations should be submitted to Berlin

before being acted upon? What would we feel like if a trade delegation came to negotiate with us and informed us that the alternative to concluding our agreement was to be incorporated in the economic system of the other party to the proposed agreement and that we could sign on the dotted line or take the consequences?[46]

He argued that, if it were not for the US, UK and French navies, there would be no freedom of the seas at this time. Could we imagine what would happen to our liberties if the world were controlled by 'the Nazi swastika and the Japanese sun'? The country, 'thinking of nothing but Ireland', had to make the biggest choice in its history: 'Having got Britain out of the country, we now stand alone in a storm-swept world. When we are taking counsel as to how Ireland's interest might best be served ... it is vital to Ireland that one side should win.' Otherwise, he said, incalculable damage could be inflicted on 'the long life that lies before the Irish Nation'.[47]

He raised the still distant possibility of the US entering the war and how Ireland would react should this happen, particularly if she were asked for port facilities. In line with contemporary military thinking, Dillon believed that the safe conduct of food, troops and supplies from the US to Europe would depend on the use of Irish ports:

Would our attitude to the United States of America, smashed by the Nazi-Japanese combine, and menaced as she may be, that we do not give a hoot, we were neutral, would take no sides, give her no accommodation, and if her ships sank, would allow just so many of her crew on our shores as could swim ashore, and then intern them here? Or would we say to her: 'You are welcome to all the hospitality of every kind that we can offer, and anybody who does not like that, anybody who has any complaint about our bidding your men welcome and giving you all the comfort and help that we can, can lump it?' Has the Government considered that?[48]

As always, he returned to the main theme, the fundamental issue:

God forbid that at this really great crisis of our independence, the first time that we faced the world in turmoil as an independent nation, any past history, any reluctance to face facts, any poverty of moral courage, should paralyse our efforts, should prevent us from doing the things we ought to do if we are to play our part in preserving, not only for ourselves, but for the whole world, liberty, decency, democracy and, above all, the right to render unto Caesar the things that are Caesar's, and to God the things that are God's.[49]

They were brave words, and unpopular. Dillon had adopted a singular stance, and the pace of events would soon require that his words be matched by deeds.

CHAPTER TEN

A SINGULAR STANCE

'We are standing out on our own in a storm-swept world, and we have
to ask ourselves, if the wind changes direction, how will we fare?'
Dillon, Dáil Debates, 2 May 1939

DILLON WAS NOT yet thirty-seven in the summer of 1939, but he was already an established and distinctive national figure. He continued to live between the family homes in North Great George's St and Ballaghaderreen. The family had by now all departed. Brian and Shawn were priests, Nano was married and living in Fitzwilliam Square with her husband PJ Smyth, a consultant at the Mater Hospital, while Myles was Professor of Celtic Studies at the University of Madison in Wisconsin. Theo had become a professor of medicine at University College, Dublin, and was living in Killiney.

North Great George's St, never a particularly cheerful house, was now something of a mausoleum, while Ballaghaderreen was not much warmer. Dillon's lifestyle had settled into a pattern, and even though politics and business dominated it, he had many other interests. Monica Duff's was now a thriving country business, well managed if somewhat old-fashioned. James still made a point of serving in the shop's various departments when he was in Ballaghaderreen – though never in the bar, of which he disapproved, and which he eventually closed largely because, he said, he hated to see farmers waste their much-needed money on market days.[1]

The Dublin of the 1940s was in social terms a small town. Apart from Horse Show week, there was no social calendar as such. The 'ascendancy', now in terminal decline, still clung to the rituals of old, its comings and goings dutifully noted in the social and personal columns of *The Irish Times*, still very much the house journal of the old order. Few Catholics had as yet made it into this stratum of society and social mixing across the religious divide was rare. Protestants stood aloof from the nationalist and Catholic mainstream, with their own university, their own schools and clubs, patronising their own shops, predominant in the worlds of banking and insurance, with Guinness all but closed to Catholics and the Masonic Order still seen as a powerful force. In politics it was generally accepted that the Protestant TDs were elected largely on the Protestant vote.

The new native rulers showed little inclination to fill the social gap left by the declining ascendancy. A professional class had emerged, and was soon to be joined by a new industrial class, but the social pretensions of both were modest. 'Losing the run of yourself' was still a particularly Irish hazard in a country which too often resented success. To a man, the new politicians were modestly middle-class in their lifestyle and aspirations. Few belonged to the old gentlemen's clubs such as the Kildare St, the University, Stephen's Green or United Services; many still went home daily for their dinner, which was always in the middle of the day. Their children went to solid Catholic schools and were rarely sent abroad. This point was well made by the Canadian High Commissioner, who prepared a series of pen-pictures of the Irish governments of the 1940s for his department in Ottawa. 'Mr and Mrs de Valera do not accept invitations nor entertain,' he wrote. Mr and Mrs Derrig 'live very quietly and do not entertain very much'. Mr and Mrs Boland 'do not entertain, nor are they much in evidence at social gatherings'. Of the government, only MacEntee and Aiken were described as 'socially active'. There is no reason to believe the pattern was very much different among their opposition counterparts.[2]

Dillon despised the pretensions of 'county' society and made no attempt to be part of it, but nor was he typical of the new political middle class.[3] He had joined the Stephen's Green Club in the early 1930s and remained a lifelong member. He was the only senior politician then or for many years to come to be an active 'clubman', even if his was the only Catholic and nationalist club of its time.[4] He also enjoyed the small embassy circuit – there were just ten embassies in all – and was a welcome guest at both the US and UK legations; he avoided, and was not invited to, the Axis ones.

Most of his social life was centred in Dublin. Dillon was unmarried and had no apparent girlfriend. A keen theatre-goer and a particular devotee of Marshall Hall, he continued to involve himself in amateur theatricals and no doubt some of what he picked up on the boards rubbed off on his parliamentary performances. He was an enthusiastic cinema-goer and went to three or four films a week, often slipping out of the Dáil for the early showings, a habit which stayed with him through most of his parliamentary career. He read voraciously: fiction, theology, history, biography, military strategy, economics, and occasionally medical textbooks.

It says much for the leisurely pace of parliamentary life that he was inveterately a late riser, though equally was rarely early to bed. His close friends included Hector Legge, then, and long after, editor of the *Sunday Independent*, and the writers Sean O'Faoláin and Frank O'Connor, the two best known and most controversial literary men of the day. They met regularly at Hector Legge's house in Ranelagh, which was frequently the scene of vigorous and heated arguments. They could agree on many things but rarely on religion, where, in the words of one mutual friend, James would 'move not an inch from the Roman collar'. Their discussions usually lasted late into the night, when James, a bad and nervous driver, would leave O'Connor home to his Sandymount house.

He was a generous and charming host. His own intake of alcohol was abstemious, generally confining himself to a sherry or a glass of wine. He liked simple food – beef, saddle of lamb and milk pudding were among his favourites. He occasionally confided to the Dáil his culinary likes and dislikes, including his total disdain for all fish, or a delight he shared with his good friend, the singer John McCormack: 'If you ask me what part of a pig is tastiest and best I would say a pig's cheek, but we have all got so grand and aristocratic that nobody would now eat a pig's cheek.'5

He was an avid radio listener and an invariable contributor to Dáil debates on the service. He was keen to see radio being used to broadcast Irish traditional music, and constantly railed against the then-current debasing of traditional music and the prominence given to what were known as 'come-all-ye's'. He wrote to his brother Myles: 'Did you ever hear of a man called Francis O'Neill of Chicago, a police captain who collected Irish music from emigrants in America? There was a programme of music from his collection on Radio Éireann last night and it was the best Irish music I have heard since Maureen Hurley sang in Ballingeary.'6

He returned to this theme in a Dáil debate in 1940 when he spoke of the 'immense mass of native music which is practically unknown. To the vast majority of people, Irish music means the intolerable tedium of the slip jig, the four-hand reel and the squealing fiddle which harass the ear.' He worried that traditional music was in danger of being lost, and urged a genuinely scholarly approach to its preservation.7

Dillon's interest in religion ran deep and he loved nothing more than long discussions on issues in philosophy, theology and morality. In Ballaghaderreen the missioners would usually stay with the Dillons, something which gave James an opportunity for late-night discussions on all matters religious, though whether the good missioners might have preferred more profane topics we do not know. His religious beliefs were orthodox, sometimes to the point of rigidity, but on some issues he could be deeply sceptical. He had little time, for example, for the phenomenon of Lourdes, but that was an exception for on almost everything else he accepted unquestioningly the official line. The idea of disobeying the laws of the Church was anathema to him, even on such matters as breaking the Church ban on attending Protestant funerals. Disobeying the Church was the vanity of vanities, the ultimate sin of intellectual pride – 'by that sin fell the angels,' he would declaim. He could be judgemental in moral terms, thinking sins against truth and charity to be the very worst of all, and he held strong views against divorce. Yet side by side with his conservative 1940s Catholicism went a deep suspicion of clerical or episcopal power when it was wielded in political matters, something he had inherited from his father and grandfather, and which sat somewhat incongruously beside his generally pious orthodoxy.

He could be gloomy and introspective – it was not unusual for him to become detached from the company he was in, lost in his own thoughts. He was a believer in original sin and inherited his father's view of the flawed nature of mankind. But he also had a strong belief in the Redemption – his favourite prayer was 'My Redeemer Liveth' – and he would frequently and approvingly quote Pastor Niemholler's observation that man cannot know the full meaning of redemption unless he knows the depths to which he can descend. With younger people, though, he had a great sense of humour, allied to a lively imagination. Absurdity greatly amused him. To many who knew him he conveyed the impression of having been born old. 'Edwardian' or 'Victorian' were words sometimes used to describe the impression he created, and indeed there was much about him of the late Victorian in his high-mindedness, his detestation of crudeness and blue stories, his sense of *noblesse oblige*, his formal and impeccable manners and his courtly treatment of women, and in his prudish views on all matters sexual. In most of these matters he was a man of his age, but as with Dillon in most things, exaggeratedly so.

It was not, however, a facade or an affectation. He had an unshakable core of fixed principle and belief. He was certain about what he believed and fearless in expressing and defending his views. As he was to show in the years ahead, he could be impervious to public opinion and accepted the consequences of unpopularity and isolation. This aspect of his character struck the journalist Robert Fisk when he interviewed him in 1979: 'a proud incorruptible man with a theological intensity that amounted at times to a form of intimidation. Dillon's monastic personality was just as dominating as de Valera's, if not more so.' Fisk commented on a certain fanaticism, 'of being governed in his behaviour by an unbending religious conviction that stayed with him all his life'.[8]

A contemporary observer, the writer Elizabeth Bowen, described Dillon in the early 1940s. Bowen, who reported to the Foreign and Commonwealth Office without the knowledge of those she interviewed, gave this picture of him in one of her reports:

> in talk he is equable and rational and shows the kind of intellect that can make the fullest use of any experience. He is less parochial in outlook than most Irishmen; in fact not parochial at all. His personality is at once monkish and

worldly. Superficially Mr. Dillon would be (from an English point of view) a very much easier man to deal with than Mr. de Valera. I say superficially ... while Mr. de Valera's fanaticism is on the surface, Mr. Dillon's, which exists quite as strongly, is deep down: it exploded once or twice towards the end of our talk – religious fanaticism of the purest kind I have met.

Later in her report Bowen commented on Dillon's ability to make enemies through his outspokenness. She described him as 'materially well off but with a contempt for "society",' and remarked that 'his nature seemed to be concentrated and his intellect powerful and precise'.[9]

But there was a lighter side, as an extract from a diary which Dillon kept while on holiday in Carna in 1941 reveals. Carna was a favourite holiday spot, and he was staying at Josie Mongan's hotel, where a year later he was to meet his wife:

August 22, 1941.
Left Westland Row on 8.00 a.m. train ... long stop at Mullingar ... going citywards was a long train with turf ... turf very precious now ... lunchtime at Lydons Cafe ... arrived Carna – Mongan's Hotel 7.30 p.m. Racing along rear beach with young Peter Legge ... bathing was delightful, water warm and with beautiful shades of green colours. Sailing and rowing boats out among the islands. Who wouldn't love Carna for holidays?

A boating party to Mweenish Island. Ran a race against a local boy. Noting how a prominent Fianna Fáil supporter from Dublin staying in the hotel had no trouble getting petrol in spite of the rationing ... heard one of the northern fishermen telling very interesting stories about birds, so interesting that I hope to get him to write some of them for publication ... played golf badly ... had a great cycle race home – two and a half miles ... won. But oh my legs!

Before going golfing spent two hours reading in the sunshine ... have finished *Wessex Wars* by A. G. Street and *Twenty Years a-Growing* by Maurice O' Sullivan ... picked buckets of apples blown down in the storm.

A wild windy and wet day for the Connemara pony show ... seeing the show for the first time I felt it could be developed into the equivalent of an RDS show of Connemara ... could become a national attraction ... went to the Ceilidhe ... no room to dance properly![10]

Foreign travel, which Dillon so much enjoyed – he had been to most European countries and had visited Australia in 1936 – was now impossible. He kept in touch with international developments, in part at least through correspondence, and especially with Myles, now in the University of Wisconsin. Writing to Myles on 15 September 1938 he had no doubt that Europe was on the verge of war, but was happy that Britain would be more than a match for the Axis: he recounted a meeting he had attended in London in mid-July where he heard impressive accounts of the level of rearmament being undertaken in Great Britain.[11]

Writing at about the same time, Myles felt that 'Hitler must be destroyed if we are to survive with any sort of dignity and freedom and it seems to be a crusade in which everyone should take part who can.'[12] Myles contemplated joining the US forces if America became involved, and on 4 September 1939, shortly after the outbreak of war, he was convinced that 'the logic of my position seems to involve my offering to serve in some capacity'. If the US stayed out of the war and Ireland remained neutral, Myles's inclination was to join the British Army in some specialist role.[13]

Writing to his brother on 16 August 1939, Dillon concluded that 'domestic politics are completely overshadowed by international affairs'. In truth, it is difficult to draw that conclusion from a study of newspapers, political speeches or parliamentary debates of the pre-war period. One of the surprising aspects of the period leading up to the outbreak of war was the almost total absence of public discussion on the issues involved and on the options open to Ireland. When the last Dáil debate on international affairs had been held in June 1939, the mood had been largely fatalistic, and Ireland's neutral position had been overwhelmingly accepted. In August, as newspapers recorded on a daily basis the worsening international situation, there was no accompanying examination of the impact these developments would have as far as Ireland was concerned, nor any attempt by politicians to prepare the public for what lay ahead. Dillon was one of the very few who sought to do so.

Speaking at an AOH rally in Killybegs, Co. Donegal, on 15 August, he said Ireland could never be a great military power 'and she does not want to be so'. He attacked 'the evils of Nazism' and told his listeners that Ireland's place 'is in the ranks of the enemies of Nazism. Ireland can never be expected to send soldiers abroad ... but our moral influence is great,' and he made it clear that Ireland should use this influence to the full against Hitler.[14] But Dillon was the only politician carrying this discussion to the public. It was as if a consensus had already been arrived at that Ireland's only hope of survival lay in non-involvement, and that talking would only cause problems.

It was in this mood that the Dáil and Seanad were recalled in emergency session on Saturday and Sunday, the 2 and 3 September 1939, just as Britain and France were declaring war on Germany. Despite a lengthy debate there was little difference of opinion among members of either House as de Valera outlined the elements of Irish neutrality. Dillon did not at this stage question the policy of neutrality. He was at pains, however, to emphasise that this did not imply any indifference on his part about the ultimate outcome of the war, and he had no doubt that 'the vast majority of Irish people placed their sympathy on the side of Poland, France and

Britain against Berlin and Moscow'.[15] Even this mild expression placed Dillon outside the mainstream. The only person to take a stronger line was Frank MacDermot – now in the Senate, having been nominated by de Valera – who wished that Ireland could openly declare itself on the side of the Allies.[16]

As yet there was no question of dissent or disagreement as the country squared up to an uncertain world for which nothing in its previous experience had prepared it. The main concern was survival, and the Dáil adjourned with the full paraphernalia of emergency legislation in place, including what was to become a draconian form of censorship. Dillon relayed his views on the unfolding situation to Myles on 9 September. After looking at global developments he referred to his own desire to help, though without specifying how. There was, he said, 'nothing very obvious to do and reasons of prudence demand that we [Ireland] should allow the first psychological shock of war to pass before entering into any commitments: it is too early yet to get the situation into perspective.' Then he turned to the domestic situation:

> Our government is finding the burdens of independence somewhat of a trial. Whereas the British government was responsible in the last war for getting supplies for this part of the then United Kingdom they have no such responsibility now and we are in the invidious position of proclaiming neutrality, but having no ships to carry or protect our supplies, so we are dependent on Great Britain for coal, petrol and all the raw materials of such industries as we have. The result is acute shortages of everything except food. The public have not felt this yet, but every manufacturer has already notified us that supplies are suspended and that they can give no date for further supplies.

Looking at the role of the IRA and the role of the Catholic Church, he thought 'Hitler's pact with Russia was a great blessing. But for it the Church was quite capable of going all wrong. They are quite all right now.' He reported to Myles his belief that 'our neutrality is a disastrous mistake.' But 'in fairness, however, I should add that had de Valera done otherwise the innate cowardice of many of our people would have reacted to war much as it did to the threat of conscription in 1918, a large number would have joined the IRA to avoid the danger of being called up and this would almost certainly have precipitated civil commotion in the state. That this is so is largely de Valera's own fault, for he tolerated the IRA, but the facts as they are must be faced ...'[17]

A false sense of calm settled on the country through the early 'phony war', and nothing had happened to change public opinion by the time the Dáil next met four weeks later. The House turned its attention to survival. Lemass, who had been made Minister of Supplies, outlined a policy which still relied a great deal on improvisation. Dillon, at this stage all pre-war skirmishing forgotten, led for Fine Gael, and relying on his business expertise showed a good grasp of the type of supply problems the country was likely to face.

The outbreak of war had prompted calls for some form of national government, but with his majority secure de Valera had no intention, then or ever, of sharing power with people such as Cosgrave or Mulcahy. What de Valera did want was strong backing and a show of national solidarity behind his government. Dillon was not among those who favoured a national government, but assured the House that Fine Gael would support the government so long as they were prepared to listen to the opposition.

The absence of any great enthusiasm for the idea within the Dáil did not lessen the insistence of *The Irish Times* that a national government was in the best interests of the country. The newspaper's campaign greatly annoyed Dillon, who felt *The Irish Times* generally sneered at the Oireachtas. Dillon had reserved his media hostility almost exclusively for the *Irish Press*, but now he let *The Irish Times* have both barrels. He accused it, 'contemptible as is the circulation of that organ', of belittling the parliamentary institutions of the country and rejected 'the claptrap about national government, that men who are honestly at variance with one another should jettison their convictions and for the purpose of pleasing the decrepit *Irish Times*, combining a futile and confused bedlam behind closed doors.'[18]

Dillon conveyed his real thoughts on the situation facing the country to his brother Myles in a letter on 3 December 1939. His early optimism about the strength and capacity of the Allies had by now dissipated: 'Europe continues to go up in flames,' he wrote. 'The invasion of Finland is a ghastly business.' He expected 'another epidemic of sinkings' of Allied shipping. He felt morale in Britain was good, with no thought of defeat, and that Germany would ultimately be defeated through internal collapse. He referred also to the new censorship which precluded any real discussion in his letter of domestic politics, though that did not inhibit him from saying that 'the Government have made every idiotic blunder they could make,' and he gave Myles news of mutual friends who had volunteered for the British forces, among them Gerard Sweetman, soon to become a Fine Gael Senator.

He also felt that the Economic War had ensured that, unlike the experience of 1914-18, Ireland would derive little benefit from this war, because 'seven years of Fianna Fáil rule have denuded the country of livestock, England is rationing her people to four ounces of bacon per week and we have practically no pigs to export! We have little or no eggs or butter either, so except for cattle and sheep we have little to offer.' Another 'remarkable achievement of the Ministry of Supply', he reported, 'was to leave us with no stores at all of India meal or other concentrated feeding stuffs and virtually no artificial manures, so we are struggling hard to get supplies, but can't get much more than half of what we require!'[19]

The false calm and the illusion of security was shattered suddenly and dramatically by the 'enemy within' when the IRA raided the Magazine Fort in the Phoenix Park on 23 December 1939 and made off with over one million rounds of ammunition. Though most of the ammunition was recovered, the incident was a major embarrassment for the government and a warning of the IRA's potential to disrupt the smooth running of the country. This setback followed a major reverse in the High Court which decided that the government did not have power to intern Irish citizens without trial under the Offences Against the State Act 1939. As a result, the government was forced to release fifty-three suspected members of the IRA who had been interned.

The upshot of this was the recall of the Dáil on 3 January 1940, when the government introduced a new Emergency Powers Bill to allow internment of Irish citizens as well as aliens. Dillon's reaction to the legislation was ambivalent. As a staunch advocate of civil liberties he warned the government not to rush to extremes to preserve stability. The day vital rights were jettisoned, he warned, 'the attackers have scored their first and most important victory against democratic institutions'. But Dillon had long argued that any democratic system worth its salt should have the wherewithal to defend itself, and on this question he had no doubts about the IRA. Their methods 'were the methods of gangsterism; they are the denial of liberty; they are the claims of a minority, not only to rule, but to tyrannise over the majority of the people'. He also feared the IRA campaign would escalate, leading eventually to political assassination.[20]

There was more to it than that. He was sceptical of de Valera's sincerity in dealing with them. Not alone was he still 'a captive to his own past', but his party was deeply ambiguous. He excluded from this charge two of de Valera's senior ministers, MacEntee and Boland, and praising their moral courage in the face of the IRA, he regretting that de Valera could not find it in his heart to use words as frank and effective as they had.[21]

Dillon's offensive on the IRA led to one of the most savage personal attacks he had yet endured. It came from Norton and reflected, in part at least, Labour's ambiguity towards the IRA, which was in some ways as deep as that of Fianna Fáil. According to Norton, Dillon's speech had been 'reeking of vengeance and malice ... and not against the people who had caused our only political problem in this country, but malice against fellow Irishmen'. Dillon, he said, could not see that 'there is no end and can be no end to our problems *vis-à-vis* Great Britain until Britain abandons her attempt to install permanently here her armed might as a challenge to the indivisibility of the Irish Nation.' As far as Norton was concerned, the IRA's main fault was that 'they have believed longer than their teachers some of the things their teachers taught them'.[22]

The operation of wartime censorship was in the hands of Frank Aiken, who decided that its rigid application was central to the survival of Ireland's neutrality. Dillon regarded Aiken as utterly unsuitable to the role of censor. He thought he had pro-Nazi sympathies and was narrow and authoritarian. In the event, he himself became an early victim of the regime and waged a wartime battle against its excesses.

This view of Aiken was not confined to Dillon and Fine Gael.[23] Mulcahy recorded a conversation with a senior Fianna Fáil figure – 'R' – a cabinet minister, and probably Ryan (to whom he was related by marriage) or Ruttledge. According to 'R', Aiken 'was removed from the Ministry of Defence because he was obstinate and ignorant and they thought the sooner they had him out of it the better, that he was a man of very little intelligence, that coming as he did of North of Ireland stock he was necessarily a bigot. Did any of them ever know a North of Ireland man who was not a bigot? Or any of them that improved in any way except MacEntee? Look at Connolly. Aiken was intolerant and dictatorial.'[24]

Not even censorship could muffle the shock caused by the lightning invasions of Norway and Denmark in early April 1940. Dillon was now more certain than ever that Irish neutrality would not be respected by the Nazis any more than they had respected the neutrality of other countries. He told the Dáil on 18 April that Nazism was 'the devil himself, with 20th century efficiency'.[25]

Matters moved from bad to worse with the invasion of Holland and Belgium, and then the invasion of France at the end of May 1940. Dillon was speaking on an Agriculture Estimate when he got word of the invasion of France and was clearly deeply moved by what was happening. He was convinced that the country was in imminent danger. He called for real national unity: 'I believe that in this hour of supreme crisis for this country one middling captain on the bridge is better than three good captains with divided counsel.' And he told the House that any criticism he was going to make would be made behind closed doors. 'We ought to show the example of refusing controversy at this present time, until the threat has passed.'[26] A week later he repeated his message that any invasion must be resisted, rather than go the 'ignoble' way of Denmark, and he urged people to enrol in one of the three branches of the defence forces.[27] Dillon himself had volunteered for the Local Defence Force on the outbreak of war but had been turned down because the government refused to allow members of the Oireachtas to join.

Dillon's speeches earned him praise from an unlikely quarter. He had never been an admirer of *The Irish Times*, and had criticised the paper trenchantly not long before, but what he had to say at this time struck a responsive chord in Westmoreland St. Editor RM Smyllie, who was weaning the paper away from its anachronistic unionism, wrote to Dillon: 'You have been rude to me, more than once; and I regret to say I have retaliated in kind; but, somehow, I never have had much stomach for our quarrels ... I have been much impressed by your attitude since the beginning of the war; and your statement yesterday that nothing matters now but the integrity of our common country expresses precisely what I feel myself. If and when the Germans come to Ireland, you and I shall be joint candidates for hanging at the first available lamp-post; so may I say now that I am sorry that we ever should have crossed swords ...[28] It was a letter Dillon much appreciated, even if it did little to change his attitude to the paper.

Dillon's emotional promise to avoid controversy, and to refrain from public criticism of the government, was soon broken. He could not hide his pro-Allied feelings, and would not refrain from criticism of day-to-day aspects of supply, rationing and the like. Elizabeth Bowen noticed that 'in Dáil debates his colleagues are at some pains to disassociate themselves from his more positive and dynamic remarks ... he is seen to err in a too extreme disregard for that general mass of opinion that, in most cases, inhibits Irishmen.'[29]

Reports of some of his speeches outside the Dáil were either censored or banned from publication in newspapers. Dillon was furious and responded by having some of them published in pamphlet form. The authorities seized the offending pamphlets, Dillon thus becoming one of the first victims of the new censorship. De Valera quickly intervened, either because he felt the censors were over-zealous or because he did not want to make a martyr of the Fine Gael TD. However, since the whole incident was itself censored, no real controversy ensued.

When the government set up the Defence Conference in May 1940, Fine Gael nominated him along with Mulcahy and O'Higgins. Fianna Fáil had Aiken, Boland and Oscar Traynor as its members, while Labour had Norton and William Davin. The Defence Conference was never a particularly happy body. De Valera had no intention of giving more power than was necessary to maintain the facade of unity, while Aiken, who was Fianna Fáil's strongman on the conference, was distrustful and graceless. Before very long the Fine Gael members, as Mulcahy put it, felt that the opposition was being 'used and smothered' and in this he took a harder line initially than Dillon, who was more prepared to take de Valera at face value.[30] Dillon soon came to share Mulcahy's mistrust. Any public complaint along these lines, however, could easily be represented by de Valera as

stabbing the government in the back and allow him dissolve the conference, and it did continue in existence until the end of the war.

In spite of Irish neutrality, the main diplomatic outposts in Dublin took
a keen and detailed interest in the ongoing political debate. Not surprisingly, Dillon's views in particular attracted the attention of the rival
legations. In early 1940 the reports of the German Minister, Dr Hempel,
referred to Dillon as a Germanophobe and noted his coolness to de Valera's
policy of neutrality. According to Hempel, nobody took Dillon seriously,
though this did not prevent Hempel himself from making formal complaints to de Valera about Dillon's statements or calling him at various
times a 'German hater', a 'Jew' and 'a bitter enemy of de Valera'.[31]

On the other hand, the British and US ministers felt they had a friend in
Dillon and developed frequent contact with him. He became personally
friendly with their respective representatives, Sir John Maffey and David
Gray. Dillon had long been regarded by many in Fianna Fáil as instinctively unsound, if not hostile to nationalism. His earlier remarks on the flag
and the anthem, his championing of the Commonwealth, his antipathy to
the IRA and his mocking of Fianna Fáil's playing of the 'green card' had
made it easy for many to dismiss him as some sort of reactionary West
Briton, and much of the criticism began and ended with that taunt. The
criticism was as unjust as it was difficult to shake off. Dillon's attitude to
Britain had been outlined in the Dáil on 14 June 1939, when he said 'there
can be in our generation no attachment to Great Britain founded on
sentiment or affection. There ought to be a relationship founded on
mutual respect and recognition by each party of the other's virtues and
qualities.'[32] Elizabeth Bowen described Dillon's attitude to England as
'guarded, calculating, satirical respectful, not hostile in even the oblique
sense'.[33]

The war came closer to Ireland in early January 1941 when German
bombs were dropped on Drogheda, Wicklow, Kildare, the Carlow–
Wexford border (where three people died) and the capital, Dublin, where
24 people were injured. When the Defence Conference met on 3 January,
Aiken wanted to say that the bombs were German but were probably
dropped accidentally. This was not acceptable to Fine Gael, and when the
German embassy had still not offered an explanation of the bombing by
the next Defence Committee meeting on 29 January, Dillon felt that the
government should make it clear to the public that the bombs had been
German, 'in order to combat propaganda that they were British, being circulated by Petersen (the German attaché) and his connections'. He claimed
that 'an official of the American embassy going through the South Circular
Road found seven out of ten people said they were British'.[34]

In April Belfast was blitzed and in May the bombing of Dublin's East

Wall killed 34 people. The country also began to experience the rigours of wartime shortages: all but essential traffic was off the roads due to the lack of petrol, there was no white bread, severe rationing of coal and tea, and in the midst of all came a devastating outbreak of foot-and-mouth disease.

Dillon, touring the country with government ministers encouraging people to aid the defence effort, was openly critical of the way in which the government was handling various aspects of the emergency. He also continued to express his concern that the policy of neutrality was morally wrong, though he knew that articulating this view politically was almost certainly suicidal.

Dillon was well aware that his voice was a minority one, that public opinion was set and that he was unlikely to change it. When, on 26 June 1940, de Valera had rejected Neville Chamberlain's offer to end partition in return for Irish co-operation during the war, Dillon told David Gray that de Valera could do no other – that the country at large would not tolerate an alliance with Britain. Even a combined appeal from de Valera and Cosgrave would not break the people's determination to stay neutral. He knew that Mulcahy believed that at best de Valera could bring half of Fianna Fáil with him, and Cosgrave maybe two-thirds of Fine Gael; that at best one-third of the country would oppose an alliance and would cause huge problems, not least from Northern nationalists whose opposition to partition made them pro-German.[35] Knowing this, Dillon was conscious of adopting an isolated position, in the knowledge that if the crunch came even his own party would not provide shelter or comfort.

Nonetheless, Dillon's Dáil scrutiny of government activities was as sharply critical as ever. He did not subscribe to the view that criticism of the government weakened the national war effort or was in some way unpatriotic. In a motion on essential supplies on 16 January 1941, he insisted that while unity on fundamentals was essential in times of crisis, a unity which covered up ineptitude or inefficiency was a menace to the state, and he claimed that the government had not come clean with the people on petrol rationing – allegations strenuously denied by Lemass.[36] In February he sought information on the bombing of Irish ships, information the government was reluctant to divulge, apparently for fear of being seen to be taking sides. Most of the attacks were from German sources, and Dillon criticised de Valera for not taking a sufficiently strong line with the German government on the matter.[37] In March he urged the government, in spite of the fact that 'our debates are proceeding in a world which is burning down around us', to address seriously the question of post-war developments. He wanted the government to invest some external assets in 'cement and iron' to provide better transport for post-war trade, better land for secure food supply; he wanted to translate the Abercrombie Report into genuine town planning schemes, with open spaces and systems of road and drainage. 'These are new times – we must prepare for a new future.'[38]

Sparring across the floor of the House with a Fianna Fáil front bench which refused to take the opposition into its confidence, Dillon's impatience with the government finally erupted. 'We have given the Government what help we could give them since this crisis came upon us, and we are prepared to give it to them right up to the end. But ... we are human ... and are not prepared to go on indefinitely getting all the kicks and none of the ha'pence.' He was angry that on the foot-and-mouth question he had given the minister damaging information privately in advance of the debate and had not mentioned it in his speech, and yet had been accused by Ryan of playing politics with the issue. 'There is a limit beyond which we cannot bring our own people and that is the limit at which our people think the Government are making fools of us.'[39]

De Valera sent Frank Aiken to the US in May 1941 to explain Ireland's position to American political leaders and Irish-American groups. Aiken saw his role as marshalling US support for Irish neutrality, but from the start it was an ill-fated mission. There was neither sympathy nor understanding for Ireland from the Anglophile Roosevelt establishment, and Aiken's chances had not been helped by de Valera's St Patrick's Day broadcast to the US, when he seemed to draw no distinction between Nazis and Allies, and which had wrongly accused the Allies of causing shortages in Ireland through the imposition of a blockade. According to historian Ryle Dwyer, 'de Valera's remarks were ill-timed and created a most unfortunate climate for the Aiken mission'.[40]

Even without this initial handicap, Aiken's dour personality was ill-suited to the delicate diplomacy his job entailed. From the start he was regarded not just as bitterly anti-British but as being pro-German. He had a blazing row with Roosevelt, and before long administration officials concluded that they could not do business with him. To make matters worse he openly consorted with some of Roosevelt's worst critics, thus involving himself publicly in domestic American politics. If the purpose of the mission had been to win US support for Irish neutrality, it was a total failure. Back in Dublin, Fine Gael warned de Valera of the damage Aiken was doing and asked for his recall, a request de Valera rejected.[41] To cap things, Mulcahy's criticism of Aiken was censored at Aiken's insistence. Aiken had ordered that nothing was to be allowed appear which might impair the success of his US trip, and in particular to prevent personal attacks and criticism of him during his absence. It was a clear abuse of his censorship powers, but far from being the only one.[42]

Dillon reacted strongly, unleashing a passionate broadside on abuses of the censorship system and the absurdities of some of the decisions taken.

He was incensed at the censoring of a pastoral letter from Pius XII, which had been reported in *Osservatore Romano*, because it had carried condemnations of Nazi persecution of Catholics in Poland, and pointed to it as just one instance of a censorship 'which had lost all sense of proportion, and ... misrepresented the scope of the discretion conferred upon it by an Act of this House'. He read details of Nazi atrocities in Poland from the censored pastoral into the record of the House, and demanded whether the government, 'the trustees of our liberties, should submit to belligerent blackmail ... in order to please a diplomat accredited to our Government'. He claimed that censorship was being used to prevent legitimate domestic criticism of the government being published – and his point was in a sense made for him when his remarks were themselves censored.[43]

Dillon was growing more pessimistic on the likely outcome of the war also. He told the Fine Gael front bench in March that he felt a British defeat was now a real possibility and warned his colleagues that a German victory 'would result in Ireland being infiltrated with Nazism. A position would be brought about in which children would never be allowed hear the word of God ... religious persecution would show itself on an unprecedented scale.' His comments persuaded Mulcahy that Dillon 'wanted to go into the war in the cause of democracy'.[44]

Dillon had reached a crisis point in his own personal position. His views on what he called Ireland's moral duty were expressed to friends with increasing passion and impatience. In spite of these signs of a crisis growing within him, Dillon's first attack on neutrality took all parties and especially his own by surprise. He began what should have been a routine speech on the External Affairs vote on 16 July 1941 with an assertion, from which he never wavered, that while he had never believed in a policy of neutrality, it was a matter for the Irish people and nobody else, and that any attack on Irish sovereignty would be resisted 'by all the forces at our disposal'.[45] This opening, however, gave little indication of what was to follow when the debate resumed at the start of the next day's business. Dillon now nailed his colours to the mast.

Neutrality was not the correct policy, he said, even though it had the support of the people, including a majority of his own party. He had not spoken out earlier because he hoped the views of government and people would change, but this had not happened: the majority of people favoured neutrality, that was a plain patent fact. He did not advocate that Ireland should enter the war, but 'we should ascertain precisely what co-operation Britain and the US may require to ensure success against the Nazi attempt at world conquest, and as expeditiously as possible to offer to the US and Britain that co-operation to the limit of our resources.' The 'limit of our resources' precluded the possibility of sending Irish troops overseas: we had neither the means nor the material. He made a long, savage attack on the nature of Nazism before returning to what support Ireland should provide: our naval and air bases, and nothing less. If Britain was not guaranteed supplies from the USA, she would be defeated, 'and the day she falls Ireland would fall too'.

This proved too much for a Fianna Fáil backbencher, Andrew Fogarty, who was moved to shout at Dillon: 'I say the Deputy should be put out of the House. I will put him out quick, the corner-boy. If he does not shut his — mouth we will shut it for him.'

Dillon would not be put off. He likened the Irish position to that of Pontius Pilate, 'asking, as between the Axis and the Allies, what is truth? and washing our hands and calling the world to witness that this is no affair of ours. We know what the truth is – that on the side of the Anglo-American alliance is right and justice and on the side of the Axis is evil and injustice.' The survival of Christianity and western civilisation was at stake, as he saw it, and a country with Ireland's traditions and values should have no doubt as to where its loyalties lay.

> I say that there is no doubt as to the right and wrong of the moral issues in this struggle that deters us from making the right decision now. It is the fear of the German *blitzkrieg* that deters us.
>
> No prudent man will minimise that danger; no just man will deride that fear. It is a terrible danger; it is a thing of which every honest public represen-tative must feel deeply apprehensive, when he thinks of bringing that danger upon the people for whom he stands trustee. It is only when he is certain that failure to face that danger now is a lesser evil than the consequences of sinking our heads in the sand, and turning our backs upon the evil, that he would be justified in the eyes of God in asking them to face it.

Nor had Dillon any doubt about the consequences of a German victory. As 'conquerors of the world, and in order to maintain that conquest, and domination over the continent of Europe and the ocean highways of the world, the first thing they will do is to demand and seize naval and air bases on our south-west coast and western seaboard.' This action would lead to a takeover of the country.

Dillon was now in full flight. The choice facing the Irish people was a choice between 'the crooked cross of Nazism and the Cross of Christ'. We would face a persecution 'beside which the worst that Oliver Cromwell did will pale into insignificance'. He based this claim on the verifiable fact that 'this has been the experience of all other countries'.

By now Dillon was speaking to a crowded and very hostile House. The heckling came from Fianna Fáil backbenches, but the antipathy was near universal. Undeterred, Dillon continued:

Ireland's action at this time may prove vital. It is a queer fate for Providence to reserve for us, that we, a small, comparatively weak country, should be fated to fill so critical a part in so unprecedented a time.

And he concluded:

I recognise the appalling nature of the responsibility. I have never said anything in my public life which I feel more sincerely or more deeply, and I believe our people are equal to their glorious destiny, equal to bear the burden and the enormous responsibility, and I pray God that they may yet find leaders who will be worthy of them in the time of crisis.[46]

Dillon's speech had taken a crowded House by surprise. Most surprised of all were his front-bench colleagues, Mulcahy and Cosgrave, who sat either side of him and to whom he had not confided his intentions. He was followed immediately by Mulcahy, who reproached his colleague gently. He told the House that Dillon had raised the subject in a rather unexpected way and the only interpretation of his speech was that Dillon wanted to declare war on the Axis powers in the interests of Christianity. Mulcahy, however, drew the discussion back to more basic matters:

I do not think it would be of assistance to this country that his attitude here should get any support. I think there is nothing that would more divide the people of this country than to be asked to take a decision on these matters at the present time.[47]

If Mulcahy was restrained, Cosgrave was not. He was angry that Dillon had not told his colleagues of his intentions, and he made it clear to the House that the matter had not been debated within the party. Neither was he impressed with the wisdom of Dillon's statement:

We are not bound to take part in a conflict of this kind. It is no part of the Christian religion or the Catholic faith to insist in our taking part in it ... The duty and responsibility of every person in public life ... lies in ensuring the security and stability and integrity of this country. If that is better served by a policy of neutrality, then it is our duty to accept and adapt that policy.

He warned against being seen to hesitate on fundamental policy. 'In a time of crisis it is advisable – it is necessary – to make up your mind rapidly, to make it up correctly and, having made it up, to stick to it like a man and to do what you can towards preserving, improving and exalting the country which it is our duty to serve.'[48]

It was an extraordinary public put-down from a party leader of his deputy leader, and it began a barrage of criticism from all parts of the House. Eamon O'Neill, a Fine Gael colleague from West Cork, perhaps best expressed the majority view, the overwhelming view of the House and probably the country:

> We are approaching the third year of war in a certain state of immunity from the horrors of that war, because of the fact that we have been able to keep up in this country, in this House and outside it, a fine decent spirit of united nationalism, and have been able to present a common front towards the world in general.

And though Dillon and O'Neill were members of Fine Gael, in his towering anger O'Neill had no hesitation in reminding Dillon of his background: 'I am not so surprised in one sense that a gentleman who, when he first came into this House said ... "A Soldier's Song was a thing of horror", could now, sitting between two men who fought and were condemned to death in 1916, gave voice to such expression as he has used today.'[49]

Mulcahy tried to calm things down by asking O'Neill to 'leave that matter to the 1916 men',[50] but to no avail. Fianna Fáil backbenchers followed up with a series of strong and very personal attacks, although de Valera took a softer line, not much different from Mulcahy's. He accepted that Dillon's views were personal and did not represent Fine Gael. He regretted them, nonetheless, and felt they could be dangerous and divisive and lead to internal dissent, and for this reason he thought Dillon's remarks should be censored – which they were. He added that while Dillon's speech was 'magnificent' it was not 'common sense'.[51]

Ominously for Dillon, Thomas Toal, Chairman of Monaghan County Council and President of Fine Gael in Dillon's own constituency, complained bitterly to Cosgrave, 'publicly disassociated [himself] from Dillon' and claimed the speech 'has caused consternation and pain among his supporters here'. It was a difficult moment for Dillon, and in a long letter to Toal he defended his position.[52] He said he had signalled his views to the constituency twelve months earlier, and he had repeatedly argued his case on the front bench. He had reluctantly agreed not to make his speech at the Árd Fheis, but felt eventually that he had only two choices: to speak out or retire from politics. 'When a man enters public life ... he knows there will be rough going in addition to the smooth and he is not entitled when the going gets rough to run away from home ...' He had not told his Fine Gael colleagues, he said, because he knew 'they would withhold their consent ... I would have to leave Fine Gael and make the speech as an Independent. I did not want to do that ... I did not believe it was in the best interest of the country or of my colleagues to do so, and accordingly on Thursday I made the speech and having made it placed in Mr. Cosgrave's hands my resignation – to accept or refuse as he thought best.'[53]

Dillon did have some few supporters. Maurice Dockrell, a former Unionist and now a Fine Gael TD, was the most explicit: 'lest it might be thought that Dillon's remarks were the vapourings of a single irresponsible madman, I should like to suggest that there is a number of deputies who – some of them – can go just as far as Dillon has gone.'[54] JJ Cole, a Protestant Independent TD from Cavan, supported the substance of his case, while James Coburn, a survivor from the Irish Party, and another Fine Gael TD, Ernest Benson, praised his courage.[55]

Outside of the Dáil he received strong support from Bishop Morrisroe of Achonry, from many sections of the AOH and from some priests. He received many letters of support from Church of Ireland rectors and elements of the Anglo-Irish community, and he got letters and telegrams from outside the country, from as far away as Kenya, Australia and the US. A bizarre endorsement came from a soap manufacturer called Dixon who sent a telegram: 'Endorse views, should start campaign, dislike you personally, enclose cheque.'[56]

But those few voices apart, there was neither support nor warmth for what Dillon had said. A Fianna Fáil backbencher, Mark Kililea, summed up what many of the Fianna Fáil party were thinking when he taunted Dillon by saying that, if he felt as he did, why did he not join the British army?[57]

Dillon insisted on having his dissent recorded when the vote was put later that evening, but the wider public remained unaware of what exactly had happened because the speech was censored. Dillon published his address in pamphlet form, hoping to ensure that his case would not go by default or be totally misrepresented. Its circulation, however, was small.

The question arises as to why Dillon chose this moment to make such a speech. He had been moving in this direction from the start of the war, but at this point he was convinced that Britain was on the brink of invasion – and that Ireland was in a position to avert such a catastrophe. This was the deciding factor: He was later to say in his *Memoir*:

I could never forget that the west coast of Ireland was littered with the bodies of dead English seamen who had been bringing supplies to us. In 1941 the Germans were flying the Cherbourg-Stavanger route up our coasts and dropping magnetic mines into the Atlantic. Britain was at a hair's breadth of being cut off from America. The British had no tanks, no oil, no means of bringing U.S. troops to Europe. I felt the time had come to take a moral stand.[58]

Dillon's speech dominated the next meeting of the Fine Gael parliamentary party, held on 23 July. The extraordinary thing is that the episode did not result in an immediate parting of the ways. Dillon ascribed this to Cosgrave and Mulcahy. In a letter to Senator John McLaughlin shortly after the parliamentary party meeting, he wrote: 'Mulcahy and Cosgrave had thrust upon them a delicate and distasteful task. Few men could have, and even fewer would have bothered to discharge it so delicately and with such splendid loyalty to a colleague against whom they had fair grounds for complaint.'[59] No record survives of the content of the debate, but Dillon's letter to Toal indicates that he placed his resignation in Cosgrave's hands and that after a long discussion 'it was decided unanimously, except for Captain Esmonde, the member for Wexford, to ask me to withdraw my resignation, which I was very glad to do'.[60] According to the party record, the meeting concluded by congratulating Cosgrave on the way in which he had handled the matter and it was decided unanimously that the episode be regarded as closed.[61] Certainly this was the impression Cosgrave conveyed to Dillon. According to Dillon's *Memoir*, Cosgrave said to him: 'Well, you've spoken your mind now, and if you don't want to return to this topic, there's no need to make it an issue!'[62]

That, however, was not the end of it, nor could it be. Dillon's feelings were passionately at variance with those of the party on the biggest issue of the day. It is strange that Dillon did not accept the logic of the incompatibility of his views and theirs, especially given his conviction that he could not stand by when the danger to the Allies was certain to escalate. The fact that he published his speech as a pamphlet showed how doggedly he believed in the rightness of his beliefs. The only conclusion is that he was less than forthright with colleagues who had treated him generously and that, in pursuit of his own sense of principle, he was prepared to risk embarrassing them again.

Dillon's speech had more impact outside the country than inside it. The foreign press put greater significance on it than was warranted, believing that as the party's deputy leader Dillon was speaking for a large body of Fine Gael opinion. This foreign press greatly irritated de Valera, who felt Ireland's position had been weakened and misrepresented.[63]

To all outward appearances, however, it seemed as if the episode was closed. When the Dáil next met on 17 September, Dillon was back to his most aggressive form, lashing out at the Minister for Local Government and Public Health, PJ Ruttledge, who was resigning as a minister to become Solicitor General to the Wards of Court. Ruttledge's resignation may have been prompted in part by de Valera's increasingly hard line against the IRA; in any case, Dillon contrasted his resigning 'in an hour of crisis, to take a soft job at £4,000 a year', with the advice being given to young men to join the army.[64] Dillon also objected strongly to a further lengthy Dáil adjournment. A month later Fine Gael's dissatisfaction with the government's working of the Defence Conference surfaced again, though the party felt it was not in a position to walk out of the committee.

The Japanese attack on Pearl Harbour in December 1941 greatly affected Dillon, who felt the last argument in favour of 'indifferent neutrality' had gone now that the US had entered the war – but he held his tongue, publicly at least. Privately, the US and UK legations were left in no doubt that he favoured making every possible help available to the Allies. Gray, the US Minister, also formed the view that Dillon would not publicly oppose the seizure of the ports and would even split his party on the issue. His assessment was very much at variance with the British understanding of Dillon's position, and with his repeated public statements that only the Irish people had the right to decide the policy of the country.[65]

Dillon nonetheless continued to plead publicly for greater non-military co-operation, and in late 1941 proposed Ireland do a barter deal with Britain, exchanging 600,000 tons of Irish-grown oats and barley in return for 400,000 tons of wheat. The government turned down the proposal on the grounds that the supply of wheat could be cut off at a moment's notice and it was safer to persist with the policy of growing supplies at home, though wheat was in short supply and of indifferent quality.[66]

His opposition to the IRA was undiminished, though he almost certainly overestimated its strength and the extent to which it had German support. Thus when the government came to the Dáil in January 1942, looking for draconian powers against the IRA, Dillon found himself in a dilemma. He excoriated the IRA, 'contaminated and sustained by Nazi help and Gestapo inspiration',[67] and he held that they 'were entitled to none of the protections of a civilised community'. However, his instinctive distrust of government was such that he wanted it to be more forthcoming on the details of the alleged IRA conspiracy and argued that the Emergency Powers Order must be temporary and subject to review.[68]

His denunciation of the IRA once again drew the wrath of the Labour Party. Dillon was 'guilty of treason by advocating an alliance with one of the belligerents', according to James Hickey, who said that Dillon 'should have mentioned British imperialism rather than Nazism as the root cause of our problem'.[69] William Davin accused him of publicly revealing information obtained at the Defence Conference.[70] Dillon also found himself under fire from the German Minister, Eduard Hempel, who formally complained to de Valera that the Ceann Comhairle had not intervened to restrain Dillon when he made his attacks on Germany, which Hempel claimed were falsely based on the 'so-called confessions of the IRA Chief of Staff, Stephen Hayes'.[71] More interestingly, when he supported the Emergency Order, Dillon found himself at odds with many of his Fine Gael colleagues. The party allowed a free vote on the Order, and lawyers like Costello, McGilligan, Fitzgerald-Kenney and others, including O'Higgins, voted against, while Dillon, along with Cosgrave and Mulcahy, supported it.[72]

Dillon's outright opposition to the IRA did not prevent him acting humanely in individual cases. The world of Irish politics was, after all, small and very personal:

> The current revival of interest in hunger strikes reminds me of a curious incident during the war years. Mr. de Valera came to have a good deal of trouble with the IRA, for whom his compromises with reality became altogether too subtle. One old comrade of his, Patrick McGrath, had been interned in late 1939 and went on hunger strike. By early December he was getting very weak. It happened that one day I came upon Mr. Cosgrave and General Mulcahy in our committee room looking very glum. I asked them why. Dick Mulcahy said that Patrick McGrath was an old comrade of his, and a man of absolute integrity, and he hated to see him die but Dev wouldn't free him for fear of what Fine Gael might say. 'Well,' said I, 'why don't you go and tell Dev that Fine Gael will make no objection?' But no, they felt they couldn't do that. 'Well then,' I said, 'I don't mind. If you have no objection, I'll go and tell Dev.' That pleased them greatly, so I went off and told Dev he would get no opposition from us if he wished to release McGrath. He was most grateful, and the upshot was that McGrath was released the next day.
>
> That, however, is not the end of the story. About eight months later, in August 1940, de Valera and I were travelling together in the Cork area, drumming up support for the national defence forces (it was customary at the time for members of both parties to pair off and to campaign together in this cause, to make it a bipartisan operation). We were actually visiting Spike Island when a message was brought for de Valera. He read it with increasing anger, and I heard him, at the end of it, mutter under his breath, 'this man must die!'
>
> What had happened was that McGrath and a companion had been caught by the guards up to no good in a house in Clontarf. There was a shootout and two policemen were shot before McGrath was captured. De Valera stuck to his intention in this case. McGrath was executed and so were a number of others later on.[73]

The war continued, but with little public discussion or open controversy. Censorship, scarcity of hard news, shortages and the infrequent meetings of the Dáil all helped lower the temperature of public debate, if not public concern. The 1942 Fine Gael Árd Fheis took place in the Mansion House against this background on Tuesday, 10 February. Like all such wartime events, it was a low-key one-day affair and the newspapers expected little controversy from the couple of hundred delegates who turned up. Ten days before the Árd Fheis, Cosgrave had issued a statement urging 'public men to preserve a discreet silence on external affairs',[74] a point he repeated in his Árd Fheis speech. Significantly, he returned to the point again: 'I am not aware of any remarkable change in the war situation which would justify alarming pronouncements. Already many of our people have felt the privation arising out of the war. Their sufferings are quite enough for them.' On neutrality he was unequivocal and almost philosophical: 'should the worst come the people would bear the crisis with fortitude, trusting as they had always done in God'.[75] Both Cosgrave and Mulcahy criticised the government's unwillingness to take the opposition into its confidence, but they stoutly defended the policy of neutrality and Fine Gael's contribution to its successful maintenance.

Dillon's speech could not have been more different. Always a crowd-puller at any public gathering, he was loudly applauded as he began to speak.

Ireland could not stand aloof from the world conflict, he said. Duty and history put it on the side of the Allies. He played the American card, and dwelt at some length, if not always convincingly, on the Irish people's historic debt to the USA. 'Whoever attacks America is my enemy, without reservation or qualification, and I say that the United States has been treacherously and feloniously attacked by Germany, Italy and Japan. These nations are, therefore, my enemies, and I would to God they were the enemies of a united Irish people.'

He continued: 'The US stands in vital peril of its existence and whatever be the consequences to my political career I hope and pray that some day we can be of help. We cannot offer more than we have got. It may be very little in the immense drama that is being enacted all over the world, but poor as it may be, it is all that we have got and in my considered judgement it is none too much to offer ...'

He warned the delegates that every effort would be made to prevent Irish co-operation with the US, that Germany would 'threaten our people with an immediate and terrible blitz, if we approach closer to the United States'. He went on:

In the desolation in which this nation will then find itself, false friends from Europe may offer new friendships to take the place of the old, and if, in some awful hour, our people commit the supreme folly of accepting in exchange for the traditional Irish-American alliance any form of co-operation from the Nazi-Fascist Powers of Europe, it will be merely the introduction to a development which will end in this country being turned into a German Gibraltar of the Atlantic.

That is the fate I feel threatening us, and while I subscribe to what Mr. Cosgrave has said in the economic sphere, my message to the delegates is this – we in this country must cling to the Irish-American alliance. No question of safety or any other consideration should make us untrue to the immense debt we owe to the United States, and I say to our friends throughout the country that their eyes should be open to the dangers that beset us, and, whatever and whenever they hear the suggestion made that the Americans are putting us in a position of embarrassment or of difficulty, let them think with me of their fathers and mothers and sisters who found safety, refuge and welcome in America when there was nowhere else they could get them, and, putting their hands on their hearts, let them answer that whatever the sacrifices, whatever America may want of us to protect her from her enemies she will get for the asking. If they do not, the name of Irish friendship will become synonymous with disloyalty and treachery.[76]

His speech met with a very mixed reception. Even US Minister David Gray, who agreed with the contents, thought it was ill-timed.[77] The British Representative was altogether warmer, and writing to Dillon on 20 February Maffey began: 'it may be undiplomatic of me to say that your courageous action strikes a very sympathetic chord in our hearts here and across oceans wide and narrow ... My hope and belief is that you have exchanged a spotlight for a beacon. At the least you have salved your conscience by telling your countrymen what you believe and what they hear from nowhere else. It had to be said and you have said it. You can stand back well content. We must wait now and watch the sweep of battle.'[78]

Dillon's words had certainly swept through the Fine Gael conference. Maffey, who was there, thought his speech was well received, but press reports – those which passed the censor – suggested considerable hostility. Several delegates criticised what Dillon had said, and one objected – unsuccessfully – to his nomination as a vice-president of the party. But vice-president or not, the official rebuke was not long in following. Sean McEoin, speaking for the front bench, said Dillon's views were purely personal; Cosgrave spoke for Fine Gael and regretted that Dillon had departed from the advice he had given to observe a discreet silence on foreign affairs.[79]

Elizabeth Bowen novelist's eye caught the fall-out in the Mansion House. 'His speech, delivered with a virtuosity – or, should one say, calculated dramatic effect – that did not detract from its effect of impassioned sincerity, had the effect of a time-bomb. There was a reaction of excited and highly emotional applause – an applause that seemed so general that I could have believed for a minute that Mr. Dillon had carried the room with him. His shots had been nicely placed. (I should say that of the people there one-third were strongly with Dillon; one-third were neutral (temporarily swayed, but due to react against him later); one-third definitely hostile.'

Bowen noticed early evidence of 'a very definite pleasure in his speech, (a) as a piece of courage, and (b) as a *tour de force*'. She noted too how 'The most bitter attacks on Dillon were to come, I am sorry to say, from the younger members of Fine Gael. These struck me as being definitely terrified of their skins.'

She paid particular attention to the reaction of Dillon's front-bench colleagues: 'Mr. Cosgrave and the rest of those on the platform, presented, during Dillon's speech, resolutely expressionless faces. Not an eyelid was batted. One elderly occupant (not recognised) took the still more cautious line of feigning sleep.'[80]

Bowen had no doubts, however, that the immediate reaction outside the Mansion House was negative. 'In Dublin after February 10, I found practically no support for Mr. Dillon. Even ex-Unionists, with their vehement sympathy for the British, either deplored or ignored Mr. Dillon's speech.' And she concluded her report to the Dominions Office with the following general observation, a point that was to change little as the war proceeded:

> Few people in the general excitement, seemed to have taken Mr. Dillon's exact point, which was not that Eire should immediately and gratuitously declare war on the Axis, as a gesture of support to America, but simply that Eire should make (with regard to German demands) a point past which she could not, consistently with her honour, continue to yield … His contention, in fact, has been that one can reach a point where dishonour is worse than war.[81]

Having made the speech, there could be no further equivocation. Dillon met Cosgrave, Mulcahy, McGilligan and O'Higgins at the party headquarters, where Mulcahy made it clear that this was a resigning matter, though he hoped that Dillon's subsequent relationship with the party would be friendly. Dillon was surprised, though why he should have been is hard to understand. A memo in the Mulcahy papers noted: 'he butted in at once that he was not going to resign; that he was not of the resigning kind'. Dillon launched into a vigorous defence of his position, 'with emphasis that all he said was that whoever struck at America was his enemy, that it would be very difficult for the Fine Gael party to explain to the country why they considered that such a statement made a man unworthy to be a member of the party.'

Dillon, unaware of or unwilling to accept that the gap between himself and his colleagues was so wide, eventually accepted the situation, saying it was a matter for the party and that his own support would be 'infinitesimal'. According to Mulcahy, Dillon said he did not want to leave Fine Gael, 'that he was a party man, but that if his colleagues did not want him that was another matter and meant a parting of the ways, that he understood the difficulties and that there need not be any unfriendliness or hard feeling'.[82]

It was arranged that Dillon's letter of resignation would be submitted to the next meeting of the parliamentary party on 20 February, but before that could happen Norton raised the matter in the Dáil, asking why Dillon's damaging speech had not been censored. His question gave Aiken an opportunity to make an assault on Dillon, claiming that foreign journalists were waiting for every word to fall from his mouth.[83] This Dáil exchange did not influence a situation which had already been resolved, but it illustrated the difficulties Fine Gael would have in maintaining a coherent position should Dillon remain. When the Fine Gael parliamentary party met, in Dillon's absence Cosgrave submitted his letter of resignation, which was accepted with regret.

The parting in fact was unusual for its warmth. Dillon wrote:

Dear Mr. Cosgrave

If it appears to you that the views expressed by me on our relations with America are inconsistent with the retention by me of the Deputy Leadership of the Fine Gael Party, I think it right to tender you my resignation from the membership of the party. I know that it is unnecessary to assure you of my continued sincere admiration and warm personal regard for yourself and the colleagues with whom I have been proud to serve for the last ten years.

Cosgrave's reply was no less friendly. In the course of a long letter he said:

My colleagues and I have given it full consideration and have reluctantly come to the conclusion that the interests of the country and the usefulness of the party to the country would best be served by acceptance of the resignation tendered by you.

A sense of duty has compelled you to pursue a particular course in relation to external policy in the Emergency of which we could not in the interests of the country approve. Like you, we are animated with feelings of cordial friendship for the United States of America, but we do not share your views as to how that friendship can best be maintained and strengthened.

We have worked together now for a number of years and I am convinced that it has been greatly to the benefit of our country. Although now in special circumstances we must part, I am happy in the knowledge that cordial relations will continue to exist between us. I assure you that is the wish of my colleagues and myself and you have certainly given us every indication that this is your wish also.

For myself I wish to express my warm affection for you and my appreciation of your unselfish, unstinted and valuable service to me.

God be with you.[84]

Neither Dillon nor Fine Gael wanted his resignation to cause a split in the party, but one member, Dillon's long-time friend Peter Nugent, felt he had to leave with him.[85]

In retrospect it can be seen that Dillon's Árd Fheis address was no spontaneous outburst: it was utterly consistent with the position he had held since the outbreak of war. The timing of the speech was dictated almost entirely by the USA's entry into the war, and his playing the 'American card' was deliberate.

Dillon had given a clear summary of his thinking in a memorandum written on 26 November 1940. In short, he thought Ireland would have 'more effectively vindicated our moral position in the world and protected our material interests in the world by declaring war in September 1939'. At this point, however, there could be no question of consenting to the transfer of the ports and air bases to Britain: public opinion would not stand for it. Nor was it acceptable that Britain should seize them by force: such an act would destroy the moral basis of her position and be little different to what Germany had done in Denmark, Holland, Norway and Belgium. The only way Dillon could see the bases being made available was through American involvement. He believed that a request from the US, especially in view of 'the aid she had consistently given Ireland for the last 250 years', and with America's safety and the future of democracy at stake, was different in kind from a British request and one which, if properly explained, the Irish people would 'cheerfully' accept.[86]

This was the thinking behind the Árd Fheis speech. It reflected well on Dillon's generosity and courage, but not on his judgement. The Pope himself would not have won a 'cheerful' response to the abandoning of neutrality or handing over of the ports in 1942. Dillon was not just on his own – his stand made no difference whatsoever to public opinion or government policy. He had, rather, embarrassed his party and rendered it suspect on the most fundamental issue of the day. He laid himself open to the charge that his speech weakened the perception abroad that the country was united at a time of crisis. There was, in addition, the certainty that in the event of a German invasion he would have been one of the first casualties, something which was not so unlikely in 1942 as it may seem almost sixty years later.

By most of the rules, his actions should have brought a promising political career to an abrupt end. He was willing to jettison his career and face into, not just the political wilderness, but misrepresentation, vilification and isolation for saying what he believed to be right. In the final analysis, whether it changed policy or not, Dillon's stand was an act of passionate moral courage.

Yet as Elizabeth Bowen wrote at the time, 'Mr. Dillon's uncompromising attitude seems to have lost him a good deal of support. The country is frightened of him. There is a widespread idea that Mr. Dillon will bring Éire into war.'[87]

CHAPTER ELEVEN

WARTIME INTERLUDE

'I am old enough to know and judge people. Do you think I would joke about so serious a matter as marriage?'

Dillon, August 1942

ILLON'S STAND ON neutrality increased his national profile, even if it did not make him more popular. In a political tableau of greys and browns he provided a touch of colour, something out of the ordinary. He was one of the few politicians who was instantly recognisable, and indeed he was a cartoonist's delight, frequently appearing in *Dublin Opinion* which, reflecting the gentler journalistic ethos of the time, treated him, as it treated all politicians, with bemused affection. His crowd-pulling oratory and mastery of language made him a favourite of journalists and, apart from the *Irish Press*, which consistently represented him as being 'pro-British' and by definition 'anti-Irish', he generally got good press.

It was, it has to be said, a time when newspapers, again with the exception of the *Irish Press*, carried very little that was personally critical of politicians and only rarely provided serious analysis of the major issues of the day. Political journalism was deferential and respectful, speeches were reported but rarely analysed, speculation was spare and careful, and the private lives of politicians were strictly off limits.

Dillon was different to most of his political colleagues in that he was unmarried, and showed little obvious interest in the prospect. He had had some girlfriends, and during his US days at least one of whom he had taken seriously and with whom he had contemplated marriage, if his letters home are any guide. Marriage had in fact been on his mind for some years. On his last visit to his uncle Nicholas at the Franciscan Abbey in Multyfarnham in 1939, the good friar had chided him about his single state and about living alone in the large house in Ballaghaderreen. On parting, James had solemnly promised to look seriously at the question. It wasn't, he said, a question of principle: he simply hadn't found the right woman yet. The approach of his fortieth birthday in September 1942 seemed to have concentrated his mind on the matter.

Dillon had always liked Connemara and was particularly fond of Josie

Mongan's hotel in Carna, a favourite holiday spot of Cosgrave's also. Mongan was a Fine Gael TD known as the 'King of Connemara', a native speaker whose Irish idiom flowed freely into his English. Dillon went on holidays to Mongan's once again in August 1942. He arrived on Friday, 13 August, and when he left four days later he was engaged to be married. The wedding took place six weeks afterwards. The story of what happened is best told by the woman he married.[1]

Maura Phelan was twenty-two in 1942. She was by all accounts attractive and vivacious and had a mind of her own. Her father had owned an old established drapery business in Clonmel and had been a supporter of the Irish Party, transferring his allegiance with some reluctance to Cosgrave in 1922, seeing him as the best of a bad lot, but his enthusiasm had obviously grown to the extent of giving his active support to the Blueshirts a decade later. Maura's mother had died in 1935 and her father in 1936, and at this stage she was legally under the protection of her guardian, her uncle, Theo Phelan, a Dublin businessman.

Maura had little interest in politics at this point and while she had heard of Dillon's stance on neutrality it meant little to her. She was holidaying in Mongan's with her sister, Kitty; Josie Mongan's wife was their first cousin. Her first experience of Dillon came before she even met him. She went to buy cigarettes (then rationed) in Mongan's shop, only to be told that there were none available. She persisted and pointed to some stocked behind the counter. These, she was told, 'were being kept for Mr Dillon,' because he smoked heavily. 'Mr Dillon,' it seems, 'was a very special person. He must have his cigarettes.' Maura was told to try her luck in the village.

It was not a good start, and neither was she impressed by her first sight of Mr Dillon, who arrived on the evening bus. Her recollection was that he was in sports-clothes, to which she felt his figure did not lend itself. And she resented the fact that because of him she was without cigarettes.

The weather was misty, and when Maura went to hire the local taxi to do some visiting the following day, she was told it was unavailable. Mr Dillon had it. He was going fishing at Lough Inagh.

They were staying in the same hotel and that night Dillon played bridge in the conservatory with his friend Lonan Murphy while the other guests assembled in the drawing-room. Dillon, apparently, was quite unaware of Maura Phelan, and certainly knew nothing of the sense of irritation he had inspired in her.

The following afternoon was still misty. Maura went swimming, came back wearing slacks, an old coat, her hair wet and wearing no make-up, and as she walked into the hotel she chatted briefly with Thelma Legge, wife of Hector Legge, and bade Dillon a formal 'good afternoon'.

As soon as she had gone, Dillon said to Thelma Legge: 'Who is that girl?

Where does she come from?'

Thelma Legge obliged with the name.

'Is she married?'

'No.'

'Is she engaged?'

'No, Mr Dillon, she is not engaged.'

'I see ... but she is wearing a ring.'

'The ring, Mr Dillon, if you look more closely, is on her right hand.' Thelma Legge explained the significance.

'I see. Well, all is fair in love and war. That is the girl I want to marry.'

And that, for the moment, was that. Thelma Legge recounted the episode later to a flabbergasted Maura Phelan. Their immediate reaction was that he must be in some way unhinged: Maura and he had not even been introduced.

Introductions in due course were made, but without any change in Maura's attitude. If anything, things got worse. In the course of conversation that evening, Dillon, in his magisterial way, dismissed 'romance' as 'an illusion of the very young', to which Maura replied, 'You know, Mr Dillon, I feel very sorry for you.'

'Why?'

'Because you must be a cynic, and I always think cynics are lonely people who don't believe in anything. Leave us to our illusions; go wallow in your cynicism.'

Dillon took this calmly enough, but the rest of the company was astonished that she should speak to him as she did.

Things improved somewhat the next day. Dillon and Lonan Murphy invited Thelma and Hector Legge and the Phelan sisters to join them in what must have been a very crowded taxi on a visit to Roundstone. The conversation, while still formal, was now somewhat friendlier.

On the Monday, Dillon (who was, incidentally, a good swimmer) was going to swim at Mweenish with Thelma and Hector Legge and invited the Phelan sisters to join them. Dillon asked permission to walk down the road with Maura, and eventually they separated from the main group. Up to this she had been Miss Phelan, but now he used her Christian name for the first time, using the Irish pronunciation 'Máire'.

His question was, to say the least, unexpected:

'Would you be very offended if I asked if I might kiss you?'

'Mr Dillon, I have been kissed many times and enjoyed every one of them.' (This was almost certainly an exaggeration, if not downright untrue.)

'That's all right then?'

'Just one thing, Mr Dillon. Treat me gently.'

It was, Maura recalled later, a very chaste kiss. However, it clearly had an exhilarating affect on Dillon. He climbed up the sand-dunes and stopped at the gate, whence he declaimed:

'Say I am gay, say I am sad

Say that health and wealth will miss me.

Say I am growing old but add

Maura kissed me.'

To which he got the cool rejoinder: 'That sounds apt, Mr Dillon, but it is not true.'

'How do you mean?'

'You kissed me. I did not kiss you.'

On the way back to Carna, with the Connemara mist enveloping them, Dillon produced his second surprise of the day.

'What would you say if I asked you to marry me?'

Maura burst out laughing. 'Mr Dillon, you must be joking! You don't know me at all and I don't know you. This is ridiculous.'

'I am old enough to know and to judge people. Do you think I would joke about so serious a matter as marriage?'

As they talked he reassured her that he was deadly serious, and pressed for an answer.

'I don't know, Mr Dillon. I would want to know you better, and in any case I couldn't say yes or no until I see my uncle, who is my guardian. If I told him I was going to marry a man whom I had just met he would say no – and I think he would be right.'

However, she agreed to think it over. She was intrigued and flattered, and they were getting on well together. When she told her sister that evening, Kitty replied instantly: 'Oh my God, I hope you said yes, because if you don't, I will.'

Later that evening, Maura was joined by Dillon as she sat reading in the conservatory. She feigned indifference.

'You know, I think you will find that book a great deal easier to read if you turn it right side up. I gather you have been considering my proposal?'

He went on to warn her of some of the pitfalls: of having to get used to living in a goldfish bowl, of guarding her opinions in public, about being followed by the press. By the end of the conversation she was clearly taking him very seriously indeed, and he pressed home his advantage by asking her, if her uncle did not exist, what would her reply be?

'I think I would say yes.'

And that, in effect, was that. It was now Monday. They had only met the previous Friday, but Dillon felt sufficiently sure to announce the news to Mrs Mongan and then at dinner took the entire company into his confidence. Hector Legge suggested an appropriate newspaper headline might read 'Dillon forsakes neutrality' or 'Dillon no longer Independent'. They had a small celebration and then all adjourned to bed. Separately, of course, and in Maura's phrase 'most properly'.

Back in Clonmel, Maura found the story of her engagement to Ireland's most eligible political bachelor had preceded her, as Dillon warned it would. There was considerable newspaper interest, so she sought the protection of a local newspaper man who guarded her confidence so long as he could be the first with the official announcement. Meanwhile, Dillon had to approach Maura's uncle, Theo Phelan. There were no problems. As Theo later told Maura, whom he had telegrammed to await his phone-call: 'He's the only TD in the Dáil worth a damn.'

The whirlwind courtship was followed by an equally fast engagement. Dillon wanted to be married before his fortieth birthday, which fell on 26 September. They were married on 30 September in St Kevin's oratory at Dublin's Pro-Cathedral by Bishop Morrisroe. His best man was his great friend, Peter Nugent, with Maura's sister, Kitty, as bridesmaid.

The marriage worked. Of that there was never to be any real doubt. But the way in which it came about tells us much about Dillon. At one level it was romantic; at another it was reckless. He was marrying a woman half his age whom he barely knew, and was doing so in great haste for no better reason than that he wanted to beat the deadline he had imposed on himself. Yet he believed himself to be a good judge of character and, thus determined, had no difficulty in embracing the concept of love at first sight.

For Maura, James's proposal brought a new sense of freedom. After her parents' death the business was run by a Miss Aylward, who ran a strict, if fair regime, but life with her was unexciting. 'The arrival of James on the scene was highly liberating.' In any event, not once in their forty-four years of married life did either he or Maura have the slightest doubt about the decision. From that point on, marriage was to be at the centre of his life. Maura grew easily into politics. She clearly idolised her husband and, not surprisingly, he changed her more than she changed him.

She took easily – enthusiastically perhaps – to the formality of his lifestyle, adopted his, rather than her friends, though her family ties, especially to her sisters, remained strong throughout her life. One of the most important things Maura brought to James was inclusion in a very close family group. Initially this was made up of Maura's sisters, Pearl, Ellie and Kitty, and her brother Michael. Kitty married Dillon's friend, Peter Nugent, who had been widowed in 1945, and family links spread further when Ellie married John Shee of Clonmel. The families kept in close contact as their children grew up. Indeed, in later years the Nugent boys were to be of enormous help to their uncle in his political campaigning.

Some friends would say later that James's influence on her was too great, that she too readily accepted his views on all public matters as being effectively the last word on the subject, and that, intellectually at any rate, she lived in his shadow. There is almost certainly some truth in this observation, but it is not necessarily surprising, given their age difference, Maura's sheltered upbringing and her lack of third-level education. But for all that, she had strong views and made sure she was informed on matters of current importance. She, too, was a good judge of character.

The lives of the newly-weds alternated between Dublin and Ballaghaderreen – Dublin when the Dáil was sitting, the rest of the time in Ballaghaderreen – where, wisely, Maura showed no inclination to upset the established staff or the settled way of doing things. Their friends there included Bay and Felicity MacDermot, the Court Clerk, Charlie MacDermott and his wife Pauline, and from time to time the local bishop. They were not in any sense a part of the local scene. Dillon was not a snob – he was a ferocious meritocrat – but his view of the world was structured and hierarchical and did not allow for spurious bonhomie or contrived intimacy. In Dublin, with North Great George's St gone – it belonged to Myles, who had sold it in the early 1940s – home was a rented flat in 36A Merrion Square and then later at 40 Elgin Rd. Cooking was not Maura's strong point so most of their entertaining was done in hotels, the Shelbourne or Gresham, or in the Stephen's Green Club. They were a self-sufficient couple, keeping in touch daily even when they were far apart, having as an article of faith that any quarrels be settled before the setting of the sun, and Dillon was particularly thoughtful, indeed sentimental, when it came to remembering and marking anniversaries or special occasions. If there had been few women in Dillon's life before Maura, there were none afterwards. Nor would such a possibility have occurred to either of them.

In July 1945 their only child, John Blake, was born. It was probably the single most important event in Dillon's life, and as John Blake grew the bond between them deepened and brought out an unexpected side to Dillon's character: his ease with children. He genuinely liked them and the liking was returned in full. He always took them seriously, answering their questions without condescension. James Nugent recalls his memories as a child and young man of his uncle, uncritically and universally admired within the family circle where 'he could let his imagination run riot – an imagination allied to a superb command of language'. James Nugent's brother, Patrick, later a robust and energetic political supporter of Dillon's, remembers how his eyes would light up when John Blake was around, showing a depth of affection which all the formality in the world could not hide.

Dillon may have been entering the loneliest phase of his political life, but he now had the comfort and security of a happy marriage, a settled domestic scene and a wife and family who adored and admired him without reservation.

CHAPTER TWELVE

THE OUTSIDER

'We are only a baby power, and the wise course for a baby power is to act like a baby and make no noise.'
Patrick Cogan, Dáil Debates, November 1943

D ILLON'S RESIGNATION FURTHER weakened a Fine Gael party already in steep decline, and put Dillon back in the political situation in which he had entered the Dáil a decade earlier. In 1932 Independent status seemed the natural, indeed the only option open to him, but now it was an irritation, and it soon became clear that he did not take easily to his newly-enforced position. In July 1942 he told the Dáil, 'I am a believer in the party system ... I am a party man and I make no concealment of the fact that it irks me to be outside party. I think Independent deputies in a deliberative assembly can do very little good.' There was, of course, greater freedom, and he felt fortunate that he need no longer worry about 'being a politically popular man'.[1] His relationship with Fine Gael remained more than cordial, to the surprise of Martin Corry who remarked during one agriculture debate that 'judging by the applause every word of his received from them [Fine Gael] today, they want to take him back'.[2]

Independence did mean some real losses. He had to give up his place on the Defence Conference, where his contribution evinced strong praise from Oscar Traynor, who said that Dillon was 'sound in everything he advised and dealt with everything in a business-like and logical way'.[3] He also lost his automatic right to priority in all debates, which a front-bench position had brought him.

Elizabeth Bowen met Dillon shortly after he returned to Dublin in July. She reported that 'his vitality and terrier-like alertness are good antidotes to the sluggishness of the Dáil ... His attitude towards vagueness and procrastination is merciless ... His new position as an Independent gives him a freer hand. In some matters, he had been inhibited by fear of embarrassing the Cosgrave party.' She felt, however, that Dillon had little support in the country: 'The reputation of being a war-monger clings to him. He is criticised for not keeping enough in touch with real feeling – for, in fact, advancing too rapidly without keeping in touch with his base.' She felt also that he was sometimes too harsh in his judgements of others.[4]

By 1943 the Dáil was coming to the end of its life. It was already the longest-running Dáil in history. Its numbers had been depleted by eleven deaths, only two of which had been replaced through by-elections. It had met less frequently than any previous Dáil and lengthy adjournments were the order of the day, something to which Dillon alone seemed to take exception. There was even a suggestion from some Independents that the life of the Dáil might be further extended rather than hold a wartime general election.[5]

Dillon's major preoccupation during the remainder of the Dáil was censorship. In the view of the author of the definitive study of wartime censorship, Donal Ó Drisceoil, Dillon was 'the most censored of all politicians, with heavy treatment given to his letters to the press and reports of his speeches in and out of the Dáil'.[6] On several occasions he locked horns with Frank Aiken on the issue. Their exchanges were personal and corrosive. Dillon alleged Aiken was misusing his powers and cited several instances where bona fide political criticism of the government by Fine Gael and Labour speakers had been censored, including parliamentary questions, criticism of government cereal policy and Norton's views on trade union legislation. Dillon thought the way his Árd Fheis speech had been censored was deliberately designed to damage Fine Gael. He repeated a charge he had made more than once before: that Aiken was biased in favour of the Axis powers, anxious to damp down anti-German feeling, and not fit to administer the affairs of the Department of Defence.[7] Dillon had the support of many colleagues from all opposition parties in saying this, and ironically too from MacDermot, whose very motives in questioning the policy of neutrality had once been categorised by Aiken as anti-patriotic.[8]

Aiken's easy use of the 'patriotic' card was echoed by many Fianna Fáil TDs and Senators, one of whom described censorship as a bulwark against the 'efforts of Quislings and the Fifth Columnists to embroil us in war'. In such a climate, Dillon worried that Aiken would abuse his powers even further, especially in an election situation, and 'when he does, it would be too late to fight back'.[9]

For his part, Aiken accused Dillon of nothing short of treachery, alleging that his speeches provided ammunition for the country's enemies: 'Dillon is the sort of crawler who says that it is treachery and disloyalty for the people of this country to take their own decisions on peace and war ... a man who has such a warped idea of loyalty cannot be relied upon when any question of honest loyalty is under discussion.' He justified censoring Dillon's speech on the grounds that 'it displayed a completely unhinged and unbalanced sense of loyalty ... contained falsehoods which, like previous falsehoods uttered by the Deputy, will, I fear, be used to prejudice our relations with foreign governments.'[10]

There was more, much more of the same. Aiken's use of censorship was heavy-handed and partisan, and in Dillon's case influenced by his personal antipathy to him. Dillon, for his part, did not see, or care to see, that his words could be misrepresented, or that he could be portrayed as expressing a more sizable body of opinion than was the case. Dillon's personal attacks on Aiken were offensive, and intended to be so, but to portray Dillon as treacherous or anti-democratic, as Aiken did, was patently false. In what he saw as the hour of supreme national danger, Aiken's response was authoritarian, if not totalitarian. It was Dillon's misfortune to be outside the national consensus, to have profoundly individual beliefs and the courage to insist on airing them.

The Dáil ended its life in this spirit of bad temper and mutual recrimination. Already the battle lines were being drawn for what would turn out to be a poisonous electoral campaign. The Dáil adjourned *sine die* on 26 May. It was not in fact dissolved, the old Dáil remaining in existence for the duration of the campaign lest the election be disrupted by a national emergency.

The 1943 election was nasty and bitter. Times were hard, the electorate was disgruntled, and its unhappiness was reflected in a swing to Labour and in the appearance of a new radical farmers' party, Clann na Talmhan. Fine Gael was in a sorry state and posed no real danger to the government, but Labour represented a threat to Fianna Fáil's urban vote, and Clann na Talmhan, with its sharp focus on the grievances of farmers, especially in the West of Ireland, hit into the party's western heartland.[11] Only this double threat can explain the performance of Sean MacEntee, who ran probably the most scurrilous and irresponsible electoral campaign in the history of the state. In a stream of frenzied vituperation which lasted until polling day, MacEntee variously accused Labour of being controlled by communists, of being in league with sinister groups determined to overthrow democratic rule, and of being 'honeycombed with agents of the Comintern'. He even ran an advertisement in the newspapers claiming that Labour had condoned the sinking of the Irish Shipping vessel, the *Irish Oak*,[12] so that the subsequent shortages would create conditions favourable to the development of 'Labour's pernicious doctrines'. Clann na Talmhan did not fare much better. According to MacEntee it was a 'totalitarian party', a party of 'spalpeens', communist in its outlook.[13]

Cosgrave, who had never been a bitter partisan, made national reconciliation the theme of this, his last election as party leader. He campaigned for the formation of a national government to ensure national unity in defence of neutrality and, he hoped, move the country a further step from Civil War politics.[14] He was wasting his time. Neither Labour nor Clann na Talmhan showed any interest and Fianna Fáil was openly contemptuous. Fianna Fáil, in an election campaign which did it no credit, now sought to make neutrality a party issue, casting doubts on the good faith and integrity of the other parties on this question – much to their justified anger.[15]

Fianna Fáil's worries about Labour and Clann na Talmhan were warranted. When the results came in, the party dropped ten seats. Fine Gael did even worse, losing thirteen, including those of Mulcahy and Costello. Clann na Talmhan won ten seats, Labour gained eight to give it seventeen, while there were twelve Independents, including a new and turbulent member for Laois–Offaly.

For Dillon it was a crucial election, his first test since resigning. Fine Gael ran a rival candidate, and though their campaign lacked conviction, Dillon could not take the support of his old organisation for granted. James Holland, one of his most influential backers, recalls that there was a great deal of questioning within the local Fine Gael party before deciding to support him. 'I remember in my own case having agonised for a week or more before deciding to follow him, even though the Dillon name meant so much to me ... I had some doubts as to whether we should divide the country on this issue, even though I was completely in favour of the Allied cause.'[16]

Most of his traditional supporters did rally round him and, as events transpired, he needed all of their support in a rough and turbulent campaign. One incident was exceptionally nasty. Dillon was due to address a meeting at Carrickmore where he was accompanied by Peter Nugent, Paddy Macklin and James Holland. The meeting was held outside the Catholic church, as was usually the case. The parish priest of Carrickmore, however, was an ardent supporter of de Valera and ferociously hostile to James Dillon. While Dillon sat in the congregation at Mass, Fr Crudden harangued him from the altar and declared that de Valera should have put him in jail.

When Mass was over Dillon went outside, mounted his chair and began his speech, loudspeaker in hand. He had barely started when Fr Crudden began to shout at him from the chapel gate, inciting the crowd not to give him a hearing. When Dillon answered, urging Fr Crudden to exercise some of 'the charity he had preached off the altar', the parish priest made a bee-line for Dillon and pulled him off the chair. The crowd rushed in and blows were aimed at Dillon. A free-for-all ensued until the presence of a few policemen helped restore order. Fr Crudden was moved away by the police, but the chorus of noise and abuse continued. Dillon was adamant that he wanted to continue the meeting, but when the police could not guarantee his safety he reluctantly agreed to leave.[17]

The Carrickmore incident was extreme, but a real reminder of the violence which lay just beneath the surface of politics. The episode showed that Dillon had physical as well as moral courage, and in a curious footnote, when he was approached by the Bishop of Clogher about Fr Crudden's role, he asked that no action be taken.

As for the election itself, Dillon was re-elected, but with a significantly reduced vote. His first-preference vote was down by 4,000 and he just about retained the third seat ahead of the Independent (Protestant) candidate, Haslett.

When the new Dáil met on 1 July, it reserved its fervour not for the election of the Taoiseach, in which de Valera beat Cosgrave by sixty-seven votes to thirty-seven, with Labour and Clann na Talmhan abstaining, but for the election of the government. All parties aired charges against Fianna Fáil, alleging jobbery and corruption in the filling of posts, but the real hostility came from Labour. Norton opposed MacEntee's renomination as a minister and attacked 'his characteristic flair for lies' during the campaign. He emphatically denied that Labour had communist links; the party, he said, was 'based on Papal Encyclicals and embraces the viewpoint of the Catholic Church in social and economic matters'.[18]

Dillon called for the formation of a national government in these 'abnormal times'. 'The election clearly signals that during this abnormal time the people want the party system suspended, but not abolished,' he argued. He predicted that if Fianna Fáil formed a government it would lead to instability – 'a protracted period of futile vacillation, culminating in a general election precipitated by the pique of Deputy de Valera' – and urged de Valera to invite Fine Gael, Labour and Clann na Talmhan into his cabinet. 'I do not believe in coalitions,' de Valera told him. 'I do not believe they will work.'[19]

The new Dáil represented a considerable break with the past. Forty-three TDs were taking their seats for the first time, and both Labour and Clann na Talmhan had a marked impact. But Labour soon lost momentum and missed the opportunity to take over as the major opposition party after its strong electoral performance. Before long it was utterly split on the question of alleged Communist Party influence. Out of it came two parties – Labour and National Labour – and the kind of personal bitterness that only an internal split can generate, as when the normally equable James Everett of National Labour accused the inoffensive William Davin of 'taking his instructions from Joe Stalin'.[20]

The initial impact in the new Dáil was made by Clann na Talmhan, which set out to show that it was not part of the established club. It had energy and anger, but little judgement, and lacked a leader of stature. Like the Centre Party of a decade earlier, one of its first targets was TDs' 'perks', in this case their tax-free allowance. Their motion on this issue merely succeeded in irritating other parties and Dillon, who had called for cuts in TDs' salaries a decade earlier, was scornful, declaring that the £9 a week he received as his parliamentary allowance meant he lost money by being a TD, a situation he thought applied to most members.[21]

Dillon had an instinctive sympathy for Clann na Talmhan's overall aims, but he soon spotted their lack of strategy and their unwillingness to press home the advantage their numbers gave them with a minority government. He had hard words for the party's abstention on the election of the government and on the re-appointment of Jim Ryan as Minister for Agriculture, a man whom Dillon regarded as a disaster in that job: 'Have you the courage to vote against him? ... At least we hard-bitten chaws are not professional weather-cocks ... Be a man, not a rabbit.' 'I expected to see volcanoes of energy in Clann na Talmhan,' he concluded: 'are you all going to die so early in your career?'[22]

Dillon saw Clann na Talmhan's potential and identified with the people who had sent them to Leinster House, the small farmers of the West, but that was not evident to the new TDs. Dillon soon found himself coming under fire from them, his stance on neutrality the target. Patrick Cogan of Wicklow called him a 'reckless, irresponsible Deputy ... who has not the physical or moral courage to take part in that conflict himself'.[23]

This and other such attacks from Clann na Talmhan did not deter Dillon from becoming involved in one of the nastiest episodes of the Dáil in December 1943, when an inexperienced Clann na Talmhan Deputy, Dominic Cafferky from Mayo, was verbally mauled by his Fianna Fáil constituency colleague, Micheál Ó Cléirigh. Dillon accused Ó Cléirigh of 'spraying Cafferky with filth', and reproached de Valera for 'keeping in hand a couple of bloodhounds'. He made an eloquent defence of Cafferky: 'The people of Mayo know Deputy Cafferky. They know his father and mother and all belonging to him ... honest people and decent neighbours.'[24]

The most spectacular new member in 1943 was Oliver J. Flanagan, elected on the Monetary Reform ticket for Laois–Offaly. Flanagan hit Leinster House and Irish politics like a whirlwind, lashing out indiscriminately, attacking all parties on his first day in the Dáil. He was a genuine populist with a flair for publicity, boundless energy, reckless and indiscriminating in his attacks – 'De Valera is bad but Cosgrave is worse'[25] – and none too scrupulous about the charges he levelled or where he levelled them. In his early days his sympathies were strongly nationalist, sympathetic to the IRA, anti-semitic and utterly anti-establishment.[26] He also had a great rapport with his constituents, an eye for local issues and an attention to local detail unknown at the time and which soon made him electorally impregnable.

There was little early affinity or common ground between Dillon and Flanagan. Flanagan was suspicious of Dillon and wasted no opportunity in insulting him, though it has to be said that Dillon was only one of many TDs who fell into this category. Dillon, he said, was the 'greatest hypocrite in the House', although in the same breath he called de Valera 'the greatest traitor ever'.[27] He spurned Dillon's well-intentioned efforts to teach him the rudiments of parliamentary procedure, a point noted by Frank Aiken one Question Time, when Flanagan seemed uncertain as to what to do next:

Aiken: 'The Deputy should get his pal Deputy Dillon to ask a supplementary question.'

Flanagan: 'Deputy Dillon is no pal of mine.'

Dillon: 'The Minister's attempt to insult me has failed.'[28]

Fine Gael had suffered more than any party in the 1943 election, and it was against this dismal background that Cosgrave resigned as party leader in early 1944. As he prepared to leave politics, he expressed his wish that the two main parties should move beyond their Civil War origins. He had signalled his intention of resigning some months earlier to enable the party arrange for an orderly succession, but that was not easy as Mulcahy, the most senior member, was not a TD at this point. Dillon's loss was now felt acutely, and in mid-December he was approached by McGilligan, who on behalf of his colleagues invited him to return to the party as leader in the Dáil; Mulcahy would be party president. Dillon considered the offer carefully but decided to turn it down. He wrote to McGilligan on 24 December 1943, telling him that while the war continued he could not return to the party, 'gladly as I would serve in different circumstances under Dick Mulcahy's leadership'.[29] When the Fine Gael parliamentary party met on 18 January 1944, Cosgrave announced his resignation and shortly afterwards Dr TF O'Higgins was elected chairman of the party and leader in the Dáil.[30]

Dillon might have accepted the offer. The whole focus of the war had now moved to the East and the question of the ports was no longer a priority with the Allies, but he felt that his views, so strongly expressed, were incompatible with leadership of Fine Gael and he could not in honour accept. It was to prove a costly decision. Had he been party leader or even deputy leader after Mulcahy returned to the front bench it is very likely that he and not Costello would have been the compromise choice as Taoiseach when the first Inter Party government was being formed.

The war continued to dominate the political agenda, and though the balance of forces tilted decisively in the Allies' favour as Hitler's armies retreated from the Russian Front, the balance of domestic opinion remained resolutely in favour of staying neutral in the conflict. Dillon's position had not changed either, and for the rest of the Dáil he would find the whole House set against him on this issue. In a major debate in November he warned of the danger of post-war estrangement between Ireland and the Allies: 'there is time yet to take measures to soften the asperity of the feelings ... we will not soften it by saying that asperity does not exist'. He feared that at the end of the war Ireland would find herself with few friends in Europe, Great Britain or the US, and would stand isolated in the post-war reconstruction.[31]

His contribution provoked outright hostility. One Clann na Talmhan TD, WR O'Donnell, told Dillon to 'set [a] good example. Get yourself killed.'[32] Cogan accused Dillon of deliberately worsening relations with the US: 'We are only a baby power and the wise course for a baby power is to act like a baby and make no noise.'[33] The most vicious attack of all came from Norton. Sabotage, malicious, insane and anti-Irish were just some of the epiteths he used. Dillon, while 'preferring comfort and smugness and complacency himself ... was willing to make his country a shambles and the homes of our people scenes of ruin and devastation'.[34]

Dillon faced up to his opponents: 'I am not one bit afraid of discharging what I conceive to be my duty in this House and so long as I stand in this House I will do it.' He did not question the right of the Irish people to choose the course they did, 'but it was my duty to define my point of view in this House and acceptance of that decision does not impose the duty of assent. I think it is wrong and that for all time it will be recorded against us as a mistake.'[35] He pointed out that de Valera was wrong to 'try to persuade deputies that there is only view about the consequences of the policy he has pursued. He did what he believed was best ... but the consequences of that policy will prove disastrous for our people ... estrangement between our people and the American people and between our people and the people of Great Britain.'[36]

De Valera was unmoved, and he bluntly accused Dillon of stirring up anti-Irish propaganda: 'As a good Irishman he should have striven to try to kill that propaganda and not to make balls for those who are opposed to us and attacking us abroad to fire.'[37] Dillon was taunted by Fianna Fáil backbenchers all through de Valera's speech, but he had his defenders, who vindicated not his views, but his right to express them. Cosgrave, in one of his last speeches in public life, called the attacks on Dillon 'hysterical' and described his contribution as 'statesmanlike'. He returned to a theme he had been touching on more and more in recent times, the need to bring Civil War differences to an end: 'In my view it would be much better, until this parliament grows up, until these two parties disappear out of public life, if international affairs were not discussed here, and in the interests of the advance of this country, the sooner that happens the better.'[38]

O'Higgins was his most staunch defender. 'He stands alone in this House and he stands alone here because he expressed views which were not in conformity with the views held by any of the parties in this House.' But O'Higgins concluded: 'if the day ever dawns when a majority here, even an overwhelming majority, attempts to gag any individual Deputy who, for expressing his own views is denounced as a malicious saboteur, then the malicious sabotage would be the responsibility of that majority and not of the individual.'[39]

One aspect of de Valera's policy which was rigorously applied during the war was internment. In all, over 500 were interned without trial and a further 600 committed under the Offences Against the State acts.[40] A number of attempts were made in the Dáil to change this policy, principally by the Labour Party, though Dillon's support for it did not waver. In April 1944 he answered Richard Corish's 'moderate and prudently worded appeal' to de Valera to release the internees by saying that 'so long as there are people, no matter how sincere, no matter how loud their protestations of patriotism may be, who claim the right to impose their will upon their neighbours by force of arms, then there will be and there should be internment'.[41]

Censorship became even more rigorous as the war entered its most decisive phase. Dillon was not to know it, but at least one telephone conversation between him and US Minister Gray was 'tapped'. The transcript revealed nothing of political significance, and it seems that it was Gray's phone which was under surveillance, but if there was one tap, there almost certainly were others.[42] Even replies to parliamentary questions were censored.[43] Dillon told the Dáil in April 1944 that Aiken's operation of censorship was 'characterised by a poisonous pro-Axis slant because the Minister's mind had been a pro-Axis mind from the start'. He attacked Aiken's 'pettiness' in refusing to allow newspapers print the name 'Kingstown' in Presbyterian Church notices – insisting that they adopt the new official name, Dún Laoghaire – and asked the Minister how using 'Kingstown' could be prejudicial to the safety of the state.[44] It was this intervention by Dillon which led Martin Corry to call for his internment: 'there are better men behind barbed-wire, men who did not do one-twentieth the harm that Deputy Dillon has done this nation this past four years'.[45]

The level of Allied pressure on de Valera intensified dramatically on 21 February 1944 when David Gray delivered a diplomatic note – the so-called American Note – to de Valera, in effect demanding the recall of the German and Japanese envoys from Ireland and the severing of diplomatic links with these countries. This message was followed by a British note a day later warmly endorsing the American 'initiative'. De Valera rejected the demand, and, looking on it as an ultimatum, put the army on alert. When the government gave no official explanation of what was happening, the country was swept by the wildest of rumours. There were reports that the Allies had invaded from Northern Ireland, that there were British battleships off the Dublin coast, that Mulcahy had been arrested and Dillon had been shot.[46] The matter only became public on 10 March when the US State Department published the note. Its publication was followed by a spate of anti-Irish hysteria in the American press. The net result in Ireland, however, was a move to rally behind de Valera in the hour of perceived national danger, significantly strengthening his political strength domestically.

The eleventh Dáil ended as Dillon has predicted. On 9 May the government was beaten by one vote on a motion to postpone the second stage of a Transport Bill until the Transport Tribunal had reported. The motion had merely sought to postpone the implementation of a Bill, and a confidence motion the next day would have secured de Valera in power, but with events moving rapidly in his favour, de Valera, after a midnight government meeting, drove to the Phoenix Park to inform President Hyde that he was dissolving the Dáil and calling an immediate general election for 30 May.[47]

The Dáil met the following day for an adjournment debate prior to dissolution. To the opposition the election was utterly unnecessary, a decision taken in pique and petulance. O'Higgins charged de Valera with constitutional sharp practice in seeking a dissolution without giving an opportunity for an alternative government to be formed. He had not consulted with the party leaders, with parliament or with the Defence Council at a time when it was clear a national government could easily and willingly have emerged. O'Higgins concluded that a 'narrow bigoted party government was not suited to the people or the nation in times of emergency'.[48] Norton charged de Valera with putting in jeopardy the unparalleled unity of the past years.[49]

As Dillon saw it, the Taoiseach should at least have allowed the Dáil to decide whether it wanted to elect a new Executive. Dillon, clearly in high good form, could not refrain from mentioning a book he was then reading: MJ McManus's uncritical *Life of de Valera*:

> The Fianna Fáil doctrine is that the Taoiseach hates politics, that he does not understand them, that he recoils from engaging in them and longs to govern this country from the Olympian calm of the Institute of Higher Studies, his dearest pride and joy, with an Olympian patience that understands everything and, understanding everything, forgives everything. Well it is a 'quare' picture of

the gentleman in a motor car, blazing through the night up to the Vice-Regal Lodge to get poor President Hyde out of his bed to sign the dissolution: the Olympian calm, the Olympian patience, the Institute of Higher Studies, and the President in his nightshirt tottering down the stairs to sign the dissolution.

At this point the Ceann Comhairle reprimanded Dillon for his reference to the President, so he turned to de Valera: 'There you are: the old warhorse is pawing the ground and sniffing the air. He thinks he is going to secure political advantage in a snap general election.'[50]

If that was de Valera's intention, he succeeded. The election which followed caught Labour divided and all the opposition parties with their resources depleted. The smaller parties ran far fewer candidates and Fine Gael failed to field any in four constituencies, including Monaghan. It was a quieter election than 1943, with Fianna Fáil making much of its resistance to the American Note and the need for a secure majority to 'protect neutrality'. Fine Gael campaigned again on a 'National Government' ticket, while the Labour campaign was as much concerned with its own internecine troubles as it was with the other parties. Dillon confined himself to one public statement on neutrality in which he defended his own position.

For Dillon, ironically, it was his best election yet. His vote increased by 3,000, he headed the poll and was elected on the first count. In getting this result he was helped by the absence of a Fine Gael candidate and of Haslett. At national level the election vindicated de Valera's judgement. Fianna Fáil gained eight per cent, with nine extra seats, while the combined Labour parties lost five seats. Fine Gael dropped a further two seats, while Clann na Talmhan and the Independents each lost one. Fianna Fáil once more had an overall majority. The only consolation for Fine Gael was Mulcahy's and Costello's return to the Dáil.

When the new Dáil met, Dillon did not oppose the election of de Valera on the basis that the people had given him a clear majority. For the first time since 1932 Labour opposed de Valera, though National Labour was part of his comfortable eighty-one to thirty-seven majority. Quiet as the election campaign had been, it had not improved the temper of the House. MacEntee's campaign had again drawn blood, and Dillon among others assailed him, to no great effect, it should be added.[51] It was almost as if there were two MacEntees: the urbane, civilised, sophisticated MacEntee of the social circuit and the bare-knuckled, unscrupulous street-fighter of electoral politics. Corry once again called for Dillon's internment. The scrapping across the floor effectively counted for little.[52] De Valera had a secure majority in a dispirited Dáil which all too accurately reflected the general temper of a demoralised country.

Hardly surprising, then, that little of note should happen between now

and the end of the war. Fianna Fáil, seemingly impervious to political pitfalls, behaved more and more as if it were the permanent administration,
impatient and increasingly imperious.

Dillon's only major intervention on the war question came during the
External Affairs debate in June 1944, which took place just as the Allies
landed at Normandy to begin their reconquest of Europe. Dillon returned
to one of his themes, the need to plan for the post-war world. He put great
emphasis on the neccessity of building a proper road network, and plan for
thirty years ahead under a single national roads authority. He also called for
an ambitious scheme of public enterprises: 'we must not shy away from
undertaking great enterprises because they appear to cost a lot. This is a
time when we should mobilise credit and use it boldly – and if necessary
repay it over the next 100 years.'[53]

Dillon took a singular line when he regretted the government's unwillingness to respond positively to the US request to exclude the German and
Japanese ministers from Ireland. He contrasted the USA and Britain's reaction to Ireland's refusal with the reaction of the Axis powers when they
had had similar requests refused in other countries – they had bombed
Rotterdam and destroyed the Dutch nation. 'Rightly, in my judgement,
they [the US] felt entitled as a sovereign government and, as they believe,
an old friend, to ask us frankly for something in our gift which they felt was
of great value to them if we were in a position to give it to them, but the
moment we indicated our reluctance ... the US instantly acknowledged our
rights.'[54]

His words angered an increasingly irritable de Valera. In spite of Dillon's
many attacks, de Valera had always retained a certain affection for Dillon,
but now de Valera was angry and accused Dillon of misrepresenting the
attitude of his government to the US. He denied that the Irish people were
indifferent to the war's outcome – a point with which Dillon agreed – but
pointed out the difficulty of his own position. 'My official duty is to say
and maintain that as a State we have adopted and are pursuing a policy of
neutrality.' De Valera then turned on Dillon personally: 'There are things
which Deputy Dillon's remarks suggest to me to say to him, but I refrain
from saying them. They have been said in this House already and, if he is
ashamed, as he says, of the attitude of our people on this particular matter,
I must say that most of us are ashamed of a person who expresses views
such as he has, and does not himself personally act in accordance with
them.'[55]

That was the last major discussion on the war for almost a year, as the
Dáil contented itself with the routine activities of parliamentary business.
From his Independent seat, Dillon hit out at all sides where he thought fit.
His relations with some of the other parties had a hard edge to them at

times, and he gave as good as he got in jousts with Fine Gael and Clann na Talmhan, but this was fencing across the chamber and never went beyond it.[56] However, an allegation by Patrick Cogan, who said Dillon had made 'a huge profit out of galvanised iron when cornering the market',[57] did cause him concern. Cogan's source, it appears, was a Roscommon Clann na Talmhan TD, John Finan, who claimed first-hand experience, but how one shop in the West of Ireland could 'corner' the market was never explained and no evidence was ever produced to back up the charge. Cogan refused to withdraw the allegation, however, while Fianna Fáil clearly saw its potential. The following year, in May 1946 a Fianna Fáil TD, Louis J. Walsh, asked Cogan why he was failing to press the issue. That December a note in Irish attached to a Dáil reply prepared for the Parliamentary Secretary to the Taoiseach suggested that if Dillon intervened the question of the galvanised iron should be thrown at him. Dillon utterly rejected the charges, but it was the beginning of a sustained acrimonious relationship with Cogan, who described Dillon as 'an evil genius', and which was to have serious consequences a few years later.[58]

Curiously too, in the light of their subsequent friendship, Dillon's relations with Oliver Flanagan showed no signs of improving as the Dáil neared its year's end. In an immediate post-war debate, Flanagan, who asked that Ireland would look after William Joyce (Lord Haw Haw) and who 'hoped Hitler was still alive', and who *inter alia* did not believe the Constitution should recognise the Jewish congregation, incurred the full force of his Independent colleague's wrath.[59]

The war ended in May 1945, but as far as the Dáil was concerned the event might as well have happened on a different planet – the first debate on the matter did not take place for a further eight weeks. Dillon, however, was quick to demand a speedy dismantling of the emergency legislation, something de Valera was reluctant to promise.[60] On 4 July a Bill was introduced ending censorship, summary trials by army personnel and the power to arrest and search without warrants, but keeping in place other sections of the legislation including the right to intern. Opposition to the new Bill was led by Dillon and Costello, who attacked de Valera's 'reluctance to trust the House or to rely on ordinary legislation, now that the war was over'. The Bill, however, passed with a comfortable majority.[61]

Now that the war was over, even if the Dáil was yet to formally acknowledge that fact, Dillon could turn his attention to other matters. These did not include any acknowledgement of the skill and diplomatic finesse de Valera had displayed in maintaining neutrality through some very difficult times, nor any appreciation of the fact that de Valera's neutrality had been heavily weighed in favour of the Allies. He was, however, generous in his praise of Lemass, whom he felt had done a good job in maintaining supplies. Not that praise came easily: 'in dealing with Fianna Fáil I am always reluctant to give praise where praise is due, because magnanimity has perished in the soul of Fianna Fáil'.[62] In fact, praise or magnanimity were rare on all sides in a surly parliament.

Dillon's emphasis on post-war reconstruction has already been mentioned, but he was also concerned with the actual status of the state, a question which had been left unanswered in the 1937 Constitution, he said. He asked de Valera repeatedly 'whether or not Ireland is a Republic?' eventually goading de Valera into his celebrated dictionary definition of the Republic. Dillon poured scorn on this, finding it 'degrading that we are obliged to deal in dictionary definitions', and declaring that he would admire de Valera 'if he would openly declare a Republic'. He did not say, however, if he would himself support such a declaration.[63]

Finally, on 17 July, the Dáil formally debated the ending of the war. For most members there was a sense of relief that Ireland's sovereignty had been respected and that the country had survived. Any foreboding there might have been about Ireland's future in a war-ravaged Europe, where few if any debts were outstanding and Churchill's scalding and scornful remarks were still fresh in people's minds, were brushed aside in the general air of self-congratulation. For de Valera in particular it was a vindication of his leadership, and of a policy which had stood the only test that mattered – success. Ireland had emerged from the war with its independence recognised, its economy intact, its people safe.

For Dillon, the lone critic of this policy, there might at this point have been forgiveness – had he sought it. Instead, he was not just unapologetic about his stand but defiant, and reaffirmed his commitment to Ireland's continuing membership of the Commonwealth of Nations, seeing it also as a means of building a bridge to Northern Protestants. He was critical of de Valera's message of condolence on the death of Hitler – 'Nazism was something loathsome – the German Minister was a representative of Nazism' – and made another attack on Aiken as having Nazi sympathies, something vehemently denied by de Valera.[64] By now de Valera had had enough of Dillon:

'I hate to say it but I think it is right I should say it, if I had the feelings personally that Deputy Dillon has I would not be asking my nation to go out and fight. I would go out and fight myself.'

Dillon: 'You said that before and it does you no good.'

'You coward!' came from a Fianna Fáil seat.

The insults hit home. Dillon was anxious to defend his honour, especially when de Valera accused him once again of 'not behaving courageously'.

Dillon: 'Does the Taoiseach not know I was the first Deputy to volunteer for the Irish Army and that my call-up papers were cancelled by the Taoiseach who expressed the desire I should not be called up?'

De Valera: 'If I have the audacity to stand up and talk about the things that were said to me in question and the duty of our people to go out and fight for these things – hang it, so long as there was no law against it, I would have gone like hundreds of Irishmen have gone.'[65]

It was probably the most bruising encounter Dillon had ever had in the Dáil. There was little friendliness or understanding of his position from any side. He was assailed from the Fianna Fáil benches by one backbencher in particular, Bernard Butler, who accused him of having Nazi sympathies, of being 'a real live Lord Haw Haw':

He stands alone; abhorred by this party, cast out by the Fine Gael party, avoided by Labour, shunned like a plague by Clann na Talmhan. He stands alone ... in abject isolation.[66]

It was a bitter moment. A lesser man might well have buckled under the pressure, especially if, like Dillon, he had other options such as law or business and was still young enough to avail of them. These thoughts, however, never seemed to have occurred to him. He had shown moral courage of a rare kind; he had defied antipathy and the loss of friends in defence of a principle, and in this darkest moment there was no question of quitting.

More than that, it was a stand which had cost much and delivered little. It had not changed policy; nor had it ever been likely to. Dillon's policy, had it been implemented, might well have made Ireland a target for German bombs, at least in the early part of the war, and split the fragile unity of the country. Dillon was realistic enough to know all this, but he knew too that in the event of a German victory, a possibility that had been very likely in 1941-42, Ireland's neutrality would count for nothing. In a Nazi-dominated world the country would find itself annexed, if not incorporated in the Reich, just as completely as France had been. Dillon had had no doubt that Quislings and collaborators would have emerged, parliament would have disappeared, the Constitution would have been suspended and a new barbarism imposed. He wanted no part in such a future, neither for himself nor for Ireland, and it was to prevent it happening that he argued Ireland should do all in its power to aid those who alone could crush Nazism. External factors ultimately ensured his fears were unrealised, but his fears were real in 1941 and 1942, frighteningly so – they were neither rhetorical nor emotional, but based on a hard reading of the international situation. He was, in all of this, neither a scaremonger nor a publicity seeker, but that rare example of a public man prepared to endure near universal odium in pursuit of the truth as he saw it.

CHAPTER THIRTEEN

SOMETHING ROTTEN
SOMETHING STAGNANT

'This is the spectacle we are being entertained to now – himself [de Valera] and the cosmic physicist sitting over in Merrion Square rise in the cosmic ether while the ignoramuses of the Fine Gael, Labour and Clann na Talmhan parties are occupying themselves with old-age pensions and cows and contemptible considerations of that kind.'
Dillon, Dáil Debates, 13 February 1947

DILLON CONTINUED TO view the post-war world from his perch high on the back benches, habitually occupying the seat to the extreme right of the Fine Gael positions, where he was strategically well placed to observe and comment on all that happened in the chamber. Not much was, however. It was a lethargic assembly, little invigorated by the influx of twenty new members in 1944 or by the arrival of Clann na Talmhan. It was a small assembly, but not particularly intimate: while the battle lines of the Civil War remained intact there was little socialising across party lines. The government regarded the opposition with outright hostility. Consultation was rare and co-operation minimal, and while Fianna Fáil ministers might occasionally consult with their own backbenchers, even on technical matters the very thought of conceding a point to the opposition was viewed as a sign of weakness.

The opposition were not seen as partners in a parliamentary process so much as enemies to be kept in their place. Starved of information and denied any real opportunity to participate, and with committees still decades away, there was little scope for opposition members to be other than negative and perennially suspicious, and political debate was usually raw, personal and bruising as a result. Conditions for TDs were primitive, too – Dillon had no office or secretary and only limited access to a phone – and the Dáil was not particularly busy. It sat for only fifty days in 1945 and much the same in 1946, and for most of this time it was in a torpor; attendances were low, with as many as half the members – many of whom were part-time politicians – absent for many votes. It was a parliament which the government, secure in its sense of permanence, took more and more for granted.

At the same time, Ireland was growing more and more isolated in a post-war world from which it had stood apart since 1939. It had been spared the physical devastation and human carnage of war, but had to endure shortages and rationing and was without much of the raw materials needed to rebuild its economy. It was an unsettled, acrimonious time, dreary with unfulfilled expectation as the population looked for a return to normality, even a taste of prosperity. Public dissatisfaction manifested itself in a series of prolonged strikes, continuing emigration, the appearance of a new political party, and a general willingness to believe that a government long grown complacent could also be tainted with corruption.

The post-war agenda was dominated by the economy. Between 1939 and 1946 the cost of living index rose by two-thirds, while the average weekly wages of industrial workers rose by just one-third. Shortages were severe, rationing continued, and increases in inflation were met by wage standstill orders. The government conveyed little sense of urgency in tackling these matters. Lemass alone exuded energy and purpose. His Department of Industry and Commerce was now an important interventionist department, with the capacity to influence industrial policy both in broad thrust and minute detail through the many controls, directives and licences it had taken in its grasp during the war years. The granting or withholding of a licence could mean the difference between profit and loss, and such were the numbers seeking them that a popular view emerged that political influence was more often than not the main factor in deciding which companies got them.

The fact that this was not so – and that the evidence suggests that Lemass and his department behaved in an objective and business-like way – was belied by the appearance of a new class of businessmen, most of whom were identified with industries which had been founded behind the wall of tariff protection, and many of whom were openly identified with Fianna Fáil. In these circumstances the opposition parties, whatever the evidence or lack of it, were prepared to concede little to the government. Neither did they offer much recognition of the enormous problems Lemass faced in finding raw materials, or giving direction to a lethargic industrial sector.[1]

Lemass was already well on the way to abandoning the core elements of his 1930s' policies, even if he still clung to the language of protection and self-sufficiency. He was now outlining an economic strategy which encouraged industrial activity based on imported raw materials, and engaging in international discussions aimed at reducing tariffs. He was also exploiting the opportunities created by worldwide scarcities to establish Ireland in international trade, and emphasising the importance of the British market for Irish exports. It was as if the *cordon sanitaire* of the 1930s had never existed and the words 'self-sufficiency' had never been uttered.

The change was highlighted by Dillon during the Industry and Commerce Estimate in early 1947, when he welcomed Lemass's conversion to 'economic orthodoxy', even if the process had cost the country dearly. Dillon wanted to go much further. He looked forward to the development of a giant free-trade area made up of the countries of the Commonwealth and the USA, which would allow for the maximum free passage of men, money and goods. He saw this as involving no infringement of national sovereignty, no interference by one state in the affairs of another, but thought such a step was essential both for the industrial countries who needed new markets and for food-producing countries like Ireland who would have 'unlimited markets for their produce'.[2]

He still saw Irish prosperity as being tied to agriculture and its exports, with little possibility of wide-scale industrialisation. For the moment, however, Dillon could only commend Lemass for moving in what he saw as the right direction, while at the same time attacking him for the sleight of hand which prevented Lemass from saying openly that his earlier policies were being quietly abandoned. Lemass, ever the realist, was not in the business of public repentance. He knew that the only way he would bring his party with him was by continuing to mouth the old verities while quietly dismantling them.

DILLON DID not easily let go of issues arising in the aftermath of the Second World War. The government's decision to ban the British Legion's Armistice Day parade in November 1945, partly at least because it feared attacks from IRA supporters, greatly angered Dillon. His protests had little impact, but on the question of Adolf Mahr he was more effective, forcing the government to reverse its position.[3]

Mahr had been Director of the National Museum up until 1939, during which time he was also a member of the Nazi party, which had a small but influential presence in Dublin. He returned to Germany when war broke out and was an enthusiastic and senior Nazi for the duration of the conflict. After his release from an Allied internment camp, where he had been ill-treated, Mahr tried to return to his old job at the National Museum; his position had remained unfilled in his absence. De Valera, who knew of Mahr's Nazi past, was nonetheless sympathetic.

Dillon had some indication of the government's intentions and raised the matter in the Dáil in December 1945. 'If this gentleman turns up tomorrow with the battle-stained flag of Nazi Germany wrapped around him,' he asked, 'will he be reinstated in this position?'[4]

At this intervention the government bade a hasty retreat, and Mahr's proposed return was aborted. The matter did not end there, however. A year later Dillon and Aiken had a bruising encounter on the issue, when Aiken accused Dillon of taking advantage of the Dáil 'to abuse everybody, right, left and centre, to kick people who are down, but I say this for that gentleman, that he went towards the fighting, unlike Deputy Dillon'. There was more in a similar vein, with Aiken asserting that Dillon had raised the issue to please 'the enemies of this country abroad', while one Fianna Fáil TD told Dillon he should have been interned during the war and another declared 'he should have been shot'.

Dillon, however, was resolute. While most Irish people might at this stage have been prepared to forgive and forget as far as Mahr was concerned, Dillon was not. He believed that some of de Valera's ministers, and Aiken in particular, were so driven by anti-English feeling as to be supporters of Hitler and the Nazis. This he was not prepared to forgive either.[5]

THE EXTENT of Fianna Fáil patronage in these years is hard to quantify, but that it existed is not in question. Opposition TDs complained loudly and frequently that representations by them to government departments were sidelined in favour of government Deputies, giving a clear message to voters that if you wanted something done the only effective route was through the Fianna Fáil organisation. Increasingly it seemed that party membership was the key to many public appointments, whether it was as a road ganger, a CIE worker, or to the judiciary. Fianna Fáil defended its position, arguing that they were merely redressing the balance of the early years of the state, and that given the level of Fianna Fáil support in the country it would be surprising if many positions were not filled by Fianna Fáil supporters, 'all other things being equal'.[6]

The reality was that Fianna Fáil was a tough, effective political machine and behaved accordingly. Having got power it was determined to hold it, and patronage was one – and only one – way of tightening its control. But at a time of fragmented opposition, of shortages, rationing and wage standstills, and with the government appearing increasingly certain of its own invincibility, it was easy for those excluded from the inner circles to feel angry and frustrated. This sense of frustration, and the generally miserable state of the country, helped give much credence to a series of events which amounted to very little individually, but together gave the impression of a government out of touch and prone to cronyism, favouritism and corruption.

The war had created the atmosphere for such a climate. Lemass may have been ruthless in dealing with black marketeers and those who abused the allocation of vital and scarce supplies, but too many people believed there was favouritism and that it was rampant. Dillon, on his Carna holiday, for

example, noted that while everyone else had to go by bike or public transport, the 'Fianna Fáil barrister' had no difficulty getting petrol. The
assumption, rightly or wrongly, was that this was so because of the 'Fianna
Fáil connection'. Dillon's observation could be multiplied a thousand
times, and there was little the government could do to counter it.

Then there were the political appointments. Dillon had protested
strongly in 1942 when Ruttledge, the Minister for Justice, resigned his
ministry and took up the position of Ward of Court, clearly an undemanding post as Ruttledge continued to hold his Dáil seat for many years later.
In 1945, when Mayo TD Mícheál Ó Cléirigh was appointed County
Registrar for Dublin, even though Ó Cléirigh resigned from the Dáil
Dillon saw the appointment as an acceptance by de Valera of standards he
would have roundly condemned a decade earlier.[7] As far as Dillon was concerned it was jobbery, no more and no less. This view was widely shared.

Another factor contributing to this general air of distrust was a series of
court cases arising out of the 1945 Seanad elections, when allegations were
made that some Senators had 'bought' votes. Court cases ensued and one
councillor was jailed. A Dáil debate on a Fine Gael motion to reform the
system followed, and during the course of that debate Davin of Labour,
among others, alleged that there could have been several other such court
cases, so widespread was the corruption. Dillon went even further: 'There
is no use in being mealy-mouthed about it; the truth of it is that the elected
Senators have among them a number who have bought their seats.'[8]

That debate did lead to a limited extension of the electorate, though that
measure was not enough for Dillon, who wanted much more fundamental
reform. The exchanges in the Dáil also gave evidence of an increasingly
fractious and bad-tempered parliament. Dillon greatly annoyed de Valera
when he disparaged the quality of his nominees to the Upper House, 'a
clutch of duds who could get neither into the Senate nor into any other
sane body in Europe by the free vote of anybody'.[9]

De Valera lashed back at Dillon, accusing him of 'exuding slime and soiling public life ... fortunately our people know Deputy Dillon ... when he
attacks us in the filthy way he does he is damaging not me, not the men
and women who have been nominated, but he is soiling the whole of our
public life.'[10]

The first TD to come under Dáil scrutiny for alleged political misbehav-
iour was Robert Briscoe, a Fianna Fáil backbencher. The Briscoe
controversy arose out of a court case in 1945, where it emerged in the
course of evidence that Briscoe had received loans from companies on
whose behalf he had made representations to various government departments. The sums involved were not large: there were ten loans of £50 each
and all had been repaid. Dillon attempted to raise the matter on several

occasions with the Ceann Comhairle on the grounds that the court evidence gave legitimate grounds for the *prima facie* suspicion that a transaction took place which was not in accordance with the standards of conduct which would be required of a Deputy. The matter was finally allowed into discussion on 15 May 1946 on a motion in Dillon's name. For Dillon, the net issue was: 'Is it becoming conduct in a Deputy of Dáil Éireann, when approached by his constituent for assistance to secure his legal rights, having heard his constituent's representations and having indicated his readiness to serve him, to say "will you lend me £50?"'[11]

De Valera agreed with Dillon that Briscoe had been unwise, but not dishonest, and that the case did not warrant a Dáil inquiry as he demanded. Dillon's motion was defeated, but no member of any opposition party supported Fianna Fáil. The debate also showed Dillon that his own behaviour was not above attack, when a Fianna Fáil TD, LJ Walsh, reopened the issue of the galvanised-steel sales. This question was to surface again before the end of the year, though no evidence was produced to substantiate the charge.[12]

The Briscoe issue was not in itself important, but it was nonetheless an embarrassment for the government. And difficult though it was, the incident quickly paled into insignificance with the appearance of the Dr Ward case, which has long since entered Irish political folklore.

Dr Ward we have met already. Tough and able, he was regarded as a formidable opponent at constituency level. He had been Parliamentary Secretary to the Minister for Public Health and Local Government since 1932 and during much of that time he was effectively in charge of the Department of Health. De Valera was now preparing to set up a separate Ministry of Health and Ward was certain to be the first minister. At a personal level, however, he appears to have had very few friends in Leinster House; his parliamentary manner was brusque and he made little attempt to accommodate opposition questioning. There was, however, universal acceptance of his competence and dedication in the health area. In *Health, Medicine and Politics,* Ruth Barrington described Ward as 'highly intelligent ... ambition matched with great energy and toughness, but his tough and abrasive personality won him few friends ... feared and respected by his officials rather than liked ... a good judge of ability, he refused to work with or support the promotion of officers whom he considered to be incompetent. He also earned the bitter dislike of the medical profession.'[13]

The controversy arose out of a falling-out between Ward and another leading Fianna Fáil supporter, Dr Patrick MacCarvill. MacCarvill was a respected physician, formerly of Monaghan but now living in Dublin. His brother, Johnny, was manager and secretary of the Monaghan Curing Company, of which Ward was the managing director. Johnny MacCarvill was also a leading member of Fianna Fáil in Monaghan, and it was Ward's decision to dismiss him from his post in the Curing Company which caused the problem.

On 22 May 1946, Dr MacCarvill wrote to de Valera making several allegations against Ward. De Valera clearly felt that they were sufficiently serious and their source sufficiently weighty to warrant the establishment of a tribunal to investigate them. Without making any apparent investigations of his own, he brought the matter to an unsuspecting Dáil on 5 June.[14]

There was considerable bad blood behind the making of the allegations. MacCarvill was a skin specialist and former president of the Irish Medical Association. He and Ward had been close friends as young men and during the Civil War had acted as locum for each other. According to Ruth Barrington, 'the bad feeling between the two was a symptom of the wider antagonism that had developed between Dr Ward and the [medical] profession. He was hated because of the high-handed way he dealt with medical issues ... The profession was particularly alarmed about the prospect of Dr Ward's becoming Minister for Health.'[15]

The allegations against Ward can be summarised as follows: he expected that he would soon be a minister and thus no longer able to continue as managing director of the Curing Company. To offset the financial loss this would cause him, Johnny MacCarvill was to be sacked and replaced by Ward's son, who would act as both manager and managing director. This, it was alleged, was the culmination of a well-established pattern of nepotism on Ward's part.

The charges then broadened out. It was alleged that there were undisclosed cash sales and that quota arrangements with the state's Pigs and Bacon Commission had been broken. A further series of allegations centred on the fact that Ward had a 'hidden system' by which he drew fifty per cent of the salary attaching to the position of Medical Officer of Monaghan, and that he had intimidated doctors who would not agree with this arrangement. A further allegation referred to the building of a local Fianna Fáil hall in Monaghan which allegedly ended up in Dr Ward's possession.

Nothing like this had happened in the Dáil before. De Valera rose in the chamber and read, first MacCarvill's letter, then letters from MacCarvill's solicitor, Darach Connolly, which amplified some of the original charges and stressed in particular Ward's failure to make proper income returns to the Revenue Commissioners.[16]

Dillon, who might have been expected to glory in Ward's discomfiture, took a totally opposite view. He angrily interrupted de Valera as he read Connolly's letter:

'What has Dáil Eireann got to do with the private activities of Dr Ward or the management of his business? ... is there anything in all these documents relevant to his conduct as a Deputy of Dáil Éireann?'

'I think so,' de Valera replied and continued reading. Dillon intervened again: 'It is detestable that in this way we should pry into these allegations on the floor of the House. Dr Ward is my colleague in the representation of County Monaghan and I ask that his personal honour be afforded the protection that would be afforded to any Deputy of this House.'[17]

De Valera agreed with Dillon on this point, and he revealed that his decision to establish a tribunal was to a great extent influenced by Ward, who had vehemently denied all the charges against him as 'a malicious libel' and asked for a judicial inquiry, and to be relieved of his duties while it was pending. Ward was also willing to issue a writ for libel and take the matter to the courts, but de Valera insisted that to do so he would have to resign as Parliamentary Secretary, which in itself would almost certainly prejudge his case.[18]

Dillon was the first speaker after de Valera. He acknowledged that Ward and himself were not on cordial terms but argued that a tribunal should confine itself to Ward's conduct as Parliamentary Secretary: 'Let us not usurp, even through a special tribunal, the function of the Court. Dr Ward's honour is untarnished unless and until these charges can be proved before a competent Court, capable of investigating them satisfactorily.'

He was also worried about procedures, and whether any set of allegations about a man's private business could now lead to a tribunal being established.[19] He felt they were establishing a precedent which could prove a bitter injury to a member of the House 'and do great harm to Ward's splendid family'.[20]

Opinion was divided among opposition members, but both Mulcahy and Norton supported the setting up of a tribunal, while Blowick and some Fine Gael TDs supported Dillon. The vote on the establishment of the tribunal reflected this difference of opinion but was comfortably carried by sixty-four votes to seventeen.

The tribunal opened on 25 June and sat for nine days. Wartime censorship had been lifted and newspapers were back to their pre-war size, with the result that the proceedings were carried with full and frequently colourful detail. As so often in cases like this, it was the smaller issues which caught the public imagination, in particular the revelation that the factory had been engaged in under-the-counter deals and that sub-standard bacon, 'tainted and covered in slime', had been sold to the army. Ward, it seemed, had not complied with regulations devised by his own government.

However, when the tribunal reported on 6 July it exonerated Ward of all the major allegations.[21] He had acted 'in what he considered to be the best interests of the Company' in dismissing MacCarvill; there had been no impropriety in the appointment of replacement doctors; the allegations of intimidation of replacement doctors 'had been made recklessly and without justification' and he had behaved with strict propriety with regard to the Fianna Fáil hall at Carrickroe. But the tribunal did find that there had been cash transactions of just under £3,000 which had not been disclosed by the company or the directors personally for tax purposes, and that sales had not been returned to the Pigs and Bacon Commission as required by law.

Though Ward had been absolved on most of the issues, it was clear the public mood was hostile to him and that his case had been damaged both by the allegations and by some of the tribunal evidence. This much was clear from de Valera's reaction. On 11 July he opened the debate on the tribunal's report by reading a letter from Ward in which he claimed he had been vindicated and in particular that it was his intention to restore the proceeds of the cash sales to the accounts of the company; he also said that, if items of inferior or damaged bacon were included in the cash sales, this was done without his knowledge or consent. Ward felt, however, that the report raised issues which might embarrass the government 'were I to continue to discharge my official duties', and he resigned.[22] His resignation was sensational, the first time in the history of the state that a minister had stepped down for alleged personal impropriety.

De Valera made no attempt to defend Ward or to comment on the letter. In effect, he threw his minister to the mercy of the opposition. There was none. Mulcahy wanted to know what the government was going to do about Ward's tax evasion and breach of the Pigs and Bacon Commission rules.[23] Norton attacked Ward's alleged abuse of ministerial privilege and the fact that he would still get a ministerial pension; the factory, he said, had been a 'cesspool of intrigue and friction from beginning to end', and he attacked the impropriety of a minister being involved with a company which dealt with a range of government departments for quotas, licences and the like. 'If we make laws for the citizens,' he concluded, 'we ought to keep them.'[24]

There was a general opinion that de Valera had handled the matter badly and should have dismissed Ward; that he should now resign from the House and not be given a pension. Only Lemass made any real attempt to defend him. He said the loss of office was a huge blow to Ward and promised that if the law had been broken then the law would take its course, starting with the state bodies, the Revenue and the Pigs and Bacon Commission. Lemass also made the point which Dillon (who did not take part in this debate) had stressed when the tribunal was being set up: that Ward was in the invidious position where he had to prove himself innocent rather than 'not guilty'.[25]

The lack of support from his own party deeply angered Ward, who was to bring his feelings of grievance and hurt with him to the grave. The debate was resumed on 11 July when de Valera, in accepting Ward's resignation as Parliamentary Secretary, further angered the opposition by confirming that Ward would get his pension, 'to which he was by law entitled'.[26] Ward, however, had had enough. On 11 September he wrote to the government Whip claiming he had been the victim of a conspiracy, and on 16 September resigned from the Fianna Fáil party. He also alleged that the government had had facts in its possession which would have vindicated him, but these had not been used. What seemed to rankle most, though, was that while MacCarvill's accusations about the way he had discharged his public duties had proved baseless, he had been treated by de Valera as if he were a public benefactor. Ward said he would be 'guided by his constituents' as to whether he would resign his Dáil seat as well as resigning from Fianna Fáil.[27] In the event he did not, but he never attended Leinster House again and did not stand in the 1948 general election.

It was a rough and brutal end to a promising ministerial career, but it was far from being the end of the matter. The Ward case had given a hungry opposition a great deal of unexpected ammunition, and the bacon, whether 'stale and musty' or 'green and slimy', was to feature large in political and public debate. Within a year, the drama and impact of the Ward case would itself be eclipsed by the Locke's Distillery issue.

THAT YEAR saw little improvement in government fortunes. The 1945 presidential election had already indicated a growing 'Fianna Fáil versus the rest' mentality, when the transfers of Independent Republican Dr Patrick McCartan went by a margin of over four to one to Sean MacEoin of Fine Gael rather than to Fianna Fáil's Sean T. O'Kelly. A decade earlier such transfers would have been inconceivable. Then in July 1946 Clann na Poblachta was launched, born out of a committee set up to help Republican prisoners during the war and fuelled by much the same type of Republican radicalism which had swept Fianna Fáil to power in 1932. It was led by Sean MacBride, a former Chief of Staff of the IRA and an old friend of Dillon's from Mount St Benedict, described by Professor JJ Lee as: 'twenty years younger than de Valera, with energy to match his boundless ambition, a highly developed self-righteousness, a somewhat exotic accent as befitted his French education, immense debating skill as befitted an accomplished barrister.'[28]

Clann na Poblachta threatened Fianna Fáil's core vote and constituted the first real challenge the party had seen in a decade, a fact Fianna Fáil was quick to recognise. Dillon thought Clann na Poblachta represented 'a sort of pure-souled version of Republicanism'. Like many other movements of that kind, 'it was so pure as to be almost incredible, but it provided a very convenient landing ground for people who all their lives had been stalwart Fianna Fáil supporters, but who were now disillusioned and yet did not wish to commit the fearful treason of voting Fine Gael.'[29]

Recognising that none of the present parties was strong enough to impress itself on the country as an alternative government, and arguing that therein lay the strength of Fianna Fáil, in September 1946 O'Higgins had raised the possibility of developing fuller co-operation between the opposition parties. He called on them to combine – if amalgamation was impossible, they could nonetheless present a common panel of candidates – and he maintained that he had never seen any major policy differences between Fine Gael, Clann na Talmhan, the farmers and Independents. Dillon and Cogan were willing to support the proposition, he said. Though he had not included either of the Labour parties or the new Clann na Poblachta in his proposal, O'Higgins had put the inter-party idea on the agenda.[30]

In general, however, it was events rather than the opposition which caused most of the government's problems. A prolonged teachers' strike from May to October left a bitter taste in the mouths of teachers. The bad weather of autumn 1946 led to a very poor harvest and was followed by the hardest winter of the century, bringing fuel shortages, power failures and bread rationing. Labour relations were poor and strikes increasingly frequent, while Lemass's sensible attempts to reorganise a fissiparous and almost anarchical trade union structure was thrown out by the Supreme Court. In Mayo, two Clann na Talmhan TDs, Bernard Cummins and Dominic Cafferkey, each served thirty days in Sligo jail in February 1947 because of their involvement in a bitter land dispute.[31] The same month, the government had to endure a re-run of the Ward case when it introduced a supplementary estimate to pay Ward's tribunal costs. Hostility against Fianna Fáil was now unrestrained. According to Norton, the estimate represented a 'brazen piece of roguery' by the government, while Ward 'was now so pouty that he will not even attend the Dáil, notwithstanding the fact that he gets an allowance of £480 per annum'.[32]

The once radical government had now become arthritic, and further paralysed by internal differences. The Fianna Fáil monolith and the absence of enquiring journalism ensured that these differences remained hidden, but by now there was a war of attrition between MacEntee and senior Finance officials on one side, and the expansionist Lemass on the other, with de Valera refusing to come down decisively in favour of either one. The net effect was an absence of direction and clarity.[33] This, combined with the hard times and the arrival of Clann na Poblachta, resulted in a poor Fianna Fáil performance in the 1947 local elections, their losses going mainly to the new Republican party.

This was the background against which the Locke case erupted. The matter first arose in the Dáil on 22 October 1947 with questions from the Meath Fine Gael TD, Captain Patrick Giles, and Oliver Flanagan about the proposed sale of Locke's Distillery at Kilbeggan. Flanagan soon introduced the Irish public to a cast of characters who would dominate political debate over the coming months. For the first time people heard the names of Maximoe, Eindiguer and Saschsell, and how a Fianna Fáil Senator, William Quirke, was said to have used undue political influence to help them get their hands on whiskey for the black market. President O'Kelly was accused of entertaining international swindlers at Áras an Uachtaráin.[34]

Located on the banks of the Brusna river in Kilbeggan, Co. Westmeath, Locke's whiskey was well known – the distillery had been in existence since 1757 – and the company well respected, in spite of the fact that it had been substantially involved in undetected illicit trading during the whiskey-starved years of the Second World War. After the war the principal shareholders, Mrs Hope-Johnstone and Mrs Eccles, decided to sell the business, prompted by the severe shortage of mature whiskey on the British market which made the stocks at Locke's extremely valuable. A syndicate called the Trans-World Trust of Lausanne, fronted by a Swiss businessman, Georges Eindiguer, and his interpreter, an Englishman called Horace Henry Smith, expressed an interest in the distillery. Eindiguer had learned of the sale from Thomas Morris, a Clonmel solicitor, with whom he had had discussions about the possibility of bringing greyhound coursing to Switzerland.

The syndicate came to Ireland in September 1947 and employed the Clonmel auctioneering firm of Stokes and Quirke to negotiate the purchase. William Quirke, who was a prominent Fianna Fáil Senator, visited the distillery with Smith, Eindiguer and Morris. Eindiguer subsequently put in a bid of £305,000 and a contract was drawn up and signed by both parties. In addition, the Department of Industry and Commerce provided what Andy Bielenberg, author of *Locke's Distillery*, called a 'sweetener' to the buyers by granting an application for an increase in the distillery's export quota from 4,000 to 8,000 gallons of whiskey.

All this was happening as a private commercial transaction, and all seemed to be in order until the £75,000 deposit was not paid by the date agreed in the contract. This failure aroused Quirke and Morris's suspicions, and Gardaí and officers from the Department of Justice were called in to investigate. Eindiguer was tracked down to the Royal Marine Hotel in Dún Laoghaire. His passport was in order and no charges were preferred, but the following day he left Ireland, never to return. Later that day Smith was picked up by the police. He had a false passport: his real name was Alexander Maximoe and he was wanted in Britain on a number of criminal charges. He was deported to England straight away, but jumped overboard from the Holyhead ferry and was presumed drowned. A chancer to the end, however, Maximoe had arranged to be picked up by a boat, and so once again escaped from the British police.

All of this had happened before the public were aware of it. Eindiguer had left Ireland on 1 October, Maximoe a day later, and the third unsavoury foreigner, Saschsell, whose role in events remained vague, had already been ordered to leave the country by the Department of Justice and left on 24 October.

So when Oliver Flanagan raised questions about the sale on 22 October it caught the press and public unaware, and at no stage was the story to lose in the telling. Dillon was quick into the fray. He called Maximoe an 'international crook', questioned Eindiguer's bona fides, referred to the fact that Maximoe, Eindiguer and Saschsell had all been entertained by President O'Kelly and alleged that Maximoe had been sheltered by people in high places before his arrest. As far as Dillon was concerned, there 'was a very serious scandal out there'.[35]

Flanagan continued his allegations that evening on the adjournment debate, his language entirely unrestrained. The government, he said, had refused the just claims of Irishmen and preferred foreigners, 'international chancers of fame'. Ministers knew all along, he said, the President's own nephew was involved, and he alleged that Eindiguer had claimed that Quirke had suggested that 'it might be a nice friendly gesture if Mr Eindiguer would bring over a gold watch and give it to the Taoiseach's son as a present in order to soften things up'. There were other allegations too, but all returned to the central theme of government or Fianna Fáil involvement in a scheme to sell off Locke's to international gangsters, so that they could then send the whiskey on to the international black market at enormous profits.[36]

By this stage many of the allegations were surreal, but two decades of closed government had not prepared the cabinet to handle the matter in an open way and its slow response to the questions being raised created the appearance of a cover-up, an idea that quickly took root. In the absence of hard information, hearsay became the order of the day, a point well illustrated by O'Higgins when he said that the allegations made in the Dáil were 'minuscule compared to the rumours throughout the country about Locke's'.[37] It was the type of situation which recurred at later times, during for example the arms crisis of 1970 and the GUBU days of 1982, when even the most outlandish rumour was believed – until it was displaced by one more outlandish still.[38] Such was the atmosphere during the Locke days.

A week later Sean Lemass went on the attack for the government. He said Flanagan had been led up the garden path by rumours inspired by the managing director of Locke's, Joseph Cooney, and added that if there was to be an enquiry it would not be the select committee which Fine Gael wanted but a public judicial enquiry, and any witness who perjured himself would face imprisonment. Lemass also explained the gold watch episode. According to his version, Senator Quirke's sister, who had failed to be cured of a serious illness in Switzerland, had come home and made a remarkable recovery due to the care of de Valera's son, Dr Eamon de Valera. Quirke wanted to offer him a gift and, admiring the gold watch worn by Eindiguer, thought to purchase a similar one for Dr de Valera. According to Quirke and Lemass there was no more to it than that, and indeed the watch was never purchased nor ever presented.[39]

Charge and counter-charge flew across the floor. Lemass defended Quirke as the person who first became suspicious of Eindiguer and brought him to the attention of the Minister for Justice. Dillon felt the watch story was no reflection on de Valera or his son, but that Quirke had been guilty of an indiscretion and that the office of the presidency had been used, unknown to the President, 'to lubricate the wheels of a somewhat unsavoury real estate deal'. Dillon claimed too that Quirke had only gone to the Minister for Justice when he felt that Saschsell was going to cut in on his commission.[40] Flanagan neither made distinctions nor showed restraint. He said he would produce witnesses to substantiate what he said and threw charges of corruption and bad faith far and wide.[41]

The debate to establish a judicial tribunal was one of extraordinary viciousness, but in the end one was announced on 30 October. The decision came on the same day as by-elections were held in Waterford, Tipperary and Dublin South-West; Fianna Fáil won only one – Waterford – the other two going to the new Clann na Poblachta, with Sean MacBride elected for the first time as a TD. Worryingly for Fianna Fáil, the opposition's votes had transferred strongly between each other.

Fianna Fáil's case had not been helped by the fact that the Locke allegations had been made during much of the by-election campaign, but more significantly, and certainly of greater long-term consequence, had been MacEntee's supplementary budget of 1947. The budget removed some important food subsidies which had been introduced as a temporary measure after the war to help the less well-off purchase essential goods at a time of high inflation, but inflation had persisted and the subsidies were eating into tax revenue, hence the supplementary and very unpopular budget.

Fianna Fáil reacted to the by-election results with a fit of pique. De Valera confirmed the threats made by Lemass during the campaigns that failure to support the government would result in a dissolution of the Dáil, and said he would be calling an election in early 1948, though he gave no definite date.[42]

The tribunal began its work in the autumn, with three judges sitting at the Four Courts under the chairmanship of Judge John O'Byrne. The proceedings were covered extensively in all the newspapers and all of the many allegations were examined in detail, but there was one curious omission from the tribunal's work, which failed to hear evidence from two of the key participants: Georges Eindiguer and Kurt Saschsell. Maximoe at this stage was presumed drowned, and an application to have the tribunal interview Eindiguer and Saschsell, outside the country if necessary, was summarily refused. It may be that judicial tribunals were relatively new, that the judges did not want to put the state to extra expense or felt they had all the information they needed, but in hindsight it appears an extraordinary decision which ensured that one part of the story would not be told.

Dillon gave his evidence on November 25 and 26. He was described by Quidnunc in *The Irish Times* as being one of the two 'star' performers, Oliver Flanagan being the other. Dillon, according to Quidnunc was 'in his most sombre mood. The effect of his diction cannot be reproduced in print. He gave the impression of taking the proceedings into his own hands from the moment that he stepped up to give his initial evidence.' What he had to say at the tribunal, however, was not particularly substantial. He had no first-hand information of his own to contribute. He had heard news of Locke's from Oliver Flanagan, who had himself heard vague rumours in his own constituency. Dillon sensed something fishy was going on and had advised Flanagan to table Dáil Questions to try to get further information, while he himself met with Cooney, the manager of Locke's, and had several sessions also with Cooney Jnr.

Dillon repeated his allegation that the Department of Industry and Commerce had favoured the new investors in its allocation of whiskey production quotas, though he admitted that he was not overly impressed by his main informant, Cooney Jnr, whom he described as 'an immature person, very excitable and rather romantic'.[43]

Like Dillon, Flanagan had no first-hand information either: the Cooneys had also been his main source. When their turn came to give evidence, the Cooneys were neither disinterested nor reliable and under pressure backed down on many of their allegations. This left Flanagan on very weak ground indeed, and doubly so since Eindiguer, Maximoe and Saschsell were not present and could not be questioned. Instead of recognising this, however, Flanagan decided to brazen it out. Quidnunc in *The Irish Times* described him as 'irrepressibly self-confident' and concluded that Flanagan 'generally emerged unscathed' from his ordeal,'[44] but unfortunately for Flanagan, this view was not shared by the judges when they came to give their report.

The tribunal held its last meeting on 11 December, on the same day the Dáil adjourned *sine die*.

The tribunal report was completed on 18 December and published a few days later.[45] On all the central issues it exonerated the government, finding that the Department of Industry and Commerce had not shown favouritism to Quirke and Eindiguer. While it was satisfied that the purchasers had intended to sell whiskey on the black market, the tribunal held that Quirke only learned this at a late stage, and when he did he immediately informed the Ministry of Justice. The tribunal found that no minister had any personal or financial interest in the sale of the distillery and neither had Quirke abused his position as Senator. The tribunal also believed Quirke's version of the gold watch story and adjudged the allegations to have been made with extraordinary recklessness. The only real point of criticism from the tribunal was directed at the President's nephew, Seamus Sweeney, who had arranged that the alleged conmen be received at Áras an Uachtaráin. The tribunal judged this to have been 'a grave indiscretion'.

The tribunal reserved much of its most scathing criticism for Oliver Flanagan. It had 'found it necessary to exercise extreme caution in dealing with his evidence ... found him very uncandid ... he contradicted himself and was disposed to shift his ground ... in respect of two matters he told us what he knew to be untrue.' It was a crushing indictment, though Flanagan seemed quite unfazed by it and took the issue to his electors. Dillon, whose own evidence was not referred to by the tribunal, felt that the main reason for Flanagan's poor performance was that his main source of information had been Cooney, the distillery's manager. According to Dillon's *Memoir*, on the night before the tribunal sat, Cooney instructed his counsel not to raise any questions or participate in any way beyond stating that they represented his interests. The reason for this, again according to the *Memoir*, was that the 'conspirators placated the wholesaler in Cork through whom the manager had been selling such stocks as he had been able to put on the market, and the wholesaler had brought pressure on the manager'. This, according to Dillon, had left Quirke and his associates something of a free field at the hearing. The record of the tribunal does not sustain this view.[46]

The tribunal thus came to an end, having generated controversy and ill-feeling out of all proportion to the issues involved. In spite of the absence of some of the principal actors, the judges had no difficulty in coming to very definite conclusions: the charges against the government were adjudged to be without substance. Dillon was not mentioned in the report, but the findings did not sustain his main allegations. He remained unapologetic about his role, however. He had good reason to believe Eindiguer, Maximoe and Saschell were crooks and the allegations about how they were granted quotas was a matter of public policy; if Senator

(Picture on previous page courtesy of the Dillon family)

Opposite: top: John Blake Dillon about 1850; centre: James Dillon's parents — left: Elizabeth Mathew, 1890; right: John Dillon, 1869 (son of John Blake);
bottom: the Dillon family in 1906 — standing (L. to R.) Theo, Jenny Plenderleith, Shawn, Myles, Maria (Lia) O'Reilly, Brian; seated: Nano and James (aged 4). (All courtesy of the Dillon family)
Above: James (left) with his father at the 1913 All-Ireland football final. (Courtesy of *The Examiner*)
Right: James with his son, John Blake, in the late 1940s. (Courtesy of the Dillon family)

Above: *Wedding portrait of James and Maura Dillon (1942). Maura's sister, Kitty, and Peter Nugent are seated.* (Courtesy of the Dillon family)
Opposite: *top — left: James and Maura's son, John Blake, and his bride, Clodagh Hickey, at their wedding in 1969* (Courtesy of *The Irish Times*); *right: James with his grandchildren, Lee and Tara, 1975; bottom: the Dillon brothers in the 1970s — (L. to R.) Fr Mathew OSB (Brian), James and Shawn.* (Both courtesy of the Dillon family)

Opposite: *The Fine Gael leader enjoys a dance with his wife at the party's Ard-Fheis.*
(Courtesy of *The Irish Times*)
Above: *In 1949, Ireland's Minister for Agriculture meets Britain's Food Minister, Mr E.J. Strachey.*
(Courtesy of the Dillon family)
Right: *Speaking at an election meeting in Patrick Street, Cork, 1951.*
(Courtesy of *The Examiner*)

Above: Liam Cosgrave addresses a Fine Gael meeting in Cork in 1946.
Left: Liam's father, W.T. Cosgrave, addresses a United Ireland meeting, Clonmel, 1933.
Opposite: Addressing the same meeting in Clonmel — top: General Eoin O'Duffy; bottom: James Dillon.
(All courtesy of *The Examiner*)

Left: *Speaking at the 1956 Ard-Fheis, as Minister for Agriculture.*
(Courtesy of *The Irish Times*)

Below: *At the opening of the Agricultural Institute. (L. to R.) Archbishop John Charles McQuaid, James Dillon, President Seán T. O'Kelly, Eamon de Valera.*
(Courtesy of RTÉ)

Bottom: *Announcing the 1961 election programme, with General Seán MacEoin and T.F. O'Higgins.*
(Courtesy of *The Irish Times*)

Opposite: *The Leader of the Opposition has a word with the Minister for Agriculture, Charles J. Haughey, in 1965.*
(Courtesy of *The Irish Times*)

"Phee-ee-e-ew! That's the second time this morning Mr. Dillon has gone through!"

"Here, Dillon, Dillon, Dillon, Dillon, Dillon!"

Cartoons from the popular Dublin Opinion *satirise the 1950s political scene in Ireland.* (Courtesy of Frank Kelly)

THE DEPARTMENT OF AGRICULTURE NEW STYLE
(As imagined by Our Grangegorman Correspondent)

Left: James Dillon
signifies 'no comment'
to reporters at the
time of the Arms
Crisis, 1970.
Below: The party
leader casts his vote
in the 1965 General
Election.
(Both courtesy of *The Irish
Times*)

Above: *The 1954 Cabinet. Seated (L. to R.): Seán MacEoin, Brendan Corish, Bill Norton, John A. Costello, Richard Mulcahy, Joseph Blewick, William Everett, James Dillon. Standing (L. to R.): Gerard Sweetman, Liam Cosgrave, Tom O'Higgins, Pa O'Donnell.*
(Courtesy of the Dillon family)

Right: *A pensive James Dillon at the Fine Gael Ard-Fheis, 1971.*
(Courtesy of *The Irish Times*)

Next page: *Waving to reporters on his discharge from hospital in 1964, accompanied by his wife.*
(Courtesy of the Dillon family)

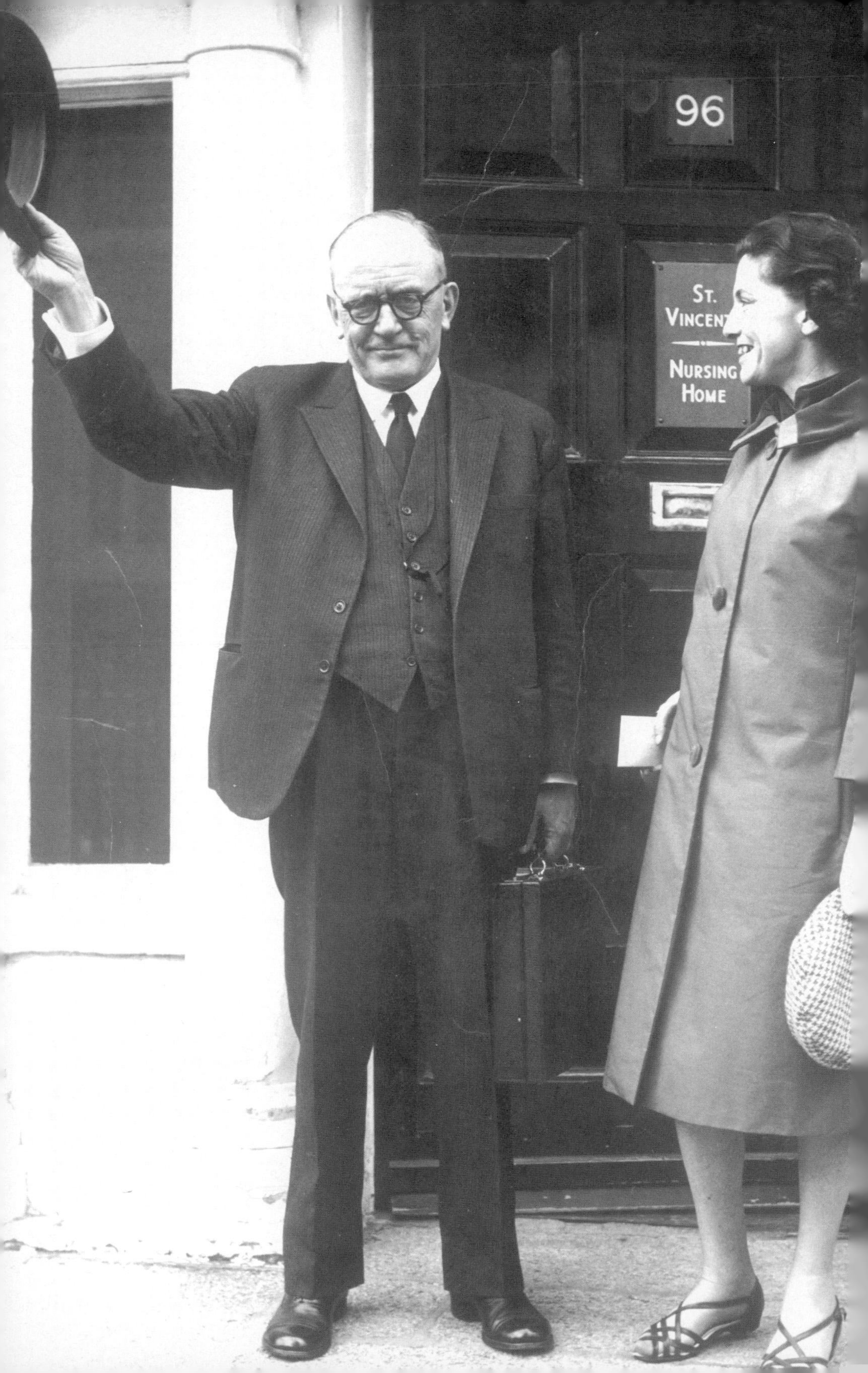
96
St. Vincent
Nursing Home

Quirke was exerting undue influence because of his political status, that too was a matter of public concern, as was his view that the President and presidency was being abused for commercial gain. In a climate of closed government, and at a time when it was widely believed that political influence was paramount in the allocating of licences and quotas, Dillon felt parliament was the only forum within which questions of such legitimate public interest could be asked, allegations made, and the truth flushed out. His opponents saw it as another example of his willingness to make serious charges without having any real evidence to substantiate them, but Dillon never regretted his role in the Locke's case and neither was he ever convinced that the full truth had been brought to light.

ANOTHER ISSUE which caught the public's attention in 1947 was the future of transatlantic travel, and in particular the future of Shannon airport, or as it was then known, Rineanna. Dillon strongly supported the government's plans for Shannon and particularly the idea of a customs-free zone, but he warned against too great a dependence on using Shannon as a transit point for passengers between Europe and the US because of developments in aircraft's flight-range. He thought 'it would be as ludicrous to suggest that in ten years time trans-express passenger services will stop at Rineanna as it would be to suggest that the *Queen Elizabeth* would stop at Castletownberehaven to take on fresh water. But there has been from the beginning, and there may yet be, a reasonable chance of making Rineanna serve as an aerial entrepôt distribution centre for the continent of Europe, provided we offer at this end adequate facilities.' By adequate facilities he meant storage and refrigeration, skilled staff for express parcel services and the best public relations to make the services known far and wide.

Dillon believed that as a point of conjunction for world passenger routes it was highly unlikely that Ireland would be used at all ten years from then – thus his concentration on Shannon as a customs-free zone – and felt it better to build up Dublin airport with a feeder service from local aerodromes in Cork, Galway, Sligo and other regions.[47]

As so often, however, he could not leave well enough alone, and during a debate on broadcasting on 1 May 1947, as he attacked the idea of a short-wave radio station to the USA (which he saw as a propaganda weapon to enhance de Valera's image) he added: 'I venture to swear that five years from today, when the rabbits start playing leap-frog below in Rineanna, the masts which are to direct the radio to the US will be converted into knitting machines to knit the wool of the rabbits from Rineanna.'[48]

While such rhetoric may have boomed through the Dáil chamber, it rebounded in the mid-west, where his remarks are sometimes still remembered even if the context and supporting arguments are long forgotten.

It was not that his arguments were wrong. Dillon had a good grasp of likely developments in the airline industry and in a broad sense he was right. What he did not have, however, was the political sense to avoid offending a wide range of local and vested interests and the ability to say what he wanted to say in a non-contentious manner. His memorable phrases lived on, and were frequently taken out of context to be used against him.

Seeing Ireland as a bridge between the English-speaking countries, Dillon was thoroughly conscious of Shannon's strategic position. His view of a post-war world order still hinged on the Commonwealth and the USA, but had developed also to include the European democracies, and proposed a degree of unity between them which was far ahead of the new international associations then taking shape.

When he spoke on foreign affairs, which was often, he reiterated his support for an expanded Commonwealth as the one institution capable of providing a framework for economic co-operation and development on a world scale. His vision of a new Commonwealth was in no way rooted in the past, and firmly rejected all elements of British imperial trappings or of continuing British hegemony. He carried on an extensive correspondence with a range of British and US writers, including the influential Arthur Knock of the *New York Times* and writers in the *Round Table*, the *Tablet* and *The Economist*, in which he argued for a new Commonwealth on an 'Anglo-American axis'. An excerpt from the then influential Washington and London newsletter, the *Whaley-Eaton Service*, summarises his proposal:

> This would take in the present Commonwealth, the United States and Ireland. It might also include other democracies in Europe sharing the same general philosophy of life. It could develop a new scheme of international collaboration, and it might form a group too strong for any predatory dictatorship to challenge .. a group 'so rich in resources and high purpose as to make the development of desert places possible and the rescue of forgotten millions in the Orient a wealth-creating crusade for a century to come.'[49]

His thinking was on the grand scale, anticipating the nature of many of the changes which would transform Europe a half-century later. Nor did he confine himself to the Anglo-American bloc. As he told the Dáil in 1947, what he wanted was that the member states form a federal union:

> each state retaining, as the federal states of the US do, full sovereign jurisdiction over its internal affairs but conceding to the union federal government the rights and duties of peace and war, of foreign policy, of tariffs and of customs, thus giving to all member states free passage for men, money and goods.

Such a union would be open to other states which accepted its fundamental principles. Dillon foresaw that it might include 'Sweden, Norway, Holland, Belgium and even some day France, Italy, Spain and Portugal ... I can see the day when such a federal union would exist here in Europe and throughout the Commonwealth.'[50]

Side by side with his advocacy of a global role for the Commonwealth was his apprehension about the encroaching menace of communism. Alone among Irish politicians he had warned about the dangers of Nazism in the 1930s; now, a decade later, he saw Soviet communism as the great threat to world peace and liberty. In his opinion there could be no compromise with communism just as there could have been no compromise with Hitler, and his strictures extended to the communist movement in Ireland. Dillon had read widely on the nature and history of communism and saw no way in which it could co-exist with democracy or Christianity.[51] On this issue, however, he found himself in the mainstream rather than swimming against the tide.

He remained in a minority on the question of how to tackle the problem of partition, however. In the External Affairs debate of June 1947, de Valera had made proposals for a worldwide anti-partition campaign which won widespread support.[52] William Norton, for example, fully endorsed it, decrying Britain as 'an occupying power in the six counties' which 'had no moral right to be there', and calling on the government to initiate a formal conference with the British and mount an international publicity campaign aimed at drawing attention to the 'suppurating sore of partition'.[53] Oliver Flanagan also supported the call, though he distrusted de Valera's sincerity: 'it serves the Fianna Fáil party and the Taoiseach to have the border there as otherwise the last trump card of the party would be played out'.[54]

Dillon was not the only person to doubt the wisdom of such an international crusade, but he was its most outspoken opponent:

If in this hour it appears before the world that Ireland, above all, is preoccupied with her own particular individual grievance to the exclusion of everything else and takes up a position among the nations of the world that, until this grievance is disposed of, we shall lend no hand in any worthy undertaking – if that be our position we are disgraced and I should be ashamed to confess abroad that I was Irish.[55]

He argued that partition was not a priority of the people and that we would be better occupied in playing a part in the reconstruction of Europe.

While he challenged some of the nationalist myths surrounding partition, he was utterly scathing of what he saw as a carefully contrived plan to create a sense of mythology around de Valera. It was an old theme but he returned to it with gusto in February 1947 when de Valera proposed to establish in Dublin an Institute for Cosmic Physics. Dillon felt the money could be much more usefully spent on the existing universities, and attributed Machiavellian motives to de Valera. It was a diversionary tactic: 'as the country grapples with a myriad of problems, the scholar Taoiseach sits there in lofty detachment, thinking only of cosmic physics'. It was more, part of a larger plot masterminded by the head of the Government Information Bureau, Frank Gallagher, to create an image of the 'scholar Taoiseach'.[56] He quoted from *Politicians by Accident*,[57] just published by a Fianna Fáil supporter – and later a judge – Leo Skinner:

> There it was described that politics were an insufferable ordeal for him: that, really, his happiness was to be detached from all mundane affairs and left free to wander in the higher realms of mathematics where few could follow him. This is the spectacle we are being entertained to now – himself and the cosmic physicist sitting over in Merrion Square rise in the cosmic ether while the ignoramuses of the Fine Gael, Labour and Clann na Talmhan parties are occupying themselves with old-age pensions and cows and contemptible considerations of that kind.[58]

There was more in the same vein, but while Dillon's words may have been colourful, he was deadly serious. He believed, and with good reason, that de Valera was not particularly well qualified in either Irish or mathematics, but that that myth had been sedulously fostered, 'paid for out of our people's money'. 'Now I know it is not fashionable to say that,' he went on, 'I know that kind of observation shocks the respectables in this country, but it has to be said.'[59]

As an old-style liberal in matters of free speech, Dillon was outspokenly opposed to the operation of censorship. He attacked the banning of Kate O'Brien's *A Land of Spices* and what he called the pernicious practice of allowing customs officials seize privately owned books: 'It is none of our business what individuals may care to bring into this country in their baggage for their own perusal.'[60] His views here received little support, either in the Dáil or from the public.

He was decades ahead of his time when he called in May 1947 for Dáil proceedings to be broadcast 'all day, every day ... on a special wavelength' so that the people could listen to and judge their representatives for themselves. He argued that 'the nearer a free people are brought to their own parliament, the more they will treasure it as a citadel of liberty'. He was certain they would realise that 'with all its faults ... this is one of the best parliaments at present functioning in the world'. Contrasting the Dáil with the pomp of some other assemblies, he felt proud of 'the plain, workaday, perhaps drab atmosphere' of Leinster House. However, his idea got little encouragement from his colleagues in the House. Patrick Beegan, a Fianna Fáil backbencher who followed him, described it as 'the most nonsensical suggestion ever made', and went on to argue that cattle prices be given greater prominence in news bulletins.[61]

IN JUNE 1947 the new Minister for Health, Dr Jim Ryan, brought before the Dáil details of a new public health scheme which had been largely prepared by his predecessor, Dr Ward. Ryan was far more conciliatory than Ward and accepted many opposition amendments, but one issue in particular caused continuing problems: the provision of health services for mothers and children. The matter was to blow into a major controversy a few years later.

Dillon had deep reservations about a provision of the Bill which made medical inspection compulsory. He thought it an 'astonishing and most undesirable proceeding' that 'every man's child ... whether his parents desire it or not, must become the responsibility of the state so far as the maintenance of his health is concerned'. The proper responsibility lay with the parents and the family, a point on which Dillon felt so strongly that he announced in the Dáil that he would petition the President to consult the Council of State on the Bill, with a view to referring it to the Supreme Court to test its constitutionality.[62]

In August, the President did consult the Council of State on the constitutionality of the Mother and Child sections of the legislation and they recommended that he sign it. Dillon refused to accept this as the last word on the matter and on 3 December issued a summons against the Minister for Health seeking a declaration as to whether the Health Act and in particular sections 21 to 28 were repugnant to the Constitution. As Dillon briefed his counsel, Costello, Cecil Lavery and McGilligan, he was not aware that the Roman Catholic hierarchy had already protested privately to the government on the same issues.[63]

There was a certain irony to the situation. By taking court action, Dillon allowed de Valera temporise on his reply to the hierarchy on the grounds that the matter was before the courts and ultimately to avoid answering the points made by the bishops. As a result, the entire problem was handed over to the new government in February 1948, with consequences that would be explosive.

The life of the government came to an effective end with the two Clann na Poblachta by-election victories in November 1947, though the general election itself was still some time off. It had been an acrimonious Dáil with tensions on one occasion spilling over into fisticuffs outside the chamber, and as it neared its end Fianna Fáil faced into its first significant electoral challenge of the decade.

The Fine Gael decline seemed to have bottomed out. It had polled respectably in the by-elections, had recruited some young and talented new members, including Alexis FitzGerald, TF O'Higgins and Declan Costello, and the party's Dáil performance could still be effective, even if the bulk of this work was being carried out by a small nucleus of members. However, Fine Gael was finding new and willing candidates, something it had failed to do for over a decade.

Overall, however, there appeared to be no credible alternative to a Fianna Fáil government. O'Higgins and Mulcahy had made various attempts to put together an alliance or at least an arrangement with Clann na Talmhan and the Independents, but with little success. Dillon had also made some efforts towards the same end. He told the US Ambassador on 25 November 1947 that he was acting as middle-man between Mulcahy and Blowick of Clann na Talmhan 'to effect a fusion of the two parties'. Dillon believed that with the support of the Independents such a party could wipe out Fianna Fáil's overall majority. He thought the new party could also count on Labour, which might even be prepared to participate in government, and win MacBride's backing if only because he was unlikely to support de Valera. Dillon also indicated to the Ambassador that his own relations with Mulcahy were cordial, and that he would be prepared to seek re-admission to Fine Gael should there be a realistic chance of the new party becoming a reality.

The principal difficulties at this stage came from Clann na Talmhan. According to Dillon, 'Blowick made decisions slowly and with difficulty,' but at this time, too, Labour was also interested in an alliance with Clann na Talmhan and this had strengthened the smaller party's hand.[64] Little real progress was made towards opposition unity, and it was their continuing disunity which prompted de Valera, who also made a none-too-subtle attempt to stifle Clann na Poblachta before it could consolidate its early gains, to dissolve the Dáil and go for an election in early 1948.

The one factor which both government and opposition seemed to underestimate was the extent to which the electorate itself was polarising into pro- and anti-Fianna Fáil positions. This shift in electoral behaviour had begun with the 1945 presidential election, but clearly had made little impact on Dillon when on 15 October 1947 he laid odds of six to four on Fianna Fáil winning all three by-elections:

> They would not win one of them if the Opposition was not scattered into four or five pieces. We would beat the heads off them if we went to the country with an appearance of solidarity out of which an alternative government could

be provided, but surely nobody but a lunatic would vote for the conglomeration which we are.[65]

The opposition, said Dillon, was like seven engines all unassembled. And despite Clann na Poblachta's success in the by-elections, he saw little possibility of that situation changing. As he faced into his seventh general election, he had little reason to believe that his description of himself as 'a backbencher with no ministerial ambitions or hopes' was likely to change. There was even less reason for optimism when the government's new electoral legislation resulted in a further reduction in the number of five-seat constituencies, a strategy specifically designed to weaken the smaller parties and maximise Fianna Fáil's potential seats.

Even before the Dáil had been dissolved and an election date set, Dillon had begun his campaign on 14 December in Carrickmacross, where he appealed to Fine Gael and Clann na Talmhan to come together as a new party. He had, he said, been working on this for the past few weeks and thought that while Fine Gael was ready, Clann na Talmhan was unwilling to change its title.[66] There was, in fact, more to it than that. Clann na Talmhan was divided on a number of issues and in no position to move towards a merger. Dillon, however, was not pessimistic and announced that in the next Dáil he hoped to establish a 'National Democratic Party'. He was tired, he said, of the futility of being an Independent and this was the last time he would run as one. Come the next election, he would go forward either as a member of a national party or not at all.[67]

CHAPTER FOURTEEN

GOVERNMENT

'I do not deny I am an optimist ... What harm is there in hoping? Many of my hopes may not come off, but a sufficient percentage of them will, to make a mighty change in the agriculture of this country, with the help of God.'

Dillon, Dáil Debates, July 1948

THE ELECTION OF 1948 was to be a watershed, though nobody called it so at the time. What made it different was the presence of Clann na Poblachta, predicted privately by Dillon to win twenty seats, by the political correspondent of *The Irish Times* to get between forty-five and seventy-five, and by MacBride 'to get an overall majority'.[1]

Fianna Fáil knew that something was wrong, even if it was not quite sure what. The signs were there. The government was unpopular as it had never been before, even among its own supporters, and the party organisation had grown sluggish and complacent. At no stage though did Fianna Fáil contemplate that it might lose office, and the well-tried formulae of previous elections were pressed into action. The 'Red scare' made its reappearance, with Labour and Clann na Poblachta as the main targets, and the public was told that there was no alternative to Fianna Fáil, that coalitions led to chaos, economic ruin, secret deals and ultimately to dictatorship. De Valera went so far as to say he thought the country would be doomed if there was government by coalition, provoking a spirited rejoinder from Dillon that 'when a politician announces that if he is not re-elected the country is doomed, it is time for him to ask himself whether he is not going daft'.[2]

Fianna Fáil had reason to be worried, though not unduly so. At the very worst, if the party did not win an overall majority a minority government could be put in place as a prelude to an early run to the country. That was the view of most commentators, and nobody, perhaps not even those involved, believed that the Fine Gael-instigated moves towards opposition unity had any hope of bringing about an alternative government. This perception was based on three not unrealistic factors: the obvious and apparently irreconcilable differences between the opposition groups; the absence of any previous experience of coalition, which, though it is the norm rather than the exception under proportional representation, was completely foreign to the Irish experience; and the fact that the main opposition party seemed to be set in irreversible decline, a trend that most observers thought would continue in the 1948 election.

There were many reasons for Fine Gael's decline, including the wartime consensus which blunted the possibilities of opposition while elevating de Valera to the status of a national rather than a party leader, the growing conservatism of Fianna Fáil and its attractions for some traditional Fine Gael voters, and the lethargy of the Fine Gael party itself, which in spite of Mulcahy's indefatigable efforts had lost much of its self-belief and will to win. There were some tentative signs of new growth. The 1946 Árd Fheis had been well attended, and it heard Mulcahy declare 'an end to Fine Gael's voluntary inactivity'. There was the party's improved performance in the 1947 by-elections, the appearance of new and able candidates, and the beginning of an intellectual debate within the party on economic and social issues and on Fine Gael's future direction. But if there were signs of a resurgence they were little noticed; instead Fine Gael was seen to suffer significant losses as a result of the sudden deaths of two of its TDs, Jim Hughes and Michael Roddy, before the campaign had started, and the death of Eamon Coogan ten days into the canvass. All three were among the party's better-performing TDs.

In Monaghan, where Fine Gael did not field a candidate, Dillon was canvassing in his seventh general election. His old adversary Dr Ward was no longer in the field, but Ward's nemesis, Dr MacCarville, late of Fianna Fáil, carried the hopes of Clann na Poblachta in the constituency. *The Irish Times* engaged the poet Patrick Kavanagh to report on the campaign. He had a good feel for local conditions:

> Monaghan deserves some credit for electing James Dillon, whose oratory adds so much colour to the Dáil. He has an enthusiastic body of supporters, many of whom are old members of the AOH, an organisation which is still alive in the county ... the dealing men of Carrickmacross to a man are Ancient Hibs and behind James. There are several strong centres of Hib life and with the remains of the Fine Gael vote and a large number of Protestants who admire Dillon's idea of a United Ireland within the Commonwealth of Nations, it is most likely that James will once more head the poll.[3]

When Kavanagh turned his attention to Dr McCarville, he detected in Clann na Poblachta 'an element of intellectualism which is not good in a rough-house brawl'. The national teachers, he noted, were strong supporters of the new party – 'small-town and small-time professional frustration is expressed' – but though McCarville had a good name in Monaghan, 'it seemed to me from hearing him he has lost the grip of the popular outlook'.

Kavanagh reported on a Clann na Poblachta meeting in Castleblayney where 'the rough elements in the town were on the side of Fianna Fáil and as good as broke up the Clann na Poblachta meeting. It struck me as strange that a new, vital and supposedly revolutionary party should have to appeal to the police for protection.'[4]

Monaghan in its way was a microcosm of the country as a whole. The Fianna Fáil vote there was down, in this case by sixteen per cent, in part due to the Ward factor; but McCarville and Clann na Poblachta failed to make their anticipated breakthrough, getting just twelve per cent of the vote. Dillon, for the second successive time, headed the poll.[5]

At a national level no party won. In a Dáil increased from 138 seats to 157 Fianna Fáil lost eight seats and saw its popular vote drop from forty-eight to forty-one per cent. It had sixty-eight seats and was still by far the dominant party, but remained ten seats short of an overall majority. Fine Gael's vote also dropped, but by less than one per cent, and it gained one seat on its 1944 figure, in the process electing thirteen new TDs. From its perspective, the decline had been stayed if not reversed, and it remained the second-biggest party with thirty-one seats. In the light of pre-election predictions, that in itself had been an achievement.

Labour and National Labour both made gains, Labour up from eight to fourteen seats, National Labour from four to five. Clann na Talmhan was down from nine seats to seven, but the big surprise was the failure of Clann na Poblachta to break through as expected – with thirteen per cent of the vote it got just ten seats, a poor result blamed in part on bad candidate strategy and inadequate organisation, but more emphatically a vindication of de Valera's pre-emptive strike and an indication of the conservatism of an electorate which had been subjected to large doses of Fianna Fáil scare tactics, especially in the closing weeks of the campaign.

From Dillon's point of view, the real significance lay in the fact that there were twelve Independents returned, of whom he was the most senior and distinguished. More than that, the mood was clearly in favour of change, and especially so among the Independents. They, not surprisingly, were strongly in favour of an alternative to Fianna Fáil. On past form, if de Valera took office in this situation he would call a new election within a year, and they were likely to be the principal casualties.

This was Dillon's own view, and at his victory celebration in Carrickmacross he said that because Fianna Fáil had been defeated by the votes of the people, the people ought to be provided with an alternative government. If nobody else took the initiative, he himself intended to invite all those who had been elected in opposition to Fianna Fáil to combine to form a government.[6]

The initiative was in fact taken by Fine Gael, which announced on 8

February that it would attempt to form a government and invited the other parties to take part in discussions.[7] Over the next week, Labour and Clann na Poblachta agreed to enter government; in the case of Clann na Poblachta the executive vote in favour was very close, but having campaigned on the slogan 'Put Them Out' the party could not support Fianna Fáil, nor could it easily stand aside. Before long the general principles were agreed – they included increased public investment, higher levels of social welfare, a new programme of afforestation and the use of Hospitals Trust funds to help eradicate TB. But policy was secondary; the importance of getting Fianna Fáil out and 'getting the country moving again' was sufficient for the day. Policy would follow power.[8]

The negotiations to form a new government were less than frenetic. Fianna Fáil stood aloof. It was willing to accept support from the Independents or any other party who wished to put a minority Fianna Fáil government in place, but there was no question of a coalition or any dilution of the principle of one-party rule. The only party remotely likely to consider such a proposition was National Labour, which Fianna Fáil believed would not enter government with its former Labour colleagues. Lemass, normally the most realistic of men, believed up to the last moment that an alternative government could not be formed because National Labour would support Fianna Fáil.[9]

Dillon, for his part, set about organising the very disparate Independents, saying that he was confident 'a non-Fianna Fáil government under a distinguished Irishman could be formed'.[10] Dillon was regarded as the leader of this group, which included some highly individualistic personalities. Oliver Flanagan was still something of an *enfant terrible*, but his earlier antipathy to Dillon had disappeared totally and in its place a close friendship had formed between them. It was, on the face of it, a strange relationship, but one which endured. In his early days in Leinster House Flanagan had frequently been critical of Dillon, and sharply so, while Dillon had not been particularly impressed with the brash young populist. But as Independents they had shared office space and with the passing of time they found, apparently, that they had much in common. Flanagan spoke especially for the 'small man' and was frequently at odds with authority and bureaucracy. He was sometimes reckless and certainly never understated, but not all that far removed from Dillon's own obsessions with the rights of the small farmer and distrust of bureaucracy, big business and red tape. Dillon tutored Flanagan in parliamentary ways and procedures, and the pair worked together in the Dáil to the extent that MacEntee dubbed Flanagan 'Dillon's political love-child'.[11]

Flanagan now played an important role in bringing the Independents together and acted as secretary to the group. They were a mixed bunch.

Amongst them were such characters as John Flynn, the 'Fiddler Flynn' as he was known, a man of reputedly seductive charm, especially where his women constituents were concerned. A former Fianna Fáil TD, he had incurred de Valera's displeasure after a highly publicised court case and lost the party Whip. In spite of this – or maybe even because of it – his Kerry constituents liked him and consistently re-elected him. More difficult for Dillon to deal with was Patrick Cogan, whose political career took him from Fine Gael to the Independent benches and then to his own National Agricultural Party, later to Clann na Talmhan, then back to the Independents, and ultimately to Fianna Fáil. Cogan, a farmer on the Carlow–Wicklow border, was outspoken, argumentative and independent, and between Dillon and himself there was a great deal of mutual dislike. There was no particular reason for it; the antipathy for the most part came from Cogan, and was later to become something of an obsession with him. Also among the Independents were the Byrnes, Alfie senior and junior, the former the last link in the Dáil with the Irish Party. There was never any question of forming a party, but for organisational reasons the Independents came together as an informal parliamentary group, with Dillon as chairman and Flanagan effectively as Whip.

By 13 February the name of John A. Costello had emerged as the probable compromise choice to lead the proposed government, and this was confirmed by Mulcahy at a meeting of party leaders called two days later. Though earlier speculation had favoured Sean MacEoin as the party's candidate for Taoiseach, the choice of Costello was not all that surprising. He was an established politician with a reputation for competence and vigour, he had little Civil War baggage, and as senior counsel to the Irish Trade Union movement for a long number of years he was acceptable to the Labour Party. He was also friendly with MacBride and Jim Larkin, son of the trade union founder. Mulcahy, whose Civil War past ruled him out, had no personal ambitions to be Taoiseach, or if he had, was prepared to forego them: in Dillon's words, he stood aside 'with the patriotism which was his outstanding quality'.[12]

This left Costello free to negotiate with both Labour parties, the Labour Party led by Norton and the National Labour Party led by James Everett. Everett had initially been instructed by his party executive to stay out of government, but eventually Fianna Fáil's record on welfare, rural workers, pensions and stand-still orders, combined with the not unreasonable view that a minority Fianna Fáil government would be short-lived, and an equally reasonable desire for office, carried the day. Soon the likelihood of a new inter-party government was being taken for granted, and newspapers began speculating about cabinet positions. Dillon was tipped for Industry and Commerce, with Blowick mentioned for Agriculture.

When the Dáil assembled it was clear that Fianna Fáil had not come to terms with the election result. For some of its members it seemed almost as if the laws of nature had been suspended, and they were convinced that the new arrangement would quickly collapse under the weight of its internal contradictions.

As outgoing Taoiseach, de Valera was nominated first, in two short, almost perfunctory speeches, both entirely in Irish. There was more flamboyance on the opposition side. Costello was proposed by Mulcahy and seconded by Norton, who described the new government as the logical corollary of proportional representation, a pooling of the nation's wisdom and energies for a policy of reconstruction, something which was a commonplace in continental Europe.[13] MacBride then spoke about his priorities in the new government, with particular emphasis on ending emigration, increasing agricultural production and eradicating TB. Clann na Poblachta, he said, would not renege on its core policies; it simply had not been given a mandate to implement them, and so 'such measures as the repeal of the External Relations Act, which are inconsistent with our status as an independent Republic, will have to remain in abeyance for the time being'.[14] Blowick and Everett followed, outlining their priorities, and then it was Dillon's turn.

He may have reflected that had he not left Fine Gael in 1942 he might now have occupied Costello's position as Taoiseach, but if he did he kept it to himself. He was in exuberant form and had no words of commiseration for his opponents. This was a great result. The House should not feel 'doomed' – 'Doomed be damned. Fianna Fáil is going out, and thanks be to God.' The election result showed that 'the country depended on no individual for its existence as a sovereign and independent state'.

Dillon's speech was extraordinarily upbeat. Unlike MacBride, 'who contemplates a long postponement of some objectives near his heart, I am more optimistic'. He wanted to see Ireland in the United Nations 'with those who seek to defend the liberty of the world from the greatest threat that has ever challenged it since history was first written'. Curiously, he did not mention the Commonwealth of Nations, but instead stressed the potential for political development within the UN: 'In accepting that invitation we may see a sovereign, independent and united Ireland delivered from the nauseating frauds of a dictionary Republic sooner than we anticipate. Call that sovereign State a Republic or what you please, sovereign, independent and standing on its own feet it will surely be ...' Dillon was later to claim that this statement presaged his willingness to leave the Commonwealth and declare a Republic, but if so it was not interpreted like that at the time.[15]

Costello was elected Taoiseach with a comfortable majority of seventy-five votes to sixty-eight. His first act was to increase the size of the new government from ten to twelve ministers (he was allowed fifteen under the Constitution). Ministers were appointed along strictly proportional party lines, each party's nominees having been agreed in advance with the party leaders. The only previous governmental experience in the new cabinet came from Fine Gael. Costello had been Attorney General in the 1920s, while McGilligan, the new Finance Minister, had been one of the successes of the Cosgrave regime in both Industry and Commerce and External Affairs.

That, however, was the limit of the cabinet's experience of government. O'Higgins in Defence had had a long career in the Dáil; MacEoin in Justice had been a War of Independence hero, the legendary 'Blacksmith of Ballinalee', and a member of the Dáil since the 1920s; Morrissey in Industry and Commerce had previously been a Labour TD, and had joined Cumann na nGaedheal in the late 1920s. Labour had two ministers. Norton, immensely experienced, streetwise and one of the best natural performers in the Dáil, was Tanaiste and Minister for Social Welfare. TJ Murphy was Minister for Local Government, while James Everett, of National Labour, was in Posts and Telegraphs.

The radicalism in the new government was expected to come from Clann na Poblachta. MacBride opted for External Affairs, a choice which at first seemed to place him on the margins, but with that department leading the negotiations for Ireland's involvement in European renewal programmes, MacBride clearly envisaged that he would have an economic as well as a political role. MacBride's other choice for ministerial office caused the greatest surprise and caught the public's imagination. Dr Noel Browne, just thirty-three in 1948, was handsome, intense, and completely unknown. He had no political pedigree to speak of; his distinction was his obvious commitment to eradicating TB.

Choosing Browne caused two problems, one immediate, the other long-term. His appointment greatly annoyed some of the more senior members of Clann na Poblachta, who felt a greater entitlement to ministerial preferment. This led to friction within the party almost from the outset, and was not helped by MacBride's lofty disdain for such worldly concerns in others.[16] The second problem was of course Browne's personality. Noel Browne was, and always would be, controversial. He had the capacity to inspire fierce loyalty, but many of those who worked with and against him over the years found him difficult, self-centred, unwilling to accept the good faith of his opponents and often profoundly unfair in his intolerance of those who disagreed with him. These judgements were, however, for the future. In 1948 Browne was simply an unknown quantity.

Dillon was appointed Minister for Agriculture. It was the job he prized most; in his *Memoir* he says that had Agriculture not been available he would not have been interested in any other office. Perhaps. But he did not have to agonise over it because, following the death of Jim Hughes, he was the only real contender.

First, however, there was the laying down of ground-rules for the new government, so utterly different in nature to de Valera's one-party regime. Costello set out to address these issues in his first speech as Taoiseach, when he reaffirmed the doctrine of collective responsibility but left room for some freedom of manoeuvre. 'The various parties who have formed this Government have sought to find, and have found, points on which they can completely agree. The Government has been formed on the basis of full agreement on all these points. Any points on which we have not agreed have been left in abeyance.'[17]

Curiously, the only areas of policy Costello addressed in his speech were industry and agriculture. As far as agriculture was concerned, he was quite clear that the new government would follow 'the policy of our late colleague, Jim Hughes ... that is our ideal'. He announced that the government had been formed around 'the fundamental principle' that 'there can be no prosperity unless agricultural production is stepped up and stepped up immediately'. The government, he promised, would 'bring agriculture back to where Patrick Hogan had left it'.[18]

The government commitment to agriculture gave Dillon plenty of scope to exercise the ideas he had until now aired in the Dáil. He entered his new department aged forty-seven and determined after sixteen years in opposition to make his mark. His mission, as he was to repeat over and over again, was to complete the work 'which my father had begun with Michael Davitt in making the small farmers of this country owners of their own land, which had culminated in the Birrell Land Acts of 1909. I felt it to be my mission in public life to make that land yield to small proprietors a decent standard of living.'[19] He was clear as to where his priorities lay: to secure every advantage from the British market for Irish produce, to increase agricultural output through land reclamation and put renewed emphasis on quality and marketing, and to free farmers from government interference and compulsion. In general, he aimed to regenerate agriculture as the driving force of economic development.

Dillon had been given a key ministry. Agriculture was the country's basic industry, employing half the labour force and providing almost all of Ireland's exports. The country could increase exports and put its external finances on a sound footing only if there were a massive expansion in agriculture. The industry also offered the only real prospect of Ireland making a meaningful contribution to the European Recovery programme.

There had been no post-war agricultural recovery in Ireland, where the depredations of the war years remained all too obvious. Whatever about its future potential, in 1948 Irish agriculture was seriously depressed. The British economic crisis had ruled out the possibility of an export-led recovery and a succession of bad winters had made matters even worse. During the war years the production of bread grain had to be greatly increased while at the same time the volume of agricultural exports, especially cattle, remained at no more than seventy per cent of their 1938 level. The volume of imports – a measure of farmers' investment in fertilisers and capital equipment – was only thirty-seven per cent of the 1938 figure. The fertility of the soil was depleted, herds and stocks were not maintained and machinery not replaced, and former export areas were allowed to run down. It had been hoped that the sterling accumulated during the war could be used to make good the damage, especially to import materials and machinery, but this did not happen because sterling could not be converted to buy commodities which were largely obtainable only from the dollar area. The inability to convert sterling into dollars made Ireland's need for aid from the US government still more urgent.[20]

Dillon quickly grasped the elements of the problem facing him, though he would add further reasons for the crisis: the depredations of the Economic War, Fianna Fáil's obsession with wheat and commodity tillage, excessive government interference and general Fianna Fáil incompetence.

> The situation with regard to agriculture in Ireland when I took office was quite remarkable. The fact was that there were fewer cattle, fewer pigs and fewer sheep on the land of Ireland in 1948 than there ever had been in the recent history of the country ... certainly since the famine. There was also a serious lack of fertility in the soil. This was by no means the entire responsibility of Fianna Fáil, but was the result of the World War, which had had the consequence that since 1939 no, or very little, potash or phosphate was available for farmers to use on the land. But above and beyond that, the Fianna Fáil administration in the Department of Agriculture had been deplorable. They were obsessed with growing wheat, and compelling farmers to grow wheat, but they had entirely overlooked the fact that they were running down the fertility of the soil, and were in fact mining the soil instead of cultivating it. When I took office, there was not in the whole of Ireland one ton of ground limestone, and yet it was true that virtually 90% of the land of Ireland was grossly deficient in lime.[21]

Dillon was only the fourth Minister for Agriculture in the history of the state, following Patrick Hogan (1922-32), Jim Ryan (1932-1947) and Paddy Smith (1947-1948). He began his new role by getting to know his department and quickly formed a high opinion of the civil servants there.

'I found about one-third of the personnel wanting to continue in their old traditions, like ancient Roman chariots going down the ruts in the stone paths, but the other two-thirds frustrated and almost despairing on occasion.'[22] Dillon believed the latter group welcomed his appointment, and that certainly is the view which has been handed down in the department's own folklore. Dillon observed: 'In those three years I had perhaps less than 10% who were quite unprepared to change radically, and I decided to let them pass out of the service in the ordinary course, which they very rapidly did ... I would say, in my whole experience ... I can only think of two civil servants who consciously and deliberately let me down. They were as rare an exception as that. Of course there were good men and bad, some brilliant men, some extremely pedestrian, but making due allowance for that, it was a joy to work there.'[23]

Dillon was in action on the first full day of the new Dáil on 25 February 1948, when he introduced a supplementary estimate for agriculture. Though the debate was restricted, he indicated at least some aspects of the policy he would follow. He proposed to extend and develop the livestock industry and end the compulsory growing of wheat, though the law in that regard would be enforced in the meantime. Having clarified these major points, he got stuck into the previous government's plans 'to adorn Connemara with glasshouses', a scheme he described as a 'disgusting fraud', but he said he would honour any commitments made by his predecessors.[24]

There were no congratulations or well-wishes on his appointment from the opposition, and it was clear from the start that Dillon was to be their principal target in the new administration. Aiken and MacEntee were quick into the attack, with MacEntee describing Dillon's wheat policy as 'gambling with the food of the people'.[25] Only Lemass, already the dominant figure of Fianna Fáil in opposition, was reasonable and measured.

In early March the new minister elaborated on his priorities at a conference of county committees of agriculture. His aim was to produce maximum quantities of fat and store cattle for the British market and to remove the price discrimination between the two types of livestock. (The British at this stage deducted 9s 4d per cwt from the basic price of cattle fattened in Ireland, as opposed to Irish store cattle fattened in England.)[26]

He was also concerned to decontrol the bacon industry. The supply and quality of bacon was regulated by the Pigs and Bacon Commission, but the system was cumbersome and the regulations governing quality were frequently flouted. Dillon indicated that he was willing to lift the controls if certain guarantees were given by the curers, but things did not turn out as simply as that and before long he found himself embroiled in his first major controversy: the Bacon War.[27]

The curers wanted things both ways. In April Dillon accused them of calling for decontrol and at the same time hoarding up to forty per cent of the supply in anticipation of making bonanza profits when controls ended, and in the meantime profiting from shortages (which their actions had created) by supplying illegal bacon at black-market prices.[28] Dillon later told the Dáil that he had discovered 'an open, defiant and rampant black market in pork'. He introduced sweeping measures to bring the curers into line, including the closure of four factories and a number of shops, the issuing of severe warnings to hotels and the suspension of seven bacon curing licences. These steps seemed to work: by May the Pigs and Bacon Commission was reporting an increase in the supply of pigs and a corresponding drop in prices.[29] With further improvements in the market that month, the commission announced that controls on the supply and distribution of bacon would end on 1 June, and in August price control ended for the first time since 1940. Prices, not surprisingly, did not come down; the curers immediately increased their prices, leading to an increase of about two pence per pound to the consumer.[30] The price was to rise twice during 1950, by two pence a pound on each occasion.

Dillon clearly loved his new job and threw himself into the work, consuming files, commissioning studies, talking to officials, and travelling throughout the country to find out about conditions for himself. Twelve-hour days became the norm, and from the start he decided to use every publicity device at his disposal to highlight his plans. He was unashamedly the 'farmers' minister'. As he told a gathering shortly after his appointment: 'We farmers are not a boastful lot, but we are constrained occasionally to remind the doctor, the lawyer and the tramp, that we, in the last analysis, maintain them all.'[31]

His impact on the Department of Agriculture was immediate and positive. Dillon had at one time dismissed the Secretary of the Department, Sean Ó Broin, as a 'desk man', but he soon reversed this assessment and established a good working relationship with him. He was an energetic minister and worked his civil servants hard. He insisted on seeing all files for himself and, unusually for the time, would frequently go down the line to talk directly to the official who was dealing with a particular issue. He usually skipped lunch and worked late in the evening. He wrote his own replies to all parliamentary questions, reminding his officials that the parliamentary question was one of the great planks of democracy. His civil servants instinctively liked him, seeing him as a serious minister and one who was quick to acknowledge their work. He was always formal in his dealings with department personnel, but at the same time thoughtful at a personal level, and marked special occasions with presents for his staff.[32]

Dillon's view of government was simple. He was a team player, prepared to fight his corner, but once a decision was taken it had his full and robust support. Loyalty to his colleagues was central, and if this meant publicly supporting a line he had opposed in cabinet, then full public support he would give. Once there was agreement on general policy he expected to be left alone to get on with his job, and he was prepared to accord to his colleagues both the same freedom from interference and the right to expect his support whenever times became difficult.

At a personal level he got on well with his new colleagues. Costello, 'a decent man who comes of decent people', he had long known and liked. Dillon found him a bad chairman, who would frequently hold up proceedings by telling protracted anecdotes, 'to the extent that one would sometimes despair of doing any business. But he was so good a man, and everyone was so personally devoted to him, that when the chips were down no one would bring him to order.'[33] This view of Costello's chairmanship is not necessarily accurate. Dillon's view failed to see his skill at avoiding or postponing decisions which might well have proven divisive. More than anybody else, Costello was conscious of the need to hold his colleagues together, even at the price of fudge and dither.[34]

Sean MacBride was an old friend whose judgement Dillon did not find impressive; in fact, on many issues he had 'the judgement of a hen'.[35] Joe Blowick, rough-hewn and warm, was the best of men but his effectiveness as a minister was, according to Dillon, lessened by his lack of formal education. Blowick, in fact, was almost illiterate.[36] Norton, with whom Dillon had many battles, especially on the question of the IRA and neutrality, he admired greatly, and the two found themselves frequently in alliance. Paddy McGilligan was probably the dominant figure in the cabinet, certainly the dominant intellectual force. Dillon had great respect for him and the two worked well together in spite of some early clashes.

Dan Morrissey he regarded as an effective Minister for Industry and Commerce, and he praised his establishment of the Industrial Development Authority. He also remembered Morrissey as a particularly fine platform orator, 'who could be heard 300 yards away without amplification'. The regard he showed for Morrissey in his *Memoir* is very much at odds with the assessment of their relationship which Noel Browne gives in *Against the Tide*, where he claimed Dillon had great contempt for Morrissey and frequently humiliated him in cabinet. Nobody else has ever made this charge. Liam Cosgrave, who attended cabinet meetings, recalls a warm and friendly relationship between the two men.[37]

The new government, describing itself as the Inter Party government, was a coalition in a country which had become accustomed to the simplicities of single-party administration, where a strict interpretation of the Westminster model prevailed. In fact, during the Fianna Fáil years the rigidities of that model had been accentuated by the party's emphasis on its absolute need to present at all times a united face to a hostile world. Even though there were often strong differences in cabinet,[38] their existence remained secret. At the very apex of the party structure, the cabinet enshrined the doctrine of collective responsibility in a way that even a politburo might have envied.

Costello adopted a much more relaxed approach. It may be that he simply accepted the inevitable in allowing differences of opinion to be aired publicly, while in the administration compromise became a way of life, postponement and deferral everyday occurrences. In the process he shocked the purists, dismayed his civil servants, and gave Fianna Fáil endless scope for displays of indignation. But by and large the Costello system worked. Through common sense and negotiating skills, he pioneered in Ireland a style of leadership which would have made him an admirable end-of-century coalition leader.

Some of the new government's working methods were ham-fisted, however. After sixteen years of Fianna Fáil there was a feeling that civil servants could not be fully trusted. This view was held most strongly by MacBride, who had a well-developed sense of intrigue, and supported by Browne, himself no mean conspiracy theorist. This suspicion led to the exclusion of the Secretary to the Government, Maurice Moynihan, from cabinet meetings. The decision was offensive and unnecessary, and had the practical consequence that notes of decisions in cabinet were often imprecise; indeed, it was not always clear when decisions were actually made. According to David McCullagh in his definitive study of the Inter Party government, *A Makeshift Majority*, this was to contribute to the confusion surrounding the two most controversial episodes of the time: the repeal of the External Relations Act and the Mother and Child scheme. Yet in spite of these difficulties, before long the new government was, according to *The Irish Times*, showing a sense of cohesion and purpose and withstanding Fianna Fáil's assaults with some ease.

Dillon's relations with his fellow Independents were not so solid, however, and this was to be a continuing feature of the government. The group met on a regular basis initially and worked together on day-to-day matters of parliamentary business, such as the allocation of committee places and the exchanging of information about forthcoming business. Liam Cosgrave, the government Whip, kept the group abreast of developments, and had an informal arrangement which ensured that sufficient Independents were always present at critical divisions to generate a comfortable majority – which was rarely lower than ten during the three-year life of the government.[39]

Dillon started well with the Independents. At their first recorded meeting on 9 March 1948, he told them that 'each had been elected as an Independent and each was entitled to maintain his independence'. Dillon assured the Independent TDs that he would always be happy to meet them, and advised them to appoint a Whip to represent their views to the government.[40] The Independents did not appoint a Whip – Oliver Flanagan liaised informally with Liam Cosgrave – and they continued to meet until the end of 1948, at which time their meetings seem to peter out. They left no criticism of Dillon in their records, but it is difficult to avoid the conclusion that his attitude to them was somewhat detached, offering them neither leadership nor intimacy. Perhaps not surprisingly, he did not see it as his responsibility to mould them into a cohesive voting bloc, but neither did it occur to him that normal political prudence would suggest that he make an effort to keep in touch and pay some attention to their concerns.

Inevitably, misunderstandings and tensions surfaced. Before long he had crossed swords with Patrick Cogan, and not long after he fell out with the Cavan Independent, Patrick F. O'Reilly. With Cogan the falling-out was perhaps unavoidable. Cogan was a man of strong views, robustly (and lengthily) expressed, and neither he nor Dillon were much given to compromise. O'Reilly's gloomy view of the world and his Cavan scepticism made him question much of what Dillon had to say and suspicious of his orotund style of saying it, while Dillon frequently remarked that listening to O'Reilly made the 'Miserere' sound cheerful.

Dillon could almost certainly have tried harder to facilitate the Independents, especially in view of the government's need to retain their support, but long before the government came to an end some of his colleagues were openly wondering how many more of the Independents he would alienate. His relationship with his Independent colleagues did, however, illustrate one aspect of Dillon as a minister. Infinitely courteous and considerate, he was not prepared to trim or be expedient, or indeed to admit to being wrong, even if it meant losing vital votes. As a characteristic it may have been admirable, but as politics it was highly dangerous, and more than once posed problems for the government Chief Whip, Liam Cosgrave.[41]

DILLON HAD set full access to the British market as one of his priorities, and within a month of taking office he made his first trip to London at the invitation of the Chancellor of the Exchequer, Stafford Cripps. The meeting was a prelude to full-scale negotiations scheduled for 17 June 1948.[42]

The Anglo-Irish trade talks were the first such negotiations for ten years. Much had happened since, and now any sustained Irish recovery depended in great part on securing a good trading relationship with Britain. The talks would have taken place no matter who was in power, but this did not prevent the new government from presenting them as its own initiative. Dillon, who was convinced that he could get a better deal than the gruff anglophobe, Paddy Smith, also saw the talks taking place in the context of significant Marshall Aid soon becoming available, much of which he expected to be channelled into agricultural development. Dillon recognised also that the international dimension of the talks – and international involvement of any sort was a rarity in those days – gave him an opportunity to convey to the farming public his own sense of excitement about the possibilities ahead.[43]

The talks opened in London on 17 June. The Irish party, eighteen in all, was the largest ever for such talks and included the Taoiseach, five ministers and the heads of all the major Departments of State. The principal object of the Irish mission was, in Costello's words, 'to get free admission to Britain for Irish agriculture and industrial produce'. Dillon, never one to lose the opportunity for the eye-catching phrase, boomed out at the press conference when the delegation arrived in London: 'We will drown you in eggs within the next two years.'[44]

In his *Memoir*, Dillon summed up his objective as getting free access for Irish produce at the same prices for Irish farmers as their British counterparts. Costello's economic adviser at this time, the economist Patrick Lynch, claims that what Dillon wanted was essentially the integration of Ireland's and Britain's agricultural economies, but 'pressure from British farm interests [was] to prevent its realisation'.[45]

In specific terms, the cabinet economic committee, meeting on 2 June 1948, indicated the objectives they were trying to achieve. The list was extensive. The government wanted to see an end to import quotas and other restrictions on Irish good. They looked for the abolition of quantitative restrictions on Irish agricultural, horticultural and fishery products; a review of the rate of supply of essential goods from the UK, including fertilisers, plant and machinery, and changes to the 1938 Anglo-Irish agreement to provide adequate safeguards against dumping. The government was also concerned to ensure adequate supplies of coal, coke and manufactured fuel from Britain. Not least, they sought to be allowed use quantitative restrictions on British goods as part of Ireland's industrial development policy.[46]

Dillon greatly enjoyed foreign excursions, and especially the opportunity to make new friends and to argue his case in new surroundings. In March he had met Chancellor of the Exchequer Stafford Cripps and British Food Minister John Strachey. The earlier talks resulted in the price for Irish cattle liveweight being fixed at the British level rather than a penny a pound lower – a not inconsiderable amount for the farmer – and Dillon had been impressed with the fairness of Cripps, who had been very supportive. Later, he recalled sitting beside Strachey at an official luncheon during the talks proper and remarking that he had come to London with a strong prejudice against Cripps because of his extreme left-wing views, 'but the more I deal with him the more I am struck by his extraordinary broad mindedness and willingness to listen to an argument and to accept it, even against the advice of his permanent officials, if he finds it convincing.' Strachey told Dillon, 'The reason Cripps is admired is that he is a perfect Christian. Stafford really asks himself what would Christ do in such a situation? And when he has decided, he does it.'[47]

The trade talks were regarded as a success by both sides, though the results were hardly earth-shattering in their consequences. Dillon was more than happy with the outcome. Henceforth the price differential of five shillings per hundredweight between Irish and British fat cattle on the British market would be abolished, and the British market would be open to the exportable surpluses of other agricultural produce. Dillon told the Dáil a few weeks later that the country was 'standing on the threshold of the greatest period of expansion in the agricultural industry. Over the next five years we can increase the volume of output by 25 per cent and up to 100 per cent in the volume of exports.'[48]

Like all such trade talks, there was no immediate way of estimating how successful they had been. In the early stages the results were difficult to see, especially since considerable detail needed to be worked out after the agreements had been signed. However, the benefit of linking Irish prices to those paid to British farmers was shown in April 1949, when British farmers got a price increase for beef which was almost immediately passed on to Irish farmers selling on the British market.[49] Export figures showed a sharp increase. In the first six months of 1948, 77,000 cattle were exported to Britain; this rose to 120,000 for the same period in 1949, while overall cattle exports to Britain increased by fifty per cent that year.[50] A new market for lamb exports was opened up and agreed prices put in place for egg exports. On butter, however, Dillon met with less success: he managed to find new markets in France and Germany, but ended up having to import butter from New Zealand and Denmark to make up for the shortfall in Irish production. Here, in any case, Britain's Commonwealth commitment to New Zealand made any substantial agreement with Ireland more difficult.

Dillon had no doubt that the talks had been a success and he was in no mood to under-sell the achievement. He told the Dáil: 'If I never achieve anything else in public life the comparatively trivial part I played in negotiating this agreement is quite sufficient to justify the fifteen years I spent pottering about this House. There is no job I would prefer in this wide world than to be Minister for Agriculture in this country ... This agreement provides for the farmers of this country a sure and certain market at remunerative prices for every conceivable product that the land of Ireland can produce.'⁵¹

That Agriculture Estimate on 9 July 1948 was Dillon's first full parliamentary outing as Minister for Agriculture. By now he had had almost five months to clarify his thoughts and order his priorities. During the debate, by far the longest of any of the estimates, Dillon set out his programme for what he hoped would be a five-year tenure, and gave his opinion on many current agricultural issues.

He told the Dáil he deliberately set high targets: 'if we fail to reach it then the fault will be largely mine, for I have no doubt that the farmers of this country will do their part, as they have always done, if given the materials, the implements and the opportunity. My job as Minister for Agriculture is to make available to them materials and instruments and to get them the opportunity to dispose of the fruits of their labour. The last I have already done [in the Anglo-Irish Agreement]. The other I am in the process of doing.'⁵²

He went down through his priorities. A rise in output would be of no use unless accompanied by increased profits for farmers, and this in turn must be accompanied by better wages for agricultural workers. On the question of wheat, he said it was a 'wartime necessity' and 'only a fool would impose on his people in times of peace the policies of war'. His own view remained that growing wheat on Irish land when supplies were available from other sources was 'a waste of land', though he respected the right of those who grew wheat and would persuade the government to guarantee the price of the crop over the next five years.

He was adamant, however, that the era of compulsion was over. This was a pet subject, touching on his hatred of state interference. 'In future the Minister for Agriculture, down to the most junior inspector, will enter on his neighbour's land by invitation or not at all.' As was his wont, he went too far in his descriptions of 'gaitered inspectors' crawling all over defenceless farms.⁵³ The inspectors were not pleased, Fianna Fáil immediately made an issue of it, and ultimately Dillon had to back-pedal.

If the Minister for Agriculture was against wheat, he was strongly for barley. He wanted 700,000 barrels of malting barley the next year and guaranteed a price of fifty-five shillings as against thirty-five to forty shillings heretofore. He wanted in fact as large an acreage of feeding barley as possible: 'grow all the oats your land will produce' was his advice.

He turned to what was to remain a major theme – the need to rehabilitate the soil. The situation was serious; since 1939 only very small quantities of potash or phosphate were available for farmers to use on land. Shortly after his appointment, Dillon commissioned a report from a New Zealand soil expert which confirmed what he already knew, that 'much of the land was virtually derelict'. The report claimed that Ireland had enormous potential for pasture production but that the capacity of the soil had been hugely damaged by the fact that compulsory tillage had been imposed on land long starved of fertilisers. Dillon promised to do everything to secure quantities of limestone, whether by import or through home production. A programme of soil testing would also be carried out with the involvement of local committees of agriculture.

He was upbeat about prospects for the dairy industry. With improved grassland and feeding for cows he saw a real future for the butter, cheese, cream, chocolate crumb, condensed milk, dried milk and baby food industries. That was all very well, but there was no way he could stop there, and so the Minister launched himself into one of the perennial controversies of the period. It is hard to believe, from a distance of fifty years, that the subject could excite such strong feelings, but excite them it did. And Dillon had no intention of not contributing his views on the matter:

> I am in favour of letting my neighbour run his farm his own way; but if he wants my opinion on the best dairy cow he can keep in this country, then it must be the dual purpose shorthorn cow.

And with total disregard for the susceptibilities of a large segment of his agricultural constituency, he ploughed on:

> I know there are a lot of old maids and cranks in this country who keep Jerseys and Guernseys and Freisians ... and they are out in the morning brushing them down and washing them with soap and water and feeding them with milk and stuffing them with little handfuls of grass and treating them as if they were Pekinese dogs. The poor old shorthorn comes in and is milked and gets a slap on the behind and is sent out on the hill for the rest of the evening. Her lactation is then compared with the lactation of the Freisan, who is fed nearly with rashers each morning ... then the Freisian is produced at the Royal Dublin Society Show and her milk is flooding the whole place and they are running for buckets to collect it and take it off. Then you find that the butter fat content is 1.4 and you begin to wonder if this is the water to wash the dairy with or milk from the cow. The poor old shorthorn comes in from the side of the hill and she is milked and out she goes again; she comes in again in the evening and she is milked and there is no respect for her at all.[54]

In short, Dillon was saying that if she were fed as well as other breeds, his department would favour the shorthorn. He could never be accused of understating his case. His remarks generated a flurry of controversy, with Fianna Fáil expressing particular outrage at Dillon's reference to Freisian owners as old maids and cranks.

This major Dáil speech included other aspects of what was to become distinctive Dillon policy during his two ministerial terms. He came back to his theme of 'drowning the English in eggs'. It had already caught the public imagination, though it was later to backfire somewhat when over-supply and the recovery of production in Britain resulted in lower egg prices. In his *Memoir* Dillon explained the origin of the phrase, which occurred during the press conference to launch the Anglo-Irish talks: 'Mr. Costello, who was a hot-tempered man, found some question which was addressed to him peculiarly provocative and proceeded to reply to the Press man with considerable emphasis. I thought that was an expedient moment to relieve the situation and I said "come gentlemen, our prime purpose in coming in here is to see you get a little of what you fancy. I imagine you'd like an egg for your breakfast these times, and you're not getting it, but if you'll pay us a fair price for eggs, we'll drown you with eggs."'[55]

Later, he was to introduce the parish plan, with the express intention of promoting self-help and self-reliance at local level, and he presaged this now, encouraging farmers to join young farmers' clubs and Muintir na Tíre. He warned that such groups must 'keep me and my likes at arm's length ... assert their absolute independence of government ... of political organisations ... of any external source of power that seeks to control them'. He advised Muintir na Tíre that one of the greatest services it could perform would be 'to make our people see and understand that the natural unit for co-operative work in rural Ireland ... is the parish'.[56] It was not until his second term as minister, however, that he really got to grips with the parish plan.

Dillon may have been a traditionalist in his attachment to the land, but he was emphatic about the need to modernise and invest in new buildings and equipment. He ran into a major row when he declared that the era of the horse was over and the sooner the tractor took over the better. His remarks were seen as elitist, anti-small farmer and anti-national, though Dillon justified what he had said on the grounds of agriculture's absolute need for greater productivity. He argued that the industrial worker had the tools of the day while the tools of the agricultural worker were seventy years out of date, and this simply would not be allowed continue. He proposed a farm building scheme, but had to admit that this would be delayed because of the shortage of cement, a shortage, he insisted, which was as real in his predecessor's time as it was now, but Smith had not told the farmers the truth.[57]

Reaction to Dillon's programme was mixed. The government and most of the Independents were enthusiastic, an opinion also reflected in both the *Irish Independent* and *The Irish Times*. Not so, however, with Fianna Fáil. With a few exceptions, including Ryan and Lemass, the opposition's reaction was abusive and personalised. Smith, at times almost incoherent with rage, called Dillon 'bats and irresponsible', a 'shorthorn fool' who 'will wreck everything with which he comes into contact'.[58] Smith was especially angry about what he called the minister's 'greatest codology – the double dairy cow, the single dairy cow and the beef shorthorn bull, crossing one with the other and expecting to retain milk here and beef there.' Smith was also very angry about Dillon's observations on the Connemara glasshouse scheme, but his dislike of Dillon ran very much deeper. He took a stab at Dillon's stance on neutrality – 'We should have put him under lock and key.' But perhaps the real reason for his hostility surfaced during Smith's five-hour speech when he claimed Dillon had called him 'a calf jobber's son', a charge emphatically and repeatedly denied by Dillon.[59] Curiously, and in spite of their frequent bruising exchanges, Dillon, the film buff, confided to his private secretary that he could never be too hard on Smith – 'he's so like Spencer Tracey'.[60]

CHAPTER FIFTEEN

AN EMBATTLED MINISTER

GALLINA SENESCENS DELENDA EST
Department of Agriculture advertisement, 1950

THE FIRST MAJOR controversy to hit the new government concerned the repeal of the External Relations Act. The subsequent writings on this question have concentrated more on the manner in which the decision was taken, and the different opinions on the matter which existed in cabinet, than on the substance of the move itself. The episode was used in particular to indicate a breakdown in normal cabinet procedures and an example of major policy being made in a spur-of-the-moment fashion. It was seized upon by opponents of the government as evidence of its inherent instability and imminent collapse.

The External Relations Act had been passed in emergency session at the time of the abdication of King Edward VI in 1936. In essence, the Act removed all references to the Crown and Governor General from the Constitution in relation to the internal affairs of the state, but reinstated the Crown's authority in external affairs. In practical terms this meant that all Irish diplomats carried letters of accreditation from the King of England, and Ireland remained a member of the Commonwealth, albeit an inactive one. De Valera justified the retention of this tenuous link with the Crown by saying that it 'might go towards meeting the sentiment of the people in the Six Counties', but the situation was probably best summed up by Sean MacEoin, who said the Act allowed Fianna Fáil to 'be in the position of being able to say down in the Bog of Allen that they are Republicans, and of being able to say in Piccadilly that they are imperialists.'[1] At the time of its enactment, Costello had described the Bill as 'a constitutional monstrosity', while Dillon had been blistering, seeing it as a massive act of hypocrisy. He constantly goaded de Valera about his 'dictionary Republic', whereby Ireland satisfied all dictionary definitions of the word 'republic', but without the word itself actually being used.[2]

By the late 1940s the External Relations Act had become a nonsense. Patrick McGilligan, Fine Gael's leading constitutional expert, had attacked it in the 1947 Dáil Estimates on External Affairs, and de Valera had long come to the conclusion that it should be repealed. He had, in fact, instructed the Department of External Affairs to prepare a repealing Bill in October 1947, and by January 1948 had a draft which referred to the state as a Republic.[3] Though only Clann na Poblachta had promised to repeal the Act in the 1948 election campaign, subsequent speeches from all parties persuaded Lord Rugby, the British Minister in Dublin, that the annulment of the External Relations Act would not long be delayed. He reported that 'no party has left the door open for any other course ... the Irish have handled it in such a way as to discredit it ... it is now clear it will not provide the bridge for closer association, as was once hoped.'[4]

Fine Gael's official position in the 1948 election, as Garret FitzGerald, who canvassed in that election, has frequently pointed out, had been in favour of continued membership of the Commonwealth, even if O'Higgins had also called for repeal of the External Relations Act. The new government, however, soon became vulnerable to attack on this particular front.

In March 1948, de Valera began a world tour to focus attention on partition, visiting the US, India, Pakistan, New Zealand and Australia. De Valera's move was highly opportunistic and fostered an even more simplistic view of the problem than had heretofore existed. It marked a further hardening and deepening of an already sterile attitude to partition, ignored Unionist rights, proposed an unworkable solution, and had little to commend it to a post-war world engrossed with its own problems. One major effect of his campaign, however, was to put the government on the defensive; Clann na Poblachta, in particular, could not afford to be 'out-anti-partitioned' by Fianna Fáil. Meanwhile, there was a real possibility that Peadar Cowan, a radical Clann na Poblachta TD who had been expelled from the party at a very early stage in the life of the government 'for disloyalty to the organisation', would introduce a Private Members Bill to repeal the Act. As a result, the government hardened its line and inaugurated the all-party anti-partition campaign, a campaign which achieved nothing except to confirm the IRA in its belief in the futility of constitutional politics. For his part, Dillon saw no value in the anti-partition campaign, nor any point in complaining about it to countries who themselves had enormous post-war problems, and simply got on with his own work.

The government, however, could not afford to be seen as lacking zeal on these issues, and in August Norton declared in the Dáil that 'it would do our national self-respect good, both at home and abroad, if we were to proceed without delay to abolish the External Relations Act'.[5] De Valera invited him to 'go ahead, you will get no opposition from us'. As Minister for External Affairs, MacBride had already begun to undermine the Act, and it is clear he had full cabinet support, including Dillon's. Notwith-standing his enthusiasm for the Commonwealth, Dillon felt that the 'ambiguity of the External Relations Act meant Éire was living a lie'. According to the leading expert on the subject, Ian McCabe, 'the pressure from the anti-partition campaign made it politically imperative that some adjustment be seen to be made to partition, or as a substitute to the External Relations Act'.[6] This was August, and in September Costello made his celebrated 'announcement' in Canada.

It is not proposed to re-hash here the circumstances surrounding Costello's decision and the events which happened subsequently. There is no doubt, and certainly Dillon agreed in his *Memoir*, that proper proce-dures were not followed. Indeed, though it appears that there had been an informal discussion and agreement round the cabinet table, the government had not taken a formal decision on the matter. The accepted procedures of consultation with Britain had not been followed and traditional courtesies had been discarded.

Costello's Ottawa announcement was almost certainly a direct result of the celebrated leak to the *Sunday Independent* that Ireland intended declar-ing a Republic. This leak, which almost certainly came from MacBride,[7] forced Costello, in his own mind at any rate, into answering the questions put to him. Just as important was the danger that the British, forewarned about Ireland's intentions, would attempt later in the year to oblige Ireland either to retain the External Relations Act or forfeit membership of the Commonwealth. Such would have made Ireland's status seem dependent on Britain, a situation Costello was keen to avoid.

Be that as it may, the new situation should have created major problems for Dillon, not because of the declaration of a Republic, but because of the decision to leave the Commonwealth. If he was perturbed, he showed no signs of it. He accepted Costello's good faith and the reality of what had been done, and was little put out by any lack of finesse or procedural pro-priety. He was helped in making up his mind by his long-stated view that Ireland was living a 'constitutional lie'; that it was neither a Republic nor a member of the Commonwealth. Thus he had no difficulties about the title and status of the new state. He had said in more than one External Affairs debate that he was happy with a Republic so long as it was honestly based and did not make reunification more difficult. Admittedly, he had at times derided the concept of the Republic, or more especially the Fianna Fáil version of it, and that party had no intention of letting him forget the fact. Fianna Fáil mocked him as a 'West Brit', while the *Irish Press* depicted him in its cartoons wearing a Union Jack apron.

More important than the state's constitutional status was the question of the Commonwealth. Dillon had long been the foremost advocate of a vigorous Irish role within the association and, as Patrick Kavanagh noted in his election coverage, this was a view which many of those who voted for him shared. Dillon should have had difficulty with the decision to with-draw from the Commonwealth, but did not. Just as he was later to support the government's determination not to seek membership of NATO because of partition, not only did he accept the government view but set about defending it with vigour. He was in the US at the Food and Agriculture Organisation (FAO) conference when the matter came before the Dáil in November, but he had been careful to make his position clear before leav-ing in a speech which was widely reported.[8]

The repeal of the Act, he said, was 'essential to the restoration of the country's self-respect'. The Act 'imposed on all our people the disgusting necessity of living a lie, pretending to be one thing inside Ireland and to be quite another outside; smuggling the diplomatic representatives of friendly foreign States into the country and dispatching their letters of credence furtively to London, while they were escorted to the Phoenix Park, and requesting our own Minister in foreign capitals to explain at endless length that, although their letters of credence spoke on behalf of the King, they represented Ireland, whose Republican Constitution admitted of no King in its machinery of government.'

He went on to argue that relations with the Commonwealth countries could now in fact be improved. They shared a common heritage based on liberty, democracy and social institutions founded upon Christian tradi-tions, and he felt a 'more enduring friendship' was possible. He hoped that they were on the brink of a new era of international collaboration, embrac-ing not just the old Commonwealth countries but also the USA, and that together they would engage in a common democratic crusade.

Dillon was to return to this theme throughout his life, though he never fully explained how leaving the Commonwealth could in fact strengthen Ireland's relations with it. He was on firmer ground, however, in arguing that the existing relationship was little more than a legal and political fiction.

In any event, his new position did not particularly displease his voters, while Fianna Fáil taunts about 'Republican James, draping himself in the habiliments of Tone' cost him no sleep. Curiously, he was to find *The Irish Times*, which felt a genuine sense of betrayal on the issue, much less forgiv-ing, and from this point on he and Costello received little praise from that paper.

DILLON WAS a genuine believer in international co-operation and saw it as nowhere so important as in his own sphere of agriculture. He had enjoyed the Anglo-Irish negotiations, and welcomed even more the opportunity to represent Ireland at the FAO conference in Washington in November 1948. The Fianna Fáil ministers had not been given to attending international conferences – because of lack of opportunity as much as anything else – but in the new government both Dillon and MacBride were enthusiastic travellers. The conference was convened to address in particular the endemic shortages of food in the post-war world. Peace, Dillon thought, was a prerequisite of food production, and then:

> Our first and indispensable step in that direction must be to stop trying to strangle one another with tariffs, exchange restrictions, quotas and other devices designed to make international exchange of goods impossible and the movement of food from areas of plenty to areas of scarcity.
>
> There is no use producing food in excess of our own national requirements if we are prevented by tariffs, quotas, exchange restrictions, etc. from selling the surplus or buying the things we want to get in exchange for our agricultural surplus.

That was straightforward enough, but he shocked many of the delegates with his next point:

> I deprecate the implied suggestion in much of what has been said that the Malthusian theory of impending disaster from excess of population is valid and that therefore one method of resolving the problem of food supplies is to reduce artificially the birth rate of mankind. This theory is utterly false and utterly evil.
>
> There is no reason to suppose that Divine Providence has ordained that the resources of this world, properly employed, shall not suffice for the requirements of mankind. To date it is manifest that these resources, had they been adequately availed of, were more than sufficient and where they have in fact failed to meet the demand, the failure was due to the follies of men rather than the insufficiency of resources.

Political correctness, even of the 1948 category, was not on his agenda. He had been genuinely annoyed by what he saw as the facile resort to an easy and, to his way of thinking, immoral solution, when there was so much that could and should be done:

> If the present population of the world had been foreseen by our forefathers in the eighteenth century, they would have been panic-stricken, and it is a chastening thought that if in their panic they had adopted the remedy of population limitation, many of the delegates here present would never have been born. Perhaps those of my colleagues here present who regret having been born would stand up and tell us why he would prefer never to have been. Here then is what we can do now.

And he followed with a list of practical suggestions, most of which would bear scrutiny fifty years later.[9]

It was Dillon's very good fortune that the US-backed European Recovery Programme (ERP) – or Marshall Aid – became available to Ireland just as he became Minister for Agriculture.[10] Ireland had been invited to participate in the Recovery Programme in 1947, not because of US good-will but because Washington believed Ireland had the potential to aid Europe's recovery by producing more food, thus reducing America's burden. In addition, it was thought that relieving Ireland's dollar problems would help to avoid an excessive drain on British hard currency reserves. There was also a fear, remote but present, that if Ireland were excluded from Marshall Aid she might be in some way vulnerable to communist influence.

Negotiations leading up to Marshall Aid had begun under the Fianna Fáil government at a meeting in Paris in July 1947, when the Irish delegation was led by the Department of External Affairs. Despite the hostility of the Department of Finance and the Central Bank to the plan, the Inter Party government was enthusiastic, if at times naive, about the possibilities on offer. MacBride, whose Department of External Affairs would administer the fund, was particularly zealous. Finance opposed Marshall Aid, not only because of its own loss of influence in a vital financial and economic area, but because of what it saw as the inevitable 'squandering' of money by politicians on useless and inflationary projects, without any thought of how the monies might be repaid.

Ultimately Ireland was to receive $128 million in loans and $18 million in grant aid, providing almost fifty per cent of total state investment between 1948-51. It was the first time since independence that Ireland benefited from an infusion of outside funding, which would help not just to boost its rundown economy, but to introduce an element of development strategy where none had previously existed.

Dillon was a keen supporter of the Marshall Plan. Having followed events on the continent, he was concerned with the need to secure the democratic structures of France and Italy, both of which were then in real danger of a communist takeover, and he praised the 'princely generosity of the American people in their approach to the difficulties of Europe'. His only regret was that the partnership was not closer.[11] He enthusiastically backed MacBride's ambitious plans for 'productive investment', not least because many of his major proposals concerned agriculture. For a new minister, this offered a real chance to make a dramatic impact.

The bilateral agreement between Ireland and the US was signed on 28 June 1948 and the first monies became available in October. 'The conservative counsels of Finance and the Central Bank to sterilise the funds' went unheeded as MacBride and Dillon flooded the cabinet table with proposals for investment.[12] Finance was deeply shocked. 'Before we have even a single ERP dollar,' a Finance memo noted, 'here are two Departments busy thinking up ways of ridding us of the prospective *embarras de riches*.'[13] The department's hostility did not worry Dillon. As we shall see later, he had a deep distrust of its leading officials' judgement and a contempt for what he saw as their Treasury-inspired conservatism.

Some historians have been critical of the handling of the Marshall Aid project, particularly the lack of a development strategy to underpin the exercise. This criticism is almost certainly unfair or at least misdirected: the new government had only just assumed office, and if Finance and the civil service was unprepared for the task, that fault, if anybody's, belonged to their predecessors of sixteen years. Bernadette Whelan takes a kinder view in her study of the way Marshall Aid was used. 'The Marshall Plan contributed to laying the ground-work not only for the subsequent emergence of the modern Irish economy, but for Ireland's participation in Europe; involvement in the OEEC developed into close association via OECD and subsequently the EC.'[14]

Dillon's proposals on agriculture were based on the fundamental need to increase productivity at all levels in order to sustain and increase export earnings, which in turn would buy much-needed fertilisers and machinery. Within that framework, his emphasis was on ensuring assured prices and guaranteed markets, improving the quality of livestock, providing better veterinary services, encouraging mechanisation and modernisation, and providing local leadership through committees of agriculture. All of these were attempted with varying degrees of success, but undoubtedly Dillon's most spectacular scheme under Marshall Aid was the Land Reclamation project.

The Land Reclamation project illustrates Dillon's style at its best. It also gives an insight into the feelings of Finance Minister Patrick McGilligan on the central question of state investment in capital projects, which was still treated with great suspicion by his department. McGilligan had himself fought bitterly against Finance in the 1920s, when as Minister for Industry and Commerce he had initiated the Shannon Scheme,[15] and he was much closer to the new Keynesian ideas now being brought to the cabinet table by Patrick Lynch and Alexis FitzGerald.[16] In fact, within the new government a quiet revolution was taking place in economic and financial thinking. Patrick Lynch, one of the main architects of this change, has written that what increasingly distinguished the Inter Party government from Fianna Fáil was its belief that capital investment by the state could best solve the basic Irish economic problem of providing jobs for the thousands who were unemployed or forced to emigrate. McGilligan in particular became, in Lynch's words, 'a formidable exponent of the relevance of employment theory to economic policy'.[17] In saying this, it must also be noted that McGilligan's flinty northernness did not desert him, and he was conscious of the cost of borrowing to the taxpayer.

Dillon's *Memoir* illustrates the point. Shortly after it was announced that Marshall Aid funds had become available, Dillon went on a characteristic 'solo run' at a meeting in Mullingar, where he declared that the funds would be used 'to replenish the entire land of Ireland with the potash, nitrogen and lime that it so urgently required'. Dillon recalled that the speech caused 'considerable confusion' in the Department of Finance. 'By the time I got to Dublin from Mullingar the whole Department of Finance was in a state of upheaval. The only calm man was my colleague, Paddy McGilligan, who, on the whole, thought it was a good idea, but felt perhaps I had spoken a little out of turn, because I hadn't had prior consultation with him, and it seemed rather odd that the Minister for Agriculture should be committing all the Marshall Aid to his own Department.'[18] Though Dillon did not admit it, the incident showed that his observance of cabinet procedures could be cavalier, if not completely out of order.

Dillon was right in his assessment of the poor fertility of much of Ireland's land. Not only had it been starved of fertiliser over the previous decade, but considerable amounts of hitherto fertile land had reverted to bog or quasi-bogland. Independent assessments put the fertility and general physical condition of the land at a very low ebb in 1947, but worse was to follow with the spread of asphosphoris, a disease in cattle caused by a lack of phosphates in the herbage. When he realised how widespread asphosphoris had become, Dillon personally drew up advertisements which appeared on hoardings and newspapers all over the country setting out the symptoms of the disease and providing simple remedies. And, as has been noted, he recruited the services of a New Zealand expert, GA Holmes, to carry out a survey of the grasslands of Ireland.[19] Holmes advised that farming's rejuvenation should be based on grass, and he thought a thorough drainage campaign, followed by liming and fertiliser, was a prerequisite for this development.

Dillon was thoroughly critical of Fianna Fáil's handling of this matter during its years in office. He claimed in his *Memoir* that they had failed to install an adequate system of soil testing, an essential step if efforts were to be made to restore the fertility of the soil. 'I remember going down to the Agricultural College in Ballyhaise in County Cavan,' he recalled, 'where I found an old man and a boy testing soil samples by a remarkable method. They had rigged up a bicycle wheel, with a medicine bottle tied to it, in which the soil sample was mixed with water. The boy turned the bicycle wheel, and thus the soil sample was tested. This was representative of the state of affairs at that time.'[20]

The New Zealand report confirmed Dillon's own assessment, and out of it was born the Land Reclamation project, a scheme which quickly captured the imagination of the agricultural community. The plan was incorporated in the Land Bill of 1949, which Dillon steered through the Dáil and Seanad in June and early July of that year. The essentials were simple; indeed, simplicity was a key objective. Form-filling was reduced to a minimum and there was no compulsion on farmers to participate. The scheme aimed at the reclamation of four-and-a-half million acres by means of draining, liming and fertilising fields, removing scrub and boulders, improving fencing and hill-grazing and reclaiming estuarine marshland. The state provided two-thirds of the cost, subject to a maximum of £20 per acre. The farmer could do the work himself or have it done by the newly established Land Project Organisation, in which case the Department of Finance paid two-fifths of the total cost subject to a maximum of £12 per acre. As far as payment was concerned, farmers could pay directly or add the cost to the annuities they paid to the Land Commission. The only caveat was that as each portion was reclaimed, if analysis showed up continuing soil deficiency, part of the grant was given as a supply of ground limestone and phosphates.[21]

The Land Reclamation project was spectacularly successful. The strongest criticism made of it was that it merely postponed the inevitable in making holdings economic that could never be so on a long-term basis, and that it would have been wiser to concentrate resources on improving farms that were already viable.[22] Perhaps. In the Ireland of 1949, at a time of universal food shortages, such a view carried little weight, and nobody then could be blamed for not foreseeing the subsequent explosion of productivity and the dramatic decline in the agricultural sector's importance to the Irish economy.

The reasons for the success of the project reflected Dillon at his best and showed him to be, in modern parlance, a 'hands-on' minister. He had an idea and nothing was going to stop him. He cut through red tape and bureaucracy to get his legislation through. He had to – and did – overcome the objections of the Board of Works, and in doing so he noted, 'I sometimes feel a little anxious in the realisation that I inclined to conservativism in my salad days and find myself becoming more radical as my hair turns grey.' It should be noted, too, that in all of this he had the staunch support of McGilligan, a fact he acknowledged in his Dáil speech of 5 July.[23]

In it he attacked Fianna Fáil for insisting that the scheme should be free of charge: 'Our people are not sycophantic paupers who can be bought by shovelling public money into their hands ... the role of the State is to make available the means of doing that which the owner of the land has never been able to do since his father bought it from the landlord, and which he never would be able to do if the community as a whole are not prepared to make provision for doing it.'[24]

There is no doubt whatever that Dillon was emotionally involved in the project and saw his work as a continuation of his father's: 'I do not deny that it gives me a certain satisfaction to have been appointed by my own people to repair the land in 1949 which the Land League recovered for our people in 1879.'[25] In fact the scheme, which was begun on a pilot basis in eight selected counties, started in Mayo on 16 August 1949, the seventieth anniversary to the day of Michael Davitt's founding of the Land League in Castlebar.[26]

With this combination of ministerial enthusiasm and simplicity of approach, good publicity and of course the help of Marshall Aid, the Land Reclamation Scheme soon became a fact of life all over the country. Farmers, used to hearing governments talk, now saw government in action. More than any other issue, it established Dillon's reputation as a minister who could deliver and confirmed him as one of the successes of the new government.

This view of the scheme, and indeed of Dillon himself, was not however shared by the Secretary of the Department of Finance, JJ McElligott, and his objections surfaced in the course of a lengthy correspondence with Dillon in early 1951. McElligott, the hard man of the Department of Finance, was critical of the administrative costs involved and was deeply sceptical about the scheme's real long-term value for money. Dillon told him that, while it would be imprudent to disregard value for money, he did not see this as the prime consideration, 'because if we can convert an uneconomic holding where a family has to be reared into an economic holding we have done something much more important than increase the national income; I suggest that what we have in fact achieved is the conversion of a family of potential paupers into a self-reliant and independent family of farmers.'

His argument cut little ice with McElligott. By this stage 28,000 farmers were availing of the scheme, but the average number of acres being reclaimed per farmer was little more than four. McElligott doubted that four extra acres would mean the difference between being 'a pauper' and an 'independent farmer'. He also pointed to a decline in the overall total of crops and pasture, comparing 1901 with 1950.

All of these criticisms were dismissed by Dillon in what must have been one of the more extraordinary letters ever to pass between a minister and the Secretary of the Department of Finance. Indeed, the fact that the correspondence took place at all was unusual, given that the normal channel was minister to minister and secretary to secretary. Only a fraction of the correspondence can be reproduced here.[27]

Dillon replied to McElligott on 10 April. He began by complimenting him on achieving 'a modest surplus' in revenue 'without the imposition of a penny's extra taxation ... how you reconcile these gratifying events with your perennial gloom is a mystery to me'. On the specific objections raised by McElligott, he argued that if administrative costs were high – which he denied – this was because they were start-up costs for a ten-year programme. Dillon pointed to the huge turnaround in renewing the fertility of the soil which had taken place in the previous three years, before moving on to what he saw as 'the heart of the matter ... the tendency of the Department of Finance to be concerned primarily with the money results immediately realisable from any financial outlay. Here is the fallacy which is, in growing measure, divorcing the Department of Finance from all reality and incidentally in growing measure depriving the government of the invaluable advice and guidance in economic affairs which it is entitled to expect and ought to have, from the experienced officers of the Department of Finance. The plain fact is that the Finance view has become so redolent of the Ivory Tower that nobody now pays the slightest attention to it, and this is a great pity, because it ought to be a valued corrective for those who are tempted to indulge in the luxury so wisely deprecated by the Marquis de Talleyrand, when he was heard to murmur *"pas trop de zèle"*.'

On the question of the decline in crops and pasture, Dillon asked McElligott why he was obsessed by the comparison between total crops and pasture for 1901 and 1950. 'These undoubtedly reveal the decline ... but if you look at the figures for 1947, 1948, 1949 and 1950 you will find the trend reversed. Is it not significant that the trend of fifty years has been reversed so quickly?'

And as for the small average number of acres being reclaimed, Dillon was totally dismissive. 'This comes strangely from one born into the kingdom of Kerry,' he told McElligott. 'Surely it is true that were we able to add four acres to every uneconomic holding in the congested areas of West Kerry we would have wrought something analogous to a miracle, and would have done much to resolve the problem of the uneconomic farmers of these congested areas.'

Dillon concluded by admonishing McElligott: 'Why sit by the Waters of Babylon to weep, when so much that deserved tears has been put an end to, and when we see ourselves surrounded by every evidence of a rising standard of living, in an atmosphere of relative calm in a world distracted by much woe.'

Dillon was prepared to borrow for socially desirable productive investment, but the concept rang alarm bells in the Department of Finance and drew criticism from Fianna Fáil, which by now had well and truly lost its radicalism of earlier decades. Dillon, however, told the Dáil in May 1950 that not only was he prepared to borrow to restore and refertilise Irish land, but he was prepared to borrow to build schools, to clear slums and to eliminate TB through the provision of sanitoria and hospitals. He was prudent, however, about the need for repayment: 'This Government is going to the task of raising the standards of living of our people with all the resources we command and we go to it telling the people that an essential concomitant of using public credit is a readiness annually to finance from tax revenue an appropriate annual sum to redeem whatever borrowing is done over an agreed term of years, which I think should rarely exceed thirty.'[28] This was not a sudden conversion on Dillon's part. He had no difficulty in reconciling his social conservativism with what he called his 'dangerous radicalism' as far as financial orthodoxies were concerned, while, among other influences, his 'browsing on the pastures of St Thomas of Aquin' had strengthened his distrust of conventional banking.

PART OF Dillon's success as a minister, and certainly his success in dealing with the land rehabilitation project, lay in his uninhibited flamboyance and showmanship. His oratory was not to everybody's taste, and there were some who argued that his penchant for the dramatic sometimes cloaked his essential message and reduced its serious intent. That said, his platform style was certain to pack in the crowds, while in the Dáil the word that Dillon was on his feet inevitably brought in an audience. There was in him an element of the actor, and he brought a sense of theatre to getting his message across in agriculture. He did it quite deliberately. He knew farmers were inherently conservative and opposed to change and he felt publicity and shock tactics were weapons which might shake them out of their old habits. He had learned about the power of advertising at Selfridges and Marshall Fields, and he personally designed posters in the campaign against asphosphoris which were highly unconventional in terms of civil service advertising in the late 1940s.

A celebrated advertisement aimed at the poultry industry bore the bold-lettered subtitle GALLINA SENESCENS DELENDA EST. 'The purpose of this was that every farmer who read the advertisement should say "what does this infernal advertisement of the Department mean?" and there would always be somebody who would say "sure, it's Latin. Go and ask the priest." The more talk you engendered about your advertisement in the parish, the better the advertisement was. So it turned out that everybody was going around saying "the aging hen must be destroyed."' The campaign aimed to persuade farmers to change old hens for new chicks, and apparently met with some success: Breandán Ó hÉithir recalled that in Gaeltacht areas day-old chicks were known for years afterwards as 'Dillons *bheaga*' – 'little Dillons'.[29]

One advantage which Dillon enjoyed, but rarely adverted to, was his friendly relationship with Independent Newspapers and in particular with the editor of the *Sunday Independent*, Hector Legge, one of his closest friends. The *Independent* was conservative and Catholic, not particularly partisan but certainly less than warm to Fianna Fáil, which had the strident support of the *Irish Press*, where Lemass was now managing director and de Valera controlling editor. Dillon had an inside track with the *Sunday Independent* and was undoubtedly a source of some of the paper's stories. It is even possible that he may have written some of its editorials: certainly that was suspected within the paper and publicly alleged by Lemass.[30]

Strangely, Dillon never came to terms with *The Irish Times* even though the paper was usually friendly in its references to him, apart from its editorial sniffiness on the question of the Commonwealth – though here it reserved most of its lasting hostility for Costello. When Sean Moylan pointed out in the Dáil that the 'chaste, virginal and pure' *Irish Times* had been praising him, Dillon replied that *The Irish Times* had placed the kiss of death on Irish politics and he placed no store on praise from that quarter.[31] Curiously, it was an attitude to *The Irish Times* common to many politicians at the time, who distrusted the sincerity of its loyalty to the new regime.

This flair for publicity may have helped Dillon with the public but did not endear him to the opposition in Leinster House. Unstinting in his efforts to spread his message to farmers, Dillon even wrote an article for the *News of the World*, which was banned in the Republic but maintained a wide clandestine circulation nonetheless. This was too much for MacEntee, who complained in the Dáil that 'This was a disgrace, even for Dillon,' and asked the Taoiseach to censure him. Dillon responded by advising MacEntee 'not to burst with sanctimoniousness'.[32]

In late 1948 he found himself immersed in a far nastier controversy with Martin Corry, from which he emerged bruised and somewhat the worse for wear. The matter arose in a debate on the Agriculture Amendment Bill in December 1948. Like so many late-night debates, exchanges were intemperate, and Dillon had been on the receiving end of some strong Fianna Fáil attacks when he himself cut loose, adopting Corry as his main target. He alleged that the Beet Growers Association, with which Corry was intimately associated, had been encouraging farmers in Galway not to buy burnt lime and that as a result the lime had been left in the factory in Tuam until Corry bought it and brought it to Cork. Corry had in fact bought the lime, but he angrily denied that there had been any collusion between himself and the BGA in the matter and before leaving the House called Dillon 'a liar and a louse'.[33]

The following day, Corry made a personal Dáil statement in which he alleged that Dillon had made charges of corruption against him. Dillon repeated the charges against Corry quite explicitly, and in the midst of a very stormy scene the issue was referred by the Ceann Comhairle to the Committee of Procedure and Privileges (CPP).[34] This did not satisfy Fianna Fáil, which felt it had Dillon on the ropes, and on 16 December Lemass called for a judicial tribunal to investigate the allegations made against Corry and the Beet Growers Association. If Fianna Fáil had had to endure the Ward and Locke tribunals, it was now Dillon's turn to face the music.

The Committee on Procedure and Privileges debated the matter at some length and, unusually, came to no agreed conclusion. The government Chief Whip, Liam Cosgrave, proposed that no further action be taken. This motion was defeated by one vote – that of Dillon's *bête noir*, Cogan – and a second motion proposed by Gerry Boland that 'the matter be investigated by a judicial tribunal' was carried by one vote.[35]

The CPP report strengthened the Fianna Fáil case and on 16 February 1949 Lemass again demanded a judicial tribunal.[36] His request was resolutely refused by Costello, but the Taoiseach added that he had no difficulty with having a select committee of the House enquire into the matter. He was adamant that this was no reflection on Dillon, who had his full confidence.

Fianna Fáil raised the matter once more on 23 March and called on the government to give effect to the recommendations of the CPP report for a judicial tribunal. Lemass admitted that Corry 'is not himself regarded as light-handed in debate or particular in his choice of weapons', but on this occasion Corry was completely in the right and Dillon was not just wrong but had persisted with his allegations. Lemass would not accept a select committee, which would have an inbuilt government majority, and insisted on a judicial tribunal. Lemass charged that this was the most 'political' Dáil in his long experience, though this argument fell somewhat flat in view of his own unrepentantly Civil War speech on the Republic of Ireland Bill a few days earlier. Costello was adamant, however, that it would be a select committee or nothing – such a committee would hear its evidence in public and the public could make its own judgement.[37]

When Dillon rose to speak he was given a hard time by Fianna Fáil and no very obvious support from his own side. He opposed a judicial tribunal because 'no body, although constituted by Dáil Éireann, had the right to require a member of this House to answer before it for anything that transpired in the course of our proceedings ... this was an absolute and unqualified parliamentary privilege.' He welcomed the select committee of the House, even if it should have an overwhelming opposition majority. In the event, the government had a comfortable seventy-two to sixty-four majority against setting up a tribunal.[38] That, effectively, was the end of the matter. It was not pursued further by the opposition and the select committee was never set up.

Fianna Fáil's antipathy to Dillon after the Corry row continued into the Agriculture Estimate of 1949, a debate so rancorous it almost had to be halted several times. The low point in the debate came when Denis Allen told Dillon, 'you have a twisted nose like a cur'. Dillon was convinced Fianna Fáil believed that if they could destroy him they could destroy the government – and it has to be said some of his own interventions invited hostility, as when he accused Fianna Fáil of 'vicious, malignant, irresponsible and aimless obstruction'.[39]

By the time of Dillon's third Agriculture Estimate in June 1950, the mood was somewhat more mellow, though only just. As the Labour TD, William Davin, pointed out: 'Instead of dealing with Dillon as Minister for Agriculture and criticising his policy in a constructive way, [Fianna Fáil] made up their minds a long time ago, the Minister for Agriculture is public enemy number one to them as politicians.'[40] Dillon had won much support during his tenure as minister. Sean Dunne of Labour, who was as ideologically different from Dillon as was possible, paid him the warmest tribute: 'while his personality may not appeal to everybody ... he has brought into agriculture a degree of vigour and imagination and virility which we have not noticed before in any Minister for Agriculture,'[41] while another new radical, Jack McQuillan, described him as 'forward-looking and courageous and willing to make mistakes'.[42] The former Clann na Poblachta and now Independent Peadar Cowan also thought that Fianna Fáil was 'determined to drive Dillon out of public life',[43] a point reinforced by some of the later Fianna Fáil contributions which described the minister as 'one of the greatest afflictions since Cromwell',[44] a rancher 'deliberately turning this country into a large grazing ranch for the purpose of producing cheaper food for England'.[45]

DILLON WAS quite willing to use the state as an agent of change when it came to rehabilitating land or eradicating TB, but on other issues he could be resolutely anti-statist, such as on the policy of compulsory Irish in schools or the compulsory growing of wheat. This anti-statism was also obvious on an issue in late 1950 which some opponents argued showed him as having double standards, or at least of being selective and inconsistent in his application of principle. This was on the question of a statutory half-day per week for agricultural workers.

Farm workers were among the most exploited section of the Irish workforce, badly paid, poorly organised and working in difficult conditions with few if any rights. Dillon had singled them out in his first major speech as people whose lot he wanted to improve. This would be done, he said, by putting farmers in the position where they could pay wages at least the equivalent of those of industrial workers. He ensured that this was the case on all state-owned farms and he was regarded as an enlightened and humane employer on his own farm in Ballaghaderreen. However, when Sean Dunne introduced a Private Members Bill to entitle all agricultural workers to a weekly half-day, Dillon disagreed with the measure.

Dillon opposed the Bill because he said it introduced an element of compulsion where persuasion should be the norm. 'There was an element of danger in too readily looking to the Legislature to effect reforms which, in the ordinary course of trade union activities, might be secured by a trade union for its members.'[46] He did not oppose the measure – in fact he supported it – but he was not going to see it brought in through legislation.

Dunne, a powerful parliamentary performer, attacked Dillon for behaving like *'Tadhg a dhá thaobh'* ('two-faced Tadhg') on the issue. 'We have arrived at the half-way mark in the twentieth century and here we are shouting our lungs out in the Parliament of the Republic for four hours for a half-day for an agricultural worker.'[47] The government allowed a free vote on the Bill and all government members except Dillon and Mulcahy supported it. Fianna Fáil abstained. After being referred to a special committee it returned to the House and was passed by eighty-six votes to eighteen, with Dillon voting against.[48]

It seems clear that Dillon's opposition in cabinet had prevented the government from adopting Dunne's Bill as a government measure: as Minister for Agriculture it could not have been taken without his support. He defended his position on the grounds that 'it seems to me the free functioning and effective participation of unions in the life of the community is put in not a little jeopardy if, instead of employing the usual methods, organisation and negotiation, the legislature seeks to disrupt that function and by statute enacts what might very much more advantageously be arranged by agreement and contract between employer and employee.'[49] His argument was convoluted. More than that, in a situation where Irish farmers were noted for their mean and in many cases exploitative treatment of their employees, and given the poor state of organisation of the rural workers, the best that can be said of Dillon's stand was that it was perhaps based on valid principle, but ill-judged in its application here.

As Minister for Agriculture, Dillon also had responsibility for fisheries, an industry which had long demanded a separate department in place of its position as 'the neglected step-child of the Department of Agriculture'. Dillon had little of the passion for this portfolio that he brought to agriculture, not because, as he told the Dáil, he had little regard for fish ('I never eat fish except on Fridays and never will, with the help of God')[50] but because he saw his role in very limited terms.

As far as Dillon was concerned, the central issue facing him was to decide between the rival claims of the inshore fishermen and those who wanted to develop a native trawling industry. Dillon quickly came to the view that the two could not co-exist. He believed that a stronger trawling industry would simply saturate Ireland's domestic market, which was of very modest proportions. 'We are not a fish-eating people. Since ninety-five per cent of us are good pious Roman Catholics we have to eat fish on Friday but we are damned if we will eat it any other day ... I would not eat fish if I could get out of it. I detest fish.'[51] He was sceptical of the industry's demands that people should be educated about the nutritional value of fish or encouraged to eat it. 'I do not want to educate anybody as to what they may want to eat. Neither do I think fish has any superior food value, that it is in any way superior to a leg of mutton or an egg.'[52]

Neither did he think that the offshore industry would be able to find export markets; rather, he believed it would wipe out the inshore fishermen – 2,000 full-time and 8,000 part-time jobs – and with them 'a way of life that is valuable and desirable to preserve for our people'. He dismissed claims by some of his Fine Gael Dáil colleagues, such as Sean Collins of West Cork and Sir John Esmonde of Wexford, that deep-sea trawling could co-exist with inshore fishing. 'My business is to see that if people want fish on their table it shall be made available to them at a fair price through the agency of the inshore fishermen, organised in a co-operative society, and that the Sea Fisheries Association will be the sole agency charged with the responsibility of furnishing the Irish domestic market with fish.'[53]

In 1949 he embarked upon a pilot scheme for quick-freezing the catch at a number of ports around the country and that year also produced a scheme to reconstitute the Sea Fisheries Association so as to help provide fishermen with boats and equipment and develop markets for their produce at home and if possible for export.[54] A year later, however, these proposals had not found their way into legislation. In the Agriculture Estimates debate on 4 July 1950 he promised that legislation would be introduced 'to ensure that the only persons allowed by law to land fish in Ireland for sale will be the Sea Fisheries Association, acting as a Statutory Co-operative of and for the inshore fishermen',[55] but that legislation had not appeared by the time the life of the government ended.

Dillon's fisheries strategy was undoubtedly conservative, in line with the approach of the previous government. Given the small size of the Fisheries Department, which had only four established officers, and the need to protect established jobs as against risking them in a new strategy, his role is defensible – though barely that. More positively, his department did play an important part in resolving the long-running dispute between northern and southern fishermen over the Foyle fisheries. With Dillon's support, one of his civil servants, JD Rushe, was a prime mover in drafting the Bill which was the basis of the solution. Passed by both Dáil and House of Commons, it established the first joint venture between North and South.

THROUGHOUT HIS career Dillon was much given to conspiracy theories, the greatest and most pernicious of which was the international communist threat. At home, he was quick to spot cartels or 'rings', well-placed groups in economic and financial circles out to corner the market against the interests of the consumer. In the 1930s he had accused Lemass of putting the Irish cement industry in monopoly hands, and he had long been convinced that the flour millers, and especially the Rank and Odlum groups, had abused their dominant position in the Irish market. In government he waged a successful battle against sections of the bacon industry which he alleged were running a black market in bacon, and went so far as to shut down a number of plants engaged in illegal curing. He also involved himself in a heated battle with Donegal potato suppliers, a controversy which generated great heat but the issues of which remain unclear. In 1949 he returned to the dominant position of the flour millers, and now took up the issue with the Secretary of the Department of Finance, JJ McElligott.[56]

Dillon had already crossed swords with McElligott on the Land Reclamation project. It is not clear why he did not seek cabinet approval for his proposals for the flour industry, which effectively called for it to be nationalised in the interests of the consumer; on the face of it, he would have enjoyed the support of Labour and Clann na Poblachta for such a move. Nor is it clear why he conducted this correspondence with McElligott. Perhaps he was bored. Perhaps he thought that if he could persuade Finance then the rest would be simple. At all events, he wrote to McElligott in October 1949 complaining about the alleged dominance of the Irish flour industry by two men, 'James Rank and Algernon A. Odlum and the ragged army of stooges who pose as independent businessmen' but who in reality were firmly annexed to Rank and Odlum. McElligott, of course, disagreed with his assessment, but did so in a quite brilliant reply which examined the philosophical and historical roots of monopoly.

McElligott saw 'another point of view on the gentlemen you mention':

> you should hand it to them for their ability, energy and irrepressible individu-
> alism, qualities you should be the last to deprecate ... are they not in themselves
> something of an answer to the overbearing authority of the modern State? ...
> would you crush the Barons of modern industry, even if they are unruly and,

in doing so, make way for what? For the servile State? For the static society, long foreseen by John Stuart Mill, where initiative and enthusiasm become stagnant and progress is arrested? ... it was not any change in climatic conditions, the fertility of their lands, or the physiology of their peoples which brought an end to Egypt, Rome or the Empire of Genghis Khan. They crumbled and withered because they had become top-heavy, and we could go on adding to the power of the State until, likewise, it topples to self-destruction.

McElligott talked further about his fear that the state in Ireland 'will soon become the chief employer of Labour, the chief owner of Capital', and he concluded: 'I am grieved to see one of our great protagonists of free enterprise and initiative turning to the facile heresy that only by investing the State with all the attributes of economic despotism can we redress any injustice arising from our own failures or shortcomings in the spheres of administration.'

Dillon replied by return.

God be praised for an interlude in the dreary round of administration ... you do not know what the net intake of the flour millers is ... all that you are ever allowed to know is that annually a quarter of a million pounds ... is thrown like a fox's body to the hounds for them to tear up and distribute among themselves at their own sweet will ... John Stuart Mill, like so many others of his persuasion, reaches his conclusions on the assumption that a personal devil does not exist; you and I know that he was mistaken and that the concept of the Economic Man was as unreal a hypothesis as that of the Rational Man on which Rousseau built the loathsome philosophy whose ultimate product has been Hitler and Lenin.

Dillon went on to attack McElligott's abhorrence of nationalisation, citing the United States, 'the citadel of free enterprise and initiative', which had nationalised or municipalised water supplies. 'I believe in private enterprise and individual initiative, but I do not believe in rapacity and exploitation, inadequately disguised to look like these things.'

The issue soon narrowed down to specifics. McElligott saw Dillon's charges as an attack on the competence of the relevant officials in Dillon's department and in Industry and Commerce, and suggested the matter could be tackled by strengthening the position of these officials.

The temptation to accompany you on a post-mortem of Egypt, Rome and Tartary and to engage further on the question of the static society is strong, but time presses. However, I must defend myself if only to the extent of pointing out that you misunderstand me completely when you see in my remarks even a measure of mixed admiration for any wasters who may have festooned themselves around the crankshafts of our flour mills. Such praise for individualism as I expressed applied merely to Rank and others of similar status and calibre and, as for the poor 'stooges', do you not agree that the toleration of such sterile organisms in society is part of the price we must be prepared to pay for the privilege of living in a liberal democracy, although, as I can well appreciate, their very existence constitutes a challenge to your strong sense of justice and efficiency?

The correspondence continued. Dillon was serious about breaking what he saw as a pernicious monopoly and the fact that 'for the past fifteen years we have been successfully bluffed out of large sums of money, for the responsible officers of Industry and Commerce who are not able to hold their own in the battle of wits with the professional accountants. The officers of the Department of Agriculture and the Minister thereof are able to do so, but are being prevented from doing so by the responsible officers of the Department of Finance.'

Dillon also made clear his views on individual initiative:

I do not admire individuals of the type of Capone, Legs Diamond or Dutch Schultz. It is of course a matter of taste, but just as I believe the Corballises and Spike McCormacks of the Animal Gang on the North Wall must be made answerable to the laws of a civilised society, so I believe the others must also be deterred from plundering the community to which they belong.

McElligott did not reply until 5 June. 'Your letter delivered some powerful punches and following Gene Tunney's sound advice I decided to take the long count before coming up again,' he told the minister. He accepted the validity of some of Dillon's points, but 'to be fully justified, the nationalisation of this industry, apart from the far-reaching social and financial implications of such a move, would, in my opinion, have to prove an absolute guarantee that the price of bread would thereby be reduced, its quality improved and its quantity increased. Nothing so far said in our correspondence warrants the conclusion that such a happy result could be counted upon.'

Only part of the correspondence is reproduced here, but there is an element of the bizarre about it all. If Dillon seriously wanted to break the alleged cartels and nationalise the flour industry, the way was open to him through cabinet, where he would have had support from Labour and Clann na Poblachta, but would have been opposed by Fine Gael. In any event, nationalisation was not on any political agenda in 1950 and the idea of Dillon as its proponent is unexpected, to say the least. He was intellectually and temperamentally opposed to monopoly capitalism and in this case he saw nationalisation as the only available alternative. It may be that he believed if he could persuade McElligott of this he would be on his way, or that at the very least a start would have been made.

IF THE correspondence with McElligott was urbane and private, happenings in the Baltinglass Post Office were far from so, and gave plenty of ammunition to the government's enemies. The facts are simply stated. The postmistress of Baltinglass, Mrs Cooke, resigned on 14 April 1950. Two candidates applied for the post: Mrs Cooke's niece, who had fourteen years experience in the Post Office, and Michael Farrell, a Labour County Councillor and supporter of the Minister for Posts and Telegraphs, who had none. When he got the job, all hell broke loose in Baltinglass. Fianna Fáil TDs Tom Brennan and Patrick Cogan raised the matter in the Dáil, where it ignited into a full-scale political row with several adjournments and many wild charges. The matter caught the public imagination and even attracted journalists from overseas; ballads were written, protest meetings held and the Farrell family virtually boycotted until, finally, Farrell resigned and was replaced by Miss Cooke.

The 'Battle of Baltinglass' was rightly seen as an act of political jobbery and damaged the moral standing of the government. The episode reflected little credit on any member of the government, all of whom would have been quick to criticise Fianna Fáil in similar circumstances, but none of whom, including Dillon, spoke up against the Minister for Posts and Telegraphs, James Everett.

Despite such clashes, the Inter Party government had passed the half-way mark in its term of office and looked increasingly secure as 1950 came to an end. RM Smyllie in *The Irish Times* took note: 'The past year, which has been so fateful for Europe and the world, has been relatively uneventful in Ireland ... The Inter Party government has been digging itself fairly comfortably in, although rumours have not been wanting that Ministers do not always see eye to eye in their government discussions ... It is remarkable that such a heterogeneous company should have held together for three years.' The credit for much of this went to Costello, according to Smyllie, while Dillon continued to be one of the more eye-catching ministers: 'the flamboyant and ebullient Mr James Dillon, having contrived to become a dyed-in-the-wool Republican overnight, has now returned to his first love ... advocating a new form of federation which would involve the creation of a vast commonwealth of nations, including, not only Great Britain and the Dominions, but also the USA.' It was, Smyllie thought, 'a nice concept ... but going nowhere.'

On Dillon's actual portfolio, however, he was unstinting in his praise: 'Dillon has unquestionably been doing some excellent work within his Department. All his officials are on their toes ... they have carried out his undertaking not to interfere unduly with the farmer and the result has been he enjoys a big measure of popularity within the farming community ... In fact, farmers have been doing pretty well... the cattle trade is flourishing, the scheme for off-the-ration butter at an enhanced price has worked out favourably.' The political correspondent predicted that the Costello government would go its full term. It was to prove a characteristically unreliable prophecy.[57]

CHAPTER SIXTEEN

LOSING THE INDEPENDENTS

'You don't understand, James. I'm a Socialist, and this is the foot in the door.'

Noel Browne, 1951

A T THE END of 1950 the omens for the long-term survival of the government were good. Fine Gael's PA O'Donnell had actually gained a seat from Fianna Fáil in the Donegal by-election the previous year, further consolidating its Dáil majority, and the Labour parties' reunification in June 1950 brought it greater cohesion. The government was also seen to be working. The Land Reclamation project was bringing tractors and bulldozers to every parish; the repeal of the External Relations Act had been safely navigated; the Industrial Development Authority had been set up, and Noel Browne's campaign to eradicate TB had caught the public imagination as no project had ever done before.

While Fianna Fáil slumbered in opposition, showing no signs of an early revival, the problems facing the government were little more than the normal wear-and-tear of an administration coming up to mid-term. Baltinglass had done harm, especially with some of the floating voters who had slipped towards Clann na Poblachta and now wanted an excuse to float away.[1] The all-party anti-partition campaign was crumbling under its own contradictions, its self-obsession captured by a delegate at the Fine Gael Árd Fheis in February 1951 who proposed that the government should 'issue a mourning stamp in black which would show to the world Ireland's wrongs under partition'.[2] Among the ministers, MacBride seemed to be losing the run of himself with increasingly exaggerated claims about the imminent demise of partition, and with it Ireland's willingness to join NATO, much to the discomfort of Costello who tried in February to tone down McBride's campaign and whose Chief Whip Liam Cosgrave publicly rebuked MacBride a few weeks later.[3] As yet the Mother and Child episode was little more than a series of behind-the-scenes wrangles and an occasional oblique rumour.

There were some problems with individual supporters of the government. Against the bonus of O'Donnell's Donegal victory had to be set the resignation from Fine Gael in September 1950 of John L. Esmonde TD. Esmonde, who had been an Irish Party MP for Tipperary, came to Fine Gael via the Centre Party, and had been a Fine Gael TD for Wexford since 1937. He had grown increasingly critical of what he saw as the dominance of Cumann na nGaedheal in the new party and the concessions given to Labour in the Inter Party government. For the moment, however, even though no longer taking the Whip, he would continue to support the government.[4]

There were other signs of eroding support. The Independent TD William Sheldon, whose backing had been consistent, wrote to Costello in December 1950 with a catalogue of complaints and said he would not necessarily support the opposition, but was reverting to being a non-aligned Independent.[5] At about the same time, PD Lehane left Clann na Talmhan because of 'lack of consultation'[6] and Cogan, whose support was erratic, declared he would not vote with the government until 'the wrong of Baltinglass is righted'.[7] Oliver Flanagan was reported as being unhappy with the rate of land division, the rising cost of living, and the extravagance of some ministers (MacBride),[8] while, most spectacularly of all, Cowan placed advertisements in the newspapers in February 1950 announcing that he was setting up a private army to bring an immediate end to partition by 'action rather than talk'. He boasted that his men were ready to move across the border and 'take possession of the six counties in a day'.[9] The northern authorities used the incident as an excuse to establish a reserve B Special unit, but while few people in the Republic took Cowan seriously, the whole episode was bizarre and the government's inability to do anything about it was a serious embarrassment.

These were the obvious signs of strain, none of them likely to bring down the government, but at another level there was a confluence of events approaching which would soon lead to the end of the Inter Party administration. The conventional analysis of this period concentrates almost exclusively on one of these, the Mother and Child controversy, which it is argued led to the break-up of the government and its subsequent rejection by the electorate. But while the controversy was spectacular and destabilising, it did not destroy the cohesion of the government or fracture the unity of a cabinet which, it must be remembered, brought its business to an orderly end, fought the election as an Inter-Party entity and then presented itself in the Dáil for re-election as a new government.

In strict fact, the government came to an end because it lost the support of a sizable number of Independents whose concerns were exclusively agricultural and local. There was nothing inevitable about their defection, but one point is emphatic: it had all to do with the price of milk and other local grievances, and little to do with the Mother and Child episode.

It was the combination of these two events which did for the government. The split in Clann na Poblachta it might have survived, but coming as it did just as the long-complaining Independents could take no more was fatal. The question has to be asked as to why the government did not make any real effort to mend its fences with the Independents, or at least to enter into meaningful discussions with them to see if a compromise was possible. The fact that this was not even attempted can in part be blamed on Dillon. He was the 'Independent' in cabinet, the issues were almost entirely agricultural, yet strangely he made no effort to broker a deal – if anything, he exacerbated the situation by bluntly rejecting the Independents' demands. Curiously, his colleagues in cabinet put no pressure on him to resolve these problems, and no attempt was ever made to blame him for them.

Yet it was the Mother and Child controversy which provided the main spectacle in the government's demise, and material for analysis and dispute over the next half-century. It is not proposed to rehearse the details of the episode here: that has been done extensively elsewhere, most dispassionately and definitively in Ruth Barrington's *Health, Medicine and Politics in Ireland 1900-1970* and in David McCullagh's *A Makeshift Majority*.

The dispute had been rumbling in the background since Browne's complex and elaborate proposals were first published. Browne proposed free (voluntary) ante- and post-natal care for mothers, as well as free medical care for all children under sixteen, without a means test. However, relations between the Minister and the Irish Medical Association declined sharply, and in early 1950 Browne's most experienced adviser, Dr James Deeney, resigned. Though he believed in Browne's reforms, he felt their plans would not succeed without the good-will of the doctors, and decried the Minister's refusal to maintain good relations with them. In October 1950 the Catholic bishops entered the fray. By March 1951, Browne was fighting desperately to save his scheme from being undermined by the bishops, the medical profession, his cabinet colleagues' lack of enthusiasm, and most of all by the open opposition of his party leader, Sean MacBride. Indeed, the handling of the Mother and Child issue is to a considerable extent the story of the poisonous breakdown in personal relations between MacBride and Browne and the effects this had on their political party.[10]

Though they persistently denied rumours of a split, Clann na Poblachta was very much divided, and it was clear that the Mother and Child issue was at the heart of it. On 3 March 1951 *The Irish Times* asked, 'why is MacBride not supporting [Noel Browne] on what is Clann na Poblachta's only major contribution to the Inter-Party programme?' A week later the paper reported that Browne was on his own, in no small part due to his own stubbornness, but 'if he goes, something clean, something pure, something rare will go too'.[11]

It was against this background that Dillon introduced his Agriculture Estimate to the Dáil on 13 March 1951. It was to be his most turbulent estimate of all and it ran parallel to the increasingly tense Mother and Child drama. By early April it was clear Browne was isolated and newspapers speculated that his resignation was imminent, but on 9 April he deferred doing so 'at the request of the Trade Union Conference'. Clann na Poblachta was almost in permanent session by this time, and in an ominous move a resolution of loyalty to the party leader was unanimously adopted on 11 April. This was seen by observers as the first step in paving the way for Noel Browne's resignation,[12] and so it was: the following day MacBride asked for and got his minister's resignation, and Costello took over immediately at the Department of Health. Browne went, it seemed, with a whimper, declaring in his statement that 'as a Catholic, I accept the rulings of their Lordships the Hierarchy without question'.[13]

Following his departure, Clann na Poblachta split irrevocably. Cowan disputed MacBride's right to request Browne's resignation, seven branches of Clann na Poblachta resigned in Dublin South-East and, a day later, Jack McQuillan, sickened by the whole episode and in particular by MacBride's behaviour, resigned from the parliamentary party.[14] That night in the Dáil the government's majority was reduced to four – with three Fianna Fáil TDs absent. The Independents were clearly uneasy also. Three days later, when the Dáil debated Browne's resignation, Oliver Flanagan said he would have preferred had MacBride gone rather than Browne: 'MacBride has his heart in Paris; his notebooks in Strasbourg, his ambitions in Washington and his intentions in the US.' Flanagan supported the Inter-Party concept, but thought the Taoiseach should go to the country for a new mandate.[15]

Dillon was absorbed in his marathon Agriculture Estimate throughout this controversy, but he was far from oblivious to the events happening around him, to Noel Browne, or to health matters generally. From his earliest days in politics Dillon had argued for a concerted national campaign against TB and the conditions which produced it, especially slum housing. The disease was widespread and its onset struck fear into the heart of communities right around the country. According to Dr Ruth Barrington, Dillon pointed straight to the core of the problem in 1942 when he criticised the 'universal lethargy' which bedevilled all attempts to tackle TB.[16] He had a very personal interest in the matter: his brother, Theo, had fallen victim to TB in his twenties. After Theo recuperated he qualified in medicine and was appointed to a Medical Chair at UCD, but he died in 1946 at the age of forty-eight. His death had a profound impact on Dillon.

Thus when Noel Browne, newly-appointed Minister for Health in 1948, made the eradication of TB an overriding national priority, he met with wholehearted supported from Dillon, who admired the energy and zeal which Browne brought to his task.

Browne took office just when a great deal of groundwork had been done by his predecessors in preparing a nationwide campaign against the disease. Restrictions on building were easing up, sites for sanatoria had been bought, engineers and architects recruited. More state money was available and considerable funding from the Hospitals Trust was coming on stream. The department was in the process of taking over beds in existing institutions to meet the immediate need for the segregation and treatment of tubercular patients.[17] What Browne brought to this work was enormous passion and drive, intense commitment and unbrookable urgency. He had flair and an uncanny sense of publicity. He used the media with skill, broadcast regularly and toured the entire country, offering a message of openness, hope and compassion. Within a year of his appointment he had become a national figure.

And he was successful. In 1948 the National Blood Transfusion Agency was set up, BCG and mass radiography reached all parts of the country, over 2,000 extra hospital places were made available and there was a significant reduction in the rate of deaths from TB. A massive hospital building programme, largely funded by the Hospitals Trust and thus avoiding the need for Department of Finance approval, was under way.[18] Perhaps most of all, Browne offered hope that a disease that had been a national epidemic was being brought under control.

However, the very qualities which made Browne so successful in waging the battle against TB were to be his undoing in the Mother and Child controversy. In his health campaign he had behaved almost independently of the cabinet, whose meetings he did not attend very often, had significant finance available from outside sources and had largely personalised the issue around himself, creating a strong – and false – impression that he had inherited, as he put it, a 'slum heritage'[19] and that little had been done before his arrival in office. The loose sense of collective cabinet responsibility allowed him scope to adopt this semi-detached role; he himself did little to build up any sense of camaraderie with his cabinet colleagues, most of whom were a generation older than him and most of whom he was ultimately to despise. Neither had he bothered much to integrate himself with his Clann na Poblachta colleagues, many of whom resented his instant promotion and his lack of party involvement.

The fairest thing that can be said about the Mother and Child scheme is that it was handled badly by everyone involved, and when the smoke had cleared it was difficult to see not so much what all the fuss had been about, but rather why the matter had not been resolved before it got out of control. The only winners, if there were any, was the Irish Medical Association, and even their victory was short-lived and incurred at the cost of years of negative esteem. It became clear that Browne, with the young man's contempt for strategy and ground-work, made no real attempt to bring his colleagues with him and totally underestimated the strength of the medical lobby. If he were to defeat the doctors, he must at least have the bishops on side, but to leave himself exposed on both flanks and without consolidating his political position was to make defeat certain.

The Catholic bishops, for their part, were never particularly clear or convincing as to the real nature of their objections. They overstepped what might reasonably have been considered a legitimate concern on a moral issue and took sides in a political dispute in which they were not particularly competent or well-informed. They displayed little subtlety, no flexibility and even less sensitivity, and if they were intent on showing who really governed – and there is no evidence that this was their intent – their stance made them seem oblivious to the real needs of poor people and did serious long-term damage to their image.

The cabinet was even worse. It failed to discuss the issues as a cabinet at any stage, and it showed neither cohesion, clarity or firmness in dealing with the bishops. Its leadership, and here Costello and MacBride were especially culpable, failed to rein Browne in at an early stage. The kindest thing that can be said of the government's final capitulation to the Catholic Church is that they took the bishops at their own estimate rather than face the issues on their merits, and in yielding to them were oblivious to the consequences of appearing to submit to the dictates of the Catholic Church. Ruth Barrington contrasts the government's handling of the situation with the robust opposition offered by the Irish Party in 1911 when the hierarchy tried to prevent the application of the National Health Insurance Bill: 'the political skills of the leaders of the Irish Party contrasts strongly with the ineptness of their political successors'.[20]

The Mother and Child episode says a great deal about the extent to which the Catholic Church's authority in Irish life had grown since independence. It should be remembered that in all of this controversy Fianna Fáil maintained a demure silence: nobody in that party was going to risk appearing 'less Catholic' than the government. De Valera, however, must have been contemptuous of the political ineptness which characterised the entire operation, and the failure to head off trouble at an early stage on an issue where compromise was possible. De Valera achieved just such a compromise subsequently.

Where did Dillon stand in all of this? In most respects he was no better, and no worse, than most of his contemporaries. He was deeply Catholic, but he also had a very clear sense of the boundary between politics and religion: he would not have been his father's son if he had not. He was critical of Sean MacEoin, for example, for being 'unduly influenced by clerical opinion' on another issue: 'There was an Adoption Bill brought before the Cabinet for discussion and I remember him coming in, after going to consult the Archbishop of Dublin on the matter, and announcing "he won't have it!" and that was the end of the matter as far as he was concerned ... it would never have occurred to him to cross the Archbishop.'[21]

At the time of the Mother and Child row, Dillon was deeply immersed in the work of his own department. The controversy broke when his Agriculture Estimate was being debated – and occupying more Dáil time and generating far more parliamentary heat than did the Mother and Child controversy up to this. For Dillon, it was a problem no more important than many of the other difficulties facing the government. In his *Memoir* he says: 'I have always found it difficult to discern what was the basis for the fuss about the scheme.'

He got involved in negotiations with the Irish Medical Association in an effort to sort out some of the earlier difficulties, though to no avail. He had, of course, opposed those sections of the 1947 Act which made for compulsory and universal application of the Mother and Child provisions. Browne's Bill was based very largely on the 1947 proposals, but Dillon felt that most of the difficulties had been sorted out early on, especially the decision not to impose charges. The reasons given for this decision vary, but are not necessarily mutually exclusive. Noel Browne says the reason was the opposition of the Labour members to universal charges and to avoid appearing to capitulate to the medical profession. Dillon's personal recollection comes to the same conclusion by a different route:

> when the matter came up in Cabinet I asked what seemed to me the obvious question, what relationship the fees payable by mothers would bear to the cost of collecting them. After some calculation, Paddy McGilligan agreed with Noel Browne that it would cost more to collect the fees than the fees would bring in, so I said 'then why on earth collect a fee? Why don't you provide the service free?' It was generally agreed at the time that that made sense both fiscally and socially. Nobody, as I recall, became excited at that or saw any great moral issue looming up.[22]

Dillon did not pay undue attention to the growing rift with the bishops. He felt the issues could be resolved: 'Noel Browne met a delegation consisting of Dr. McQuaid, Dr. Browne of Galway and other bishops on a number of occasions in October 1950 to discuss the problems they discerned. Now, I liked McQuaid, but he was a very orthodox person, and Browne of Galway was a very rough customer, but, rather to my surprise, after a number of meetings, Noel told me that their differences had been resolved.'[23]

Dillon attached greater significance to the deteriorating situation between MacBride and Noel Browne. He was highly critical of MacBride, especially when he attacked the Minister for Health, at a particularly sensitive time in Browne's discussions with the Catholic bishops, over the fact that he was pictured with the Protestant Archbishop of Dublin on 29 January 1951.

Dillon, who always saw himself as a pragmatist and a problem solver, sought to act as an unofficial mediator between Browne and the bishops, in large part because he continued to believe the matter could be resolved:

> Sometime before the row became public in March 1951, I paid a visit to the Archbishop of Tuam, Dr. Walsh, and put it to him that Noel Browne seemed to be at loggerheads with their lordships of Dublin and Galway, though no matter of substance seemed to me to be at issue between them. I asked him if he could be willing to have a word with Noel. 'Certainly, James,' said he. 'Ask him to call on me and I will be delighted to talk over the whole thing with him, quietly and off the record. Then I can have a word with McQuaid and Browne, and see if we can't settle it.' I reported this back to Noel Browne when I returned to Dublin and he said that he would be delighted to go and talk to the Archbishop. I learned subsequently that, without ringing and making an appointment, Noel got into his car and drove down to Tuam. When he arrived in Tuam, he found that the Archbishop was out on the Aran Islands administering confirmation. Thereupon, since he was in the area, he made the catastrophic decision, since he couldn't see the Archbishop, to call on Dr. Dignan, the Bishop of Clonfert.[24]

There is no record of Browne having called to see Bishop Dignan at this time, and Browne makes no reference to it in his memoir, *Against The Tide*. This does not mean the meeting did not take place, and Dillon, who would have no reason to invent such a story, is emphatic that it did. He thought Dignan was the last person Browne should have spoken to, if it was compromise he was seeking. According to Dillon, Dignan was 'a lunatic' who had been appointed by the Pope in the late 1920s to put manners on the Irish bishops.[25]

Dillon's characterisation is unfair. Dignan was an advanced social thinker, whose ideas 'had made an important contribution to the debate on the future shape of the Irish health services'.[26] For this he had been lambasted by MacEntee, and if the Irish hierarchy in 1951 had an 'outsider' it was Dignan. Noel Browne does say, without giving a date, that Dignan had 'remained a firm friend and had warned me of the futility of taking on the Bishops'.

Dillon's *Memoir* continues:

> At any rate when Noel came back from the West he was like a raging lunatic.

As a result of confronting Dignan, he was ready for battle with all and sundry. I remember remonstrating with him in his room, asking him what was the point of having this battle when things could still be settled by diplomacy, and he saying to me, 'You don't understand, James. I'm a Socialist, and this is the foot in the door.' He seemed to be thirsting for a fight.[27]

Dillon had pressing business of his own on hands. His Agriculture Estimate was introduced on 17 April. By that time the government's majority was crumbling. It had already lost Cogan, Lehane and Sheldon, and on 11 March the Fine Gael TD Josie Mongan had died. John Esmonde, who had resigned from Fine Gael in December, left the Dáil itself in late April following the nomination of his brother, Anthony Esmonde, as the Fine Gael candidate in Wexford.[28] Clann na Poblachta's ten was now seven, with the departure first of Cowan and then of Browne and McQuillan.[29] At this stage the government still had seventy-one votes as against Fianna Fáil's seventy, but its majority was gone. It was dependent on the increasingly fissiparous Independents and dissidents.

The situation worsened on 27 April when Patrick Finucane resigned from Clann na Talmhan because of the way Dillon had treated the milk producers. Dillon, he said, had been 'unreasonable and unsympathetic'.[30] Two days later Patrick Halliden resigned from the party for much the same reason,[31] and by now there were serious question marks over some of the other Independents too. Effectively the government was in a minority. The collapse of its support had far more to do with bread-and-butter agricultural issues than with the Mother and Child scheme, a point quickly grasped by Fianna Fáil, which chose Dillon's Agriculture Estimate as the battleground for its showdown with the government. Very few TDs wanted to talk about the Mother and Child scheme, least of all the rural and highly conservative Independents. The survival of the government soon developed into a game of parliamentary cat and mouse, with the government seeking to keep the debate on agriculture going and avoid a vote while essential business, and especially the budget, was attended to.

There was as a result an air of unreality about the debate on the Agriculture Estimate. Cowan summed it up when he said 'the atmosphere surrounding the debate has been artificial and unreal ... Deputies have been marking time ... larger issues have been painfully protruding themselves ... dwarfing into insignificance the routine mechanism of parliamentary procedure.'[32]

Nevertheless, Dillon ploughed on, outlining the extent to which his policies of the previous three years had been successful. His achievements were impressive, especially given that he was only half-way through the period against which he expected to be judged. Exports for 1950 were up, even if the base of 1947 was a low one against which to estimate: cattle exports were up from £15.6 million to £22.7 million; poultry from £1.926 million to £3.916 million; eggs from £1.574 million to £5.146 million; chocolate crumb from £472,000 to £2.785 million. The livestock population had increased – cattle from 3.53 million to 3.91 million, sheep from l.626 million to l.949 million, pigs from 369,000 to 530,000. He could also point to a series of major initiatives – an all-out attack on disease, arterial drainage and land rehabilitation, the extension of water supplies, a co-operative scheme for marketing apples and a new board for marketing potatoes, and proposals for a parish plan and for a new agricultural institute, both of which had fallen behind schedule but which he would return to.

The debate on agriculture may have seemed unreal to Peadar Cowen, for whom 'larger issues were painfully protruding themselves', but it was not so for the Independent TDs – Finucane, Halliden, Lehane, Sheldon, Cogan and O'Reilly – all erstwhile supporters of the government, whose fate now lay in their hands. The issue, when it came, was simple and uncluttered. The Irish Creamery Milk Suppliers Association wanted an increase of from four to six pence a gallon on the prices paid for milk, which was set at 1s 2d per gallon between May and October and 1s 4d between November and April. Dillon, with government backing, was offering an increase of one penny and no more.

The Independents' support for the government was there for the asking once the price was right, but Dillon, who felt their demands – essentially the demands of the ICMSA – were too high, made no real effort to meet them or win them over. In fact, Dillon wanted to reduce the price of milk to a flat rate of 1s per gallon all year round in order to save £3m in annual subsidies. He expected farmers to maintain their income by increasing milk production and saw no room for compromise on the issue. He made no real effort to placate the Independents or to deal diplomatically with the major farm organisations, especially the ICMSA, whom he said he would not meet 'at the end of a forty foot pole'.[33]

His attitude is astonishing given what was at stake. Neither did his colleagues in government put him under any pressure to change his stance. It is important to make this point. There was, as has been noted, nothing inevitable about the collapse of the government after the Mother and Child crisis. It had the wherewithal to stay in office, at least in the short to medium term, had it so chosen. It chose otherwise, and in so doing it was not helped by Dillon's handling of matters under his political remit.

As the Agriculture Estimate's debate continued it became a series of judgements on the minister and his policies. Smith, as usual, led the attack. Dillon, he claimed, had removed the ban on the cross-border export of pigs because of pressure from the 'Molly Maguires' (the AOH) in Ballybay, a 'corrupt and secret organisation'. Smith had no evidence for this but he was on stronger ground when he said that Dillon had insulted the milk producers – Dillon had, among other things, described the ICMSA as a 'Fianna Fáil ramp'.[34] Aiken declared that Dillon was simply a liar who had been 'mischievous ever since he appeared in public life in this country',[35] while Tom Walsh of Fianna Fáil avowed that 'his one sole ambition is to see this country subject to Britain again'.[36] Cogan was equally intemperate, saying that the minister 'treats farmers like serfs'. Perhaps more to the point was the charge that he 'has not met his fellow Independent Deputies once in Council ... he will meet an individual Deputy and talk down to him ... he acts like a dictator.'[37]

Dillon, however, was not fazed. MacEntee's vitriol he attributed to the good weather – 'it is the spring cockerel season ... he was bound to crow'[38] – while O'Reilly was as usual, 'woe, woe, universal woe ... intoning the "Miserere" in E flat'.[39] Neither did he lack for supporters, often from unlikely quarters. The taciturn William Sheldon, a Protestant Independent from Donegal whose intervention in debates was economical, was almost enthusiastic about Dillon: 'My respect almost always goes to anyone who can show enthusiasm, and I would prefer a man to go ahead in the wrong direction than to sit down and do nothing. That is something ... the Minister will not do. He will frequently go in the wrong direction but at least that is better than sitting still, waiting for everything to happen around him.' Dillon, he saw as a 'catalyst' moving the conservative agricultural community 'along a modernising path'.[40] Sean Collins of Fine Gael noted that Fianna Fáil 'hated Dillon with an undying hatred because scheme after scheme envisaged by the broad vision of the Minister is now coming into effect', a point supported by TDs from Clann na Talmhan.[41] Most significant of all perhaps was the fact that Cowan, who was going to vote against the Estimate because of the Mother and Child issue, told Dillon this was no reflection on him: 'One of the most amazing matters in our public life over the past three years has been the sustained campaign of abuse and bitterness which has been directed against the Minister for Agriculture.' As far as Cowan was concerned, 'no man could have worked harder or worked better on behalf of the farmers than he has'.[42]

The debate continued as the life of the Dáil ebbed away. Fianna Fáil missed an opportunity to bring the whole thing to an end when Smith was suspended on 26 April, losing them the vital majority needed to topple the government. According to *The Irish Times*, Smith, 'either exasperated by the urbanity of Dillon, or annoyed because the government would not close the debate, told Dillon he was a liar', and 'since it ill becomes Mr. Smith's style to retract', he was suspended.[43]

From this point on, however, it was simply a question of tactics and time.

On 30 April the Agriculture Estimate was deferred. On 2 May, the 'Family Man's budget' was introduced and, under the shadow of impending dissolution, the Agriculture Estimate was talked out, with Flanagan in possession for over two hours. That night, in the last act of the life of the thirteenth Dáil, the Adjournment Debate fell to Dillon, on a motion in Corry's name to do with ground limestone. It was a nasty, fractious debate, dominated by personal insults. Dillon, Corry said, was a 'brother of Ananias', while Dillon held that Corry's 'conduct and language are as mischievous as those of a Gibraltar monkey'.[44]

There was little more that could be usefully done. The Dáil had run its productive course. The government had lost its working majority and on the following day Costello announced the Dáil would be dissolved at the weekend and polling would take place on 13 May.

The Inter Party government may have lost control of its destiny, but its break-up was reasonable and orderly. After putting the budget in place, the government, minus Noel Browne, held together with near total solidarity. It maintained this cohesion through the election campaign, and presented the electorate with a clear choice between two blocs – Fianna Fáil or the Inter-Party alternative – each capable of forming a government. Personal relations between the party leaders were also warm and mutual respect between the five parties' TDs was now the norm.

Faced with a united opposition and a sustained assault from the *Irish Press*, the Inter Party government had not only held together but cohered. Though its operational methods had been untidy and loose, its relationship with senior civil servants naive and mistaken, it did have some important achievements to its credit. Through Norton it had tackled the backlog of social welfare reform, its economic policy marked a crucial and innovative stage in the transformation of the economy – the IDA, in particular, was a tribute to the government's foresight – and the sham of a 'dictionary' Republic was no more. Most of all, it had shown that there was a viable alternative to Fianna Fáil, and in its own way it had taken the novel concept of coalition and made it a reality. As subsequent elections would show, a significant proportion of the electorate was persuaded to support the idea whenever they were given an opportunity.

From Dillon's point of view, it had been an exciting and fulfilling three years. He was, by universal regard, one of the real successes of the government, a fact celebrated by his friends and confirmed by Fianna Fáil's deep antagonism. He had fought hard for agriculture at the cabinet table and ensured its interest would never go by default. His successive initiatives, from land reclamation to agricultural education and better marketing, and his flair for publicity, had brought agriculture onto centre stage. He had also safely navigated the jump from Commonwealth to Republic, and he had enjoyed himself. He could face into his eighth general election in good heart. In the words of one of his senior civil servants, 'he had put agriculture on the map, just as Lemass had done for industry and commerce'.[45]

CHAPTER SEVENTEEN

NOTHING NEW
NOTHING DIFFERENT

The same old nasty politics.
John Healy on Dáil Eireann in this period.

THE 1951 GENERAL election was Dillon's eighth in nineteen years and the first one he fought from the vantage point of government. He was fighting, too, from a position of some security: he had a particularly high profile, his reputation was established, and once again Fine Gael was giving him a free run in Monaghan. More than that, there was every reason to believe that Inter Party solidarity would translate into higher transfers and offer, for the first time in a decade, a real alternative to Fianna Fáil.

Their cohesion was dramatically illustrated by the joint advertisement signed by Costello, Norton, MacBride, Blowick and Dillon, asking for a return of the government on the basis of its record and urging their voters to transfer their votes to other Inter Party candidates. The presence of an alternative was about the only novel aspect of the election – there was no question of new ideas or new policies. Fianna Fáil was uncharacteristically quiet; it made no real effort at providing specific policies and the declaration of a Republic had taken some of the wind out of its republican sails. The Mother and Child controversy was barely an issue in the campaign and received scant attention from party platforms or newspaper coverage. While it may have assumed epic proportion in later years, it was largely ignored at the time.

Dillon came in for criticism from *The Irish Times*, which said, somewhat sourly, that he had 'campaigned unashamedly against declaring an isolated Republic in 1948, and look what happened'.[1] The newspaper's words caused him little worry. His personal popularity was evident at the coalition parties' final rally in O'Connell St, Dublin, where he received the loudest welcome and attracted the most heckling. Dillon loved hecklers. He provoked them and then met their remarks with a dramatically uttered put-down. The relevance of the put-down didn't much matter in what was still an unsophisticated age; nor did it matter that the same phrase had served its purpose on many previous occasions. In O'Connell St he detected some sporadic booing from the edge of the crowd – 'You hear that low moaning sound ... the voice of the ghosts of Mr de Valera's slaughtered calves' – and once more it worked.[2]

The campaign may have been lacklustre, with the parties trying – and failing – to accentuate policy differences,[3] but the result at least was close. Dillon headed the poll in Monaghan with a healthy surplus, and for the most part the government parties did well. Fine Gael was the big winner with forty seats and its popular vote up almost thirty per cent, from 262,000 votes to 342,000. The reunited Labour Party lost four seats, Clann na Talmhan gained one, while Clann na Poblachta, which had six seats at the dissolution, was reduced to two, and MacBride suffered the ignominy of waiting until the last count before scraping home in Dublin South-West. Fianna Fáil moved hardly at all. Its popular vote was up almost thirteen per cent but it gained only one extra seat, still five short of an overall majority.[4]

Two aspects of the election were particularly significant. The first was that the electorate had clearly accepted the idea of a coalition government as an alternative to Fianna Fáil, a point emphasised by the degree of transfers between these parties. The second aspect was the continuing strength of the Independents. Their number was down from seventeen to fourteen, but these included Noel Browne, Jack McQuillan and Peadar Cowan (whose election campaign was characterised by a complete absence of canvassing, but who still won the last seat in Dublin North-East), all formerly of Clann na Poblachta. Elected also was a politically unknown Dublin doctor, Michael ffrench O'Carroll, a disciple of Noel Browne. Dillon's great friend, Oliver Flanagan, got another huge vote, but the Independents also included his *bête noir* Patrick Cogan. The main Independent casualty was another of Dillon's protagonists, Patrick O'Reilly from Cavan.

In the days immediately after the election the press assumed that a majority of the Independents would support Costello.[5] On 3 June MacBride formally proposed a four-party government of Fianna Fáil, Fine Gael, Labour and Clann na Talmhan, an option which was a non-starter,[6] but things changed dramatically the following day when Fianna Fáil made it known that it was prepared to form a government. It went even further than that: the party produced a programme for government, something it had neglected to do during the election campaign. The programme jettisoned some of the party's traditional policies, including compulsory tillage, and promised to continue a number of Dillon's plans for agricultural education, reclamation and land fertilisation. It also promised to persist with MacBride's policy on afforestation, and to implement new Social Welfare and Mother and Child bills. The programme was a shopping list to attract the Independents; its appearance showed that Fianna Fáil had learned that power was not something to be assumed automatically, but had to be fought for.[7]

Fianna Fáil's energy contrasted starkly with the government's lethargic approach towards winning the Independents. From the outset Browne, Cowan and Flynn were unlikely to support Costello; ffrench O'Carroll was likely to be influenced by Noel Browne; while Cogan, enjoying his role as kingmaker and taking the opportunity to settle a few old scores, laid down his conditions on 7 June, the principal one being that Dillon must not be Minister for Agriculture.[8] It was taken for granted that Jack McQuillan would vote against the Inter Party government, and that, it seemed, would be that.

It was not, however, quite so clear-cut. When the Dáil met on 13 June, de Valera announced that the outgoing Ceann Comhairle, Frank Fahy, who had held the position for the previous nineteen years, would not be seeking re-election.[9] This, of course, meant an extra vote for Fianna Fáil, and two extra votes if his successor came from the Inter Party side. Costello duly proposed a Labour TD, Patrick Hogan, who was elected Ceann Comhairle, thereby depriving his own side of a vital two votes. Given the figures, it would have made greater political sense for Costello to have offered the position to one of the Independents, especially one likely to oppose him, but that option was not even contemplated. The government thus began two votes down.

Even with that, the outcome was uncertain as the Independents made the most of their opportunity. Cogan pinned his colours to the mast in a rancorous speech: the Inter Party group sought to 'buy' the independent votes, he said, but he was not for buying. He would vote for de Valera, and he gave his reasons: the Labour Party was a danger to the nation's defences and associated with international communism, Dillon had sabotaged agriculture and Everett was a national disgrace.[10] Cogan relished the occasion while, in the words of one observer, 'the Fianna Fáil party looked on with the embarrassed air of a school prefect who finds himself being saved from drowning by a Third Form boy'.[11] Subsequently, ffrench O'Carroll promised his conditional support to Fianna Fáil, while Browne, in a low-key speech, said that while the Inter Party government had been good in many ways, it had been weakened by its profound ideological differences.

Dillon followed Browne with what *The Irish Times* called one of his best ever parliamentary speeches.[12] He had no intention of adopting Browne's understated approach. Indeed, what he had to say set the tone for an acrimonious relationship with the Independents who supported de Valera which was to last the entire parliament.

He dismissed Browne's remarks out of hand. 'What ideological differences, if words retain their meaning, divide any two Deputies on any side of this House? The last government was at one in its fight against poverty, there were no ideological differences in government.' And he carried on:

> I give him the charity of thinking that that is the folly of childish inexperience and lack of capacity to appreciate the nature of his acts. But people on all sides of this House who know the developing reverberations of the tale he purported to tell all over the world, wherever there are enemies of Ireland, or wherever there are enemies of the Catholic Church, cannot say grandiloquently, 'it is all over as far as we are concerned'. The echoes have only begun to roll and not all the eloquence of every Deputy can catch up with the mighty army of lies which is marching behind that standard at this moment all over the world to prove that in Ireland it is true what Salisbury, what Balfour, what Carson said was true – that Home Rule was Rome Rule.

Browne's misrepresentations, he said, would help those who wanted to prove that 'to be free men you must destroy the Church'.[13] He then turned to Cogan, who had indicated that the outgoing government had sought to 'buy' the Independents' support. Dillon vehemently denied it: 'We reasoned with, argued with, asked them to lend us a hand ... but it was Fianna Fáil who has slandered the Independents by suggesting they were purchasable.' He was sanguine about the prospect of opposition: 'if the decision of the House requires us to leave down the work we are just beginning, so be it. That is the fortune of politics and only a fool engages in politics if he is not prepared to take the rough with the smooth.'[14]

Cowan, about whose vote there was little doubt, gave his support to Fianna Fáil. There was a certain irony in this: it was not so long since MacEntee had singled him out for a particularly nasty series of attacks in the *Irish Press*, describing him as the 'Red Pope' and a 'crawling communist' – even a 'sort of abortion'.[15] McQuillan, who had been expected to follow his friend Noel Browne into the Fianna Fáil lobby, provided the first major surprise. Despite the fact that he had left Clann na Poblachta because MacBride and others had 'ratted' on Browne and the Mother and Child scheme, he had no faith in Fianna Fáil's sincerity, nor their seeking support on the basis of a seventeen-point programme which had not been available before the election. He was not happy, but he would vote for Costello.[16]

And so it continued as each Independent stated his case. The tension was finally broken when John Flynn told the House he would vote for de Valera. He was soon to rejoin his former party.

Costello was first proposed and lost by just two votes, seventy-four to seventy-two – the change of Ceann Comhairle had made the difference. De Valera was then proposed and was elected with a comfortable five-vote majority when three of the Independents who had earlier voted for

Costello – Sheldon, Finucane and Lehane – abstained.

The Dáil then moved on to the formation of a government, and with the exception of Costello's speech, the tone of the debate was rancorous. Costello dwelt instead on the solidarity and trust that had been forged in his government. MacBride he described as 'an old friend and a loyal colleague'. As for Labour:

> it was a matter of profound satisfaction that I worked, and worked in the clos-est harmony with a unified policy, with no dissensions and no divisions, and no bargaining with the members of the Labour Party; that we in Fine Gael who are supposed to be conservative, the close-fisted party, the representatives of the rich men, if you please, were able to work and find ourselves in close sympathy with the representatives of the working people of this country.

And having praised all his former colleagues he left till last 'perhaps the outstanding person, James Dillon ... the work he has done will prove of lasting value'.

> He has left the mark of his genius, his constructive imagination and fertile brain on the agriculture of this country ... but we who have sat with him day after day know that he gave a far more valuable contribution than his contri-bution to agriculture, because his mind, his experience and his integrity, were always at our disposal in the very difficult problems we had to face.[17]

After that it was all bitterness and personal antagonism, and the Independents who had supported Fianna Fáil found themselves most often in the opposition's firing line. Dillon was quick to dub the five 'Fianna Fáil's busted flush – four wild west diamonds and one bleeding heart.' The bleeding heart, apparently, was ffrench O'Carroll, but the appellation in one form or another was to attach itself to the five TDs for the rest of the session. From a tactical point of view the line taken by opposition parties made no sense. They went out of their way to alienate the Independents when a change of mind on the part of one or two of their number was all that was needed to put Fianna Fáil out of office. Clearly, feelings ran too deep even to contemplate such a move.

DE VALERA'S 1951-54 government has been characterised as his worst ever administration. There was no indication that it had learned much during its period in opposition, and in spite of the fact that several new members were elected in 1948 and 1951 the cabinet was still dominated by the men of de Valera's first administration – seven of the twelve ministers had been members of the 1932 government.

After the new government was in place, Dillon found himself once more on the opposition benches. With the loss of his ministry went the loss of his ministerial Dodge, and his salary dropped from £1,500 per year to £350. One of the first pieces of advice he gave to the new government was to increase ministerial salaries. He argued then and throughout his political life that politicians were seriously underpaid, and was one of the few politicians prepared to make this point publicly.[18] Resuming his seat on the second row of the Dáil on the opposition side, he continued to be an assiduous contributor during the next three years, principally on agricultural issues but having his say at some stage on almost every topic before the House. By now he was a senior statesman. As an Independent he was spared the chore of travelling to party meetings throughout the country, but it was assumed almost from the beginning that it would only be a matter of time before he rejoined Fine Gael. His attitude to Fianna Fáil had not altered.

The Dáil had some new faces, the most notable being Declan Costello, PJ Hillery and Sean Flanagan, but there was little evidence of new thinking, and the government resumed more or less where it had left off in 1948. Dillon was right when he said there was little ideological difference between members of the House, and McQuillan was equally correct when he said that there was little to distinguish Fianna Fáil's policies from Fine Gael's, or indeed from the other parties'.[19] Debates continued along well-worn tracks as the new parliament got under way. Soon Dillon was back in the wars. For the first and only time he was expelled from the House, an event which arose, as these things often do, out of nothing. It happened on the election of a new Leas Ceann Comhairle in July 1951, when the Ceann Comhairle, mistakenly assuming that the debate was concluded, refused to allow Dillon to speak. Dillon persisted in the midst of enormous disorder, then refused to leave the House until eventually he was 'named' and expelled.[20]

He allowed his successor as Minister for Agriculture, Kilkenny farmer Thomas Walsh, an easy start in the Agriculture Estimate in June, and then, after ridiculing Fianna Fáil's abandonment of compulsory tillage, insisted that the industry should be above party. In July Dillon strongly defended the fledgling IDA, then under threat from Lemass. He thought the organisation should be focused exclusively on creating new industry and was best relieved of bureaucratic responsibilities, and he wanted it, too, to be 'outside of politics', so it would enjoy the confidence of business people. He made the shrewd point that one of Lemass's reasons for proposing to disband the IDA was not based on any hostility to industrial policy *per se*, but because Lemass's position in cabinet, especially *vis-à-vis* Walsh in Agriculture, gave industrial policy a dominant place within government and he was not willing to share the making of that policy with a new agency.[21] In fact, Lemass soon became a strong supporter of the IDA.

Dillon also returned to one of his earliest themes, his belief that Irish language policy had been a sham. He pointed out that Irish was very much less used outside the schools now than it had been thirty years earlier, and recalled his own enthusiasm for the language at the age of twenty, when he set about learning it for its own value. He argued that Irish had been diminished by the fact that it had become an instrument of corruption – a means of procuring preference. It had disgusted him in government, he said, to see highly qualified people lose out in appointments and promotions because of their lack of competence in Irish. He made the radical proposal of 'free education in terms of real scholarships for those who can benefit from them rather than the universal and compulsory teaching of Irish to those who would never benefit'.[22]

At around this time, MacEntee in Finance began attacking the financial record of the Inter Party government, accusing it of having spent recklessly and borrowed improvidently, and leaving it to their successors to pay. McGilligan thought he saw in MacEntee's attitude 'the answer to a question that had been puzzling me' – the whereabouts of the statue of Queen Victoria, recently removed from the front of Leinster House. 'She is quite clearly now installed in the Department of Finance and we are going to have Victorianism rampant.'[23] There was substantial truth in his remarks. The 'old guard' in Finance used the change of government to wrest control back from the 'young Turks' – Patrick Lynch and Alexis FitzGerald – and in MacEntee they had an unrepentant fiscal conservative. Dillon was in favour of capital expenditure for productive or social purposes and had never been afraid to borrow, and he took issue with MacEntee's financial doctrine: 'No business, no nation stands still, it either goes forward or it goes backward.' He regretted MacEntee's domination by the Department of Finance, though in reality their relationship was a marriage of minds.[24]

In general, however, the 1951 parliamentary year ended as it had begun, in a welter of personality clashes and recriminations. Dillon was very much at odds with the Independents who supported Fianna Fáil. Cowan was his first target, after Cowan had proposed in July 1951 'if partition is to be ended in our time it can only be ended by the enforcement of our will on the will of our fellow citizens in the Six Counties'.[25] He also sparred with Fianna Fáil, especially after Walsh told him in November that the government was not going to go ahead with the Parish Plan he had instituted as Minister for Agriculture.[26] Later that month he described Fianna Fáil's proposed undeveloped area scheme as a ploy to win back rural support which had been lost in the election, and he laced his attack with charges of corruption which he did not back up.[27] This was only one of several abuses alleged by Dillon and, coming on top of his continual sniping at the

Independents, it brought Cowan to the brink of rage: 'Every patriot of our generation has felt the venom, the bitterness, the pent-up hatred, innuendo and false suggestions of Deputy Dillon.' Dillon, he ranted, was 'unbalanced … a megalomaniac … with a sinister hostility to Ireland.'[28]

This was parliamentary overkill, but a deeper bitterness seemed to lie between Noel Browne and Dillon. There had been rumours in October that Browne was about to form a new party, in part as a defensive measure to prevent the Independents being picked off one by one by government or opposition. Those mentioned as potential members were essentially the rump of Clann na Poblachta – Cowan, McQuillan, Noel Hartnett (now a Senator) and ffrench O'Carroll – though nothing came of it.[29] By now Browne's strictures were comprehensive, embracing many members of the Labour Party and all members of the outgoing cabinet, particularly Norton. Browne had become and was to remain obsessed with the Mother and Child episode, and was beginning to show signs of what *The Irish Times* – generally his most uncritical supporter – called 'that *saeva indignatio* which can become as wearisome as the conversation of a man with a grievance'.[30]

Dillon thought Browne was guilty of gross disloyalty to his former colleagues, and in a November debate accused him of as much. Browne hit back, accusing Dillon of trying to have him sell his soul to the medical association. 'You do not have to worry,' he spat, 'you will get free treatment for a long time for your services.' Dillon replied: 'The temptation to get into the gutter with the doctor is well nigh irresistible.'[31] It was one of many such ugly exchanges, and while Dillon's attitude to Browne mellowed with the years and his references to him in his *Memoir* are neutral or friendly, the reverse was the case with Browne in his book, *Against the Tide*.

The government's dependence on the Independents' votes made for insecurity, especially given the volatile nature of some of those involved and their past attitude to Fianna Fáil, but, as de Valera calculated, the Independents had made their bed and were bound to lie in it. When the Dáil resumed in February 1952 after the Christmas recess, the government adjourned the House for a further two weeks for the simple reason that there was no legislation available. Their handling of the adjournment summed up Fianna Fáil's attitude both to the Dáil and opposition. Lemass, as Leader of the House, did not even tell the opposition Whips about his decision; he simply told the Dáil of the government's intentions and then voted the adjournment through.[32]

It had been suspected that the hard men of Finance were now back in control, and MacEntee's budget in April confirmed those fears with a vengeance. The budget put one shilling in the pound on income tax and raised the price of virtually all commodities. It was, as one commentator said, so sharply punitive it confirmed even the most pessimistic of prophets. The newspapers dubbed it 'the butchery of the taxpayers'.[33]

MacEntee had, admittedly, inherited a financial deficit, due in part to the rise in the price of imported raw materials following the devaluation of the Irish pound in line with sterling in 1949, and the stockpiling of goods as a result of the Korean War in 1950. It was argued that these were one-off measures and that the situation was already righting itself, but this was not the view of MacEntee or Merrion St. Professor JJ Lee has argued that 'McElligott needed a crisis to purge the economy of Inter-Party promiscuity'. MacEntee was a willing aide.[34]

The MacEntee budget was introduced at an unprecedently early date – 2 April – no doubt on the grounds that if there were to be harsh measures, the sooner the government got them over with the better, especially when the Independents would not relish an early election. The severity of the budget, however, was almost certainly excessive and a miscalculation in economic and political terms. In Lee's judgement it 'probably contributed significantly to both the reality and the atmosphere of depression'. He contends that 'the relentless pursuit of deflation in 1953 and 1954 further accentuated the slump'. This 'deflationary crusade ... discouraged investment in manufacturing industry and may have inhibited export development'.[35]

Politically, the budget was the defining moment in the life of the government, generating a wave of unpopularity from which it never recovered. Four days later, at a Labour Party protest meeting in Dublin, riots erupted and over seventy people were hurt.[36] This type of street protest was to recur more than once over the coming years, and while never approaching anything on the scale of French street riots, it signalled people's deep resentment at the government's rigorous handling of the national finances. The government had, however, judged correctly the reaction of the Independents: three of Dillon's 'busted flush' – Browne, Cogan, and Cowan – voted with Fianna Fáil on the budget, while ffrench O'Carroll abstained. Browne's support ruled out any possibility of his joining Labour and effectively made Fianna Fáil his only possible political home, should he or his colleagues seek to remove themselves from the increasingly isolated zone which had become the abode of the Independents.

THE BEGINNING of the realignment of the Independents, which was to see their numbers reduced from fourteen to eight during the lifetime of the Dáil, began, however, with Dillon. In May he was approached by Costello to rejoin Fine Gael, 'since the issue on which I had parted from them was no longer a live one'.[37] Dillon had no hesitation about accepting the invitation.

While in some ways he was the epitome of an Independent TD, Dillon had from his earliest days been a believer in party. His participation in government had erased any residual anger over his wartime stance and he had remained on good terms with his Fine Gael colleagues subsequently. In addition, Fine Gael had not opposed him in Monaghan, treating him to a real extent as one of their own. When his return to Fine Gael was announced on 11 May by Mulcahy[38] (who was still party leader, despite Costello's being leader of the opposition) the move had a major psychological effect on other Independents. A week later Flanagan followed Dillon into the party, leading to Sean MacEntee's celebrated jibe that Flanagan was 'Dillon's political love-child whom he had fostered on Fine Gael'. Charlie Fagan, once of the Centre Party, then Fine Gael, and latterly an Independent, followed suit.[39]

1952 also saw the first of the eight by-elections of that relatively short parliament. In April, Denis Burke, a Limerick Fianna Fáil TD, died, followed in May by Mrs Bridget Redmond, the widow of Captain Willie Redmond and inheritor of the still significant Redmondite vote in Waterford. Five days later PJ Ruttledge died. The subsequent by-elections saw no overall change in party strength, but what was significant was the consistency of voting transfers between the non-Fianna Fáil parties, which made it clear that the Inter Party arrangement was secure in the short-term at least. Later in the year this was demonstrated more emphatically when an Independent candidate, Thomas Byrne, won the seat of his late brother, Alfie Byrne Jnr, with almost double the Fianna Fáil vote. In fact, Fianna Fáil's vote in this by-election was down forty per cent in a working-class Dublin constituency, further evidence of the damage wrought on the party's popularity by MacEntee's budget.[40]

De Valera, meanwhile, was suffering from increasingly bad eyesight, and he was out of the country for the last third of the year, attending an eye clinic in Utrecht. His long absence and virtual blindness, during which time Lemass was effectively Taoiseach, fuelled speculation that he would soon retire as leader of Fianna Fáil, but, not for the first or last time, de Valera had no notion of obliging. Otherwise, 1952 offered little of note, apart from the continuing bad temper in the Dáil. The first months of the year had seen a bout of fisticuffs in the restaurant, when John Flynn, now back in Fianna Fáil, hit Oliver Flanagan, claiming that Flanagan had maligned him during a debate on adoption.[41] In July, a bout of name-calling resulted in Fianna Fáil's Mark Killilea crossing the floor to strike Sean Collins of Fine Gael who had sorely provoked him, with Martin Corry urging them to full fisticuffs outside the chamber.[42] A day later Sean Collins found himself in another incident in the hall of Leinster House when he was physically assaulted by the Minister for Education, Sean Moylan.[43] No sooner had apologies been proffered and accepted for this incident than

Dillon was obstructed on the main staircase by the Leader of the Senate and veteran of the Locke Tribunal, Senator William Quirke, who knocked the cigarette from Dillon's mouth and verbally assaulted him. Eventually Quirke made a full apology to the Senate, which was then conveyed to the Dáil.[44] None of these incidents was serious in itself, but together with the personalised attacks and general abusiveness of so many Dáil debates, they pointed to an underlying sourness in the general atmosphere. Dillon himself took a sinister view – he saw the incidents as part of the Fianna Fáil conspiracy to intimidate opposition members – while the teetotal Flanagan saw them as a good reason to close the Dáil bar.[45]

On rejoining Fine Gael, Dillon had resumed his agricultural spokesmanship. It might have been wiser of him to seek an alternative portfolio rather than confining himself to one area, but his heart was in agriculture. In truth, he found little to fault the government on during 1952. When the Agriculture Estimate was introduced in July he was fully in agreement with its policies, which he said in many respects were a continuation of his own. His only major difference was on the re-organisation of the Advisory Services, which he wanted based on the parish rather than the county. He admitted with unusual parliamentary candour: 'I have moved to refer back this estimate and to tell you the honest truth I am damned if I know why I did. I think the only grounds is that the Minister appears to me to be a great deal more somnolent than he ought to be ... wake up. That is my principal admonition to the Minister for Agriculture. Wake up and throw your weight about because if you do not, others will.'[46]

He used his speech to reassert the fundamental importance of agriculture to the overall development of the country, attacking the 'city outlook' which failed to appreciate its dependence on rural Ireland, and attacking especially 'the whole crazy structure of tariff industries ... built on the foundation of the agricultural industry'. He stood against artificial development based on protection, not against industrialisation *per se*, but clearly he saw little prospect of worthwhile industrial development in Ireland.[47]

Dillon spoke on most estimates. He was one of the most full-time members of the Dáil, invariably present at Question Time and for the Order of Business. His performances still drew people to the House, and his language was as colourful as ever. He derided one particular proposal in July 1952: 'since Eusebius the Eunuch put up the provincial prefecture of the Roman Empire of the East for sale, I do not think any more indecent proposal has been brought before Dáil Eireann.'[48] He could be provocative, revelling in the short-arm combat of parliamentary debate, and had few scruples about being offensive. He liked to portray Lemass as a gambler – 'Monte Carlo, close your doors when you see the Tanaiste arrive; the greatest bluffer, the best poker player that ever stood in Irish politics,'[49] and on a proposal from Lemass which he regarded as a diversion, he lambasted him for introducing a red herring: 'after twenty years he has them fresh and he has them stale; he has them smelly and he has them stinking, for calling upon when the situation demands'.[50] Lemass, of course, could and did hit back, but it appears there was little personal ill-will in their relationship. Incomprehension yes; bitterness no. Dillon admired Lemass's drive and energy; in the 1952 budget debate he praised his sense of public service, his ambition and his desire for power, qualities which Dillon thought were estimable in any serious politician.[51] Erskine Childers, however, continued to annoy him, especially his long pontificating speeches and his tendency to lecture the House on Irish history, something which got on Dillon's nerves: 'It ill behoves a Childers to tell me how I should conduct myself in an Irish parliament.'[52]

Around this time, MacEntee accused Dillon of trying to imitate Churchill. 'Mr Churchill wears a peculiar and funny hat; so does Mr Dillon. Mr Churchill smokes a cigar; Mr Dillon smokes a cigarette. Mr Churchill speaks in orotund phrases ...'[53] It was hardly the greatest put-down, though the charge of aping Churchill was frequently made later. Dillon did indeed admire Churchill and there was occasional correspondence between them – Churchill had admired John Dillon in the old House of Commons days and this provided the basis for their good, if slight relations. But the charge that Dillon imitated Churchill was without foundation: Dillon's style had been well established long before Churchill became Prime Minister. If he did have a model in this regard it was Franklin D. Roosevelt, who had long been the politician he most admired.

His relationship with Frank Aiken was never to improve. The memory of the heavy-handed wartime censorship he had suffered still troubled him, and he continued to charge Aiken with Nazi sympathies in those years:

> I can remember when the Minister was the familiar of the Nazi Embassy in this country. I remember when the Minister's friends used to pass through the corridors of this House inquiring if you would like an invitation to dine with the Nazi Minister in Dublin. I remember a time when we knew he loved Nazism and hoped to see it win, because he felt that was the way to govern ... absolute power ... There was one in this House who aspired to it ... who saw himself cast in the role of the *Gauleiter*, if that power should ever come to Ireland.[54]

Dillon was suspicious of Fianna Fáil to a degree where he saw conspiracies when none existed, but his image of a network of patronage designed to keep the party in power was not far short of the mark: after twenty years in government, Fianna Fáil had nailed down almost every position which could be attached to the party. Dillon, however, went further still. He believed that Fianna Fáil lacked some of the essentials of a democratic party, especially in not allowing freedom of speech to its opponents. It was this belief which encouraged him to transform Dáil incidents into political intrigues and made him almost pathologically suspicious of Fianna Fáil's actions and utterances.

It was not an uncommon conviction among non-Fianna Fáil politicians at the time, especially those in Fine Gael. Equally there were many in Fianna Fáil whose attitude to Fine Gael was just as uncompromising. While Dillon could be on the best of terms with individual Fianna Fáil TDs, there was little doubt that this fixation made it impossible for him to see good in anything the party did. His obsession probably damaged him as a politician, limiting his own appeal and at times casting doubts on his judgement. It would be wrong, however, to think of Dillon at this or any other period as being abrasive or uncivil. Outside the chamber he was the most civil and courteous of men. He valued loyalty to his Fine Gael colleagues as amongst the highest of virtues – it was Noel Browne's lack of loyalty which he regarded as his greatest sin. In fairness, Browne had of course a different view of who had been loyal to whom.

The victory of the Inter Party candidate, Thomas Byrne, in the Dublin Central by-election in November 1952 led to further calls on the government to resign and go to the country. Dillon also called for an election, arguing that the government was being sustained in office by Independents who had no mandate to do so, since none had campaigned on the basis of keeping Fianna Fáil in power. Dillon did not spare the increasingly vulnerable Independents, even offering to help them out – 'give the four poor satellites some compensating consideration' – and appealing to the government: 'If you make the proposition that the price of your going now would be to put the four tulips in the Seanad, we will go a long way to try to meet you.'[55]

De Valera returned at year's end from Utrecht and almost immediately convened a meeting of his parliamentary party, the first such meeting in five months and a clear indication that, in spite of age and blindness, the Chief had no intention of retiring.[56] This new resolve did little to improve the economic situation. Unemployment grew to 90,000, prices rose and industrial unrest, especially among civil servants and the unemployed, expressed itself in mass protests in Dublin. As the year progressed, the revival in Fine Gael fortunes was signalled by victories in two by-elections in June 1953. In East Cork, a seat formerly held by Labour was won by Dick Barry, where Fine Gael's vote was up by 3,500, while in Wicklow Mark Deering caused a major surprise by winning the Fianna Fáil seat formerly held by Thomas Brennan.[57] The government and opposition each had sixty-nine seats, with the balance held by the nine Independents.

Fianna Fáil had lost in five of the six by-elections since 1951, but de Valera had no intention of buckling under. Deciding that attack was the best form of defence, he called for a confidence vote in early July, in effect issuing a challenge to the Independents to keep him in office or face a general election. To no one's surprise, the Independents were not for turning and the government survived by two votes. Its victory was of course helped by Fine Gael's decision to attack rather than sway the Independents. Cogan's bitterness to Dillon was again much in evidence when he described him as a 'political Christie' (a reference to the then notorious multiple murderer) 'with a cupboard full of skeletons'.[58]

De Valera pressed home his advantage a few weeks later, after the death of Frank Fahy, the former Ceann Comhairle. Normally the by-election would wait until the autumn session, but South Galway was an impregnable Fianna Fáil fortress and after three successive by-election losses de Valera needed an electoral boost. The Dáil sat into August and on 1 August, just a fortnight after Fahy's death, the writ was moved. The tactic worked inasmuch as Fianna Fáil won the seat with fifty-four per cent of the vote, but ominously for them it was the Fine Gael vote which increased, while theirs remained static.[59]

In October 1953 the pro-Fianna Fáil Independents accepted the inevitable and formally joined Fianna Fáil. Browne, Cogan and ffrench O'Carroll were joined in signing the party pledge by Noel Hartnett, augmenting Fianna Fáil numbers and introducing a new element of stability, short-lived though it proved to be.[60]

When two further by-elections arrived in early 1954 as a result of the deaths of Fine Gael TDs Dr TF O'Higgins and George Coburn of Louth, it was clear from the start of the campaigns that their outcome would determine the future of the Dáil. If Fianna Fáil did well, it was expected that a number of wavering Independents would follow Browne into the party, thus ensuring the government's life. If they did badly, the life of the Dáil was effectively over. In the event, Fine Gael did not just win both seats but headed the poll in each with Labour transfers running at eighty per cent; the Fianna Fáil vote was down significantly. De Valera, although describing the result as a 'freak', decided on an early, though not an immediate election. *The Irish Times* assured its readers it would be his last: 'the time of his useful service has come to an end'.[61]

The die was cast. Nominating conventions were summoned and parties took up predictable positions on whether or not they would enter government. Almost the last act of the Dáil was the budget on 21 April – not surprisingly a mild budget, with tax concessions and a lowering of beer duties. It caused little stir and did nothing to erase the memory of

MacEntee's earlier draconian measures.[62] Finally, on 24 April, a Dáil that had been fractious, undistinguished and unproductive came to an end.

Its one achievement of note had been the skilful salvaging of the Mother and Child scheme by de Valera and the Minister for Health, Jim Ryan, when it looked as if the bishops and the Irish Medical Association might once again scupper it. For long periods following the publication of Ryan's White Paper in July 1952, it seemed as if neither group had learned from the earlier débâcle, but Ryan managed to keep the controversy clear of open confrontation and made small concessions while winning all the points of substance. De Valera then forced the bishops into a last minute re-think at a crucial moment, and effectively brought policy-making on health matters back into political hands. It was one of de Valera's finest political performances, and in spite of the later reservations and strictures of Noel Browne, it was a clear victory for de Valera over both the bishops and the doctors. It was, however, a victory de Valera preferred to celebrate privately. One further aspect of the affair which was intriguing was de Valera's secret meeting with Cardinal D'Alton which took place in Áras an Uachtaráin, a clear indication that President O'Kelly was not totally above party politics.[63]

The election campaign was well under way before the dissolution. The Inter Party group campaigned as a bloc, offering an alternative government, its core programme contained in a ten-point plan. In addition, Costello announced that Dillon's Parish Plan would be a major part of Fine Gael's policy in government, and he endorsed Dillon's proposal to establish an institute of agriculture and veterinary science. In what proved to be a lacklustre election campaign, one of the few controversies was the defection of an entire Fianna Fáil cumann in Dublin to Clann na Poblachta, apparently because some British army officers had been received at the Curragh and their visit had been endorsed by the Department of Defence. More significant was the endorsement of Fianna Fáil by *The Irish Times* for the first time, and the paper's strong attack on Fine Gael, whose 'good faith' it could no longer trust after the Commonwealth episode.[64]

The election was an emphatic endorsement for the Inter Party group. Fianna Fáil's number of seats dropped to sixty-five, Fine Gael's rose to fifty, Labour gained four seats, giving it nineteen, Clann na Talmhan had five, Clann na Poblachta now had three (and this time MacBride was comfortably elected) and there were just five Independents. Dillon again headed the poll in Monaghan, where he was elected on the second count, while Fine Gael gained able new TDs such as Tom Finlay (later Chief Justice) and Patrick J. Lindsay. What was significant, however, was the defeat of all of Dillon's 'busted flush' — Browne lost in Dublin South-East, where Costello's surplus won a second Fine Gael seat; Cowan, ffrench O'Carroll and Cogan were all casualties. Only Jack McQuillan of the old Clann na Poblachta, the most independent of Independents, survived.[65]

The post-election period saw a certain amount of manoeuvring as the parties went through the motions of forming a government. *The Irish Times* put the government's defeat down to bread-and-butter issues, and noting Fianna Fáil's transformation into a 'party of big business', urged the formation of a Fianna Fáil–Labour government. Labour, it argued, was closer to Fianna Fáil, but the real reason for this advice was a continuation of its anti-Fine Gael mood: 'Such a pact assuredly would dish the whigs in style.'[66] Labour thought differently. It called a special delegate conference on 13 May when, on the basis that Labour would have significant economic clout and that reducing prices would be at the heart of government policy, the 700 delegates gave their unanimous agreement to a new Inter Party arrangement. Fine Gael gave its approval to the ten-point programme a day later, and on the morning of the new Dáil Clann na Talmhan decided that it, too, would sign on. McBride remained outside the agreement, however: he would support the new government but would not participate in it.[67]

When the Dáil met on 2 June, the atmosphere was very different from the excitement of 1948 and 1951. There was no uncertainty: de Valera was quick to accept that the electorate had sent him into opposition, though not for long, he said, and it would inevitably come looking for his return. Costello was elected by seventy-nine votes to sixty-six, and his clear-cut victory ensured a good-humoured handover of power, something that had been notably absent for some time.

CHAPTER EIGHTEEN

BACK IN GOVERNMENT

Quod ab initio nihil fit non firmatur tractu temporis.[1]
Bishop Browne to Costello, July 1955

OSTELLO'S CABINET WAS a blend of experience and new blood. Norton was Tanaiste once again, though this time with responsibility for Industry and Commerce. Mulcahy, Everett, Blowick, MacEoin and Keyes of the old cabinet all returned; McGilligan turned down Finance, but remained at the cabinet table as Attorney General. Liam Cosgrave and Brendan Corish, who had been parliamentary secretaries from 1948 to 1951, were promoted to External Affairs and Social Welfare respectively. The three newcomers were Gerard Sweetman in Finance, TF O'Higgins in Health and PA O'Donnell in Local Government. In his autobiography, O'Higgins captures the almost casual way in which the government was put together. Up until the morning the government met he had no indication he was to be a member. 'On that morning I attended the courts as usual ... as I was leaving the Library I met Mr Costello. He was on his way from a court appearance ... He stopped me and said, "Tom, I want you to join the government ... I want you to take health out of politics."'[2]

And that was that. O'Higgins was an important appointment; open-minded with a good grasp of economics and liberal instincts. He was to be a key modernising influence in Fine Gael over the coming years. Sweetman, the new Minister for Finance, was a forceful personality, charming or ruthless as the occasion demanded but always vigorous in expressing his deeply-rooted conservative beliefs. His conservatism was to a great extent doctrinaire, and differed in its depth of intellectual conviction from the instinctive conservatism of so many of his colleagues. He was not a man to make easy concessions and his style of debate left little room for compromise. There was a degree of distrust between himself and the new Attorney General, McGilligan, which long predated the formation of the government.[3] Costello found him a difficult colleague, and there was little about him to assure Labour ministers, not to mention the party's backbenchers, that he was sympathetic to their concerns, as McGilligan had been when he held the Finance portfolio in the previous Inter Party government.

Dillon, as was widely expected, was reappointed to Agriculture. Whether he would have been wiser to broaden his experience does not seem to have occurred to him or to anybody else. As far as he was concerned, there was unfinished business at Agriculture, and he got what he wanted. He was joined in the department by his great friend, the scourge of Fine Gael in the 1940s, Oliver Flanagan, newly appointed Parliamentary Secretary. It was to prove a happy partnership.

Dillon quickly found, however, that being a party member rather than an Independent had several drawbacks. As an Independent he was free to come to cabinet with the policies he preferred, and this is what he had done, failing for the most part even to consult with his Independent colleagues, and thereby, as we have seen, contributing to the break-up of the government. Now, however, he was a party member, and 'I had to bring them first to the party, where every jealousy and cross-current could be manifested, and every mischief-maker and pest busied himself to make difficulties. One had to fight one's way through the party, and then go through the whole procedure again in cabinet. So I did not so much enjoy being a Fine Gael Minister.'[4]

That said, there was good reason to expect that the new government would be more cohesive than its Inter Party predecessor. With only three parties, greater experience and a comfortable majority, there was reason to be confident. The members of cabinet all knew each other and personal relations appeared to be good, while in the Fine Gael parliamentary party the emphasis at its first meeting was put firmly on the need for discipline and proper consultation with the other parties in government.[5]

MacBride had declined the invitation to continue where he had left off in External Affairs. The Clann na Poblachta national executive opposed participating in government and McBride would have run into difficulty had he accepted the offer. He said that he felt the party's small number of seats hardly entitled it to a cabinet place, but that he would give the new government 'critical support'. Had he been a free agent, the chance of being back in office would have been hard to resist.[6]

The two problems which dominated and eventually destroyed the government surfaced within weeks of its taking office. On 11 June, Sweetman told the Dáil that MacEntee 'had scraped the bottom of the barrel' and left virtually no financial reserves. It was not the first time an incoming Finance Minister set the scene by blaming his predecessors – MacEntee had made much the same claim three years earlier – but Sweetman believed what he was saying. He made this clear in an early memorandum he submitted to the government: 'Current outgoings should be met from current revenue; exchequer borrowing requirements are excessive and there is an urgent need for swingeing cuts in public expenditure ... the overall objective should be to secure a substantial easement of the tax burden.'[7] This message was to remain at the core of Sweetman's subsequent policy and be a source of major strain in government.

The second of the government's problems surfaced two days later on 13 June, when a brazen raid on Armagh Barracks by fifteen IRA men netted 300 rifles and resulted in the B Specials and army being put on the alert. It was the first evidence of a revival in IRA activity and an ominous sign of things to come.[8]

The government was conscious that Fianna Fáil's electoral defeat had been due primarily to its inability to control the rising cost of living, and had promised to make this question a priority. One of its first decisions, therefore, was to reduce the price of butter by sixpence a pound, the cost to be met by a state subsidy which would add £2m annually to Sweetman's already worrying deficit. In addition, a number of public service pay increases, refused by the Fianna Fáil administration, were sanctioned at a cost of an additional £1m.[9] Whatever about the long-term consequences, peace, at least of a temporary nature, had been bought and gave the government some room to manoeuvre.

Dillon served with Costello, Norton and Sweetman on the key financial Estimates Committee, and by the end of 1954 he had been given leave by the cabinet to introduce seven different pieces of legislation, none of them major but all of a reforming nature, dealing with such issues as destructive pests and insects, the control of animal remedies, the worrying of livestock. Seven more Bills followed in 1955 and four in 1956, making him in legislative terms one of the busier ministers of the period.[10] He continued to play a full part in all cabinet discussions, and Costello, Cosgrave, O'Higgins and a new minister, Lindsay, commented positively on his contributions. Lindsay recalled Dillon's insistence on the need to examine all aspects of any major proposal before the cabinet, and if he were not happy he sounded what he called his 'three-bell warning'. When he did, Lindsay said, 'we all listened with respect and in the majority of cases accepted his judgement'.[11]

Dillon's second term was more focused than the earlier period. In his judgement, the land reclamation scheme was now a reality, the British market had been secured and a farm modernisation scheme was in place. He saw his mission as completing some unfinished business, and he had two priorities: to establish an agricultural institute and to put in place his 'parish plan', an idea about which he felt passionately and which had been one of the key planks in Fine Gael's electoral programme.

On the face of it, the need for an agricultural institute seemed quite straightforward in a country which gave such importance to farming, but Dillon was to find, as did de Valera subsequently, that the concept offended a wide variety of vested interests, not all of them agricultural, and at one stage raised the possibility of a re-run of the Mother and Child controversy, with a full confrontation between the government and the Catholic bishops.

Meanwhile, at a personal level this was one of the happiest periods in Dillon's life. He had a job which he loved and was doing work he regarded as worthwhile, a fact acknowledged by friends and opponents. Family life rotated as ever between Ballaghaderreen and Dublin – the rented house in St Mary's Rd and later the basement flat in Elgin Rd, where the broadcaster Gay Byrne and his wife Kathleen were later to be friendly neighbours. His son, John Blake, was now attending St Gerard's School in Bray, and the warmth between father and son was strong and secure. And whatever the whirlwind nature of his courtship, the relationship between Maura and himself had matured as their married life continued.

THE IDEA of establishing an agricultural institute arose from conversations between Dillon and JE Carrigan in 1949. Carrigan, who had been Dean of an agricultural college in Vermont, was the senior official dealing with Marshall Aid in Dublin, where he and Dillon became close friends. He was an important influence on Dillon's thinking, especially in his passionate advocacy of education for farmers and of providing them with the most advanced research as a means of improving the quality and volume of agricultural production. Dillon was keenly conscious of the absence of any worthwhile scientific research in agricultural and veterinary matters, something he felt was essential if the industry was to develop. What research there was – and there was very little – was carried out either by the Faculty of Agriculture in University College, Dublin, or in the Dairy Science department of University College, Cork. The Department of Agriculture also had a few experimental stations of its own, though, as we have seen, their facilities were minimal. For its part, the department felt university research did not respond to the real needs of agriculture, while the universities blamed the government for chronic underfunding. Both were right.

Dillon's early approach, whether through ministerial inexperience or impatience, was unorthodox. What he wanted was an independent, degree-giving institute for agricultural and veterinary research, and he was assured by Carrigan that such a proposal would find favour with the American Marshall Aid authorities. So keen was Dillon to ensure that the proposal would fall within American funding guidelines that he had the first draft critically evaluated by Carrigan, who suggested a number of amendments. Dillon also engaged in early discussions with the universities and with the Department of Finance. After a meeting in May 1950 with McGilligan and the President of UCD, Michael Tierney, Dillon felt he had the essentials of his scheme in place.[12]

Dillon's proposal at this point was to establish, by statute, an institute of agricultural and veterinary science, its buildings and equipment paid for out of the Counterpart Fund created by the $3m grant received the previous year under Marshall Aid. Dillon wanted the institute located on a property at Brownstown near Clondalkin in Dublin; it would be a recognised college of both the National University of Ireland and Trinity College; students would spend two years studying fundamental science at one of the universities and then transfer to the institute for two years further study. He also proposed that it should absorb the Albert College and UCC's Dairy Science department, and that Carrigan should be the institute's first president. He then asked Michael Tierney to prepare the heads of a Bill to give effect to these proposals, and the parliamentary draftsman to put these heads in the form of a draft Bill.[13]

Immediately the draft was prepared, Dillon approached Costello for approval in principle for the scheme and for permission to appoint Carrigan. A day later he had Costello's approval in principle on condition that he talk to Professor Alfred O'Rahilly, President of UCC, and Provost Alton of Trinity,[14] and on the following day, 12 May 1950, the institute was put on the cabinet's supplementary agenda and approved by them.[15] It was extraordinary that no documentation had been furnished and the cabinet had almost no prior notice of the matter, but Dillon's arguments clearly carried the day with his colleagues as they had earlier with McGilligan and Costello. This was the genesis of the agricultural institute proposal, and the circumstances were such that de Valera (who strongly supported the idea) would later say when difficulties arose: 'the origins of the proposal are shrouded in mystery'.[16]

Persuading the cabinet was, however, the easiest part of the operation. After it was agreed that the monies would come from the American grant counterpart special account,[17] the remainder of 1950 up to the change of government in 1951 was spent fleshing out the plan before putting it to the Americans. By the end of 1950 the Americans were happy with the proposals, but these inevitable delays, however, gave those whose patch was being threatened time to prepare their cases. The veterinary profession united in opposition to any proposal which would in effect merge teaching and research facilities in a new institute separate from both Trinity and UCD. University College, Cork, was alarmed at the loss of its Dairy Science faculty. There were murmurings within the National University about the apparently equal status about to be accorded Trinity, especially with regard to the proposed governing authority for the new institute.[18] As a result, progress on the institute slowed down and the drafting of the Bill was still not completed when Dillon left Agriculture in 1951. It was one of his great regrets on leaving office.

The change of government did not mean a change of policy, but it did give the Department of Finance an opportunity to kill the scheme, which it reckoned did not warrant the spending of American money on what it termed 'additional commitments'. The money was not, of course, an 'additional commitment' – it had been sanctioned by cabinet in August 1950 – but Finance continued to fight a rearguard action, even though its opposition was doomed because of de Valera's personal interest in the proposal. In fact, though Walsh was Minister for Agriculture, it was effectively de Valera who drove the project through the lifetime of the 1951-54 government.[19] Like Dillon, he appreciated its intrinsic importance, but also, as an academic *manqué*, he enjoyed the opportunity it gave him to dabble in academic politics and reshape an important area of higher education. At a meeting in late August 1951 his department made it clear that the agricultural institute was 'the most important project for Grant Counterpart monies', and there would be no turning back on the plan.[20]

De Valera's ill-health may have been the reason, but 1952 saw little progress. Perhaps because he was overshadowed by de Valera, or because he was a relatively junior minister, Walsh did not take control of the project and it languished in a kind of inter-departmental limbo. A sub-committee which de Valera had established failed to come to any decisions, much to the annoyance of Lemass who was acting Taoiseach, and in January 1953 it required a rebuke from de Valera to get the sub-committee moving. It did, however, make recommendations on most of the main issues, proposing that the new institute incorporate the Veterinary College, the Albert College and UCC's Dairy Science department, and affiliate to both the NUI and Trinity College, but there would not be a central campus as Dillon had wanted.[21]

This hard-won agreement in government was, however, matched by growing external opposition. University College, Cork, insisted on keeping its Dairy Science faculty and sent a delegation, whose members included the Roman Catholic Bishop of Cork, Dr Lucey, to see de Valera. In succeeding weeks Macra na Feirme, the vets and a range of other bodies expressed their concerns. De Valera treated these groups, and especially UCC, which tended to express itself in a particularly truculent way, with a mixture of courtesy and threat; it is clear from the minutes of their meetings that he was not going to allow a national project be scuppered by vested interest.[22] His position was strengthened by the news in early 1954 that the US House of Representatives had approved the project for funding and that the US Senate was about to do so shortly. Meanwhile, UCC had raised the stakes and began to press for its own faculty of agriculture.[23]

At this point the government changed. Back in office, Dillon found on his desk UCC's request for its own agricultural faculty. Similar requests were to follow from Galway and Trinity. They were all turned down, but out of the blue a new actor now entered the fray.

The standing committee of the Catholic hierarchy met in January 1955, at which meeting the question of the new agricultural institute was discussed. The matter clearly agitated their Lordships, because immediately afterwards they requested an urgent meeting, not with Dillon, but with the Taoiseach. Costello agreed to meet at short notice with Michael Browne of Galway and Cornelius Lucey of Cork.[24] They made their concern brutally clear: the position of the National University of Ireland, about which they felt proprietorial, 'must not be impaired', and Trinity College 'must not have a say in the teaching of agriculture in the new institute'.

Theology and turnips did apparently mix, but if the bishops felt they were in for a re-run of 1951 they were wrong. As far as Costello was concerned there was no question here of 'faith and morals'. He told the bishops their objections were belated, that 'the association of Trinity with the institute was already agreed in principle, and was now an accomplished fact'. He revealed that he had been assured by de Valera that Fianna Fáil was anxious to secure continuity of policy as regards the institute, and he reminded the bishops that when de Valera had met the Cork deputation, which included Bishop Lucey, no specific objection had been raised about Trinity College. Costello was adamant that Trinity would be associated with the agricultural institute and asked why the bishops had not brought their concerns to his predecessor, to which he got no answer. It was clear, however, that the bishops' central objection was to the equality of status accorded to Trinity, and on this they got no satisfaction whatsoever. Costello told them that, in dealing with the college, the government would 'not do anything which would give material for unfriendly persons to make charges against us of intolerance or unfairness towards the Protestant minority'. The meeting ended with little satisfaction for the bishops other than that they would be consulted as events proceeded, as would all other interested parties. It is hard to resist the interpretation that the bishops, having failed with de Valera, felt Costello would be a softer touch. On this issue, at least, they were wrong.[25]

A more serious and well-founded objection came in April from the President of UCD, Michael Tierney. Tierney was unusual in university politics in his ability to think ahead and take major decisions, but the agricultural institute proposals were now causing him difficulties, too. He cited the uncertainty surrounding the 'removal of one of the most successful of our faculties', and said the long delay in getting the institute established made long-term planning at the university virtually impossible. Tierney wanted a decision.

Dillon felt he could carry his original proposals, and in July 1955 announced that he would be presenting a Bill before Christmas along these lines.[26] On 29 August 1955 the cabinet gave approval for the draft outline of such a Bill. Dillon did not expect an easy ride, and nor should he have. Opposition within the universities was simmering and it was only a matter of time before it flared into the open. Nor was Bishop Browne of Galway giving up easily. In a peremptory and unfriendly letter to Costello at the end of July, he began, '*Quod ab initio nihil fit non firmatur tractu temporis* ... as the proposed Institute violates the University settlement of 1908 not even the agreement of yourself and Mr de Valera could heal its fundamental defect.'[27] Browne's epistle presaged another intervention from the Catholic hierarchy, which came in October. It was preceded by a public attack on the government's proposal in September by Bishop Lucey in one of his Confirmation broadsides. Lucey described the proposal as 'socialism of a gradual, hidden and underhand' kind, while Trinity College, 'if not wholly Protestant, is free-thinking or indifferent as regards religion' and therefore should not have a position of equality with the NUI colleges.[28] Lucey's offensive greatly angered Dillon. He told the Cork writer, John J. Horgan, that 'the plain truth is that the intervention of individual bishops in public controversy is becoming a serious evil, and if it continues irretrievable damage will be done'. Dillon felt that not only were the bishops arrogant in tone, invariably wrong in their facts, but 'their antics' stimulated others 'to even wider extravagances'. As to why he did not take them on publicly, Dillon was both old-fashioned and practical: 'if one exposes this kind of irresponsible criticism it involves a public denigration of bishops which, though perhaps justified, carried with it the possibility of consequences in a wider field out of all proportion to the advantage which is served by their public correction.'[29] More than anything else, he did not want to damage or delay his plans for the new institute.

Within the hierarchy, Archbishop Walshe of Tuam supported the institute, but his was a lone voice.[30] In October the secretary to the hierarchy, Bishop Fergus of Achonry, wrote to the government criticising the agricultural institute plan as 'another incursion of the state into the sphere of higher education'. Among other things, it lacked 'the essential qualities of academic freedom ... it would do grave injury to the National University of Ireland ... it would transfer Catholic students to a purely secularist institute ... it was a serious setback to the historical efforts of the Irish Catholic people to secure higher education'. Moreover, the proposal would involve the 'forcible injection into the university of extraneous and hostile elements'.

At this stage the real agenda became clear. 'We regard with serious misgivings the trend in recent years to allocate to Trinity College a state subsidy out of proportion to the number of Protestants in the state ... even though Trinity has an extensive endowment originating from the confiscation of state property.' Their lordships then widened the attack: 'it is a serious matter for the Irish Catholic taxpayer to be asked to endow an institution which is prohibited to Catholics as intrinsically dangerous and it raises issues of very serious importance to us who are charged with the defence of the Catholic faith'.[31]

Costello's response was angry and spirited, and backed by the entire government. On 4 November he sent the bishops a detailed rebuttal of the many claims they had made. He rejected totally the charge of 'another state incursion', and asked what the previous incursions had been. He dismissed the suggestion that places for Trinity on the institute's board meant 'an injection of external and hostile elements', and went on to detail the errors of fact in the bishops' letter before finally addressing the central issue: 'the proposal of representation to Trinity College, Dublin, is not a question which can be decided on the basis of the number of Protestants in the twenty-six counties;' the government had to take into account 'broad conditions of the national interest' and 'cannot close their eyes to the fact that Protestants amount to twenty-four per cent of the population of Ireland as a whole, and that the ending of partition is a primary aim of national policy'. The letter concluded by assuring the bishops that the government would try to meet the views of the hierarchy and all other interested parties 'to the utmost extent that may appear compatible with the general interest of the country as a whole'.[32]

This reply was not designed to please, nor did it. After their next meeting, Bishop Fergus wrote to Costello, saying that the bishops expressed deep regret at the tone and content of the letter, and alleging that none of the main objections had been answered. The government, however, was not particularly upset. At a meeting of the cabinet on 24 January, 'the view was taken that the letter does not call for a reply'.[33]

By now, however, and as might have been predicted, the level of opposition to change had intensified within the universities. Nor were the farming organisations much better. Most of them were showing signs of having been 'got at' by the various institutions, but most notably by those defending UCC's position. The various pressure groups – Macra na Feirme and the National Farmers Association – wanted, in effect, the best of all worlds. They were not opposed to the institute but they wanted no diminution in existing services; UCD and UCC should remain unchanged and there should be new agricultural faculties in Cork, Galway and Trinity. A variety of local lobbyists, especially in Cork and Galway, joined in, adding to the confusion. The danger now was that the project would collapse under the weight of the incoherent demands being piled on it.[34]

At this stage Dillon was thinking in terms of a separate agricultural university with its own charter. The longer the debate went on, however, the more Dillon recognised the intractable nature of the opposition, and in October 1955 he confided to Canon Hayes of Muintir na Tíre that he was looking at a compromise where the universities would remain the degree-awarding bodies, while the institute would concentrate on research.[35] By July 1956 he had made up his mind that his original proposals would be unlikely to succeed, and if he wanted his institute he had no option but to settle. At an off-the-record discussion with the National Farmers Association that month, he outlined the difficulties he faced, 'especially the wasteful, jealous competition between universities'. Instead, he proposed a research institute which would be independent of the universities, with its own staff and authority to carry out or co-ordinate agricultural research. He found the NFA broadly in agreement with this proposal, and though it fell very far short of his own ideal, it represented what was politically attainable. This was the outline he broadly followed, and on 30 November 1956 the Agricultural Institute Bill was finally ready for the Dáil.[36]

It was not left to Dillon, however to implement it. That fell to his Fianna Fáil successors, Sean Moylan and Paddy Smith, but the Act which finally set up the institute differed little from Dillon's proposals. The main change was the provision of a part-time chairman and full-time director. Moylan, who knew that Dillon had been obliged to drop the teaching element in his original proposals, sought briefly to restore it, but he, too, failed, or felt the battle was too costly, and reluctantly accepted the situation.[37] The agricultural institute finally came into being in 1958.

THE PARISH PLAN was Dillon's second great project. It was an issue about which he felt passionately, and was a major plank in Fine Gael's 1954 election programme, but it never saw anything like its full realisation, and was in fact eventually abandoned by Fianna Fáil after the party returned to office in 1957.

The plan's fundamental aim was to provide farmers with information and expertise through a series of parish agents, who would all be agricultural science graduates. Under Dillon's proposal, there would be an agent for each group of three parishes (300 agents in the country in all) and, as Dillon told a class of agricultural science graduates in 1955, 'the Parish Plan is based on the parish and works with the people of the parish. It is completely educational in character and is based on the voluntary co-operative efforts of the farmers of the parish. It is provided only when the people of the parish ask for it and express the readiness to make a very material contribution to the operation of the plan in their parish.' The 'material contribution' was not intended to be financial – that would be borne by the state – but a readiness to co-operate in agricultural development.

Dillon felt strongly that Irish agriculture was backward because of the low level of scientific and marketing expertise available to farmers, and because of the inability of communities to work together. He argued that the county committees of agriculture, whose remit included agricultural education, were inadequate when it came to educating farmers in the latest developments and had little success in encouraging them to work together.[38] Dillon's thinking was influenced by two men for whom he had very high regard. Canon John Hayes, the founder and leader of Muintir na Tíre, had long advocated the idea of a plan for rural development based on the parish, which he saw as the core unit of Irish society. The other influential figure was Carrigan, who argued the virtues of the American Land Agent schemes and whose thinking coincided with Dillon's own preference for local rather than central involvement in community development.

When he first took office in 1948, Dillon had lost little time in bringing the matter to cabinet and was given permission to proceed with his plans on a pilot basis in three selected parishes. At a meeting of all Inter Party TDs and Senators in January 1949 Costello endorsed the scheme, which, he said, would be undertaken in conjunction with Muintir na Tíre and would be extended nationwide if it were successful.[39] Later the cabinet took the unusual step of allowing Dillon recruit to his department Dr Harry Spain, one of the founders of Macra na Feirme, to implement the proposals. Spain became closely identified with the Parish Plan, and he toured the country with missionary zeal, urging communities to take part in it.[40]

The three pilot schemes were soon established: in Bansha, Co. Tipperary, (Canon Hayes own parish), in Tydavnet (in Dillon's constituency) and in Co. Limerick. However, the plan soon ran into major obstacles, the first and most formidable coming from the Department of Finance, which led to the only serious row Dillon ever had with McGilligan. Dillon's proposal was ambitious, but Finance's reply had traces of arrogance and overkill which went so far as to effectively assume responsibility for formulating agricultural policy.

McGilligan was concerned that Dillon's proposals would weaken the county committees of agriculture's capacity for local leadership; they were 'a blow to the system of representative local government and a notable step further to the direction of a highly centralised state'. Given the extent to which local authorities were spancelled and starved of funds by the Department of Finance, this argument was tendentious at best; undeterred,

McGilligan went on to tell Dillon how he could achieve equally good results at a fraction of the cost – through, for example, 'well-written articles placed free of charge in provincial newspapers', the provision of local courses, expert lectures and summer schools.

The real bite came when McGilligan lectured Dillon on the reasons for the 'backwardness of Irish farmers – and your proposal amounts to an admission that after half a century of effort by the Department of Agriculture they still are very backward indeed'. After this swipe at Dillon's officials, McGilligan gave his analysis of the reasons for agriculture's 'backwardness':

> the state policy of liquidating large holdings – the only holdings which offer an inducement to farmers to get their sons highly trained in agriculture for any purpose but that of becoming instructors and inspectors – and the multiplicity of state spoonfeeding schemes. The former has gone far towards depriving farmers of leadership in the technical development of their industry ... what the farmers need is practical evidence that progressive methods pay. That is what no government official can give them. As to spoonfeeding, it has largely destroyed the self-reliance and initiative which in no industry is more necessary than in farming.[41]

Dillon was incandescent with rage. The reply confirmed his already strong aversion to the negativism of the Department of Finance, and in this case it was the officials rather than McGilligan who took the brunt of his anger. The episode, in fact, prompted Dillon to write a memo to all government members on the negativity which he claimed characterised the thinking of these officials.[42]

Dillon won that particular battle, and on 4 November 1949 he got sanction from Finance for the establishment of three parish schemes in each of four counties. The rider, however, was that if the scheme was not seen to help improve productivity it would not be extended. Under Spain's leadership sufficient progress was made for Dillon to get sanction for twenty-seven further appointments to be made in 1950. The positions were duly advertised and the candidates chosen, whereupon Dillon ran into further problems when the Agricultural Science Association advised the graduates selected not to accept the positions until the terms of their employment were significantly improved. Given that the terms had been clearly stated in the advertisement, Dillon was furious, and accused the Agricultural Science Association of effectively sabotaging the whole scheme. The matter had not been resolved when the government left office in 1951, leaving Dillon with little enough to show for his efforts.[43] When the new Fianna Fáil government took over it dropped the scheme, in effect, while blaming the lack of progress on the shortage of properly qualified graduates.

Back in office in 1954, Dillon's enthusiasm for the Parish Plan was unabated, and he set to work to achieve what had earlier eluded him. By now, however, a considerable body of opposition had built up. The hostility of the county committees of agriculture was predictable, especially those controlled by Fianna Fáil, which viewed the scheme as a direct encroachment on their territory. Dillon had a poor view of these committees; the vast majority 'were utterly hopeless', he thought. As a result 'agricultural advisers did little or nothing. They simply circulated around about half a dozen farmers whom they knew and filled up their diaries at the end of the week.'[44]

Dillon announced at the Fine Gael Árd Fheis in February 1955 that the Parish Plan would be launched within a month, though he was well aware of the extent of opposition against it.[45] Macra na Feirme was set against the fact that parish agents would be appointed by the civil service commission: Macra President PI Meagher told Spain that 'the Parish Plan was state controlled and they would oppose it'.[46] This line was also taken by Bishop Lucey, who used the pulpit to attack the project: 'it would be far better for a parish to pay its own instructors than to take one who would dance to the departmental tune'.[47] This was all very well, except that there was no evidence that parishes had either the will or the ability to do as much. Dillon was thoroughly critical of Lucey's role in the affair. He alleges in his *Memoir* that Lucey, who was President of Muintir na Tíre, told Canon Hayes that unless the organisation disassociated itself from the Parish Plan he would resign as president, because in providing agricultural instruction directly from the Department of Agriculture when the county committees were available for this purpose, the plan violated the doctrine of the 'hierarchy of authority'. Dillon wrote: 'I urged Canon Hayes to go and see the Archbishop of Cashel and get him to tell Bishop Lucey to take a running jump for himself, but the Canon said "That's all very well for you to say, Mr Dillon, but I am only an old country parish priest and I cannot take on the Bishop of Cork." So Muintir na Tíre withdrew from co-operation. It was plain to me that the Bishop's theological scruples had been to some degree provoked by representations to him from various county committee members, but it would have served little purpose to say so.'[48]

Dillon was forced to recognise the realities. His *Memoir* continues:

The farming communities were widely split on the issue. Muintir na Tíre's initial enthusiasm had been tempered by Lucey's opposition. Macra na Feirme was also opposed, and other farming organisations, including the National Farmers Association, joined in the opposition to the scheme, to the great dismay of the saintly Canon Hayes, who despaired at so much opposition, much of which he found to be 'dishonest'.[49]

From this point on the project began to run out of steam. In spite of Spain's enthusiasm and Dillon's unflagging support, progress was slow. In 1956 there were forty-three agents in place, a long way short of Dillon's target of 300, even if it did mean 129 parishes were involved.[50] Had Dillon remained in office, some of this opposition might have been broken down, but it was always going to be difficult to make headway in the face of so many self-appointed experts such as Lucey, the entrenched opposition of vested interests such as the county committees of agriculture, the political hostility of Fianna Fáil and the chronic inability of Irish farming organisations to co-operate – not to mention the quasi-theological fears of 'state interference' in rural development. In the event, the new Fianna Fáil government quickly abandoned the scheme.

In later years Dillon took some modest comfort from an unlikely source. Charlie Haughey – in Dillon's opinion 'an extremely good Minister for Agriculture' – set up a system 'which was in fact a renewal of the Parish Plan'. Dillon recalled asking Haughey: '"On what basis do you propose to establish this plan of yours?" He looked at me quite blandly and said: "On the basis of three parishes." And then he winked.'[51]

THE FIRST eighteen months of the new government's life went reasonably smoothly. Dillon fought hard for the farmers at cabinet, especially those beset by flooding, and did succeed in getting a series of low-interest loans established. In 1954, in the face of a glut of wheat in the market, he got a guaranteed price for the crop, even if it was lower than what the farmers wanted. He hoped that cheaper wheat would mean cheaper bread, and survived a Fianna Fáil attempt to reverse his policy with a comfortable Dáil majority in December 1954.[52]

The year ended on a positive, if uneasy note. In its end-of-year review *The Irish Times* concluded that 'economically the new government has been successful ... prices have been kept stable, apart from the problem of tea, unemployment has declined ... the first loan was an outstanding success, trade has been good and the economic indices augur well.' There was, however, one significant caveat: 'thoughtful minds are uneasy at some financial omens'.[53]

And indeed they should have been. The following year prices began to spiral: meat went up seven pence a pound in January due to the huge increase in cattle exports, bacon was up two pence a pound in February, tea up two shillings a pound in October, while in the same month stout and tobacco also rose. For a government elected to control prices the omens were not good, even if the budget on 4 May provided some marginal relief for pensioners and taxpayers.[54]

There were ominous portents, too, from Northern Ireland, and the widening of a rift on policy which would ultimately lead to the fall of the government. In 1954, Clann na Poblachta supported a motion in the name of Jack McQuillan to introduce legislation to allow elected representatives in Northern Ireland take their seats in Dáil Eireann. Costello laid out the government's opposition to the proposal in a speech which strongly condemned the use of force. The debate concluded in a highly unusual way. Firmly directed by de Valera, Fianna Fáil supported the government line, while four Labour TDs, including the Tanaiste, William Norton, voted against the government. The government won easily by 100 votes to twenty-one.[55]

Northern Ireland returned as an issue in 1955 after the B Specials killed an innocent man at Keady in March, and the abstentionist Sinn Féin Westminster MP and convicted IRA man Tom Mitchell was elected, seated and unseated in a series of legal battles, and eventually re-elected in mid-Ulster. There was an IRA raid in London in August and on the RUC barracks in Roslea in November. Faced with this, the government's tough anti-IRA stance seemed to carry the support of the opposition.[56]

Apart from these difficulties, the year ran relatively smoothly. Fianna Fáil won the only by-election of the year, held to fill the Limerick West seat vacated on the death of the Fine Gael TD, DJ Madden, but the votes were virtually identical to the general election, and the Fine Gael vote showed no sign of erosion.[57] 1956 was very different. In international terms, it was the year of Suez and the invasion of Hungary. At home, it was the year of scarce money, rising unemployment, greatly increased IRA activity, sustained by-election losses and swingeing budget impositions.

Little of this unease surfaced in the early part of the year. The Clann na Poblachta candidate won her late father's seat in North Kerry with full Inter Party backing in March, and in May the Independent candidate, Paddy Byrne, won his father Alfie Byrne's seat in Dublin North-East, beating off Charles Haughey by 4,000 votes.[58] That same day, however, the first real by-election warning surfaced for the government when the seat held by William Davin for Labour in Laois–Offaly since the foundation of the state was lost in a straight fight between Labour and Fianna Fáil. The Inter Party vote was down by 8,000; a majority of 7,000 was turned into a deficit, and the explanation of 'reluctance on the part of Fine Gael farmers to vote Labour' was seen by most political commentators as being only part of the explanation for what was a severe government reverse.[59]

The economy did little to boost the government's fortunes. A marked deterioration in the balance of payments resulted in a deficit of £35m in 1955, while the net external assets of the banks fell by almost the same amount in the same period. In March 1956, Minister for Finance Gerard

Sweetman felt the crisis to be such that special import levies on sixty-eight 'non-essential' goods were imposed. The budget two months later brought further heavy increases on petrol and cigarettes, and in July there were yet further increases in import levies and a £5 million cut in government spending.[60] Unease at the government's performance surfaced at the Labour Party conference in April and initiated a long and gloomy debate on the inevitability of national collapse,[61] a foreboding fuelled by the results of the census of population published in June, which showed the population of the country to be the lowest ever recorded.[62]

The appointment of TK Whitaker as Secretary of the Department of Finance, and Sweetman's stated determination to modernise the department, made little counter-impact.[63] By July, one of Clann na Talmhan's Deputies, Patrick Finucane of Kerry, repeated the pattern of 1951 by making his support for the government conditional on concessions being made on some local issues.[64] In early August Fine Gael got its biggest electoral rebuff yet, when Fianna Fáil held its seat in Cork with no great increase in its vote, but with Fine Gael down 9,000 votes on the general election figure.[65] The pattern showed electoral support draining away from the government, though as yet not moving to Fianna Fáil. The government still had a secure majority, but a newly aggressive opposition was exploiting the unease so palpable among government supporters, and this unease was further increased by the death of veteran Fine Gael TD, PS Doyle, whose seat was highly vulnerable, and exacerbated further by a ten per cent rise in electricity prices.[66]

The government was shaken, and then galvanised into action in late September 1956 when James Larkin TD attacked the government's economic measures at a Labour Party meeting. His central point was simple: government policy was obsessed with cuts and economies instead of taking positive measure, especially greater capital investment, to resolve the problems. Larkin was taken seriously, and his views clearly reflected trade union dissatisfaction with government policy. *The Irish Times* political correspondent noted that the criticism made it more difficult for the government to solve its many problems in accordance with its present policy of 'disinflation, restriction and economy', and pointed to impending difficulties in cabinet over Dillon's determination to increase the price of milk paid to farmers and his resistance to duties on the importation of agricultural implements.[67]

Larkin's intervention sparked off a frenetic bout of activity. Labour called for capital investment projects and other means of expanding employment. Sean McBride demanded a ten-year national plan, while O'Higgins won Costello's support in cabinet for a change in policy to face the current crisis. A recovery plan was prepared by O'Higgins, not Sweetman, who was reluctant to depart from the guidelines he had laid down, but who was by now in a minority at the cabinet table.[68] Dillon enthusiastically backed this new development and his own input was significant.

The government also instructed O'Higgins to consult with MacBride and his two parliamentary colleagues to ensure that they were fully behind the new proposals.[69] The plan was ready within a month and O'Higgins had it endorsed by MacBride before it was presented by Costello at a special meeting of Inter Party Deputies and Senators (including Clann na Poblachta TDs) on 4 October. Costello was enthusiastically received; his presentation was described as 'dynamic'. Larkin welcomed the thrust of the proposals, as did McBride, who proposed a motion of confidence in Costello and in the 'new policy for production'. Costello was accorded a standing ovation.[70]

The government's new strategy was based on a number of key principles. It gave precedence to investment in agriculture above all, though it sought also to encourage private savings and investment and provided for a range of incentives to increase exports. It offered grants of £50,000 for new factory buildings, established an Industrial Advisory Council and a Capital Investment Committee of experts (drawn from outside the civil service) to advise on public investment, set up an agricultural investment council and promised the immediate establishment of the agricultural institute. The plan also provided for the establishment of a Committee on Income Tax and for the granting of independence to Radio Éireann. Agriculture featured large in the programme for recovery. Greater investment in agricultural education, a £1m campaign against bovine TB, short-term credit facilities for small and medium farmers, government guarantees of stable prices for beef, wheat, milk, barley and grade A pigs were just some of the major proposals.[71]

The plan met with a particularly negative response from de Valera, but otherwise won widespread and genuine praise. *The Irish Times* thought it was 'magnificent' – 'Not only was it practical, it must be put into practice.'[72] Sweetman, his early reservations set aside, now tried to do just that, and on 22 October sent Whitaker a list of matters which needed implementation. With Whitaker he was pushing an open door.[73]

In other circumstances the plan might have succeeded, but its timing could hardly have been less propitious. Within weeks of its publication the Soviet invasion of Hungary and the Suez crisis had erupted, creating the most unstable international situation since the late 1930s, while at home the IRA stepped up its campaign in Northern Ireland. The balance of the Dáil also shifted, when in mid-November Fianna Fáil won two further by-elections, holding its seat in Carlow–Kilkenny and taking a Fine Gael seat in Dublin South-West.[74] Clann na Poblachta now held the balance of power, though given that McBride had lately endorsed the National Plan there appeared to be no immediate threat to the government, which enjoyed a comfortable majority with his support. This perception was strengthened when McBride indicated that he meant to further his policies for long-term planning, credit creation and forestry.[75]

Events, however, were moving rapidly, and not in the government's favour. Suez led to petrol rationing and price increases. IRA raids were now a weekly occurrence and the government had to threaten the severest measures yet against that organisation. On New Year's Day 1957 an *Irish Times* editorial summed up the year: '1956 is gone and few of us lament its going ... a curiously discomfiting year, during which money has become scarcer, while unemployment, poverty and emigration have increased.'

Unfortunately for the government, 1957 did not start off any better. On 1 January, Sean South and Feargal O'Hanlon died in the Brookborough raid. As the month went on, IRA men were arrested and sentenced both north and south of the border while raids and bombings continued, and the Dublin Regional Council of the Labour Party (which was always to the left of the party) urged Labour to quit government unless immediate measures were taken to relieve unemployment.[76] The real bombshell came on 28 January, when McBride tabled a Dáil motion of no confidence in the government.

MacBride's volte-face was hard to explain. 'When he was with you, he was forceful and charming,' O'Higgins later wrote, 'but when the sun went in, he was a different man.'[77] The sun had indeed set for MacBride, at least as far as domestic politics were concerned. He himself knew that de Valera would be far more harsh with the IRA than Costello, that MacEntee was even less expansionist than Sweetman, and that he was handing the political advantage to a Fianna Fáil party he had come to detest. The reality, however, was that his influence in Clann na Poblachta had seriously diminished and, against his advice and that of the other TDs, the national executive instructed them to put down the motion of no confidence.[78] MacBride could have fought it, and, given his recent support for the economic programme would have been justified in doing so. He chose otherwise, and probably deserved the verdict of *The Irish Times* editorial writer that 'the curious and obviously studied opportunism of MacBride coincides just too nicely with the operations of the illegal organisation against the Six Counties; it fits in just too comfortably with the wave of resentment which seemed to be overcoming the decent people of the Twenty-Six counties.'[79]

The Dáil was not due to reassemble until 13 February. With the recent death of Tom Derrig the voting position in the Dáil was tied at seventy-two each.[80] The casting vote of the Ceann Comhairle would sustain the government, though as against that there was doubt about the intentions of some government supporters. Dillon's view was that it was all to fight for. With two weeks in hand before the resumption, there was still time to address the government's difficulties, and with an economic strategy in place it might just survive. Dillon, who was anxious above all to implement the agricultural institute legislation, and O'Higgins, whose Bill establishing the Voluntary Health Insurance Board was to be the last Act of this parliament, felt the fight was worth making, but Costello, anxious to avoid a defeat he thought inevitable, felt otherwise and thought it better to take the fight to the country before being forced out of office.[81]

Dillon believed Costello's decision was a misjudgement. He thought the economic plan provided a sound basis for a recovery and in agriculture in particular the revenue prospects were good. He felt in the end that 'Jack Costello had become weary of the business of governing. The death of his wife had been a sad blow to him, and it seemed to me that his heart was no longer in the business after that.' According to Dillon, Costello had made up his mind to go to the country if any of the government's supporters brought a motion of no confidence. Dillon believed that if MacBride had known Costello's mind he would have withdrawn his motion,[82] but this was not to be, and on 4 February the government announced that the Dáil would be dissolved on the 12th and an election held on 5 March. It would be, said *The Irish Times*, an election 'nobody really wanted'.[83]

History's verdict on Costello's second administration is harsh. It lacked the sparkle and enthusiastic unpredictability of his first government, its life dominated by economic crisis, international uncertainty and IRA violence. Sweetman's economic line set a forbidding tone, much as MacEntee's had done for Fianna Fáil a few years earlier, while the government's recovery programme came too late to retrieve the ill-effects of his cutbacks. The government's failure to stand and fight its corner, rather than rushing precipitately to the country, created an ineradicable impression of a government fleeing in face of problems with which it could not cope. Dillon's instinct to stay and fight was probably the right one. By going against his advice, Fine Gael was about to suffer a major and to some extent self-inflicted wound.

The second Inter Party government ended not because of anything done by Fianna Fáil, but because of external economic and political factors and the volte-face of Clann na Poblachta, factors outside of its control. But at a deeper level it ended because some of its parts had suffered an erosion of will – Costello in his haste to take the issue directly to the people, and the Labour Party, or sections of it, in its loss of faith in the very concept of coalition. The record of Costello's second government was no better and no worse than that of the de Valera governments which preceded or followed it, but the way in which it came to an end had about it an aura of failure, which was exploited to the full by its opponents and certain to linger in the public memory. It was not a confident performance, nor could it be in the climate of economic and political gloom which prevailed. The experience was to damage all the parties involved and to lead to the soul-searching in Labour which resulted in that party's abjuring of coalition for most of the next two decades. From Fine Gael's perspective, and from Dillon's especially, though he was not to know it at the time, that was possibly the most significant political consequence of all.

CHAPTER NINETEEN

IN WAITING

Although Dillon pictures himself as a champion of rural life, he is in
fact more of a country squire – urbane, witty and a good companion.
US Embassy, Dublin, to State Department, October 1959

D E VALERA'S VICTORY IN 1957 was his most emphatic in thirty
years, and he achieved it almost without trying. The government
was caught in an economic maelstrom and had lost public confidence in its ability to handle it; all Fianna Fáil had to do was present itself
to the electorate. It gained thirteen seats to bring its total to seventy-eight,
an overall majority of nine and in reality a majority of thirteen when the
abstentionist Sinn Féin seats were taken into account. Fine Gael lost ten
seats, Labour seven, Clann na Poblachta was reduced to one and MacBride,
regarded by the government as the election's perfidious architect, lost his
seat, effectively ending his domestic political career. Sinn Féin won four
seats and there were nine Independents, including Noel Browne, who having been denied a Fianna Fáil nomination by MacEntee in Dublin
South-East subsequently pushed him into third place in that constituency,
while in Dublin South Central the mood of disaffection was expressed in
the election of an unemployed non-party candidate, John Murphy. Dillon
was comfortably re-elected in Monaghan, again heading the poll.

On the surface very little changed in Irish politics between 1957 and
1959. Fianna Fáil had an impregnable majority and de Valera continued as
Taoiseach, giving no hint that a change of direction might be necessary or
that he himself might think of retiring; indeed, he reacted irritably if the
suggestion were even made. He did introduce some new blood into his
cabinet – Neil Blaney, Kevin Boland, Micheál Ó Móráin – but for the most
part the emphasis was on continuity, not change.

Fine Gael was shocked by the result of the election. With forty seats and
a number of talented young TDs, the party was in fundamentally better
shape than it had been in the 1940s, but the mood was gloomy and there
was little thought of renewal. Apart from Mulcahy, Dillon and Cosgrave,
very few of the leading members were full-time politicians, and the burden
of parliamentary work tended to fall inordinately on their shoulders. In

addition, the party leadership continued on its two-headed way, with Costello as leader of the party in the Dáil and Mulcahy as party leader. Some of the bad feeling generated during the last government also carried over. Sweetman was resentful of his treatment by Costello and wary of the influence of McGilligan.[1] He opposed a future alliance with the Labour Party, where Norton still continued as leader.

Dillon decided to carry on as Fine Gael spokesman on agriculture, and neither he nor anyone else contemplated his moving to another portfolio. To most people it was his natural place. In his earlier years in politics he had spoken on all major issues, and in the 1940s he had of course taken his singular stance on neutrality, but from 1948 on he had been identified almost exclusively with agriculture, and had become the great defender and advocate of the rural way of life. At a time when the economy was shifting from agriculture to industry and the country from rural to urban, it might have been wiser for Dillon, with his agricultural reputation established beyond question, to have broadened his appeal by becoming spokesman for industry and commerce, finance or foreign affairs. But he was happy in agriculture and that is where he stayed, thus confirming the popular impression that this was where his priorities lay, as indeed they did.

There was little evidence of change in the atmosphere of the Dáil itself. The debate on the nomination of the Taoiseach on 20 March 1957, and subsequent debates on the formation of the government, illustrated the generally mean air of so much of the Dáil's business. Normal courtesies were still the exception rather than the rule, and it was rare even to see a new minister being congratulated by the opposition on his appointment. Motives were always questioned, good faith doubted and memories of the Civil War – or, more accurately, its poisonous aftermath – were still dominant.

Yet important changes were taking place, some in the Dáil itself, and there was a fundamental shift in economic policy and in Ireland's attitude to the European Economic Community – the Common Market. The Dáil witnessed the foundation of the National Progressive Democrats by Noel Browne and Jack McQuillan in May 1958, and though it was never more than a two-man band, for long periods during 1958 and 1959 it supplied the most effective opposition to the government, scoring direct hits with a series of embarrassing, well-researched questions. Browne and McQuillan's fresh energy showed up the lacklustre, part-time and essentially routine approach of the bigger opposition parties.

In economic terms, the event which is seen as the harbinger, if not necessarily the cause of change, was the publication in November 1958 of two documents, *Economic Development* and the *First Programme for Economic Expansion*. There was nothing revolutionary in the notion of the government of the day presenting a detailed economic strategy, but what was new was the appearance of the new programmes as a civil service initiative rather than a party or government plan. More significant still was the documents' implicit rejection of much of Fianna Fáil's basic economic strategy – which, as Dillon was quick to point out, was one of the reasons for the way the new plans were presented.[2]

The new approach proposed a major shift from protection to free trade and an active policy of encouraging foreign investment. It gave a central role to agriculture, with the emphasis on export-oriented production, but made it clear that industrial development was no longer of secondary importance. These publications, forever associated with TK Whitaker, sparked off a debate on economic development which cut across traditional party lines, and whatever their defects, and they have been variously criticised for being too conservative and for the quality of their methodology, they marked an important turning point, best summarised by Lee as 'a radical initiative whose sheer quality comes through more luminously with the passage of time'.[3]

Even before the publication of these economic reviews, Dillon had been uncomfortable with what he saw as an official tendency to give primacy to industrial over agricultural development. He did not see large-scale industrial development in Ireland as a real possibility – a view which was not indefensible at the time. It was, he argued in May 1957, essentially a question of natural resources:

I think we have to face the fact that we will never be rich in this country ... we are primarily an agricultural economy whose natural resources consist of 12 million acres of arable land and the people who live on it. That will never provide in terms of money and goods the same standard of living as is available in the great industrial economies.[4]

Without a prosperous agricultural sector, he felt industry could not flourish. The future depended upon producing agricultural produce for export.

Dillon had long recognised that Lemass was trying to escape the straitjacket of Fianna Fáil's traditional policies, and in this Dillon encouraged him. He urged Lemass to seek out the major US corporations and invite them to establish manufacturing bases here. Lemass could do little in this direction without repealing the Control of Manufactures Acts, which prohibited foreign investors from having majority control in enterprises based in Ireland, but the Act was at the very heart of Fianna Fáil's protectionist strategy and any open attack on it, even from Lemass, meant serious trouble. Dillon argued that protected industries should be helped to become competitive, but their existence should not be the dominant concern. 'I often grow weary of the codology that goes on in this House. Either Fianna Fáil wants foreign capital or it does not want foreign capital. If it wants it, it should open its doors to it.'[5] Lemass did not rule out foreign investment, but held that 'Irish industrial progress would come more speedily from the extension of the activities of existing concerns rather than the establishment of new concerns by new companies.'[6] On this issue at least, Dillon's was the better judgement.

Dillon welcomed the *First Programme for Economic Expansion*, and argued that it had its genesis in the Inter Party government's plans in 1956. He bade good riddance to the economic policies – self-sufficiency and protectionism – which in his view had done such sustained harm over the previous thirty years. In his celebrated biography of de Valera, Tim Pat Coogan notes that de Valera insisted the new programme did not represent the ditching of Fianna Fáil's economic doctrines, but was rather a long continuation from the time when 'We set out these policies in 1926 at the formation of Fianna Fáil.' It was, said Coogan, another example of 'de Valera fact'. Things were as he said them to be.[7]

As a parliamentarian, Dillon was outraged that the programme was never debated in the Dáil, and he had no doubt as to the reason why: Lemass's reluctance to face his own party with such a complete volte-face. He was also critical of the break with tradition which the attribution of authorship of the document to Whitaker represented: 'heretofore the most sacred principle of the public service was that anything appearing from government sources was the responsibility of the minister ... who had to take the blows and accept the laurels appropriate to whatever a permanent official of his department did or left undone'. This was an important convention which he thought should not have been breached, and he was sure Fianna Fáil would use it to its advantage. 'The government will use this grey book as a kind of grey umbrella under which it will shelter and claim immunity from attack,' and by so doing violate one of the cardinal principles of governmental accountability to parliament. 'Where do we go from here? There is one place we certainly cannot go and that is to the author of the grey book. His public life, like that of the swan in the fable, begins and ends with his swan song and he can make no further contribution to the ensuing discussion.'[8]

While Dillon saw much good in the new document, he was critical of the detail. He argued strongly, for example, for a much higher investment in education than was being provided, and continued to complain about the downgrading of agriculture: 'out of £220m investment over five years, less than £50m is for agriculture ... all the rest is for airplanes, railways, shipping, fuel and power, phones, industrial credit, tourism, airports ...'[9]

Dillon's thinking continued to be dominated by the centrality of agriculture in economic development, by his general scepticism about the viability of industrial growth, and by his old distrust of excessive state involvement in economic activities. In this he was not just differing from the government's – or at any rate Lemass's – thinking, he was diverging, too, from the thinking of the most influential younger figures in his own party, particularly Declan Costello, Tom O'Higgins and Michael O'Higgins. Declan Costello, for example, argued in December 1959 that since the private sector was not capable of driving economic development, the public sector would have to intervene on an ever-increasing scale. He also maintained that the public sector was not adequate for these tasks, and 'if we are to get proper economic development it must be planned on a much more extensive scale than heretofore'. He thought the banks needed to play an active rather than a 'frustrating part' in aiding economic growth, and saw a need for a social as well as an economic dimension to such development. In short, Costello urged Fine Gael to move to the left of conventional thinking.

Costello's views were delivered to a meeting of the Fine Gael Research and Information Centre, recently set up by Costello, Tom O'Higgins and Alexis FitzGerald to modernise and develop party policy, especially on social and economic issues. Dillon replied to the paper and the exchange between Costello and himself is significant; it was the first of the many policy disagreements that would characterise their relationship.[10] He treated Costello's paper as in some way an attack on the record of the Inter Party governments and for that reason felt the need to be unduly defensive, but then got to the nub of their differences:

> I feel no sympathy with his exhortation to move openly and firmly to the Left. As a lifelong Radical, I believe in attacking the forest of practical problems tree by tree, always resolved to preserve individual liberty and never to sacrifice it in order to achieve short-cuts at excessive costs. I believe we should be ready to do anything, consonant with the law of God, to surmount the problems that confront this country, but I believe that neither requires us to move to the right nor to the left, but straight ahead in the developing and elaboration of policies which have achieved so much in the six years of Inter-Party government ...[11]

It was not then, nor was it going to be, a meeting of minds.

IRELAND'S ENTRY to the Council of Europe in 1949 and to the UN in 1954 signalled the beginning of a move away from the isolation of earlier years. There was little debate on Ireland's options, and neither did the government do anything to stimulate public discussion, but for a small number of TDs participation in the Council of Europe offered a first-hand glimpse of what was happening on the continent. By 1959 the political parties were at last having to give serious attention to future decisions on European integration. Fine Gael proposed that a select Dáil committee should be set up to keep TDs informed on events in Europe, but this suggestion was flatly rejected by Lemass. His decision was in some ways surprising, since Fine Gael broadly supported his approach and might well have been useful allies against the more suspicious nationalists of his own party, but evidently the political style of the day dictated that the opposition should have no meaningful involvement, even where that involvement might be helpful to the government.

The dynamic of European integration was novel to most people in 1958-59. Dillon, who had long advocated membership of an essentially English-speaking commonwealth including the USA, had not been thinking much in terms of a major European involvement. He was sceptical of developments on the continent and slow to abandon his own proposition. For the moment, however, he was conscious that Britain's intentions would seriously affect any Irish decision. If Britain joined the new EEC, then, given Irish dependence on the British market, the country had no real alternative but to follow. He felt, however, that if we did enter into negotiations or arrangements with other Common Market countries, our relationship with our 'next-door neighbour' should remain the first priority.[12]

Though the fundamental issues were already beginning to engage politicians' thinking, the big debate on Europe was still in the future. At home, meanwhile, Fianna Fáil's majority guaranteed the government a trouble-free Dáil. Most opposition politicians gave the impression of 'marking time', a not uncommon phenomenon when a government has a rock-solid majority. There was also that sense of flatness which often descends on politicians who have lost office and who must take up anew their business or professional lives. Few of the Fine Gael politicians could afford to be full-time, with the result, as has been said, that Mulcahy, Cosgrave and Dillon shouldered a disproportionate amount of the routine work. There was some dissatisfaction, though not yet articulated, at the fact that Costello, who was a busy barrister, had to ration the amount of time he could devote to leading the parliamentary opposition.

The Browne and McQuillan partnership, by contrast, was enjoying its new-found parliamentary role. Browne had no reason to distinguish between the major parties as targets, but because Fianna Fáil was in power most of his shafts were directed in its direction. On one issue in particular, he and McQuillan succeeded in wounding de Valera in a way he had never before experienced. This was their exposure of de Valera's day-to-day relationship with the *Irish Press* while he held the office of Taoiseach and the manner in which his family had obtained ownership or control of a majority of the newspaper's shares. Their attack was carried out by means of a Private Member's motion which ensured the matter had to be the subject of a full parliamentary debate.

Dillon had long regarded de Valera's relationship with the *Irish Press* as highly improper. He described the paper as the 'Fianna Fáil *Pravda*' – 'the instrument of Fianna Fáil falsehood in this country ... the instrument of the Taoiseach who uses it for the propagation of Fianna Fáil propaganda ... their principal channel of falsehood.'[13] But Dillon, no more than any of his Fine Gael colleagues, had never drawn blood on this issue, much to his frustration. Browne, however, managed to get hold of vital information which had eluded earlier protagonists. He was given a present of one *Irish Press* share, and this gave him access to the company's records, which showed who had bought and sold *Press* shares over the years. The information he found contradicted the picture of ownership and control which de Valera presented.

The situation was bizarre, or certainly would be by the standards of the later twentieth century. De Valera had been controlling director of the *Irish Press* while he was Taoiseach of the country. The job was not, as de Valera claimed, merely nominal. The articles of association of the *Press* made it clear that the controlling director 'shall have sole and absolute control of the public and political policy of the company and of the editorial management thereof ... he may appoint at his discretion, remove or suspend all editors, sub-editors, reporters, writers, contributors of news information and all such other persons as may be employed in or connected with the editorial department and may determine their duties and fix their salaries and emoluments.' Browne said that this represented a clear and indefensible conflict of interest with de Valera's role as Taoiseach.[14]

De Valera's Dáil defence was weak and self-righteous. He claimed he had never attempted to hide the fact that he was involved in the *Irish Press* – it was well-known. However, he had no financial interest in the *Irish Press*, he took no salary, and he claimed that his duties as controlling director had not 'conflicted in any way with the full and proper exercise of my duties as Taoiseach'.[15] His position, he insisted, was no different to that of a farmer or a doctor or a teacher who also happened to be Taoiseach.[16]

The debate continued sporadically from November 1958 to mid-January 1959, when Browne produced an even more damning case against de Valera. Unravelling the financial basis of the *Irish Press*, he recalled that in 1933 the Fianna Fáil majority in the Dáil had voted, against strong opposition, to channel some of the Republican loan money previously raised in the US into the *Irish Press*; in other words, public money was voted by de Valera into a private institution in which he had a major and undeclared financial interest. Browne also showed that the American shareholders' funds no longer existed, while the de Valera family now had up to 150,000 shares; the Fianna Fáil party held just ten. Browne's summing up on 14 January was relentless. De Valera, he said, 'had used his joint positions to create a very prosperous commercial entity, a very solid nest egg for the days of his retirement'. Three of the six *Irish Press* directors were de Valera family members and, Browne claimed, that as controlling director de Valera had taken steps to see that the newspaper's shares had not been quoted on the Dublin Stock Exchange, with the result that they had been made available to the de Valera family at a grossly undervalued price. 'In refusing to allow quotations on the Dublin Stock Exchange they have deprived these poor shareholders of the dividends which Mr de Valera told them must come soon.' In effect, Browne accused de Valera of stealing the *Irish Press* from the shareholders, of 'depriving the shareholders of the right to whatever assets are payable should this company go into liquidation, and he has misled the House when he said "I have no financial interest in the *Irish Press*."'[17]

Browne had struck a raw nerve. Fianna Fáil reacted with a mixture of outrage, bluster and personal attack. MacEntee accused Browne of 'singling out the people who are leading the independent development of this country as outcasts and pariahs'. Browne had no right to raise the issue at all, he said: 'the matter is not a fit subject for Dáil debate, but rightly belongs to a meeting of shareholders'. In any event, 'the *Irish Press* is not an ordinary national newspaper, but is, along with Fianna Fáil, part of the national movement'. He went on: 'The friends of Ireland ... who supported the Republican cause entrusted their savings, many of them their life's savings, to Eamon de Valera as controlling director of the *Irish Press*, to see established here an organ which would influence public opinion and keep the nation on the right path.'[18]

The motion – 'a slimy Private Member's motion', in MacEntee's words – was defeated by seventy-one votes to forty-nine, but even so, Browne and McQuillan had inflicted more damage on de Valera than the combined efforts of the entire opposition. De Valera's biographer, Tim Pat Coogan, is convinced that it was this debate, and especially the likelihood of it being repeated as the other opposition parties got in on the act, which increased the pressure put on de Valera at senior level in Fianna Fáil to quit active politics and run for the presidency, where he would be 'above' party politics. Coogan's assertion is no more than that, but de Valera's decision to contest the presidency was announced the day after the Dáil vote, on 15 January 1959. His declaration dominated the news, relegating the *Irish Press* story to the margins. Neither was it followed up subsequently by the main opposition parties or by the newspapers, who had little appetite in those days for such stories.[19]

Shortly after announcing that he would run for the presidency, a position he was certain to win, de Valera also proposed changing the electoral system from proportional representation to a straight vote. De Valera, like every prime minister before and since, had come to view the PR system with disfavour. Among his reasons for seeking its abolition was his not unreasonable expectation that, without his presence, proportional representation would do in Ireland what it did elsewhere and produce a multiplicity of parties leading to the end of Fianna Fáil's hegemony. It was an attempt to change the rules before they became unfavourable, and the conventional wisdom dictated that a combination of the de Valera name and the proposal to change the electoral system would be unbeatable.

The best laid plans do not always work out. From the outset Fianna Fáil mishandled its case, largely because the party had no understanding of the word 'consensus'. Had Fianna Fáil sought Fine Gael agreement to a modification of PR, perhaps to the single seat single transferable vote system, such co-operation would certainly have been examined. Dillon, for example, was opposed to the changes proposed by Fianna Fáil, though not necessarily to all change. He had no doubt about the purpose of the Bill – it was consistent with Fianna Fáil policy since 1935, when every electoral reform had reduced the size of constituencies for the purpose of damaging the electoral prospects of minority groups. 'If you advise minorities with deeply held convictions that the electoral system is being so reconstructed that they will be swept aside and denied a voice in the House, what do you expect them to do?' he asked. He was open to other variants of proportional representation – he had a preference for the single seat transferable vote – and declared himself willing to sit down with Fianna Fáil to discuss these options, but clearly Fianna Fáil was not in the business of compromise, and Dillon's offer, along with a number of others, went unheeded.[20] Fianna Fáil was to learn the hard way that winning a referendum in Ireland requires a wide degree of cross-party support. The end result, in fact, was to unify the opposition, which now had a real issue on which to campaign, and to alienate many neutrals from Fianna Fáil. The government suffered an embarrassing defeat in the Seanad and ultimate defeat at the hands of the people.

FIANNA FÁIL lost the referendum on June 17, the day de Valera won the presidency. A week later Sean Lemass was elected Taoiseach and Leader of Fianna Fáil.

De Valera's departure signalled the end of a political era. It was going to be difficult to imagine politics without him, but Lemass's election was so smooth, so inevitable, that few at the time could anticipate the degree of change his leadership would eventually precipitate. There were many who were sceptical about the new leader. He was seen as a city man, an industrialist, a friend of big business; a superb organiser but not a visionary or a man who would stir people's passions. The fact that de Valera had tried to change the electoral system implied that he lacked confidence in the new Taoiseach's election-winning appeal, and there were question marks over his ability to assert his authority on a cabinet where he would be, at least to begin with, *primus inter pares* rather than the 'Chief' of old. This is not to say that Lemass was under-rated: his record of achievement was second to none, he was a devastatingly effective parliamentarian, his intellect was razor sharp, and he had the energy of a man half his age. For the moment, though, many commentators were reserving their judgement on how he would fare as Taoiseach.

Dillon's reaction to Lemass's election was not generous. Dillon may have been following his own dictum that 'in this House antagonism is not between individuals but between the policies for which they stand ... you identify the individual with the policy he seeks to sustain and for the convention of debate your attack is directed on the Deputy who advocates a certain argument ... if Parliament becomes too polite in all its deliberations, Parliament will cease to function.'[21] Dillon had strong feelings where Lemass was concerned, and his speech was negative and devoid of any personal warmth. It contrasted sharply with the conciliatory attitude of John A. Costello, who welcomed Lemass as the harbinger of a new era in Irish politics. Dillon concentrated instead on Lemass's record on the economy and the jaded complexion of his cabinet. If Lemass was offended he showed no signs of it, shrugging off the attacks of Dillon and others: 'personally I have a liking for the rough and tumble of party conflict, and indeed I do not think it does harm to the national interest'. Lemass did, however, hope that from that point on the political parties would compete in their ability to plan constructively for national progress rather than in personal disparagement. His intention, he said, was to avoid saying 'any word which could be regarded as being personally offensive to anyone'.[22]

Lemass's arrival wrought a change in parliamentary style. De Valera had been a remote and distant Taoiseach, frequently absent from the Dáil, and with little instinctive feel for the mood and vagaries of parliamentary life. Lemass was a natural 'hands on' parliamentarian and he signified this on his first working day as Taoiseach by taking the Order of Business, something de Valera had not done for many years. While Lemass thus indicated that, in addition to being Taoiseach, he would also act as Leader of the House, the humour of the House seemed also to be improving. Yet old habits died hard. *The Irish Times* political correspondent noted in July that 'there was a slight tendency among Deputies to spar with one another at Question Time ... MacEntee attempted to deliver one of his noted barbed cracks, only to be told by Oliver Flanagan, "You're supposed to be good now, under the new-look procedure."'23

Lemass began his tenure as Taoiseach vigorously, clearly determined to stamp his own personality on the government. On 14 July he met British Prime Minister Harold Macmillan at 10 Downing Street to discuss the possibility of a new trade agreement and to review developments in the Common Market. A week later he presaged the beginning of a new policy on Northern Ireland with an offer of greater economic co-operation with the North, and in October he made his celebrated address to the Oxford Union which, with its theme of 'unity by agreement', marked a dramatic shift away from traditional Fianna Fáil thinking. Already the Lemass persona was coming to the fore, bringing with it an emphasis on a practical, no-nonsense approach to all problems, the focus firmly on pragmatism rather than ideology. Phrases like 'economic development', 'modernisation' and 'European integration' were beginning to replace the traditional nationalist mantras.

There was a certain paradox in Lemass, the architect of protectionism, the apostle of economic self-sufficiency, now dismantling his own handiwork without a backward look. It was one of Lemass's great achievements that he concealed, at times even denied change, while at the same time he promoted it vigorously. Not all in his own party were happy with the new direction and their worries surfaced from time to time, enough to cause concern in private, but never sufficient to derail progress.24 Under Lemass, Fianna Fáil was assuming a leadership role at a time when Ireland was experiencing its first taste of economic prosperity. In particular, the limitations of agriculture as an engine of growth were becoming more and more evident, the notion of economic self-sufficiency was increasingly threadbare, and the clear message was that foreign investment, major structural changes and massive modernisation were all needed if Ireland was to survive and eventually prosper. Such a message had its dangers in a deeply conservative country just emerging from decades of isolation. It was Lemass's particular talent that he was passionate about the need for change but never overestimated the pace of what was possible.

Lemass's assumption of leadership was not good news for Fine Gael. The party's hybrid system still remained in place and continued to operate unsatisfactorily. Mulcahy was party leader and had lost none of his conscientious sense of duty, but he was seventy-two years of age at this stage, a 1916 veteran, with forty-five years of active political service behind him. Even at the best of times his austere, almost monastic persona had about it a quality of remoteness; he had never been a good vote-getter, and this was not likely to change. Costello continued to act as leader of the opposition and party leader in the Dáil. He was still a formidable parliamentary performer, visionary and forward-looking when he chose to be, capable of forensic brilliance at committee stage of a Dáil debate, and capacious on the major issues. But he was a part-time leader, with a busy legal practice, and his Dáil attendance was poor. His front bench functioned only sporadically, and there was no serious evidence of attention being given to policy development, recruitment of new members, or restructuring of the party organisation. The situation was causing growing concern among the more ambitious members of the parliamentary party, but while there was no open expression of dissatisfaction, the appearance of Fine Gael as a party of part-timers, of comfortable farmers and solid businessmen, of lawyers arriving in the Dáil after a day's work in the courts, stood in sharp contrast with Fianna Fáil's active leadership, even if the bulk of that party's parliamentary representation remained set in a conservative mould.

There was a restlessness within Fine Gael during 1958 and 1959, and what one US diplomat characterised as 'bickering', especially on the question of leadership.[25] The election defeat of 1957 had been demoralising, but a year later the party should have been getting itself back into shape. It was not, and Dillon was among the foremost critics of those who were not pulling their weight. He was particularly critical of the poor attenders among the TDs and Senators and urged that discipline be tightened and sanctions imposed. He was impatient with the failure of the front bench to give an explicit lead and called on Costello to outline policy in succinct terms so that party members could then put it to the wider public.[26] Dillon was on firm ground in making his criticisms. He himself was an assiduous Dáil attender and happy to accept invitations to address meetings in all parts of the country. Curiously, however, he was not so much concerned with the content of policy as with its vigorous expression, along with the relentless harrying of the government in the Dáil. To a great extent he agreed with Sweetman that 'a distinctive policy was not so important when we were so far from a general election', and he also tended to conclude that Fine Gael's problems were essentially to do with 'morale and finance.[27]

The problems were in fact deeper. In his autobiography, *A Double Life*, TF O'Higgins reflected on the endemic difficulties to do with morale, direction and personal relationships at this time. 'Personal problems ... and a general air of despondency permeated the party ... a situation prolonged by the fact that there was no clear picture of what the party's future might be. The Inter-Party idea was under attack and in decline, and the situation was exacerbated by a dogged antagonism which Gerard Sweetman now displayed to any idea of future co-operation with other parties. At times this antagonism was directed toward Jack Costello and was a continuation of their bad personal relationship in government since 1956.'[28]

However, the change in leadership in Fianna Fáil brought matters in Fine Gael to a head. Mulcahy had been contemplating his own retirement for some time, and in October 1959 he confided his intentions to some close colleagues. A meeting of the front bench was held on Saturday 17 October, at which Mulcahy announced this decision. When it became clear that he would not change his mind, Costello told the meeting that the dual leadership structure should be abandoned. Others, including Dillon, MacEoin, Mulcahy and Michael Hayes, the leader in the Senate, agreed that the party should have a single leader, but insisted that the new leader must be full-time.[29] This appears to have been the majority view, and had Costello accepted these conditions he would almost certainly have been the automatic successor to Mulcahy, but he was not prepared to accept the role full-time, and was genuinely taken aback that such a condition should now emerge. Costello was confident that if he had the full backing of the front bench he could effectively lead the party in the Dáil and in the country. Clearly, however, others in the party had discussed the matter and come to a contrary conclusion. Mulcahy, who was himself a full-time politician, was adamant on this point and had long been critical of the poor performance of some front-bench colleagues. It was this conviction rather than any personal animosity to Costello which was the deciding factor. In fact the two remained lifelong friends, and their disagreement on this matter never became personal.[30]

When the parliamentary party met at its routine meeting on the following Wednesday, Mulcahy formally announced his retirement – the first many members had heard of his decision. Mulcahy told the meeting he saw the change providing the party with a chance to make a new start, and that, now that the recent focus on the presidential elections and the question of proportional representation was past, the development of social and economic policies should be given priority.

After Mulcahy's announcement, a letter was read from Costello, who, oddly, was not present at the meeting. Costello reaffirmed what he had decided at Saturday's front-bench meeting: that he would be willing to lead the party and assume the full leadership, but he would not do so unless he could also continue his practice at the bar. He did not think that the party leader should necessarily be full-time: 'My carefully considered opinion was, and is, that it is wrong in principle in a small democracy, where average incomes are low, that a leader of a party in opposition should necessarily be a person whose economic circumstances permit him to devote his whole time to party and parliamentary work. Others may legitimately hold different views, but it is not a matter on which to make a serious issue. My own circumstances are such as not to permit withdrawal from my professional practice.'

However, he told the meeting that since most of his colleagues were clearly of the opinion that a wholetime leader was essential, after careful thought he had concluded that 'I should, as I do now, relinquish my position as leader of the opposition. The decision is final.' He hoped, he said, to continue 'in the dignified if unaccustomed position of a backbencher'.

Fine Gael did not have any set standing orders for the election of its leader. Technically, the Árd Fheis elected the party president and the parliamentary party the leader in the Dáil, but in practice the Árd Fheis merely confirmed the vote of the parliamentary party. There were no apparent rules about nominations or other procedures: the party had never had to have a contest to elect its leader before, so in effect the parliamentary party made it up as it went along. Thus, after Mulcahy's announcement and the reading of Costello's letter, and the tributes to both men, the question of what to do next arose. MacEoin wanted the matter decided there and then; Michael O'Higgins, a supporter of Costello, saw no problem with dual leadership and asked for time for reflection, while Maurice Dockrell felt that to ask one person to assume party and parliamentary leadership was 'an appalling burden to ask of one man', and he also wanted time to reflect.

Dillon, by contrast, got to the point very quickly. The party must proceed, he said, on the assumption that both Mulcahy's and Costello's decisions were irrevocable. Then he put down his marker: the party must have a leader who would devote himself full-time to the task. As far as he was concerned that narrowed the field down to two people: Cosgrave and himself. And even though he was senior and willing to serve, he felt that Cosgrave had on his side youth, a great name, and parliamentary and ministerial experience. Thus he proposed Cosgrave for the leadership.

Dillon, in his turn, was proposed by Sean MacEoin and seconded by Michael Hayes. What his uncle Nicholas would have made of this endorsement by two leading figures from old Sinn Féin hardly bears thinking of, but the fact that Dillon had the support of Mulcahy, Hayes and MacEoin made him the 'establishment' candidate, and this impression can only have been strengthened when it became clear that the party Whip, the influential Gerard Sweetman, was also supporting him.

The debate as to whether or not to finalise matters that evening continued. A majority of those present favoured an immediate decision, but at Mulcahy's request the matter was deferred until the following evening, when the party was due to meet at 10.30 pm.[31]

Fifty-four of the party's fifty-seven members were present at this meeting, while two of the three absent members had entrusted their completed ballot papers to Mulcahy. Michael O'Higgins sought at the outset to have Costello change his mind, but Mulcahy quickly headed off this line of argument and said that Costello's decision was final. He then asked for any further nominations. At this point matters were complicated somewhat when McGilligan disagreed with having any nominations before the meeting at all. 'Every name was before the meeting,' he insisted, so it was agreed that the ballot papers would contain the names of all the party's TDs.

Mulcahy was the sole scrutineer and after twenty minutes he returned with the news that Dillon was the new leader.[32] The voting figures were not announced (a tradition which Fine Gael still maintains), and the news release after the meeting indicated that Dillon's election had been unanimous; it failed even to mention the fact of Cosgrave's candidacy. It would not do, apparently, to let the public think that Fine Gael had engaged in anything as vulgar as an election contest.[33] Dillon himself had no doubt his election had been by a comfortable margin, and on enquiring from Mulcahy was told he had got sixty-six votes as against twenty-six for Costello and six for Cosgrave. These figures do not make sense, since no more than fifty-six people voted, but other sources confirmed that Dillon's margin was comfortable.[34]

What is intriguing, at least from Mulcahy's figures, is that a substantial section of the party still favoured a Costello leadership – even on his own terms. What was most significant were some of those who did not vote for Dillon. Even though McGilligan had asked Dillon to accept the leadership in 1943, he now supported Cosgrave, while those who wanted to move the party towards new economic and social policies, such as the O'Higginses and Declan Costello, did not vote for him either. To Tom O'Higgins, he was the first Fine Gael leader from outside the Sinn Féin tradition: 'for the first time what was basically a Sinn Féin party had a leader from an entirely different tradition. It was inevitable that such a change, even if its full significance was not immediately realised, would tend to alter the party's outlook.'[35]

Differences would indeed surface, and, as O'Higgins was to write later, 'the six years of James Dillon's leadership were years in which a quiet struggle took place in Fine Gael'.[36] Little of this was evident in the leadership contest, which was gentlemanly in the extreme. There were no policy statements, no obvious canvassing of votes, no campaign managers, no press 'leaks' and little outside speculation, though some journalists later claimed that Dillon's 'campaign' had been managed by Sweetman. In any event, the way in which the campaign was conducted does not suggest a Dillon hungry for power. He saw the leadership more in terms of a duty, a responsibility to be shouldered rather than the fulfilling of a long-cherished ambition. He realised there was a problem with finding a new leader: Costello was the obvious choice but was not prepared to take a full-time position; Cosgrave was seen by some colleagues as still being too young.[37] In the circumstances, Dillon felt he had no option, and there is no reason to doubt his claim in his *Memoir* that 'oddly enough, I never wanted to be Taoiseach. My interest was in being Minister for Agriculture.'[38]

Dillon had nonetheless come into his political inheritance, even if few in 1959 saw it as a particularly promising one, and more than one observer wondered whether Dillon was the man to exploit it to the full, or whether he had come to it too late.

CHAPTER TWENTY

LEADERSHIP

The lot of leader of the opposition I did not find a happy one.

Dillon, *Memoir*

ILLON, A US diplomat commented in 1959, was 'cast in an Edwardian mould'. His description summed up the perception of Dillon as a man out of his time, redolent of the values and manners of an earlier period, and concerned more with 'completing the work my father began'[1] than with finding new worlds to conquer. This impression was to persist throughout his leadership, a time which saw Dillon grappling with problems for which he had little empathy, and engaging in a process of political modernisation for which he had little appetite.

Dillon himself would probably dispute this judgement. He would argue that in politics, as in business, he had always been a moderniser, but that the central issues of politics were unchanging: individual liberty, the rule of law, the supremacy of parliament, and, as he told Declan Costello, tackling the forest of practical problems tree by tree. It was his misfortune to be cautious of change at a time of unprecedented change, to be suspicious of dogma at a time when some of the brightest and most eager minds in his own party hungered for a more ideological or schematic approach, and, most of all, to have as his principal political foe the forward-looking and vigorous Lemass, who not only captured but in some ways embodied the new mood. As a result, Dillon's time as party leader was not particularly satisfying, and he himself was to admit he enjoyed it very much less than he did his years in agriculture.

He inherited a party in a fractious mood, uncertain of its role, sluggish and lethargic in the performance of its duties. It was set to fight a long war of attrition as rival wings fought a battle to determine not just the party's future direction but its very *raison d'être*. For many of the younger members the Civil War was no longer a defining issue of party allegiance. New times needed new policies, but there was no consensus as to what these should be, or indeed whether change was necessary or desirable. The forces in Fine Gael in 1959 were such that a battle along these lines was probably inevitable. It was an inheritance for which Dillon was almost certainly unprepared.

Meanwhile, at an operational level Dillon did not have the freedom to appoint his own front bench, which at this stage was elected by the parliamentary party. He noted in his *Memoir*:

> I was saddled with a number of gentlemen whom I certainly would not have chosen ... they were no good, and it was not often possible to get them to turn up to deal with the business falling within their sphere of responsibility. Very frequently I had to go down myself and hold the fort for one or other of them, or ask Gerard Sweetman or Liam Cosgrave to do so.[2]

There was no secretarial or other backup available to him or his party colleagues; research, in so far as it existed, consisted of newspaper clippings gathered from local and national papers by the party's general secretary, Colonel Dineen, and heavily underlined in blue pencil. The official allowance barely paid for a typist; everything else had to be provided by the party, and little really was. Eventually Senator Ben O'Quigley, one of the brighter young lawyers in Fine Gael, began to act as unpaid secretary and co-ordinator of the front bench, but for the most part Dillon was left to his own devices. As leader of the opposition he had to deal with the whole legislative programme in the Dáil with not a fraction of the civil service assistance available in government departments. He was not the first or the last opposition leader to experience the frustrations of that office. As he noted in his *Memoir*, 'the lot of the leader of the opposition I did not find a happy one'.

Dillon had been ungracious in his response to Lemass's election as Taoiseach. Lemass now returned the compliment in kind and added a mischievous sting in its tail. Speaking at the Fianna Fáil Árd Fheis shortly afterwards, he opted to see Dillon's election as an opportunity to restore what he called 'pre-Treaty unity'. Now that the Treaty controversy was dead, he said, Fine Gael knew what it was doing when it elected Dillon, 'the embodiment of the old Irish Party'. Fine Gael, he thought, 'should develop the characteristics and outlook which Dillon seems to personify and the natural alignment should be between the "Republican movement" and those who support the old Irish Party'.[3] It was a nice try by Lemass and mischievously intended. There was no possibility of any realignment, but Lemass had struck a sensitive chord, and both he and many in Fine Gael knew it.

Dillon began his leadership vigorously. As if to emphasise the era of change which was at hand, the week after Dillon's election saw the accession of Pope John XXIII to the papacy and the unleashing of the greatest transition in the Catholic Church this century. These changes, many of which Dillon was decidedly unenthusiastic about, were to impact powerfully and unexpectedly on Ireland in the coming years.

To begin with, Dillon put his front bench on a more formal footing. Meetings which had been irregular were now formalised, proper records were kept, and front-bench members were instructed to give a lead in Dáil attendance and the development of policy. He also stressed the need to re-organise the party in readiness to fight a general election.

His first major policy statement was not long in coming. Fine Gael's first objective, he said, would be to expand the output of the land, 'our prime source of wealth', and find profitable markets for its produce. This was the foundation on which to build industrial development. The truth was, he did not believe that a country with few natural resources could sustain such development on a large scale, and he was sceptical about the extent of foreign investment available. In taking this line his thinking was at one with most of the economic and financial establishment, which still held that a prosperous agricultural sector must form the basis of any plan of economic resurgence.[4] Lemass, of course, was moving in another direction.

This is not to say that Dillon was obsessed with agriculture or did not seek to broaden the party's policy base. Within a month of becoming leader, he organised a weekend study conference for the parliamentary party at Malahide out of which a number of significant initiatives emerged. Agriculture again took centre stage, but the need for industrial development was also highlighted. It was argued that the lead here should come first from the private sector, 'stimulated by tax concessions and other fiscal inducements to stimulate production of goods for export'. The importance of factories established by foreign capital and using modern technology to produce goods for export was also stressed. However, if the private sector was not adequate, the 'Government should not hesitate to establish efficient industrial units and procure the personnel to operate them efficiently and economically'. The policy statement looked not so much to the Common Market for its future – at least not yet – but wanted 'greater integration of the economies of Ireland and the UK', and as a first step 'a reciprocal trade agreement which would give Ireland a link with their prices in respect of cattle, sheep, pigs and bacon'. Other aspects of this first policy included a commitment to eradicate bovine TB, the revival of the Parish Plan, and greater popular involvement at all levels of education culminating in free university education for 'all those capable of benefiting from it'.[5]

Dillon had moved quickly to fill Fine Gael's policy vacuum, but ironically this had the effect of highlighting how little difference there was between the major parties on most issues. It was no comfort to Dillon to be told by *The Irish Times* that this was partly because Fianna Fáil had stolen some of Fine Gael's clothes, or that the present party alignments were doomed to die out with the Civil War generation.[6] To a growing number of people, the main difference between the parties was that Fianna Fáil was in power and in a position to implement its new policies; Fine Gael could only talk about them. Already Lemass was more credible as an advocate of economic and industrial change than was Dillon, who still exuded a predominantly rural and agricultural persona. And this in spite of the fact that, as Lemass's biographer, John Horgan, has noted, in cabinet Lemass was 'quite often at loggerheads with some members of the government, especially on agricultural and rural matters, and his emphasis on a more modern approach to the creation of wealth'.[7]

The point was emphasised when Dillon addressed his first Árd Fheis as party leader in February 1960. Once again he underlined the main elements of his policy, with agriculture at the centre, despite the emphasis on industrial development. One observer wrote of him:

> Beneath the parliamentary flamboyance he has always displayed a matter-of-factness, a cold sense of reality which is required for the present generation of political leaders. Fine Gael lacks a policy to differentiate it with sufficient sharpness from Fianna Fáil ... the speech yesterday was comprehensive and carefully composed, with very little in it that could not have been said by Lemass at a Fianna Fáil Árd Fheis ... integrate our economy as closely as possible with Britain – but Lemass is doing this already ... encourage foreign enterprise to set up ... perhaps new and major issues will appear, but, if not, Fine Gael will find it hard to maintain the role of a dynamic opposition, even under so dynamic a leader.[8]

The third act in the changing party scenario came on 26 February 1960, when William Norton announced his resignation as leader of the Labour Party. Norton had held the position since 1932. After twenty-eight years as party leader and two spells in government, he was tired, but more than that there was a certain restlessness within the party, and he had been publicly criticised for accepting a company directorship a short while earlier. He was identified, too, with the Inter Party concept, and after the 1957 election the Labour Party was divided on whether to continue to seek coalition partners or to 'go it alone'. The election of Brendan Corish a week later was, among other things, a victory for the 'go it alone' policy, which was to be the crucial factor in determining who would govern for the next decade, a theme which will be developed later. For the moment, Corish's election confirmed that the old Inter Party relationship was over and that a period of possible party realignment had begun.

The term 'possible' is important here. *The Irish Times* political correspondent might talk of parties starting to take up new positions on a political spectrum: Fine Gael 'reverting to the classical conservative policies of its founders;' Fianna Fáil moving 'left of centre', and Labour 'commanding the left'.[9] Making such things happen was another matter, and the Labour Party of 1960 was as ill-equipped for this as the electorate was unready to allow it take place. As John Horgan observes in *Labour – The Price of Power*, the party 'exhibited many of the tendencies of a political organisation which had become very set in its ways ... the party could not hold a candle to its competitors in organisational, financial or professional terms. The party was not in fact organised at all in the accepted sense of the word, in that it had no central register of members, no income worth speaking of, and a tiny staff.'[10]

In spite of these circumstances, Corish moved quickly to consolidate his leadership and set the party on his chosen course. He won an important battle when he agreed an alliance with Noel Browne, in spite of Norton's antipathy to the arrangement.[11] At the party conference in October 1960 he declared Labour's determination to 'weld together all progressive forces', though, ever cautious, he warned that this was not 'a general invitation to people with queer political ideas to shelter under the umbrella of the Labour Party'. Nonetheless, the conference adopted a resolution pledging that Labour would not join in coalition with either of the two 'conservative' parties.[12] This decision was to determine the course of Irish politics for more than a decade to come.

As IRELAND entered the 1960s, the reality was that between Dillon and Lemass there were now few real differences of policy. There were differences of emphasis, of ethos and style, and most of all differences of perception. The contrast was well caught by a parliamentary sketchwriter in May 1960. Dillon, he wrote, 'delivered stirring, often highly emotional pieces of oratory with some deft and cutting phrases aimed at some of the government's dafter industrial projects ... the finish had the touch of the maestro; dramatic lowering of the voice that brought a tense silence as Mr Dillon, in his most intense tone, proclaimed his credo ... the future of the country must lie in the exploitation of its greatest national resource, the land.' Lemass, by contrast, 'gave a crackling, fast-moving speech ... the sharp-witted technocrat of Government, talking in terms of industrial production rather than save-the-land slogans'.[13]

On issues of substance there was little to differentiate the two leaders. Dillon had long opposed the Control of Manufactures Act – the legislative framework of protection – and campaigned for its total abolition. 'Surely the time has come to take our courage in our hands, abolish the whole fraud and acknowledge that we want foreign capital in this country, that we want foreign technology, that our principal concern is to get employment for our own people in their own country ... does it matter a hoot who runs the show?'[14] He was, however, conscious of the downside of such invest-ment, particularly the vulnerability of offshore plants in the event of recession, realising that in such cases the Irish plants would be the first to close. However, on the principle of outside investment he was at one with Lemass, indeed was less guarded and, unlike Lemass, articulating a view he had long held.

Dillon believed Irish membership of the Common Market was probably inevitable. He was apprehensive rather than enthusiastic about it. When Lemass said in the Dáil in July 1960 that it was still too early to think of joining the European movement, that the British trade agreement was still 'the keystone of our external trade structure' and despite 'anything which may emerge from discussions about European trade ... the preservation of the chief characteristics of that agreement must be a main objective of our policy',[15] he was simply stating in unequivocal terms what Dillon had long been saying, but what had never before been admitted so openly by a Fianna Fáil leader. Nor were Dillon and Lemass far apart when in the same speech Lemass stressed the need to secure access for Irish products to the markets of Western Europe, though Lemass was clearer and less concerned about the drastic structural changes in agriculture which this would neces-sitate, and in particular the consequences for the family farm.

A year later, in the Dáil adjournment debate of August 1961, Lemass was closer to taking a decision to apply for membership of the Common Market. He was clearly excited by the prospect, and more aware than he cared to admit that the implications were greater than merely economic and that political union could well be further along the road. For the moment, however, it was the 'economic and not the political aspect of the Rome Treaty which should be our prime concern'.[16]

Dillon accepted the Lemass analysis, albeit without enthusiasm. For a start, it was not the type of international alliance he had envisioned, an English-speaking alliance involving the Commonwealth countries and the USA. He had less natural affinity with the countries of Europe. He was also pessimistic about the capacity of Irish industry to survive and adapt, though he accepted that if Britain joined the Common Market, Ireland had no alternative but to follow because of the close integration of the two economies. He claimed, and with justification, that Lemass was not frank with the Dáil on the full political implications of the Rome Treaty, and was one of the few politicians conscious of the loss of parliamentary sovereignty involved:

In signing this Treaty we authorise the authorities in Brussels to tell us in respect of certain matters what Oireachtas Éireann may and may not do. We limit our discretion in a variety of matters relating to social services, employment practices relevant to certain measures which we have heretofore employed to stimulate employment.[17]

He accepted that such was 'part of the price we pay', and in a memorandum in August 1961 he offered two reasons why we should accept it. The first was agriculture:

We simply cannot afford to have the tariffs on agricultural produce levied against us in the British market. Free access to the British market is vital to the agricultural industry of Ireland, and the agricultural industry provides employment directly and indirectly for three-quarters of the people of Ireland. It is the foundation of our whole economic life, and unless it can be made to prosper, Ireland could not provide a reasonable standard of living for her people.

The second reason was his old theme of the defence of freedom and liberty:

The future of the Common Market itself depends on its ability successfully to resist the challenge of Communist Imperialist aggression. At the present moment West Berlin depends for its survival on the United States of America. If the United States withdrew its support tomorrow, the presence of France and Great Britain would not long protect West Berlin from being overwhelmed by the Cominform. If the prosperity and freedom of West Berlin today excites the hatred of the Soviet and its satellites, how much more would a free and prosperous Europe excite it tomorrow?

Nor was he going to give up on his wider and long-held vision:

Ultimately, if the forces of evil are to be successfully resisted, the whole concept of the Common Market must be expanded to include not only the nations of Western Europe, but the United States, Canada, Australia, New Zealand, and all other freedom-loving countries in the World. Ireland can have a great role in this Association of free nations, in encouraging its expansion and development so that all the free people of the world, combining their resources, spiritual and material, may establish a secure citadel in which freedom can survive. And, at the same time, such an Association can deploy its vast resources to help the new nations emerging in Africa and Asia to achieve a reasonable standard of living for their people, and free institutions which can only flourish when hunger and destitution have been successfully overcome. As the restrictions on the free passage of men, money and goods disappear, the Border which divides our country will become progressively more absurd, and

out of this Common Market adventure, Ireland may well yet realise her destiny as a united nation, extending her hands between the Old World and the
New, to bring into existence a great new world force for freedom, individual
liberty, and a philosophy based on the Christian concept of the dignity of
man.[18]

Yet, even if elements of it were visionary, Dillon's endorsement of Europe
was expressed with a sense of reluctance. It had none of Lemass's barely
suppressed sense of enthusiasm when in the same debate he declared 'the
emphasis is now on change and innovation in every sphere of national
activity ... this is a time for new ideas ... personally I find the prospect exciting and stimulating ... the work of Government must now be directed to
the preparation for the momentous years ahead ... we must look with cold
objectivity on the national assets and the national deficiencies so that we
can plan properly together to exploit the one and remedy the other.'[19]
Lemass's passion for Europe had another aspect to it. He knew that his
enthusiasm was not shared by all his colleagues in government, and in seeking public and, more critically, party endorsement for Ireland's application,
he tied it into the nationalist aim of Irish unity. In the words of John
Horgan, 'he was writing a scenario in which economic and political objectives were deliberately linked; the final abandonment of the national aim of
economic self-sufficiency would deliver the political aim of unity'.[20] It was
Lemass at his political best.

A DEFINING event of the new decade was the government's decision to
establish a national television service, Telefís Éireann. An avid cinema-goer,
Dillon was keenly aware of the new service's potential and he participated
fully in the debate on the legislation which put it in place. He agreed that it
should be under the control of a government-appointed authority, 'believing that the power of television as a medium of communication is so great
that we could not with equanimity contemplate it being divorced from all
control by the Oireachtas', and supported them in making the appointments. 'I take the view that in the last analysis the government cannot
escape responsibility for them ... somebody must choose ... better the
responsibility should be squarely set upon the government who must
answer to this House and ultimately to the country.'[21] He did, however,
want full disclosure of any possible conflict of interest which could lead to
abuses, and was later very critical of the appointment of Eamon Andrews as
first Chairman of the Authority on this very principle: 'It is a bad principle
that any man should be charged with the responsibility of presiding over
the TV authority at a time when it was universally known that he is in a

very large way of business, offering material to the Authority of which he is Chairman. If that principle is generally accepted in our public and private lives there will have been a very serious lowering of standards.'[22]

Dillon vigorously opposed the inclusion in the Act of the controversial Section 31 which gave the Minister for Posts and Telegraphs the power to direct the authority to refrain from broadcasting any particular matter or matters of any particular class. This section was to attain controversial status later when it was used to ban the IRA and kindred organisations from the airwaves, though this was not foreseen by Dillon in 1960. He saw it as a potential threat to free speech and open to abuse by a future government which wanted either to censor its opponents or propagandise to its own benefit. In arriving at this view he had, no doubt, painful memories of the unsubtle censorship used by Aiken during the war years.[23] His objections, however, made little impact on the debate.

One area where the difference between Fine Gael and Fianna Fáil might have been underlined was the question of Northern Ireland, or partition, as it was more usually called, but Lemass's ongoing efforts to move Fianna Fáil away from its traditional anti-partition stance headed off this option. Lemass called for greater co-operation with the North while at the same time reassuring his supporters that national unity remained the ultimate goal. It was a delicate balancing act and Lemass's shift in policy, especially as outlined in his Oxford Union speech, worried many both inside and outside Fianna Fáil.[24] For the most part, the North was an issue all the major parties tended to treat with caution, not least for fear of stirring up problems in their own organisations.

The smaller groups had no such inhibitions. The most immediate reaction to the Oxford speech came in a Dáil motion in the name of an Independent TD, Frank Sherwin, debated on 10 November 1960. Sherwin's message was simple and unreconstructed. The people in Northern Ireland 'were planted and given certain functions to perform ... Lemass should try to unify all national forces, invite the people of Sinn Féin and IRA to join it.' He wanted 'an active policy', and though the activity was not defined it was not difficult to guess what it might have contemplated.[25]

Lemass answered that the path to unity lay in removing barriers and promoting greater contact between North and South. Dillon's line was not much different. He, too, wanted greater co-operation: an attempt at force would amount to civil war. He felt the onus was on the Unionists to end discrimination against Catholics, and that ending partition would mean a stronger, freer, more independent Ireland. Lemass and Dillon's closeness on this topic led to an extraordinary outburst from Dillon's old colleague, Michael Donnellan of Clann na Talmhan. 'What we have, we hold!' he thundered. There was 'no such thing as a government of Northern Ireland' as Lemass and Dillon had said; rather there was 'a junta set up at the behest of the British government'. He disagreed with Dillon – 'nothing was ever got except what was fought for ... Northern Ireland be damned. It is not Northern Ireland ... it is just a corner ... six counties, nothing else.'[26] Donnellan's line echoed much of Fianna Fáil's traditional thinking, but little of this was evident now, certainly not publicly.

In 1960 Fianna Fáil produced a new electoral Bill which discriminated in favour of western and rural constituencies on the grounds of the heavier work-load and longer distances to be travelled by their TDs compared with urban Deputies. It was no coincidence that these were the constituencies where Fianna Fáil support was strongest, and there was little attempt to conceal the political motivation behind the Bill. In the event, in one of the first instances of judicial review, the legislation was successfully challenged in the High Court by a member of Dillon's front bench, Senator John O'Donovan. His objection was not appealed by the government, which was now obliged to bring in a new and more equitable Bill.

Dillon was not impressed with the new draft any more than the first. His view, that the government had done its best to draw the boundaries to the advantage of Fianna Fáil, was justified. Lemass's biographer, John Horgan, tells us that the Taoiseach took personal charge of the project and 'made every effort to adjust it in Fianna Fáil's favour'.[27] Redistribution, Dillon argued, 'is a very integral part of our whole system of representative government, and it really reaches the nadir of absurdity and disruptiveness when we have a map erected in the Custom House with members of the Fianna Fáil party gathered around it like bees or wasps around a honey pot to see what they can do.' This was a blatant attempt at gerrymandering, he said, and he called instead for an independent system, rather than having the Act 'drafted by a succession of Fianna Fáil TDs visiting the Custom House to explain their personal hopes, aspirations and fears to those responsible for drawing the line of the new constituencies'.[28] Dillon had been prepared to discuss with Fianna Fáil the possibility of a compromise between the parties preferred electoral systems in 1959. He had been rebuffed then and in spite of his reservations now the new Bill as proposed was enacted. Liam Cosgrave was to meet the same situation in 1968.

Change and talk of change was in the air in the 1960s, and extended to the possibility of new political alignments and the final disappearance of the battle lines of the Civil War. Within Fine Gael the lead in such discussion was taken, not by one of the younger politicians, but by the party's senior statesman, John A. Costello, who in May 1961 was predicting that 'there will be a break-up in the old political positions over the next ten years'. Costello went so far as to predict that the 'left wings' of Fianna Fáil and Fine Gael 'might even unite with Labour to form a new party'.[29] Dillon, however, had little time for such speculation. He was finding that being party leader was about mundane matters like finance, organisation, and the management of people as much as policy.

Financially, the party was in difficulties, and one of Dillon's first decisions was to impose a levy of £400 on each constituency to deal with the immediate crisis. Organisationally, the party had a nationwide network of branches, district executives and constituency executives, but in many cases the branches had little more than a notional existence and no active role, coming to life generally only at election times to carry out the time-honoured rituals of canvassing, postering and manning the polling stations. The local organisation invariably played second fiddle to Fianna Fáil in terms of numbers, fervour and local presence. It may be that Fianna Fáil, so long in office, saw its local cumainn almost as a branch of government, the eyes and ears of the party, and still retained some of its militaristic approach to questions of organisation, which gave it an edge over all other parties. Dillon had never been a great believer in tightly disciplined party structures. In Monaghan he did not encourage its development and generally operated almost at arm's length from the party, depending on a loose network of traditional supporters for his local work. No national recruitment campaign had been undertaken to increase the membership, nor was there any serious examination of the role and function of party structures.

The onus of developing party policy fell on the front bench, but getting them to involve themselves in this area was proving a difficult task. The front bench had nineteen members, five of whom were Senators. They were elected, not chosen, and their quality and commitment was very uneven. One Senator attended only three of the forty front-bench meetings held in 1960-61; another managed only ten.[30] Not all frontbenchers were willing to get down to the business of producing draft policies for discussion, and on a number of occasions Dillon had to appeal to those who were falling down in this regard to admit it and let someone else do the job. Admittedly, the front bench had no research or secretarial help, and no resources to hire any, but for some members policy was almost a luxury, while others found it beyond their capacity. There was the inevitable problem, too, of being in opposition to a government which was appropriating most of the best lines. The temptation was to be negative and critical, to wait for the government to make mistakes so as to trumpet its inconsistencies. Sean Lemass was scornful of Fine Gael on this point:

> There is a modern idea that parties win elections not so much because of the programmes they offer to the public and the speeches made by their leaders as by the image of themselves they succeed in impressing on the public mind.

What image of themselves do the Fine Gael party think they are impressing on the public mind? A lost tribe wandering in the wilderness, running around in circles. They will never get out of the wilderness unless they make up their mind to go in a straight line in some direction.[31]

Declan Costello was one of the first to grasp this point. He had been among those who set up the Research and Information Centre study group shortly after the 1957 election, and had later established a newspaper, the *National Observer*. Fine Gael's young politicians, aware of developments in Europe, were anxious for new ideas and intellectual underpinning at a time of intellectual and political aridity, and while the group never made a major impact on the rank and file of the party, it did have significant influence on some key figures, helped attract new members and was a welcome sign of positive thinking in an otherwise indifferent climate. Dillon fully supported the Centre, even if he was not intimately involved in its activities. This support, however, did not extend to Sweetman, who deeply distrusted Costello's 'left wing' proclivities, especially his support for state involvement and social investment in the economy. Sweetman was thoroughly conservative, and articulated what was probably a majority view in a parliamentary party dominated by business and farming interests – and in some cases by inertia. Pat Lindsay, a radical in some respects, summed up his opposition to the Costello line: he was, he said, 'a conservative small-holder from the West of Ireland', and outraged by proposals 'borrowed from a number of failed systems abroad'.[32]

Declan Costello had been elected to the Dáil in 1954. He was different to many of his colleagues – intense, intellectual, shy and unclubbable – and passionately interested in Fine Gael's need to develop its sense of identity, which he believed should move the party significantly to what was then regarded as the conventional left. Between Dillon and himself there was always courtesy and guarded mutual respect, but never any great warmth or affection. The first of what was to be a long-running series of difficulties between them emerged in mid-1960. In a letter to Dillon that July, Costello called for an urgent meeting of the front bench 'to discuss the policy of the party'. Costello felt very strongly that Fine Gael was going nowhere, while Fianna Fáil was as strong as ever in the country and had recovered in Dublin. Costello pointed out that 'in order to form even a minority government after the election next year, we must win at least twenty seats'. He saw no prospect of this happening. The next election would not be won 'by enthusiasm engendered three or four weeks before polling day or by a hurriedly constructed policy statement issued at that time'. What he wanted was a clear statement of policy 'on the many urgent social and economic problems which face us'. He submitted a list of specific policy issues and invited Dillon to respond to them. 'I am satisfied that we can only fulfil our duty to the country,' he concluded, 'by clearing our minds and making decisions on these urgent problems.'[33]

Dillon wasted no time in replying, but clearly there was no meeting of minds between him and his front-bench colleague. 'I believe that an excess of optimism is unjustified, but it is certainly not as pernicious as an excess of pessimism.' Dillon went on to express his own optimism that 'the tide is flowing strongly against Fianna Fáil'. His chief difference with Costello was that, while he agreed that we must 'clarify our minds on outstanding matters of policy', he did not see any fundamental problems. There was much to be updated and certain matters best not followed, such as the question of NATO membership, but he challenged Costello to say, if there were a socialist party in Ireland along the lines of Gaitskill's Labour Party, 'would you feel a duty to support it?' Dillon ended this letter with an extraordinary admission, which must have raised some doubts in Costello's mind as to the depth of his leader's commitment to actually winning power. He felt confident that after the next general election 'Fine Gael will be the largest party in Dáil Éireann. I admit that this is rather an alarming prospect, but it is one that I do not suppose we can avoid facing if it arises.'[34]

Costello was in no way mollified. His reply a month later revealed a deeper sense of unease within the party than might have been suspected. Costello was adamant that Fine Gael did not have, as Dillon claimed, a 'comprehensive policy'; nor was it clear as to what it would do if elected to government. He cited the divisions which were evident to him at the most recent parliamentary party meeting: one senior colleague claimed he did not know what the policy of the party was on any issue; another said 'there was no difference between us and Fianna Fáil'. A third agreed but said 'this didn't matter'. Another (Maurice Dockrell) thought that 'the main thing was that we were decent fellows and our opponents weren't'. Costello continued: 'no one present could say in what way we differ from our opponents ... what disturbed me about the meeting was that this did not seem to cause a great deal of concern'.[35]

Costello had one further point to make. The party had supported the retention of proportional representation, and the logic of PR was that coalitions were the norm, overall majorities an exception. Fine Gael had shown that coalitions could work, 'and if we wanted to repeat it in the future, then we must have our own minds clear upon the things we want to do and we must be trying to get support for these objectives in outside parties'.

As to where Fine Gael should be on the political spectrum, Costello was equally clear: it should not be 'a conservative party, but should move to the left'. He would support Mr Gaitskill: 'I think that Christian Social principles as applied to this country, require us to accept the full implications of the Welfare State and the increased role the government must play in promoting economic activity.'[36]

This simmering disagreement surfaced again in November 1960, when Costello declined to take through the Dáil a Bill for which he was responsible, the Rent Restrictions Bill, because he disagreed with the party line on the issue at hand. Dillon responded by taking the Bill himself.[37]

The burden of pulling together the various strands of policy and of arbitrating between competing views fell to him, and, given the difficult circumstances in which he operated, the surprising fact is that so much rather than so little policy was developed at this period. When it came to the question of managing his colleagues, Dillon's approach was conciliatory, almost avuncular. In appealing for a full effort at a by-election campaign in 1961, he told the parliamentary party, 'it was not in my make-up to dragoon members into playing their part, but that I expected full loyal co-operation'. Sadly for him, it was not always forthcoming. Not all TDs and Senators bothered to attend the two-day policy conference held in Malahide which Dillon had called; many TDs entered into 'private' pairing arrangements and frequently absented themselves from Dáil attendance, some frontbenchers did not even turn up in the Dáil to deal with their own portfolios. The predominance of lawyers on the front bench created such a problem that Dillon contemplated having one of the lawyer TDs act as an informal Whip in the Law Library in an attempt to improve matters. Sanctions generally counted for little: Dillon depended on the good-will of his colleagues. Mulcahy made the point at a presentation made by the parliamentary party to mark his retirement. Attendance at Leinster House was 'a disgrace and could not go on. The time has come for Deputies to consider retiring ... the present position imposed a task on a small minority that cannot be performed.'[38] Dillon did what he could in such circumstances, and led by example and exhortation, but, as he was to note in his *Memoir*, the role of the leader of the opposition is one of the most arduous and least rewarding tasks of politics.

DILLON'S FIRST electoral test came in late June 1960 with the by-election in Carlow–Kilkenny and local elections nationwide. The by-election was caused by the death of a Fine Gael TD, Joseph Hughes, and while the Fine Gael candidate lost, the Fine Gael vote was up by 3,000, the Fianna Fáil vote down by 8,000, and the margin of victory a mere 129 votes. It was a good result for Dillon, but somewhat ominously just one-third of the Labour transfers went to Fine Gael, only slightly more than went to Fianna Fáil. The local government results also had little to say. According to the newspapers, the Fine Gael campaign showed greater effort and discipline than before, but not enough to make a significant difference.[39] In March 1961, Dillon finally scored his first real victory. This was a by-election in Sligo–Leitrim, and in a straight fight with Fianna Fáil, Joseph McLaughlin won the seat with a 600-vote margin. It was encouraging news for Dillon, even if it did not indicate a new trend.[40]

By mid-1961, the general election was fast approaching. Lemass had indicated in August that he would dissolve the Dáil between September and mid-October, thus giving all parties ample opportunity to get into shape. Dillon immediately set about getting Fine Gael policy finalised. Progress had been somewhat slow; there was still a poor response to Dillon's call for policy papers even in March 1961, but by May the main points were emerging, and the front bench considered a full draft in July. The programme was comprehensive but had little that was new: most points had been outlined by Dillon in his Árd Fheis speech.

Of most interest was the new thinking on education, promising to revive the Irish language through 'inducement rather than compulsion', to provide more and better scholarships, and to extend university education 'to all those capable of benefiting from it'. *The Irish Times* attributed much of these ideas to Dillon, who 'showed himself to be genuinely concerned with the scandalous lack of scholarships'.[41] In health, the party sought to provide a choice of doctor scheme if that was possible. However, the draft policy ran into trouble at the outset when Declan Costello indicated that 'he wished to be regarded as not being in agreement with the document ... he thought it was inadequate for election purposes and that the proper emphasis was not on the matters he considered to be important, such as full employment and the means whereby that would be achieved, the social programme, education etc.'[42] Costello played no further party in policy formation and effectively sidelined himself for the duration of the campaign.

The prelude to the 1961 election was livelier than the country had been accustomed to. The opening of the Patrician year in June was perhaps the last mass outpouring of Catholic pietism in the country, with all political leaders kneeling in traditional deference to the Papal Legate. At another level, the new presidential style of John F. Kennedy was making an impact, and one optimistic observer noted a 'new intellectual curiosity' in trade unions and young farmers' clubs, 'university societies were more lively, while the new Institute of Public Administration and the intellectual group, An Tuairim, were pioneering a new scientific examination of political problems'. The writer concluded, however, that the 'Dáil itself showed little if any reflection of the new ferment of thought in the country', though he qualified this by saying that whatever changes may come 'would be within the existing parties' as a result of the 'infiltration of new ideas from the younger generation'.[43] New ideas from a younger generation did not, however, make much impact on an all-too-familiar philistinism, with the proposal from the Electricity Supply Board to demolish its Georgian buildings in Fitzwilliam St, Dublin. Dillon vehemently opposed these plans, though without success.

More worrying from the government's point of view was a strike by ESB electricians in August which led to widespread power-cuts and threatened the entire national system. The Dáil was recalled in emergency session on 1 September to pass legislation forcing the striking ESB workers back to work, a measure supported with reluctance by Dillon. Four days later a new wage offer was made, and accepted on 7 September. The general election was called the following day.

Yet while this was the first major test of all three new party leaders, the election campaign itself was dull. Lemass campaigned hard, but there was no sense of excitement to what he did; he adopted a safety-first policy of reassuring his own supporters and scaring the non-committed with the message that 'only Fianna Fáil can govern'. Labour was determined to go it alone, unwilling to say what it would do or which party it would support in the event of a 'hung' Dáil. The party's line was that there was as much onus on the bigger parties, between whom there were no great differences, to combine in that event as there was on Labour to 'prop up' either party.

Fine Gael nominated ninety-five candidates, a signal that it intended to form a Fine Gael government, and Dillon stoutly maintained his belief that this was a realistic target. But the door was not entirely closed on a post-election alliance: the front bench agreed that campaign criticism should be focused entirely on Fianna Fáil and that they would not alienate other groups. If they subsequently found themselves in a position to form a government, the party leader 'should have the utmost freedom in the formation of it'.[44]

The election campaign was almost devoid of policy-driven debate. The only real spark of controversy came from Fine Gael's policy on Irish, described by *The Irish Times* as 'realistic and idealistic' and by Fianna Fáil as 'irresponsible and anti-national'.[45] Lemass admitted privately that Fine Gael had struck a responsive chord with the electorate on the issue, and as a result put pressure on Tomás Ó Fiaich and the long-sitting Commission on the Revival of the Irish Language to hurry up with its recommendations. Up to now Lemass had shown little interest and no facility in Irish, but he knew it was an issue on which no Fianna Fáil leader could afford to be wrong-footed, so the pragmatist in him called for specific plans, while the politician assailed Fine Gael's proposals as a 'policy of retreat'.[46]

The campaign was described by the press as 'the quietest ever' – a description which had been applied to virtually every campaign since 1933. When the results came in, there were no clear winners. Fianna Fáil dropped 80,000 votes and was reduced to seventy seats, three short of an overall majority; Fine Gael gained 50,000 new votes and won seven seats on its 1957 figure, including three extra seats in Dublin; Labour won sixteen seats, an increase of four; Clann na Talmhan had two, Clann na Poblachta one, the NPDs held their two seats and there were six Independents. For Dillon personally it was a good result: he headed the poll in Monaghan, beating Erskine Childers into third place.

Under normal circumstances the 1961 election would have represented a significant victory for Dillon, but now it was a hollow triumph. While his party had gained seven seats and seen Fianna Fáil lose eight, the possibility of forming a government seemed to be out of the question because of Labour's singular policy. When the Dáil met on 11 October, Labour proposed Corish as Taoiseach and called on Fianna Fáil and Fine Gael to merge. The party's decision ensured Lemass's election. Even more worrying from Dillon's point of view were the contributions of the various Independents, who effectively held the balance of power. Frank Sherwin, James Carroll and Joe Leneghan all opted for Lemass as representing the best hope of stability, while Joe Sheridan, formerly a Fine Gael member, and who ran as an Independent after his failure to get the party nomination, abstained. The Independents had no desire to return to the hustings and opted, without too much soul-searching, for Lemass.[47]

Though the election campaign had been humdrum and the election of Taoiseach robbed of any real drama as a result of Labour's stance, the speeches which followed Lemass's election were different in kind from anything that had been heard on similar occasions over the previous forty years. Dillon can claim much of the credit for this. He began by pouring scorn on those journalists, especially from the *Guardian* and *The Times*, who predicted a period of instability for the Republic because no party had a clear majority. Dillon answered: 'Ireland will have at the hands of this Dáil one of the most stable governments in Europe.' He went on: 'we have formidable problems, domestic and external, to surmount. Instead of paralysing our capacity with the crocodile tears of self-pity, because our people have preferred democracy to authoritarianism, let us take off our coats and get on with the job of leading our people through whatever perils may beset us.'[48]

Nor was Dillon subscribing to the then fashionable view that the two major parties were outdated. He attacked the notion that 'there is not a sufficiently violent difference between us in the House, or we are all engaged in political play-acting because none of us is prepared to repudiate the fundamental beliefs we all hold in common'. He was contemptuous of the idea that politics had grown dull, 'as if this Oireachtas were a peep show for the edification of any panic mongerer or agent of the yellow press which seeks to find diversion in our proceedings'. He decried those who wanted Ireland to follow the ideological spectrum found on the continent, arguing quite accurately that there was no basis in Irish society for such divisions, and making the valid if inconsequential point that 'the differences between Fianna Fáil and Fine Gael are as wide as those that divide the Republicans and the Democrats in the US'.[49]

Dillon's assertion was strengthened rather than weakened by Brendan Corish's speech. Corish was at pains to point out that Labour's policy was deeply rooted in Christian Socialism, and quoted copiously from papal encyclicals to buttress his assertion. And for once there was agreement between Lemass and Dillon on this question. Lemass agreed that 'except in some very obvious and important matters the apparent similarity between the position of Fine Gael and Fianna Fáil is superficial only, and conceals the fact that both parties reached the positions they now hold by somewhat different routes'.[50]

After this calm start it was only a matter of time before normal political hostilities were restored, but there was a new maturity, even a mellowness about the exchanges, underlying which was a fundamental faith in the ability of the system to survive without a single-party majority.

The new Dáil gave Dillon an opportunity to reshuffle his front bench, yet in spite of his good electoral performance and the need for a strong parliamentary display to test the new government, he was curiously hesitant, almost diffident, in his approach to this question. He had complained in the past that some of those elected by the parliamentary party would not have been his first choice if he had a free hand in selecting the shadow cabinet, but instead of seeking to revert to the pre-1957 situation, when the party leader had nominated his own front bench, he made a series of compromise proposals to the parliamentary party. He proposed that the party TDs would nominate ten members, five would be nominated from the Senate, and Dillon could then co-opt such other members as he needed to make an effective front bench. The strange thing was that there was very strong support from rank-and-file members of the parliamentary party for a return to the old position. Dillon did not push the matter; he simply exhorted members to give him men he 'could lean on and have full confidence in', and went ahead with the old system. When the front bench was completed it had fifteen Dáil members, so Dillon had added five of his own choice, though who they were was not disclosed. At his instigation the parliamentary party also invited Richard Mulcahy, who was no longer a TD, to sit on the front bench, which he agreed to do, and in fact attended front-bench meetings from time to time during the remainder of Dillon's leadership.[51]

Back in the Dáil, the first attempt to test the strength of the new government came in late November 1961. Fine Gael moved a motion calling for compensation for farmers who had been particularly badly hit by falling wheat prices as a result of adverse weather conditions. Fine Gael's aim was to embarrass the rural Independents into voting against the government, thus destabilising or even defeating it, but in the event the intention backfired. For a start, Lemass raised the temperature by personally intervening, thus making the issue one of confidence in his administration. He declared he would not be pressurised by party political considerations and would not buy his way out of trouble, a clear message to the Independents that they could find themselves facing an early election if they weren't careful. Secondly, Dillon's speech, vivid though it was, pitched Fine Gael support on the narrow ground of one section of the farming community, and the matter was made worse through Sweetman's truculent refusal to broaden the issue to include all farmers on an amendment from Browne and McQuillan. Thus when the vote came it was easily defeated, with all the Independents absenting themselves and Browne and McQuillan spurned. Worst of all for Dillon, only thirty-nine of Fine Gael's fifty-four TDs actually voted. Lemass had won the first skirmish and had done so largely thanks to a badly-chosen motion, ineptly handled.[52]

The growing authority of Lemass and his government was confirmed by a successful Fianna Fáil Árd Fheis in January 1962, which had a vigorous and youthful air to it, and an openness of debate hitherto lacking at gatherings of this sort. Lemass captured or directed the mood with a speech which placed his party in the forefront of change, and laid ownership in particular to the European issue, which he sold to the Fianna Fáil faithful as a promise of future prosperity and a means of ending partition.[53]

Two weeks later Dillon put in an equally vigorous performance at a meeting of his party's central branch when, according to an *Irish Times* editorial, he was beginning 'to show himself as the kind of leader who might at last fulfil the hopes of those who do not want to see Fianna Fáil in permanent power'. But Fine Gael, it said, had yet to find a policy which was coherent, popular and distinctive from that of the government.[54] Nor did Fine Gael's Árd Fheis three weeks later show much evidence of serious debate among delegates, or signs of a new policy emerging.

The budget of 1962 put no real strain on Lemass's survival, and as the year progressed Dillon and his party marked time. The belief that the minority government could easily be displaced had given way to a feeling that it could go quite a distance, especially since two of the Independents, Sherwin and Leneghan, were now almost permanent fixtures in the government lobby. This in turn reflected itself in an increasingly lethargic Dáil performance by Fine Gael.

Dillon had decided in April to become the party's chief delegate to the Council of Europe in order, he told the parliamentary party, 'to offset

Lemass's claim to be the only one to be properly informed'.[55] It was a responsibility he took very seriously, attending Strasbourg and reporting back in detail to both front bench and parliamentary party on developments in Europe. He canvassed a diversity of opinion from other countries as to the future shape of the Common Market. Despite his reservations, he had decided early on that membership was in the national interest and that it would be irresponsible to embarrass the government in the midst of crucial negotiations. He rejected demands from some members of the parliamentary party that he should adopt a more critical line and capitalise on the difficulties Lemass was encountering. For this he was attacked by *The Irish Times* in November 1962, which described his attitude as 'fresh evidence of the negative approach to politics which has characterised his party since the EEC debate started. He has let Lemass make all the running and has failed to secure a full national debate.' Dillon's reply was restrained. He could have been niggling, he said. He could have made much of the NATO kite flown by Micheál Ó Móráin, or of some of Brian Lenihan's provocative remarks, but he did not as it 'would have been against the vital national interests of the country'.[56]

1962 was also a year in which the style of politics was changing. Lemass was impatient to introduce new blood to key positions in his own party, but not nearly as impatient as some of the new bloods themselves. There was a new arrogance abroad, a pushiness best exemplified in the personae of some of Lemass's favourite sons. The new prosperity began to manifest itself, most notably in the property markets, in the building and redevelopment programmes, in the establishment of new industry and in the emergence of a more ostentatious style of living among some of the new high-flyers in business and some of the politicians associated with them. Charles Haughey, appointed Minister for Justice at the age of thirty, had bought his first racehorse in 1962 and was already a controversial figure – 'no doubting his ability and intelligence,' said *The Irish Times* in its end of year review, 'but inexperience or lack of judgement or an inherent psychology or public relations deficit militate against popularity in the House and outside.'[57] In his book *The Best of Decades*, Feargal Tobin recalls the growing anxiety that 'Fianna Fáil was becoming identified in the public eye with an unsavoury get rich quick cabal ... with men of considerable property who were uninhibited in the way they flaunted their wealth ... the sleek Mercedes, the mohair suits, the expensive monthly fundraising lunches in the Russell Hotel.'[58]

Two episodes which jarred most that year were the setting of police dogs on Noel Browne and Jack McQuillan during a demonstration outside the US Embassy in November, an incident captured dramatically in newspaper photographs and for which the Justice Minister was reluctant to offer an early or full apology.[59] However, when Fianna Fáil's Donogh O'Malley drove drunkenly up O'Connell St on the wrong side of the road, there was an attempt to cover up the case, and the Garda who had taken the prosecution was harshly treated.[60] Subsequent events showed that many in Fianna Fáil were unhappy with the new style as personified by Haughey, O'Malley and to a lesser extent Brian Lenihan, but open disquiet was for the future.

In December 1962, Dillon took great exception to the awarding of a state contract to the accountancy firm of Haughey Boland, of which Haughey had been a founding partner, along with a brother of Fianna Fáil minister Kevin Boland. Dillon did not say the firm in question should not have been awarded the contract, but did demand a public explanation as to why this particular firm had been preferred:

> I rightly conceive that, simply because we do enter into public life, we must not be asked to abandon our ordinary means of life, but the fact that we do enter public life puts on us certain obligations, one of which is to avoid the possibility of the imputation of allowing our position in public life to secure for us any sort of preference at the hands of the government, or anybody controlled by the government.

The matter should have been notified to the Dáil: 'failure to do that and the persistent silence in regard to it lowers the tone of public life and gives rise to justifiable *malaise* in the public mind'. His protestation was brushed aside and no explanation of the procedures used or justification of the decision was given.[61]

By the beginning of 1963, Lemass had escaped de Valera's shadow and was establishing his own style and personality. Many, including Garret FitzGerald, then an economics writer with *The Irish Times* and a disaffected Fine Gael supporter, acknowledged him as a man whose personality and economic expertise were in tune with the needs of the time. Dillon, by contrast, was seen by many – including FitzGerald – as a somewhat anachronistic figure. A political commentator wrote of him:

> still the supreme parliamentarian, giving the House the glamour and splendour and high purpose of a hundred years before, and maintaining in relation to Noel Browne and Jack McQuillan, whose policy he detests, the philosophy of Voltaire, of hating what they say, but being ready to give his life for their freedom to say it. One sometimes thinks of him as a statesman born a century too late, but quite often he draws bouquets for his oratory, even from a cynical press gallery.[62]

The same writer noted that under Dillon's leadership Fine Gael 'has become more integrated, more disciplined and more informed'. That, however, was not to be enough, and 1963 was the year when the debate simmering about the party's *raison d'être* finally came to the boil. The year was to find the party riven down the centre between the modernisers, led by and personified in Declan Costello, and the conservative, though not necessarily traditional wing, led by Sweetman and Senator EA McGuire. Dillon found himself holding the middle ground, like many party leaders before and since, putting party unity ahead of a decisive outcome which, whatever way it went, would alienate significant sections of the party.

The early months of 1963 offered a number of issues which could have proved beneficial to the opposition. A pay pause in the public service was imposed; the Singer case and especially the performance of the Attorney General continued to embarrass the government;[63] industrial unrest remained a worrying factor, with an acrimonious bus strike in April. Most promising of all from an opposition perspective was the announcement in February, confirmed in March, that a sales tax was inevitable and likely to be permanent. The turnover tax, as it would be called, duly made its appearance in the April budget. Moreover, Lemass's hopes of early entry to the EEC looked more and more unlikely because of de Gaulle's hostility to Britain's membership. At home, the government's decision to allow the Electricity Supply Board demolish Georgian buildings at Fitzwilliam St drew attention to its insensitive approach to environmental matters. In face of these growing problems, especially industrial unrest, Lemass's only positive response seemed both feeble and futile, when in February he arranged to meet with employers and unions in the hope of securing a national wage agreement.[64]

The budget should have been a godsend to the opposition, imposing as it did a new turnover tax of two-and-a-half per cent on all sales, including food and other essentials, but the opposition – Fine Gael, Labour, even Browne and McQuillan – failed to see its full significance and concentrated most of their fire elsewhere. The full implications of the tax began to emerge only weeks later. The lapse was not indicative of a vigilant opposition, or one with its eye to the main chance politically.

Declan Costello's frustration surfaced once more in March 1963. He attempted to revive the debate he had started two years earlier by submitting a memo to the front bench. He recalled for Dillon that he had forwarded a document on economic and financial policy to the front bench as far back as 1959, but after some discussion 'an answering memo' was circulated by Sweetman and after some further discussion the matter simply lapsed.

Costello pointed out that, in the public mind, there seemed to be very little difference between the financial and economic policies of the two main parties, and as a result 'Fine Gael was open to the charge of shadowboxing in the economic and financial debates which have and will take place.' He put forward three proposals to enable Fine Gael advocate a distinctive policy which would materially assist the economic development of the country. The first was the need for proper economic planning, as distinct from the 'programmed' nature of the *Programme for Economic Expansion*, which underpinned the government's economic policy and which Costello believed to be seriously defective. Looking at the role of the state, particularly in providing fixed capital formation, he argued that 'to increase capital formation, the role of the state must be increased and if necessary the state must itself originate capital projects'. He wanted especially to see an increase in social expenditure and greater participation by the government in providing housing and new schools. His third key point concerned banking. 'One of the most important determinants of economic development is the credit policy of the commercial banks. The government should have control of this policy. It has not. Accordingly it is suggested that, as in other countries, the Central Bank can control the commercial banks and the government can effectively control the Central Bank.'[65]

Costello saw his proposals as a starting point, not the last word. What he wanted from the front bench was a clear indication as to whether or not they were satisfied with present policy, whether they agreed with Costello's proposals, or whether they would put forward their own suggestions. He concluded by putting his propositions directly to the front bench. The debate did not move on to the parliamentary party and no word of it leaked out, but if Costello was looking for a decision he was once more to be frustrated. The front bench had two discussions on the matter and discussed it again on 15 May at their pre-Árd Fheis meeting, when Dillon, as was his wont, sought to reconcile the differing views. He gave the meeting an excerpt from his Árd-Fheis speech dealing with these matters, which he felt summed up the consensus. Costello, however, was emphatic that his proposals did not go far enough; Sweetman thought they went too far.[66]

Dillon's Árd Fheis speech concentrated on his sensible and increasingly popular proposals for removing the compulsory element in the teaching of Irish. The remainder focused on well-worn Dillon themes, and had little to suggest any real awareness of the rapid changes happening socially and economically, much less offer a plan to deal with or lead these developments. There was no evident input from Costello, or any real reflection of his concerns.[67]

However, if Dillon was looking for confirmation that all was well with the party generally, he got it a week later when his candidate, Patrick Belton, had a comfortable victory in the Dublin North-East by-election caused by the death of his brother, Jack Belton. Fine Gael got over forty per cent of the first-preference vote as against thirty-three per cent for Fianna

Fáil and eighteen per cent for Labour, and the result undoubtedly strengthened Dillon's hand within the party.[68] The by-election was followed by a
period of intense political work as Dillon sought to build on this success by
undermining Fianna Fáil in the Dáil. This turn of events rattled Lemass in
a way he had not been up to now, and he replied with a strong and petulant
attack on the opposition for being so 'irresponsible' as to try to defeat his
government and 'throw the country into chaos'.

Lemass had reason to be worried, for by now the turnover tax issue had
exploded into a damaging controversy, and on 25 June – the eve of President
Kennedy's visit to Dublin – his government survived on that section of the
Finance Bill by only one vote. Realising that the tax was an issue on which
the government was perhaps even fatally vulnerable, depending as it did on
the support of Independents who would have to bear the brunt of public
anger on the issue, as soon as the Kennedy visit was over (a visit that confirmed Dillon in all his admiration for things American, and in truth he,
no less than Lemass, had been bowled over by the US President's charm
and energy), Dillon relaunched his assault. But while traders and house-
wives may have engaged in sporadic protests, anyone expecting a Poujadist
reaction was to be disappointed:[69] the government won a further division
on 11 July, again by just one vote, during the committee stage of the
Finance Bill. Fianna Fáil looked increasingly jittery over the next weeks as
one Fine Gael speaker after another hammered at the Independents,
Sherwin and Leneghan, knowing that without their support Lemass could
not survive. The debates were vigorous, personal and at times nasty.
Leneghan made an unsubstantiated allegation that he had been offered a
£5,000 bribe by Fine Gael to vote against the government, and Sherwin
added another, presumably unsubstantiated allegation, that 'one of the
frontbenchers in Fine Gael is living like Profumo'.[70]

With government nerves frayed and a realistic chance of victory in the
offing, Dillon and Sweetman were at their parliamentary best. Sweetman
in particular, revelling in the clash of parliamentary exchanges and using all
his tactical guile, had the government under severe pressure. However, it
was to be their last real chance, and the government was let off the ropes by
the arrival of the summer recess in late July, and of course by the sustained
fidelity of Lemass's two Independent supporters.

What followed next was in some ways extraordinary. The summer recess
seemed to signal an end to political activity as far as most people in Fine
Gael were concerned: the front bench met only once during the summer
and the parliamentary party not at all. No attempt was made to sustain the
momentum which over the previous weeks had nearly put paid to a
nervous government. For the next ten weeks the newspapers were devoid of
news about Fine Gael, while Lemass made his celebrated Tralee speech,

effectively recognising the reality of partition, took a tough line with Post Office strikers, set up the National Industrial and Economic Council with the high-profile Frederick Boland as chairman, published the *Second Programme for Economic Expansion*, and followed all this in early October with a highly successful visit to the USA, where he was warmly welcomed by Kennedy and received extensive press and television coverage.[71]

The first sign of Fine Gael activity came in October, when the party announced it would oppose the new pig levy,[72] and later that month, after the death of a Fianna Fáil TD for Cork, John Galvin, let it be known it would press for an early by-election. Once again the party chose the turnover tax as the issue on which it would do battle, and put down a Dáil motion calling for its suspension.[73]

Faced with the prospect of a defeat which would precipitate an election, Lemass launched a spirited counter-attack. The omens should have been favourable for Fine Gael, especially with the farmers in a disgruntled mood and beginning a series of protests,[74] but curiously it was Labour which turned up the heat. Even though the turnover tax was by now law, Labour put down a motion of 'no confidence' in the government, with the tax occupying centre place in its attack. Then, anticipating the possibility of a tied vote, Labour quite improperly wrote to the Ceann Comhairle, Labour TD Patrick Hogan, instructing him as a party member to vote against the government in the event of a tie.[75] It was an unprecedented move, indicative more than anything else of the fact that Labour had been sidelined in the debate up to now and was trying desperately to take the initiative. It was also an unrealistic strategy, since in the event of a government defeat Labour was not going to participate in the formation of a new government anyway. Fine Gael sat back at this stage and let Labour inflict what damage it might.

In the event, there was none. Sherwin and Leneghan were committed to Fianna Fáil and would remain so. Neither wanted an election and the barrage of taunts they had endured was unlikely to commend the opposition to them. Joe Sheridan, another Independent, professed himself happy with the new government grants for heifers and farm buildings[76] and had developed a warm personal relationship with Lemass, while a fourth Independent simply voted for the government and kept his own counsel. The government had a majority of four, and as the tension evaporated it was clear the overall situation had changed. Lemass had scared the Independents, his predictions of instability and a series of indecisive elections had unnerved them, while Dillon's speeches offered neither inducement nor menace. This was Lemass the street-fighter, the gut politician. It was bare-knuckle stuff, and neither Dillon nor Labour were any real match. From this point on the spectre of an early election vanished.

For the moment it was Labour which took the fight to Lemass, and though the party had no greater success, it appeared to be gaining in strength. In November Sean Dunne rejoined the party and two weeks later Noel Browne and Jack McQuillan applied for and were accepted as members. Despite tensions over Browne's acceptance – Corish, among others, was opposed to the move – Labour seemed to be in a healthy mood, though it suffered a loss that winter with the death of its former leader, William Norton.[77]

Norton's death meant two by-elections were now pending, and could not be delayed long into 1964. Given the government's minority status, they assumed enormous importance, becoming effectively a judgement on whether Fianna Fáil should continue in office or not. Three factors would prove decisive in the by-elections. Against the odds, or at least in the face of conventional wisdom, Lemass had opened the way for a national wage agreement in November. The political commentators gave him little chance of success,[78] but by January 1964 Lemass had delivered, and delivered not just an agreement but an unprecedentedly high deal of twelve per cent – or in the case of lower-paid workers a rise of £1 a week.[79] The second factor in the by-election was the revitalised Fianna Fáil electoral machine. The organisation had swept all before it in the 1930s; by the late '40s it was complacent, tired and aging, and the '50s were little different, but now under the control of Neil Blaney, Kevin Boland, Charles Haughey and Brian Lenihan it was professional, innovative, ruthless, arrogant and utterly effective in its ability to mobilise and deliver votes. It was run with military precision, and when it hit the constituencies of Cork and Kildare it was to make not just a major impact, but to create a psychological sense of electoral invincibility which demoralised its opponents.

The third factor, of course, was the perception of Fine Gael, and of Dillon in particular. The tide had turned. Dillon had failed to overcome Fianna Fáil in spite of the sustained pressure of the previous months. He could argue that if Sherwin and Leneghan were stuck, limpet-like, to the government there was little he could do about it, and in this he was right, but the criticism ran much deeper. Lemass, while holding much of the conservative ground, had laid claim to sections of the centre and the left. On the big issue of joining the European Community, Dillon had no option but to follow the national interest, which he did willingly; on domestic issues, however, he was offering nothing that was new. One influential journalist, John Healy, an admirer of Lemass but nonetheless a sharp and at times mordant observer, summed it up in late 1963 by saying that the great difference between Fianna Fáil and Fine Gael was one of 'Amateurs and Professionals'. Many in Fine Gael were 'successful in their own walks of life, to whom politics seems to be an interesting sideline'. This was in marked contrast to Fianna Fáil, 'where, for almost all, politics is a professional career'. There was, he wrote, 'no evidence of a lust for power or passion for government burning in the collective bellies of Mr Dillon's party'.[80]

It was a fair observation. Fianna Fáil did have the collective resources of the civil service behind it, but in Lemass and some of his younger ministers it also had a team determined on change and modernisation and it had taken care to revitalise its organisation and electoral machine. Fine Gael, by contrast, spent much of 1963 agonising over whether or not to appoint a full-time public relations officer (which it did not). No sustained attempt had been made to address the organisation's weaknesses and the parliamentary party continued to be fitful in its attention to Dáil duties. This was the burden Dillon carried; at the same time, these were the difficulties he as leader had not adequately addressed, in part because he did not see them as problems, in part because he was too soft a taskmaster. He, however, was more and more being blamed for the party's ills.

The Cork and Kildare by-elections accentuated the differences between Fianna Fáil and all other parties, Fine Gael in particular. The government's trump card was produced early. Whatever the reservations of economists and employers, the national wage agreement captured the public imagination sufficiently to make a political difference. Fine Gael's attempt to produce detailed policies fell at the first hurdle, largely because the party refused or was unable to cost them, and as a result spent most of the election defending their proposals from Fianna Fáil's robust and at times contemptuous criticism. 'Anybody can draw up elaborate schemes,' Lemass taunted, 'but what about the costing, the specific revenue proposals?'[81] Dillon was forced to fall back on generalisations about buoyancy, increased revenue and unspecified savings, but whatever advantage his proposals might have had was immediately lost. His best card, his promise to abolish the two-and-a-half per cent turnover tax, while identifying no alternative source of revenue, held little credibility against the twelve per cent pay rise already finding its way into workers' pockets. To make matters even worse, the Fine Gael effort in the constituencies looked feeble compared to Fianna Fáil's electoral juggernaut.

In strict terms, the result did offer some consolation to Fine Gael: the party held its vote in Cork and was down only slightly in Kildare. But Fianna Fáil won both seats and won them decisively. Its vote was a massive fifty-three per cent in Cork – up seven per cent – and the win in Kildare brought an extra seat and guaranteed Lemass's position in the Dáil.[82]

The price of victory for the economy may have been high, but it was a resounding victory at a psychologically important time. Subsequently, the national wage agreement disturbed a whole series of wage differentials and this, combined with the cumulative effects of tariff reductions made in 1963 and 1964, accentuated the erosion in the competitiveness of Irish goods and led to an increasing balance of payments problem. Lemass's gamble had worked, but the price would be heavy. Fine Gael, however, got little public thanks for pointing that out.

It was a black moment for Dillon. On this occasion the party's disappointment ran deeper than before. Fine Gael had promised much during 1963, when its leaders had been assuring members of the imminent demise of 'this unstable government'. The by-election defeats did what years of prodding from Declan Costello and others had failed to do – brought Fine Gael face to face with the enormity of the problems facing it if it wanted to be seen as a serious contender for government. Suddenly the party was in crisis, and Dillon found himself facing questions over his leadership.

Press reaction was harsh and singled Dillon out for criticism. *The Irish Times* political correspondent thought his personality, was 'a negative factor for Fine Gael', especially when contrasted with the 'confident, relaxed, decisive Lemass'. The paper's editorial likened Fine Gael to the old Irish Party: 'fade away it will for lack of cohesion and drive if something radical is not done soon'.[83] The by now fashionable charge of Fianna Fáil professionals showing a clean pair of heels to Fine Gael's amateurs was much in evidence. Not all the blame fell on Dillon. John Healy wrote about the search being on for a scapegoat: 'I will remind them that Mr Dillon is the soul of integrity, the essence of kindness and a parliamentarian without equal. Two of these virtues – his integrity and his kindness – are the besetting sins which, in part, may one day be written into political history as the factors which led to the decline and fall of the Fine Gael party.'[84]

Healy pointed out that Dillon was dependent on support which, in the main, was not forthcoming. 'He could have been unkind by raising the whip across their flanks ... he did not ... believing his loyal attendance would inspire his men. It did not.' Healy's advice to Dillon was blunt. He must be abrupt and harsh. He needed new blood. 'The young Turks who have been made unwelcome by a section of the front bench' must be given their head.[85]

CHAPTER TWENTY-ONE

THE JUST SOCIETY

'Young men dreaming dreams and seeing visions.'
Dillon, Fine Gael Árd Fheis 1964

T HOUGH FINE GAEL was badly shaken by the by-election results in Cork and Kildare, talk of Dillon's leadership being under threat was premature. There were murmurings and a great deal of unhappiness and some of this was repeated in the press, but the reality was that there was no move against Dillon and no rival seeking to unseat him. Nevertheless, there was deep unease and the issues were vented in full at a meeting of the parliamentary party on 26 February 1964. Perhaps because he felt secure, or because he felt the issue had to be brought into the open, Dillon began the meeting by putting his leadership at the top of the agenda. He defended his record but made it clear that he was willing to go should the party so desire. No such demand was evident: in fact his intervention was met with a standing ovation. For the moment, at least, there was no further talk of the leadership, and from that point on most of the meeting's criticism was aimed at the front bench and its poor Dáil performance; there were also calls for reorganisation and a drive to encourage new members.

There was general agreement on these issues, but the differences on the fundamental direction of the party were at last leading the debate. The two opposing views were put to the meeting by Dillon and Costello. Dillon's position was that there was nothing wrong that could not be put right within the existing framework. There was no crisis. The election had been lost because of the national wage round; the party had lost no seat; its finances were sound. Fine Gael was still the only alternative to the present government. He was critical of the poor support and lack of performance in the House and admitted that their targets needed to be more focused, but that, essentially, was that. There was no need to panic or to rush into radical change simply for the sake of change.

Declan Costello put the alternative view. Two very different constituencies had expressed increased support for the government: why had Fine

Gael got it so wrong? He repeated his argument that Fine Gael had no credible alternative to the government's economic programme and had failed to persuade people that it could provide an alternative administration. Fine Gael had to admit it could not win an overall majority: the corollary of this was that the party must accept the consequences of proportional representation and effectively work for an alliance with Labour. And this – he brought the thesis full circle – could only be done if the party had new and radical policies.

Most of those who spoke supported Costello, but what was significant was the number who did not speak. It seemed that a majority of those on the right did not respond, while those in the centre stayed their hands. Matters, however, could not stay as they were, and at the end of the meeting Dillon agreed to come back with proposals for organisational and policy reform.[1]

In fact, the core of Costello's strategy had been expressed by Garret FitzGerald an article in *The Irish Times* on the day of the party meeting. FitzGerald was blunt: 'Fine Gael does not understand what is meant by the formulation of economic, social and cultural policies under modern conditions.' The party was not making use of study and research groups, did not realise the electorate expected professionalism from its politicians, and Fine Gael's policies in the by-election consisted of 'a large number of unintegrated and in some cases superficial proposals, many worthwhile, but none (excluding health) showing signs of research or serious thought'. FitzGerald, ever helpful, concluded with a whole range of areas needing reform to which the party could turn its mind.[2]

Dillon brought his proposals for re-organisation to the following week's parliamentary party meeting. He proposed setting up two committees, one to deal with organisation and propaganda which would be chaired by Sweetman, and a committee on policy under Cosgrave.[3] Sweetman and Cosgrave were regarded as being on the conservative wing of the party. Both were hardworking, Sweetman renowned for his energy and organisational ruthlessness and Cosgrave astute and widely trusted, but there was little to indicate any new departure along the lines proposed by Costello coming from the new committees, and Costello himself was not on either. In short, the *malaise* was likely to remain. Such was the media consensus, and it was an accurate reflection of the reality.

At this stage Fianna Fáil, in the person of Frank Aiken, presented Fine Gael with what one journalist called 'a lifeboat to keep it afloat'[4] – a booklet called *Facts About Ireland* published by the Department of External Affairs. Fifty-six thousand copies were distributed, and for the most part the booklet contained much useful information about the country. There was a problem, however, with the historical section. Quite simply, it set out to misrepresent the circumstances surrounding the foundation of the state and effectively rewrite the history of that period. No mention was made of Griffith or Collins and there was no reference to WT Cosgrave or his governments of 1922-32. The founding of Fianna Fáil was put forward as a key event in history; there was no reference to the founding of the national parliament. The Civil War was 'lost by those who wished to maintain the Republic', while the foundation of the state itself was not covered. The only politician who appeared in the booklet was Eamon de Valera.[5]

The government was castigated for what was seen as 'petty' and 'shabby' behaviour. There was honest outrage in Fine Gael, all the more so when the publication coincided with another episode, almost certainly innocent in character, but badly handled by the government. This was the removal of the portraits of Griffith, Collins and O'Higgins from Leinster House, ostensibly for cleaning, but also it was said to allow the Committee on Procedure and Privileges to hang other portraits. The coincidence of these two events persuaded many in Fine Gael – and some outside the party – that something sinister was afoot, and the matter was not helped by Lemass's strangely defensive and hostile attitude to Dáil questions on the issue. Lemass was always a team player and defending his own side came naturally to him, but his stance contrasted strongly with the reasonable, almost statesmanlike approach later adopted by Donogh O'Malley, the minister responsible for the removal of the portraits.

In spite of Lemass's best efforts to prevent it, and his unworthy assertion that Dillon was seeking to revive the controversies of the Civil War, the debate on the publication of *Some Facts About Ireland* was uncomfortable for the government.[6] Dillon charged the government with a futile effort to pervert the truth and falsify history – 'a piece of unseemly Fianna Fáil propaganda' – and asked that the whole chapter be left to the detached study of future historians.[7] A number of speakers sought to revive memories of the Civil War, but the debate was marked by a sense of tolerance and understanding. In a low-key speech, Liam Cosgrave paid tribute to the generosity of Donogh O'Malley, who had broken with Fianna Fáil convention and paid eloquent tribute to both Collins and Griffith.[8]

The whole episode was, in Declan Costello's words, 'shabby', but the truth of how it had happened was perhaps pointed up by McQuillan: 'I believe that this booklet is a product of an element in the Fianna Fáil party led by Frank Aiken. I am satisfied that the Taoiseach is gnashing his teeth at being walked into the embarrassing situation which has arisen from this publication.'[9]

The *Facts About Ireland* controversy gave Dillon a temporary respite from his internal difficulties, as the party's Dáil performance improved dramatically in the following weeks and the new committees got down to their business. This time, however, Declan Costello decided to play the game by his rules, and in late April he side-stepped both the policy committee and the front bench and circulated all the members of the parliamentary party with a set of principles which he felt should underlie the work of the committee in the formulation of policy. Costello was blunt about his reasons for going over the heads of the front bench: 'I am sure that you are already aware that I have held the views expressed in this motion for some considerable time. Equally I am sure you know they are not shared by the majority of my colleagues in the front bench. I would very much welcome a decision as to whether or not they are acceptable to the party and if necessary I will ask that a formal vote be taken.'10 Costello asked his colleagues to treat the matter as confidential and to refrain from leaks to the press, which, astonishingly as it may seem, they did.

Dillon's immediate reaction was to refer the Costello document to the policy committee and he proposed this measure to a meeting of the parliamentary party on 29 April, but Costello was not going to be so easily disposed of, and now he appealed directly to the parliamentary party. He wanted Deputies to have full and direct knowledge of what he proposed so that the party could decide whether his views were 'right or wrong', and on that basis direct the front bench to draw up a statement of party policy.11

Costello's bold appeal to the backbenchers caught Dillon and his supporters by surprise. Dillon assured the meeting somewhat lamely that Costello's earlier views had not gone unrecognised – two of the major points in his own Árd Fheis speech had been based on them. He did not add, though he could have, that these two proposals dealt with external affairs, Costello's front-bench brief, and not with economic matters. Sweetman, however, was less equivocal. He rejected Costello's proposals outright – 'the country needs alternative governments rather than alternative policies' – and called for incentives rather than the type of controls which Costello proposed. Maurice Dockrell was even more categorical in his opposition, while an attempt by Sean MacEoin to add Costello to the policy committee was rejected by Costello himself, who was determined to retain his initiative. At this stage, however, McGilligan intervened in favour of Costello. It was the most important support he had yet received.12

When McGilligan indicated he wished to make a lengthy contribution, the meeting adjourned for a week, during which time not a single line appeared in public. The debate up to now had been entirely behind closed doors and, extraordinarily, this secrecy was maintained for another two weeks. When the discussion resumed on 5 May, McGilligan threw his weight firmly behind Costello. This was so was not surprising. McGilligan had always had a radical streak, was widely read on economics, had a strong social commitment, and was temperamentally and indeed personally antagonistic to Sweetman's conservatism. Indeed, though it was not widely known at the time, his thinking had been one of the factors influencing Costello in the first place.

McGilligan's support for Costello's views was total. He argued that one of the primary objectives of the party should be to secure full employment and to raise living standards. He asked what Fine Gael would have done had they taken over government after the last election, and in answer said he did not believe the party's stated policy would achieve the necessary volume of employment to reach their targets. He advocated social investment in addition to normal capital investment, and price control in certain areas to alleviate hardship and prevent exploitation. He argued that control of the credit policies of the commercial banks should be examined; he did not necessarily want nationalisation, but he regarded the banks as obstructive to economic development (a view he had held since his attempts to finance the Shannon Scheme in the 1920s) and he wanted change. He said it was inevitable that there would be more government interference in the private sector and he urged the establishment of a new Ministry of Economic Planning 'to combat the non-forward policies of the Department of Finance'.[13]

McGilligan's passionate and eloquent intervention proved to be crucial. Dillon quickly grasped the significance of what had happened: the balance of power within the parliamentary party was changing. Though he disagreed with McGilligan on some points, he described his contribution as being 'of priceless value'. Costello now had the initiative and he pushed home his advantage, telling his colleagues that they must face the facts and avoid any spurious compromises between Sweetman's views and his.[14]

Costello wanted a decision, but it was not to be made that evening, for just after Costello spoke the Dáil division bells rang and the discussion was postponed until the next scheduled meeting of the parliamentary party a week later.[15] It seems extraordinary that the urgency of the issue did not dictate an early resumption of the debate, but apparently that was the way things happened in the Fine Gael parliamentary party at that time. Or it may have been that the delay was welcome to those who opposed Costello and wished to buy time. And, as things transpired, the discussion did not resume a week later, because that meeting was cancelled due to the death of a party colleague, the TD for Roscommon, James Burke.[16]

In the meantime, however, the 'Costello Plan', as it was now being called, continued to divide the party as nothing had before. Costello's message was that Fine Gael had to modernise or die, though his supporters also argued that Fine Gael was uniquely well placed to become the party of modernisation – not least because of its current agnosticism on so many of the issues central to organising a rapidly industrialising and expanding economy.

Garret FitzGerald, who supported Costello's initiative, pointed out that:

> Fianna Fáil is inhibited from rethinking its basic ideas by a number of factors
> – the continuing strength of its out-of-date nationalism which the present
> Taoiseach has only partly submerged; the character of a political organisation
> built on the grassroots local cumann, which provides an assurance of a good
> turnout on election day but which inhibits both the nomination of first-class
> candidates and the rethinking of basic policies, and finally the fact that it is at
> present the government party and for twenty-six of the past thirty-two years
> has been ensconced on the government benches with the advice of the Civil
> Service and no encouragement to think for itself.[17]

That was one view. The rival view of Fine Gael's role in Irish politics was
given its most lucid expression in a letter written to Dillon by Senator EA
McGuire. McGuire, a patrician figure, owner of Dublin's major store,
Brown Thomas, a bank director and influential businessman, had long
been a powerful, largely behind-the-scenes figure in Fine Gael, widely liked
and much respected and an important figure in the party's modest
fundraising activities. He was conservative, deeply so, and Costello's plans
were totally unacceptable to him: 'they are pure socialism of the most
dictatorial kind, under which all planning and power would lie in the
hands of the state, which is presumed to be all-wise and all-knowing'. The
Costello Plan was impractical and undesirable: 'The Irish Labour Party
already advocates these proposals as its policy and Fine Gael ought to have
no truck with the ill-digested ideas which they contain.' He accused
Costello of seeking to 'adopt policies rather for their popularity-gaining
value than because we believe in them'. His letter continued:

> I have been associated for over forty years with the Fine Gael party, which I
> look to as the party of freedom. Initially, it stood against the dictatorial and
> undemocratic attitudes of de Valera and Fianna Fáil, and it has continued to
> stand for freedom for the farmers, individual freedom and the right of owner-
> ship of property and private enterprise, generally. It stood for the duty of the
> state to provide the infrastructure for the economy and for agricultural and
> industrial prosperity. It stood for the establishment and operation of state
> enterprise where and when necessary. It stands today for the progressive devel-
> opment of that policy, but in conformity with modern conditions.
>   I reject the idea that social and economic growth is only to be found in
> socialist planning by the alleged all-powerful and all-knowing state, which is
> really to say that a few politicians and a large number of Civil Servants are
> competent to achieve the perfect society.
>   It is not correct to say that there is no difference between Fine Gael and
> Fianna Fáil policy, and even if it is thought by Declan Costello that there is
> none, it is no solution for us to adopt the Labour Party's policy, as he suggests

we should do. Merely because enough people will not support our policy is no reason that we should change our philosophy of freedom merely to gain power, unless the winning of power is the sole purpose of our being in parliament. As a matter of fact, if we radically change our philosophy, we will, I think, destroy our party. We have as supporters people of all classes, including very large numbers of what are known as 'the working class' who do not vote Labour and will not vote Labour even when we call a Labour socialist policy Fine Gael policy.

As the President has already shown, all the powers that will be necessary to plan and guide the growth of the economy already exist in our policy without resorting to a freedom-killing system in every phase of our national life.

McGuire continued with a lengthy defence of the role of the banks: 'even on Paddy McGilligan's showing, the Government have at present all the powers it requires over the banks'; an attack on the proposals for increased direct taxation: 'the ill-effects of such a policy would be felt in the industrial sphere where we now rely so heavily upon a tax incentive policy to attract new capital, both native and foreign'; and insisted that 'artificial price control is impossible unless we adopt a full totalitarian communist system ... there is no future to price control except in the minds of inexperienced and impractical persons'.

McGuire concluded with this:

It seems to me the question for consideration by the party is this. Is this party to enunciate a policy of state control over every facet of our national life that will outdo Fianna Fáil and even Labour? There is nothing proposed by Declan that is not already being proposed by the Labour Party. There is in this proposal a confusion of thought which thinks that it is only in the all-powerful, omniscient state with anonymous officials in control of everything, that progress is to be found. Such a line, in my opinion, will gain us few new supporters and lose to Fianna Fáil the large bulk of those who have supported us over the years.

It would have been much simpler and more honest to merely say that we should adopt Labour Party policy and eliminate the Fine Gael party, as has been advocated by *The Irish Times*.[18]

Costello now had the debate he wanted, but at this time, however, Dillon, reacted rather than led. Intellectually, the Costello ideas did not engage him. He was distrustful of state intervention in economic matters and sceptical of economic planning. He still looked to agriculture and was ill at ease with an industrialising society. On top of that, he was closer personally to Sweetman than to Costello. Yet he had always argued for increased social investment, whether it be in education, health or housing; he shared McGilligan's distrust of the banks, and he was conscious that he lived in a time of rapid and dramatic change. He tried to explain this to a Fine Gael man, Denis Burke, a leading Tipperary businessman and long-time party supporter, who wrote to Dillon complaining about Costello's memorandum, which, he said, was causing 'undoubted unease' in the country. Dillon's reply was philosophical. He hoped that

> we can reconcile all our views in a sensible manner to all our supporters and at the same time demonstrate that, like Pope John, we are prepared to adjust ourselves to a changing world. The plain truth is that the impact of Pope John and President Kennedy on the rising generation has been very great, and it is a good thing to make it manifest that none of us is indifferent to the things that these two remarkable men have done, and asked all of us to do, and I know that you will agree that so long as we keep in step with their thoughts we won't go far wrong.[19]

The nub of Dillon's problem was that as party leader he was leading a divided party, the unity of which it was his responsibility to maintain. He knew, too, that to adopt a new line would mean difficult personal choices: if the Costello Plan were accepted, the job of selling it would fall to Sweetman, the party's financial spokesman, and as John Healy noted in *The Irish Times*, Sweetman would not be credible in the role. Given what Healy characterised as Sweetman's 'vote-repelling image', he urged Dillon to drop him. Because Sweetman had been loyal to Dillon, however, Healy doubted that he would have the stomach to do so.[20] He was right.

The parliamentary party had not yet reconvened by the time of the party's Árd Fheis on 19 May. By now the issues were out in the open and the subject of intense media speculation, and the Árd Fheis delegates had a right to expect leadership or at the least guidance from Dillon. They were disappointed. Dillon could have ignored the matter and told the Árd Fheis he did not wish to pre-empt the parliamentary party's deliberations, or he could have addressed the issues directly, but he did neither. He made no direct reference to the policy controversy but instead went out of his way to praise Sweetman, and went on to speak with patronising eloquence of 'young men dreaming dreams and seeing visions' and disparaging all who sought 'political short-cuts'.[21]

Dillon may have been reacting instinctively in defence of a close and hard-working colleague, now being cast as a reactionary, or perhaps he was seeking to slow down or derail the Costello initiative, but one way or another he came across as hostile to the move for change. Moreover, if party unity was his main concern, he had done little for that cause; in fact, he had angered many of the younger members and not shown particularly good political judgement. And he had left a leadership vacuum, which was immediately filled by Liam Cosgrave, who argued that negative criticism of Fianna Fáil was not enough and that Fine Gael must move to the left of centre, albeit without embracing doctrinaire socialism.[22] Cosgrave's intervention seemed to catch the mood of the Árd Fheis, a point not lost when the parliamentary party finally got down to discussions the next day, 20 May. The fact that both Cosgrave and McGilligan were seen to be backing the Costello proposals was now having a real influence on some of the hitherto reluctant senior members and backbenchers.

A week of frenetic activity was to follow before matters were finally resolved, but the battle was effectively won at this post-Árd Fheis meeting. Once again the key speakers were McGilligan, passionate and intellectually dominant, and Cosgrave, who asked that the Costello proposals be put to the policy committee for immediate attention. TF O'Higgins gave his complete support to Costello, and Mark Clinton was equally enthusiastic. Some, inevitably, still had reservations, but Costello, sensing victory, was happy to have his proposals referred to the policy committee on the understanding that it would broaden its membership and complete its work over the coming weekend.[23] When the committee met again, Dillon himself became directly involved in the drafting process, as did Declan Costello, Sweetman, Cosgrave, Michael O'Higgins and Michael Hayes. The drafting was done first in Leinster House, and when the House closed the group moved to Power's Hotel, where much of the weekend was spent setting out the principles which would underlie party policy.[24]

There is evidence to suggest that those opposed to change made one final attempt to reverse the process, but it was clear now that Costello was in the ascendant and that Dillon had left himself in the minority position on the most crucial issue of his leadership. In particular, he had misjudged not just the mood of the Árd Fheis, but the mood within his own parliamentary party. John Healy reckoned that if the matter had been put to a vote Costello would have won by thirty-five votes to twenty-five, and when Dillon realised this he became resigned to the inevitable. Healy concluded: 'James Dillon must seriously question the accuracy of the advice of those surrounding his throne. They left him curiously exposed in this crisis.'[25]

When the parliamentary party reconvened on 26 May the battle was over. The party leadership accepted the Costello principles with little change of substance. The first six points were virtually identical to Costello's original memo: economic planning in both public and private sectors; a Ministry of Economic Affairs; greater control of the commercial banks, especially on the question of credit policies to the Central Bank; increased government investment in industrial development; greater social capital investment; a change in taxation policies, though without endorsing a higher level of direct taxation; an element of price control. A final point,

on the development of agriculture and rural areas, was seen by some as a
sop to Dillon.

Dillon, in fact, moved the resolution at the parliamentary party meeting,
which, in addition, enjoined the policy committee 'to give absolute priority
to the preparation of the detailed policy document to be prepared in accordance with the foregoing principles', and in the discussion which followed
he was uncharacteristically impatient. When some members sought to re-
open the debate, especially Sweetman, who made it clear that his
interpretation of the principles might not always coincide with Costello's
and that in effect the practical detail had yet to be worked out, Dillon was
having none of it. The debate, he said, could not be allowed to go on inter-
minably, and he brought the proceedings to a close.[26] To a close, as it
turned out, but not to a conclusion.

Dillon put a brave face on the outcome, claiming that the programme
was close in many ways to the policies he had outlined at the last two Árd
Fheisanna – if de Valera could claim the Whitaker proposals as his own,
Dillon could do likewise with Costello. The task of translating the Costello
principles into detailed schemes still lay ahead, and from the attitude of
Sweetman and some others in the parliamentary party, it was apparent that
this was not going to be easy.

It is difficult to know how Dillon felt. He had been defeated on the decisive issue of party policy, but he had maintained the unity of Fine Gael. He
had gone against his own instincts, pragmatically recognising the
supremacy of numbers. He was aware of the momentum of change and at
a late stage had asserted control over the debate – not in substance, but in
guiding it to a conclusion. In a letter to McGuire shortly afterwards, he
sought to present the outcome in the most benign way possible: 'as a result
of careful consideration and discussion, the original document submitted
by Declan Costello was withdrawn and an entirely new resolution was submitted, from which the objectionable proposals were eliminated. I think
this was a good result, and bearing in mind our three hundred and seventy-
five thousand supporters, I rejoice that they have not been deprived of the
united leadership which they are entitled to expect from us.'[27]

Yet no matter how Dillon might represent it, Costello had won his victory,
and in the process had created an opening for Fine Gael. Garret FitzGerald
summed it up thus:

> the mere fact that singlehanded and without much preparation Declan
> Costello has been able to win substantial support for his radical ideas within
> Fine Gael is a clear demonstration of the extent to which this party is open to
> a transformation of this kind and proof enough that its policy vacuum pro-
> vides a possible method of introducing new ideas into Irish politics today.

Costello's eight points are pragmatic rather than ideological in character, strongly influenced by their author's huge social conscience and deep concern about immediate ills, and they represent a symbol of revolt against complacency, rather than deeply thought ideology.[28]

That was probably as fair a summing up as was possible.

FOR THE moment the crisis was over. Dillon had emerged shaken but still in control. It had been an unconvincing performance, however, and as events were to show, those who opposed the basic thrust of the Costello proposals were not going to give up easily. Their chance came soon enough in the Roscommon by-election. Fine Gael had a good candidate in Joan Burke, the widow of the late Deputy James Burke, and the parliamentary party was united behind her. Sweetman, too, was determined to prove a point. The result was an uncharacteristically energetic Fine Gael campaign. Seasoned observers were taken by surprise at the ferocity of the party's assault on Roscommon. One wrote: 'of course there was a Fine Gael machine. The very phrase itself looks almost indecent but it is the only phrase I know to describe the Fine Gael effort which, in my long memory of political battlefields, I never saw before!'[29] The result was a massive increase in Fine Gael first-preference votes and a comfortable second-count victory for Joan Burke.

Roscommon was a welcome boost for Fine Gael, but it came with a price-tag. Exhausted by the strains of the previous months, Dillon was ordered by his doctors to rest, and spent much of July in hospital recuperating and undergoing tests. The truth of Roscommon was that it was won on the back of traditional loyalties, a sympathy vote, a good candidate and hard campaigning. The 'Costello Plan' was not a factor. As *The Irish Times* noted: 'Roscommon was the first real opportunity for Costello's ideas to be tested. That little or no attempt was made to test them means that either they were considered not to be applicable to a mainly rural constituency or that Mr Costello's plan is in cold storage. It is disturbing to accept the first and difficult to accept the latter. Whatever satisfaction Fine Gael may derive from the Roscommon victory, it is clear that the transition period for the party is not yet over.'[30]

This assessment was at least partly unfair: Roscommon was a deeply conservative constituency, its voters not those most likely to be influenced by Costello's ideas. Suspicions about a slow transition from policy principles to party practice were, however, all too accurate. The Roscommon result went a long way towards confirming the belief of Sweetman and others that proper organisation, professionalism and good candidates were more important than academic analysis and left-leaning doctrine when it came to winning elections.

Very little progress was made on developing the Costello principles during the summer of 1964. It may be that, after a hectic period culminating in the Roscommon victory, most TDs were tired, and unused to working during the summer recess. Or there may have been a deliberate delay. In any case, as the weeks went on it became clear that there was an element of dissatisfaction with Dillon's leadership growing in some quarters. In July, John Healy reported a whispering campaign against Dillon, 'nothing specific', he said, but it was there.[31] A month later Healy repeated the point and accused Dillon of living in an ivory tower: 'Your reputation as a gentleman shields you ... your charm disarms; the critical barbs never reach you. No one wishes to hurt a Dillon ... but in the quiet snuggeries of men, in the elegant chatter of cocktails and in the political salons, there are a variety of ways of saying the same truths. James is not leading.'[32]

Healy wrote what others preferred to leave unsaid, and his articles almost certainly reflected the reality that Dillon was personally remote from some of the younger members of his party, that his style was seen as out of tune with the times, and that he was unlikely to change. For the moment, however, the Roscommon victory had given Fine Gael a sense of buoyancy, and the intense political debate within the party declined as the policy committee promised and then failed to bring forward more detailed plans. Lemass, meanwhile, had turned the potentially embarrassing resignation of Paddy Smith on 8 October into a public relations triumph by appointing Haughey as Minister for Agriculture, and his government continued to operate vigorously, if not always sensitively, as when in October it finally sanctioned the Electricity Supply Board's demolition of its Georgian houses in Fitzwilliam St.[33]

Fine Gael's mood of well-being, which began with Roscommon, was confirmed when Sweetman persuaded the captain of Galway's All-Ireland winning football team, John Donnellan, to run on the party ticket in the by-election caused by the death of his father, Michael. Michael Donnellan had died during the 1964 All-Ireland final just as his son was leading the county to victory. Under normal circumstances, East Galway was one of the safest Fianna Fáil constituencies in the country, but by persuading Donnellan to run, Sweetman not alone brought some of the remnants of Clann na Talmhan into the party, but produced a candidate whose electoral appeal transcended all traditional allegiances. Sweetman was in his element as he directed the campaign, and again the party machine, augmented by hundreds of Donnellan's personal supporters, outperformed Fianna Fáil. It was a famous victory. Donnellan turned a deficit of 7,000 into a majority of almost 2,000, and following so soon after Roscommon, it led many Fine

Gael speakers to proclaim that the tide was now running in its favour.[34]

The reality, however, was different. East Galway had been won by the exceptional and emotional circumstances of John Donnellan's candidature and by a determined electoral performance. The party machine had worked well, but the conclusions Fine Gael took from the result were unwarranted. Even so, it strengthened the position of Sweetman and others, and newspapers were soon speculating that this group was holding back progress on the Costello Plan.[35]

1964 ended with yet another by-election following the death in December of the Labour TD for mid-Cork, Daniel Desmond. Even the advent of the mid-Cork by-election did not speed up progress on the new policy, which still remained unpublished. Critics were growing impatient. 'A political party must be judged by its ability to get things done' said *The Irish Times*, noting Fine Gael's failure to complete this task.[36] Thoroughly frustrated, Costello wrote a letter of complaint to Dillon on 6 February 1965. By now, he said, most of the detailed work involving economists and other experts had been completed, but the parliamentary party's decision on the final document had yet to be taken. Costello had good reason to be concerned. He felt that the memoranda from the policy committee would go directly to the front bench, which would then present its recommendations to the parliamentary party in the form of summaries. Strictly speaking, the front bench would have been within its rights in so doing, but Costello knew he did not have its full support and he feared his plans would be watered down or delayed even further. Dillon replied two days later, saying that there was 'no sinister design to have a protracted discussion on the policy papers at front bench', whose recommendations, he felt, would speed up the entire process.[37]

This reply seems to have angered Costello. He wrote to Dillon again on 13 February, pointing out that exhaustive discussions had already taken place and those with contrary views had not put forward alternative policies, in spite of having been given every opportunity to do so. 'Further front bench discussions will not just delay the whole process but will result in a further hardening of positions, without any alternative being offered.' Costello warned that he would feel free to express his dissatisfaction to the parliamentary party and concluded: 'please do not think I am insensitive to the difficulties you have as leader. Like you, I am vitally concerned for the interests of the party. I believe that if we can adopt a progressive new dynamic policy our prospects of electoral success are very great. If we stumble or compromise now I cannot see us beating Fianna Fáil at the next election.' Costello had also noted that 'the press have been extraordinarily patient in not criticising our dilatoriness: we cannot rely on this forbearance indefinitely'.[38]

Whatever about the press, the protracted delay was clearly irking some of Fine Gael's own supporters, and just a week later the first direct attack on Dillon came at a seminar organised by the group Dillon had taken to calling the 'Young Tigers' – the University College, Dublin, branch. The strongest attack came from a student of economics and politics, Vincent Browne, whose message to Dillon was blunt. 'Over the last number of years Fine Gael has failed to rise to the problems of modern democracy; the party has either failed to put before the people the fundamental issues of government in a comprehensive fashion or has distorted these issues and thereby misled the public.' He accused Dillon of failing to recognise the undoubted economic progress of recent years and of exaggerating the balance of payments crisis. Except in the area of health, Fine Gael, he said, had failed to put forward comprehensive policies. Browne in fact summed up the frustration felt by many of the younger members of the party when he accused Dillon of ignoring the changes that were taking place, and the plan which 'has inspired the hope that Fine Gael would offer the country progressive, intellectual and detailed policies on all aspects of government activity; above all the plan has given hope for a new and vital leadership which Fianna Fáil is incapable of providing.'[39] But Dillon, aware of these criticisms, chose to ignore them.

The mid-Cork by-election was a trap in waiting for Fine Gael. Lemass's image remained high, boosted especially by Northern premier Terence O'Neill's visit to Dublin in early February, so he was well placed to call a quick election. The likelihood that he would increased with the death of MJ Kennedy, Fianna Fáil TD for Longford–Westmeath, on 14 February. With a ready-made candidate in Senator Gerry L'Estrange, Fine Gael could reasonably be expected to win here, and as a result the mid-Cork by-election assumed even greater importance: if Fianna Fáil were to lose this contest, Lemass would have little incentive to wait around for another defeat in Longford–Westmeath. Characteristically, however, he gave little away, one day dismissing talk of an election, a few days later threatening one should Fianna Fáil lose in mid-Cork. With the focus now firmly on Cork, Fine Gael decided not to publish its new policies until after the by-election.[40] Those who believed that organisation and not policies were what really counted had won once again.

Fianna Fáil lost mid-Cork to Labour, with Fine Gael in third place, as many observers had predicted. Lemass wasted no time in calling an immediate general election for 7 April. Fine Gael's failure to produce its policy document and the obvious divisions in the party were undoubtedly factors in Lemass's decision, as was the likelihood of defeat in Longford–Westmeath and, more positively, the general sense of well-being in the country. 'You can't buck prosperity,' John Healy wrote. However, all was not as it seemed.[41] The economic prospects for 1966 looked uncertain and had given Lemass cause for concern; his biographer, John Horgan, has written that Fine Gael's contention that 'things were getting out of control, particularly in relation to the balance of payments, was more accurate than Lemass cared to admit'.[42] For the moment, however, these worries were kept from view, and with a general election in the offing, the spotlight focused instead on Fine Gael. The party had to make up its mind one way or another where it stood on future policy. In reality, there was no contest. The parliamentary party had already approved the Costello proposals, the policy committee had fleshed them out, and there was no alternative on offer. The question was why the delay, and whether the new policy would be stifled at birth.

Costello's supporters moved quickly to have the new policy published, and a week into the election campaign the *Just Society* programme was launched. There were difficulties right to the very end: one observer was not joking when he described the operation as 'a Caesarean delivery after a very difficult labour period which started on Friday, resumed on Saturday morning, and when the Dáil closed at midday the front bench moved to Power's Hotel where the birth took place'.[43] The pace all weekend had in fact been frenetic: the committee had had six different documents to assess before the composite *Just Society* could be approved.

The *Just Society* document was formally accepted by the parliamentary party on 18 March and published that day. It was an eloquent and well-written text, proposing the establishment of a Department of Economic Affairs, a free medical service, an incomes policy which would ensure continuous and orderly growth of incomes, control over the credit policies of the commercial banks, a domiciliary welfare service, better treatment for the mentally handicapped, higher expenditure on housing and social amenities, 'equality of opportunity to be the objective as far as access to education was concerned', and abolition of the old dispensary system and means test in health. There was more, but at last the policy had been produced, and for the most part it had been costed, with the estimates as professionally done as electoral costings ever are.[44]

The *Just Society* did catch the popular imagination, not least among younger voters unimpressed by the arrogance and insensitivity of some Fianna Fáil ministers, and undoubtedly it was a seminal document as far as the development of Fine Gael under Garret FitzGerald a decade later was concerned. Moreover, it put Fine Gael back centre stage in the 1965 election. The document had its defects, not least its late arrival, with the campaign already well under way. Much more damaging, however, were the doubts about the extent to which the party, and especially its leadership, was intellectually and emotionally committed to the new line.

The truth of the matter was that Declan Costello had effectively carried out a coup. The policy had not sprung organically from within the party but had been foisted on it. The policy vacuum, and the hunger of some of the younger members for a political purpose suited to the changing times, facilitated its acceptance, but sections of the party were indifferent or uncomprehending, and others were still hostile. The genuine adherents to the new policy were a minority. Most damaging of all, however, was the position of the leadership. Dillon accepted the new programme as the price he must pay to maintain party unity. He did so as a professional and in the belief that in a time of change Fine Gael must change also. But he had little sense of conviction or enthusiasm about it, and neither did he want old friends and supporters marginalised in the future. Thus on the day the *Just Society* policy was announced, he assured journalists that Fine Gael was and remained 'a party of private enterprise'.[45] He was right, and indeed the *Just Society* would not prevent it from so being, but his remark was taken as a clear signal that the document was a flag of convenience rather than the genuine espousal of new ideas.

Doubts about the degree to which Fine Gael really accepted the new document carried within the party and to the broader public. Garret FitzGerald, who had been thinking of seeking a nomination in Dublin South-East, now decided against it. His principal reason, he told Dillon, was 'the failure of the party to adopt a positive policy in relation to the social security system, which is crucial to social progress'. And, he added: 'the whole process of policy-making in the party in recent months has been quite extraordinarily dilatory and leisurely'. FitzGerald told Dillon that he would 'probably only be an embarrassment to the party in present conditions', and so would remain 'most reluctantly' on the sidelines for the moment.[46]

The Irish Times pointed out that 'a radical policy required a radical leader',[47] and even those commentators who saw much of value in the new proposals argued that the 'wrong' party was proposing them. Much of this criticism was predictable: *The Irish Times,* for example, had consistently supported Lemass and would continue to do so. In spite of press scepticism, the *Just Society* was making an impact where it counted most – with the electorate. Costello's personality, his idealistic and principled approach, was easy enough to contrast with the rugged pragmatism of Lemass and, more tellingly, with the ostentatious materialism of some of his ministers. Fine Gael's new programme was having an effect, to the extent that Lemass announced on 2 April that he was considering a social development programme, a tacit admission that economic growth also needed a social dimension, and that the Costello Plan was having considerable influence.[48]

Dillon willingly agreed to make use of the plentiful supply of young supporters during the campaign, many of whom had been drawn to the party by the Costello debate. The result was the most professional Fine Gael election campaign for decades, including the establishment of a full-time Press and Information Centre at Power's Hotel, and an aggressive style that had not been seen for years, though the campaign poster of a sombre-looking Dillon was unlikely to appeal much to younger voters. Dillon, as usual, did a nationwide tour, though neither he nor Lemass managed to generate any great excitement.

The Labour Party programme published on 23 March was similar in many respects to Fine Gael's, though Labour could claim to have held that particular ground for some time. The points of similarity between them contrasted with the policies offered by the government, and ensured that issues featured in the election debate to a much greater extent than previously. Social and economic issues were all very well, however, but there was one fundamental political fact which would prove decisive: the formation of a new government. Lemass knew this was both his only fear and his trump card, and on 24 March he threw down the gauntlet to Labour, saying that in the event of a hung Dáil Fianna Fáil would not enter coalition with them.[49] Nobody, least of all Labour, had made such a suggestion, but Lemass knew what he was doing and, as he hoped, Labour rose to the bait. Corish responded the following night at Tullamore by saying that Labour would not enter a coalition under any circumstance. Labour, in pursuit of independence, would not take part in government.[50] Since Fine Gael could not conceivably win an overall majority, Corish was effectively clearing the way for Fianna Fáil's return to power, and doing so in spite of Costello's best efforts to produce policies acceptable to the Labour Party.

Lemass's fear of a Fine Gael–Labour alliance had disappeared overnight. From that point on, Dillon's slim hopes of forming a government were dead. Lemass pushed home his advantage subsequently, but Corish's Tullamore speech was the decisive factor. It vindicated the points made earlier by Costello, O'Higgins and others, that the logic of proportional representation decreed that Fine Gael should have sought common ground with Labour to ensure that an alternative government might be put in place. Labour, however, in its then phase, was little interested in such discussion, and indeed much of its own policy development was still at a primitive stage. Even if the party's leaders had been willing to talk, they would have received little warmth from Sweetman and others.

It was in some respects a curious campaign. Media observers seemed to agree that Fine Gael and Labour had succeeded in stressing social justice issues in a way which had not happened previously; but Fianna Fáil had won the debate on the type of government which could be formed. In its eve of poll editorial, *The Irish Times* wrote that 'an inter-party government is not on the cards, and this reinforces the need to give Sean Lemass a firm mandate'.[51]

Lemass cruised through the election, though he still did not get his over-all majority. With seventy-two seats and three compliant Independents, his position was, however, secure. The Fine Gael popular vote was up two per cent to thirty-four per cent, but it won no new seats, staying at forty-seven; Fianna Fáil, for all its clear run, managed only two seats more than it had in 1961. The main winner was the Labour Party, which gained six seats to bring it to twenty-two, but among its casualties were both Noel Browne and Jack McQuillan, neither of whom were ever to be re-elected as Labour TDs. Dillon once more headed the poll in Monaghan.

Journalists had been predicting that Dillon's leadership would face chal-lenge in the event of his not forming a government, but there was no evidence of manoeuvrings in the immediate aftermath of the election and when the front bench met on 13 April it decided to propose Dillon as Taoiseach.[52] When the Dáil met to elect a Taoiseach on the 21st there was little sense of drama about the occasion. Lemass was nominated in an almost perfunctory manner by MacEntee and a backbencher; Dillon was nominated in similar fashion by Cosgrave and Lindsay. Only Labour, proposing Corish, felt the need to make speeches, and even these were short. Lemass was elected by seventy-two votes to sixty-seven and came back with a government of which only he and Aiken were survivors of the first Fianna Fáil administration in 1932. Lemass had his own government at last.

Dillon's contribution to the debate on the appointment of Taoiseach was uncharacteristically brief. He ended his speech: 'I do not know how long this government are likely to last; the shorter the better it will be for the country. But, in the meantime, I suppose we can all be unanimous in one sentiment: "God save Ireland".'[53]

Dillon convened a meeting of the front bench almost immediately after the vote. What he had to say took most – if not all – of those present by surprise. He was resigning the leadership with immediate effect. His reasons were straightforward: he was now sixty-two and would be sixty-seven by the time of the next election, and that, he felt, would be too old to lead Fine Gael into government. The party needed to be reorganised and, 'having discussed his own position with some of his close friends and advisers, he had decided irrevocably to retire from the leadership of the party, and he asked the front bench and the party to engage at once in the selection of a new leader, which should be done that night or the following morning. He thought the sooner a new leader was elected the better, and he hoped that the choice would be unanimous if at all possible.'[54]

A number of attempts were made to dissuade him, but he insisted that his decision was irrevocable. The party then moved with uncharacteristic haste, uninhibited by anything so awkward as standing orders, to elect its new leader. A meeting of the parliamentary party was summoned, at which Dillon formally announced his resignation and recommended that a new leader be appointed without delay. The meeting acceded to his wishes: Cosgrave was proposed by Sweetman, seconded by Michael O'Higgins, and elected unanimously.[55]

Dillon did preside over the parliamentary party one more time. When WT Cosgrave died six months later, Dillon took the chair to pay warm tribute to a man he greatly and genuinely admired.[56]

The speed of Dillon's resignation led to speculation about the circumstances surrounding the decision, but there was little real doubt that the reasons he gave were genuine. As he wrote in his *Memoir*: 'the whole of Europe was littered with old gentlemen who regarded themselves as indispensable ... and I didn't want to be another piece of flotsam and jetsam floating about'.[57] He had a hard edge of realism, knew he faced problems of discontent and party reorganisation, and possibly even a move against him. He had been in the political front-line continuously for thirty-three years, and he was no longer in tune with the popular mood. Every good reason told him it was time to go. In a telling aside, he had confided after a party rally in Limerick to his nephew John Dillon, who along with Patrick Nugent had accompanied him throughout the campaign: 'It's all very well to bore other people, but when you begin to bore yourself, it is probably time to quit.'[58] Having made his decision, he saw no reason to delay further.

One question which does arise is whether he moved quickly so as to affect the outcome of the succession; certainly he left no time for alternative candidates to emerge. His decision does not seem to have been designed to catch Costello unprepared and thus facilitate Cosgrave's election; there is no reason to believe Costello was interested in the leadership, or would have been temperamentally suited to it. He was a shy, private person with little liking for many of the necessary tediums and intrusions of political life – the glad-handling, the endless round of party functions, the sorting out of local squabbles, the inevitable personality clashes – all of which are part of the baggage of leadership. Cosgrave was the obvious choice. He was a full-time politician, had played a key part in bringing the *Just Society* into existence, and he was trusted by the more traditional sections of the party. He also had the support of key figures like Tom O'Higgins, who replaced Sweetman as party spokesman on Finance. Dillon's timing simply recognised the inevitability of Cosgrave's election and facilitated his orderly accession to the leadership.

Dillon's resignation from the leadership of Fine Gael passed without comment in the Dáil. There was no tribute from Lemass, nor any welcome for Cosgrave as the new leader of the opposition. In its public manifestations, at any rate, it was still an ungracious age, with neither side ready to show much by way of magnanimity to the other. Privately, however, things were different. Once the news of his going became public, hundreds of letters poured in from those who had supported him down the years and from many who had disagreed with him politically. Garret FitzGerald wrote in praise of his 'unselfishness in voluntarily deciding to retire ... few people in politics would have acted with such complete disregard for personal interest, and in this action, as throughout your political life, you have set an example of the highest standards of integrity and self-abnegation, which is an answer to all who say that politicians cannot be people of integrity.' Frank MacDermot wrote from Paris telling of his sadness, and there was a warm message in Irish from Cearbhall Ó Dálaigh. But the letter which must have pleased him most came from his old friend and lifelong political opponent, Todd Andrews, which concluded: 'I have always regarded you – as indeed I did your father – as a great and specially decent patriot.'[59]

After his resignation came the assessment of his career as leader. In factual terms, he assumed leadership of a party which had twenty-six per cent of the vote and forty seats in 1957. In 1961, his first election, Fine Gael got thirty-two per cent of the vote and forty-seven seats, and in 1965 its share was up to thirty-four per cent and forty-seven seats. In historical terms he had brought the party back from its 1957 low and stabilised its popular vote at its highest point since the 1930s. The years of continuous decline were well and truly over – even *The Irish Times* had stopped predicting the imminent demise of the party, without necessarily ceasing to hope for such. In many other ways, too, he left the party in much better condition than he inherited it. Fine Gael had shown real vigour in a series of by-elections and was better organised in 1965 than it had been in previous general elections. The party had also set the agenda for much of the political debate of the 1960s, and for the first time had begun to attract new and young members in significant numbers.

He had, of course, failed to make the breakthrough which would have brought the party into government, though this failure had as much to do with Labour's strategy as it had to do with Dillon's leadership. It was his lot to preside over the party during a particularly fractious period, when he was expected to lead changes with which he was not always in accord and to provide a coherence which was not always internally sustainable. He worked hard and led by example, even when that example was not followed by others. His leadership was solid, methodical and principled. It was not crowned with success, but it was far from being a failure. Had he had the options open to his successors, Liam Cosgrave, Garret FitzGerald and John

Bruton, of forming a coalition, then James Dillon would have been Taoiseach in 1965, rather than retiring to the back benches. Politics, however, is never an exact science; timing and luck are vital ingredients and cannot be prescribed. They come in their own time or not at all.

CHAPTER TWENTY-TWO

THE LATER YEARS

'Are you not a very foolish man to be opening your mouth and crossing swords with Deputy Dillon? In your short term in this House you should have learned that.'
Sean Dunne to a Fianna Fáil TD, Dáil Debates, February 1968

RESIGNING AS PARTY leader lifted the daily burden of leadership, but it did not mean the end of politics. Dillon remained in the Dáil until 1969, and showed every sign of enjoying his last four years on the back benches. He had the freedom to speak on any and every issue, and did so, though he was totally and unambiguously loyal to Liam Cosgrave, in private as well as in public. He had come to see WT Cosgrave – 'sniper' Cosgrave of his uncle Nicholas's day – as probably the greatest politician since Independence, and had taken an avuncular interest in Liam Cosgrave from his earliest days in the Dáil. It would never have occurred to him to upstage or give less than full support to any leader, but especially not to one for whom he had such a genuine fondness.

As a former leader he found himself cast as an elder statesman, a role that came easily to him. Not that there was any mellowing where his opponents were concerned: here it was business as usual, and if hard things had to be said, they were. His interventions on the 1965 budget drew Lemass's ire: 'The Deputy has been retired and should stay retired!'[1] Dillon spoke on every major issue, and not just on the broad sweep of second-stage debate but contributing to the detailed analysis of committee stage, the testing ground of the true parliamentarian. Thus, for example, he was fully involved in the committee stage of the Extradition Bill, the Succession Bill (which was largely rewritten on the floor of the House by John A. Costello), the Finance Bill and much else. This detailed probing of major issues set the pattern for the remainder of his parliamentary career, but he also used parliamentary questions to highlight matters concerning Monaghan and invariably he sat through all of each day's Question Time, sprinkling the exchanges with his own observations and frequently helping inexperienced colleagues to get the most out of the procedural possibilities open to them.

He was a stickler for proper procedures and took a dim view of the casual way some of the new ministers treated the established conduct of the House. He had sharp words with Charles Haughey, accusing him of treating the Dáil in a cavalier manner by failing to provide information to which it was entitled. Haughey reacted angrily, telling Dillon he was being personally abusive.[2] This was not the only time the two men crossed swords. In November 1965, in the course of a long speech which drew a full House, he wrongly accused Lemass of having 'a strange, almost daft obsession' about 'passing on to his son-in-law the post he at present occupies'. Haughey responded humorously that Dillon was 'ruining' him. Dillon's reply illustrated a deeply ambivalent attitude to Haughey, one he had formed early on and never changed: 'I would not want to do that. The Minister for Agriculture is a highly intelligent young man. I would not wish to ruin him. I would wish to reform him. The difference is I do it in public, his colleagues do it behind closed doors.'[3]

Some of the views he had held in his younger days had altered over time. His antipathy to trade unions changed to the extent that in 1966 he described them as 'highly responsible, sensible, tough and honourable', and he criticised the low salaries they paid their own officials, arguing that unless they were prepared to pay decent salaries they would not attract people of a high calibre. The Labour TD James Tully misinterpreted this as an attack on the reputation of union personnel and rounded on Dillon, accusing him of denigrating the entire movement. Dillon was unperturbed: 'I am quite in the habit of saying things in this House which vex people, and it is not going to put me off one bit if I alarm Deputy Tully.'[4]

In spite of the passing years, Dillon never managed to establish anything approaching a personal relationship with Lemass. There was neither trust, affection nor mutual understanding between the two, each of whom lived with a fixed and unfavourable view of the other. Neither man made any effort to break down the barriers, but even so there was a degree of courtesy between them, and when Lemass came to resign in November 1966, Dillon wished him well and expressed his pleasure that Lemass was going for 'purely political reasons' and not for any considerations of health or age. (In this, Dillon, like everybody else, was at least partly wrong.) Concluding his personal tribute to Lemass, who had always behaved with 'diligence and industry', Dillon wished him 'and his gracious lady many long years, to enjoy for the rest of his life his release from the burdens he has carried'. Politically he was deeply critical of Lemass's timing, a position which he did not know was also shared by Sean MacEntee, who condemned Lemass for 'washing his hands' of responsibility for the country's affairs, of 'letting us all down' and 'squandering the party's heritage'. Dillon's point was different from MacEntee's. Lemass, he said, had campaigned a year earlier under the slogan 'let Lemass lead on'. Now he was breaking faith with the people by opting out, leaving behind the problems he had promised to solve.[5]

Whatever the reasons for Lemass's going, he did so in a way which brought about confusion and bad feeling over the election of his successor. Dillon, like the rest of the country, looked on with fascination, disbelief and a certain distaste as the Fianna Fáil succession race developed. He liked Jack Lynch, whom he called 'a young man of integrity', and respected George Colley as 'an honest upright man', but he had no doubt both were expendable in the eyes of the group he called the *Camorra* – Haughey, Brian Lenihan, Neil Blaney, Kevin Boland and Donogh O'Malley – who would 'relentlessly pursue their leadership ambitions' whatever the outcome of the contest between Lynch and Colley. The battle, he said, had started already: 'there is not an hour, or a day, or a week until they break his [Lynch's] heart, that the clash of knives will not be heard in the corridors of Fianna Fáil.' Lynch, he said, 'was as expendable as an old shoe; and he is too decent a man to be treated in this way. I do not despair that our people will recoil with loathing from the prospect of replacing a man of integrity, as I believe Deputy Jack Lynch to be, with one of the *Camorra*, who are now sharpening their knives and whirling their tomahawks, not only for their enemies but for one another.'[6]

Dillon's parliamentary career continued right to the end of the 1965-69 Dáil, and with the zest and commitment of a man experiencing parliament for the first time. In some ways he was at his best, able to range widely over all topics, drawing not just on his thirty years experience but on the memories inherited from his father also. He could be repetitious, and some of his stories and phrases had a well-practised air to them, but they rarely lost in the telling and he continued to be one of the few politicians capable of attracting a sizable 'House'. His one, indeed only political regret continued to be Brendan Corish's decision not to enter coalition in 1965, and as he watched with distaste the growing influence of some of Fianna Fáil's ambitious and aggressive young ministers, his sense of regret grew sharper. He began one speech with a rebuke to Sean Dunne, who was by now a good friend. 'If it were not for a speech made by his Leader in Tullamore, Fianna Fáil would not be the government of this country today. If the Labour Party were prepared to accept their part of the burden I was prepared to undertake, that crowd would never have got in. We are paying a bitter price for the decision enunciated at Tullamore ... if Bill Norton, the Lord have mercy on him, had still been with us, he would have faced that responsibility with the same valiance as he did in 1948 and in 1954.'[7]

As the 1960s brought forth new issues and revived old difficulties, Dillon kept a watching brief on the major topics as they came before the House. He saw the government's second attempt to abolish proportional representation as 'a sordid plot to destroy the Labour Party', and though he and

Fine Gael were prepared to consider variants of the PR system as they had been a decade earlier, once again no approach was made by the government. He used his external affairs contributions to call for greater vigilance in the face of the threat of world communism, a well-worn theme but one sharpened by events in Eastern Europe and by some of the student radicalism nearer home. His last major Dáil intervention was at committee stage of the Criminal Justice Bill in May 1969. It was a badly drafted Bill which had been virtually rewritten in the House, to the extent that an exasperated Dillon called on the minister to 'withdraw this blooming Bill. It has got too riddled with amendments.'[8]

By now, May 1969, Dillon knew he was at the end of his parliamentary career. A general election had been called, and if Dillon was downhearted at the prospect of not taking part in it, he showed no sign; indeed, his good humour was noted by his old adversary Martin Corry, who, in probably the only civil exchange they ever shared, confessed that Dillon seemed to have become 'kind of good-natured in his old age'. His last intervention in debate was on 20 May, the day before the eighteenth Dáil was dissolved. He had spoken on his first day in the seventh Dáil in 1932, and on his last day but one, thirty-seven years later.

In his last political year, Dillon continued to be conscientious in carrying out party responsibilities, whether at parliamentary party meetings or Árd Fheisanna, and keeping in regular contact with his constituents in Monaghan. It was no secret that he would not be running again, but he was annoyed that his announcement, made in late January 1969, came in response to a question from the *Sunday Independent* rather than directly to his constituents. As soon as the general election was announced he spoke at Fine Gael meetings right across the constituency, thanking not just those present for their loyal support and generosity over the thirty-two years he had been their TD, but remembering also 'the many old friends who have gone to their eternal reward, but who were in the van of battle when the going was very tough and stormy thirty years ago'.[9] He campaigned vigorously when the election started, reminding his constituents that Fine Gael had amassed enough votes in 1965 to win two seats and now was the time to make sure of them. To his great satisfaction, the constituency returned two Fine Gael TDs for the first time, John Francis Conlon and Billy Fox.

Dillon's retirement raised one important question: whether the Dillon tradition of political involvement would continue into the fourth generation. Many of those who wrote to James at the time expressed such a hope, but he left the matter entirely up to his son, John Blake, advising him simply that he should only contemplate a career in politics if he were sufficiently independent to walk away if circumstances required. In the event, John Blake, who was by now successfully launched on his career as a chartered accountant, opted to follow his chosen profession.

Of the many who wrote wishing Dillon well in retirement, only one disputed his decision – his brother Shawn, now a parish priest in Chapelizod. In several letters Shawn urged his brother not just not to resign, but to wrest back the leadership of the party from Declan Costello and Garret FitzGerald, 'the latter being as great a disaster in public life as Pope John XXIII was in ecclesiastical'. Shawn then admitted his growing regard for Fianna Fáil, especially Brian Lenihan and Neil Blaney, and told James that if he did not return to politics he himself would probably vote for Fianna Fáil in the election. Not for the first time, Dillon courteously declined his older brother's advice.[10]

The 1969 election, which brought Fianna Fáil back into power under Jack Lynch, marked the official end of Dillon's political career. He returned only once thereafter, to attend the 1970 Árd Fheis. His last party appearance was at a function in the Mansion House, Dublin, in April 1983 to celebrate the 60th anniversary of the founding of Cumann na nGaedheal, of which his family had so disapproved, and the 50th anniversary of the founding of Fine Gael, in which he had played a major part. Introduced to the strains of 'A Nation Once Again', standing between his successors Liam Cosgrave and Garret FitzGerald, both of whom became Taoisigh, his performance that evening stole the show. He recalled that it was sixty-six years since he had first stood on a political platform, and recounted the stormy days of the 1930s when freedom of speech had to be fought for, and was won, 'no thanks to those who were opposed to us'. He proclaimed that politics was a true vocation, not a profession, 'and if you don't feel that, get out of politics as quickly as you can'. Characteristically, he ended his short speech with a ringing endorsement of FitzGerald, who was going through a particularly difficult period, and called on the party to stand four-square behind him: 'I give him my hundred per cent loyalty, and I exhort you to do the same.'[11]

Television arrived too late for Dillon as a practising politician, and he had strong reservations about its likely impact on political life, but in 1967 he did a lengthy interview with RTE. The face-to-face encounter with Patrick Gallagher, filmed in black and white, took a cigarette-smoking Dillon through his background and career, and clearly he enjoyed his reminiscences enormously. 'Mr Dillon enjoys his politics,' *The Irish Times* television critic Ken Gray commented afterwards. 'He treats the whole business with a relish that some people reserve for food and drink.' The *Evening Press* critic thought Dillon's performance merited a Jacobs Award, and letters of congratulation came in considerable volume, including a particularly warm note from Declan Costello. One letter was quite unexpected: it came from Donal Ward, a son of the late Dr Ward of Monaghan. 'I do not know what my late father would have thought about your comments on freedom of speech in County Monaghan in the 1930s,' he wrote, 'but I feel sure that somewhere he gave a wry smile.'[12]

Dillon's departure from politics was not quite final in that he continued to be involved in the Ancient Order of Hibernians right up until his death. He was its National Vice-President and subsequently its National President. Though the Order was run effectively by another formidable member of the Nugent family, Kathleen Nugent, and Dillon's responsibilities as National President were not onerous, he took his duties seriously. He presided over meetings of the Order's governing body, the Board of Éireann, spoke at meetings in Ireland and Scotland, and in general gave benign guidance in the modest affairs of an aging organisation which had long ceased to have any real relevance in Irish life, a fact Dillon accepted but which loyalty and sentiment prevented him from taking to its logical conclusion.

When trouble erupted in Northern Ireland the AOH was placed in an invidious position, especially when it was described as the Catholic equivalent of the Orange Order. Dillon had thought hard about this, and his ambition was to position the AOH in such a way that a person could say they were a member and be accepted as a genuine nationalist while being utterly opposed to the IRA and its activities. As a result, he was deeply angered when he was approached in June 1967 by the leader of the Nationalist Party, Eddie McAteer, who urged him to encourage the AOH to disband, in the hope that this 'would encourage the Orangemen to take a step or two along the same road'. McAteer told Dillon that he knew that the AOH 'does not purport to hold any kind of political power analogous to that exercised by the Orange Order', but that 'the general public can see some external common denominators in the two Orders'.[13]

Dillon's temper was not helped by the fact that the idea had come originally from Ernest Blythe, for whom he had scant regard, and he dismissed the proposal out of hand. He told McAteer that he had no doubt his suggestion would be enthusiastically received by the Orange Order, 'who will rejoice to have it even implied by someone like yourself that we in the Ancient Order of Hibernians have promoted acrimony and ill-will, as the Orange Order undoubtedly have, while the exact reverse is true of the Ancient Order of Hibernians'.[14]

As the decade drew to a close, Dillon was free to spend more time in Ballaghaderreen and was happy to be able to do so; Ballaghaderreen had always continued to be 'home'. He dabbled in the business, dealing with customers but free from any real responsibility. He had not, in fact, been involved in an executive capacity since 1948. When he had entered government he decided that, as a bonded wholesaler, having prior knowledge of changes in the rates of duty would constitute a conflict of interests, and he had divested himself of all involvement in the running of the business and handed the management over to Michael Cawley.[15] This arrangement remained in place throughout his political career, so that when he retired to Ballaghaderreen in 1969 business became a hobby. Like many others of his generation, retirement did not mean any lapse in formality. He still wore a black three-piece suit with a white shirt and dark tie, occasionally changing his black hat for a Harris tweed cap. The easy informality of the seventies and eighties was completely foreign to him.

He found time to do some book reviewing, including books on CP Scott, Robert Menzies, Neville Cardus, GK Chesterton and Michael Davitt, and some works on American politics, including biographies of Martin Luther King, books by Robert Kennedy, and a book which intrigued him, *The Selling of the President* by Joe McGinnis: its theme of the triumph of style over substance disturbed him.[16]

He was invited by Bishop Fergus to represent the diocese of Achonry on the newly constituted National Council for the Apostolate of the Laity, and took on the task with enthusiasm. He was irritated by the new generation of theologians who had emerged since the second Vatican Council; he had attacked the trend in a speech in 1968: 'it seems to me as a Catholic layman that the theologians have taken it into their heads that it is their business to run the Church and that the bishops are no longer to be trusted to discharge the duties of their office.' He went on: 'I venture to hope that the authorities of all Christian churches will remind the theologians that their sphere is research and discussion but the government of the Christian churches is a matter for the accepted authority of these churches, and the sooner the theologians awake to that fundamental fact, the better it will be for Christianity the world over.' This was the spirit in which he undertook his duties, while making it clear that his role was to offer advice, which the bishops might heed or not as they thought best.[17]

Retirement gave more time for family and friends. The one serious personal rift in his political career had been with Frank MacDermot. Dillon had been critical, even bitter about MacDermot's treatment of his colleagues and the detached, superior attitude he had had at that time. MacDermot regretted this, and wrote to Dillon in 1937 describing their estrangement as 'damned nonsense', adding that, even though it was Dillon who had 'renounced friendship', he was 'not afraid of risking dignity' if that brought about a rapprochement between them.[18] Dillon refused this olive branch, and despite a further effort by MacDermot his long silence continued. It was Maura Dillon who took the initiative in restoring good relations. She began a correspondence with MacDermot, and in the late 1960s the two families holidayed together. They met whenever MacDermot visited Dublin thereafter, but Dillon still retained a certain prickliness, and in 1973 MacDermot scolded him lest 'the revival of ancient political controversies should create any coldness between us'.[19] A year later, in July 1974, MacDermot's wife died. His feelings for Dillon were well summed up when he wrote in reply to Maura's letter of sympathy: 'Elaine had for you and James as much affection as I have, and that is saying a great deal.'[20] Frank MacDermot died in 1975.

Dillon's son, John Blake, had married Clodagh Hickey in 1969, and their daughters, Tara and Lee, were born two and four years later. Like all grandfathers, Dillon indulged them, and they adored him in turn. To the children he was 'a large grown-up' who always wore a three-piece suit 'of ample volume and endless pockets'. Tara recalled sitting on his 'spacious lap':

> His voice was booming but not alarmingly so. He would sometimes read us stories about a boy called 'Black Sambo'; seven or eight books (which would now be deemed politically incorrect!) were kept in a small compartment beneath shelves of daunting tomes and exotic bookends. They had turquoise covers and his favourite part of all the stories was the bit where the boy would surprise his ailing grandmother with a regular supply of mangoes, her favourite food.

She also remembered the timeless routine of daily life in Ballaghaderreen, its 'well defined ritual and a certain anachronistic tradition'.

> In the late morning he would oversee the making of the breakfast tea at the long dining-room table. The kettle was an old dimpled brass affair, which stood on a spit-like stand over a methylated spirit flame. Like the pocket watch it is an integral part of my mind's eye image of GranPaw. The evening equivalent was an even more battered cocktail shaker in which his pre-dinner drink of gin and martini was regularly shaken and stirred.
>
> He had a deep smoker's laugh, often heard, and a Churchman's cigarette packet was never far from his fingertips. When we arrived in Ballagh for a weekend he greeted us with breath-squeezing hugs and soggy kisses on our cheeks. As he grew older and less strong his hugs became arm-clasps; not for the feeble-armed nevertheless!

And she recalled his tenderness, a quality not often seen in public:

> I remember vividly the one time I saw he and my grandmother openly embrace. He had got up from the dining-room table after dinner and was heading for the drawing-room and coffee. Unexpectedly he stopped beside my grandmother at the other end of the table, clasped her round the shoulders and kissed her warmly. The energy and youth of this gesture stands out in my memory.[21]

The family circle was small and closely knit. Patrick and James Nugent, who had frequently campaigned with him in Monaghan, and their brother, Andrew, a Benedictine monk who had also been a political helper at one time but was now more interested in matters spiritual, visited frequently and enlivened Dillon as few others could. Myles's son, John, Professor of Greek at Trinity College and the only one of the next generation to have been seriously tempted by politics, persuaded Dillon to record his memoirs in 1982. James had also remained close to Maura's sisters. Ellie had married John Shee of Clonmel; Kitty had married his greatest friend, Peter Nugent, after Peter had been widowed in 1945, and he took enormous pride in the achievements of Pearl, now Sister Joseph Ignatius of the Irish Sisters of Charity, a pioneer of the hospice care movement and honoured for her work in 1983 as a national 'Person of the Year'.

But growing old also meant the loss of people he had been close to, and one by one the ranks of his family and friends began to thin. Theo had been the first brother to die. He had spent much of his early life in sanitoria, suffering from TB, in spite of which he achieved excellence in his medical studies at Vienna, was appointed Professor of Pharmacology and Therapeutics at UCD in 1932 when he was just thirty-four years of age, and had published widely in professional journals. Theo died in 1946.

Shawn was probably the most eccentric of the family, outspoken and intemperate like his uncle, Fr Nicholas. Shawn had been ordained in 1923 as a priest of the Dublin archdiocese, where, according to a biographical note in a book edited by his nephew, John M. Dillon, 'he never rose high in the hierarchy, mainly due to a certain degree of laziness and eccentricity'. He ended his career as parish priest of Chapelizod and died in 1970. Myles, two years older than James, had won a travelling scholarship to Germany in 1922 and his vivid account of those days has been published recently.[22] He lectured in Trinity and UCD until 1937, when he got the Chair of Irish at the University of Wisconsin, which he held until 1946. He later lectured at the universities of Chicago and Edinburgh before returning to Ireland as senior professor at the School of Celtic Studies at the Dublin Institute of Advanced Studies. James was a frequent visitor to tea on Sunday at Myles's house in Portmarnock, when the two brothers would engage in challenging discussions on theological and political questions. Myles died in 1972.

James was closest to his brother, Brian. After qualifying as a lawyer, Brian opted instead for the priesthood, and studied at the Beda College in Rome where he was ordained in 1933. A year later he became a Benedictine monk at Glenstal Abbey, where, as Father Matthew, he was headmaster for many years. When he died in October 1979, James was devastated. He was the sole surviving brother now, all the familiar points of reference no more to hand. By this stage his only sister, Nano, was living in the US. After the death of her husband, PJ Smyth, in 1958, she had gone to live in Washington, close to her son Nicholas and daughter Roma. Nano was five years older than James and while they were very fond of one another there was also a certain tension between them – Nano never quite ceased to be the elder sister directing her sometimes precocious younger brother, who in her eyes could occasionally forget his place in the family scheme of things. Nano survived him, dying in September 1986.

Retirement and its attendant tranquillity gave him time to reflect upon his life, and especially its political dimension, and he put some of his thoughts together in an essay, 'The Politician as Christian Witness', published in 1972.[23] In it he reaffirmed his lifelong debt to Thomas Kettle and urged any young person entering politics to read and re-read Kettle's essay, 'The Philosophy of Politics', which Dillon himself had done throughout his political career. As Dillon saw it, politics was essentially about a simple concept: freedom – 'free to think whatever we want to think, free to protest against anything we believe to be wrong, free to organise to take over the government by the consent of the majority of our fellow citizens'.

It gave him great satisfaction to record that he had never regretted a single moment of his political activity. In politics 'I found what I am convinced I was meant by Providence to attempt.' Politics had given him 'ample scope to use whatever gifts I was endowed with, and whether I adequately availed of this opportunity or not is irrelevant, because if my performance was unsatisfactory the fault was wholly mine, it was not for any lack of opportunity.'

He set out in the essay the simple but inflexible rules of conduct which he felt should govern a career in politics:

The first relates to Wisdom itself – wisdom cannot be acquired from anyone, however wise he or she may be, it is available only in the hard school of experience, where you must learn it by trial and error.

The second rule is that in the long run, quite apart from the moral aspect, it never pays to tell lies; ephemeral success may be secured by a liar, but sooner or later he will be found out and judged accordingly.

The third rule in politics is to avoid becoming a chronic resigner. Every politician must satisfy his own conscience on the question of whether an issue is a fundamental matter of principle, or merely a question of expediency as to how best a desired end can be reached effectively.

If a fundamental principle is involved, and this is rare, resignation from one's party is really the only course if your view does not prevail. But on questions of expediency, you should accept the opinion of the majority and work with your colleagues to make the best you can of the policy agreed upon.

The fourth rule is do not allow an experience to make you cynical – Tom Kettle has said all that needs to be said on this subject in his 'Philosophy of

Politics'; read it carefully and you will never be guilty of 'this last treachery, the irredeemable defect'.

The fifth rule is to be on your guard against Utopianism, which means you should realise that you cannot create heaven on earth by making laws: you can and should keep trying to improve the human condition and always be on the lookout for opportunities to do this through appropriate parliamentary action ... the Duke of Wellington said to his officers at the most critical moment of the Battle of Waterloo: 'hard pounding, this, gentlemen; try who can pound the longest now.' It is good advice for a young politician.

Lastly, young politicians would do well to remember the precepts of an Irishman who is famous worldwide as a great statesman, Edmund Burke – his words will suitably conclude this sketch of politics as it should be practised by Christian men and women: 'Falsehood has a perennial spring – this means that you must be prepared to put falsehood down year in, year out, as the farmer cuts the weeds which, unlike crops, can grow and flourish no matter how often they are cut and burned. All that is necessary for evil to prevail is that good men should do nothing. When bad men combine, the good must associate; else they will fall one by one, an unpitied sacrifice in a contemptible struggle.'

And when the radio, television and the press combine to tell you what ought to be done, and how far short of their standards they think you have fallen, you can turn to Edmund Burke again for the appropriate reply: 'Applaud us when we run; console us when we fall; cheer us when we recover; but let us pass on – for God's sake, let us pass on.'[24]

James Dillon had enjoyed good health through most of his long life, but he had been a lifelong and habitual smoker and in his early eighties he began to suffer from emphysema. As his breathing became more difficult, his energy waned. His granddaughter, Tara, recalls him 'sitting silently in the navy chair in the drawing-room in Ballaghaderreen, his oxygen supply on, fingertips together, gazing into the fire.' She added: 'I never asked him what he was contemplating. I wish I had.'[25]

It was clear he was failing, but fortunately his mental faculties and his interest in life remained with him right to the end. On the day before he died he had a vigorous theological discussion with his nephew, Peter Dillon, a monk of Glenstal, when he reaffirmed his certainty of the truth of his favourite prayer, 'My Redeemer Liveth'. His granddaughter, Lee, has a poignant memory of the last time she saw him. It was 2 January 1986 and the family were preparing to return to Dublin. James was too weak to wave them off from the front steps of the house, as he and Maura always had done.

In the hall, I turned around to look at Granpaw, and he was sitting there, with the oxygen pipe hooked up, staring in front of him. And I remember this feeling so clearly. I just knew that this would be the last time I would see him. We were just leaving and I went back into the room and went over to him and I think I told him that I loved him. And I hugged him – gently. And he looked at me and he smiled and I think I remember him squeezing me back. I think he might have known too – I'm sure he knew what I thought at any rate. I was twelve. This is one of the clearest memories of my life.[26]

The end, when it came, was sudden and merciful. He died in Ballaghaderreen on 10 February 1986. He was buried in the family plot in Ballaghaderreen, where he was joined in July 1991 by Maura.

CHAPTER TWENTY-THREE

ENVOI

*'In what spirit should one approach the actual work of politics? I speak
only for myself, but I think one should take enthusiasm for the driving
force, and irony as a refuge against the inevitable disappointments.'*
Tom Kettle, quoted by Dillon to Young Farmers' Club, 1954

IN JANUARY 1951, at a time when Dillon was at his busiest in the
Department of Agriculture, and ill into the bargain, he received a letter
from Colonel Richard Butler Charteris. The Colonel was a substantial
landowner in Co. Tipperary and very nearly owned the town of Cahir. He
was annoyed with the monthly fairs which crowded the streets with animals,
and the inevitable mess which had to be hosed down and cleaned at a cost
borne by the ratepayers, of whom the Colonel was one. He was not happy,
and wanted the Minister to ban the holding of fairs on the streets of Irish
towns.

Most ministers receive letters of this kind from time to time. Usually they
are simply acknowledged or sometimes, if the petitioner is a constituent,
the minister may pen a polite response or say the matter was really the
responsibility of another department and arrange to have the letter passed
on. Not so with Dillon. He had a policy of personally reading all letters
addressed to him and gave this one his full attention.

Will you forgive me if I am quite frank on the subject about which you wrote
to me? I know that my view is somewhat unorthodox, but I cannot help feeling that it has some merit to commend it. First, in this regulation-ridden
world I have a horror of pushing people about, and having spent most of my
life in rural Ireland, I know the irrational passion which small farmers have for
showing their stock to what they think is best advantage. Comparing the
background of the street, with what to them seems the vast anonymity of the
fair green, they instinctively believe that the former background presents a
more flattering setting for the jewels they display. I am told that Hatton
Garden diamond merchants sooner retire from business than display diamonds on any other background than black velvet, though in the last analysis
they know that no skilful jeweller will suffer his judgement to be finally ruled
by the first blaze of glory which diamonds on black velvet present. I am afraid
that the railings in the square of Cahir are for the small farmers and their

modest wares all and more than black velvet is to the merchants of Hatton Gardens.

There followed a discussion on the role of publicans in the fair-day scheme of things before Dillon returned to his central theme:

Rural life in Ireland has much of tedium in it, and I am convinced that the monthly fair is for many of our people all that the spectacle of the Place de la Concorde, as one comes out from the Crillon, is for those fortunate enough to have experienced this recurrent delight. I know that I should not stay at the Crillon nor indeed go to Paris at all, because I cannot afford the one nor the other, but I do and life would become well nigh intolerable if prudence confined me (which it ought to do) perpetually to the four shores of Ireland. And so, I have never felt myself justified in denying to my neighbours on the grounds of unanswerable prudence and reason their irrational joy in displaying their wares everywhere they should not display them; in wasting £15 a month of the ratepayers money washing streets that they should never have soiled; in glorying in their right to buy from itinerant 'hand-me downs' the raiment that they should buy from me in the respectable and orderly atmosphere that obtains in my venerable shop.

All this flight from reason seems to me the apotheosis of freedom, and all my annoyance at trying to drive my car through multitudes of bullocks and their proprietors evaporates in the realisation that in your country and mine there are no uniformed representatives of authority to push the people about, but rather that on this day they push me and I push them in friendly but vociferous assertion of exclusive rights which neither of us really have any title to at all.

I hope that this devotion to liberty at the cost of order will not shock you, but I know you will wish me to give you the facts as I see them.[1]

Dillon's response to Colonel Charteris tells us much about the man and his politics. He believed in straight talking for a start. He was a defender of tradition and a champion of the small man, and because the fair day was a time-honoured part of rural life, Dillon was going to defend it against so-called progress or administrative tidiness. His reply reflected an idealised and slightly anarchic view of rural life, one not far removed from the Old England of Chesterton and Belloc in its evocation of sturdy traditional values – and not all that far away either from de Valera's idealised Ireland of athletic youths and comely maidens, even if Dillon's island did allow for the existence of public houses and the excesses that flowed therefrom. His devotion to 'liberty at the cost of order' and his attachment to the values of the past, mark him out as a troubadour, a man who for all his solemnity saw life in terms that were in part romantic, instinctively individualistic, and antipathetic to the increasingly regulated and corporate world in which he lived.

And that, in its own way, was part of Dillon's problem as a political leader. In many people's eyes he was a man who looked back rather than forward, somebody who felt there was as much to be lost as to be won in the bright new world of the 1960s, a leader who conveyed a lack of enthusiasm for change at a time when many of his party and the electorate saw change in terms of liberation. It was his misfortune, too, to be confronted through his entire time as leader of Fine Gael by Sean Lemass, who gloried in implementing policies he had excoriated decades earlier.

Dillon's and Lemass's periods of leadership overlap almost exactly, and it is Dillon's historic fate to be forever compared to him. History will judge Lemass to have made the more significant contribution. While de Valera's reputation has waned, his earlier and later career suffering particularly, Lemass has grown in stature and in most respects rightly so. He was a leader in tune with his time who generated and managed change as no other politician had before. But if his success was spectacular, it involved jettisoning many of the policies he had devised and executed, often with an intolerant zeal, over a period of thirty years: economic protectionism, industrial self-sufficiency, isolationism, the elimination of the cattle industry in favour of tillage, and Fianna Fáil policy on Northern Ireland. In the end, there was little of lasting substance to show for the twenty-one years of Fianna Fáil rule which preceded Lemass, a great deal to show for the six years during which he led. Even this had its downside: there was an official philistinism, questionable links with big business and a new ethos of self-aggrandisement. The legacy which resulted from allowing 'low standards in high places' still casts a long shadow over Fianna Fáil and Irish public life.

In electoral terms Lemass inherited a party with a fourteen-seat majority; he himself never got an overall majority. Dillon inherited a party divided and with little appetite for power; under him it won four of the eight by-elections it contested (as against three for Lemass), increased its popular vote and its seats in the Dáil. Had there been a coalition arrangement, Dillon could well have been Taoiseach. There was none, and history can only judge him on what he did, not what he might have done.

The balance sheet will show a man who brought colour and sparkle to an often drab political scene, a politician who was passionate about the central importance of politics to people's welfare, a parliamentarian who used parliament to scrutinise the expansive and intrusive tendencies of all governments. He was a nationalist, one who saw no contradiction in maintaining friendship with England or membership of the Commonwealth. He believed in Irish unity, and – long before it became fashionable – unity by consent. He was a liberal who hated censorship or compulsion in any form but was prepared to suspend liberties if he felt the safety of the state was threatened. He was an effective and flamboyant minister and probably the best orator of the century. Most of all he was a truthful man, one who showed unflinching moral courage on issues he believed fundamental.

He will be remembered, too, as somebody who was ill-suited to the role of party leader. Under his leadership his party stabilised but did not prosper. Not all of the fault was his; his parliamentary party in particular were more culpable than he, but ultimately he was too gentle a man to crack the whip, too remote a man to understand the nature of the changes he saw around him but did not fully comprehend, too archaic a man to establish an easy rapport with his electorate, and too intellectually honest to embrace with enthusiasm policies which, while politically necessary and essentially unthreatening, he found unconvincing and uncongenial. He was, in a true sense, a man born out of his time, who nonetheless travelled a long political road and did so with distinction, even if the ultimate prize always eluded him.

But perhaps the final word on Dillon is a simple word, expressed by his old friend and political foe, Todd Andrews. 'I have always regarded you – as indeed I did your father – as a great and specially decent patriot.' Dillon himself would have asked for no more fitting epitaph.

NOTES

INTRODUCTION
1 Thomas M. Kettle *The Days Burden* 16

CHAPTER 1
1 *Memoir* 3, JMDP
2 ibid. 3
3 ibid. 4 and FSL Lyons *John Dillon* for a good account of Elizabeth Dillon: Ch. 9 'A Short Happy Life'
4 ibid. 7
5 ibid. 5
6 Professor John M. Dillon recalls regular visits by his father, then a professor at the Dublin Institute of Advanced Studies, James, leader of Fine Gael, and Brian, headmaster of Glenstal, to Lia in her very old age, where all three accorded her great deference and affection.
7 *Memoir* 5
8 Information from Dr Patrick Nugent, nephew and close friend of James Dillon.
9 Details on Dillon family from family records (JMDP), Lyons op. cit. 1-10 and Brendán O'Cathaoir *John Blake Dillon: Young Irelander* 5-14
10 For interesting portraits of Mrs Deane see Wilfred Scawen Blunt *The Land War in Ireland* (London 1912) 59-60 and Sophie O'Brien *My Irish Friends* (London and Dublin 1937)
11 O'Cathaoir op. cit.
12 ibid. 60
13 William Dillon *Life of John Dillon* Vol. II, 249-62
14 Charles Gavan Duffy *Young Ireland* Vol. I, 38-9
15 Details from an unpublished autobiography of William Dillon, written for his family and dated 1932, JMDP
16 Lyons op. cit. 480-1
17 *Memoir* 8
18 Maura Dillon to author, 1990

CHAPTER 2
1 *Memoir* 11, JMPD
2 Much of what follows is taken from an unpublished history of the school, 'Adventure in Education' by Matthew Dillon OSB (1981), JMDP
3 ibid. 7
4 *Memoir* 12-16
5 ibid.
6 Dillon op. cit. 8
7 *Memoir* 12-16
8 ibid. 17-18
9 ibid.
10 ibid.
11 ibid.
12 ibid.
13 ibid.
14 ibid.
15 FSL Lyons *John Dillon* 392-403
16 *Parliamentary Debates* vol. 82 cols 935-51
17 James Dillon to John Dillon, 11 November 1916, JMDP

18 JMDP
19 *Memoir* 25
20 ibid. 25-6
21 JMDP
22 *Memoir* 20
23 ibid.
24 CS Andrews *Dublin Made Me* 128
25 ibid. 175
26 J. Meenan (ed.) *The Literary and Historical Society* 165
27 JMDP
28 JMDP
29 Diaries and letters, JMDP
30 Andrews op. cit. 128
31 John Dillon to TP O'Connor, 8 February 1923
32 *Memoir* 26

CHAPTER 3
1 FSL Lyons *John Dillon* 456
2 John Dillon to James Dillon, 3 January 1921, JMDP
3 ibid. 12 December 1922
4 *Memoir* 30, JMPD
5 John Dillon to James Dillon, 2 December 1922, JMDP
6 ibid. 6 January 1922, JMDP
7 Lia O'Reilly to James Dillon, 8 March 1922, JMDP
8 *Memoir* 30
9 ibid.
10 James Dillon to John Dillon, 9 January 1921, JMDP
11 ibid.
12 ibid.
13 ibid. 7 July 1922
14 John Dillon to James Dillon, 20 July 1922, JMDP
15 James Dillon to John Dillon, 21 July 1922, JMDP
16 *Memoir* 31
17 Shawn Dillon to James Dillon, 24 Novembert 1921, JMDP
18 ibid. 2 September 1923
19 John Dillon to James Dillon, 12 December 1922, JMDP
20 Theo Dillon to Myles Dillon, TDP
21 *Memoir* 30
22 Diary entry, 24 April 1923, JMDP
23 *Memoir* 33
24 Diary entry, 26 February 1923, JMDP
25 ibid.
26 ibid. 1 March 1923, JMDP
27 Cohalan to Dillon, 7 November 1923, JMDP
28 Crawford to Dillon, 19 June 1923, JMDP
29 Theo Dillon to John Dillon, November 1923, TDP
30 Diary entry, 3 March 1923, JMDP
31 ibid. 3 July 1923
32 ibid. 22 March 1923
33 *Memoir* 36
34 ibid. 38

CHAPTER 4
1 James Dillon to John Dillon, 30 October 1924, JMDP

2 Theo Dillon to John Dillon, January 1925, TDP
3 Details of these changes are found in a weekly, and sometimes daily, series of letters from James Dillon to John Dillon at this time, JMDP
4 *Roscommon Annual* 1990
5 The correspondence of John Dillon at this time in *The Correspondence of Myles Dillon* has many references to the 'crisis' in the business.
6 Detailed correspondence, newspaper cuttings and contemporary leaflets dealing with the strike in JMDP
7 Original in JMDP. Interestingly, Hunt was reluctant to engage in direct conflict with John Dillon for whom he retained great respect. James, however, in Hunt's words was 'inexperienced, and youth is ever-inclined to be extreme'.
8 *Roscommon Herald* 25 April 1925
9 Lyons op. cit. 474
10 JMDP
11 The business accounts were very kindly made available to the author by Brian Kelly of Ballaghaderreen, and analysed by Laurence Crowley, executive chairman of the Smurfit Graduate School of Business at UCD.
12 James Dillon to John Dillon, 23 October 1924, JMDP
13 *Memoir* 19, JMPD
14 James Dillon to John Dillon, 24 September 1926, JMDP
15 ibid. 12 December 1926
16 ibid. 17 February 1927
17 ibid. 21 March 1927
18 *Irish Independent* 7 June 1927
19 James Dillon to John Dillon, 30 June 1927, JMDP
20 Dermot Keogh *Twentieth-Century Ireland* 46-48
21 JMDP
22 *Memoir* 39
23 *Irish Independent* 5-10 August 1927
24 Lyons op. cit. 478
25 Text in JMDP
26 Hugh Kennedy to James Dillon, 22 December 1930, JMDP
27 George Gavan Duffy to James Dillon, 23 December 1930, JMDP
28 Department of President of Executive Council, S5983/52, NAI
29 Royal Society of Antiquaries of Ireland to James Dillon, 20 February 1931, JMDP
30 Fr Nicholas to James Dillon, 1 November 1931, JMDP
31 ibid. 11 December 1931
32 *Memoir* 44
33 William Dillon to James Dillon, 25 February 1928, JMDP
34 ibid. 9 December 1931
35 Fr Nicholas to James Dillon, 12 June 1931, JMDP
36 ibid. 24 November 1931
37 ibid. 11 January 1932
38 *Irish Independent* 25 January 1932
39 Full text of election address, JMDP
40 ibid.
41 *Irish Independent* February 11, 12, 1932
42 *Memoir* 41
43 Fr Nicholas to James Dillon, 8 March 1932, JMD
44 *New York Times* 15 February 1932
45 ibid. 14 February 1932
46 ibid. 19 August 1928
47 ibid. 21 February 1932
48 JMDP

CHAPTER 5

1 The best contemporary account of these developments is in Warner Moss *Political Parties in the Irish Free State*
2 See *Irish Press* 9 February 1932 and Moss op. cit. 183
3 *Memoir* 42, JMPD
4 See Conor Brady *Guardians of the Peace* 73
5 *Memoir* 43
6 *Dáil Debates* 42, 9 March 1932, 26
7 Thomas Jones *A Diary with Letters*
8 *Irish Independent* 12 March 1932
9 *Irish Times* 23 March 1932
10 *Parliamentary Debates* CC1XV, 1914
11 *Dáil Debates* 42, 27 April 1932, 628-631
12 ibid.
13 For a full discussion see D. O'Sullivan *The Irish Free State and its Senate*
14 *Dáil Debates* 42, 27 April 1932, 631 et. seq.
15 ibid.
16 ibid.
17 ibid. col. 1404. The copy of this debate in the Oireachtas Library is much marked and well thumbed, indicating frequent recourse by political opponents.
18 *Memoir* 25
19 *Dáil Debates* 43, 4 August 1932, 1608 et. seq.
20 See K. Hancock, *Survey of British Commonwealth Affairs* Vol. 1, 334-50
21 *Dáil Debates* 43, 15 July 1932, 1183
22 *Dáil Debates* 43, 22 July 1932, 1316-21
23 ibid. 1366, 67
24 *Statistical Abstract 1932*, 1933
25 *Dáil Debates* 42, 8 June 1932, 791
26 *Dáil Debates* 42, 15 June 1932, 1318
27 ibid.
28 *Dáil Debates* 44, 11 November 1932, 1530
29 *Dáil Debates* 44, 28 October 1932, 743 et. seq.
30 *Dáil Debates* 44, 27 October 1932, 613
31 *Dáil Debates* 44, 15 November 1932, 1695-1704
32 ibid.
33 For a full account of MacDermot's background see interview with Patrick Gallagher and David Thornley, RTE archives
34 K. O'Higgins to MacDermot, 18 May 1927, 1065/1/1/ NAI
35 ibid.
36 RTE op. cit.
37 See *Irish Independent* for July-September 1932 and 17 September 1932
38 Dillon to MacDermot, 19 September 1932, JMDP
39 Cumann na nGaedheal parliamentary party minutes, 17 November 1932, UCDA
40 ibid. 18 November 1932
41 ibid. 24 November 1932
42 For detailed discussion of this period see Maurice Manning *The Blueshirts* 38-44
43 *Irish Independent* 3 October 1932
44 See Manning op. cit. 21-27 and M. Cronin *The Blueshirts and Irish Politics* 17-38
45 *Dáil Debates* 50, 31 January 1934, 900
46 *Irish Independent, Irish Times* 2 January 1933
47 ibid. 3 January 1933
48 Cumann na nGaedheal standing committee minutes, 2 January 1933, UCDA
49 Cumann na nGaedheal parliamentary party minutes, 3 January 1933, UCDA

50 Cumann na nGaedheal standing committee minutes, 3 January 1933, UCDA
   and *Irish Independent* 4 January 1933
51 *Irish Independent* 5 January 1933
52 ibid.
53 ibid. 6 January 1933
54 ibid. 18 January 1933
55 ibid. 7 January 1933
56 ibid.
57 See Manning op. cit. 46-52
58 *Irish Independent* 16 January 1933
59 ibid. 17 January 1933 and 19 January 1933
60 ibid. 18 January 1933

CHAPTER 6
1 *Dáil Debates* 46, 8 February 1933, 22
2 ibid. 26
3 *Dáil Debates* 46, 1 March 1933, 178
4 ibid. 186
5 ibid. 187
6 ibid. 192
7 ibid. 193
8 *Dáil Debates* 46, March 1933, 1885-6
9 ibid. 1897
10 ibid. 1940
11 ibid. 1990
12 See Maurice Manning *The Blueshirts* 23-63
13 *Irish Independent* 23 February 1933
14 *Dáil Debates* 46, 14 March 1933, 782 et. seq.
15 *Irish Independent* 15 May 1933
16 ibid. 22 May 1933
17 *Dáil Debates* 47, 1 June 1933, 2184-5
18 See Manning op. cit. 23-63
19 See J. Bowyer Bell *The Secret Army* (London 1971) 101-109
20 Dáil Debates, 48 13 July 1933, 2769-70
21 *Irish Independent* 20 July 1933
22 ibid. 1 August 1933
23 ibid. 3 August 1933
24 ibid. 24 June 1933
25 *Dáil Debates* 48, 23 June 1933, 1173-4
26 *Dáil Debates* 49, 28 September 1933, 1980-1905
27 Vincent to Tierney, Tierney papers, LA30/340/2, UCDA
28 Tierney papers LA30/340/2, UCDA
29 Most of these details were provided by Cosgrave, *Irish Independent* 9 September
   1933
30 *Irish Independent* 31 July 1933
31 ibid. 1 August 1933
32 *Dáil Debates* 49, 1 August 1933, 1043
33 ibid. 1060-67
34 See Manning op. cit. 78-87
35 *Dáil Debates* 49, 9 August 1933, 1577
36 *Dáil Debates* 49, 1 August 1933, 1065 et. seq.
37 ibid. 1067 et. seq.
38 *Irish Independent* 9 August 1933
39 *Dáil Debates* 49, 9 August 1933, 1546 et. seq.

40 ibid.
41 *Irish Independent* 11 August 1933
42 ibid.
43 ibid. 14 August 1933
44 Manning op. cit. 78-87
45 *Irish Times* 18 August 1933
46 *Memoir* 44; MacDermot interview, RTE archive
47 This impatience with Cosgrave is expecially evident in the letters exchanged at this time between Tierney and James Hogan.
48 MacDermot correspondence, JMDP
49 MacDermot claims that Arthur Cox, who was solicitor both to him and O'Duffy, persuaded him that O'Duffy could be an effective leader. JMDP
50 *Memoir* 45
51 See especially MacDermot interview, RTE archive
52 *Irish Independent* 9 September 1933
53 Hogan to Tierney, September 1933, Tierney papers LA30/363(i) UCDA
54 Belton to O'Duffy, Tierney papers LA30/347 (12) UCDA
55 *Irish Independent* 2 September 1933
56 National Farmers and Ratepayers League, p39/min. UCDA
57 *Irish Independent* 9 September 1933
58 ibid.
59 Tierney papers LA/30/363 (i) UCDA
60. There was a conflict between the Centre Party and Cumann na nGaedheal over the choice of name: the Centre Party wanted the name United Ireland Party while Cumann na nGaedheal wanted an Irish name. The compromise adopted was Fine Gael–United Ireland Party. Fine Gael – 'Tribes of the Gael' – was first used at the Irish Race Convention in Paris in 1923.

CHAPTER 7
1 Conor Brady *Guardians of the Peace* 73
2 Maurice Manning *The Blueshirts* 64-68
3 *New York Times* 10 September 1933
4 ibid. 17 September 1933
5 Figures from Secretary's report to each party's Árd Fheis 1934
6 Manning op. cit. Ch. 6
7 For a full discussion of the political ideas of Hogan and Tierney see Manning op. cit. Ch.13 and M. Cronin *The Blueshirts and Irish Politics* Ch. 4
8 Tierney papers 4A30/363/(i) UCDA
9 *Irish Times* 30 November 1933
10 *Irish Independent* 16-20 September 1933
11 ibid. 14 September 1933
12 ibid. 25 September 1933
13 ibid. 27 September 1933
14 *Dáil Debates* 49, 28 September 1933, 1890
15 ibid. 1900 et. seq.
16 ibid. 1904
17 ibid. 1930 et. seq.
18 *Irish Independent* 2 October, 9 October 1933
19 Coughlan's vivid account of this episode was given in an RTE radio documentary *Episodes of his Career*, 1 October 1990, RTE archive
20 *Irish Independent* 7-8 October 1933
21 *Irish Times* 9 December 1933
22 ibid. 23 October 1933
23 ibid. 5 January 1934

24 *Irish Independent* 13 October 1933
25 General Purposes Committee of Fine Gael, 4 January 1934, FG papers p39/1/2, UCDA
26 *Dáil Debates* 50, 15 November 1934, 170 et. seq.
27 *Dáil Debates* 50, 28 February 1934, 2313 et. seq.
28 For a full account of these events see Manning op. cit. 114-127
29 ibid. 114.
30 Fine Gael papers p39/1/2, UCDA
31 Tierney papers 4A 30/363/1, UCDA
32 ibid.
33 Fine Gael papers p39/1/2, UCDA
34 ibid.
35 ibid.
36 *Irish Times* 1 February 1934
37 *Dáil Debates* 50, 7 February 1934, 1187 et. seq.
38 *Dáil Debates* 50, 23 February 1934, 2227
39 *Dáil Debates* 50, 28 February 1934, 2293
40 *Dáil Debates* 50, 1 March 1934, 2486 et. seq.
41 *Dáil Debates* 50, 28 February 1934, 2299 et. seq.
42 *Dáil Debates* 50, 1 March 1934, 2367 et. seq.
43 *Dáil Debates* 50, 28 February 1934, 2238 et. seq.
44 *Dáil Debates* 51, 18 April 1934, 1862 et. seq.
45 ibid. 1864
46 ibid. 1970
47 ibid.., 1999
48 See especially O'Sullivan *The Irish Free State and its Senate*
49 *Irish Times* 21 March and 4 April 1934
50 For a good political and economic discussion of the Economic War see Cronin op. cit. 136-167
51 *Irish Independent* 25 June 1934
52 ibid. 4-6 July 1934
53 See Manning op. cit. 135-45
54 *New York Times* 9 July 1934
55 JMDP and McDermot papers 1065/4/1-5, NAI
56 ibid. This letter shows a peevishness on MacDermot's part to his new colleagues, especially Cosgrave and McGilligan.
57 McDermot papers 1065/4/1, NAI
58 McDermot papers 1065/2, NAI
59 *Cork Examiner* 1 September 1934
60 McDermot papers 1065/4/2, NAI
61 ibid.
62 *Cork Examiner* 2 September 1934
63 Public Records Office, FO/800/310, 'Notes on Eire' 9 November 1940
64 Dillon to MacDermot, 15 September 1934. McDermot papers 1065/2/3, NAI. There are in fact two letters. The first on 15 September is in the MacDermot papers; the second, ten days later, is a more comprehensive account and is in the Dillon papers.
65 ibid. 25 September 1934. Copy in JMDP
66 ibid.
67 Letter of 15 September, McDermot papers 1065/2/3, NAI
68 Dillon to MacDermot, 22 September 1934, McDermot papers 1065/2/3, NAI
69 Minutes of meeting, Fine Gael papers, UCDA
70 Dillon to MacDermot, 22 September 1934, McDermot papers 1065/2/3, NAI
71 Dillon to MacDermot, 25 September 1934, JMDP

72 ibid.
73 Manning op. cit. 172, 199, 202-7
74 Dillon to MacDermot, 22 September 1934, McDermot papers 1065/2/3, NAI
75 Dillon to MacDermot, 25 September 1934, JMDP
76 Tierney to MacDermot, 4 October 1934, McDermot papers 1065/4/5, NAI
77 Dillon to MacDermot, 17 October 1934, McDermot papers 1065/2/6, NAI
78 ibid.

CHAPTER **8**
1 *Irish Press* 4 October 1934 and 31 October 1934
2 Ibid 20 November 1934, *Irish Times* 18 May 1935, *Irish Independent* 10 June
  and 15 June 1935
3 For a full account see M. Cronin *The Blueshirts and Irish Politics* 145-55
4 *Dáil Debates* 62, 28 May 1936, 1313
5 Maurice Manning *The Blueshirts* 182-195
6 *Irish Independent* 22 and 23 March 1935
7 *Dáil Debates* 65, 25 February 1937, 1116
8 Fine Gael select committee, UCDA
9 *New York Times* 15 August 1933
10 Fine Gael parliamentary party minutes, 31 October 1934, UCDA
11 *Irish Independent* 16 March 1935
12 *Dáil Debates* 50, 31 January 1934, 1036
13 ibid. 1204
14 *Dáil Debates* 66, 31 March 1937, 96
15 ibid.
16 *Dáil Debates* 50, 31 January 1934, 1020
17 ibid. 1027
18 *Dáil Debates* 63, 24 June 1936, 253
19 Report of Joint Committee on Temporary Accommodation of the Oireachtas
  1924, Oireachtas Library
20 ibid.
21 For further deails of Fianna Fáil attitudes at this time see E. O'Halpin
  'Parliamentary party discipline and tactics: the Fianna Fáil archives 1926-32,'
  IHS Vol. XXX No. 120, November 1997
22 *Dáil Debates* 52, 2 May 1934, 270 et. seq.
23 *Memoir* 49
24 *Irish Independent* 7 January 1935
25 *Dáil Debates* 54, 28 November 1934, 501
26 ibid. 502-507
27 *Irish Independent* 9 January 1935
28 ibid. 22 February 1935, 6 March 1935, 9 March 1935
29 ibid. 28 February 1935
30 ibid. 3 May and 1 July 1935
31 ibid. 27 March 1935 and 30 March 1935
32 ibid. 1 July 1935
33 ibid. 19 and 22 July 1935
34 ibid. 20 July 1935
35 Fine Gael select committee, UCDA
36 *Irish Independent* 6 June 1935
37 *Dáil Debates* 61, 24 March 1936, 52 et. seq.
38 *Dáil Debates* 55, 27 February 1935, 32 et. seq.
39 *Dáil Debates* 56, 3 May 1935, 500 et. seq.
40 *Dáil Debates* 59, 12 December 1935, 2618 et. seq.
41 ibid. 2630

42 *Dáil Debates* 56, 4 June 1935, 2189
43 *Dáil Debates* 58, 25 July 1935, 1042
44 ibid. Carey was the informer whose evidence convicted the 'Invincibles' after the Phoenix Park murder.
45 *Dáil Debates* 56, 3 May 1935, 393
46 *Memoir*, 44
47 JMDP
48 ibid.
49 *The Times* 21 July 1934
50 ibid.
51 JMDP
52 ibid.
53 ibid.
54 ibid.
55 McDermot papers 1065/4/4, NAI
56 ibid. 1065/4/5 NAI
57 *Irish Independent* 17 September 1935
58 Fine Gael parliamentary party minutes, UCDA
59 Fine Gael select committee, 4 October 1935, UCDA
60 *Irish Independent* 5 October 1935
61 ibid. and JMDP
62 *Dáil Debates* 65, 24 February 1937, 1014
63 *Dáil Debates* 59, 12 December 1935, 2645
64 *Dáil Debates* 59, 6 November 1935, 486 et. seq.
65 *Dáil Debates* 55, 11 April 1935, 2455
66 *Dáil Debates* 59, 26 February 1936, 1273 et. seq.
67 *Dáil Debates* 59, 14 December 1935, 2391 et. seq. and *Irish Independent*
68 *Dáil Debates* 61, 23 April 1936, 1411 et. seq.
69 for example *Dáil Debates* 61, 24 March 1936, 125 et. seq.
70 for example *Dáil Debates* 61, 23 April 1936, 1430 et. seq. and *Dáil Debates* 66, 31 November 1937, 66
71 *Hibernian Journal* September 1937
72 ibid.
73 *Dáil Debates* 65, 19 February 1937, 689 et. scq.
74 ibid.
75 ibid.
76 JMPD
77 *Dáil Debates* 63, 23 June 1936, 33
78 ibid. 38
79 *Dáil Debates* 63, 23 June 1936, 38 et. seq.
80 *Dáil Debates* 62, 18 June 1936, 2672.
81 *Dáil Debates* 63, 23 June 1936, 38-40
82 ibid. 38 et. seq.
83 ibid.
84 ibid.
85 ibid.
86 ibid.
87 ibid.
88 *Dáil Debates* 63, 3 June 1937, 1697
89 *Dáil Debates* 63, 4 June 1937, 1860. See Hogan G. 'The Constitution Review Committee of 1934' in Ó Muircheartaigh (ed.) *Ireland in the Coming Times* 342-69

CHAPTER 9

1 For an excellent account of politics in Monaghan see Ann Carville 'The Impact

of Partition: a case study of County Monaghan 1910-26,' UCG 1990. Also interviews with James Holland , Paddy Macklin, JF Conlon at various dates.

2 This point was made to the author by a number of survivors.

3 Carville op. cit. 246 et. seq.

4 *Memoir* 49, 50

5 ibid. 51

6 ibid. 53

7 Fine Gael parliamentary party minutes, UCDA

8 *Dáil Debates* 69, 7 October 1937, 1554 et. seq. – debate on report of the special committee

9 *Dáil Debates* 70, 2 February 1938, 36

10 *Dáil Debates* 71, 24 April 1938, 185 and JJ Lee *Ireland 1912-1985: Politics and Society* 214

11 ibid. and Mary E. Daly *Industrial Development and Irish National Identity* 102

12 *Dáil Debates* 70, 23 March 1938, 774 et. seq.

13 For a full and balanced discussion of these issues see Daly op. cit. esp. Ch. 9

14 ibid. 172

15 *Dáil Debates* 71, 27 April 1938, 422

16 ibid. 190

17 ibid. 187

18 *Dáil Debates* 71, 29 April 1938, 316

19 *Dáil Debates* 72, 30 June 1938, 19 et. seq.

20 *Dáil Debates* 82, 13 March 1941, 652

21 *Dáil Debates* 73, 23 November 1938, 928 et. seq.

22 ibid.

23 *Dáil Debates* 73, 30 November 1938, 1147

24 *Dáil Debates* 73, 7 December 1938, 1353

25 *Dáil Debates* 73, 30 November 1938, 1200

26 *Dáil Debates* 81, 11 December 1940, 358

27 *Dáil Debates* 74, 15 February 1939, 494

28 ibid.

29 *Dáil Debates* 79, 10 April 1940, 1092

30 *Dáil Debates* 75, 2 May 1939. 1453

31 *Dáil Debates* 76, 14 June 1939, 878 et. seq.

32 ibid.

33 *Dáil Debates* 72, 14 July 1938, 833 et. seq.

34 ibid. 840

35 ibid. 798 et. seq.

36 *Dáil Debates* 74, 16 February 1939, 670 et. seq.

37 ibid.

38 ibid. 682

39 *Dáil Debates* 74, 2 March 1939, 2000

40 ibid. 1295

41 ibid. 1440

42 ibid.

43 ibid.

44 Fine Gael parliamentary party minutes, UCDA

45 *Dáil Debates* 74, 3 March 1939, 1454 et. seq.

46 *Dáil Debates* 75, 2 May 1939, 1454 et. seq.

47 ibid.

48 ibid.

49 ibid.

CHAPTER **10**

1 Information from Patrick Lindsay
2 Canadian National Archives, Ottawa, Minister of External Affairs papers RG25, Vol. 8519 file 6605-J-40C
3 Much of the material in this and subsequent paragraphs is based on interviews with Hector and Thelma Legge, Maura Dillon and other members of James Dillon's family.
4 For an account of Stephen's Green Club, see CF Smith and B. Sharp *Whigs on the Green* (Dublin 1990)
5 JMDP
6 JMDP. I am grateful to Ciarán MacMathúna for his analysis of O'Neill's work. See also Breandán Breathnach, 'Francis O'Neill, Collector of Irish Music,' *Dal gCas* No. 3, 1977, and article by Bill Meek, *History Ireland* Vol. 7, No.1 1000. It is important to note that Dillon recognised O'Neill as a serious scholar well before this became an accepted academic view.
7 *Dáil Debates* 79, 10 April 1940, 1098
8 Robert Fisk *In Time of War* 364
9 FO/800/310 Public Records Office
10 JMDP
11 ibid.
12 ibid.
13 ibid. Myles did not specify what such role might be.
14 *Irish Independent* 16 August 1939
15 *Dáil Debates* 77, 2 September, 1939, 13
16 SD 23, 3 September 1939, 1029
17 JMDP
18 *Dáil Debates* 78, 4 January 1940, 1532 et. seq.
19 JMDP
20 *Dáil Debates* 78, 3 January 1940, 1381-2
21 *Dáil Debates* 78, 4 January 1940, 1531
22 ibid. 1544
23 For a full discussion on wartime censorship see D. Ó Drisceoil's excellent study *Censorship in Ireland 1939-45*
24 Mulcahy papers, UCDA
25 *Dáil Debates* 79, 18 April 1940, 1612 et. seq.
26 *Dáil Debates* 80, 28 May 1940, 1097
27 *Dáil Debates* 80, 5 June 1940, 1528
28 JMDP
29 DO/130/28 Public Records Office
30 Mulcahy papers, memo 24 May 1940, UCDA
31 See JP Duggan *Neutral Ireland and the Third Reich* 135, 146
32 *Dáil Debates* 76, 14 June 1939, 874
33 FO/800/310 Public Records Office
34 Mulcahy papers, 29 January 1941, UCDA and Fisk op. cit. 317
35 See T. Ryle Dwyer *Irish Neutrality and the USA* 64
36 *Dáil Debates* 81, 16 January 1941, 1347
37 *Dáil Debates* 81, 5 February 1941, 1740 et. seq.
38 *Dáil Debates* 82, 13 March 1941, 634 et. seq.
39 ibid.
40 Ryle Dwyer op. cit. 110 et. seq.
41 ibid. and Mulcahy papers, UCDA. Also *Dáil Debates* 82, 3 April 1942, 1437 et. seq.
42 Ó Drisceoil op. cit. 266
43 *Dáil Debates* 82, 3 April 1941, 1437 et. seq.

44 Mulcahy papers, 4 March 1941, UCDA
45 *Dáil Debates* 84, 16 July 1941, 1858 et. seq.
46 *Dáil Debates* 84, 17 July 1941, 1864 et. seq.
47 ibid. 1872 et. seq.
48 ibid. 1878 et. seq.
49 ibid. 1884
50 ibid. 1885
51 ibid. 1907
52 This correspondence is in the possession of Eamon MacHale who very kindly made it available to me.
53 24 July 1941. Original in MacHale collection
54 *Dáil Debates* 84, 17 July 1941, 1887
55 ibid. 1888-1894
56 Correspondence in MacHale collection
57 *Dáil Debates* 84, 17 July 1941, 1892
58 *Memoir* 51
59 MacHale collection
60 ibid.
61 Fine Gael papers, UCDA
62 *Memoir* 51
63 Joseph T. Carroll *Ireland in the War Years* 116
64 *Dáil Debates* 84, 17 September 1941, 2549
65 Mulcahy papers, UCDA, Ryle Dwyer op. cit. 149 and 220-21
66 Dillon memorandum, S11394, NAI
67 *Dáil Debates* 85, 28 January 1942, 1541
68 ibid. 1549
69 ibid. 1554
70 ibid. 1598
71 Duggan op. cit. 170
72 The order was passed by 71 votes to 20. *Dáil Debates* 85, 29 January 1942, 1600
73 *Memoir* 53-4
74 *Irish Times* 1 February 1942
75 *Irish Times* 11 February 1942
76 ibid.
77 T. Ryle Dwyer *Strained Relations* 47
78 JMDP
79 *Irish Times* 11 February 1942
80 DO/130/28, 20 February 1942, Public Records Office
81 ibid.
82 Mulcahy papers 7a/217, 17 February 1942, UCDA
83 *Dáil Debates* 85, 19 February 1942, 2054
84 Fine Gael papers, UCDA
85 ibid.
86 JMDP
87 DO/130/28. 20 February 1942, Public Records Office

CHAPTER 11

1 Much of the information in this chapter is based on interviews with Mrs Maura Dillon and her sisters, Ellie, Pearl and Kitty, with Hector and Thelma Legge and on Dillon's own account in his *Memoir*, 52-53. I am also grateful to Professor John Dillon who recorded Mrs Dillon's account and made it available to me.

CHAPTER 12

1 *Dáil Debates* 87, 1 July 1942, 2123 et. seq.
2 *Dáil Debates* 86, 16 April 1942, 701
3 *Irish Independent* 26 March 1943
4 DO/130/28 Public Records Office
5 *Dáil Debates* 89, 18 February 1943, 700 et. seq.
6 Ó Drisceoil *Censorship in Ireland 1939-45* 264
7 *Dáil Debates* 87, 2 July 1942, 2284 et. seq.
8 See especially Ó Drisceoil op. cit. 211
9 *Dáil Debates* 88, 9 July 1942. 1015
10 *Dáil Debates* 87, 2 July 1942, 2316 et. seq.
11 For a good account of Clann na Talmhan see Varley and Moser, *History Ireland* Vol. 3, No. 2, 1995
12 The *Irish Oak* was sunk by a U-boat in May 1943
13 *Irish Independent* 4 June 1943, 21 June 1943
14 ibid. 4 June 1943
15 ibid.
16 Interview with author
17 James Holland, interview
18 *Dáil Debates* 91, 1 July 1943, 26-39 et. seq.
19 ibid. 30
20 *Dáil Debates* 93, 20 April 1944, 1206
21 *Dáil Debates* 92, 16 December 1943, 1050
22 *Dáil Debates* 91, 1 July 1943, 79
23 *Dáil Debates* 91, 8 July 1943, 397
24 *Dáil Debates* 92, 16 December 1943, 1050
25 *Dáil Debates* 91 1 July 1943, 38
26 See for example *Dáil Debates* 92, 23 February 1944, 1547
27 *Dáil Debates* 97, 17 July 1945, 2615
28 *Dáil Debates* 92, 23 February 1944, 1516
29 McGilligan papers, p35/207, UCDA
30 Fine Gael parliamentary party minutes, UCDA
31 *Dáil Debates* 91, 11 November 1943, 2026 et. seq.
32 ibid. 2038
33 ibid. 2049
34 ibid. 2051-55
35 ibid. 2026
36 ibid. 2035
37 ibid. 2106
38 ibid. 2059-60
39 ibid. 2055-58
40 JJ Lee Ireland *1912-1985: Politics and Society* 220-3
41 *Dáil Debates* 93, 18 April 1944, 953
42 For a full account of this episode see Maurice Manning *Irish Press* 2 January 1991
43 *Dáil Debates* 92, 1 March 1944, 2010
44 *Dáil Debates* 93, 25 April 1944, 1476-1530
45 ibid. 1542
46 See J. Carroll *Ireland in the War Years* 147, Ryle Dwyer *Strained Relations* 117 et. seq.
47 *Irish Independent* 10 May 1944
48 *Dáil Debates* 93, 10 May 1944, 2475
49 ibid. 2470
50 ibid. 2482-4
51 *Dáil Debates* 94, 9 June 1944, 10

52 ibid. 10-153
53 *Dáil Debates* 94, 14 June 1944, 501
54 *Dáil Debates* 94, 28 June 1944, 1337 et. seq.
55 ibid. 1350 et. seq.
56 *Dáil Debates* 96, 19 April 1945, 2291, and 20 April, 2366.
57 *Dáil Debates* 97, 18 May 1945, 694
58 *Dáil Debates* 101, 17 May 1946, 345 and Department of Taoiseach S14029, NAI
59 *Dáil Debates* 97, 18 May 1945, 694 et. seq.
60 *Dáil Debates* 97, 17 July 1945, 2615
61 *Dáil Debates* 97, 4 July 1945, 1879-2138 and 13 July 1945, 2470 et. seq.
62 *Dáil Debates* 97, 20 June 1945, 1327 et. seq.
63 *Dáil Debates* 97, 17 July 1945, 2594
64 The view that Aiken was at the very least pro German was shared by at least one of his cabinet colleagues – Boland. See Fisk op. cit. 366
65 *Dáil Debates* 97, 17 July 1945, 2743-8
66 *Dáil Debates* 97, 17 July 1945, 2659

CHAPTER 13
1 For a full account of Lemass in this period see John Horgan's superb biography *Sean Lemass The Enigmatic Patriot*
2 *Dáil Debates* 105, 17 April 1947, 800 et. seq.
3 *Dáil Debates* 98, 6 December 1945, 1660
4 ibid. 1551.
5 For a full account of this incident see David O'Donoghue *Hitler's Irish Voices*
6 A phrase attributed to Donogh O'Malley, but probably in currency before then.
7 *Dáil Debates* 98, 10 October 1945, 261
8 ibid. 123 et. seq.
9 ibid.
10 ibid. 11 October 1945, 285 et. seq.
11 *Dáil Debates* 101, 15 May 1946, 353
12 ibid.
13 Ruth Barrington *Health, Medicine and Politics* 115
14 *Dáil Debates* 101, 5 June 1946, 1319. Many of the subsequent details are contained in the report of evidence to the inquiry and in the Dáil debates
15 Barrington op. cit. 134
16 *Dáil Debates* 101, 5 June 1946, 1319 et. seq.
17 ibid. 1329, 1331
18 ibid. 1332
19 ibid. 1334
20 ibid. 1336
21 Report of Judicial Tribunal into Locke's Distillery 1947, Oireachtas Library
22 *Dáil Debates* 102, 11 July 1946, 610 et. seq.
23 ibid. 620
24 ibid. 638 et. seq.
25 ibid. 650 et. seq.
26 *Dáil Debates* 102, 16 July 1946, 849 et. seq.
27 *Irish Independent* 17 September 1946
28 JJ Lee *Ireland 1912-85: Politics and Society* 296. For two good studies of Clann na Poblachta see E. MacDermot *Clann na Poblachta* and Kevin Rafter *The Clann*
29 *Memoir* 58, JMPD
30 *Irish Independent* 9 September 1946
31 *Dáil Debates* 104, 14 February 1947, 1168 and 105, 26 March 1947, 166

32 *Dáil Debates* 104, 25 February 1947, 1225 et. seq.

33 See Horgan op. cit. Ch. 4

34 For a full account of this saga see A. Bielenberg *Locke's Distillery*

35 *Dáil Debates* 108, 22 October 1947, 682 et. seq. and *Memoir* 54-8

36 *Dáil Debates* 108, 22 October 1947, 830 et. seq.

37 ibid.

38 GUBU – Grotesque, Unbelievable, Bizarre, Unprecedented. Used to describe political events where if anything can go wrong, it will, and even if it does not, people will still believe the worst.

39 *Dáil Debates* 108, 29 October 1947, 986 et. seq.

40 ibid. 1103

41 ibid. 1116 et. seq.

42 *Irish Independent* 31 October 1947

43 *Irish Times* 26 November and 27 November 1947

44 ibid.

45 Report of Judicial Tribunal into Locke's Distillery 1947, Oireachtas Library

46 Memoir 54-8

47 *Dáil Debates* 104, 12 February 1947, 835 ct. scq.

48 *Dáil Debates* 105, 1 May 1947, 1908.; *Dáil Debates* 105, 1 May 1947, 1903 et. seq.

49 JMDP

50 *Dáil Debates* 101, 19 June 1947, 2186 et. seq.

51 *Dáil Debates* 106, 20 June 1947, 2327 et. seq.

52 *Dáil Debates* 106, 20 June 1947, 2346 et. seq.

53 *Dáil Debates* 107, 24 June 1947, 26 et. seq.

54 ibid. 66

55 *Dáil Debates* 106, 20 June 1947, 2346 et. seq.

56 *Dáil Debates* 104, 13 February 1947, 980 et. seq.

57 Liam Skinner *Politicians by Accident*

58 *Dáil Debates* 104, 13 February 1947, 995 et. seq.

59 ibid.

60 *Dáil Debates* 98, 7 November 1943, 787 et. seq.

61 *Dáil Debates* 105, 1 May 1947, 1903 et. seq.

62 *Dáil Debates* 107, 27 June 1947, 470 et. seq.

63 For a full discussion of this episode see Barrington op. cit. 183-4

64 Airgram no. A-78, US Legation Dublin, 20 November 1947; 841D.00/11-2047 USNA (College Park MD)

65 *Dáil Debates* 108, 15 October 1947, 480 et. seq.

66 *Irish Independent* 15 December 1947

67 ibid.

CHAPTER 14

1 *Irish Times* 13 January 1948

2 *Irish Times* 19 and 23 January 1948

3 *Irish Times* 30 January 1948

4 ibid.

5 ibid. 7 February 1948

6 ibid. 9 February 1948

7 ibid.

8 For a full and vivid discussions on the formation of the government see David McCullagh *A Makeshift Majority* 29-41 and Eithne MacDermot *Clann na Poblachta* 69-75

9 ibid.

10 *Irish Times* 13 February 1948

11 Minutes of meetings of Independent TDs in JMDP
12 *Memoir* 59, JMPD
13 *Dáil Debates* 110, 18 February 1948, 23
14 ibid. 26
15 ibid. 27, et. seq.
16 See especially MacDermott op. cit. 75 et. seq.
17 *Dáil Debates* 110, 18 February 1948, 69
18 ibid. 70
19 *Memoir* 60
20 For a good account of the agricultural situation see C. Ó Gráda *A Rocky Road* Ch. V and McCullagh op. cit. 157-64
21 *Memoir* 61
22 ibid.
23 ibid.
24 *Dáil Debates* 110, 25 February 1945, 100 et. seq.
25 ibid. 112
26 *Irish Times* 3 March 1948
27 ibid. 13 April 1938
28 ibid. 22 April 1948
29 ibid. 6 May 1948
30 ibid. 17 August 1949
31 ibid. 15 March 1948
32 based on interviews with former departmental officials
33 *Memoir* 70
34 See McCullagh op. cit.
35 ibid. 70-1
36 ibid.
37 Interview with author
38 See Horgan *Sean Lemass: The Enigmatic Patriot*
39 Interview with author
40 JMDP
41 Interview with Liam Cosgrave
42 *Irish Times* 24, 25 March 1948
43 The rationale behind the trade talks is elaborated in Foreign Trade Committee report 1946-9, S14767 A SPO
44 *Irish Times* 18 June 1948
45 Nowlan and Williams *Ireland in the War Years and After* 191
46 Minutes of meeting 2 June 1948, S14293, NAI
47 *Memoir* 60
48 *Dáil Debates* 111, 9 July 1948, 2587 et. seq.
49 *Irish Times* 11 April 1948
50 ibid. 2 September 1948
51 *Dáil Debates* 112, 5 August 1948, 2252 et. seq.
52 ibid.
53 ibid. 2593
54 ibid. 2603 et. seq.
55 *Memoir* 64
56 *Dáil Debates* 111, 9 July 1948, 2610
57 *Dáil Debates* 112, 15 July 1948, 594
58 *Dáil Debates* 111, 9 July 1948, 2625
59 *Dáil Debates* 112, 13 July 1948, 55 et. seq.
60 Information from department officials

CHAPTER 15

1 *Dáil Debates* 113, 24 November 1948, 395. The two best accounts of this episode are in Ian McCabe *A Diplomatic History of Ireland 1948-49* and David McCullagh *A Makeshift Majority* Ch. 3

2 *Memoir* 72, JMPD

3 Public Records Office, DO 35/3955, 27 October 1947 and McCabe op. cit. 21

4 Public Records Office cab 134.118. Rugby to Mochtig 27, 28 January 1948, 55-56

5 *Dáil Debates* 112, 7 August 1948, 2500 et. seq.

6 McCabe op. cit. 35

7 Most authorities, including MacBride's private secretary, Louie O'Brien, believe MacBride was the source of the leak, but Mike Burns, who later worked in the *Sunday Independent*, claims Dillon leaked the material and cites Hector Legge as his source. In an interview with the author, Hector Legge denied that this was so.

8 *Irish Times* 26 October 1948

9 Text in JMDP and interviews with departmental officials

10 For a good account of Ireland's Marshall Aid experience see B. Whelan, 'Ireland and the Marshall Plan,' 49-70

11 JMDP

12 JJ Lee Ireland *1912-85: Politics and Society*

13 Ronan Fanning *The Irish Department of Finance 1922-58*

14 Whelan op. cit. 69

15 Manning and McDowell *The ESB* Ch. 3

16 For a good account of Alexis FitzGerald see Lynch and Meenan *Essays in Memory of Alexis FitzGerald*

17 Lynch and Meenan op. cit. 186-7

18 *Memoir* 45

19 Holmes GA, 'Report on the Present State and Methods for Improvement of Irish Land,' Stationery Office, Dublin 1949

20 *Memoir* 64

21 Full details of scheme in JMDP

22 See especially Lee op. cit.

23 *Dáil Debates* 117, 5 July 1949, 115

24 ibid. 130

25 *Dáil Debates* 116, 8 June 1949, 281

26 *Irish Independent* 17 August 1949

27 The full correspondence is in JMDP; departmental references

28 *Dáil Debates* 120, 9 May 1950, 2020

29 Breandán Ó hEithir *The Begrudgers Guide to Irish Politics* and *Memoir* 66

30 Information from Mike Burns who subsequently worked with the *Sunday Independent*. Lemass's charge: see *Dáil Debates* 123, 23 November 1950, 1212

31 *Dáil Debates* 121, 22 June 1950, 2225

32 *Dáil Debates* 124, 13 March 1951, 1674

33 *Dáil Debates* 113, 14 December 1948, 1506 et. seq.

34 *Dáil Debates* 113, 15 December 1948, 1534 et. seq.

35 Minutes of meeting of CPP, 16 February 1949

36 *Dáil Debates* 114, 16 February 1949, 360 et. seq.

37 *Dáil Debates* 114, 23 March 1949, 1550 et. seq.

38 ibid. 1557 et. seq.

39 *Dáil Debates* 115, 12 May 1949, 1083 et. seq. and 20 May, 25 May

40 *Dáil Debates* 121, 15 June 1950, 1825

41 *Dáil Debates* 121, 20 June 1950, 2034

42 *Dáil Debates* 122, 27 June 1950, 38

43 *Dáil Debates* 122, 28 June 1950, 168
44 *Dáil Debates* 121, 21 June 1950, 2174
45 *Dáil Debates* 122, 28 June 1950, 294
46 ibid. 474
47 *Dáil Debates* 123, 29 November 1950, 1500 et. seq.
48 *Dáil Debates* 123, 6 December 1950, 1869 et. seq. and 124, 21 February 1951, 300
49 *Dáil Debates* 123, 29 November 1950, 1521
50 *Dáil Debates* 112, 15 July 1948, 663
51 *Dáil Debates* 115, 25 May 1949, 1991
52 ibid. 1992
53 ibid.
54 *Dáil Debates* 115, 24 May 1949, 1851
55 *Dáil Debates* 122, 4 July 1950, 541
56 Correspondence in JMDP; departmental references
57 *Irish Times* 1 January 1951

CHAPTER 16
1 Eithne MacDermot *Clann na Poblachta* 143-4
2 *Irish Times* 7 February 1951
3 ibid. 8 February and 20 March 1951
4 ibid. 21 September 1950 and 27 March 1951.
5 ibid. 2 December 1950
6 ibid. 13 December 1950
7 ibid. 9 December 1950
8 ibid. 28 February 1951
9 ibid. 4 February 1950 and S14850 NAI
10 See especially MacDermot op. cit. 146-52
11 *Irish Times* 10 March 1951
12 ibid. 12 April 1951
13 ibid. 13 April 1951
14 ibid. 13 and 14 April 1951
15 *Dáil Debates* 125, 17 April 1951, 940
16 Ruth Barrington *Health, Medicine and Politics in Ireland* 130, 131
17 ibid. 197-201
18 ibid.
19 Noel Browne *Against the Tide* Ch. 8
20 Barrington op. cit. 220
21 *Memoir* 73, JMPD
22 ibid. 75
23 ibid.
24 ibid.
25 ibid.
26 Barrington op. cit. 152
27 *Memoir* 76
28 *Irish Times* 2 May 1951
29 ibid. 29 March 1951
30 ibid. 28 April 1951
31 ibid. 30 April 1951
32 *Dáil Debates* 125, 26 April 1951, 1630
33 *Dáil Debates* 125, 4 April 1951, 23
34 *Dáil Debates* 125, 17 April 1951, 876 et. seq.
35 *Dáil Debates* 125, 18 April 1951, 1074 et. seq.
36 ibid. 1130

37 ibid. 1168 et. seq.
38 ibid. 1514
39 ibid. 1513
40 ibid. 1587 et. seq.
41 ibid. 1637
42 ibid. 1600
43 *Irish Times* 27 April 1951
44 *Dáil Debates* 125, 2 May 1951, 2016 et. seq.
45 Interview with author.

CHAPTER 17
1 *Irish Times* 16 May 1951
2 ibid. 29 May 1951
3 ibid. 12 May 1951
4 ibid. 2 and 3 June 1951
5 *Irish Times* and *Irish Independent* 2 and 4 June 1951
6 *Irish Times* 4 June 1951
7 *Irish Times* 5 June 1951 and Brian Farrell *Sean Lemass* 88
8 *Irish Times* 8 June 1951
9 *Dáil Debates* 126, 13 June 1951, 1
10 ibid. 30
11 *Irish Times* 14 June 1951
12 *Dáil Debates* 126, 13 June 1951, 37, 38
13 ibid. 44-48
14 ibid.
15 *Irish Press* 10 May 1951
16 *Dáil Debates* 126, 13 June 1951, 54-57
17 ibid. 85-92
18 ibid. 48
19 ibid. 54-57
20 *Dáil Debates* 126, 4 July 1951, 824 et. seq. and 17 July, 1749 et. seq.
21 *Dáil Debates* 126, 12 July 1951, 1595
22 ibid. 1723
23 ibid. 27 June 1951, 691
24 ibid. 18 July 1951, 1921
25 ibid. 19 July 1951, 2264
26 *Dáil Debates* 127, 15 November 1951, 889
27 *Dáil Debates* 128, 29 November 1951, 30
28 *Dáil Debates* 131, 20 May 1952, 1981
29 *Irish Times* 5 October 1951
30 ibid. 24 April 1952
31 *Dáil Debates* 127, 15 November 1951, 940 et. seq.
32 *Irish Times* 2 February 1952
33 ibid. 3 April 1952
34 JJ Lee Ireland *1912-85: Politics and Society* 322
35 ibid.
36 *Irish Times* 7 April 1952
37 *Memoir* 48
38 *Irish Times* 12 May 1952
39 ibid. 22 May 1952
40 ibid. 28 June 1952 and 14 November 1952
41 ibid. 1 February 1952
42 *Dáil Debates* 133, 23 July 1952, 1578
43 *Dáil Debates* 133, 24 July 1952, 1758

44 SD 40, 30 July 1952, 1959-61
45 ibid. 1880 and *Dáil Debates* 134, 22 October 1952, 57
46 *Dáil Debates* 133, 16 July 1952, 1073 et. seq.
47 ibid.
48 ibid.
49 *Dáil Debates* 130, 3 April 1952, 1336
50 *Dáil Debates* 127, 15 November 1951, 959
51 *Dáil Debates* 130, 3 April 1952, 1334
52 *Dáil Debates* 129, 5 March 1952, 2223
53 *Dáil Debates* 130, 25 March 1952, 394
54 *Dáil Debates* 138, 29 April 1953, 829 et. seq.
55 *Dáil Debates* 135, 4 December 1952, 835
56 *Irish Times* 15 January 1953
57 ibid. 22 June 1953
58 *Dáil Debates* 140, 2 July 1953, 450
59 *Irish Times* 13 July, 1 August, 24 August 1953
60 ibid. 28, 29 October 1953
61 ibid. 5, 6, 10 and 12 March 1953
62 ibid. 22 April 1953
63 Barrington op. cit. 239 et. seq.
64 *Irish Times* 17, 18 May 1954
65 ibid. 20, 21 May 1954
66 ibid. 22 May 1954
67 ibid. 31 May 1954

CHAPTER **18**
1 'What has no validity from the beginning is not made firm by the passage of
    time.'
2 TF O'Higgins *A Double Life* 185
3 Conversations with Patrick McGilligan, various dates in early 1970s
4 *Memoir* 79, JMPD
5 Fine Gael parliamentary party minutes, 3 June 1954, FGA
6 Anthony Jordan *Sean MacBride* 145-6
7 F200/8/54, NAI
8 *Irish Times* 14 June 1954
9 ibid. 16 June 1954
10 Not all of these 18 bills were enacted during Dillon's term, but all did eventu-
    ally find their way onto the statute book.
11 Patrick Lindsay *Memories* 167-8
12 Details in minute to Costello from Dillon, S14815A, NAI
13 ibid.
14 Costello to Dillon 11 May 1950, S14815A, NAI
15 Cabinet minutes 12 May 1950, Item 2, NAI
16 S14815B, NAI
17 Cabinet minutes 18 July 1950, Item 3, NAI
18 Details of opposition in S14815B, NAI
19 S14815 A/2, NAI
20 ibid.
21 ibid.
22 S14815B, NAI
23 S14815C, NAI
24 Meeting 19 January 1955, S148a5C, NAI
25 ibid.
26 Cabinet minutes 29 July 1955

27 30 August 1955, S14815E, NAI
28 *Irish Times* 17 September 1955
29 JMDP
30 29 July 1955, S14815E, NAI
31 11 October 1955, S14815E, NAI
32 S14815F, NAI
33 S14815G, NAI
34 Memo to government 23 October 1956, S14815G, NAI
35 S14815G, NAI
36 Memo to government April 1957, S14815H, NAI
37 S14815 I, NAI
38 Text in JMDP
39 *Irish Times* 27 January 1949
40 S11832B, NAI and interview with Dr Spain
41 Correspondence JMDP
42 Memorandum re Existing System of Treasury Control, JMDP
43 JMDP
44 *Memoir* 80
45 *Irish Times* 2 and 3 February 1955
46 Meagher to Spain, February 1955, JMDP
47 *Irish Times* 17 September 1955
48 *Memoir* 80-81
49 ibid.
50 Department of Agriculture figures
51 *Memoir* 82
52 *Irish Times* 3 September, 15 October, 22 October, 27 October, 13 November, 22 November 1954
53 *Irish Times* 1 January 1955
54 *Irish Times* 8 January, 15 February, 5 May, 26, 31 October 1955
55 *Dáil Debates* 28 October 1954
56 *Irish Times* 7 March, 28 May, 13 August, 17 August, 6 October, 28 November, 1 December 1955
57 *Irish Times* 15 December 1955
58 ibid. 2 March 1956 and 1 May 1956
59 ibid. 2 May 1956
60 The best account of the financial crisis is to be found in Ronan Fanning *The Irish Department of Finance 1922-58* 500 et. seq.
61 *Irish Times* 25 April 1956
62 See especially J. O'Brien *The Vanishing Irish* published at this time
63 Fanning op. cit. 504
64 *Irish Times* 20 July 1956
65 ibid. 4 August 1956
66 ibid. 6 August, 7 September 1956
67 ibid. 27 September 1956
68 O'Higgins op. cit. 186
69 ibid.
70 *Irish Times* 5 October 1956
71 ibid. 6 October 1956
72 ibid.
73 Fanning op. cit. 505
74 *Irish Times* 16 November 1956
75 ibid.
76 ibid. 2, 3, 15, 16, 17 and 19 January 1957
77 Interview *Irish Times* 7 October 1991

78 Jordan op. cit. 150
79 *Irish Times* 30 January 1957
80 ibid. 20 November 1956
81 O'Higgins op. cit. 184
82 *Memoir* 82
83 *Irish Times* 5 February 1957

CHAPTER **19**
1 See TF O'Higgins *A Double Life* 185-7
2 *Dáil Debates* 173, 10 March 1959, 819
3 JJ Lee *Ireland 1912-1985: Politics and Society* 342-8
4 *Dáil Debates* 161, 15 May 1957, 1357
5 *Dáil Debates* 166, 19 March 1958, 430 et. seq.
6 *Dáil Debates* 166, 25 March 1958, 837
7 TP Coogan *De Valera* 671
8 *Dáil Debates* 173, 10 March 1959, 819 et. seq.
9 ibid.
10 Text of speech JMDP. Costello spoke on similar lines, *Dáil Debates* 178, 10 December 1959, 1380 et. seq.
11 ibid.
12 *Dáil Debates* 178, 10 December 1959, 1342
13 *Dáil Debates* 164, 5 December 1957, 1603
14 *Dáil Debates* 171, 12 December 1958, 2179 et. seq.
15 ibid. 2193 et. seq. and 172, 7 January 1959, 128
16 *Dáil Debates* 171, 12 December 1958, 2168
17 *Dáil Debates* 172, 14 January 1959, 586 et. seq.
18 ibid. 585 et. seq.
19 Coogan op. cit. 674-7
20 *Dáil Debates* 172, 20 January 1959, 826 et. seq.
21 *Dáil Debates* 181, 19 May 1960, 1635 et. seq.
22 *Dáil Debates* 176, 23 June 1959, 134 et. seq.
23 *Irish Times* 17 July 1959
24 John Horgan *Sean Lemass: The Enigmatic Patriot* 194 et. seq.
25 USNA, College Park, Md RG59 740A 00/2 2960
26 Fine Gael parliamentary party minutes, 16 July 1958, FGA
27 ibid. 9 July 1958
28 O'Higgins op. cit. 185-6
29 Fine Gael front bench minutes, 17 October 1959, FGA and *Memoir* 83-85
30 Risteárd Mulcahy *Richard Mulcahy, A Family Memoir* 345
31 Fine Gael parliamentary party minutes, 20 October 1959, FGA; *Memoir* 83-85
32 ibid. 21 October 1959
33 *Irish Times* and *Irish Independent* 22 October 1959
34 *Memoir* 84
35 O'Higgins op. cit. 188
36 ibid. 188-9
37 Patrick Lindsay was one of those influenced by the age factor: *Memories* 172, and in discussion with author
38 *Memoir* 83

CHAPTER **20**
1 *Memoir* 87, JMPD
2 ibid. 84. Ben O'Quigley was appointed secretary to the front bench in October 1960. FG front-bench minutes, FGA
3 *Irish Times* 11 November 1959

4 ibid. 23 October 1959. Dillon's views on the primacy of agriculture were at one with much of the establishment thinking of the time. See for example *Economic Development,* successive Central Bank reports and I*rish Banking Review*.
5 *Irish Times* 30 November 1959
6 ibid.
7 John Horgan *Sean Lemass: The Enigmatic Patriot* 194
8 *Irish Times* 24 February 1960
9 ibid. 26 February 1960
10 John Horgan *Labour: The Price of Power*
11 *Irish Times* 11 October 1960
12 ibid. 10 October 1960
13 ibid. 4 May 1960
14 *Dáil Debates* 178, 10 December 1959, 1352
15 *Dáil Debates* 183, 20 July 1960, 1917 et. seq.
16 *Dáil Debates* 191, 2 August 1961, 2573
17 ibid. 2598
18 text in JMDP
19 *Dáil Debates* 191, 2 August 1961, 2563
20 Horgan *Sean Lemass* 220
21 *Dáil Debates* 180, 16 March 1960, 637 et. seq.
22 *Dáil Debates* 181, 19 May 1960, 1626
23 *Dáil Debates* 180, 16 March 1960, 638
24 See Horgan op. cit. 254-8
25 *Dáil Debates* 184, 10 November 1960, 893
26 ibid. 922
27 Horgan op. cit. 198-0
28 *Dáil Debates* 188, 12 April 1961, 204
29 *Irish Times* 2 May 1961 and 1 October 1961
30 Fine Gael front bench minutes, FGA
31 *Irish Times* 17 January 1962
32 Patrick Lindsay *Memories* 190-1
33 correspondence in JMDP
34 ibid.
35 ibid.
36 ibid.
37 Fine Gael front bench minutes, 2 November 1960, FGA
38 Meetings of Fine Gael parliamentary party 18 November 1959, 8 February 1961, FGA
39 *Irish Times* 25, 26 June 1960
40 ibid. 3 March 1961
41 ibid. 14 September 1961
42 Fine Gael front bench minutes, 26 July 1961, FGA
43 *Irish Times* political correspondent, 2 May 1961
44 Fine Gael front bench minutes, 7 October 1961, FGA
45 *Irish Times* 14 and 28 September 1961
46 Horgan op. cit. 305-7
47 *Dáil Debates* 192, 11 October 1961, 13 et. seq.
48 ibid. 37
49 ibid.
50 ibid.
51 Fine Gael front bench minutes, 15, 22 November 1961, FGA
52 *Irish Times* 28 November 1961
53 ibid. 17 January 1962
54 ibid. 5 February 1962

55 Fine Gael front bench minutes, 28 March 1962, FGA
56 *Irish Times* 13 and 15 November 1962
57 ibid. 1 January 1963
58 Fergal Tobin *The Best of Decades* 159, 160
59 *Irish Times* 24 October, 1 November 1962
60 ibid. 18 and 25 June 1962
61 *Dáil Debates* 198, 13 December 1962, 1331
62 *Irish Times* 1 January 1963
63 For a good account of Singer, see Tobin op. cit. 67-71
64 *Irish Times* 21 February 1963
65 correspondence in JMDP
66 Fine Gael front bench minutes, 20 March, 22 March, 2 April, 15 May 1963, FGA
67 *Irish Times* 22 May 1963
68 ibid. 1 June 1963
69 ibid. 4,5,6 July 1963
70 ibid. 19 July 1963
71 ibid. 30 July, 22 August, 18 September, 28 September, 7 October 1963
72 ibid. 10 October 1963
73 ibid. 14 and 17 October 1963
74 ibid. 28 October 1963
75 ibid. 30 October 1963
76 ibid. 31 October 1963
77 ibid. 28 November and 5, 7 December 1963
78 ibid. 13 December 1963
79 ibid. 1 January 1964
80 ibid. 28 December 1963
81 ibid. 14 February 1964
82 ibid. 21 February 1964
83 ibid.
84 ibid. 22 February 1964
85 ibid.

CHAPTER 21

1 Fine Gael parliamentary party minutes, 26 February 1964, FGA and *Irish Times* 28 February 1964
2 *Irish Times* 26 February 1964
3 Fine Gael parliamentary party minutes, 2 March 1964
4 *Irish Times* 7 March 1964
5 *Some Facts About Ireland* Department of External Affairs 1964
6 *Dáil Debates* 203, 12 March 1964, 861 et. seq.
7 ibid. 868
8 ibid. 914
9 ibid. 892
10 Fine Gael parliamentary party minutes, 29 April 1964, FGA ,and JMDP
11 ibid.
12 ibid.
13 Fine Gael parliamentary party minutes, 5 May 1964. FGA
14 ibid.
15 ibid.
16 *Irish Times* 14 May 1964
17 ibid. 27 May 1964
18 Correspondence in JMDP
19 ibid.

20 *Irish Times* 16 May 1964
21 ibid. 20 May 1964
22 ibid.
23 Fine Gael parliamentary party minutes, 20 May 1964, FGA
24 ibid.
25 *Irish Times* 30 May 1964
26 Fine Gael parliamentary party minutes, 26 May 1964, FGA
27 JMDP
28 *Irish Times* 27 May 1964
29 John Healy, *Irish Times* 11 July 1964
30 *Irish Times* 10 July 1964
31 ibid. 18 July 1964
32 ibid. 22 August 1964
33 ibid. 7 October 1964
34 ibid. 5 December 1964
35 ibid. 2 January 1965
36 ibid.
37 Correspondence JMDP
38 ibid.
39 *Irish Times* 22 February 1965
40 JMDP
41 *Irish Times* 13 March 1965
42 Horgan op. cit. 207
43 *Irish Times* 15 March 1965
44 ibid. 19 March 1965; Fine Gael parliamentary party minutes, 18 March. FGA
45 *Irish Times* 19 March 1965
46 JMDP
47 *Irish Times* 20 March 1965
48 ibid. 3 April 1965
49 ibid. 25 March 1965
50 ibid. 26 March 1965
51 ibid. 6 April 1965
52 Fine Gael front bench minutes, 13 April 1965, FGA
53 *Irish Times* 22 April 1965
54 Fine Gael front bench minutes, 21 April 1965, FGA
55 Fine Gael parliamentary party minutes, 21 April 1965, FGA
56 ibid. 17 November 1965, FGA
57 *Memoir* 86
58 Interview with author
59 correspondence in JMDP

CHAPTER 22
1 *Dáil Debates* 215, 13 May 1965, 1309
2 *Dáil Debates* 218, 19 November 1965, 2033
3 *Dáil Debates* 218, 10 November 1965, 1566
4 ibid. 223, 29 June 1966, 1520
5 *Dáil Debates* 225, 11 November 1966, 898 and John Hogan *Sean Lemass: The Enigmatic Patriot* 337-8
6 ibid. 898-918
7 ibid. 897
8 ibid. 240, 14 May 1969, 1166
9 Text of speeches JMDP
10 JMDP
11 Text in RTE sound archive

12 JMDP
13 Text of correspondence JMDP
14 ibid.
15 information from John Blake Dillon.
16 Texts of reviews, JMDP
17 JMDP
18 JMDP
19 ibid.
20 ibid.
21 Text supplied to author.
22 Fischer and Dillon *The Correspondence of Myles Dillon 1922-25*
23 JMPD
24 ibid.
25 Text supplied to author.
26 ibid.

SOURCES AND BIBLIOGRAPHY

1. *James Dillon Papers* (JMDP)
This collection of James Dillon's personal and political papers was made available to the author by John Blake Dillon. The collection includes correspondence with John Dillon, Fr Nicholas, William Dillon, Myles, Shawn, Brian and Theo Dillon, Hugh Kennedy, Charles Gavan Duffy, Thomas O'Donnell of the National League, Judge Coholan, Lindsay Crawford, Declan Costello, Garret FitzGerald, Ernest Blythe, Eddie McAteer, Denis Bourke, John Horgan (of the *Round Table*), the Mathews family, Lia O'Reilly, Frank MacDermot, RM Smyllie, Sir John Maffey.

It includes also school correspondence, poems from schooldays, social letters during his London and US sojourns, a US diary and a diary of a Carna holiday; election material, speeches and songs of the 1932 election; AOH speeches and correspondence; articles and correspondence on the Commonwealth of Nations, Atlantic Alliance, EEC; memos and correspondence on the *Just Society*; copies of *Forum* (FG magazine 1944-48); various departmental papers including files on the Parish Plan, agricultural institute, correspondence with JJ McElligott, land rehabilitation, 1948 agricultural policy; draft article 'The Philosophy of Politics'; correspondence on Apostolate of the Laity; letter to Col. Charteris; letters on resignation as leader and retirement from politics; minutes of Independent Group of TDs 1948-49; copies of book reviews and various miscellaneous material.

2. *James Dillon Papers* (JDP) Trinity College, Dublin
Mainly speeches, newspaper cuttings and miscellaneous business records.

3. *Theo Dillon Papers*
Correspondence between John Dillon and Theo Dillon, in possession of Theo Dillon's daughter, Mrs Marie-Therese Farrell.

4. *Eamon MacHale Papers*
Mainly correspondence relating to Dillon's resignation in 1942, in possession of Mr MacHale.

5. *Unpublished Ms.*
Memoir. Dictated to Professor JM Dillon, prepared and edited by him in consultation with James Dillon; 88pp
Adventures in Education: Father Sweetman and Mount St Benedict by Matthew Dillon OSB (1981); 46pp
Biographical Notes on William Dillon and the Irish Connection by William R. Dillon (1992); 206pp
The History of the Dillon Family and Monica Duff and Co. Ltd, JMPD

6. *Archive Material*

Frank MacDermot papers	National Archive of Ireland (NAI)
Ernest Blythe papers	University College Dublin, Archives (UCDA)
Desmond FitzGerald papers	UCDA
Michael Hayes papers	UCDA
Hugh Kennedy papers	UCDA
Sean MacEntee papers	UCDA
Sean MacEoin papers	UCDA
Patrick McGilligan papers	UCDA
Richard Mulcahy papers	UCDA
Cumann na nGaedheal papers	UCDA
Fine Gael papers	UCDA and Fine Gael Archive (FGA)
RTE Archive	

7. *Official Records*
(a) National Archives of Ireland: cabinet and departmental material
(b) Public Record Office; London: Foreign and Dominions Office
(c) United States National Archive, Washington DC: State Department
(d) Public Archives of Canada, Ottawa: Department of External Affairs

8. *Parliamentary and Official Reports*
Dáil Debates
Seanad Debates
Judicial Inquiries into Locke's Distillery and Dr Conor Ward

9. *Newspapers and journals*

Cork Examiner	*New York Times*
Irish Independent	*Round Table*
Irish Press	*Forum*
The Irish Times	*National Observer*
Sunday Review	*Hibernia*
Sunday Independent	*Dublin Opinion*

10. *Other material*
Financial records of Monica Duff's, Ballaghaderreen, made available courtesy of
Mr Brian Kelly.

SELECT BIBLIOGRAPHY

Andrews, CS *Dublin Made Me* (Cork 1979)
— *Man of No Property* (Dublin 1982)
Barrington, Ruth *Health, Medicine and Politics in Ireland 1900-1970* (Dublin 1987)
Bew, Paul and Patterson, Henry *Sean Lemass and the Making of Modern Ireland 1945-66* (Dublin 1982)
Bielenberg, Andrew *Locke's Distillery: A History* (Dublin 1993)
Brady, Conor *Guardians of the Peace* (Dublin 1974)
Bowman, John *De Valera and the Ulster Question 1917-73* (Oxford 1983)
Callanan, Frank *Tim Healy* (Cork 1997)
Carroll, J. *Ireland in the War Years 1939-45* (Dublin 1975)
Carville, Ann, 'The Impact of Partition; Monaghan 1910-26,' MA thesis University College, Galway, 1990
Collins, Stephen *The Cosgrave Legacy* (Dublin 1996)
Coogan, Tim Pat *De Valera: Long Fellow, Long Shadow* (London, 1993)
Cronin, M. *The Blueshirts and Irish Politics* (Dublin 1998)
Cronin, S. *Washington's Irish Policy 1916-86* (Dublin 1987)
Daly, Mary E. *Industrial Development and Irish National Identity* (Dublin 1992)
Davis, Troy D. *Dublin's American Policy* (Washington 1998)
Deeney, James *To Cure and to Care: Memoirs of a Chief Medical Officer* (Dublin 1989)
De Vere White, T. *A Fretful Midge* (Dublin 1957)
Devoy, John *Recollections of an Irish Rebel* (Dublin 1969)
Dillon, William *Life of John Mitchell* 2 Vols (London 1888)
Dunphy, Richard *The Making of Fianna Fáil Power in Ireland* (Oxford 1995)
Dwyer, T. Ryle *Irish Neutrality and the USA, 1939-47* (Dublin 1981)
— *Strained Relations: Ireland at Peace and the USA at War 1941-5* (Dublin 1988)
Earl, Lawrence *The Battle of Baltinglass* (Oxford 1994)
Fanning, Ronan *The Irish Department of Finance 1922-58* (Dublin 1978)
Farrell, Brian *Sean Lemass* (Dublin 1991)
Farrell, Brian (ed.) *The Irish Parliamentary Tradition* (Dublin 1973)
J. Fischer and J. Dillon (eds) *The Correspondence of Myles Dillon 1922-25* (Dublin 1998)
Fisk, Robert *In Time of War* (London 1983)
Foster, Roy *Paddy & Mr Punch* (London 1993)
Garvin, Tom *1922: The Birth of Irish Democracy* (Dublin 1996)
Gaughan, JA *Thomas Johnson 1872-1963: First Leader of the Labour Party in Ireland* (Dublin 1980)
Girvan, Brian *Between Two Worlds: Politics and Economy in Independent Ireland* (Dublin 1989)
Gray, Tony *Mr Smyllie, Sir* (Dublin 1991)
Grott, AJ *Democracies Against Hitler* (London 1999)
Gwynn, DR *Life of John Redmond* (Dublin 1932)

Hancock, K. *Survey of British Commonwealth Affairs* Vol. 1 (Oxford 1937)

Harkness, D. *The Restless Dominion* (Dublin 1969)

Healy, John *Healy, Reporter* (Dublin 1991)

Hogan, James *Could Ireland Become Communist?* (Dublin 1935)

Horgan, John *Labour: The Price of Power* (Dublin 1986)

— *Sean Lemass: The Enigmatic Patriot* (Dublin 1998)

Jones, Thomas *Whitehall Diary* Vol. 3 (London 1971)

Keogh, Dermot *The Vatican, The Bishops and Irish Politics 1919-39* (Cambridge 1986)

— *Twentieth-Century Ireland: Nation and State* (Dublin 1994)

Kettle, Tom *The Day's Burden* (Dublin 1910 & 1937)

— 'The Philosophy of Politics' (Dublin 1906)

Lee, JJ *Ireland 1912-1985: Politics and Society* (Cambridge 1989)

Lindsay, Patrick *Memories* (Dublin 1992)

Longford, Earl of, and O'Neill, TP *Eamon de Valera* (London 1970)

Lynch, Patrick and Meenan, James *Essays in Memory of Alexis FitzGerald* (Dublin 1987)

Lyons, FSL *John Dillon* (London 1968)

Lyons, JB *The Enigma of Tom Kettle* (Dublin 1983)

McCabe, Ian *A Diplomatic History of Ireland 1948-49* (Dublin 1991)

McCagne, Eugene *Arthur Cox 1891-1965* (Dublin 1994)

McCullagh, David *A Makeshift Majority* (Dublin 1998)

MacDermot, Eithne *Clann na Poblachta* (Cork 1998)

McMahon, D. *Republicans and Imperialists: Anglo-Irish Relations in the 1930s* (Yale 1984)

McManus, F. *The Years of the Great Test 1926-39* (Cork 1967)

MacManus, MJ *Eamon de Valera* (Dublin 1962)

Manning, M. *The Blueshirts* (Dublin 1971)

— *Irish Political Parties* (Dublin 1972)

Manning, M. and McDowell, M. *Electricity Supply in Ireland: A History of the ESB* (Dublin 1985)

Maye, Brian *Fine Gael 1923-87* (Dublin 1993)

— *Arthur Griffith* (Dublin 1997)

Meenan, James *The Irish Economy Since 1922* (Liverpool 1970)

— *Centenary History of the Literary and Historical Society 1855-1955* (Tralee 1957)

Moss, Warner *Political Parties in the Irish Free State* (Harvard 1933)

Mulcahy, Risteárd *Richard Mulcahy (1886-1971). A Family Memoir* (Dublin 1999)

Murphy, JA and O'Carroll, J. (eds) *De Valera and his Times* (Cork 1983)

Nowlan, KB and Williams, TD (ed.) *Ireland in the War Years and After* (Dublin 1969)

O'Brien, Conor Cruise *Parnell and his Party 1880-1890* (London 1957)

Ó Broin, Leon *No Man's Man: A Biographical Memoir of Joseph Brennan* (Dublin 1982)

Ó Cathaoir, Breandán *John Blake Dillon: Young Irelander* (Dublin 1990)

O'Donoghue, David *Hitler's Irish Voices* (Dublin 1998)

Ó Drisceoil, D. *Censorship in Ireland 1939-45* (Cork 1998)

O'Duffy, Eoin, 'Why I Resigned from Fine Gael,' Dublin 1935

Ó Gráda, C. *A Rocky Road: The Irish Economy Since the 1920s* (Manchester 1977)

— *Ireland: A New Economic History 1780-1939* (Oxford 1994)

O'Halpin, Eunan *Defending Ireland: The Irish State and its Enemies Since 1922* (Oxford 1999)

Ó hEithir, Breandán *The Begrudgers Guide to Irish Politics* (Dublin 1986)

O'Higgins, TF *A Double Life* (Dublin 1996)

Ó Muircheartaigh, F. *Ireland in the Coming Times: Essays to Celebrate TK Whitaker's 80 Years* (Dublin 1997)

O'Sullivan, Donal *The Irish Free State and its Senate* (London 1939)

O'Sullivan, Michael *Sean Lemass: A Biography* (Dublin 1994)

Rafter, Kevin *The Clann: The Story of Clann na Poblachta* (Dublin 1996)

Raymond, RJ 'The Marshall Plan and Ireland, 1947-52' in PJ Drudy (ed.) *The Irish in America* (1985)

Share, Bernard *The Emergency: Neutral Ireland 1939-45* (Dublin 1978)

Skinner, Liam *Politicians by Accident* (Dublin 1946)

Tobin, Fergal *The Best of Decades: Ireland in the 1960s* (Dublin 1996)

Valiulis, MG *Portrait of a Revolutionary: General Richard Mulcahy and the Founding of the Irish Free State* (Dublin 1992)

Walsh, Dick *The Party* (Gill & Macmillan)

Whelan, B. 'Ireland and the Marshall Plan,' *Irish Economic and Social History* Vol. 9 (Dublin 1992)